APPLIED INDUSTRIAL ECONOMICS

Applied Industrial Economics is a student reader which presents the seminal research published in industrial economics over the last ten years. In an extensive introduction Louis Phlips synthesizes the recent major developments in the field and surveys the current state of industrial economics. *Applied Industrial Economics* is intended for advanced undergraduate students and graduate students in applied economics, industrial economics, and business studies.

Louis Phlips is Professor of Economics at the European University Institute in Florence. He was President of the European Economic Association in 1995. His publications include *The Economics of Price Discrimination* (Cambridge University Press 1983), *The Economics of Imperfect Information* (Cambridge University Press 1989) and *Competition Policy: A Game-Theoretic Perspective* (Cambridge University Press, 1996).

Edited by

Louis Phlips

APPLIED INDUSTRIAL
ECONOMICS

CAMBRIDGE
UNIVERSITY PRESS

PUBLISHED BY THE PRESS SYNDICATE OF THE UNIVERSITY OF CAMBRIDGE
The Pitt Building, Trumpington Street, Cambridge CB2 1RP, United Kingdom

CAMBRIDGE UNIVERSITY PRESS
The Edinburgh Building, Cambridge CB2 2RU, United Kingdom
40 West 20th Street, New York, NY 10011–4211, USA
10 Stamford Road, Oakleigh, Melbourne 3166, Australia

First published 1998

Printed in the United Kingdom at the University Press, Cambridge

Typeset in Times 9.5/12.5 pt [CE]

A catalogue record for this book is available from the British Library

Library of Congress cataloguing in publication data

Applied industrial economics / edited by Louis Phlips.
   p.   cm.
Includes index.
ISBN 0 521 62054 6 (hb). – ISBN 0 521 62954 3 (pb)
1. Industrial organization (Economic theory)   I. Phlips, Louis.
HD2326.A657   1998
338.5–dc21   97–25537   CIP

ISBN 0 521 62054 6 hardback
ISBN 0 521 62954 3 paperback

For Astrid and Elisabeth

and in memory of Octavie, their great-grandmother

Contents

Preface

I wanted to give this book the title 'Applied price theory'. Unfortunately, none of my referees liked it. Nor did my editor, Patrick McCartan. They all thought it was old-fashioned, vague, imprecise and whatnot. So I gave in and went for 'Applied industrial economics', hoping that my readers will realize that I, as always, am interested in the links between 'theory' and 'reality', where 'reality' refers to observed behaviour as well as antitrust policy, while 'theory' refers to particular products or markets.

My introduction is rather long and aims at explaining the logic behind my choice of contributions. Since I am aiming mainly at advanced undergraduates, I tried to start from scratch and define the basic concepts and results in a totally non-technical way. Yet, I did not try to unify the notation of the chapters, nor did I delete technical appendices or proofs: students must learn to switch from one notation to another and should be given the opportunity to work themselves through the technicalities. Intuition is not enough.

I am grateful to John Sutton for encouragement and moral support and to Andrew Lewis, Andrea Lofaro, and Stephen Martin for comments on my introduction.

Jessica Spataro, my secretary, had the brilliant idea of scanning the papers. As a consequence, she had to retype all the maths and unify the typographical presentation. She was fast and efficient as always. Our computer freak Marcia Gastaldo came in to help (when all the computers had broken down) without ever losing her smile. I thank them both.

Louis Phlips
Florence, April 1997

Introduction

The chapters in this book all concentrate on the analysis of particular markets or critically evaluate policy measures taken in the US or Europe to promote market competition. In that sense they are 'applied'. Yet, they are also 'theoretical' in that they elaborate or test theories about the functioning of markets. The chosen contributions follow a partial equilibrium methodology, recognizing 'the fact that a few relationships are usually dominant with respect to the prices and outputs of particular goods' as emphasized by Stigler in the last chapter of his *Theory of Price* (where he explains why he neglected the theory of general equilibrium).

Consider the UK market for salt. The main questions to be answered are the following. Why are there just two producers of salt in the UK, not more nor less? In what precise sense can one say that there is room, today, in that market for just two producers, so that entry of new firms would not be expected? Is this to say that there exist 'barriers' to entry? Knowing that there were many producers of salt at the beginning of the century, why did they disappear and how? Why did some producers give up and close down while others merged with competitors?

But then, why didn't the remaining two producers of salt merge to enjoy a monopoly position? Intuition suggests that they could cash in on monopoly profits by colluding. However, collusion is illegal so that secret arrangements seem to be called for. On the other hand, applied game theory shows that 'tacit' collusion can work without there being agreements or direct communication, as long as there is some common pricing practice. For example, the salt producers individually announced price changes well in advance so as to give their competitor time to adopt the same price change. Is this practice of so-called 'parallel pricing' conducive to monopoly profits? What if advance notification of list-price increases is combined with the use of (a) contractual provisions which ensure the buyer of obtaining the lowest price (available on the market) and/or (b) discriminatory delivered prices? Do such practices replace an explicit price agreement successfully? This immediately raises the question of how the authority responsible for antitrust policy can detect tacit collusion or rather how you, dear reader, could help the authority – as an economic expert – make up its mind. A financially more interesting alternative, though, might be for you to help tacitly colluding competitors hide this by misinforming the authority about some key parameters that determine market outcomes.

Instead of colluding, two competitors may indeed prefer to merge, which in turn is likely to raise prices and profits. Today, an additional merger in the UK market for salt would transform a duopoly into a monopoly. Yet, some mergers are necessary for survival, as in the days when there were too many salt producers in the UK. Where is the borderline between a 'good' and a 'bad' merger? How can price theory produce sound guidelines for merger control?

Fortunately, in many cases the authority can and should reduce the burden of collusion detection by exempting practices that look collusive but in fact are not. Theory shows that cooperation in R&D and through franchising are cases in point.

This example has illustrated the four basic topics covered in this book. First, one has to explain the observed structure of the market under study, in particular the degree of market concentration (which is typically oligopolistic). Second, market structure is not independent of the degree of price competition (which helps determine how many producers can make a profit). How can oligopolists find a competitive price while avoiding price wars (that would force some or all of them to exit?). Third, how can competition policy operate in a world where oligopolists can tacitly collude? Fourth, how can competition policy be complemented by merger control so as to prevent monopolization?

This introduction aims to help the reader find a coherent answer to these questions, at putting the papers into perspective and – where necessary – at giving intuitive definitions and explanations for the technical terms or game-theoretic techniques used by the authors. These techniques have now become so standard that they cannot be ignored.

1   Market structure

John Sutton (chapter 1) constructs a theory capable of explaining why market structure is as observed at a particular moment in time in a particular market. The term 'market structure' designates the number (N) of producers in that market and their relative strength, as measured by an index of market concentration such as $1/N$ (the higher the N, the less the market is concentrated) or the concentration ratio.

To explain why N is equal to 2 in the UK market for salt amounts to showing that N = 2 is an equilibrium of a game the salt producers are supposed to have been playing. Sutton's basic assumption is, indeed, that a number of potential producers of salt are players in a game that has two stages. In stage 1, they determine for how many salt producers there is room in the UK market, taking account of the degree of competition that is likely to result in stage 2 and of the implied profits. In stage 2, this equilibrium number of firms sell their salt in a more or less competitive way and realize the equilibrium profits.

1.1   A two-stage game

Why suppose that this game has two stages? Why not suppose that the investments in setting up the equilibrium number of firms and the degree of competition are determined in a one-stage ('one-shot') game? The formulation of this question is possibly a bit confusing, in that it may suggest that the two-stage game is solved in two successive steps. So let me emphasize right from the start that the players of such a game solve its successive 'subgames' or steps *before* the game is actually started, as is the case with a one-shot game. (We shall see a bit later how the solution is found.)

The advantage, then, of distinguishing two stages is to disentangle the long-run and the short-run aspects of the problem without separating them. The first step, in which the investments or disinvestments (by entry into or by exit from the industry) are decided, is the long-run aspect of the problem. The second step, in which the profits that motivate the entries or the exits are determined, is the short-run aspect. The latter determines the former. But the former is 'long-run', since it is more difficult to change an investment decision than to change a price.

Since my undergraduate days, I have struggled with the distinction between the short run and the long run, which I encountered for the first time in Alfred Marshall's *Principles* (1952, book V, chapter V, section 6). I quote:

To sum up then as regards short periods. The supply of specialized skill and ability, of suitable machinery and other material capital, and of the appropriate industrial organization has not time to be fully adapted to demand; but the producers have to adjust their supply to the demand as best they can with the appliances already at their disposal . . . In long periods on the other hand all investments of capital and effort in providing the material plant and the organization of a business, and in acquiring trade knowledge and specialized ability, have to be adjusted to the incomes which are expected to be earned by them: and the estimates of these incomes therefore directly govern supply.

My interpretation is that Marshall's distinction is analytical rather than chronological. It hinges on what is (supposed to be) given and what is (supposed to be) changeable. The 'long run' is not to be confused with a 'long term' that lasts longer in chronological time than a 'short term'. The long run does *not* come after the short run. The long run implies that the variables under study can fully adjust. Static theories therefore are long run. The short run implies partial adjustment. Dynamic theories are therefore short run.

Sutton's two-stage game fits perfectly with such a Marshallian approach, which suggests that the short-run problem (stage 2) has to be solved first, analytically, for any given value of N. Once this solution is worked out, it becomes possible to find out for what values of N the second-stage profits allow to pay for the costs of setting up these N firms. In other words, the first-stage equilibrium number N sustains the second-stage equilibrium profits. One implication is that if the second stage is (or becomes) very competitive so that profit margins shrink, this will induce the players to prefer a more concentrated market structure (reduce the number of firms existing in the market).

Consistency between the short and the long run is thus achieved by what game theory calls a 'subgame perfect' or simply 'perfect' equilibrium. Solving the second stage first, you get 'estimates of these incomes' (as Marshall calls the subgame equilibrium profits) which 'directly govern supply', that is, which allow you to find the equilibrium N^* (in the first stage). If this game were actually played, N^* plants would be put in operation (there being one plant per firm by assumption, to simplify) and they would provide profits that confirm that choosing N^* was the right decision (all other things being equal, of course).

Note that if the game had stages corresponding to successive time periods, finding the perfect equilibrium by backwards induction starting from the equilibrium of the *last* time period T and moving to the equilibrium of the subgame starting at period $T-1$, then the subgame starting at $T-2$, etc. until today, would generate intertemporal or time consistency. The decisions taken in any time period would be confirmed at the next period as being the right ones, all other things being equal. Such games are considered in chapters 3, 4, and 5. Note that in Sutton's two-stage game there is no succession of time periods: the equilibrium N^* is found by a static reasoning. In the real world, there may exist an observed number of plants (which were perhaps an equilibrium in the past) that are now, say, too large: $N > N^*$. Perhaps market demand declined over the years or a long-lasting price war has eroded profit margins too much. Whatever the reason, the industry has to be restructured. How? By the disappearance of some plants, obviously. But which should exit first: the big ones or the small ones? Instead of disappearing, the big ones should perhaps be progressively reduced to the size of the smaller ones? These are the sort of questions multi-stage games, where each stage is a time period, can answer. They thus provide additional results which nicely complement Sutton's static approach.

After these preliminaries, I examine Sutton's model more closely.

1.2   Exogenous sunk costs

Salt is a homogeneous commodity. So there is no point in organizing advertising campaigns to promote a particular brand nor is there in investing in R&D outlays to improve the quality of salt. In the absence of fixed costs for advertising and R&D, the only fixed costs salt producers have to care about are the costs of setting up their plant. These costs (σ) are exogenously given to them and cannot be recovered: they are sunk costs and therefore play no role in the day-to-day pricing policy.

To be more precise, σ is the cost of acquiring a single plant of minimum efficient scale, net of resale value. In the first stage of the game, the entry decision is taken at this cost σ, which is treated as a fixed parameter in the second stage (so that prices do not depend directly on it). To justify entry, σ must be recovered *ex post*, so entry decisions depend on the interplay between σ and the intensity of competition. If competition turns out to be too intensive, then some existing plants have to be closed. (To make sure that the second-stage equilibrium prices are compatible with σ and the corresponding market structure, the game is solved backwards as explained above. However, once the game is actually played and circumstances change, inconsistency may indeed arise and lead to a restructuring of the industry.)

Sutton (1991, chapter 2) constructs the following example. Suppose market demand can be specified as $X = S/p$ where X is the total quantity of salt demanded and p is its price, so that S is the total expenditure on salt. S can thus be interpreted as the size of the market, while the price elasticity is supposed to be -1. (This specification has the advantage that we can make the market for salt grow or decline by simply letting the parameter S grow or decline.) Suppose also that there is a price p_0 above which sales are zero.

Then we can let the intensity of competition differ in a precise way by considering three games with different second-stage subgames: (1) one with a monopoly subgame in which the sum of the profits of all potential producers is maximized (joint-profit maximization); (2) one in which the potential salt producers use so-called Cournot strategies[1] in the second stage, that is, they determine the optimal *quantities* (to produce and sell) in a non-cooperative way, while the market price for salt results from putting the sum of these optimal quantities in the inverse market demand function (which stipulates how the market price is determined by the total quantity sold and purchased); and (3) a third game in which the potential producers use Bertrand or price strategies and compete by undercutting each other's price. Competition is more intense in the second than in the first subgame, and also more intense in the third than in the second subgame. Because of that, these three games have very different subgame-perfect equilibrium market structures.[2]

When the monopoly profit, say Π_0, can be obtained jointly, it does not change with the number of entrants, it being the sum of the profits of whoever establishes itself as a salt producer. Then the equilibrium market structure (N^*) is such that each production covers its set-up cost, or $\sigma N^* = \Pi_0$ or $N^* = \Pi_0 \sigma$. There will be as many producers as set-up cost allows, given Π_0.

In the subgame with Cournot strategies, the second-stage profit for each potential producer is $\Pi = S/N^2$. So being in the salt business is profitable as long as $S/N^2 - \sigma > 0$. At a subgame-perfect equilibrium, $N^* = \sqrt{S/\sigma}$. So if the size of the market increases relative to the set-up cost (S/σ increases), the equilibrium number of firms N^* increases and market structure becomes more fragmented.

If competition were even more intense so that the potential salt producers consider

---

[1] A number of important characterizations and applications of the Cournot equilibrium are collected in the book of readings edited by Daughety (1988).
[2] The second-stage subgames have different price equilibria, needless to say. These equilibria will be discussed in section 2 of this introduction.

undercutting each other's price, this mutual undercutting would stop only at the point where the price would be equal to the marginal cost of producing salt. At that (equilibrium) point, however, each producer would make a net loss of σ. It would therefore only make sense to enter the salt business if one were sure that nobody else would enter. More precisely, for any $\sigma > 0$, $N^* = 1$: exactly one firm enters in equilibrium and sets the monopoly price. We get the perhaps surprising and apparently paradoxical result that the most intense competitive pressure leads to the most monopolistic market structure. However, this is neither surprising nor paradoxical: why would producers willingly engage in price wars to kill each other? If they can avoid it, they will.

We can now establish a relationship between the degree of market concentration (measured by $1/N$) and market size (measured by S) and show how this relationship depends on the intensity of price competition. In the absence of any such competition, that is, when fully collusive monopoly profits can be obtained, there will be as many producers as there are firms that could cover σ with their profit share, given the size of the market. This is the case represented by the lowest of the three curves in figure 1. Market concentration falls monotonically as S/σ goes up. When the potential competitors envisage Cournot competition, $1/N$ again goes down as S/σ increases, but the degree of concentration is higher for any given value of S. On the contrary, when price cutting is to be expected, monopoly is maintained throughout because entry is totally deterred by the fact that just one entry, leading to a duopoly, would push the price down to marginal cost and thus lead to negative net profits.

The three curves in figure 1 suppose that the different types of competitive behaviour are compatible with an increasing number of firms, there being no feedback of N on the intensity of price competition. For example, full collusion is supposed to remain possible when the number of firms increases with market size. The three cases are simply maintained alternative hypotheses to give a precise content to the idea that the intensity of competition differs. To determine which degree of competition (or collusion) is compatible with a given market is another type of problem which will be taken up in part II. What Sutton wants to emphasize is that the intensity of competition affects market structure in the long run in such a way that there is a trade-off between tough price competition and equilibrium concentration levels.

Coming back to the currently existing salt duopoly in the UK, I infer from this theory that the very existence of a duopoly (rather than a monopoly) suggests that price competition cannot be that intense. On the other hand, the fact that this duopoly resulted from a series of mergers suggests that price competition must have been intense in the past. That this was indeed the case is well documented in Sutton (1991, chapter 6): the homogeneous nature of their product made the numerous salt producers of the late nineteenth century very vulnerable to price cutting. Since attempts at collusive pricing had failed repeatedly at the beginning of this century, the industry came to realize that stopping entry and reducing N was the only solution in the long run that could guarantee profitability.

In the preceding analysis, the good put on the market was assumed to be strictly

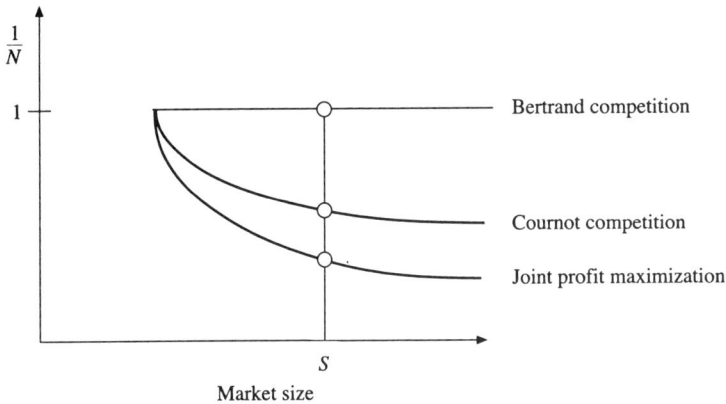

Figure 1 Concentration–market size relationship
Source: Sutton (1991, figure 2.2).

homogeneous. In reality, even salt is somewhat differentiated, if only because different sellers put it on the market in different wrappings with different brand names. Different 'varieties' of the same commodity (with the same quality) then coexist. In the literature, this is called horizontal product differentiation, as opposed to vertical differentiation,[3] which implies quality differences.

Shaked and Sutton (1987 and 1990) show that the presence of horizontal product differentiation (a) shifts the concentration-market size curve downwards and to the left and (b) transforms this curve into a lower bound. Indeed, if each firm were to produce only one variety, then market structure would become more fragmented as market size increases. On the other hand, if firms could produce several varieties (a more realistic assumption), then multiple equilibria would arise, some with many producers each offering one single variety and some with a small number of firms each offering several varieties. Adding a new variety to one's list of products may increase sales at given prices and thus give a larger market share without engaging in price competition. Conversely, when a given number of varieties is offered by a larger number of sellers, tougher price competition results so that entry is discouraged. There also may be economies of scope due to a broader product line. Finally, adding new varieties to one's product line may be a strategic move to forestall entry by potential competitors. Schmalensee (1978) described this tactic as monopolization by product proliferation, typical of the US ready-to-eat breakfast cereal industry. Each of these four effects may lead to a degree of market concentration represented by a point that lies above the concentration-market size curve, which thus becomes a lower bound.

---

[3] On this distinction and the use of the Hotelling model to describe horizontal differentiation, see Phlips (1983, pp. 203–12).

1.3   Endogenous sunk costs

In Sutton's terminology, endogenous sunk costs are those incurred with a view to enhancing consumers' willingness-to-pay for a specific firm's product. Implicit is the assumption that there are quality differences (or vertical differentiation) which the firms want to advertise or develop. So these costs are (mainly) advertising and R&D costs. They increase with u, an index of perceived quality. On the consumers' side, their willingness-to-pay is a non-decreasing function of u. Markets with these characteristics are what Schmalensee calls type II markets in chapter 2.

The natural thing to do is to take the two-stage game discussed above and insert an intermediate stage in which the firms that decided to enter (at cost σ) in the first stage choose a value of u (and therefore an advertising level or an R&D effort) at a sunk cost $A(u)$ to be added to σ. In the third stage, then, the vector $\{u_i\}$ is given and firms compete (à la Cournot for example).

If advertising leads to sufficient increases in demand, then firms will increase their advertising costs $A(u)$ and thus increase total sunk costs $\sigma + A(u)$. Such an escalation of costs raises the equilibrium level of total sunk costs, which has now become endogenous. The end result is that there will not be room in the market for more and more firms as market size increases: market structure does not become more and more fragmented as S increases, in sharp contradiction with type I markets.

All this hinges on the degree of demand responsiveness faced by the individual firms to increases in their advertising or R&D outlays or, in terms of costs, on the returns to these outlays. Sutton (1991, chapter 3) uses the convenient specification

$$A(u) = \frac{a}{\gamma}(u^\gamma - 1), \qquad \gamma > 1.$$

Putting $u = 1$, we have $A(1) = 0$ and $A'(1) = a$. So a small initial outlay at $u = 1$ produces a return corresponding to an expense a, which is the cost per message. On the other hand, a higher γ implies more rapidly diminishing returns. The total fixed outlays function (which can thus be interpreted as the advertising response function) is then

$$\sigma + \frac{a}{\gamma}(u^\gamma - 1).$$

It turns out that market concentration no longer decreases monotonically with market size when set-up cost σ is smaller than a/γ in equilibrium. On the contrary, as of a certain market size concentration increases!

The Cournot equilibria are depicted in figure 2 which is to be interpreted as follows. The dotted curve is the locus of the points at which there is a switch from a non-advertising to an advertising regime. When $\sigma = a/\gamma$ (represented by σ_2 in the figure), an increase in S does not change the number of firms to the right of the dotted curve. When $\sigma > a/\gamma$ (σ_1 for example), market concentration decreases monotonically as in type I markets. But when $\sigma < a/\gamma$ (σ_3 or σ_4 for example), then a further increase in

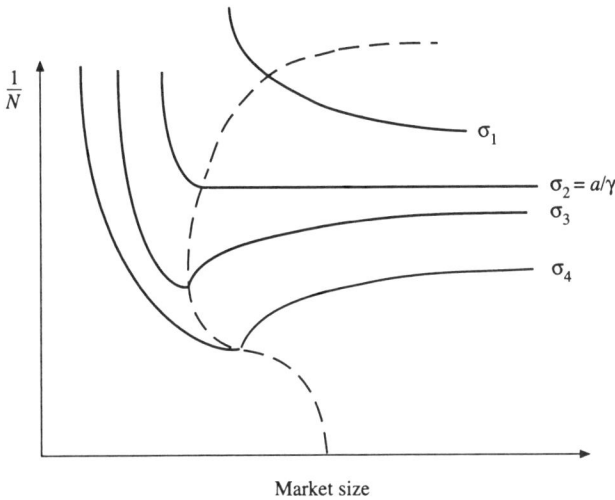

Figure 2 Concentration and market size for various values of σ, where

market size *increases* market concentration. On the one hand, advertising (or[4] investing in R&D) becomes profitable only when a certain minimal market size is attained, as represented by the dotted curve. On the other hand, once a market is on the right-hand side of that curve, rising outlays may become very large compared to σ and firms which survive this escalation break the fragmented structure.

In his review article, Schmalensee reduces the three-stage approach just outlined to a two-stage model, in which firms decide to enter and, if they enter, choose the level of $A(u)$ in the first stage. This is not a fundamental modification of the model, since what counts is that both σ and A be treated as sunk costs in the last stage. However, precisely on this point Schmalensee raises a number of objections to the two-stage approach. First, he says, while 'product designs are typically longer-lived than prices, advertising budgets are regularly revised in light of short-term changes in market conditions, for instance, while prices are sometimes rigid for very long periods'. Here, there is a confusion between the short (or long) term and the short (or long) run: long-run decisions analysed in a first stage of a game do not necessarily take more time than the second-stage short-term decisions. In the same vein, the effects of advertising on demand do not have to be more long lived than the effects of prices for a two-stage modelling to be justified. Third, while it is true that the entry deterring effect of advertising costs is not different from that of any other form of non-price competition, this is not a difficulty since advertising is only one example of sunk costs: $A(u)$ can be interpreted in many other ways. Finally, it is true indeed that two stages are not

---

[4] A more specific analysis of the impact of R&D investment on market concentration is developed in Sutton (1996). For example, the equilibrium number of firms is smaller when R&D aims at improving the quality of existing varieties rather than introducing new varieties.

necessary to show that N^* converges to a positive constant: see the discussion of Schmalensee's equation (8). Yet, a two-stage approach clarifies the economics involved.

Matraves' (1996) recent study of the pharmaceutical industry nicely complements[5] Sutton's historical analyses of different food and drinks industries. The latter are characterized by high advertising outlays leading to horizontal differentiation. The former is both advertising and R&D intensive. Matraves finds that (a) the advertising to sales ratio has remained constant since 1981 while sales increased and (b) the R&D to sales ratio increased during the same period. As market size has been increasing, advertising expenditure increased at the same rate and R&D at an even faster rate. The theory predicts that market concentration should also have increased. This prediction is confirmed at the world level (in terms of market shares of the top ten firms world-wide). However, it is not confirmed at the national level inside the European Union nor at the level of the Union. This suggests that competition is taking place in pharmaceutical markets at the global level or, at least, that the theory is relevant for the competitive relations that exist at that level.

1.4   Dynamics of market expansion and contraction

Chapters 3, 4, and 5 look into the dynamics of how market structure changes over time. The two preceding chapters showed how to determine the equilibrium number of firms N^*. Now the problem is to figure out how N is going to be increased when $N < N^*$, for example when market demand is expanding and the potential producers have come to the conclusion that there is room for additional capacity. The alternative problem is to take the case of a contracting industry in which the producers have come to the conclusion that $N > N^*$ and to ask how the industry's capacity is going to be reduced.

Both cases will be studied with the help of a so-called 'timing' game, that is, a game in which the players have to decide at what point in time they will do something. In the case of two players, they have to decide for example who will be first to make an announcement, to decide, to start producing or whatever. Our problem is: which firm will be first to invest in new capacity when demand expands and to close down or divest when demand contracts over time.

In chapter 3, Ghemawat tells the story of Du Pont's capacity expansion strategy in the US titanium dioxide industry and shows that it accords with the predictions of a timing game between two firms. Firm 1's cost of constructing a new plant is lower than firm 2's. These two firms are participating in a public auction[6] in which they alternate in making bids about the dates at which they are willing to add capacity between time 0 and time T. One firm makes the first bid promising to add new

---

[5] And so does the paper by Robinson and Chiang (1996) which uses PIMS (Profit Impact of Market Strategies) data. They include a heterogeneous sample of consumer *and* industrial goods markets that can have intensive R&D spending as well as intensive advertising spending.

[6] A rather non-technical introduction to auction theory can be found in chapter 4 of Phlips (1988).

capacity at time t_j^*. If the other firm does not announce an earlier date before the end of the auction, that's it. Alternatively, the other firm can announce that it will invest earlier in period $t_j^* - s$, and thus 'undercut' the previous bid. This undercutting goes on as long as the resulting additional profit covers the cost of adding capacity. This profit is the present value of the profits that will be made as of the point in time at which the undercutter would add capacity if he were not undercut himself. Who will be the first to stop this bidding? The first player for which this profit is smaller than the cost of adding capacity (discounted to the present). This must be firm 2: the firm with higher capacity costs will be the first to stop bidding. Consequently, the low-cost firm will find it profitable to pre-empt the others in adding new capacity.

This reasoning is based on the assumption that the evolution of demand is known by both players with certainty, so that future profits can be computed without error. If demand is uncertain, so that the price of the product is a random variable whose distribution has variance σ_{t*}^2, where $t*$ is the date from which future profits are estimated, then one has to correct the previous reasoning to take account of the risk involved in putting up new capacity and possibly of the degree of risk aversion of the players. Since only the costs differ between the players, it suffices to correct the cost of adding capacity by adding the increase in risk due to increasing firm i's capacity from K_i to $K_i + 1$. The risk associated with having capacity K_i is measured by Ghemawat in the usual way as $\phi K_i^2 \sigma_{t*}^2$, where ϕ is the constant measure of risk aversion. The increase in capacity from K_i to $K_i + 1$ then increases risk by $[\phi(K_i + 1)^2 \sigma_{t*}^2 - \phi K_i^2 \sigma_{t*}^2]$, which is to be added to the discounted cost of putting up an additional unit of capacity $C_i(K_i + 1)e^{-rt*}$. Now firm 1 will no longer pre-empt the other firm if the latter's capacity K_2 is small enough compared with K_1 and its cost disadvantage not too big or if ϕ and σ_{t*}^2 are high enough. This is what Ghemawat means when he writes that 'demand uncertainty acts as the great leveller in tending to equalise firms' costs . . .'. So demand uncertainty may prevent the lowest-cost producer from pre-empting its competitors. This result is illustrated by the fact that Du Pont had to postpone the creation of new plants and expansions of existing plants.

Resource constraints also tend to reverse the pre-emption outcome. For example, there was a lag of at least four years between Du Pont's decision to construct and the date on which the plant could be started up. On the other hand, pre-emption by firm 1 is more likely if it is better informed about costs or demand, for example, if it has more knowledge of the new technology to be used or if it has a more efficient marketing department than its competitors. All this is directly relevant to the story of the timing of Du Pont's decisions between 1972 and 1977 and the eventual start-up of its US plant at DeLisle in 1979.

Let us now consider a declining industry whose demand is shrinking regularly over time. In their elegant 1985 paper on 'Exit', Ghemawat and Nalebuff (GN) only consider the cost of maintaining existing capacity in operation. In addition, the only way to reduce capacity is simply to 'exit', that is, to close down. The game is a Cournot game between two firms that break even at the beginning of the planning horizon (t = 0) and are facing continuously shrinking demand. Which of the two will close down first?

The two firms have the same marginal cost so that attention now concentrates on differences in revenue. The firm with the smaller output has the greater marginal revenue. It will exit at the point in time where its average revenue is equal to the cost of maintaining its capacity. As soon as one firm exits, the other firm is a monopoly and as such will continue to operate until its price is equal to its cost. This period is longer for a small firm than for a big firm, because its average revenue is higher so that it takes more time to get this revenue down to the level of cost (with the same shrinking demand).

In subgame-perfect equilibrium, the bigger firm exits first because the small firm can credibly commit to remaining in the market longer. Indeed, the small firm can use its prospective monopoly profits as a commitment to remain a loss-making duopolist, if necessary.[7]

This perhaps surprising result was obtained using stringent assumptions, and was not confirmed empirically in a convincing way (see Lieberman's contribution, chapter 5). So GN did their homework again in their 1990 paper on 'The devolution of declining industries' which is included in this volume as chapter 4. The same basic logic is followed as in the 'Exit' paper but the exit decision is changed by allowing firms to continuously reduce their capacity. This implies that capacity is now a function of time, that is, $K(t) = [k_1(t), \ldots, k_n(t)]$ in a discrete sense using time periods of duration Δ. Initially firms have ordered capacity levels by assumption, that is, $k_1(0) > k_2(0) > k_n(0)$. Δ is then allowed to get arbitrarily small to simulate the continuous equivalent. The main result is that now the largest firm continuously reduces capacity until it is of the same size as the next largest and then the two together reduce capacity until they are of the same size as the third largest, etc. Finally all firms are of the same size (the smallest originally) until the market no longer supports the oligopoly and they all exit.

The intuition behind the result is that smaller firms, by definition, face higher marginal revenue and therefore have no incentive to reduce output. Marginal revenue is also decreasing in output and therefore the bigger firms have a greater incentive to reduce capacity. Note that future monopoly profits of the surviving firm play no part here given that the firms, by reducing capacity, can all be of the same size should they so desire.

The case study of the synthetic soda-ash industry by GN makes chapter 4 a very impressive one. As their figure I shows, the pattern of closure of plants supports their predictions in two respects: 'First, each of the three multi-plant firms closed a plant before either of the two single-plant operators. Second, none of the five firms dropped out of the market until all firms were down to one plant apiece.' Some empirical

---

[7] Fishman (1990) extends the GN exit model to include an entry stage, while Londregan (1990) studies the whole life of an exogenously growing and then declining industry when firms are able to exit and then re-enter. On the other hand, Whinston (1988) assumed that some firms may operate with several different sized plants which they can dispose of as they choose. Dierickx *et al.* (1991) introduced different cost structures. In general, there is no direct generalization of GN's small firm survival result in these papers.

support can also be found in Lieberman's careful analysis of 30 chemical products (see chapter 5).

Restructuring an industry, in particular by closing down some plants, is often done through mergers. The analysis of mergers will be taken up in connection with a discussion of merger control in section 4: it is postponed until then because one first has to have a theory of pricing with a given market structure. This theory is discussed in the next section, which thus takes a closer look at the price equilibria obtained in the second-stage subgames of Sutton's (two-stage) game.

2   Industrial pricing and pricing schemes

Consider a market with a given oligopolistic structure. The simplest case is a duopoly. It is good research strategy to simply consider $N = 2$, since the results obtained are often generalizable to a larger number of firms. In such markets, there is strategic interaction: what one firm does affects what its competitors do. What sort of price equilibrium is to be expected if these firms do not collude? What if they do collude?

2.1   Non-collusive price equilibria

A large majority of economists – in my personal experience – think that if sellers announce, post or publish their (non-collusive) prices, they *therefore* use Bertrand strategies and *thereby* reveal that the Bertrand model is the appropriate one to use. Some even go as far as to argue that the Bertrand model has descriptive value. In my opinion, this reasoning is mistaken and results from a misunderstanding of the Cournot model. I shall indeed argue that it makes perfect sense to use Cournot strategies to explain real-world pricing.

Let us have a closer look at Sutton's example of a Cournot subgame (presented above in section 1.2). Market demand is $X = S/p$. There are N identical firms, selling a homogeneous good, with profit function

$$\Pi_i = (p - c)x_i$$

where $p = S/X$. Let $X = X_{-i} + x_i$, where X_{-i} is the sum of the outputs of all i's rivals. Then this profit function becomes

$$\Pi_i = \left(\frac{S}{X_{-i} + x_i} - c \right) x_i$$

and

$$\frac{\partial \Pi_i}{\partial x_i} = \frac{-Sx_i}{(X_{-i} + x_i)^2} + \frac{S}{X_{-i} + x_i} - c = 0$$

are the first-order conditions. Because of the symmetry assumption, $x_i = x$ for all i and these conditions become

$$\frac{-Sx}{(Nx)^2} + \frac{S}{Nx} - c = 0$$

or

$$\frac{S(N-1)}{N^2 x} = c$$

or

$$x = \frac{S}{c} \cdot \frac{N-1}{N^2}$$

implying

$$X = Nx = \frac{S(N-1)}{cN}.$$

The equilibrium price is obtained by putting this equilibrium aggregate quantity in the inverse demand function $p = S/X$

$$p = \frac{cN}{N-1} = c\left(1 + \frac{1}{N-1}\right).$$

Hence equilibrium profits are

$$\Pi_i = \left(\frac{cN}{N-1} - c\right) \frac{s}{c} \cdot \frac{N-1}{N^2} = \frac{S}{N^2}$$

as mentioned above.

Notice that in this Cournot procedure, each firm first determines its optimal quantity in a non-collusive way. Then these quantities are added up and their sum is inserted in the inverse market demand function to find the equilibrium price. It is relatively easy to visualize a situation where each firm simultaneously puts the partial derivative (with respect to its *own* quantity x_i) equal to zero: the result is a system of N equations (reaction functions) whose solution gives the N equilibrium quantities. But who does the adding up? Who computes the equilibrium price? All Cournot says is that it 'will be convenient' to use the inverse demand function (Cournot, 1838, chapter 7, p. 89). Implicit is the idea, it seems to me, that the firms – after having determined their production rates – will charge a price they think 'the market will bear', that is, compatible with their collective production decisions.

It remains to be explained, though, by what mechanism or 'pricing scheme' competitors find such a price. This is precisely what d'Aspremont, Dos Santos Ferreira and Gérard-Varet do in an abstract and very technical way in their 1991 paper on 'Pricing schemes and Cournotian equilibria'. They argue that more or less explicit customs are followed in real life. These customs, called 'pricing schemes', play the same role as the computation of the equilibrium price using inverse demand (and have thus the same status as auctions or bidding mechanisms). Only formal representations are discussed, namely abstract pricing schemes such as taking the arithmetic mean of a number of price signals, or their harmonic mean, or their geometric mean, or picking the lowest or the highest price signal as the common price. These examples are used to show how they can lead to a unique equilibrium price to which corresponds a vector of quantities which are the Cournot quantities. We are interested in understanding how these schemes look in practice and especially whether they lead only to non-collusive (Cournot) outcomes or also to collusive profits – in which case they deserve to be called 'facilitating practices'. This is the purpose of chapters 6, 7, and 8.

2.2   Pricing schemes

Before tackling their collusive aspect, I want to describe the functioning of a few pricing schemes that are frequently observed.

The Monopolies and Mergers Commission noted in its 1986 report on white salt that over the period under investigation the price of the two UK producers followed a pattern of 'parallel pricing'. Every time there was a price change, one of the firms announced it while the other firm followed within a couple of weeks with an identical change. You might expect the bigger of the two firms to have been the price leader, but that was not the case: the smaller firm led eight times and the bigger firm led only five times. Notice that whoever took the initiative for a price change, informed the competitor a month in advance, and the latter would then inform the leader of a proposed identical change within that month. This is perhaps the most straightforward example of a pricing scheme as defined by d'Aspremont *et al.* (1991). There being only two firms and one taking over the price of the other, there is no need, really, to compute an average price. But the logic is the same: price signals, that is, announced prices are turned into one single price valid for all competitors.

The theoretical underpinning of the experiment on parallel pricing conducted by Harstad, Martin, and Normann (see chapter 6) is taken from MacLeod (1985), who supposes that n firms follow a custom (called a 'social convention') which is to react to an announcement of a price change (by any competitor) according to an alignment rule. This rule says that firm j should adopt price changes equal to those announced by i, whoever i is. MacLeod applies this rule to differentiated as well as homogeneous goods, while d'Aspremont *et al.* (1991) consider only the original Cournot case of a homogeneous good, for which the producers must charge the same price in equilibrium. That is why the experiment is based on the assumption that the experimental subjects sell differentiated commodities.

MacLeod imagines the following strategy: (1) when a price increase is announced by a competitor, follow it if it is profitable to do so and if the others do the same; otherwise, do not change your price; (2) when a price decrease is announced by a competitor, follow it as long as it does not lead to prices lower than the prices that would obtain in a static non-collusive Nash equilibrium; (3) if any rival firm does not behave according to (1) and (2), announce the static non-cooperative Nash equilibrium price. Then there exists a non-cooperative equilibrium with prices higher than the non-collusive Nash prices but lower than those which would maximize the joint profit.

The experiment confirms this. When (in the so-called treatment II) players may make announcements, prices rise above their static Nash equilibrium levels. When they are forced to match their competitors' announcements (see treatment III) prices are still higher. The same is true when the players are experienced, that is, have played the game before.

Parallel pricing occurs in the time domain, in which practically all firms operate. The producers of heavy goods, for which the cost of transportation (to the location of the customers) represents a non-negligible part of their total cost, simultaneously operate in the space domain. There, too, an equilibrium price has to be found. But this price has to be determined, at a given point in time, for all possible locations in which sales occur. Again, pricing schemes are used for that purpose. Look at the sales conditions printed at the back of invoices or on the cover of price catalogues of antiquarian bookshops. You'll sometimes find that shipping costs will be added to the price (for orders of less than so many pounds or francs). More often than not, especially for heavy industrial products such as steel plates or cement, you'll discover that they will be delivered to the buyer's premises at the same price (valid, say, for all of Belgium) as if differences in location and therefore in transportation costs did not matter. Very often, however, you will be surprised to read that the actual price to be paid on *delivery* – the 'delivered' price – is a strange sum of a base price valid at some announced 'basing point' (a particular town, for example) plus the official railway tariff, as if the actual distance between the plant where the steel plate was made (*not* located in the basing point indicated) and the delivery point, as well as the actual means of transportation (a company truck rather than the railway) did not matter.

Taking a closer look, you may even find out that the basing point used by seller *i* to compute the delivered price is the location where this seller's *competitor* has its plant. If all competitors in a market use a spatial alignment rule which says that they will all – whatever their location – use the same base price, the same unit transportation cost and the distance from the same basing point to determine their delivered prices in any point in space, then the analogy with the intertemporal alignment rule in case of parallel pricing becomes evident. The uniqueness of the delivered price in any point in space is obtained by adopting the convention that all competitors must charge, at every delivery point, the *lowest* combination of a base price plus freight to that point (from the different basing points to which the base prices relate). This scheme is nothing other than the multiple basing point system that is applied in the European steel industry. It amounts to picking the lowest price signal as the common price, since each possible combination of an announced base price plus freight can be interpreted as a signal.

In chapter 7, Thisse and Vives begin their analysis of spatial pricing schemes (which they call 'price policies') with the observation that the economics literature has not paid enough attention to the logic behind these schemes. Indeed, whoever is familiar with the running of a business or is involved in antitrust proceedings, must be impressed by their pervasiveness. Yet, when interviewed, business managers will typically (and probably honestly) answer that there is nothing special or irregular or illegal with the particular scheme they are using, because that is 'the custom of their trade'. When pressed, they are unable to explain why the custom is what it is and would be very surprised indeed to hear that they need this to find their Cournot equilibrium price (or, even worse, to sustain a collusive equilibrium in a repeated game, as we shall argue later).

Thisse and Vives have the merit of taking spatial pricing schemes seriously and analysing their choice in a duopolistic environment in which strategic considerations are of primary importance. Right from the start, they distinguish between the choice of a particular pricing scheme and the choice, given a pricing scheme, of a particular price. Their general conclusion is that price discrimination by all firms in the market emerges as the unique equilibrium outcome. The discrimination results from the fact that the net price received by the sellers, after deducting the transportation cost from the delivered price, differs among buyers on the basis of their location. My only query with the Thisse–Vives approach is about their use of Bertrand strategies, which gives the (wrong) impression that duopolists necessarily undercut each others' price until the market price is down to the (highest) marginal cost. In fact, this undercutting is no more than a possibility[8] which the pricing scheme aims at preventing![9]

After the time domain and the space domain, I finally consider pricing schemes in what I call the income domain. Having different incomes, consumers differ in their willingness to pay and therefore in their search for a lower price in the market place. Sellers are tempted to respond by giving some customers a price discount. Are there pricing schemes which prevent competitors from giving discounts such that the market price would drop below the Cournot equilibrium price? So-called 'best-price' policies can have this effect, when combined with advance notification of price changes.

This is the important message of Holt and Scheffman in chapter 8. They build a two-stage model in which n firms select a common list price to announce in advance in a first stage, and then decide whether to undercut this common price in a non-cooperative way in the second stage. Considering each possible common list price in turn, it turns out that the Cournot price is the highest price that will not be undercut by individual firms if the list-price contracts include provisions that are 'best-price'. Such provisions give buyers both meet-or-release and most-favoured-customer protection. The first type of protection is a guarantee with respect to other sellers: it entitles a customer who finds another seller offering a lower price to demand this same lower price or to be released from his contractual obligation. The most-favoured-customer clause is a guarantee with respect to other customers: it guarantees that the buyer is receiving the lowest price offered to anyone by the seller. In the second stage, the sellers are supposed to use Bertrand strategies, which allows them to behave very competitively (as was the case in the Thisse–Vives paper). Yet, for first-stage announced list prices up to the Cournot price, no undercutting (that is, no 'non-selective discounting') will take place in equilibrium, while undercutting will drive effective prices down (below the announced common list price) until the Cournot

---

[8] As I pointed out in my 1993 paper on 'Basing point pricing, competition and market integration'.
[9] This point is further developed in the next section on tacit collusion.

price corresponding to the Cournot equilibrium quantity vector is realized. Why is this?

The intuitive reason is that, when all competitors have a best-price clause, and a general discount given by firm i is met by all other firms, then offering a (small) discount *does not take sales away from anybody*. Consequently, using this clause allows all competitors to stick to their desired sales quantities, which are the Cournot quantities. This being the case, the only reason for a firm to actually undercut the common price is the possibility of making *new* sales by a unilateral output expansion. However, such an expansion is not profitable by definition at the Cournot vector of sales quantities, while it always *is* profitable (for some firm) when aggregate production is *below* the Cournot aggregate quantity, that is, at a list price *above* the Cournot equilibrium price.

The reader will notice that all three models constructed in order to analyse pricing schemes in the time domain (parallel pricing), in the space domain (discriminatory delivered pricing) and in the income domain (best-price clauses) include a two-stage model. In the first stage, a common price is announced and determined: the price of the first mover in case of parallel pricing, the lowest delivered price in case of spatial alignment, or the lowest of the announced list prices in case of best-price clauses. In all schemes, each seller adjusts his price to that of his competitors in a very precise and well-determined way. This makes it possible to enforce the equilibrium price in the second stage.

2.3   Tacit collusion and repeated games

The next question is whether these pricing schemes are not, also, 'facilitating practices' which make it possible to enforce tacitly collusive Nash equilibria. In fact, these pricing schemes are facilitating practices in the sense that, *if there is tacit collusion*, then the common use of the scheme facilitates the enforcement of the collusive outcome. But the converse statement is not true: the fact that one of these pricing schemes is being used is not proof of collusion. Indeed, we just discovered that their use may simply facilitate the enforcement of a non-cooperative Cournot equilibrium.

In chapter 13, I define tacit collusion as collusive outcomes that are sustained as equilibria of a non-cooperative repeated game. A repeated game is such that the *same* one-period game is repeated period after period and represents the circumstance when the same firms meet over and over again in the market place. In such a game, an equilibrium that implies profits between the Cournot profit and the joint-profit-maximizing profit can be sustained, although there is no cooperation between the players. Game theory thus offers an answer to the vexing question, which arises so often in antitrust proceedings, of how firms can collude without making agreements and even without contacting each other.

Collusion is sustained through credible threats of punishments of any cheater. Such threats are credible if all players have an individual interest in carrying these out. A first example was worked out by J. Friedman (see chapter 8 in his 1977 textbook), who imagined that any deviation from the joint-profit-maximizing outcome in period

t would be punished, in period $t+1$, in the following way: all players would shift to the Cournot equilibrium quantities. This is credible, because the Cournot equilibrium is a Nash equilibrium nobody wants to deviate from. Given such strategies, each firm will compare the discounted value of its profits if it cheats (and is then punished forever) with the discounted value of its profits if it stays at the initial collusive outcome. It will discover that cheating is not worthwhile (or, in other words, tacit collusion works) if the discount factor $1/(1+r)$ is large enough (that is, if the market rate of interest r is small enough). Loosely speaking, if enough weight is put on future benefits and losses, the immediate gains from cheating will be outweighed by subsequent losses.[10]

Consider the basing point systems. Thisse and Vives (chapter 7) ask whether the single basing point system can be given a competitive interpretation using the assumption that the players have Bertrand strategies. Their answer is no and confirms the conventional wisdom that simple basing point pricing facilitates tacit collusion. They reach the same conclusion for the multiple basing point system: it ensures market sharing which gives it 'a non-competitive flavour'.

At this point I must report an afterthought. I have already emphasized the analogy between the intertemporal alignment of prices in case of parallel pricing and the spatial alignment of prices in the case of multiple basing point pricing. It occurs to me that the latter is also analogous to a combination of 'meet competition' and 'most-favoured customer' clauses, since the alignment: (a) is on the perfectly known *lowest* combination of a base price plus freight, (b) is applied by *all* sellers in a particular delivery point, and (c) is applicable to *all* customers located in that point. In addition, the purpose of the alignment rule is to freeze existing trade patterns and thus leave market shares unchanged: it ensures that a price cut does not take sales away from anybody, exactly in the same way, it seems, as a best-price clause. One could not exclude the possibility, therefore, that the Holt–Scheffman analysis would apply, so that no undercutting takes place in equilibrium for delivered prices up to the Cournot price, while undercutting drives delivered prices down (below the announced base price plus freight) until the Cournot price is realized but not any further. This could be a convincing rationalization of what happens when a basing point system is said to break down because regional price wars occur. Such a regional price war could be interpreted as 'non-selective discounting' (in the sense of Holt and Scheffman) bringing the delivered price in a particular location down to the Cournot level corresponding to the Cournot market shares (in that location). Again, using a best-price clause or a spatial alignment rule changes the Bertrand analysis of the profit-ability of price cutting into a Cournot problem.[11] Or, assuming Bertrand strategies

---

[10] Instead of a punishment forever, one can imagine punishments for a specified number of periods and sophisticated punishment paths such as the ones considered by Rees in chapter 12 in his study of collusion in the UK white salt market. One can also make the punishment proportional to the deviation, as in Slade (chapter 11).

[11] Holt and Scheffman's comment on their equation (3) is here applied to a particular point in geographical space.

with product homogeneity does not imply price undercutting until the price is equal to marginal cost, when an alignment rule is adopted by all players.

Vertical restraints

Until now I have discussed horizontal strategic relationships between sellers of a homogeneous good, so that the emphasis was on Cournot strategies. (Price strategies were introduced only in the form of price cutting (or discounting) in order to see how they could be avoided.) We now consider vertical relationships between producers and their retailers in markets with differentiated products. For such products, Bertrand strategies do not imply that prices go down to marginal cost and are best suited to analyse competition at the production as well as the retail level.

A preliminary question is: why does a duopolist have an advantage in selling his product through an independent retailer (vertical separation) rather than directly to consumers (vertical integration)? Assume the two goods are imperfect substitutes (at the consumption level) and strategic complements[12] (at the retailer level). Then the answer is:

Vertical separation with wholesale prices in excess of production costs is profitable when there are fully extracting franchise fees for the following reason. By raising his wholesale price, manufacturer 1 causes the price charged by retailer 1 to rise. Given our (rather mild) assumptions on demand, the reaction function of seller 2 in price space is upward sloping and, therefore, the price of retailer 2 rises too, which benefits manufacturer 1. Starting from a position where wholesale price equals production cost, the effect upon profits of a small increase in wholesale price due to the change in p^1 is negligible, whereas that due to the induced change in p^2 is distinctly positive. Hence the overall effect is beneficial. (Bonanno and Vickers, 1988, p. 263)

In fact, both producers are better off so that vertical separation is in their collective interest.

Chapter 9 on vertical restraints[13] is a direct continuation of this analysis. Suppose that the producers have assigned exclusive territories to their retailers, so that intra-brand competition is eliminated and each retailer (of a given brand) enjoys mono-polistic power over a fixed fraction of final demand. Exclusive dealing leads to higher equilibrium retail prices *and* wholesale prices. The mechanism is essentially the same as the one described in the preceding paragraph: exclusive dealing leads to higher retail prices (in the different territories) for a particular brand; this induces the retailers of the rival brand to increase their retail prices, which benefits the producers.

The existence of exclusive dealing arrangements inside the European common market makes arbitrage between the national markets costly if not impossible. Geographical market segmentation persists and differences in the price elasticity of demand between countries provide an incentive to price discriminate. Chapter 10 is an

---

[12] According to Bulow *et al.*, (1985), there is strategic complementarity on a retail market when it is in retailer 2's interest to react to an increase of p_1, the price of retailer 1, by increasing his price p_2. This implies that the reaction curves in (p^1, p^2)-space are upward sloping.

[13] An extended version of this chapter can be found in Rey and Stiglitz (1995).

impressive econometric analysis of the much discussed question why car prices are so different across European countries. The answer is clear.[14]

Empirical studies of tacit collusion and the relevant market

In her pathbreaking work on tacit collusion in the Vancouver retail gasoline market, Slade (chapter 11) directly compares the collusive and non-collusive outcomes of constituent (or stage) game of a repeated game between several strategic subgroups of gasoline stations. In my chapter on the detection of collusion and predation (chapter 13) to which the reader is referred, I list the exceptional circumstances which she was able to create by collecting daily data on the spot. The model is a direct application of the definition of tacit collusion, given above. The collusive outcome sustained as an equilibrium of the repeated game turns out to be well below the joint-profit-maximizing profit – but above the non-cooperative one-shot Nash equilibrium, exactly as predicted by the theory. The outcome is secured by two different types of punishment strategies: on the one hand, discontinuous reversion to Nash behaviour for the one-shot game (called 'example one'), and, on the other hand, continuous strategies such that small deviations (from the collusive outcome) trigger small punishments and large defections trigger large punishments ('example two'). The latter imply intertemporal reactions to previous-period price changes initiated by a competitor (i.e., another subgroup of gasoline stations) which can be tested and seem to be the most appropriate for this market.

Ray Rees' testing of tacit collusion in the UK market for white salt (chapter 12) has the unique feature that it uses yearly data for only five years (1980–4) – because these are the only data collected by the Monopolies and Mergers Commission. So standard econometric techniques cannot be used. Yet, the chapter shows that most interesting results can be obtained. It is possible to compute the gains and losses the salt producers would have incurred if they had deviated from a collusive outcome and had been punished (in a theoretically well-defined way) and to check whether these gains and losses are such that it is in the producers' interest not to deviate. This amounts to testing whether the assumption of collusive behaviour is consistent with the theory on which the computations are based. Rees' answer is positive. Is this then proof of collusion? In chapter 13 I argue that it is not, because the equilibrium the producers are not deviating from is not shown to be a collusive one. Since they had adopted the pricing scheme of parallel pricing, this equilibrium could have been the non-cooperative Cournot equilibrium. The observed absence of deviations during the period 1980–4 could simply be rationalized as compatible with the latter equilibrium. Proof of collusion implies a direct comparison between a collusive and a non-collusive outcome. That is why I propose the Osborne–Pitchik detector which is derived from such a comparison. My table 13.1 makes me believe that the UK salt producers *had* reached a collusive outcome with the help of parallel pricing.

At this point, I want to elaborate somewhat on the difference between the Slade and the Rees approaches and the standard empirical methods of identifying and measuring

---

[14] Other empirical studies of price discrimination are discussed in Kirman and Phlips (1996a).

market power (described in a non-technical way in Baker and Bresnahan (1992) and in a technical way in Bresnahan (1989)). The former directly use game theory to define and measure collusion. The latter, it is fair to say, refer to general equilibrium theory in that they aim at measuring departures from competitive equilibrium defined as price equal to marginal cost. These departures imply the ability to raise price by reducing output. A particular firm or a group of firms may have this power when it can pass on a cost increase through a price increase without losing a great deal of market share or when the demand for its product is price inelastic. The focus is thus either on one firm or on a group of colluding firms: strategic interaction between oligopolists is supposed always to imply the desire to collude. The possibility that a group of firms may reach a non-cooperative Nash equilibrium and may react to a common cost increase by a common non-collusive price increase is not even considered. Anything that is not the competitive equilibrium of general equilibrium theory is called 'market power' or 'monopoly power' or 'collusion'. The subtleties of our distinction between a non-collusive and a collusive Nash equilibrium are lost. One wonders to what extent the results of such econometric exercises could be relevant in antitrust cases of alleged tacit collusion.

The potential dangers of using the Bresnahan techniques to define the 'relevant market' empirically should also be pinpointed. Indeed, they define markets with reference to substitute goods, not with reference to strategic relationships (such as strategic substitutability or complementarity) between rivals. The following quotation from Baker and Bresnahan (1992, p. 8) is revealing:

The empirical methodology of residual demand estimation, developed for identifying the market power of a single firm, has also been applied to define markets. The experiment proposed by this application raises cost simultaneously for all the firms selling in the proposed market – for example, all the manufacturers of carbonated soft drinks – without raising costs for firms selling possible demand substitutes excluded from the proposed market, such as juice, coffee, milk and other beverages. If the soft drink producers collectively would respond to a soft drink industry cost increase by raising price, despite the threat of lost sales to the producers of other beverages, it is likely that a soft drink cartel would raise price and, thus, likely that soft drinks form a product market.

Such a reasoning leads to a broad definition of the relevant market, that includes products which could appear as independent according to today's theory of strategic interdependence. I therefore prefer the exogeneity test employed by Slade (1986) in a study of geographic market boundaries of petroleum products. Applied to Bresnahan's example of soft drinks, it implies testing the exogeneity of the price of one variety of soft drinks with respect to the price of another variety of soft drinks. I can imagine that Coca-Cola and Pepsi could turn out to belong to the same market while exogeneity might show up between Coca-Cola and Perrier as well as between Pepsi and Perrier.

3   Competition policy

It must seem strange to have papers on 'competition policy' presented separately from papers on 'merger control'. Merger control is of course (part of) competition policy.

The partition reflects the following historical evolution of the European Commission's antitrust policy. In the early sixties, it was not at all clear whether articles 85 and 86 of the Treaty of Rome, which govern competition policy in the European Union (as explained in my chapter 13), were applicable to mergers. In 1966, a committee of four professors was asked this question by the Commission. In my minority report I gave a negative answer, arguing that article 85 makes explicit and tacit collusion (with a given market structure) illegal but does not apply to structural changes such as those resulting from mergers. At most, a merger could be construed to be an abuse of a dominant position under article 86 in particular circumstances (such as a hostile takeover leading to a monopoly position). For 20 years, this was the prevailing opinion inside the Commission.[15] It was abandoned after the Philip Morris judgement of the European Court of Justice of 17 November 1987 (*British American Tobacco Company Ltd. and R.J. Reynolds Industries Inc. v EC Commission*, European Court Reports, p. 4487). The court held that in the case concerned, when the cigarette manufacturer Philip Morris had acquired some voting rights in its competitor Rothmans International, such an acquisition can lead to the coordination of the market behaviour of the acquirer and the target, so that article 85 can be applied to it. This re-opened the debate and led to the Council Regulation No. 4064/89 of 21 December 1989, which allowed the Commission to set up a merger control system run by a special branch of Directorate General IV. The implementation of this policy has led to many criticisms and conflicting views (which are reflected in chapter 23). At any rate, merger control is still considered something apart by most Europeans.

My chapter 13 is far from giving a comprehensive overview of antitrust policy. For one thing, it completely ignores vertical restraints (for example between producers and distributors). Hence we have the expository paper by John Kay (chapter 14), which is self-explanatory[16] and is followed by a chapter taken from the OECD report on *Competition Policy and Vertical Restraint*, whose main authors are Patrick Rey and Steven Brenner. On the other hand, the seminal paper by d'Aspremont and Jacquemin (chapter 16) gives a theoretical justification for the Commission's policy of granting a block exemption to joint R&D ventures on the condition that the products resulting from these cooperative R&D investments be sold in a non-cooperative way.

The objectives of competition policy

The reason why I did not want to elaborate on the objectives of antitrust policy is clear: the question is controversial and therefore not suitable for an official public lecture.[17] It is controversial, as soon as one enters into technical details. Of course, the ultimate and indisputable objective of competition policy is to improve consumers'

---

[15] See the Commission's memorandum *Le problème de la concurrence dans le Marché Commun*, CEE, Série concurrence, no. 3, 1966.

[16] A selection of more technical papers on vertical relationships can be found in the special issue of the *Journal of Industrial Economics*, vol. 39, September 1991, edited by John Vickers and Michael Waterson.

[17] Chapter 13 is my Presidential Address to the Prague Congress of the European Economic Association.

welfare. The interesting question is, however, to what extent one wishes to push this concern, given that consumers' welfare cannot generally be increased without hurting the producers, that is, without reducing profits. More precisely, there is probably general agreement that antitrust authorities should do what is necessary to get prices down towards marginal cost. But how far should they go down? Until they are equal to marginal cost?

'Price-equal-marginal-cost' is indeed what results from the theorems of welfare maximization based on general equilibrium theory. Define social welfare as the sum of consumers' surplus and producers' surplus. In general, the maximum of a sum of functions is not the sum of their maxima. This is unfortunately the case here: the maximum of social welfare, thus defined, is not the sum of the highest possible consumer surplus and the highest possible profits. (Unconstrained) social welfare maximization implies 'price equal marginal cost' and this in turn implies (a) zero profits when marginal cost is constant, (b) positive profits when marginal cost is increasing and (c) negative profits (losses!) when marginal cost is decreasing. Cases (a) and (c) are more likely to occur in the real world than case (b). I don't know of any antitrust authority in the world that would wish (or dare) to drive the firms under investigation into the red. Yet, an occasional statement that a price 'closer to marginal cost' is desirable can be found and is probably in the back of most economists' minds. So let us consider this in more formal terms.

An antitrust authority has among its main tasks to decide on (α) which cases of alleged collusion or predation to prosecute and (β) which fines to impose. It should be possible to determine the optimal combination of (α) and (β) by maximizing the authority's objective function.[18] Suppose this function is the social welfare function $W = S + \Pi$, where S is consumer surplus and Π represents profits. The immediate implication of maximizing W is that this authority should distrust quantity strategies (since the Cournot equilibrium price is above marginal cost) and do whatever is necessary to induce the firms under investigation to adopt Bertrand strategies. This authority should not only be sympathetic to firms that cheat on collusive agreements but also prosecute and fine any behaviour (such as information sharing) that makes cheating difficult. Price wars should be welcome, knowing that rational firms would not price below marginal cost. Any spatial pricing scheme other than fob-mill pricing should be forbidden (since they all imply price discrimination) as should parallel pricing and best-price policies.

The philosophy of the contributions collected in part II is different. If I was Director-General of DG IV, I would be very happy if my policy induced the firms under investigation to end up in a Cournot equilibrium. On this point, I received unexpected support from d'Aspremont and Motta (1994). They remark that excessive price competition may cause exits or bankruptcies – as happened in the US salt industry – leading to an increase in concentration which is not beneficial. Referring to the Sutton model of part I, they first consider a homogeneous good industry

---

[18] Besanko and Spulber (1989) do this under the assumptions that the authority does not know an industry's marginal cost and maximizes the consumer surplus.

composed of two firms facing the market demand function $X = S(1-p)$, where S measures market size as before. In a Cournot equilibrium each firm sells $S/3$ at a price of $1/3$, so that the producer surplus is $2(S/9)$. The consumers' surplus is $\frac{1}{2}\left[2\frac{S}{3}\left(1-\frac{1}{3}\right)\right] = \frac{2}{9}S$, so that $W = \frac{4}{9}S$. If the enforcement of competition policy forces these firms into Bertrand competition, short-run profits are driven to zero. Only one firm can survive, selling $S/2$ at the price $1/2$, making profits of $S/4$. The consumers' surplus is only $\frac{1}{2}\left(\frac{S}{2}\cdot\frac{1}{2}\right) = \frac{S}{8}$ and $W = \frac{3}{8}S$. Welfare has decreased since $\frac{4}{9} > \frac{3}{8}$! These sorts of changes in welfare, taking the market structure consequence of the intensity of price competition into account, is what should motivate anti-trust authorities (rather than welfare theorems based on instantaneous welfare maximization).

The example just given is overly simple. That is why d'Aspremont and Motta generalize it to a product differentiation model and show conditions under which Cournot competition allows a larger number of firms to operate in the industry than Bertrand competition. It turns out that total welfare is again higher under Cournot than under Bertrand, which should be no surprise if one remembers figure 1 above and my comment that excessive price cutting (Bertrand competition) forced the UK salt industry to reduce the number of producers and stop entry.

4   Mergers and merger control[19]

Although Salant, Switzer, and Reynolds (chapter 17) use special assumptions such as symmetry, linearity of market demand and constant marginal cost, their contribution deserves to come first, because it triggered off a fruitful debate on the effects of mergers and directly inspired a series of papers culminating in Farrell and Shapiro (chapter 18), who not only use general cost and demand functions but also discuss the special cases that result from the assumption of linearity on the demand or cost side (section 3.3) or relaxing it (see their sections 3.4 and 3.5). Their contribution is directly relevant for an evaluation of the US Merger Guidelines of 1984 and their discussion with G. Werden, a member of the Antitrust Division of the US Department of Justice (chapters 19 and 20), provides a better understanding of the guidelines and the insights given by theory. The two last chapters (22 and 23) make it possible to draw parallels between the actual enforcement of merger control in the US and in the European Union. Chapter 21 is devoted to vertical mergers.

In what follows, I want to briefly summarize what I have learned about the welfare effects of mergers and finally to raise the question of the possibility of monopolizing an industry through acquisition.

---

[19] I resisted the temptation to include papers that can be found in the Symposium on 'Horizontal Mergers and Antitrust', *Journal of Economic Perspectives*, Fall 1987, pp. 3–54 and in the special issue on 'Merger' of the *International Journal of Industrial Organization*, March 1989.

Effects of horizontal and vertical mergers

Two aspects of the Farrell–Shapiro chapter are of particular interest. First, the effects of mergers are analysed in terms of their impact on the *equilibrium* of the industry in which they occur, taking all interactions into account – both among the merging players and between the new firm and the non-participants. Second, this approach makes it possible to evaluate changes in welfare for the outsiders and the consumers, without having to measure the internal effects of a proposed merger, that is, the alleged internal efficiencies resulting from internal reorganization leading to 'synergies'. The practical enforcement of merger control could thus be drastically simplified, since the authority would not have to go into the inevitable efficiency arguments (economies of scale, economies of scope . . .) which the partners of a proposed merger come up with.

The effect on market prices, in equilibrium, of a horizontal merger is clear. In Werden's words, 'mergers that do not lower costs always raise price' and 'mergers that lower costs still raise price unless they lower costs quite a lot'. Inevitably then, if marginal cost is constant, as in the Salant–Switzer–Reynolds model, a merger raises the market price.

This result is valid for a market in a closed economy such as the US. In Europe, where the same good is sold in several markets (which are separated by vertical restraints – as explained above – if not by artificial trade barriers), the question arises how a merger in one market affects the price in these different markets through its effect on the extent of the pass-through of a devaluation on an appreciation of the currency of one of the markets. Kirman and Phlips (1996b) answer this non-trivial question in the framework of the Salant–Switzer–Reynolds model, which has the advantage of reducing a merger to a change in concentration (if two firms merge, the new firm is treated as a collection of plants under the control of one player in the same game with the number of players reduced by one), so that one sees the 'pure' effect of a change in the number of players. They consider two markets for a commodity, market 1 and market 2, separated by barriers other than tariffs and transportation costs. Market structure is oligopolistic in each: n firms located in market 1 and m firms located in market 2 each sell a commodity which is homogeneous within each market (but may differ between markets). All firms sell on both markets. Each market has its own currency. The market demand functions differ. Under these assumptions, it is shown that a merger increases the pass-through of an exchange-rate change in the market where this merger occurs if market demands are linear (so that all firms regard their product as a strategic substitute for their competitors' in both markets). For example, a merger in market 1 increases the pass-through of an appreciation of currency 2 in market 1, so that the post-merger equilibrium price increases more than the pre-merger price. This is consistent with the basic result that a merger 'raises the price'. Note that the same merger (in market 1) decreases the pass-through (of the devaluation of currency 1 which corresponds to the revaluation of currency 2) in market 2, where the post-merger equilibrium price decreases less than the pre-merger price.

Next consider an appreciation of currency 2 combined with a merger in market 2.

Then the post-merger equilibrium price increases less in market 1, which is compatible with the empirical finding that more-concentrated exporting industries lower their price markup more than less-concentrated industries when there is an appreciation of their domestic currency.

As for the welfare effect of horizontal mergers, ΔW is positive – where ΔW is the 'external' welfare effect, that is, the effect on the profit of the outsiders and on the consumers – if the aggregate market share of the insiders (participating in the merger) is smaller than the aggregate market share of the outsiders weighted by their individual responses (λ_i) to changes in industry output. In a linear world, $\lambda_i = 1$ for all outsiders, so that a horizontal merger is desirable (on this criterion) if it includes at most half the industry. On the other hand, a horizontal merger is profitable in this linear world only if more than 80 per cent of the firms in the industry take part in it. In practice, this means a merger to monopolize the industry.

Note that with vertical mergers everything is simple (or so it seems). Indeed, these mergers are not considered to be anticompetitive, because a merger of successive monopolists results in a reduction of the final good price by eliminating the double marginalization, as already noticed by Cournot (1838, chapter 5). However, this is valid only if the monopolist produces only one good, as pointed out by Salinger in chapter 21 with reference to Edgeworth's paradox.

Monopolization of an industry

The philosophy behind merger control is to prevent the 'monopolization' of an industry. So the ultimate question is: can mergers indeed result in such monopolization?

A first interpretation of this question is to ask whether a merger facilitates explicit collusion. An answer can be found in Selten's result that '4 are few and 6 are many': if there are less than five competitors in a market, they will all find it profitable to collude; if there are more than five, it becomes more advantageous to stay out of a cartel formed by others. Clearly, if a merger reduces the number of firms in an industry below five – and one accepts the linearity assumption of the Selten model – the remaining firms will all find it profitable to join a cartel, while before the merger only partial cartellization was profitable.

Another question is to ask whether a merger facilitates tacit collusion. The Selten result is not applicable here because it characterizes the equilibrium of a static game, while tacit collusion (as I define it) arises as the outcome of a repeated game. So one has to check how a reduction of the number of players affects the sustainability of a collusive outcome, which in turn depends on whether the players have an incentive to deviate from it. Deviation does not occur when it leads to future losses, due to retaliation, which are larger than the immediate gains from deviating. Here the discount factor used to evaluate future losses comes in: we know that no cheating will occur when that factor is high enough. If this limiting value is increased when the number of firms is reduced, then mergers make tacit collusion less likely, that is, more difficult to sustain as an equilibrium. Davidson and Deneckere (1984) show that this is indeed the case. If the punishment strategy is to produce Cournot–Nash quantities when cheating is detected, then the outside firms make higher profits at the Cournot equilibrium because of the merger. Thus, the losses due to the retaliation decline after the merger, the condition on the discount factor is strengthened and outsiders are more likely to cheat.

Finally, the most natural interpretation of the question whether mergers facilitate monopolization is to ask whether competitive acquisition of firms by their rivals can result in complete monopolization of an industry. The answer given by Kamien and Zang (1990), after a rather considerable amount of computations, is that complete monopolization is limited to industries with relatively few firms. They thus strengthen proposition F of Salant, Switzer, and Reynolds (chapter 17) that it is unprofitable for a given fraction of the industry to merge when n gets large and demand is linear. With non-linear demand, merging will also not occur when n is large enough even if the merged entity makes more than the separate entities did before the merger. The reason is *not* that numerically large industries are difficult to coordinate or that departure from agreed upon levels of output is more difficult to monitor. The reason is that each of the merged firms will want to make at least what it could by unilaterally abandoning the merger.

In the special case of linear market demand for a homogeneous good, three is the number of firms as of which only an equilibrium, in which the original industry structure is retained, can occur. Kamien and Zang (1990, pp. 470–2) illustrate this with the following example (of what they call a 'centralized game', that is, the case in which an owner possessing several firms operates them as one entity). The assumption is that each owner of a firm makes offers or bids for every other firm *and* announces an asking price at which he would sell out. I quote:

To crystallize our results, we offer the following example. Suppose that the inverse demand function is $P = 20 - Q$, where Q refers to total quantity sold, and that production is costless. It is not difficult to establish that a monopolist's profit in this case would be 100, a duopolist's profit would be 44.44, that each firm in a three-firm oligopoly would realize a profit of 25 at the Cournot equilibrium, 16 if there were four firms, and 11.11 if there were five.

[. . .]

We now turn to the outcomes that can arise in the centralized game if there are three firms in the industry. First note that, as in the case of $n = 2$, if the asking prices of all three owners are sufficiently high, say 37.5 or above, and their bids on all the others' firms are sufficiently low, say 25 or below, then no player will have an incentive to unilaterally change his asking price or bids, and consequently a three-firm oligopoly will prevail. Consider now the possibility of a monopoly equilibrium in this game. More specifically, suppose that the first owner acquired the firms owned by the other two. Note that the first owner, by lowering his bids for the two other firms below their asking prices, can refrain from buying them. Thus, he can guarantee himself at least the single-firm profit of 25 in a triopoly. If he acquires the two other firms and becomes a monopolist, he will make 100. Hence he will not be ready to purchase the other two firms for more than the difference, of 75, between the monopoly profit and the single-firm profit in a triopoly. Consider now the situation of a seller. If the first owner seeks to purchase all three firms, an owner, say the third, can raise his asking price above the bid he received from the first owner. If he does so unilaterally, then the first owner will purchase only one firm, own two, and operate only one. The industry will then turn into a duopoly. Thus, each seller can unilaterally assure himself 44.44, the single-firm profit in a duopoly. To prevent this and achieve a monopoly, the buyer has to pay each seller at least 44.44 or altogether 88.88 to the two of them. This is more than the 75 he can afford to pay. Thus, a monopoly equilibrium cannot obtain in this case. Using a similar argument, it is possible to show that an equilibrium, in which one owner purchases only one other firm turning the industry into a duopoly, also cannot arise. Indeed, in this case the buyer can afford to pay the seller no more than 44.44 − 25, while the seller can make 25 by deviating and raising his asking price.

In general, when the demand function is nonlinear and the number of firms in the industry is sufficiently large, a monopoly equilibrium cannot occur in the centralized game. The main reason for this is the combination of the potential buyer's unwillingness to pay more than the monopoly profit with the ability of each potential seller to guarantee himself the duopoly profit, when acquisition of all other firms took place.

For cartels, four are few and six are many. For mergers, two are few and four are many.

References

Baker, J.B. and T.F. Bresnahan (1992), 'Empirical methods of identifying and measuring market power', *Antitrust Law Journal*, 61, 1, 3–16.

Besanko, D. and D.F. Spulber (1989), 'Antitrust enforcement under asymmetric information', *The Economic Journal*, 99, 408–25.

Bonanno, G. and J. Vickers (1988), 'Vertical separation', *Journal of Industrial Economics*, 36, 257–65.

Bresnahan, T.F. (1989), 'Empirical studies of industries with market power', in R. Schmalensee and R. Willig (eds.), *Handbook of Industrial Organization*, vol. I, North-Holland, chapter 17.

Bulow, J.I., J.D. Geanakoplos, and P.D. Klemperer (1985), 'Multiproduct oligopoly: strategic substitutes and complements', *Journal of Political Economy*, 93, 488–511.

Cournot, A. (1838), *Recherches sur les Principes Mathématiques de la Théorie des Richesses*, Paris, Hachette.

d'Aspremont, C., R. Dos Santos Ferreira, and L.-A. Gérard-Varet (1991), 'Pricing schemes and Cournotian equilibria', *American Economic Review*, 81, 666–73.

d'Aspremont, C. and M. Motta (1994), 'Tougher price-competition or lower concentration: a trade-off for antitrust authorities?', CORE Discussion Paper no. 9415.

Daughety, A.G. (ed.) (1988), *Cournot Oligopoly, Characterization and Applications*, Cambridge.

Davidson, C. and R. Deneckere (1984), 'Horizontal mergers and collusive behaviour', *International Journal of Industrial Organization*, 2, 117–32.

Dierickx, I., C. Matutes, and D. Neven (1991), 'Cost differences and survival in declining industries', *European Economic Review*, 35, 1507–28.

Fishman, A. (1990), 'Entry deterrence in a finitely-lived industry', *Rand Journal of Economics*, 21, 63–71.

Friedman, J.W. (1977), *Oligopoly and the Theory of Games*, Amsterdam, North-Holland.

Ghemawat, P. and B. Nalebuff (1985), 'Exit', *Rand Journal of Economics*, 16, 184–94.

Kamien, M.I. and I. Zang (1990), 'The limits of monopolization through acquisition', *Quarterly Journal of Economics*, May, 465–99.

Kirman, A. and L. Phlips (1996a), 'Empirical studies of product markets', in B. Allen (ed.), *Economics in a Changing World*, vol. II, London, Macmillan and St Martin's Press.

(1996b), 'Exchange-rate pass-through and market structure', *Journal of Economics*, 64, 129–54.

Londregan, J. (1990), 'Entry and exit over the industry life cycle', *Rand Journal of Economics*, 21, 446–58.

MacLeod, W.B. (1985), 'A theory of conscious parallelism', *European Economic Review*, 27, 25–44.

Marshall, A. (1952), *Principles of Economics*, Eighth edition, London, Macmillan.

Matraves, C. (1996), 'Advertising, R&D, and market structure: The EU pharmaceutical industry', Wissenschaftszentrum, Berlin, mimeo.

Monopolies and Mergers Commission (1986), *White Salt: A Report on the Supply of White Salt in the United Kingdom by Producers of Such Salt*, London, HMSO.

Phlips, L. (1983), *The Economics of Price Discrimination*, Cambridge University Press.

(1988), *The Economics of Imperfect Information*, Cambridge University Press.

(1993), 'Basing point pricing, competition and market integration', in H. Ohta and J.-F. Thisse (eds.), *Does Economic Space Matter? Essays in Honor of M.L. Greenhut*, St. Martin's Press, pp. 303–15.

Rey, P. and J. Stiglitz (1995), 'The role of exclusive territories in producers' competition', *Rand Journal of Economics*, 26, 431–51.

Robinson, W.T. and J. Chiang (1996), 'Are Sutton's predictions robust?: empirical insights into advertising, R&D, and concentration', *Journal of Industrial Economics*, 64, 389–408.

Salop, S.C. (1986), 'Practices that (credibly) facilitate oligopoly coordination', in J.E. Stiglitz and G.F. Mathewson (eds.), *New Developments in the Analysis of Market Structure*, London, Macmillan.

Schmalensee, R. (1978), 'Entry deterrence in the ready-to-eat breakfast cereal industry', *Bell Journal of Economics*, 9, 305–27.

Selten, R. (1973), 'A simple model of imperfect competition where four are few and six are many', *International Journal of Game Theory*, 2, 141–201; reprinted in R. Selten, *Models of Strategic Rationality*, Kluwer Academic Publishers, 1988, pp. 95–155.

Shaked, A. and J. Sutton (1987), 'Product differentiation and industrial structure', *Journal of Industrial Economics*, 36, 131–46.

(1990), 'Multiproduct firms and market structure', *Rand Journal of Economics*, 21, 45–62.

Slade, M.E. (1986), 'Exogeneity tests of market boundaries applied to petroleum products', *Journal of Industrial Economics*, 35, 499–516.

Sutton, J. (1986), 'Vertical product differentiation: some basic themes', *American Economic Review (Papers and Proceedings)*, 76, 393–8.

(1991), *Sunk Costs and Market Structure*, Cambridge, MA., MIT Press.

(1996), 'Technology and market structure', *European Economic Review*, 40, 511–30.

Whinston, M. (1988), 'Exit with multiplant firms', *Rand Journal of Economics*, 19, 568–89.

Part I

MARKET STRUCTURE

Chapter 1

Game theory and industry studies
An introductory overview

John Sutton

1.1 A statistical regularity

Many authors have observed that the ranking of industries by concentration level tends to be closely similar from one country to another: an industry that is dominated by a handful of firms in one country is likely to be dominated by a handful of firms elsewhere too.[1] This 'statistical regularity' has occasioned a wide range of response in the literature. The large majority of studies argue in favour of the existence of such a regularity and interpret it as a reflection of the fact that the pattern of technology and tastes that characterize a given market may be expected to be similar across different

---

This chapter previously appeared as chapter 1 of John Sutton's *Sunk Costs and Market Structure: Price Competition, Advertising, and the Evolution of Concentration*, MIT Press, 1991, and refers to other chapters in that book.

[1] The issue was raised by Bain (1966). An ambitious early study by Pryor (1972) covered 12 countries. That study suffered from one serious limitation, however, insofar as it used official statistics on concentration ratios that involved different levels of aggregation for certain industry groups, in different countries. Phlips (1971) avoided this problem by taking advantage of the newly available statistics for EEC countries, which were based on a common set of industry definitions. A similar approach was followed by George and Ward (1975). More recently, Connor *et al.* (1985) have carried out comparisons for industries within the food and drink sector over OECD countries. All these authors conclude that a high degree of correlation exists, whether comparisons are made on a pairwise basis (regressing UK concentration levels on US levels, etc.) or otherwise. Many studies indicate an unusually wide disparity of experience between the United Kingdom and the United States; the relatively poor correlation obtaining in this case was emphasized by the early study of Shepherd (1961).

countries. For this reason, the industry's equilibrium structure may in turn be similar from one country to another. While some authors have regarded this similarity of structure as rather trivial and of little interest, many, if not most, authors have seen it as providing considerable encouragement for the view that the underlying pattern of technology and tastes strongly constrains equilibrium structure (Scherer, 1980; Caves, 1989; Connor, *et al.*, 1985).

Closely related to this empirical regularity is an important strand in the traditional literature on industrial structure, which aims to explain differences in concentration across industries by reference to a small number of candidate explanatory variables that are taken to reflect basic industry characteristics. Typically, the degree of scale economies, the intensity of advertising, and the level of R&D expenditure have been regarded as key variables. This study attempts to develop a new approach to this issue.

Most of the existing empirical work on cross-sectional differences in structure is based on an appeal to the structure/conduct/performance paradigm of Bain (1956). Within that paradigm, it is supposed that a one-way chain of causation runs from *structure* (the level of concentration) to *conduct* (the degree of collusion), and from conduct to *performance* (profitability). Structure, in this setting, is explained by the presence of certain barriers to entry, whose height can be measured by the degree of scale economies in the industry and by observed levels of advertising and R&D outlays relative to industry sales. This approach has for example motivated various empirical studies that seek to explain structure by regressing observed concentration levels on measures of scale economies, advertising intensity, R&D intensity, and so on (see chapter 5).[2]

Bain's pioneering studies laid the foundations for a generation of subsequent work. His approach, however, has been subjected to considerable criticism both by empirical researchers during the 1960s and 1970s and by contributors to the game-theoretic literature of the past decade. The approach taken in this study, like many contributions to the recent game-theoretic literature, differs sharply from that of the Bain paradigm. The key theoretical differences between the two approaches are set out in section 1.4.

This volume also differs from much of the earlier literature in terms of its empirical focus. Here the starting point of the analysis lies in an alleged tendency for a given industry to be less concentrated, in those countries in which the size of the market (as measured by the total volume of sales) is larger. This negative relationship between market size and concentration has been noted by several authors (Phlips, 1971; George and Ward, 1975; Schmalensee, 1989), but it has not received much attention in the past. After all, it seems a 'natural' result and one that can be immediately explained by reference to traditional ideas. Put loosely, we might expect that given any particular configuration of barriers to entry, an expansion in the size of the market will raise the profitability of incumbents and so induce more potential entrants to surmount that barrier, thus leading to a fall in concentration.

---

[2] Please note that the chapters referred to are chapters in Sutton's book, not this publication!

This relationship between market size and market structure stands at the center of my analysis, which is developed in three steps. The first step lies in describing a new theoretical rationale for the appearance of a negative relationship between market size and concentration, which is quite different to that embodied in the post-Bain literature. The second step involves the central claim of the present study. It says that this size–structure relationship, which has traditionally been seen as holding across industries generally, is in fact only valid for a certain group of industries. Most important, it is not valid for those industries in which advertising and R&D outlays play a significant role. In this latter context, it is argued that the negative relationship between market size and concentration levels breaks down for reasons that are quite fundamental.

The third step in the argument lies in developing some implications. Once the mechanisms leading both to the appearance of this negative relationship and to its breakdown in advertising and R&D-intensive industries is understood, we are led to a new way of organizing many long-standing ideas regarding the determinants of cross-industry differences in structure. Those few empirical relationships that have emerged consistently in earlier empirical work now emerge as corollaries of certain relationships implied by the present theory. At the same time, we are led to a series of new approaches to a wide range of phenomena, noted in earlier empirical work, and to some new insights regarding a number of long-standing controversies.

But why should the relationship between market size and market structure merit such attention in the first place? The reason for this lies in the fact that the present characterization of the size–structure relationship represents one of the relatively few robust theoretical results to have emerged from the recent game-theoretic literature. To see the point of this remark, it is necessary to digress a little.

1.2   Game-theoretic model

Within the recent game-theoretic literature, numerous authors have sought to examine the long-run issues surrounding the determination of industrial structure (see Dasgupta and Stiglitz, 1980; Shaked and Sutton, 1982; and Vickers, 1986). One feature basic to this game-theoretic literature, however, is that the results of such analyses tend to depend delicately on the precise form of the underlying game.

Game-theoretic oligopoly models employ various simple building blocks that carry key distinctions of empirical interest. For example, we may capture the notion of the toughness of price competition by distinguishing a 'Bertrand' formulation, a 'Cournot' formulation, or a 'joint-profit-maximization' formulation. Again, we may capture the presence or absence of some strategic asymmetry in the firms' relations to each other by contrasting a sequential moves formulation with a simultaneous moves formulation.

But these distinctions can often be mapped into empirical categories only in a rather loose and informal way. We may be willing to accept some particular formulation as a reasonable representation for some specific market, at least in the sense of a 'prior' or null hypothesis. But if we aim to investigate statistical regularities that are presumed to hold across a range of different industries, between which the toughness of price competition or the degree of strategic asymmetry may vary, it may be extremely problematic to identify any measurable market characteristic that can act as an adequate proxy in capturing such distinctions.

Many researchers have come to feel that a natural response to such difficulties is to focus analysis on some specific market, or some set of virtually identical markets, so that we can tailor-make the oligopoly model to fit that specific context. The 'ultra-micro' work to which we are led along this route is now one of the most lively areas of empirical research in industrial economics.[3]

These observations have led to a growing skepticism about the value of searching for statistical regularities that hold across a broad run of different industries. After all, if current theory indicates that most results are delicately dependent upon certain factors that are liable to vary widely across different industries and we cannot measure or proxy these in any satisfactory way, then the basis of running cross-industry regressions might appear to be somewhat dubious.

A central thesis of the present study is that this currently popular view is unduly pessimistic. Moreover, a too-rigid adherence to such a view runs the risk of abandoning a central part of the traditional agenda of the subject, which concerns the investigation of regularities of behaviour that hold across the general run of industries.

The point of departure lies in the observation that a fundamental trade-off exists between the degree of precision of predictions that obtain across a class of models and the breadth of applications of that class. Tight predictions may demand quite stringent a priori restrictions on the model(s); but it may nonetheless be possible to find some (necessarily weak) predictions that are robust in the sense that they hold across a wide class of models and so lend themselves to implementation across a correspondingly broad set of different industries.

The approach taken in what follows, then, is to begin by looking to such robust predictions as will hold across a wide class of reasonable models, and to use these predictions as a basis for cross-industry regressions. What kind of results can be obtained at this level of generality? It turns out that certain robust results can be obtained that relate to the specification of a *lower bound* to the equilibrium level of concentration as a function of the size of the market. The properties of such bounds are studied in detail, and their role is examined empirically by reference to cross-country comparisons of industry structure. A number of ancillary results are also obtained at this general level, which again can be investigated by reference to cross-country comparisons.

In parallel with the development of this general framework, various special cases within the theory are investigated, and these may be used as a vehicle both for tracing

---

[3] For a selection of such studies, see the *Journal of Industrial Economics* symposium of June 1987. Influential contributions include Hendricks and Porter (1988) on the auctioning of offshore oil leases, Slade (1987) on gasoline price wars, and Bresnahan and Reiss (1990) on the relationship between the size of towns and the number of retail outlets.

the evolution of particular industries and for generating a richer menu of testable predictions appropriate to a correspondingly narrower domain. The next three sections are devoted to providing a chapter-by-chapter summary of the study as a whole.

1.3   An outline of the theory

The theory developed below derives from the recent vertical product differentiation literature. The starting point of this analysis, as developed by Shaked and Sutton (1982, 1987) and elaborated in Sutton (1989a), lies in the observation that advertising and R&D can both be thought of as sunk costs incurred with a view to enhancing consumers' willingness-to-pay for the firm's product(s). Focusing attention on this relationship makes possible a simple unified treatment of these two contributory factors. Now R&D and advertising outlays are choice variables to the firms, and so their levels must be determined endogenously as part of the specification of industry equilibrium. The role of scale economies, on the other hand, can be introduced by treating the acquisition of a single plant of minimum efficient scale as involving an element of sunk cost that must be incurred by all entrants, and whose level is determined exogenously by the nature of the underlying technology.

The central focus of the present theory lies in unravelling the way in which these *exogenous* and *endogenous* elements of sunk cost interact with each other in determining the equilibrium pattern of industrial structure. This theoretical framework is set out in detail in chapters 2 and 3. In what follows, a brief description of the main features of the theory is presented, as a prelude to summarizing the contents of later chapters.

Exogenous sunk costs (i)

The way in which the central notion of *sunk costs* is captured in the present study is by modelling industry equilibrium in terms of a two-stage game. At stage 1 of the game firms incur fixed outlays, which are associated with acquiring a single plant of minimum efficient scale (set-up costs), and developing and establishing a product line (possibly incurring advertising and R&D outlays). These fixed outlays incurred at stage 1 of the game are treated as sunk costs in analysing price competition at the second stage of the game. In the latter stage of the game, all firms are assumed to operate at the same constant level of marginal cost.

Consider first the case in which the only sunk costs involved are the exogenously given set-up costs. Within this case it is useful to distinguish two subcases. The first subcase is that in which the various firms produce a homogeneous product. In this setting, as the size of the market (measured by the population of consumers) increases, the equilibrium number of firms entering the market increases, and so concentration declines indefinitely. To see this, note that entry occurs up to the point at which the (stage 2) profits of the last entrant cover the sunk cost incurred on entry at stage 1. But, for any given level of concentration in the industry, any increase in the size of the market will tend to raise these profits and so induce further entry. Thus concentration declines indefinitely as market size increases (except under very special circumstances; see chapter 2).

This case, then, corresponds to some familiar limit theorems of the standard theoretical literature; and it offers one way of characterizing the traditional idea that scale economies become unimportant as a constraint on equilibrium structure in large economies. What may be less obvious is the way in which this process is affected by the nature of price competition at stage 2 of the game. When analysing stage 2, concentration is taken as fixed – being inherited as a result of decisions made at stage 1, which are now irreversible (i.e., they embody sunk costs). Now this means that we can properly build into our analysis of this stage of the game (i.e., the stage 2 subgame) the traditional Bain hypothesis on conduct: that prices (and so unit margins) decline as concentration falls. Within the present theory, this notion is embodied in the form of a *function* linking concentration to prices or unit margins. This *function* will be affected by such features of the market as the physical nature of the product (homogeneous versus differentiated products) and the climate of competition policy (a strict or acquiescent approach to price coordination by firms). In what follows, references to the 'toughness of price competition' in a market will always refer to this *function* – and *not* to the level of prices or unit margins observed at equilibrium. (In other words, differences in the toughness of price competition across two different markets relate to the way in which margins *would* differ between those markets where concentration held at the same arbitrary level in both.)

It is shown in chapter 2 that according as price competition is tougher in this sense the equilibrium level of concentration will be correspondingly *higher*. The intuition underlying this result is simply that the anticipation of a tougher competitive regime makes entry less attractive, thus raising equilibrium concentration levels. One of the main attractions of the two-stage game formulation is that it allows a neat unravelling of this latter effect from the traditional Bain effects (higher concentration implies higher margins, and higher profitability). To sum up: where sunk costs are exogenous, and where firms offer a homogeneous product, the equilibrium level of concentration declines with the ratio of market size to set-up cost and rises with the toughness of price competition.

Exogenous sunk costs (ii)

The next subcase to be considered is that in which firms offer products that are differentiated, but in which sunk costs are still exogenously determined. This case has been widely explored in the horizontal product differentiation literature; the archetypal example arises in simple locational models of the Hotelling kind (a brief description of these standard models is provided in chapter 2). In these models, consumers are spread over some geographic region, and they incur (psychic or transport) costs in purchasing from distant suppliers. Each firm may establish any number of plants, incurring a given set-up cost per plant. Consumers thereafter make their purchases from the lowest-cost supplier, where the cost to the consumer consists of the price paid to the firm plus a transport cost that increases with his distance from the supplier.

In models of this kind, multiple equilibria are endemic. In general, for any given market size, we may find fragmented equilibria, in which a large number of firms each sell at one location, and concentrated equilibria, in which a small number of firms each sell at many locations. In chapter 2 the factors underlying the appearance of these two types of equilibria are set out; these factors are likely to vary widely from one industry to another. Thus, if we are interested in finding properties robust enough to be of interest in cross-industry studies, we cannot constrain possible equilibrium configurations here, beyond saying that the bound corresponding to the most fragmented configuration (single-product firms) forms a *lower bound* to equilibrium concentration. This bound declines with market size in the manner of the schedule described above for the homogeneous product case.

The case, then, is that in which the present theory *least* constrains the data; and so this set of industries provides the first of several illustrations of the inherent limitations of this theory, insofar as robust predictions appropriate to a broad cross-section of industries are involved. It is perhaps worth remarking, therefore, that even in this case the theory *does* in fact yield some quite sharp predictions. But these predictions depend in all cases upon market features that are likely to vary widely from one industry to another and that are difficult to measure or proxy in many instances (Shaked and Sutton, 1990).

Bringing together these remarks on the two subcases, then, a central conclusion for the *exogenous sunk cost* regime may be phrased as follows: an increase in the size of the market relative to set-up costs may lead to the appearance of indefinitely low levels of concentration in these industries. It is precisely this property that breaks down once we turn to the next case.

Endogenous sunk costs

We now turn to the case of *endogenous sunk costs*. These cost components may be of various kinds; the two most obvious examples, though not the only ones, are advertising and R&D outlays (see chapter 14). Suppose that, by incurring greater advertising (or R&D) outlays at stage 1 of the game, a firm can enhance the demand for its product at stage 2 (i.e., for any prices set by other firms, the demand schedule of the firm in question shifts outward). Then it is fairly obvious that the game played at stage 1 might involve a competitive escalation of outlays by firms and so lead to higher sunk costs being incurred at equilibrium. It is also fairly obvious that the larger the size of the market – and so the profits achievable at stage 2 – the greater might be the sunk costs thereby incurred at equilibrium.

What is not obvious is that this is not merely a *possible* outcome; rather, on examining a range of different oligopoly models, an unusually robust result arises in this case, which runs contrary to that found in the exogenous sunk cost case. This result says that under very general conditions a lower bound exists to the equilibrium level of concentration in the industry, no matter how large the market becomes.

The level of this lower bound depends on the degree of demand responsiveness faced by an individual firm to increases in its fixed (advertising or R&D) outlays at stage 1 of the game. The higher the degree of responsiveness, the higher will be the lower bound to equilibrium concentration levels in the industry.

The central assumption of this study, then, is that across a certain range of industries, advertising works; loosely stated, it is postulated that the degree of responsivenesss of demand to advertising outlays for any one of a number of competing firms always exceeds some minimal level. An exact statement of this assumption must be deferred to chapter 3.

Under these circumstances, increases in market size cannot lead to a fragmented market structure as the size of the market increases. Rather, a competitive escalation in outlays at stage 1 of the game raises the equilibrium level of sunk costs incurred by incumbent firms in step with increases in the size of the market – thus offsetting the tendency towards fragmentation.

The importance of this simple but basic result lies in the fact that it holds over an extremely wide class of oligopoly models. For example, the result holds independently of whether each firm offers a single product or a range of products. It holds independently of the form price competition takes at stage 2 of the game (Bertrand, Cournot, etc.). Furthermore, it is not affected by altering the sequence of moves in the entry stage of the game (simultaneous entry, sequential entry, etc.). The degree of robustness of this result to changes in model specification makes it a suitable candidate for investigation in a cross-industry setting.

The above comments on the *exogenous* sunk costs case imply that, if we confine attention to some set of industries in which advertising and R&D outlays are insignificant and examine how concentration varies with the size of the market across different countries, then we should expect the lower bound to observed concentration levels to fall as the size of the market rises relative to the set-up costs incurred in entering the industry. The central prediction of the theory is that this relationship should break down among advertising-intensive industries. The precise way in which the relationship fails, and the testable implications of this result, are developed in chapter 3.

Further themes explored in chapter 3 include the question of how exogenous sunk costs *interact* with endogenous sunk costs in determining industrial structure. Attention is also directed towards various special cases arising within this general theoretical framework. The most important of these special cases relates to the role played by 'first-mover advantages' in determining equilibrium structure and to the factors leading to the evolution of dual structure – in which a small number of leading firms spending heavily on advertising and enjoying large market shares coexists with a possibly large fringe of non-advertisers who sell on price.

Econometric tests

The theoretical framework developed in chapters 2 and 3, then, leads to a basic prediction about the way in which the market size/market structure relationship will vary between industries in which sunk costs are exogenously given and those in which endogenous sunk costs such as advertising or R&D play a significant role. This book is concerned with exploring this and other predictions of the theory within the context of a group of advertising-intensive industries.[4] In chapter 4, the rationale underlying the selection of this group of industries is set out in some detail. Broadly, the aim was to find a group of cognate industries in which R&D played an insignificant role and in which levels of advertising intensity were high on average, but varied widely across different industries within the group. Based on these criteria, the food and drink sector provided an obvious choice. This sector, which comprises about one-eighth of all manufacturing industry in the countries studied, has both the highest level of advertising intensity among all two-digit SIC groups and is among the lowest of all such groups in terms of R&D intensity.[5] This study is based on the experience of 20 narrowly defined food and drink industries across six countries (France, Germany, Italy, Japan, the United Kingdom, and the United States). These industries divide into two groups. In the first group, advertising outlays are extremely low in almost all cases; and these industries provide a benchmark case corresponding to the exogenous sunk cost case of the theory. In the other group of industries, the levels of advertising intensity are moderate to high; and the evolution of this group is examined by reference to the endogenous sunk cost case.

In chapter 5, a cross-sectional econometric analysis of observed concentration levels is presented, the results of which are consistent with the theory. These results, moreover, are *not* consistent with the alternative view, that observed advertising levels can be regarded as exogenously given, that is, determined by product characteristics and other factors, independent of market size.

A second important theme developed in chapter 5 is that those few statistical regularities that have emerged more or less consistently in the earlier literature in this area can be shown to follow as a *consequence* of the basic regularity identified here. Thus the present theory, as well as generating new findings, appears successfully to provide an explanation consistent with these well-known empirical relationships.

Cross-industry regression results always invite alternative interpretations, however,

[4] There are good reasons to divide the task of implementing the theory in this way, in spite of its emphasis on the similarities of the advertising and R&D cases. In the case of advertising-intensive industries, a great deal can be learned from cross-country comparisons of structure, since the sunk costs incurred by a firm in advertising its product in one country do not carry over to other countries. (Its brand image must be established anew in each country.) This is not so for R&D outlays, and most R&D-intensive industries are best treated as unified global markets. It is also worth remarking at this point that even at the theoretical level, the case of R&D is somewhat more complex than that of advertising, and an adequate treatment of the R&D case requires some extensions of the theoretical framework developed here (see chapter 14).

[5] In the United States, for example, the food and drink sector accounted for 12 per cent of the total value of production in manufacturing in 1980 (Connor *et al.*, 1985). The level of private R&D expenditure as a proportion of sales was lowest, equal with textiles and apparel, at 0.4 per cent in 1975 (Scherer 1980, p. 410). The level of advertising expenditure relative to sales far outruns that of any other sector. Food and tobacco advertising accounted for 32 per cent of advertising of all manufactured products in the United States in 1979, but for only 12 per cent of all sales of manufactures (Connor *et al.*, 1985, p. 80).

and in the following industry studies an attempt is made to probe the validity of the interpretation offered here by investigating whether the pattern of evolution of structure in these two industry groups exhibits those different qualitative features implied by the theory.

Industry studies

The core of this book consists of a matrix of industry studies, which has been compiled using a combination of published market research reports and a lengthy programme of meetings with senior marketing executives in the industries concerned. An attempt was made, whenever possible, to provide accounts of the industry that were complete relative to the theory. One aim of this exercise is to provide the appropriate background information to readers who may wish to explore alternative explanations for the statistical regularities of chapter 5.

By building up a detailed profile of each industry, it was possible to go much further in probing the validity of the theory than would have been possible solely on the basis of a cross-sectional econometric analysis. Apart from directly testing the implications of the theory, moreover, these industry studies make possible a number of ancillary exercises. The presentation of these studies has, for expositional reasons, been arranged around a number of major themes.

Testing the theory I : two mechanisms

The central idea of the theory lies in the claim that two qualitatively different mechanisms operate to prevent certain fragmented configurations from persisting over time – the claim is that such configurations are not (Nash) equilibria, that is, they will be broken because, in such a configuration, it will always be optimal for one firm to deviate in a way that destroys that configuration.

(i) With the exogenous sunk costs model, a too fragmented configuration will break down because it is impossible to maintain price-cost margins sufficient to generate a normal rate of return on the set-up costs incurred in establishing plants; and while this is perfectly possible in the *short run*, it is not consistent with a *long-run* equilibrium situation in which obsolete plants need to be replaced periodically. Attempts by firms to coordinate prices to a degree sufficient to recover these outlays will fail unless a level of concentration is achieved that exceeds the lower bound consistent with equilibrium (see chapter 2 for details).

(ii) Within advertising-intensive industries, a second mechanism operates to exclude the persistence of certain fragmented configurations. In this setting, as has already been noted, the mechanism involves a competitive escalation of advertising outlays in the initially fragmented industry.

The first theme explored in the industry studies lies in examining whether the histories of these two groups of industries provide any evidence for the alleged operation of these two distinct mechanisms. Although these mechanisms recur throughout many of the chapters that follow, the contrast between them is best illustrated by reference to chapters 6 and 8.

Chapter 6 is devoted to the application of the exogenous sunk cost model to a study of the salt and sugar industries. These two industries are characterized by a high degree of product homogeneity and a fairly high level of set-up cost relative to market size. The theory predicts that, in this setting, a process of free competition will lead to a highly concentrated structure. The experience of the salt industry offers a striking example of this mechanism. In the case of US and British industries, whose history is relatively well documented, the market was initially quite fragmented. Both industries were characterized by strong price cutting, especially in periods of declining demand and repeated attempts to bring about price coordination among the many firms ended in failure. In each case, poor profitability led to a mixture of exit and of merger and acquisition activity, and it was this process which in turn led to a consolidated industry structure within which unit margins were stabilized and profitability recovered. Current concentration levels in these industries greatly exceed those levels that have been considered 'warranted' by previous observers (the traditional notion of warranted concentration levels is discussed in the next section).

The central novelty of the present theory in this context is that the equilibrium level of concentration is argued to depend inter alia on the toughness of price competition in the market. The theory predicts that if institutional factors cause price competition to become less tough (in the sense that higher unit margins can be sustained at any *given* level of concentration), then the *equilibrium* level of concentration will be correspondingly lower. The obvious way to probe the validity of this argument is to look to cases in which institutional factors impinge to varying degrees on the free play of competition in different markets. Except where state monopolies exist, the salt industry has in most cases operated with minimal intervention by the authorities. Policy measures in the industry have for the most part been 'pro-competitive', in that they have involved no more than occasional attempts to limit or prohibit price fixing. But the sugar industry, in contrast, usually enjoys the support of a strong agricultural lobby, and the authorities' approach to price determination in the industry has varied widely, both across countries and over time. In some cases, the authorities have favoured unfettered competition; in others they have effectively determined industry margins, with a view to either stabilizing or rationalizing industry structure. In others, policy has varied sharply in different periods.

In contrast to the salt industry, which is highly concentrated everywhere, the sugar industry shows a wide divergence of structure across countries. In chapter 6, it is argued that these differences in structure can be traced directly to the differences in policy regime in a manner consistent with the theory.

The cases of salt and sugar, then, illustrate the way in which the toughness of price competition impinges on the determination of structure in those industries where set-up costs are high in relation to market size. The evolution of concentration in these two industries stands in sharp contrast to the pattern observed in advertising-intensive industries.

44   John Sutton

Chapter 8, a pivotal chapter, begins the exploration of advertising-intensive industries by examining the evolution of structure in the frozen food market. This case is of special interest, as this is one of the rare examples of an advertising-intensive industry within the food and drink sector whose origin is both recent and sharply defined. The industry's beginnings can be traced to the development of certain freezing processes in the 1930s, and the early history of the industry, especially in the United States and the United Kingdom, is well documented.

The themes explored in chapter 8 provide a clear illustration of the mechanism postulated in the present theory as applying to industries that exhibit endogenous sunk costs. The set-up costs incurred in entering the frozen food industry are quite low; and the market includes both a retail segment (within which advertising is quite effective) and non-retail segments in which buyers choose suppliers almost wholly on the basis of relative price. Under such circumstances, the theory predicts that increases in market size may lead to an indefinite expansion in the total number of firms, but that the (advertising-sensitive) retail sector will remain concentrated, while advertising outlays by leading sellers in the retail sector expand in step with the size of the market. (The theoretical basis for the evolution of this dual structure is described in chapter 3.) A competitive escalation of advertising outlays will necessarily lead to a situation in which only a small number of firms survive and dominate the retail segment of the market.

This process is well illustrated by the history of the frozen food industries of the United States and the United Kingdom. In each case, it is possible to pinpoint the exact phase at which firms became partitioned into two discrete groups: a high-advertising group selling primarily to the retail sector, and a non-advertising group selling solely to the non-retail sector. Indeed, it is possible to trace the way in which firms situated between these two groups faced declining profitability until this split was achieved.

While the frozen food industries provide an unusually clear-cut illustration of this process, the same process can be seen to operate in a wide number of instances explored in later chapters. In many of these cases, however, the appearance of the high advertising group can be traced to the turn of the century, and documentation of the structure of the industries at that time is often sparse. Moreover, the partitioning of firms into two groups appears to have taken place in a more gradual and less dramatic fashion than in the case of the frozen food industry. This may in part reflect the lesser scale and effectiveness of advertising prior to the advent of television. These qualifications apart, however, the same process appears to have operated across a wide range of those advertising-intensive industries that are explored in later chapters.

Testing the theory II : comparative static predictions

A central issue concerns how the exogenous and endogenous elements of sunk costs *interact*. How does a higher level of set-up costs affect equilibrium advertising outlays and equilibrium structure, other things being equal? Since other things are rarely equal, examining this question empirically poses considerable difficulties. As far as theoretical predictions are concerned, chapter 2 shows that a rise in set-up cost will lead to a more concentrated equilibrium structure; this modest result, however, is the only robust comparative static result within the endogenous sunk cost model. In respect of advertising, a rise in set-up costs from an initially very low level will at first imply a rise in the advertising–sales ratio. As set-up costs continue to rise, however, the advertising–sales ratio may continue to rise, or it may fall. The outcome will depend delicately on the details of the model – and most importantly on the extent to which increases in total *industry* advertising affect total *industry* sales. This feature of the market will differ sharply across different industries, so that no robust result is available.

Investigating such comparative static properties is made difficult, in general, by the presence of a multitude of industry-specific characteristics whose effect may be extremely hard to quantify. The analysis of chapter 12 takes advantage of the fact that two pairs of industries within the present sample offer an unusually helpful context in which to examine this issue, for in each case the two industries in question have set-up costs that differ by a very large factor, while the other economic characteristics of the industry are closely similar. The production of instant coffee involves set-up costs very much greater than those incurred by the typical producer of ground (or roast and ground) coffee. Within the confectionery industry, the set-up costs incurred by producers of mass-market chocolate confectionery items exceeds by an order of magnitude the costs incurred by the typical producer of sugar confectionery. In each of these cases, we find that the industry with the higher set-up costs is more highly concentrated. Furthermore, differences in set-up costs vary across different market segments; and a detailed analysis of how concentration differences mirror these differences in the pattern of market segmentation offers further support to this interpretation. Finally, it is shown that, within the confectionery sector, the high set-up cost (chocolate confectionery) industry displays a systematically higher advertising–sales ratio. This is not true within the coffee industry, however: here the advertising–sales ratio in the instant coffee market may be higher or lower than the ratio obtaining in the ground coffee market. While considerable caution is needed in interpreting these differences in experience, they appear in part to reflect the extent to which *total* advertising outlays for instant coffee are likely to expand total instant coffee sales (at the expense of total sales of ground coffee) as the present theory implies.

Special cases: first-mover advantages

One important role played by the industry studies that follow lies in allowing an exploration of various special cases arising within the general theoretical framework. One such special case arises in respect of 'first-mover advantages': to what extent do strategic asymmetries between early entrants to an industry and firms that enter later impinge on the equilibrium pattern of structure? Here, the results of a game-theoretic analysis suggest that the outcome depends delicately on the details of the model; and so in this context the focus is *not* on testing theory, but is merely exploratory. The aim is to examine on the basis of industry histories how such influences may play a part in accounting for the often wide divergence of structure in the same industry from one country to another.

It is often extremely difficult in practice, however, to decide whether or not a particular firm enjoys this kind of strong strategic asymmetry relative to its rivals. But there are some instances in which the historical and institutional background point to a sharp asymmetry between firms, of a kind that can reasonably be represented by a simple sequential entry model. Chapter 9 examines three industries in which a very clear-cut first-mover advantage was present and traces the apparent consequences of this strategic asymmetry for the evolution of structure.

In the prepared soups industry the contrast between the United Kingdom and the United States is of particular interest, as the same two firms dominate each of these markets. Their roles in the two markets are precisely reversed, however, with the US market leader Campbell filling the same role in the United Kingdom market as does the UK market leader Heinz in the US market. This similarity of roles extends to such areas as the two firms' pricing policy, their decisions as to whether to supply retailers' own-label products, and so on; and these differences can be traced to the fact that each country's current market leader enjoyed a first-mover advantage over its rival in that country. In this case, the structure of the industry is closely similar in both countries, and only the roles of the leading players differ.

A second example illustrates how the presence or absence of first-mover advantages may exert an apparently profound effect on the overall structure of the industry. In the margarine market, Unilever enjoyed a strong first-mover advantage in the various European markets, where it still enjoys a leadership position. In the US market, however, a strong agricultural lobby effectively stifled the development of the margarine market until the 1950s, by which time a number of major US food producers had developed a position in the industry. Thus, no one firm had a first-mover advantage on the eve of the rapid takeoff in margarine sales, which coincided with the growth of television as the dominant advertising channel during the 1950s. The outcome was a less-concentrated overall structure, in which Unilever competes on a more or less equal basis with two major indigenous food producers (Kraft and Proctor & Gamble).

A third example of a first-mover advantage arises in the soft drink market. The Coca-Cola Company and Pepsico enjoy rough parity in the US market, and the escalating competition between the two has played a central role in shaping the evolution of the US industry. In Europe, however, a sharp asymmetry exists between the two, which can be traced to a series of events that took place during the Second World War. In return for its commitment to 'put a Coke in the hand of every US serviceman' for 10 cents, the Coca-Cola Company was made exempt from wartime sugar rationing, and the resulting ubiquity of Coca-Cola set the stage for the continuing dominance of Coca-Cola over Pepsi throughout post-war Europe. It is argued in chapter 9 that this asymmetry may be one of the contributory factors underlying the wide divergence in structure in this industry in the United States and Europe.

The limitations of the theory

Another theme that runs through the industry studies relates to the limitations of the theory – indeed, one of the main virtues of constructing such a matrix of industry studies is that it provides an unusually detailed feel for both the strengths and the limitations of the theory. The limitations are of two kinds:

1 The theory predicts only a *lower bound* to equilibrium concentration levels. The lower this minimal equilibrium level, the less the theory constrains the data.

   This implies an inherent limitation in the theory, the importance of which varies across different groups of industry. This issue is explored in chapters 7 and 8.

2 The usefulness of this theory rests on the assumption that the advertising response function depends only on certain (unspecified) product characteristics, which may be assumed similar across countries, and on *observable* institutional factors, which may differ across countries.

While this assumption appears, on the basis of the evidence, to be broadly reasonable, occasional instances arise in which idiosyncratic factors peculiar to certain firms or markets profoundly influence the extent to which advertising 'works'. A good illustration of this kind of effect, which highlights a potentially serious limitation to the value of theories of this kind, is provided by the experience of the mineral water market. Perrier's success in the French market, and its competitors' reaction to that success, transformed the structure of the industry within a few years. In no other country has Perrier, or any other company, achieved a similar success. Indeed, in the three main European markets (France, Germany, Italy), apparently closely similar market conditions coexist with levels of concentration that diverge very widely from one country to another (chapter 11) .

Controversial cases

The final theme explored in the industry studies relates to the re-examination of some cases that have received heavy emphasis in the recent literature in terms of the present theoretical framework.

One of the most crucial US antitrust cases in recent years was that brought by the Federal Trade Commission (FTC) against the Kellogg Company and its main rivals in the ready-to-eat (RTE) breakfast cereals industry. The case was interpreted in some quarters as constituting a test for a new departure in antitrust practice – a departure in favour of government intervention in markets on the basis of an examination of structural features (concentration) per se, independent of any observed anticompetitive practices. Under these circumstances, it is not surprising that the case attracted an unusual degree of interest among industrial economists, and the causes of concentration in the industry became a much debated issue. The most popular theory to emerge was that proposed by Schmalensee (1978), who proposed that Kellogg's dominant position could be traced to a process of monopolization by product proliferation. By taking advantage of its status as a first-mover, Kellogg could allegedly fill all available product niches, leaving little scope for rivals to enter.

How does this view fit in with the present theory? In chapter 10, it is shown that the strategy of product proliferation can be seen as a special case of the general framework developed here; but placing it within this setting introduces as an additional and primary mechanism the same competitive escalation of advertising outlays that appears across the general run of advertising-intensive industries. It is argued that this difference in interpretation has possible implications for the effects of the type of remedy proposed by the FTC.

The evolution of concentration in the beer industry is the subject of the last of the industry studies presented in part II. Few industries have been more intensively studied; and particular attention has been focused on the US industry, in which a steady rise in concentration over the past generation has led to a situation in which the emergence of a triopoly was becoming evident by the late 1980s.

The causes of this massive and sustained rise in concentration have been variously explained. Two lines of argument stand out in the economics literature. One emphasizes changes in brewing and bottling technology, which have led to a substantial rise in the minimum efficient scale of operation (m.e.s). Another view emphasizes the role of escalating advertising outlays by the major brewers and the consequent pressure on small and medium-sized firms. Some authors take an eclectic view, arguing that both of these factors have contributed to the changes in industry structure.

The central theme of chapter 13 is that within the context of the present theory, these two contributory factors, while both relevant, are not independent. Rather, they both play a part within the same unified mechanism that underlies the evolution of all of the advertising-intensive industries studied here. Under this interpretation, the exogenous changes in technology that have raised the minimum efficient scale – and so the level of set-up costs – have thereby stimulated and fueled the concomitant increases in advertising outlays, thereby accentuating what would otherwise have been a comparatively modest trend towards higher levels of concentration.

A central implication of this analysis relates to the likely effect of recent changes in technology, which appear to favour the relative efficiency of smaller breweries. It is argued in chapter 13 that such a reversal of earlier trends towards higher m.e.s. levels will *not* tend to lead to a dilution in industry concentration.

The Bain paradigm revisited

It may be of interest to readers familiar with the earlier literature to see how the ideas set out above relate to the Bain paradigm. Two points of difference are obvious. The first point relates to difficulties arising with the chain of causation story. As noted earlier, the Bain paradigm posits a one-way chain of causation running from structure to conduct to performance. The determination of structure, in this setting, is explained by reference to various barriers to entry, whose nature is taken to be exogenously given. It is not only within the recent game-theoretic literature that one finds the adequacy of such a story challenged: various early empirical studies drew attention to the need to consider a possible reverse link from conduct or performance to structure; but this was often presented as an econometric issue, in the sense that it might be dealt with by writing down a simultaneous equations system linking structure, conduct, and performance. This line of response did not prove very fruitful, however (see Schmalensee, 1989 for a review). Within the present framework, the problem is tackled by looking rather to a reformulation of the basic theoretical model. The key contribution of the two-stage game formulation is that it offers a neat way of unravelling the two-way link between structure and conduct.

The second point of difference with the Bain paradigm lies in its treatment of observed advertising levels as a barrier to entry, whose level might be appealed to in explaining industry structure. This view of advertising as a barrier to entry was taken to its logical conclusion in a series of studies that regressed observed levels of (or changes in) concentration on a series of explanatory variables, including the level of scale economies, the level of advertising intensity, and so on. (See chapter 4 for a comparison of the results of such studies to this study.)

Within the present approach, observed advertising levels are endogenously determined. This difference is of fundamental importance, and it raises some serious questions about the way in which the barriers to entry concept is commonly used. The role of this concept in the post-Bain literature lay in providing a rationale for why apparently high profits could be consistent with an absence of entry. If the height of such a barrier is endogenously determined, however, then considerable care is needed in formulating explanations of why observed concentration levels are high, or why high measured profit levels do not seem to stimulate new entry in certain industries.

Beyond these two rather obvious differences, however, there are a number of further ways in which the present approach departs from the traditional literature. One such feature relates to the relationship between product differentiation and advertising. In the traditional literature, these were often closely identified; advertising intensity was in fact widely used as a proxy for the degree of product differentiation. Such an approach is highly dubious on purely empirical grounds: many industrial sectors (such as engineering) involve both a high degree of product differentiation and minimal advertising. Within this study, a sharp analytical distinction exists between the effects of product differentiation per se and the effects of advertising outlays. In making this distinction, the concepts of horizontal and vertical product differentiation outlined above turn out to be extremely useful (section 3.5).

There is one final difference between the present approach and the earlier empirical literature that deserves a relatively full remark. This relates to the way in which a lower bound to industry structure was introduced by some contributors to the traditional literature, in the guise of a warranted level of concentration. The idea ran as follows: Consider an industry in which advertising and R&D play no role, so that a firm's costs may be identified with the (fixed and variable) costs of production alone.

Imagine that each firm operates subject to an average cost schedule that declines up to some critical level of output (the minimum efficient scale (m.e.s.) of operation) and is flat after that point. Any firm operating at a level of output below this point will suffer a competitive disadvantage, and at equilibrium the industry will be populated by a number of firms operating at a level of output at or above the m.e.s. Thus a lower bound to industry concentration exists, corresponding to a configuration in which the industry consists of a number of firms operating at a level of output *equal to* the m.e.s. level. The associated level of concentration is referred to as the warranted level of concentration throughout much of the empirical literature of the 1960s and 1970s (see Anderson *et al.*, 1975).

It was noted by many observers, however, that actual concentration levels seem to lie far above the levels warranted on the basis of such arguments (see Scherer, 1980, and for a specific example, Anderson *et al.*, 1975), whether the m.e.s. level used in calculating such bounds came from estimates of median plant size, or from independent engineering studies (see chapter 4).

How does this relate to the present approach? A strict formulation of the preceding argument depends necessarily on the assumption that the average cost schedule becomes perfectly flat once the m.e.s. level of output is exceeded. In applying the idea empirically, however, it was (and remains) customary to adopt an arbitrary definition of m.e.s. as corresponding to the level beyond which further increases in output would lead to a reduction in average cost of no more than 10 per cent. Engineering studies would otherwise often imply an implausibly high value for m.e.s., and one that might lie far above those generated by the other popular measure of m.e.s., viz., the size of the median plant operating in the industry. It was in terms of these definitions that the warranted levels of concentration were seen to be very low compared with actual levels. While this procedure may lead to plausible answers, it actually hides the central analytical issue behind an empirical guess, for it rests upon a judgment as to the size of cost disadvantage a firm may suffer without being driven from the market.

But such questions obviously depend on the intensity of price competition in the market, and this will depend in turn not only on product characteristics (the degree of product differentiation) and on the state of competition policy, etc., but also on the degree of concentration in the industry. But if this is so, it would appear that there is no escaping an explicit analysis of the kind undertaken in chapter 2.

Within the present approach, it is assumed that the firm's average cost (including the contribution of sunk outlays incurred in setting up production) are declining, so that the m.e.s. level – on a strict definition – is infinite. On the other hand, the toughness of price competition is considered explicitly, and the equilibrium level of concentration is ground out by the interplay between set-up costs, market size, and the toughness of price competition.[6]

---

[6] Thus, the warranted degree of concentration does not figure in the present scheme. The use of m.e.s. levels, as estimated from either engineering studies or median plant size, enters only insofar as it is assumed that differences in the cost of establishing a single m.e.s. plant, as defined along traditional lines, may provide a very rough proxy for differences in the level of set-up cost across different industries (see chapter 4).

References

Anderson, K.B., M.P. Lynch, and J.D. Ogur (1975), *The Sugar Industry*, Washington, DC, US Federal Trade Commission.
Bain, J. (1956), *Barriers to New Competition*, Cambridge, MA, Harvard University Press.
  (1966), *International Differences in Industrial Structure: Eight Nations in the 1950s*, Connecticut, Greenwood Press.
Bresnahan, T.F. and P.C. Reiss (1990), 'Entry in monopoly markets', *Review of Economic Studies*, 57, 531–53.
Caves, R. (1989), 'International differences in industrial organisation', in R. Schmalensee and R. Willig (eds.), *Handbook of Industrial Organisation*, Amsterdam, North-Holland.
Connor, J.M., R.T. Rogers, B.W. Marion, and W.F. Mueller (1985), *The Food Manufacturing Industries: Structure, Strategies, Performance and Policies*, Lexington, MA, Lexington Books.
Dasgupta, P. and J.E. Stiglitz (1980), 'Industrial structure and the nature of innovative activity', *Economic Journal*, 90, 266–93.
George, K. and T.S. Ward (1975), *The Structure of Industry in the EEC*, Cambridge, University Press.
Hendricks, K. and R.H. Porter (1988), 'An empirical study of an auction with asymmetric information', *American Economic Review*, 14, 301–14.
Phlips, L. (1971), *Effects of Industrial Concentration: A Cross-Section Analysis for the Common Market*, Amsterdam, North-Holland.
Pryor, F.L. (1972), 'An international comparison of concentration ratios', *Review of Economics and Statistics*, 54, 130–40.
Scherer, F.M. (1980), *Industrial Market Structure and Economic Performance* (2nd edn), Chicago, Rand McNally.
Schmalensee R. (1978), 'Entry deterrence: The ready-to-eat breakfast cereal industry', *Bell Journal of Economics*, 9, 305–27.
  (1989), 'Inter-industry differences of structure and performance', in R. Schmalensee and R. Willig (eds.), *Handbook of Industrial Organisation*, Amsterdam, North-Holland.
Shaked, A. and J. Sutton (1982), 'Relaxing price competition through product differentiation', *Review of Economic Studies*, 49, 3–13.
  (1987), 'Product differentiation and industrial structure', *Journal of Industrial Economics*, 36, 131–46.
  (1990), 'Multiproduct Firms and Market Structure', *Rand Journal of Economics*, 21, 45–62.
Shepherd, W.G. (1961), 'A comparison of industrial concentration in the United States and Britain', *Review of Economics and Statistics*, 43, 70–5.
Slade, M. (1987), 'Interfirm rivalry in a repeated game: An empirical test of tacit collusion', *Journal of Industrial Economics*, 35, 499–516.
Vickers, J. (1986), 'The evolution of market structure when there is a sequence of innovations', *Journal of Industrial Economics*, 35, 1–12.

Chapter 2

Game-theoretic models of market concentration
Sunk costs and market structure: a review article

Richard Schmalensee

Every serious student of industrial economics should read John Sutton's *Sunk Costs and Market Structure: Price Competition, Advertising, and the Evolution of Concentration*.[1] This massive (577 pages overall), masterful, innovative, and thought-provoking study sets out to derive and test robust implications of game-theoretic models of free-entry equilibrium for the dependence of minimum viable levels of seller concentration on market size, set-up costs, and other factors. Empirical analysis is based on an extraordinary set of detailed, often fascinating histories of 20 food and drink industries in the six largest industrial economies. Formal econometric techniques and international comparisons are carefully and cleverly exploited.

The analysis in *Sunk Costs* distinguishes sharply between what I will refer to as type I and type II markets; advertising competition is important only in the latter. It is argued that models of type I markets generally imply that the lowest viable concentration declines to zero as market size increases, while models of type II markets generally imply that this lower bound converges to a strictly positive value. Empirically, six industries with low advertising–sales ratios are taken to be of type I,

This article first appeared in *The Journal of Industrial Economics*, June 1992, Vol. 40, pp. 125–34.
I am indebted to Stephen Davis and Bruce Lyons for exceptionally helpful comments on an earlier draft and to John Sutton for correcting a significant error in that draft, but I cannot share with them responsibility for the opinions expressed in this article or for any defects it may contain.
[1] Unless otherwise indicated, all chapters and page citations in what follows refer to this book, which will itself be referred to as *Sunk Costs*.

while the remaining 14 advertising-intensive industries are taken to be of type II. Cross-section relations between concentration and market size are estimated for these two groups of industries. Focused international and interindustry comparisons are employed mainly to explore the corresponding processes of market consolidation and evolution.

1   Type I markets

In what follows a number of simple models of one-dimensional rivalry are presented, none of which appear in *Sunk Costs*. These models, which are intended to complement the analytical framework developed in *Sunk Costs*, depict an industry with free entry and N *ex ante* identical firms, in which the profit of a typical firm *i* is given by

$$\pi_i = (P_i - c_i)q_i - A_i - \sigma \tag{1}$$

where P_i is firm i's price, c_i is its constant per-unit cost, q_i is its unit sales, A_i is its advertising or other demand-shifting expenditure, and σ is its technologically fixed set-up cost. Chapter 2 indicates that the defining feature of what one might call pure type I markets is that the A_i can be properly treated as exogenous. Thus in a symmetric model we can set $A_i = 0$ for all i.

In the simplest sort of type I market, ex post identical firms produce a homogeneous product, so that $c_i = c$, $P_i = P$ and $q_i = S/NP$, where S is total spending on this product. To derive an illustrative solution, let me suppose that S is a constant and that the percentage markup, $(P - c)/P$, can be well approximated by k/N^a for $k > 0$, $\alpha > 0$ and $N \geq 1$. Setting $\pi_i = 0$ in (1) and treating N as continuous, we can solve for the free-entry equilibrium number of firms

$$N^* = [k(S/\sigma)]^{1/(1+\alpha)}. \tag{2}$$

Here (S/σ) measures the effective size of the market, and α measures what *Sunk Costs* calls the toughness of price competition. The case $\alpha = 1$ corresponds to Cournot behaviour with constant elasticity demand; the larger is α, the more rapidly entry erodes margins. The key implication of (2) is that for any positive α, $N^* \to \infty$ as $S \to \infty$, so that any measure of concentration tends to zero as market size increases. Doubling S less than doubles N^*, since increasing the number of firms increases pressure on margins. Finally, $\partial N^*/\partial \alpha < 0$: tougher price competition results in higher equilibrium concentration because it gives rise to greater gaps between pre-entry and post-entry margins.

Chapter 2 also discusses models of horizontal (spatial) differentiation with exogenous sunk costs. The least concentrated equilibria in such models involve one-brand firms, each earning exactly zero profit. As the size of the market increases without bound, so does the number of such firms. These models generally have other more concentrated free-entry equilibria, some of which involve multi-brand firms and strictly positive profits. Thus in the case of horizontal differentiation, one can only say that the *lower bound* on concentration declines to zero as market size increases.

Symmetric (representative consumer) models of differentiation are not considered in *Sunk Costs*, but these also generally imply that $N^* \to \infty$ as market size increases. Consider, for instance, a variant of the price competition model presented in Schmalensee (1986)

$$\pi_i = (P_i - c)S\left[P_i^{-e} / \sum_{j=1}^{n} P_j^{-e}\right] - \sigma \tag{3}$$

where S is now total unit sales, assumed fixed, and the quantity in brackets is firm i's market share. Well-behaved symmetric Nash equilibria in the P_i exist for all $N \geq 2$ if $e > 2$, and the zero-profit value of N is given by

$$N^* = \frac{c(S/\sigma) + e}{e - 1}. \tag{4}$$

As before, $N^* \to \infty$ as $S^* \to \infty$, doubling S less than doubles N^*, and $\partial N^*/\partial e < 0$. Here e determines the toughness of price competition: the more sensitive market share is to price, the lower is the Nash equilibrium markup, and the smaller is N^*.

Chapter 5 presents econometric results consistent with these predictions. The lower bound on the four-firm concentration ratio, C_4, declines as (S/σ) increases in type I markets.[2] In addition, in regressions of C_4 on industry and country dummies and the logarithm of market size relative to the US market, the coefficient of the relative market size variable is negative and highly significant.

Scatter diagrams reveal considerable variation in C_4 for each value of (S/σ) in type I markets. The models discussed above and those in *Sunk Costs* imply that apart from disequilibrium or measurement error, differences in concentration in type I markets can only reflect differences in (S/σ), in the toughness of price competition or in the equilibrium selected in markets in which horizontal differentiation is important.

Chapter 6 argues that the histories of the salt and sugar industries are consistent with this implication. Both industries have small values of (S/σ). Price competition in salt has nowhere been suppressed, and concentration is everywhere high. In contrast, international differences in concentration in the sugar industry mirror differences in the extent to which governments have suppressed price competition.

The discussion of the remaining four type I industries (flour, bread, meat packing, and canned vegetables) in chapter 7 suggests the importance of factors omitted from the theoretical analysis. These industries have relatively large values of (S/σ) and exhibit large variations in concentration, but chapter 7 concludes that differences in the toughness of price competition are not helpful in explaining these variations. In one of these industries (bread), horizontal (geographical) differentiation is clearly important, and international differences in concentration plausibly reflect the exist-

---

[2] As Chapter 4 indicates, market size, S, is typically measured by total physical output. The key ratio (σ/S) is estimated by the product of the share of US output accounted for by the median plant and the industry capital-output ratio. It is argued that within the food and drink sector, engineering estimates of minimum efficient scale, where available, correlate well with median-plant size.

ence of multiple equilibria. But horizontal differentiation does not appear to be important in the other three industries.

In these industries, as in most discussed in *Sunk Costs*, sellers vary considerably in size. Indeed, as a general matter C_4 tends to be more closely related to measures of size inequality than to numbers of sellers. One of the merits of the historical approach in *Sunk Costs* is that size differences can often be traced to particular strategic decisions or innovations that apparently provided long-lived competitive advantages. On the theoretical side, it is relatively easy to construct asymmetric free-entry Nash equilibrium models in which, for instance, unit costs differ. The resulting equilibria are generally more concentrated than those of symmetric models, and they predict that firms with competitive advantages earn positive economic profits. It thus makes both empirical and theoretical sense to stress competitive asymmetries as a generally important determinant of concentration, even though the development of such asymmetries is endogenous, poorly understood, and hard to predict. But, apart from occasional allusions to first-mover advantages, *Sunk Costs* avoids this point in theoretical discussions.

2   Type II markets

In chapter 3, rivalry in type II markets is modelled as a two-stage game. In the first stage, firms decide whether or not to enter and, if they enter, choose levels of advertising spending – the A_i in equation (1). In the second stage, the A_i are sunk costs, and only price (or output) competition occurs. Reflecting this modelling approach, type II markets are generally described in *Sunk Costs* as having endogenous sunk costs. An illustrative two-stage model built on a vertical differentiation framework is shown to have the property that N^* converges to a strictly positive constant as $S \to \infty$.[3] In a more general analysis (following Shaked and Sutton, 1987), it is shown that if payoffs in the second-stage subgame are sufficiently sensitive to changes in the A_i (and if some other conditions are satisfied), the market share of the largest firm is bounded away from zero as S increases.

I have long believed that markets in which advertising plays a major role differ in important respects from other markets, and the empirical work in *Sunk Costs* confirms and informs that belief. But, for reasons I outline below, I am not persuaded that the two-stage approach is either plausible in this setting or necessary to obtain results of the sort just described. I also address a related issue that arises because theoretical work in *Sunk Costs* deals only with pure type I industries, in which advertising is exogenous, even though advertising is a business decision variable in all real industries. Thus strict exogeneity of advertising cannot be necessary for concentration to follow the Type I pattern observed in *Sunk Costs*. There must be some structural

---

[3] In a nice extension of this basic model, equilibria with two sets of consumers having differing sensitivities to advertising are shown to exhibit some key features of real industries with retail and non-retail segments; one can hear echoes of Caves and Porter (1977).

feature that determines whether firm choice of advertising outlays leads to type I behaviour or type II behaviour at the industry level.

On the issue of plausibility, it is worth noting that the models in *Sunk Costs* are descendants of those in the vertical product differentiation literature (see especially Shaked and Sutton, 1983), in which product characteristics are chosen in the first stage and prices are chosen in the second. Since product designs are typically longer-lived than prices and are typically more expensive to change, a two-stage framework seems appropriate in this setting. But the dynamic differences between price and advertising are much less clear. Advertising budgets are regularly revised in the light of short-term changes in market conditions, for instance, while prices are sometimes rigid for very long periods.[4]

An alternative defence of the two-stage approach might rest on advertising's long-lived effects on demand. But, as a general matter, one would also expect price to have durable effects on demand – particularly if purchase experience influences behaviour. Moreover, most empirical work suggests that advertising's effects are not in fact very long-lived (Berndt, 1991, chapter 6).

Sutton's response (*Sunk Costs*, p. 315) to this last point is that, 'What is at issue here is not the rate of depreciation of advertising, which might be rapid, but rather the difference between the flow of expenditure an incumbent needs to maintain his position and that required of an entrant in establishing a similar position.' In the simplest 'goodwill stock' framework, the distinction that this passage at first seems to assert does not exist. That is, as the rate of depreciation of goodwill increases, the difference between the advertising cost of maintaining any given goodwill stock over any positive period and the cost of acquiring that stock from scratch goes to zero. Alternatively, one might read this passage broadly as arguing that tough advertising competition may deter entry even though *ex ante* identical incumbents are profitable. But this would appear to be potentially true for *any* form of non-price competition and would not appear to have anything to do with whether the associated costs are in any sense sunk.

Turning to the issue of necessity, two simple one-stage models appear to illustrate the range of possible relations between the toughness of non-price competition and free-entry concentration. In the first model, the A_i in equation (1) are zero, price is fixed (perhaps in an earlier stage of the game), and both quality and market share can be increased by spending more on each unit produced. Let the profits of a typical firm i be given by

$$\pi_i = (P - c_i)S\left[c_i^e / \sum_{j=1}^{N} c_j^e\right] - \sigma \tag{5}$$

where e is a constant. One might think of the market share function in brackets as the output from a random utility model. Well-behaved, symmetric, zero-profit Nash equilibria in the c_i exist for all $e > 0$, with the number of firms given by

---

[4] Compare, for instance, Berndt (1991, chapter 6) and the references he cites with Carlton (1986).

$$N^* = \frac{P(S/\sigma) + e}{1 + e}.$$ (6)

As before, $N^* \to \infty$ as $S \to \infty$; non-price competition that focuses on unit cost resembles price competition in the limit. The higher is e, the more sensitive market share is to quality, the tougher is quality competition, and the smaller is the equilibrium number of firms.

The second model, a variant of the advertising competition model in Schmalensee (1976, 1986), shows by example that the two-stage approach in *Sunk Costs* is not necessary for N^* to converge to a positive constant as S grows. What does seem to be necessary is that market share be sufficiently sensitive to variations in *fixed* costs, so that rivalry is both tough and focused on fixed outlays, not on per-unit price–cost margins. In this model, P and c are exogenous, and market share can be increased by spending more on advertising

$$\pi_i = (P - c)S\left[A_i^e / \sum_{j=1}^{N} A_j^e\right] - A_i - \sigma$$ (7)

where S and e are again positive constants. The market share function in brackets may be thought of as arising from a random utility model, or the whole first term may be thought of as approximating the return to advertising in the second stage of a two-stage game. Well-behaved symmetric Nash equilibria in the A_i with non-negative profits exist for $0 \leq e \leq 2$. The larger is e, all else equal, the higher are advertising outlays per firm and the lower are profits.

The condition that profit be zero reduces to

$$T \equiv (1/N^*)(1 - e) + (1/N^*)^2 e - (\sigma/S)(1/(P - c)) = 0.$$ (8)

For $e \leq 1$, the single positive value of N^* that satisfies (8) increases without bound as $S \to \infty$. In this case advertising competition is not particularly tough, and concentration again converges to zero as the market grows. It is thus possible to have type I behaviour ($N^* \to \infty$ as $S \to \infty$ and relatively low advertising–sales ratios) with endogenous advertising if market shares are not too responsive to advertising outlays. When $e = 1$, it is easy to see that $N^* = [(P - c)S/\sigma]^{1/2}$. Doubling market size less than doubles the number of firms, so that advertising per firm must increase without bound as the market grows in order to maintain zero profits.

For $1 < e \leq 2$, this model yields the sort of type II behaviour stressed in chapter 3: $N^* \to N^{**} \equiv [e/(e - 1)]$ as $S \to \infty$. In this case, advertising competition is so tough that no more than N^{**} firms can earn non-negative profits no matter how large the market becomes. It follows that advertising per firm must grow even more rapidly with the market than when $e = 1$. While it is difficult to obtain results of this sort when rivalry involves price or unit cost, such results seem to arise easily when rivalry involves fixed cost.[5]

---

[5] For instance, suppose market shares are proportional to u_i and that $A_i = (a/\gamma)[(u_i)^\gamma - 1]$, with $u_i \geq 1$. This combines the $A(u)$ function used in the illustrative type II model in *Sunk Costs*

Now suppose that $(P - c)$ in (7) is some decreasing function of N because of price competition. If $(P - c) > 0$ for some N, the last term in (8) goes to zero as $S \to \infty$ for that N. Thus if $1 < e \leq 2$ and $(P - c) > 0$ for all $N \leq N^{**}$, N^* will still converge to N^{**} as the market grows. If price competition drives margins to zero with $N^{***} < N^{**}$ firms, as in the Bertrand case, N will of course never rise above N^{***}. This at least suggests that the key type II result – concentration is bounded away from zero whenever advertising competition is sufficiently tough – is robust to alternative approaches to modelling competition that involves both price and advertising. Since it is unclear (to me, at least) how such competition should be modelled in general, this is a source of some comfort.

Sunk Costs devotes considerable attention to the careful empirical analysis of type II industries. The cross-section econometric results for type II markets presented in chapter 5 differ sharply from the results for type I markets and seem broadly consistent with the theory above and in chapter 3. The lower bound on concentration in type II markets does not appear to decline to zero as (S/σ) increases, nor does mean concentration decline significantly with relative market size.

One can use the data in chapter 4 to examine the impact of market growth on advertising intensity in type II markets. If concentration remains essentially constant as these markets grow, there is no reason to expect margins to shrink. Then if advertising competition holds profit to zero, advertising–sales ratios must increase with market size. To see this, consider a symmetric zero-profit equilibrium by setting $q = S/NP$ in equation (1), where S is total spending in the market. Rearranging the resulting equation yields

$$\frac{NA}{S} = \frac{P - c}{P} - \frac{N\sigma}{S}. \tag{9}$$

If N and the percentage markup are unchanged as S increases, the industry advertising–sales ratio, NA/S, must rise to hold profit to zero.

Regression analysis of the data in tables 4.3 and 4.4 of *Sunk Costs* does not support this prediction, however.[6] Regressions of industry advertising–sales ratios on industry and country dummies and relative market size, using a variety of functional forms,

---

(pp. 48–9) with the 'us/(us + them)' market share specification used here; the smaller is γ the more sensitive market shares are to differences in advertising spending. In general, $u_i = 1$ for small S, and N^* rises with S over this range. If $\gamma \geq 1$, we have type I behaviour with $N^* \to \infty$ as $S \to \infty$; if $\gamma < 1$, $N^* \to 1/(1 - \gamma)$ as $S \to \infty$ and the model exhibits type II behaviour. In the latter case if $[\sigma - (a/\gamma)]$ is negative (positive), N^* falls (rises) as S increases beyond the value at which the u_i first exceed unity. Thus, as stressed in chapter 3, concentration may rise in type II markets with increases in market size over a significant range.

[6] The regression analysis in chapter 5 may have employed additional data. Three type II industries are omitted without explanation from table 4.3, which presents estimates of C_4 and (S/σ) and no usable data are presented for two others. There are 46 usable type II observations in this table and table 4.4 gives advertising–sales ratios for all but one. While chapter 5's scatter diagrams of C_4 versus (S/σ) (pp. 114, 118) show 46 type II points, 58 observations are reported (p. 122) to have been used in regression analysis of the relation between these variables. [The 58 datapoints include twelve observations for the frozen food and margarine industries in each of the 6 countries. The

yield coefficients of relative market size that are negative and insignificant.[7] These results suggest that either economic profit generally grows with market size in type II markets, or some form of non-advertising competition restrains profit growth. Profit growth is consistent with the view that advertising creates entry barriers,[8] but it is also consistent with free entry as long as tough price or non-price competition implies non-positive profit for any additional entrant.

In many ways the richest and most interesting part of *Sunk Costs* is the discussion of the evolution of 11 of the 14 type II industries in chapters 8–13.[9] Unfortunately, this is much the hardest part of the book to treat adequately in a brief essay, but I cannot resist noting a few highlights.

Chapter 8 shows how the emergence of intensive advertising competition in frozen foods led to high concentration even though (S/σ) was generally relatively large. An interesting feature of the consolidation process in this industry and in some others is that market followers often lost share even with somewhat higher advertising–sales ratios than market leaders. This is consistent with scale economies in advertising of the sort present in equation (7) with $e > 1$: if firm A spends k times as much on advertising as firm B, its advertising–sales ratio will be k^{1-e} times firm B's. Since $e > 1$ is necessary and sufficient for type II behaviour, type II behaviour and scale economies in advertising are equivalent in the model of equation (7).

Chapter 11 observes that a similar pattern of consolidation by advertising competition occurred in the French mineral water market but not in the apparently otherwise comparable markets of Germany or Italy. In France, Perrier came up with a very effective advertising campaign, but nothing similar occurred in Germany or Italy. This points up an unavoidable problem with international comparisons in markets for consumer products. Because culturally based taste differences cannot be ruled out in such comparisons, it is essentially impossible to tell whether differences of the sort observed in mineral water markets reflect historical accidents or essentially inevitable responses to differences in actual and potential demand conditions. In particular, Perrier's success may have been an accident – and similar accidents may be waiting to happen in Germany and Italy – or it may reflect differences in consumer preferences and susceptibilities to advertising that are not directly observable.

A similar problem arises in chapter 10, in which evidence from the UK RTE cereal

---

data for these is taken from the market share tables in the Appendix. The regressions reported in Sutton's Table 5.2 are for the full dataset of 58 points that include these twelve observations. Editor's note.]

[7] When C_4 is added to this regression, its coefficient is positive and sometimes significant; when both C_4 and $(C_4)^2$ are added, neither coefficient ever approaches significance.

[8] *Sunk Costs* attacks the notion of advertising as an *exogenous* entry barrier at several points (e.g., pp. 78–80) but only by arguing that advertising must be treated as an endogenous variable. The hypothesis that there is a structural link between advertising and competitive advantages of incumbents is dealt with only by dismissing the classical structure–conduct–performance tradition within which this hypothesis arose. But clearly the endogeneity of advertising is not *logically* inconsistent with a structural link of this sort, whatever the facts of the matter may be.

[9] Perhaps for reasons of space, three type II industries are described only in appendices, though one (biscuits) is cited in the text (p. 310) as a 'key example'.

market is employed to argue that advertising competition is more important in the US market than in the model of Schmalensee (1978). It is hard to dispute this conclusion, since advertising is treated as exogenous in Schmalensee (1978). But it has never been clear to me that the UK market, which has long been dominated by Kellogg's Corn Flakes, has demand conditions that are usefully similar to those in the US market, which has long been highly fragmented at the brand level. It is thus unclear how much one can learn about the US market from studying the UK market.

Chapter 9 provides an interesting discussion of apparent hysteresis effects in three industries and indicates that ancient differences in strategies have had permanent impacts on the US and UK soup markets. Chapter 13 argues persuasively that escalating advertising competition played a role in the consolidation of the US beer industry at least comparable to the role played by increases in scale economies in brewing. Finally chapter 12's analysis of sugar versus chocolate confectioneries and instant versus roast and ground coffee supports the prediction that higher values of (σ/S) are associated with higher levels of concentration, all else equal, even in type II markets.

3   Conclusions

The game-theoretic revolution in industrial economics has taught us that unobservable details of market structure may have large effects on conduct and performance. With *Sunk Costs*, John Sutton has shown that one can nonetheless sometimes obtain robust game-theoretic predictions that depend only on observables. *Sunk Costs* also shows that such predictions can be usefully confronted with a mixture of econometric analysis, industry histories, and international comparisons. This book deserves to have a long-lived impact on methods of empirical research in industrial economics.

In this chapter I have concentrated on relatively general issues, particularly those on which I found the arguments in *Sunk Costs* most provocative. But *Sunk Costs* is primarily an empirical study, and one with the rare virtue that potentially important facts are not omitted because they cannot be reduced to numbers or cannot easily be reconciled with the author's favourite model. While I am not fully persuaded that *Sunk Costs* completely answers all the important questions it addresses, the intelligence, energy, and care it embodies entitle it also to have a long-lived impact on the agenda of empirical research in industrial economics.

References

Berndt, E.R. (1991), *The Practice of Econometrics: Classic and Contemporary*, Reading, Addison-Wesley.

Carlton, D.W. (1986), 'The rigidity of prices', *American Economic Review*, 76, 637–58.

Caves, R.E. and M.E. Porter (1977), 'From entry barriers to mobility barriers: conjectural decisions and contrived deterrence to new competition', *Quarterly Journal of Economics*, 91, 241–61.

Schmalensee, R. (1976), 'A model of promotional competition in oligopoly', *Review of Economic Studies*, 43, 493–507.

(1978), 'Entry deterrence in the ready-to-eat breakfast cereal industry', *Bell Journal of Economics*, 9, 305–27.

(1986), 'Advertising and market structure', in J.E. Stiglitz and G.F. Mathewson (eds.), *New Developments in the Analysis of Market Structure*, Cambridge, MA, MIT Press.

Shaked, A. and J. Sutton (1983), 'Natural oligopolies', *Econometrica*, 51, 1469–1484.

(1987), 'Product differentiation and industrial structure', *Journal of Industrial Economics*, 36, 131–46.

Sutton, J. (1991), *Sunk Costs and Market Structure: Price Competition, Advertising, and the Evolution of Concentration*, Cambridge, MA, MIT Press.

Chapter 3

Expanding markets
Capacity expansion in the titanium dioxide industry

Pankaj Ghemawat

Recent attempts to apply industrial organization to the analysis and shaping of competitive strategy suggest that the approach of focusing on the static determination of prices in homogeneous industries is inadequate in explaining many competitive interactions. More fruitful is a combination of industrial organization and the industry history approach taken at business schools. In other words, micro-economic analysis has to be wedded to detailed consideration of strategic moves and counter-moves, sufficiently broad coverage of firms' interactions along a number of different dimensions, and recognition that firms' resource endowments can frequently be varied only in the medium to long-term – and even then, only at a cost.[1]

In this chapter, I use a hybrid approach to study the capacity expansion process in capital-intensive industries. In section 1, I develop a theoretical model that leads to the conclusion that where costs differ significantly across firms, the lowest cost producer will tend to pre-empt the others in adding new capacity. But two factors can reverse this outcome: resource constraints which are likely to occur during periods of very heavy investment, and uncertainty about demand. Conversely, concern about supply coordination failures and most sorts of informational asymmetries among

This article first appeared in *The Journal of Industrial Economics*, 1984, vol. 33, pp. 145–63.
The author is indebted to Richard E. Caves, Stacy Dick, Marvin B. Lieberman, Michael E. Porter, A. Michael Spence, and two referees for their comments and to the Division of Research at the Harvard Graduate School of Business Administration for financial support.
[1] For a more detailed exposition, see Porter (1980).

firms are likely to favour pre-emption by the lowest-cost producer, as is a desire to dominate the industry in order to restrict output.

The model also suggests that if the less-efficient producers are financially constrained or suffer from informational asymmetries, the lowest-cost producer has an incentive to price strategically by holding prices artificially low until new capacity comes on-stream and then raising them. Another prediction of the model is that licensing is unlikely to be profitable if pre-emption occurs. Therefore, we expect the lowest-cost producer to show more interest in licensing its technology overseas than to domestic competitors.

Section 2 examines capacity expansion in the US titanium dioxide industry in the context of these theoretical predictions. Du Pont's strategy in titanium dioxide over 1972–7 accords with the predictions from section 1 but also highlights some of the risks of pre-emption.

1   Theory

1.1   The basic model

For our purposes, two types of cost difference among firms are of interest: absolute cost disparities and dynamic scale economics; the latter are familiar to economists as 'learning by doing' (Arrow, 1962). Their effects can most readily be discerned in a market served by two firms. Assume that at time 0, firm 1 (the 'leader') operates K_1 units of capacity and firm 2 (the 'laggard') K_2 units. The plants can be operated forever at zero variable cost so that firm i's costs of producing at the rate K_i, are entirely sunk.[2]

Capacity is added in increments of one unit. The cost disparity between the two firms comes into play here. We assume that as the *net* result of learning and absolute cost differences, firm 1's total costs of constructing a new plant are lower than firm 2's.[3] Symbolically,

$$C_1(K_1 + 1) < C_2(K_2 + 1). \tag{1}$$

Finally, let the market be expanding so that given total capacity, K,

$$\frac{\partial p(K, t)}{\partial t} > 0 \tag{2}$$

where p stands for the real price of the product and t denotes time.[4] In particular,

---

[2] This assumption, although somewhat unattractive, lets us avoid getting bogged down in the mechanics of price and output determination in the short run.

[3] Although it is more usual to explain learning on the basis of cumulated output, convenience dictates that the model focus on cumulated gross investment – for which there is also some empirical support. (see Sheshinski, 1967).

[4] Without demand growth, p would hold steady for any given level of capacity, K, because cost reductions are assumed to occur only through new investment.

assume demand is such that over the planning period (time 0 to T), only one unit of capacity will be added. With non-cooperative behaviour, which firm will build it?

To find the answer, recast the problem as an auction in which the firms alternate in making public 'bids' about the dates at which they are willing to add capacity. The bidding continues until one firm makes a bid that its rival is unwilling to match. That bid takes effect and the firm that made it adds the new unit of capacity at the promised date. (In view of the bidding process, this outcome is the rational expectations equilibrium.)

Let firm j start the bidding. Denote the first bid as t_j^*. If firm i lets this bid stand, its total profits are

$$\int_0^{t_j^*} K_i p(K,t)e^{-rt}dt + \int_{t_j^*}^T K_i p(K+1,t)e^{-rt}dt \tag{3}$$

where r is the discount rate. The alternative of undercutting firm j's bid by s leads to profits of

$$\int_0^{t_j^*} K_i p(K,t)e^{-rt}dt + \int_{t_{j-s}^*}^T (K_i+1)p(K+1,t)e^{-rt}dt - C_i(K_i+1)e^{-r(t_j^*-s)}. \tag{4}$$

Since firm i can make s arbitrarily small, the limiting profits from undercutting are

$$\int_0^{t_j^*} K_i p(K,t)e^{-rt}dt + \int_{t_j^*}^T (K_i+1)p(K+1,t)e^{-rt}dt - C_i(K+1)e^{-rt_j^*}. \tag{5}$$

Comparing equations (3) and (5), we can see that firm i will undercut any bid t_j by firm j as long as

$$\int_{t_j}^T p(K+1,t)e^{-rt}dt > C_i(K_i+1)e^{-rt_j}. \tag{6}$$

From equation (6), the laggard, which has higher capacity costs, will be the first to stop bidding and the leader will find pre-emption profitable.

Three points about the model are worth noting. First, the pre-emption result is robust *vis-à-vis* the cost function assumed. It can allow for exogenous technical progress so long as the leader's capacity costs are lower than the laggard's and accommodate spillovers of learning across firms if the leakage is less than total.[5] Second, the analysis can be extended to allow for any number of firms and for demand profiles requiring the construction of more than one unit of capacity (Gilbert and Harris, 1981). Finally, non-zero variable costs can provide another rationale for pre-emption by the leader if they make operation below capacity profitable, since the

---

[5] However, spillovers are likely to decelerate the pace of capacity expansion. See Ghemawat and Spence (1982).

leader augments its ability to restrict output by adding capacity itself rather than farming it out to competitors.

1.2   Uncertainty

Uncertainty varies in its impact on the pre-emption result depending on the form that it takes. The most obvious sort, demand uncertainty, tends to blur cost differences among firms. To demonstrate this point, I modify the basic model by letting the market price be a non-deterministic function of capacity and time; the indeterminacy, in this context, is a consequence of uncertain demand. Then the net present value of revenue per unit of capacity from time t^* onwards, assuming that total capacity remains K, is

$$\int_t^T \bar{p}(K, t)e^{-rt}dt \tag{7}$$

with a variance of σ_t^{*2}.[6]

Replicating our earlier analysis (see equation (6)), we find that the incremental expected revenue from adding a unit of capacity at time t^* is the same for both firms and can be ignored. Assuming, as a descriptive matter, that managers care about variance rather than covariance with the market, the incremental risk-adjusted cost of a new unit to firm i is

$$C_i(K_i + 1)e^{-rt*} + \phi(K_i + 1)^2 \sigma_{t*}^2 - \phi K_i^2 \sigma_{t*}^2 =$$
$$C_i(K_i + 1)e^{-rt*} + \phi(2K_i + 1)^2 \sigma_{t*}^2 \tag{8}$$

where ϕ is the risk-aversion coefficient.

The implication is that demand uncertainty acts as the great leveller in tending to equalize firms' costs, and therefore their market shares.[7] More exactly, demand uncertainty is likely to overturn the pre-emption result when the laggard has much less capacity than the leader but only a slight learning-related cost disadvantage and when the risk aversion of the two firms and the variance of the revenue stream are high.

Another form of uncertainty that may rule out pre-emption by the leader is the legal sort. US courts have never resolved whether cost-based pre-emption is a legitimate business practice (Beckenstein and Gabel, 1981). Since the costs of legal conflict can be high, such uncertainty should blunt the incentive for the leader to pre-empt.

On the other hand, some uncertainties favour the leader at the expense of the laggard. Consider a situation in which the leader, by virtue of its greater experience, has better information than the laggard about a cost or demand characteristic relevant to post-expansion profits – as may well happen when the laggard has less experience

---

[6] To simplify the argument, let this variance be independent of K.
[7] This result is far from new. Chandler (1980) reports that such considerations had begun to influence Du Pont's strategy as early as 1903.

than the leader with the technology that the new plant is to use, or is highly diversified and thus faces considerable costs in gathering information about a particular market.[8] In both cases, the leader's ability to pre-empt is likely to be enhanced.

Another impetus to the leader to pre-empt relates to what Smith (1981) has called supply coordination failure. Smaller firms are likely to have less accurate forecasts about each other's expansion plans than about the leader's since the latter is the obvious candidate for adding capacity. Consequently, if the leader fails to exercise its dominance and abandons the field to smaller rivals, the probability of miscalculations in capacity expansion will increase. In the form of overcapacity, these can hurt each firm's profitability.

1.3   Resource constraints

Students of business policy have long recognized that a firm's strategy is constrained by the resources available to it. Such constraints can take a multiplicity of forms: organizational, managerial, financial. Although I shall focus on the effects of limited financial resources, the conclusions concerning the pattern and pace of capacity expansion (although not those about margins) can easily be shown also to hold in the presence of organizational and managerial limitations as well.

To elucidate the effect of imperfect financial markets, I modify the basic model in several ways. First, I assume that capacity expansion has to be entirely self-financed.[9] Second, the leader is now allowed to choose a non-negative level of variable costs, a, that the laggard must match to stay competitive.[10] Finally, convenience dictates the restriction that a be small enough in relation to marginal revenue for the two firms to keep operating at capacity.

Now, the earliest date, t_i, at which firm i has the capital to build a new plant is given by

$$I_i + \int_0^{t_i} K_i(p(K, t) - a)e^{-rt}dt = C_i(K_i + 1)e^{-rt} \qquad (9)$$

where I_i is its initial resource endowment. Replicating our earlier analysis (and

---

[8] The latter sort of situation seems quite frequent given the prevalence of portfolio planning in large companies. See Haspeslagh (1982).

[9] A similar analysis holds in the presence of debt as long as there is an upper bound on leveraging.

[10] This somewhat artificial device, introduced as an analytically convenient way of letting the leader strategically set margins, calls for some elucidation. First, a is an expense incurred at the leader's discretion. Second, it plays no role in expanding demand for the product; instead its role is purely rivalrous in requiring matching commitments (per unit sold) by each firm if it is to sell its output. (Competitive advertising that would cause buyers to shift from one seller to another without increasing aggregate demand is one possible example.) Third, a could be assumed to be subject to learning-by-doing. This complicates the notation but does not reduce the incentive to pre-empt. Fourth, after the capacity expansion has been completed, the leader will always set a to zero, i.e., minimize costs. It is only prior to the expansion that the leader *might* choose to set a greater than zero in order to affect other firms' ability to expand.

remembering that a will always be set to zero after expansion), the earliest date at which firm i would be willing to build, t_i, is given by

$$\int_{t_i}^{T} p(K+1,t)e^{-rt}dt = C_i(K_i+1)e^{-rt}. \tag{10}$$

Then with financial constraints, firm i's earliest bid will be

$$t_i'' = \max(t_i, t_i'). \tag{11}$$

The new unit will be added by the firm with the lowest t_i''.

Several points emerge from this way of setting up the problem. First, financial constraints may retard capacity expansion, but they never accelerate it. Second, the leader will not always be able to pre-empt. For instance, during periods of rapid demand growth or technological obsolescence, the magnitude of capacity expansion required makes it likely that the laggard will be able to add at least some of the capacity that needs to be brought on-stream. Third, although we cannot, at this level of generality, derive sufficient conditions for the leader to choose, prior to expansion, to set a greater than zero, it is likely that this would require inelastic demand (which gives the leader an incentive to delay construction) and capacity costs that are large compared to the laggard's initial resource endowment and earning streams (which make it likely that the laggard is financially constrained).[11]

If, as mentioned in the last section, the laggard has much less information about the industry than the leader, the latter will have yet another reason to manipulate margins. In some circumstances, the leader will then find it worthwhile to invest in sending costly signals (i.e., setting a at a positive level) to make the laggard unwarrantedly pessimistic about the expansion that it would otherwise like to under-take.[12]

Finally, when a is set greater than zero, perverse changes in the margins may be observed at the date at which the new capacity goes on-stream. At that instant, the margin changes from

$$p(K,t) - a \tag{12}$$

to

$$p(K+1,t). \tag{13}$$

Hence margins may actually increase as quantity supplied goes up.

---

[11] In the context of capital market imperfections, the Kuhn–Tucker conditions can be used to show that for a to be set greater than zero, it is necessary that firm 2 be financially constrained.

[12] Although it seems counterintuitive to think that strategic pricing (setting a greater than zero) can succeed in deterring expansion by laggards who know that the leader is contemplating such strategic behaviour, rigorous analysis of competitive interactions as games of incomplete information shows that such deterrence *can* work (Milgrom and Roberts, 1980).

1.4   Licensing

When a market is structurally disposed to pre-emption by the leader, licensing will not occur.[13] To see this, recall that the revenue term that the leader and the laggard factor into their construction decision is the same. With licensing in the form of equalization of efficiency, the costs of adding capacity are also equal. The licenser (firm 1 – the leader) and licensee (firm 2 – the laggard) are then equally matched and will compete the incremental profits from a new plant down to zero. So the maximal royalty that firm 2 can afford to pay firm 1 is zero. As a result, with licensing, firm 1's incremental profits, gross of revenue losses on existing plants but net of royalties received, are also zero. This is clearly dominated by the no-licensing equilibrium at which the corresponding profit term for firm 1 is positive. Therefore, firm 1 will forego licensing and add the new plant itself.[14]

However, uncertainty and financial constraints can, as we have seen, invalidate the predicted pre-emption result. In this case, licensing may be to the leader's advantage.

These considerations lead us to predict that less licensing will occur among firms in the same country than across national boundaries, since the latter situation typically involves greater uncertainty and resource constraints.[15]

2   Empirical evidence[16]

Titanium dioxide is a commodity chemical used in paints, paper, and plastics. The analysis here treats the United States as the relevant geographic market; international linkages seem inconsequential because imports from Europe would face cost disadvantages amounting to 12–20 per cent of the US selling price [CX 209] while the US market itself is unified by compelling scale economies and relatively low transport costs.[17]

The first three parts of this section of the chapter provide background material on the events that, in 1972, conferred a substantial cost advantage on Du Pont over other US titanium dioxide producers. The next three parts trace the implications for Du Pont's titanium dioxide strategy over the five succeeding years.

---

[13] Market failures in the arm's-length transfer of knowledge reinforce this conclusion.

[14] For a more detailed discussion see Ghemawat (1982).

[15] Available empirical evidence (Caves, 1981) supports this hypothesis.

[16] This analysis draws on publicly available data from FTC Docket No. 9108. The abbreviations used to refer to sources are:
    CX Complaint Counsel's Exhibit
    RX Respondent's Exhibit
    AB Complaint Counsel's Appeal Brief
Other discussions of the industry can be found in Gilbert (1978), Shepherd (1979), (1980a), (1980b) and 'E. I. du Pont de Nemours & Co. – Titanium Dioxide' (1981). The footnotes will indicate that Gilbert's is the only account of which I have made some use.

[17] Transport costs amounted to only 1.3 per cent of product value over 350 mile hauls (CX 21) – a modest figure compared with Scherer *et al.*'s (1975) calculations for 12 other products. Scale economies are the focus of the next section.

2.1   Technology

There are two ways to manufacture titanium dioxide: batch process sulfate technology which uses ilmenite feedstock, and continuous process chloride technology, which can be adapted to handle either ilmenite or rutile.[18] The second process exhibits much stronger static scale economies than the first; engineering average cost estimates given by equations (1) and (2) in table 3.1 indicate that each doubling of plant size cuts manufacturing costs for the sulfate process by 7.5 per cent and for the chloride process by 14.3 per cent.[19]

Table 3.1 *Static and dynamic scale economies*

Equation	(1) Sulphate plants	(2) Chloride plants	(3) All Du Pont plants	(4) New Johnsonville
Time period	–	–	1955–70	1959–70
Dependent variable	LSULFA	LCHLOR	LDPCOS	LJVCOS
Independent variables				
Constant	5.609^a	5.837^a	6.499^a	5.277^a
	(0.033)	(0.056)	(0.372)	(1.826)
LEXP			-0.329^a	-0.287^b
			(0.068)	(0.162)
LCAP	-0.110^a	-0.223^a	-0.243	0.095
	(0.008)	(0.013)	(0.206)	(0.396)
LCU			-0.304^b	-0.408^b
			(0.084)	(0.266)
R^2	0.93	0.93	0.95	0.96
F	210	302	82	65
D-W	–	–	1.50	2.37
D.F.	16	23	12	8

Note: Standard errors are given in parentheses. Levels of statistical significance (one-tailed test) are $a = 1$ per cent, $b = 10$ per cent.

[18] Ilmenite ore contains less titanium dioxide than rutile ore and therefore requires more complex processing.
[19] Two points should be made here. First, Du Pont had operating experience with both processes over a wide range of scales so that these particular engineering cost estimates are probably more reliable than most. Second, although the regressions present estimates of the elasticity of cost with respect to output, it aids the intuition to talk in terms of the slope, which is defined by $S \equiv 2^{-m}$ where S is the slope and m the elasticity. The figures cited above in the text are equal to $1 - S$.

Table 3.2 *Variable definitions and sources*

Variable	Definition	Sources
LSULFA	Logarithm of deflated average manufacturing costs for the sulfate process at capacity operation.	CX 381
LCHLOR	Logarithm of deflated average manufacturing costs for the chloride process at capacity operation.	CX 40Z
LDPCOS	Logarithm of Du Pont's average cost of sales (current figures deflated by the wholesale price index).	CX 109Z14
LJVCOS	Logarithm of average labour costs at Du Pont's new Johnsonville plant (current figures deflated by the wholesale price index).	CX 109Z12
LEXP	Logarithm of cumulated titanium dioxide tonnage at all Du Pont plants (regression 3) and at New Johnsonville (regression 4).	Ghemawat (1982)
LCAP	Logarithm of capacity at the relevant plant (regressions 1, 2, and 4) and of weighted average capacity at all Du Pont plants (regression 3).	Ghemawat (1982)
LCU	Logarithm of capacity utilization at all Du Pont plants (regression 3) and at New Johnsonville (regression 4).	Ghemawat (1982)

Industry sources also indicate that learning effects are present. Du Pont's calculations, based on data from 1950 to 1970, indicate a learning rate (i.e., elasticity of average costs with respect to cumulated output) of 0.322, or a slope of 80 per cent [CX 1 09Z14]. My estimates, based on the 1955–70 period because of reports of disequilibrium until the mid-1950s, are presented in equation (3). The learning rate turns out to be 0.329, which is very close to the Du Pont figure. The aggregate static scale economy coefficient of 0.243 – corresponding to a slope of 84.5 per cent – meshes well with the estimate in equation (2) (as it should, because all of Du Pont's expansion over this period was chloride based) but is not statistically significant. Finally, for given levels of experience and capacity, greater capacity use lowers costs.

To alleviate anxiety about the level of aggregation used in equation (3), I also calculated a learning rate for labour costs at Du Pont's New Johnsonville plant. The coefficient of 0.287 in equation (4) corresponds to a slope at 82.0 per cent and indicates, I think, the adequacy of an 80–5 per cent learning curve as a ballpark figure.[20]

The absolute cost positions of titanium dioxide plants depend not just on scale economies but also on such process-related factors as investment required per ton of

[20] A referee also voiced misgivings that equations (3) and (4) might be misspecified. In testing for first-order autocorrelation, the Durbin–Watson statistic tended to fall into the inconclusive region (which tends to be large for small sample sizes). This leaves open the possibility that cost reductions were based on exogenous technical progress – although sustained interfirm differences in production efficiency then become quite difficult to explain.

Table 3.3 *Costs in 1972 cents/Lb*

	Chloride-Ilmenite	Chloride-Rutile	Sulfate
Ore	2.5	3.5	2.5
Other ingredients	3.9	2.9	3.7
Energy	1.5	1.5	2.9
Labour	1.9	2.9	3.7
Miscellaneous	4.6	4.6	4.1
Capital	3.0	2.5	4.0
Waste disposal	0.2	0.1	0.3
	17.6	18.0	21.2

Sources: [CX 23], [CX 28] and various other documents.

capacity and the costs of ingredients and waste disposal. Table 3.3 presents some rough pre-1970 estimates for 50,000 ton per year plants operating at capacity and drawing on similar pools of learning but using different technologies.[21] The data indicate that, at that scale and date, the rutile and ilmenite chloride processes were at rough cost parity but enjoyed a 15–17 per cent cost advantage over the sulfate process.

2.2   Industry history

National Lead began production of titanium dioxide in the United States in 1918. Du Pont entered the industry through acquisition in 1931. By 1955, American Cyanamid and Glidden (to be acquired later by SCM) had joined their ranks.

Until the mid-1960s, all firms with the exception of Du Pont used the sulfate process. While expanding its sulfate units in the 1930s, Du Pont had become aware of problems with the process [AB, p. 6] and in 1941 it began work on a manufacturing process using chloride technology. (The decision to chlorinate ilmenite rather than rutile was made simply because little rutile was available at the time whereas Du Pont had captive stocks of high-quality ilmenite [CX 16].) A process of learning-by-doing at progressively larger scales culminated in the successful operation of the 35,000 ton chloride unit at Edge Moor in 1951. This was followed by the 1958 start-up of a plant at New Johnsonville, Tennessee, that had an initial capacity of 45,000 tons but was expanded to 100,000 tons by the end of the 1960s.

The low costs and superior product of the New Johnsonville plant inspired the other producers (who now included New Jersey Zinc, subsequently to be acquired by Gulf & Western) to undertake their own experiments with chloride technology. These differed from Du Pont's early essays in one important respect. By the late 1950s, rutile ore had been discovered in large quantities in Australia. The ore's low price combined with the lower investment costs of the rutile process and its relative simplicity and

---

[21] I have tried to eliminate accounting distortions.

Table 3.4 *Relative mill costs*

	1972	1973	1974	1975	1976
Ilmenite Chloride vs. Rutile	0.69	0.74	0.69	0.88	0.81
Ilmenite Chloride vs. Sulfate	0.70	0.67	0.69	0.88	0.80

Sources: [CX 182T, U].

cleanliness to make rutile the economically preferred route for any plant built between 1961 and 1969 [RX 20A]. Thus all firms, including Du Pont, based their new units in the 1960s on the rutile chloride technology. That Du Pont entered the 1970s with a substantial amount of ilmenite chloride capacity was simply an historical accident.

2.3   Disequilibrium

The years 1970 and 1971 saw a jump in ore prices and the introduction of new pollution control legislation that sharply increased waste disposal costs. These developments undercut the positions of the rutile chloride and sulfate producers respectively (table 3.4).[22] As the only producer using ilmenite chloride technology (which accounted for 70 per cent of its total capacity in 1972), Du Pont profited from these events. Combined with its greater average scale per plant and learning, they gave it total costs 21–23 per cent lower than its competitors'.

Du Pont reacted in the way section 1 predicted. In a May 1972 report to Du Pont's Executive Committee that was based on analysis of competitors, the head of the Pigments Department observed that Du Pont was 'in a unique position to increase its share of the market by a substantial amount. Sulfate producers, with the exception of NL Industries (National Lead) will be unable to cope with waste disposal problems and will shut down. (Rutile) chloride process operators probably will continue operations but it is difficult to see how they can cope with waste disposal and generate sufficient funds for major expansion' [CX 26C].

Du Pont's internal discussions indicate that the growth strategy, as the programme for pre-emption was called, was decided upon for the reasons discussed in section 1.1: Du Pont was the lowest-cost producer and it thought that margins would be higher in the long run if it pre-empted and then exercised its market power to restrict output.

Du Pont did not perceive the uncertainties that might work against pre-emption as being very significant. Demand had grown steadily since 1955 so that major fluctuations were not expected [CX 182L]. And the shutdown of three of the competitors' sulfate units did appear inevitable; the 1972 ROI on each was under 1 per cent and the parents seemed to lack either the debt capacity or the inclination to make the heavy anti-pollution investments necessary for continued operation [CX 23, 28, 246].

---

[22] Table 3.4 understates the cost advantage of the ilmenite chloride process for several reasons, including the fact that over 1972–6, Du Pont incurred heavy start-up expenditures that were expensed unduly rapidly [CX 680, P].

Table 3.5 *1972 Capacities*

Firm	Total capacity (Kilotons)	Sulfate process (%)
Du Pont	265	21
National Lead	180	100
American Cyanamid	110	64
SCM	75	67
Gulf & Western	65	62
Kerr-McGee	45	0

Source: [CX 23, 26].

In contrast, uncertainties that encouraged pre-emption were very much in evidence. Du Pont thought that the dominant share resulting from pre-emption would reduce the long-term risk of supply coordination failures – of no small importance in an industry where efficient scale was very high (at least 12 per cent of 1972 US demand) and 35 per cent of total costs were fixed even at capacity operation [CX 2Z23, 114].

At a more immediate level, the technology that competitors would have had to use to expand (rutile chloride) was more sensitive to ore prices than Du Pont's ilmenite technology; in 1972, ore accounted for 30 per cent of total cost for the former but only 18 per cent for the latter [CX 23]. So the uncertainty attending ore prices cast less of a burden on Du Pont than on other firms.[23] In fact, there is evidence that over 1972–4, competitors postponed expansions and tried to resolve the uncertainty about ore prices by developing artificial rutile with costs similar to those of natural rutile [CX 16B].

Financial constraints also seemed to weigh more heavily on its competitors than on Du Pont. The sulfate plants required especially large investments – approximately $60 per ton of capacity at 1972 prices – to meet the new pollution controls [CX 51]. Since the sulfate process accounted for a smaller fraction of total capacity for Du Pont than for any other producer except Kerr-McGee (table 3.5), its major competitors suffered more from lack of capital for expansion.

For all these reasons, the perceived profitability of the growth (i.e., pre-emption) strategy was high [CX 29K, 0]. The following sections describe its original objectives and implementation over 1972–7.

2.4   Investment policy

The growth strategy originally called for total pre-emption. In 1972, Du Pont estimated that by the end of the 13–year planning period, demand for titanium dioxide would have risen by 377,000 tons. It also assumed that apart from National Lead, all competitors would have closed their sulfate units by then, eliminating 160,000 tons of existing capacity. These developments were expected to create room

---

[23] I owe this observation to Gilbert (1978).

for 537,000 tons of new capacity, of which Du Pont intended to add 94 per cent. The target market share for 1985 was 65 per cent [CX 26].

Du Pont paid little attention to adverse uncertainties in devising this plan. Since the revised investment programme called for a tenfold increase in investment over 1972–9 compared with the earlier business plan [CX 259X], rather more attention was focused on possible capital constraints. Simulations indicated that the largest (undiscounted) cumulative cash flow shortfall of the titanium dioxide business would occur in 1978 as the second line of a new plant went on-stream, and would amount to roughly $55 million [CX 322]. This seemed a small enough part of the $410 million budgeted investment expenditure for Du Pont to feel that financing it would present no special problem [CX 23, 259].

But there was one practical barrier to total pre-emption, and that related to physical constraints on the rate of investment. For a plant with an annual capacity of 150,000 tons, there is a lag of at least four years between the decision to construct and the date on which the plant can be started up [CX 40I, I78F]. Existing plants can be expanded more quickly. Therefore in 1972, Du Pont decided to expand in two phases. Until 1975, incremental capacity was to be obtained by expanding ('reaming out') existing facilities to their practicable limits. Construction work on a large new plant was projected to begin in 1975.

These plans first began to go awry when shortages of titanium dioxide developed in 1973–4 and looked set to persist until 1977. In response, Kerr-McGee announced in mid 1974 that it would build a 50,000 ton plant at Mobile [CX 178L]. Du Pont could do little to thwart this move since it was in no position to increase the amount of capacity that it planned to add over the next four years. However, to dissuade other firms from emulating Kerr-McGee, it issued a press release that referred to the magnitude of the expansions at existing Du Pont plants and announced (falsely) that it had decided to begin construction of the 130,000 ton first line of a new plant at DeLisle, Mississippi [CX 54A, 159F].

Because of the economic downturn and unexpectedly high price sensitivity, the demand–supply imbalance for titanium dioxide began to reverse itself in 1974.[24] By early 1975, a number of factors dictated revision of the capacity plans that Du Pont had made in 1972. First, demand was expected to lag the 1972 forecasts at least through 1980 [CX 178C]. Second, the uncertainty now perceived to surround demand projections made attempts at total pre-emption seem very risky [CX 182D]. Third, unexpected leniency in the enforcement of pollution controls had let competitors' sulfate units continue to operate [CX 182E]. Fourth, low capacity utilization and sharp increases in chlorine and construction costs led planners to realize that the cash flow from the titanium dioxide business over 1975–8 would be at least $100 million below 1974 predictions [CX 54K, 75S, 254]. Since there was a corporate shortage of

---

[24] Du Pont estimated that the price elasticity of demand for titanium dioxide lay between -0.22 and -0.44 [CX 99]. My simultaneous equations model of supply and demand over 1955–70 suggests a price elasticity of -1.399. Details will be provided on request.

Table 3.6 *The implications of different DeLisle start-ups*

Strategy	Start-up date	Du Pont's 1985 share	Others' expansions: 1975–81	Du Pont discounted cash flow: 1975–84*
Maintain	Postponed	43 per cent	160,000 tons	$14 million
Growth: A	1979 Q3	< 55 per cent	110,000 tons	$53 million
Growth: B	1978 Q4	55 per cent	50,000 tons	$73 million

Note: * The cash flow is discounted at the rate of 10 per cent. Higher discount rates do not affect the rankings of the three strategies. Sources: [CX 755, 109F, 111B, 213B, C, D].

capital ('E.I. du Pont de Nemours & Co. – Titanium Dioxide', 1981), financial constraints were beginning to pinch.

Consequently, a number of major decisions were taken in February 1975. The second line at DeLisle and a 110,000 ton plant in Europe were postponed indefinitely, and expansions of existing plants that were to have been completed by 1975 were staggered until 1977 [CX 26, 172, 178E, F].

The major strategy question that Du Pont continued to wrestle with concerned the timing of the 130,000 ton first line at DeLisle. Because of reduced demand projections and capital constraints, start-up in 1977 was no longer attractive. Key managers of the Pigments Department spent five months in 1975 simulating the effects of the three scenarios listed in table 3.6. They knew that delaying DeLisle would reduce the cash outflow over the critical 1975–8 period but would also let competitors raise prices. Using estimates of these short-term price rises, competitors' costs, and the rates of return that their respective parents were known to demand on new investment projects, Du Pont calculated the amount of capacity that competitors were likely to add. Feeding the effects of these expansions back into the long-run prices (see table 3.6), it found that start-up in the third quarter of 1978 would be the most profitable choice *if* demand recovered as expected.

However, demand continued to trail forecasts. By October 1977, it was clear that Kerr-McGee had deferred its expansion plans indefinitely, so that no major competitive expansion would occur before 1982 [CX 178]. The need for capacity expansion no longer dictated the immediate start-up of DeLisle. But numerous factors – prior commitment of 77 per cent of the project cost and apprehensions about cost escalation, the ability to renew environmental permits and future credibility [CX 188T, 1969] – ensured that further delay was not advantageous so the DeLisle plant was started up in 1979.

2.5   Pricing policy

In 1972, Du Pont had decided 'to maintain prices at a point to provide cash for Du Pont expansion but limit competition's ability to expand' [CX 76D]. The price in the

Table 3.7 *1972 Returns at alternative prices*

	26 c/lb.		28 c/lb.		
	Net income ($ million)	ROI %	Net income ($ million)	ROI %	Debt capacity
Du Pont	17.9	13	23.2	16	Ample
National Lead	4.4	4	8.0	8	Marginal
American	1.6	2	3.8	5	Ample
Cyanamid	0.6	1	2.1	4	Marginal
SCM	1.3	4	2.2	7	Ample
Kerr-McGee	0.0	0	0.8	3	Marginal
Gulf & Western					

Sources: [CX 23, 28E, 246A, D, C].

first half of 1972, 26 cents/lb., seemed satisfactory on both counts. Escalated to cover inflation, it appeared adequate to let the Pigments Department self-finance all but $55 million of $410 million of investment budgeted for 1972–9 [CX 26I, 290]. By contrast, table 3.7 shows that the higher cost competitors would be unable to pay for an efficient 50,000– 100,000 ton chloride unit (at an investment cost of at least $1,000 per ton of capacity) out of their titanium dioxide operations [CX 98, 175E]. Because of this and lack of favourable operating experience with the chloride process, immediate expansion by National Lead and Gulf & Western seemed unlikely. American Cyanamid had the requisite debt capacity, but given the low ROI on its existing titanium dioxide operations, apparently did not wish to commit more resources to that industry [CX 246H]. Du Pont considered Kerr-McGee and SCM (in that order) the competitors most likely to expand [CX 213B].

Kerr-McGee moved first by initiating a 2 cents/lb. price increase in July 1972. Despite the prospect of a $10 million annualized increase in operating earnings, Du Pont refused to acquiesce because both Kerr-McGee and SCM had told major customers (who had promptly relayed the message to Du Pont) that the price increase was needed to justify their expansion plans [CX 28A]. This refusal did not immediately force competitors to back down; in 1972 Du Pont's excess capacity amounted to only 3 per cent of total industry demand so that it lacked the leverage to force a price cut.[25] As a result, an unusual two-tier price structure prevailed in the industry for nearly a year.

In 1973 and (especially) 1974, widespread shortages and rapid increases in costs led to a steep climb in price (table 3.8). Since it was operating at capacity, Du Pont had to accept these increases even though they led Kerr-McGee to announce plans to build a 50,000 ton plant.

The weakening of demand in early 1975 initially led Du Pont to adopt a tougher stance. In January, it used its excess capacity (which now accounted for 12 per cent of

[25] Gilbert (1978) also makes this point.

Table 3.8 *Du Pont's titanium dioxide cost and price indices*

	1972	1973	1974	1975	1976	1977
Ingredient, fuel and waste disposal costs	100	116	169	209	197	208
Price	100	108	140	163	178	184

Source: [CX 182P].

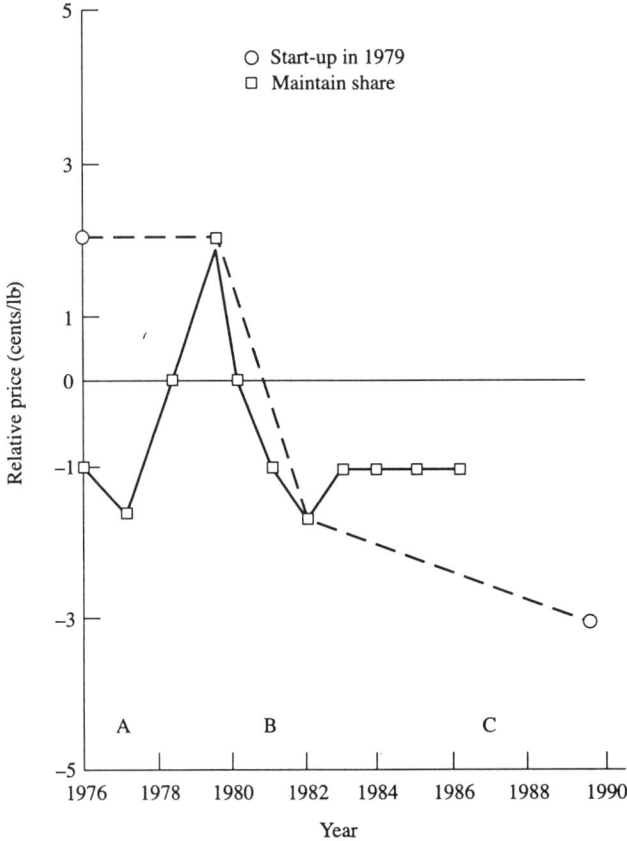

Figure 3.1 Price relative to the base case of start-up in the third quarter of 1978

industry demand) to force Kerr–McGee to roll back a 5 cents/lb. increase that it feared would encourage other competitors, especially SCM, to expand [CX 1780].

But as the full impact of the recession became clear, Du Pont realized, as we saw in the section on investment policy, that pre-emption was a risky and perhaps unattractive strategy. Accordingly, it analysed the effects on price of the three capacity strategies listed in table 3.6. The results are depicted in figure 3.1.

Consider first the implications of the maintain strategy. In phase A, the announcement that DeLisle was being abandoned was expected to let competitors take
advantage of tight supply to raise the price by 2 cents/lb. In phase B, temporary
oversupply would erode prices until in 1982 they stood at 2 cents/lb. lower than in the
base case. In phase C, competitors would descend their 80 per cent chloride learning
curve with the result that in 1990, their costs would be 4–5 per cent lower than in the
base case. This cost reduction was expected to translate into a price differential of −3
cents/lb. [CX 109Z 14].

Second, examine the perceived effects of delaying the DeLisle start-up to 1979.
In phase A, Du Pont would initially have to hold prices low in order to 'protect'
the market for DeLisle, but prices would climb in 1979 as Du Pont began operating
at capacity and lost control. In phase B, competitors would scramble to fill their
new capacity, leading to drops in price. Finally, in phase C, the industry would
return to equilibrium but competitors would have reduced their costs by learning
so that the industry price would be 1 cent/lb. lower than in the base case [CX 213
C].

These price projections were, as we noted above, used to calculate the discounted
cash flow from the three strategies over 1975–84. Thus they were instrumental in the
end-1975 decision to bring DeLisle onstream in 1978 if demand recovered – which it
did not [CX 178R].

2.6   Licensing policy

Beginning in 1972, Du Pont received a 'large number' of enquiries about licensing,
particularly from National Lead [CX 33C]. But Du Pont seemed to be aware of the
implications of licensing for the pattern of capacity expansion in the industry (section
1.4.) and rejected domestic requests without even calculating the royalties that might
be generated.

As predicted, overseas licensing presented a different picture. No requests for
licences from European producers were entertained, presumably because of Du Pont's
interest in competing directly in the West European titanium dioxide market. But Du
Pont carefully explored licence applications from countries outside its zone of interest
– Brazil, China, Japan, and the USSR. The Japanese proposal advanced to the
negotiating stage but was shelved in autumn 1977 because of weak demand [CX
180E].

The remedy proposed by the FTC in the antitrust case that it brought against Du
Pont in 1978 also agrees with our analysis. The FTC's appeal brief [p. 65] notes that:

Royalty-free licensing would 'break the chain' of this pre-emptive process by immediately
placing competitors in a position of cost parity with Du Pont . . . Licensing with royalty
fees would not be nearly as effective in upsetting the Du Pont 'growth strategy', since the
effect of requiring royalty payments would be to maintain the Du Pont cost advantage
over time. Competitors would continue to be at a cost disadvantage by the amount of
royalty payment.

3   Conclusion

Du Pont's formulation of its growth strategy agrees well with our discussion of pre-emption driven by cost asymmetries. The results are of general interest because the same process appears to drive capacity expansion in many other industries. For instance, petrochemical producers in oil-rich countries enjoy significant cost advantages based on cheap feedstock and subsidized access to capital.[26] They are expected to use their lower costs to increase their share of installed global capacity.

Also thought-provoking, though, are the results of Du Pont's strategy. They suggest that pre-emption is a hazardous process in which miscalculations can depress profitability – for the entire industry – for years to come. The moral is perhaps 'caveat pre-emptor'.

References

Arrow, K.J. (1962), 'The economic implications of learning by doing', *Review of Economic Studies*, 29, 155–73.

Beckenstein, A.R. and H.L. Gabel (1981), 'Experience curve pricing and the antitrust laws', mimeo, University of Virginia.

Caves, R.E. (1981), 'Multinational enterprises and technology transfer', mimeo, Harvard University.

Chandler, A.D. Jr. (1980), *The Visible Hand: The Managerial Revolution in American Business*, Cambridge, MA, Belknap Press.

'E. I. Du Pont de Nemours & Co.—Titanium Dioxide', 1981, Harvard Case Services.

'Federal Trade Commission vs. E. I. Du Pont de Nemours Company', FTC Docket No. 9108, Washington, DC.

Ghemawat, P. (1982), 'The experience curve and corporate strategy', Ph.D. dissertation, Harvard University.

Ghemawat, P. and A.M. Spence (1982), 'Learning curve spillovers, shared experience and market performance', mimeo, Harvard University.

Gilbert, R.J. (1978), 'Pre-emptive competition in the titanium dioxide industry', mimeo, University of California at Berkeley.

Gilbert, R.J. and R. G. Harris (1981), 'Investment decisions with economies of scale and learning', *American Economic Review*, 71, 172–7.

Haspeslagh, P. (1982), 'Portfolio planning: uses and limits', *Harvard Business Review*, 60, 58–73.

Milgrom, P. and J. Roberts (1980), 'Limit pricing and entry under incomplete information: an equilibrium analysis', mimeo, Northwestern University.

Porter, M.E. (1980), 'Strategic interaction: some lessons from industry histories for theory and antitrust policy', mimeo, Harvard University.

Scherer, F.M. *et al.* (1975), *The Economics of Multi-Plant Operation: An International Comparisons Study*, Cambridge, MA, Harvard University Press.

Shepherd, W.G. (1979), 'Anatomy of a monopoly (1): Excess capacity and the control of price', *Antitrust Law and Economics Review*, 11, 103–16.

(1980a), 'Anatomy of a monopoly (II): the power to control prices', *Antitrust Law and Economics Review*, 12, 73–92.

[26] For a useful but dated discussion, see Turner and Bedore (1977).

(1980b), 'Anatomy of a monopoly (III): costs, prices, and innovation', *Antitrust Law and Economics Review*, 12, 93–106.

Sheshinski, E. (1967), 'Tests of the 'Learning by Doing' hypothesis', *Review of Economics and Statistics*, 49, 568–78.

Smith, R.L., II (1981), 'Efficiency gains from strategic investment', *Journal of Industrial Economics*, 30, 1–23.

Turner, L. and J. Bedore (1977), 'Saudi and Iranian petrochemicals and refining: trade warfare in the 1980s?', *International Affairs*, 53, 572–86.

Chapter 4

Declining markets
The devolution of declining industries

Pankaj Ghemawat and Barry Nalebuff

1   Introduction

Models of dynamic competition generally take a rosy view of time: markets expand; better technologies become available; information improves. In this preoccupation with time as an engine of progress, environments in which time is an agent of regress have been shunted aside. Yet, declining industries form an important part of developed economies: more than 10 per cent of the United States' 1977 manufacturing output was accounted for by industries whose real output had shrunk over the 1967–77 period.[1]

In declining industries the important competitive moves pertain to disinvestment rather than investment. An industry facing decline must reduce its capacity in order to remain profitable. Capacity reduction, however, is a public good that must be provided privately.[2] Each firm would like its competitors to shoulder the reduction: a firm may even maintain excess capacity – and sustain losses – in order to force competitors to withdraw sooner. The question arises: Who gives in first?

The timing game in a declining industry is therefore a war of attrition rather than a

This article first appeared in the *Quarterly Journal of Economics*, 1990, Vol. 105, pp. 167–86.
We are very grateful for comments provided by John Londregan, Mike Whinston, and two anonymous referees.

[1] This estimate is based on Bureau of Labor Statistics Data for 95 'Economic Growth' industries. The estimate would be even higher at a lower level of aggregation.

[2] For a discussion on motivating private provision of public goods, see Bliss and Nalebuff (1984).

race to pre-empt. In the original model of the war of attrition (Maynard Smith, 1974), each competitor chooses between continuing to 'fight' at a pre-specified level of intensity or conceding; the competitor that hangs in the longest wins the prize. Ghemawat and Nalebuff (1985) applied this model, with its dichotomous choice, to declining industries by restricting production to be an all-or-nothing decision for each firm. This chapter, in sharp contrast, allows firms greater strategic flexibility by letting them continuously adjust their capacities as demand declines.

We show that with continuous adjustment, there is a unique subgame-perfect outcome to the battle over declining markets. The Davids cut the Goliaths down to their own size: large firms are the first to reduce capacity, and they continue to do so until they have shrunk to the size of their formerly smaller rivals. *Ceteris paribus*, survivability is inversely related to size. This prediction appears to fit with recent empirical findings.

The chapter's outline is as follows. Section 2 discusses theoretical work on declining industries and introduces our results. Section 3 offers corroborative empirical evidence. Section 4 presents the formal model and its equilibrium. Section 5 provides a brief conclusion. The appendix contains the proofs of all lemmata.

2   Theoretical literature

Our previous paper examined market decline in a highly stylized setting (Ghemawat and Nalebuff, 1985). Firms were perfectly informed about their competitors' costs and capacities. Re-entry was not allowed after exit. Demand declined continuously and deterministically. Exit was an all-or-nothing decision. Under these four assumptions, there was a unique subgame-perfect equilibrium: the smaller of two equally efficient duopolists forced its larger rival to exit as soon as duopoly profits turned negative.

Does the smallest firm continue to enjoy a competitive advantage in a more general setting? It is useful to recapitulate what we know about the effects of relaxing our previous assumptions.

Incomplete information

In a paper concurrent with our first model, Fudenberg and Tirole (1986) examine the exit decision in an environment of incomplete information where each firm is uncertain about its rival's costs. They provide conditions for the existence and uniqueness of sequential equilibrium in duopoly. When expectations are symmetric, if exit occurs, it is the less-efficient firm that leaves.

Re-entry

Londregan (1987), in a model of the industry lifecycle, allows for the possibility of re-entry after entry and exit. He shows that if re-entry costs are positive, there is a unique subgame-perfect equilibrium in the all-or-nothing exit game with complete information: smallness continues to be an advantage during decline and, by backward induction, also during the growth phase (see also Fishman (1989) for the effect of decline and exit on entry deterrence).

Probabilistic decline

Fine and Li (1986) consider a market that is declining probabilistically. In each period the probability distribution of demand is stochastically worse than before. If the intervals between decisions are sufficiently short, there is a unique subgame-perfect equilibrium in which the smaller firm outlasts its larger competitor.[3] Huang and Li (1986) study exit decisions in a model with random drifts in demand. Because demand may not decline, there is no endgame to work backwards from. Even so, if the state space is continuous so that demand changes smoothly, there is again a unique subgame-perfect equilibrium in which the smaller firm will never be forced out by its larger rival.

Capacity adjustment

Whinston (1987, 1988) examines an oligopoly in which capacity is adjustable in lumps equal to plant size. In this framework he shows that it is difficult to reach any general conclusions about the pattern of plant closures. When each firm controls several differently sized plants, there is no theoretical prediction about the order of exit. There are several complications. A firm that withdraws a small plant now may be at a strategic disadvantage later if its remaining plants are large. Or a firm with many small plants may find this flexibility disadvantageous against a larger firm with one big plant. Thus, it is hard to separate out the effect of flexibility versus size. To focus on size alone, Whinston considers a special case when all plants are equally sized. There is still a complication; who moves first to break a tie between the two largest firms? The structured pattern of exit returns when the equilibrium play is independent of the tie-breaking rule (a quasi-markov equilibrium) – only the largest firms reduce capacity. Following the proof of theorem 1, we discuss the relationship between our results in greater detail.

In the present analysis we prefer to maintain the assumption of complete information: in the typical declining industry competitors are well acquainted, and the production technologies embodied in extant investments are common knowledge. The payoffs to allowing re-entry or stochastic demand trajectories are probably limited: the papers cited above suggest that smallness continues to be a competitive advantage with these generalizations.

We believe that there is a large payoff in extending the models of exit beyond the all-or-nothing production technology. Although such technologies characterize some industries with large, inflexible plants such as alumina refining (see Ghemawat and Nalebuff, 1985), firms usually shrink continuously as demand declines (soda ash, rayon, baby foods, vacuum tubes, cigars, and electric coffee percolators are some of the many examples: see Harrigan, 1980). We study competition under the opposite of

---

[3] In their paper they argue that probabilistic decline allows the possibility of multiple equilibria. The multiplicity, however, is an artifact of the long time periods between decision making. Imagine that the time interval between decisions is sufficiently long that only one decision is made for all time. Then, we are in the traditional one-shot or static Nash equilibrium model where we know multiple solutions are possible. It is possible to extend the Fine and Li model to prove that if the decision periods are sufficiently short, there is a unique sequential equilibrium in which the smaller firm always outlasts its larger rival.

all-or-nothing adjustment; we focus on production technologies where capacity is continuously adjustable. This allows us to model the effect of size differences without the complication of differential flexibility.

Allowing variable capacity is an important extension for an additional reason: it represents a significant generalization of the standard war of attrition. Wars of attrition, as usually formulated, allow only two actions: fight or concede. The possibility of variable capacity corresponds to allowing variable levels of concession, which considerably complicates calculating equilibrium. To our knowledge, this chapter and one by Whinston (1987, 1988) are the first to characterize the equilibria in a war of attrition with variable response possibilities. The cost of this extension is that we must confine our attention to a highly stylized oligopoly with uniform and constant marginal costs.

We demonstrate that given continuous capacity adjustment, there is a unique subgame-perfect equilibrium in declining industries. In this equilibrium the largest of several equally efficient firms will reduce capacity alone until its market share is equal to that of its next smallest rival. Once parity is reached, the two largest firms reduce capacity together while all others maintain capacity. Then, when they reach the size of the third biggest firm, all three start to shrink at an equal rate, and so on.

The motivation behind this result is that marginal revenue is inversely proportional to firm size. Firm i's marginal revenue equals $Q_i P'(Q) + P(Q)$; this is a declining function of Q_i since a bigger firm suffers more from a decline in price. In the absence of economies of scale, bigger firms have, therefore, a greater incentive to reduce capacity. The force of this marginal revenue argument is quite distinct from the level that operates when capacity decisions are all-or-nothing. In the all-or-nothing environment the survivor of competition among equally efficient rivals is the firm that has the longest profitable tenure as a monopolist.

To help illustrate the novel results of this chapter, consider a duopoly where firm 1 operates four machines and firm 2 operates two machines.[4] If the firms must make a dichotomous choice between operating at full capacity or exiting in toto, Ghemawat and Nalebuff (1985) demonstrate that the capacity vector evolves from (4,2) to (0,2) to (0,0) as the industry declines. In contrast, if firms may withdraw machines continuously, the only subgame-perfect equilibrium for the industry capacity vector is (4,2) to (X,2) to (2,2) to (Y, Y) to (0,0), where X falls smoothly from 4 to 2 and Y falls smoothly from 2 to 0. In words, the larger firm reduces capacity until its size equals that of its smaller competitor. Once parity is reached, the firms shrink together.

The move towards equalization of market shares provides the testable hypothesis that large firms undertake a disproportionate share of the capacity reductions during decline. Empirical support for this hypothesis is marshalled in the following section. The formal propositions are then proved in the context of the stylized model presented in section 4.

The available empirical evidence on decline suggests that firms with larger market shares experience greater pressures to shrink as an industry devolves. Herein, we provide a review of three case studies and relevant cross-sectional evidence.

---

[4] The machines are all of equal size and equal efficiency.

Company	Plant capacities in 1967 (kilotons)	1968	1969	1970	1971	1972	1973	1974	1975	1976	1977	1978
Allied	450	——X										
	800	———————————————————X										
	1000	——————————————————————————————→										
Olin	400	—————————————————————X										
	410	———————————————X										
PPG	250	——————————————————————————X										
	600	——————————————X										
Diamond Shamrock	800	—————————————————————————X										
BASF Wyandotte	800	——————————————————————————X										

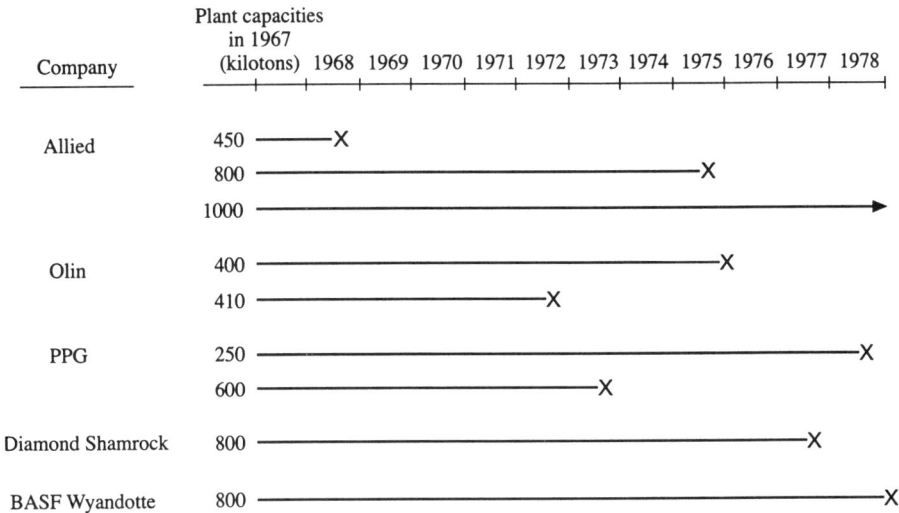

Figure 4.1 Plant closures in the synthetic soda ash industry
Source: Harrigan (1980, chapter 5).

The first case describes the decline of the US synthetic soda ash industry over the 1967–78 period (see Harrigan, 1980, chapter 5). In 1967 almost three-quarters of the soda ash consumed in the United States was synthesized from limestone and salt. Five firms (listed in figure 4.1) accounted for 99 per cent of the domestic synthetic soda ash capacity. All five employed the mature and very capital-intensive Solvay process. The remainder of the US soda ash market was supplied by natural reserves that had begun to be mined in Wyoming in the 1950s. Natural soda ash cost significantly less to 'produce' than did synthetic soda ash; the costs of transporting it, however, were higher because most soda ash customers were located east of the Mississippi, closer to the synthetic soda ash capacity.

Under pressure from natural soda ash, synthetic soda ash producers operated at 89 per cent of their capacities in 1967 – an amount probably just below their break-even level. Over the next decade the tide continued to turn against synthetic producers. Wyoming relaxed its regulations governing the mining of natural soda ash. Higher energy costs and stricter environmental regulations undercut the Solvay process because it was more energy and emission intensive. Since the Solvay capacity required substantial reinvestment to be kept operational, the stage was set for plant closures.

Over the next decade the output of synthetic soda ash fell by nearly two-thirds. In 1978 only one Solvay plant, out of the original nine, remained operational.[5] Figure 4.1

---

[5] The sole survivor, Allied Chemical, operated the largest plant in the industry. Harrigan (1980, pp. 136–7) notes that it benefited from the most advanced Solvay technology, access to a saline lake (which facilitated waste disposal), and the eastern-most location of any synthetic soda ash plant (which gave it the biggest advantage in terms of transportation cost over producers of natural soda ash).

depicts the devolution of that industry. The pattern of closures supports our predictions in two respects. First, each of the three multi-plant firms closed a plant before either of the two single-plant operators. Second, none of the five firms dropped out of the market until all firms were down to one plant apiece.[6]

Our second example is based on Baden-Fuller and Hill's (1984) case study of the UK steel castings industry. The demand for UK steel castings declined by 42 per cent over the 1975–81 period, and the industry's return to sales ·dropped from 11 per cent to 1 percent. Competitors adjusted their capital stocks by closing foundries. Executives of the two largest firms, F.H. Lloyd and the Weir Group, 'felt that they had borne the brunt of the costs of rationalization' (Baden-Fuller and Hill, 1984, p. 23). They accounted for 41 per cent of industry output in 1975, but for 63 per cent of the capacity that was withdrawn over the 1975–81 period; this reduced their combined market share to 24 per cent. Some of the Lloyd and Weir foundries that were closed had been more efficient than foundries that their competitors continued to operate.

The US integrated steelmaking industry provides a third example of devolution. During the 1960s and 1970s, imports and minimills (which recycle steel scrap) intensified the pressure on integrated steelmakers. Deily (1985) studied the contraction of the eight largest integrated steelmakers which together accounted for 90 per cent of US capacity in 1960. Because they faced large barriers to exit, Deily focused on their replacement investments over the 1962–79 period. After controlling for plant efficiency and reinvestment requirements, she concluded that (p. 125) 'firm size seemed to have a negative impact on *all* major investments during these years. It is possible that some of the laggardness reflected the strategic behaviour described by Ghemawat and Nalebuff (1985)'. It is worth adding that the eight-firm concentration ratio in steelmaking fell from 90 per cent in 1960 to 76 per cent by 1979.

In order to ascertain whether the market-share effects identified in these case studies hold up more broadly, Ghemawat (1985) used Harvard University's PICA database to analyse the determinants of changes in four-firm concentration ratios over the 1967–77 period in 294 four-digit US manufacturing industries. Since it is difficult to control for intra-industry differences in efficiency based on publicly available data, the basic specification did not attempt to do so. This omission is likely to bias the results towards the null hypothesis – that declining demand does not decrease concentration – in proportion to one's prior belief that size is positively correlated with efficiency.

Ghemawat found that even in the absence of controls for cost differences, a dummy variable indicating declines in real industry output over the sampled period was positively associated, at the 5–10 per cent level of statistical significance, with decreases in industry concentration. When the rate of decline was introduced as a continuous independent variable, again he found a significant correlation: the higher the rate of decline, the greater the observed rate of decrease of concentration.

---

[6] Note that some of this evidence goes against the predictions of Ghemawat and Nalebuff (1985) that the order or exit should follow plant size. Of course, the smaller firms may be producing below efficient scale. Or, they may be producing for a market niche so that their fate will be less affected by the great winds blowing against the industry.

Lieberman (1989) offers the most careful and comprehensive cross-sectional tests of the predictions implied by the theoretical models of exit and devolution. His results are based on a sample of 30 chemical products, each of which experienced chronic declines in output lasting five years or longer. 'In general in declining industries, it appears that small producers suffer disproportionately high mortality rates whereas large-share firms make more frequent incremental reductions of capacity. When analysis is limited to survivor firms in steeply declining industries, there is significant evidence that firm size convergence is due to more rapid divestment by the largest producers' (p. 17). Specifically, of the 15 products in Lieberman's sample that experienced declines in capacity of 40 per cent or more, 12 exhibited convergence in the sizes of the survivors. This evidence, together with the cases discussed above, is suggestive of a tendency for market shares to converge during decline.

4   Model specification

The formal structure of our model consists of the following notation and assumptions:

(A1) There are m competitors in the market. Initially, firm i has a capacity level of $k_i(0)$. The industry capacity vector at time t is represented by $K(t) \equiv [k_i(t), \ldots, k_m(t)]$.

(A2) For each firm i the flow cost of maintaining its capacity is C per unit. There are no other operating costs. Production is constrained by capacity; set-up costs preclude the addition of new capacity or the reintroduction of previously withdrawn capacity.

(A3) Capacity can be adjusted continuously. Reductions are irreversible.

(A4) Time is quantized into periods of duration Δ. Period n begins at time t^n. An approximation of the continuous time solution is the equilibrium in the limit where Δ approaches zero.

(A5) A withdrawal of capacity is effected at the beginning of the relevant time interval and is reflected immediately in cost reduction. Withdrawal decisions are made simultaneously.

(A6) Firm i's cost of withdrawing capacity is S per unit. This cost will be positive if exit costs (e.g., severance payments) predominate or negative if the retired capacity has a sufficiently large salvage value. If the output price is zero, exit costs are not sufficiently large to prevent firms from withdrawing capacity: $rS < C$, where r is the discount rate.

(A7) Each firm's output is a perfect substitute for every other firm's output. Define total output at t by $Y(t) \equiv k_1(t) + \ldots + k_m(t)$. The price to firm i is $P(Y(t), t)$.[7]

---

[7] We are implicitly assuming that firms produce at full capacity. Although this simplifies the exposition, the results generalize directly to the case where firms may produce at less than full

(A8) The inverse demand function $P(Y,t)$ is well defined and continuous for all $Y \geq 0$. $P(0,t)$ is bounded, and $P(Y,t)$ equals zero for some finite Y. Furthermore, $P(Y,t)$ has continuous second derivatives and is downward sloping: $P'(Y,t) \equiv dP(Y,t)/dY < 0, P''(Y,t) \equiv d^2 P(Y,t)/dY^2$ is continuous.

(A9) Firm i's marginal revenue at any Cournot–Nash equilibrium output level (k_i^*) is a non-increasing function of total industry output: $P'(Y,t) + k_i^* P''(Y,t) \leq 0$ for all possible Y. Hahn (1962) demonstrates that this condition ensures the stability of the Nash equilibrium.[8]

(A10) Demand is declining towards zero for exogenous reasons. For any $\varepsilon > 0$ there exists a T such that $P(0,t) < \varepsilon$ for all $t \geq T$.

(A11) Marginal revenue at full capacity, $P(Y,t) + k_i P'(Y,t)$, is a strictly decreasing function of t for all Y. Assumptions A10 and A11 are both satisfied, for example, if $P(Y,t) = P(Y)e^{-gt}$.

These assumptions lead to a unique subgame-perfect equilibrium. The firms with the largest capacity are the first to shrink. When the formerly larger firms shrink to the size of their smaller rivals, the latter join in subsequent reductions of capacity.

Although the arguments are technical, the intuition is simple. Imagine that all firms act 'myopically'; i.e., each firm seeks to maximize only its current period profits. This behaviour leads to a sequence of period-by-period Cournot–Nash equilibria. Since marginal costs are equal, the firms with the smallest outputs have the greatest marginal revenue. This implies that the smallest firms never act first to reduce capacity.

This sequence of period-by-period Nash equilibrium strategies is the unique subgame-perfect equilibrium. When each firm acts myopically, any deviation in output must lower current period profits. The only reason to deviate, therefore, would be to raise future profits. In lemma 2 we show that maintaining capacity in excess of the myopic equilibrium has no effect on future outcomes. Since demand is declining, the firm will already have some excess capacity; extra units of excess capacity do not convince competitors to further reduce their output. In lemma 4, we show that a reduction of capacity below the myopic solution also fails to increase future profits; it may even decrease profits by encouraging competitors to increase their future outputs (i.e., temper their reductions). This intuition is now made rigorous.

---

capacity. The reason is that production costs depend only on capacity. Thus, in a one-period problem, no firm would maintain excess capacity. We then show (theorem 1) that the unique subgame-perfect equilibrium follows the sequence of period-by-period maximizations. This remains true whether or not there is the option of maintaining idle capacity.

[8] Note that Hahn (1962) makes an a priori assumption that there is a unique Nash equilibrium. Since we are also interested in proving uniqueness, his condition must be modified so that the stated inequality holds at any Nash equilibrium. The general condition will be satisfied if $YP'(Y,t)$ is a declining function of Y.

Lemma 1

There exists a unique *Cournot–Nash equilibrium to the single-period problem where each firm maximizes its current flow of profits subject to the constraint that no firm produces above its capacity:* $k_i(t^n) \leq k_i(t^{n-1})$.

Proof of Lemma 1   See the appendix.

The output at this Cournot–Nash equilibrium is denoted by $k_i^*(K(t^{n-1}), t^n)$. We refer to the strategy of maximizing current profits as *myopic* behaviour.

Definition 1

$K^*(K(t^{n-1}), t^n)$ *is the vector of myopic Nash strategies*[9]

$$K^*(K(t^{n-1}), t^n) \equiv \left[k_1^*(K(t^{n-1}), t^n), \ldots, k_m^*(K(t^{n-1}), t^n)\right].$$

The *sequence* of myopic Nash equilibrium strategies is then defined by calculating the myopic Nash equilibrium level in period t^n, where the initial capacity vector is given by the myopic Nash equilibrium from period t^{n-1}. Proposition 1 states that in this sequence of myopic Nash equilibrium strategies, only the largest firms reduce capacity.

Proposition 1

Order the firms so that $k_1(0) \leq k_2(0) \leq \ldots \leq k_m(0)$. *In the sequence of myopic Nash equilibria, each period there exists some* $k^*(t^n)$ *such that all firms with initial capacity below* $k^*(t^n)$ *remain at their initial capacity and all firms with initial capacity above* $k^*(t^n)$ *have reduced their capacity to* $k^*(t^n)$:

$$K^*(K(t^{n-1}), t^n) = [k_1(0), k_2(0), \ldots, k_j(0), k^*(t^n), \ldots, k^*(t^n)]$$

where $k_j(0)$ *is the maximum initial capacity less than* $k^*(t^n)$.

Proof of Proposition 1   Define $k^*(t^n)$ by

$$\int_0^\Delta \left\{k^*(t^n)P'(K^*, t^n + \tau) + P(K^*, t^n + \tau) - (C - rS)\right\}e^{-r\tau}d\tau = 0$$

where K^* is shorthand for the industry's unique, myopic Cournot–Nash equilibrium level of output in period t^n. All firms with capacity $k^*(t^n)$ are maximizing current period profits. Because P' is negative, all firms with $k_i(0) < k^*(t^n)$ have positive marginal profit at full capacity utilization. In the myopic solution all such firms are capacity constrained. Hence, $K^*(K(t^{n-1}), t^n)$ is a Cournot–Nash equilibrium for period t^n, and by lemma 1 this equilibrium is unique.   ∎

To calculate a subgame-perfect equilibrium for this model poses no theoretical difficulties. We proceed using the logic of dynamic programming and backward

---

[9] For notational consistency, let $K^*(K(t^{-1}), t^0)$ equal $K(0)$, the initial capacity vector.

induction. The primary conceptual issue is to characterize the nature of the solution. We show that for equally efficient oligopolists, only the largest firms reduce capacity in response to declining demand. This characterization of the subgame-perfect Nash equilibrium coincides with the description of the sequence of myopic Nash equilibrium strategies proved in proposition 1, as we now show that the two solutions are the same.

Theorem 1

Under assumptions A1–A11, $K^*\left(K\left(t^{n-1}\right), t^n\right)$ is the unique subgame-perfect equilibrium capacity vector in period t^n for all n.

Proof of Theorem 1   The proof is based on backward induction. We first show that the result is true past some time T. Then by assuming the result from period t^{n+1} onwards, this implies that from time t^n onwards there exists a unique subgame-perfect equilibrium which coincides with the myopic Nash equilibrium in each period. Intermediate steps in the argument are provided by lemmata 2–5, which are stated and proved in the appendix.

Since demand is declining towards zero, eventually all firms will cease to produce, even as a monopolist. Lemma 5 shows that there exists a time T such that once $t^x \geq T$, the unique myopic solution coincides with any subgame-perfect equilibria: all firms have zero capacity.

The inductive hypothesis tells us that over $\left(t^{n+1}, \infty\right)$ there is a unique subgame-perfect equilibrium which coincides with the sequence of period-by-period Cournot–Nash solutions. We need to extend this back one period to t^n. By lemma 1 the myopic Nash equilibrium in period t^n is unique. To demonstrate that this is also the unique subgame-perfect equilibrium, it is sufficient to show that producing either more or less than $k_i^*\left(K\left(t^{n-1}\right), t^n\right)$ results in lower aggregate profits over $\left[t^n, T\right]$. Any deviation away from k_i^* lowers profits over $\left[t^n, t^{n+1}\right]$, since k_i^* is the one-period profit-maximizing strategy. The only reason to deviate, therefore, is that it might produce higher profits over $\left[t^{n+1}, T\right]$. In this interval the inductive hypothesis allows us to consider the sequence of period-by-period Cournot–Nash solutions as the unique subgame-perfect equilibrium. We show for this sequence of myopic Nash equilibrium strategies, any deviation away from $k_i^*\left(K\left(t^{n-1}\right), t^n\right)$ cannot raise profits over $\left[t^{n+1}, T\right]$.

Consider the payoff to a firm that deviates and chooses to produce more than the myopic level, $k_i' > k_i^*\left(K\left(t^{n-1}\right), t^n\right)$. Because firm i is able to produce more than k_i^*, it is obviously not constrained by capacity in the period t^n myopic Nash equilibrium. In the sequence of myopic Nash equilibria that follow, lemma 2 shows that all unconstrained firms produce a strictly smaller output each period. As a result, from period t^{n+1} onwards, the subgame-perfect equilibrium in each period is unchanged: $K^*\left(K'\left(t^n\right), t^{n+1}\right) = K^*\left(K\left(t^n\right), t^{n+1}\right)$. The additional capacity of firm i held at t^n is eliminated immediately in period t^{n+1} and does not affect profits over $\left[t^{n+1}, T\right]$.

Consider, alternatively, the payoff to a firm that deviates and chooses to produce $k_i' < k_i^*\left(K\left(t^{n-1}\right), t^n\right)$. In this case the subgame-perfect equilibrium from periods t^{n+1} onwards may change. Lemma 3 implies that the new subgame-perfect equilibrium involves firm i producing no more and the other firms producing no less than at the no-deviation benchmark. This outcome leads to (weakly) lower profits for firm i by lemma 4. Intuitively, the reaction curves are negatively sloped so that excess capacity reduction by firm i encourages its rivals' production and thus reduces its own profits.

We have shown that any output other than $k_i^*(K(t^{n-1}), t^n)$ in period t^n results in strictly lower profits in period t^n without any possibility of future gain in the continuation equilibrium. Thus, $k_i^*(K(t^{n-1}), t^n)$ is the unique subgame-perfect equilibrium output in period t^n. By induction this is true for all n. The sequence of myopic Nash equilibrium strategies is the unique subgame-perfect equilibrium.

Remark 1

One might be tempted to argue for uniqueness more directly. Subgame-perfection is a stronger condition than Nash equilibrium. Since every subgame-perfect equilibrium is *a fortiori* Nash, if there were multiple subgame-perfect equilibria there would have to be multiple Nash equilibria. It might therefore be argued that since lemma 1 establishes uniqueness of the Nash equilibrium, there can be at most one subgame-perfect equilibrium. This argument is flawed. Lemma 1 only establishes the uniqueness of the *myopic* Nash equilibrium in each period. If firm i lowers its capacity below $k_i^*(K(t^{n-1}), t^n)$, this can change the sequence of subsequent myopic Nash equilibria. The full Nash equilibrium of the multi-period problem is *not* unique.

Remark 2

If capacity reductions are reversible, the result remains true, and the argument is even simpler. In each period there is a unique 'myopic' Cournot–Nash equilibrium, and this equilibrium is not affected by the previous play (since reductions are reversible). The uniqueness of the single period-by-period Nash play together with a finite horizon immediately implies that there is a unique subgame-perfect equilibrium.

Remark 3

Weaker conditions that also lead to lemmata 1–5 will provide a generalization of theorem 1. For example, the market can decline stochastically, as in Fine and Li (1986).

There is no direct generalization of theorem 1 when firms have heterogeneous costs. The reason is that without equal marginal costs, we can no longer order marginal revenue by output. As a result, the decline in demand affects firms differentially depending on both size and marginal cost. Even if there remains a unique subgame-perfect Nash equilibrium, there is no longer a simple characterization result (such as proposition 1) describing an orderly pattern to the capacity reductions.

A comparison with Whinston (1988) suggests that the assumption of continuous capacity adjustment is essential to our result. If capacity adjustment is subject to an integer constraint, the proof of theorem 1 breaks down. The problem arises in lemma 1; because of integer constraints, there is no guarantee of a unique solution even in the one-period myopic problem.

It is worth pinpointing the source of difficulty. If capacity lumps come in different sizes, multiple equilibria are a generic problem. But, if capacity lumps are all equally sized, multiple equilibria arise in the one-period problem only to break ties. When there are two equally large firms, which one reduces capacity first? A tiebreaking rule is needed. Because the rule may depend on the earlier play of the game, it can contaminate the entire characterization of the previous play. Whinston solves this problem by restricting firms to 'super-markov' strategies; the resolution of ties cannot depend on earlier play. With this additional restriction, he shows that with equally sized lumps of capacity, only the largest firms reduce capacity.

Our result is a limiting case of the discrete model. In the passage to continuous time we do not require super-markov strategies. For intuition, consider the sequence of period-by-period myopic Nash equilibrium strategies. With lumps of any size one of two equally sized firms must move before the other. With continuous capacity adjustment there is no tension between equally sized firms; they reduce capacity together. There is a unique myopic equilibrium in every period which then coincides with the subgame-perfect solution.

5   Conclusions

We have demonstrated that in situations where equally efficient oligopolists start out with asymmetric market shares, larger firms will bear the brunt of capacity reductions until their market shares equal those of their smaller competitors. Once shares do equalize, all competitors with identical capacities reduce together.

Although some empirical corroboration of these conclusions is available, we still face obvious gaps in our understanding of how industries actually decline. One important item on the research agenda concerns the impact of cost differences (arising, possibly, from economies of scale) on shrinkage patterns. An additional agenda item is to expand firms' strategy spaces to permit cost-reducing investment. The considerable amount of theoretical and empirical work that remains to be done in this area suggests that the study of exit will continue to be a growth industry.

Appendix

This appendix provides the proofs for lemmata 1–5.

Lemma 1

There exists a unique Cournot–Nash equilibrium to the single-period problem where each firm maximizes its current flow of profits subject to the constraint that no firm produces above its capacity, $k_i(t^n) \leq k^i(t^{n-1})$. The output at this Cournot–Nash equilibrium is denoted by $k_i^*\left(K(t^{n-1}), t^n\right)$

$$k_i^*\left(K(t^{n-1}), t^n\right) \equiv \underset{k_i}{\mathrm{argmax}}$$

$$\int_0^\Delta k_i\left[\left(\sum_{j\neq i} k_j^*\left(K(t^{n-1}), t^n\right) + k_i, t^n + \tau\right) - (C - rS)\right] e^{-r\tau} d\tau$$

subject to

$$k_i \leq k_i(t^{n-1}).$$

Proof of lemma 1   Assumptions (A8) and (A9) provide sufficient continuity to prove the existence of at least one myopic Nash equilibrium (see Friedman, 1977). Here we concentrate on proving uniqueness.[10] At any myopic Nash equilibrium marginal profit for firm i equals[11]

$$M\Pi_i = \int_0^\Delta \left\{ k_i P'(K^*, t^n + \tau) + P(K^*, t^n + \tau) - (C - rS) \right\} e^{-\tau} d\tau \geq 0. \quad (1A)$$

Let there be two distinct myopic Nash equilibria, with total capacity levels K_A^* and K_B^*. Without loss of generality, $K_A^* \geq K_B^*$. Since K_A^* and K_B^* are distinct, there must exist some firm i such that $k_{iA}^* > k_{iB}^*$. The fact that $k_{iA}^* > k_{iB}^*$ implies that firm i is not capacity constrained in B, and hence $M\Pi_{iB} = 0$. For firm i in the Nash equilibrium K_A^*, $M\Pi_{iA} \geq 0$. Therefore, $M\Pi_{iA} - M\Pi_{iB} \geq 0$. This leads to a contradiction because

$$M\Pi_{iA} - M\Pi_{iB} \qquad (2A)$$

$$= \int_0^\Delta \left\{ k_{iA}^* P'(K_A^*, t^n + \tau) + P(K_A^*, t^n + \tau) \right.$$
$$\left. - \left[k_{iB}^* P'(K_B^*, t^n + \tau) + P(K_B^*, e^{-r\tau} t^n + \tau) \right] \right\} e^{-\tau} d\tau \qquad (3A)$$

$$\leq \int_0^\Delta \left\{ k_{iA}^* P'(K_B^*, t^n + \tau) - k_{iB}^* P'(K_B^*, t^n + \tau) \right\} e^{-r\tau} d\tau \qquad (4A)$$

$$\leq 0. \qquad (5A)$$

Equality (3A) follows by cancelling the cost terms $(C - rS)$. Inequality (4A) is based on (A9), which states that each firm's marginal revenue $k_i P'(K, t) + P(K, t)$ is a non-increasing function of industry output, K; this implies that $k_{iA}^* P'(K_A^*, t) + P(K_A^*, t) < k_{iA}^* P'(K_B^*, t) + P(K_B^*, t)$ over the interval $t \in [t^n, t^{n+1}]$. The final inequality follows as $P'(K_A^*, t)$ is negative (by (A8)) and $k_{iA}^* > k_{iB}^*$.

---

[10] At any Nash equilibrium the second-order conditions for a maximum will be met as

$$\frac{d^2 \Pi_i}{dk_i^2} = \int \left\{ 2P'(K, t^n + \tau) + k_i^* P''(K, t^n + \tau) \right\} e^{-r\tau} d\tau$$
$$< \int \left\{ P'(K, t^n + \tau) + k_i^* P''(K, t^n + \tau) \right\} e^{-r\tau} d\tau \leq 0$$

by (A9).

[11] Firm i's marginal profit may be positive if it is capacity constrained.

Definition 2

$\Pi_i^*\big(K(t^{n-1}), t^n\big)$ *is the present value of firm i's profits over the period t^n to t^{n+1} in the sequence of myopic Nash equilibria.*

The myopic Nash equilibrium outputs in period t^n, $K^*\big(K(t^{n-1}), t^n\big)$ are a function only of the previous period's capacity vector; thus, $K(t^{n-1})$ determines the profits in period t^n.

Definition 3

Firm i is capacity constrained *in the myopic Nash equilibrium $K^*\big(K(t^{n-1}), t^n\big)$ if $k_0(0) < k^*(t^n)$, where $k^*(t^n)$ is as defined in the proof of proposition 1. For all capacity-constrained firms, $k_i^*\big(K(t^{n-1}), t^n\big) = k_i(0)$.*

Lemma 2

In the iterated sequence of myopic Nash equilibria, each firm that is not capacity constrained in the period beginning at t^n reduces its output in the next period

$$k_i^*\big(K(t^{n-1}), t^n\big) = k^*(t^n) \Rightarrow k_i^*\Big(\big(K^*(K(t^{n-1}), t^n)\big), t^{n+1}\Big) < k^*(t^n).$$

Proof of lemma 2 Imagine to the contrary that in the unique equilibrium $K^*\big(K(t^n), t^{n+1}\big)$ there exists some unconstrained firm i with $k_i^*\Big(\big(K^*(K(t^{n-1}), t^n)\big), t^{n+1}\Big) = k_i^*\big(K(t^{n-1}), t^n\big) = k^*(t^n)$. Since in any myopic Nash equilibrium $MR_i \geq 0$, it must be true at t^{n+1} that

$$\int_0^\Delta \Big\{ k^*(t^n) P'\big(K^*(K(t^n) t^{n+1}), t^{n+1} + \tau\big)$$
$$+ P\big(K^*(K(t^n), t^{n+1}), t^{n+1} + \tau\big) - (C - rS)\Big\} e^{-r\tau} \geq 0. \tag{6A}$$

This implies that no firm would want to reduce capacity below $k^*(t^n)$ in period t^{n+1}; any firm with a lower capacity would have strictly positive marginal revenue and could only be in equilibrium if it is capacity constrained. By proposition 1 all firms have capacity less than or equal to $k^*(t^n)$ and hence maintain their capacity. But if no firm reduces capacity between period t^n and t^{n+1}, $K^*(t^{n+1}) = K^*(t^n)$. The inequality in (6A) now contradicts (A11) which states that if K is held constant, $k_i P'(K, t^n) + P(K, t^n)$ is a strictly declining function of t; this is zero averaged over t^n to t^{n+1} and hence cannot be greater than or equal to zero when averaged over t^{n+1} to t^{n+2}.   ∎

Next, we show that if a firm reduces its output, this encourages its competitors to raise their production in the future. As a result, such a firm earns (weakly) smaller profits in each subsequent iteration of the myopic Nash equilibrium.

Lemma 3

Let $K(t^n)$ and $K'(t^n)$ differ only in that firm i has less capacity in K' than in $K: k'_i(t^n) < k_i(t^n)$ and $k_j(t^n) = k'_j(t^n)$ for all $j \neq i$. This implies that

$$k_i^*(K', t^{n+1}) \le k_i^*(K, t^{n+1}) \text{ and } k_j^*(K', t^{n+1}) \ge k_j^*(K, t^{n+1}).$$

Proof of lemma 3 If $k_i^*(K', t^{n+1}) = k_i^*(K', t^{n+1})$, then the constrained optimization problem that defines the Nash equilibrium is unaffected by the fact that $k_i^*(K', t^n) < k_i^*(K', t^n)$: the equilibrium following K' and K are identical. By the same token, it would be impossible for the equilibrium following K' to have $k_i^*(K', t^{n+1}) > k_i^*(K', t^{n+1})$; any Nash equilibrium following K' is also feasible following K, and this would contradict the uniqueness result of lemma 1. It remains to show that if $k_i^*(K', t^{n+1}) < k_i^*(K, t^{n+1})$, then $k_i^*(K', t^{n+1}) < k_i^*(K', t^{n+1})$ leads to a contradiction. An argument parallel to the derivation of equation (6A) shows that firm j cannot be capacity constrained in $k_i^*(K', t^{n+1})$; its marginal revenue must be zero in the K' solution. This leads to the inequality

$$\int_0^\Delta \left\{ k_j^*(K, t^n) P'(K, t^{n+1} + \tau) + P(K, t^{n+1} + \tau) \right\} e^{-r\tau}$$

$$\ge \int_0^\Delta \left\{ k_j^*(K', t^n) P'(K', t^{n+1} + \tau) + P(K', t^{n+1} + \tau) \right\} e^{-r\tau} d\tau. \tag{7A}$$

This implies for all firms other than i, that $k_j^*(K', t^{n+1}) \le k_j^*(K', t^{n+1})$. And for firm i, this is true by assumption. Aggregating across firms reveals that $K^{*'}(t^{n+1}) < K^*(t^{n+1})$. But the function $k_j P'(K, t^{n+1}) + P(K, t^{n+1})$ is decreasing in both K by (A9) and k_j (holding K constant) by (A8): this contradicts the inequality in (7A).

On a more intuitive level, (A9) insures that the reaction curves are negatively sloped

$$dMR_i(K(t^{n-1}), t^n)/dk_j = \int_0^\Delta \left\{ P'(K^*, t^n + \tau) + k_j P''(K^*, t^n + \tau) \right\} e^{-r\tau} d\tau \ge 0.$$

As a result, a reduction by firm i moderates the future reductions by all other firms.

Lemma 4

Let $K(t^n)$ and $K'(t^n)$ differ only in that firm i has less capacity in K' than in K. Then for all $t^x \ge t^n$

$$\Pi_i^*(K'(t^x), t^{x+1}) \le \Pi_i^*(K(t^x), t^{x+1})$$

where $K'(t^x)$ and $K(t^x)$ are the two myopic Nash equilibria that evolve in period t^x given capacity levels $K'(t^n)$ and $K(t^n)$, respectively, in period t^n.

Proof of lemma 4 To consider the effect on firm i of moving from $K(t^n)$ to $K'(t^n)$, we break up the change into two parts. First consider the effect of firm i moving from $k_i^*(K(t^n))$ to k_i' when all other firms remain at $K(t^n)$. Because $K(t^n)$ is a myopic Nash equilibrium, firm i strictly lowers its current profit by moving to k_i'. Next, consider the effect on firm i of the other firms' movement from $k_j^*\big(K(t^n), t^{n+1}\big)$ to $k_j^*\big(K'(t^n), t^{n+1}\big)$. By lemma 3, all the other firms either maintain or increase their output. Because goods are perfect substitutes, this can only reduce the price and thus further hurt firm i. The same argument applies to all periods past t^{n+1}. ∎

Our final lemma establishes the trivial uniqueness of the subgame-perfect equilibrium once the market price is sufficiently low that all firms have $k_i = 0$ as a dominant strategy.

Lemma 5

There exists some time T such that in any subgame-perfect equilibrium all firms have zero capacity for $t^n \geq T$. This coincides with the myopic Nash equilibrium, $K^*(K(t^{n-1}), t^n)$.

Proof of lemma 5 Downward-sloping demand (A8) implies that a firm could never earn more than the price at zero aggregate supply

$$\Pi_i\big(K(t^n), t^n\big) \leq k_i(t^n)\Big[P(0, t^n) - (C - rS)\Big]/r.$$

Let $\in = [C - rS]$. By A6, $\in > 0$. Then by A10 there exists some T such that $P(0, t) < \in$ for $t \geq T$. Hence, for $t^x \geq T, \Pi_i\big(K(t^x), t^x\big) < 0$ for all $K(t^x)$ and for all firms. Maintaining any positive capacity is dominated by exiting in toto.

References

Baden-Fuller, C. and R. Hill (1984), 'Industry strategies for alleviating excess capacity: the case of the Lazard scheme for UK steel castings', Centre for Business Strategy, London Business School, August.

Bliss, C. and B. Nalebuff (1984), 'Dragon-slaying and ballroom dancing: the private supply of a public good', *Journal of Public Economics*, 25, 1–12.

Deily, M.E. (1985), 'Capacity reduction in the steel industry', Ph.D. thesis, Harvard University.

Fine, C. and L. Li (1986), 'A stochastic theory of exit and stopping time equilibria', Working Paper 1755–86, Sloan School of Management, MIT.

Fishman, A. (1989), 'Entry deterrence in a finitely lived industry', Foerder Institute for Economic Research, Tel-Aviv University, Working Paper 5–89.

Friedman, J.W. (1977), *Oligopoly and the Theory of Games*, Amsterdam, North-Holland.

Fudenberg, D. and J. Tirole (1986), 'A theory of exit in duopoly', *Econometrica*, 54, 943–60.

Ghemawat, P. (1985), 'Concentration in decline', Working Paper, Graduate School of Business Administration, Harvard University.

Ghemawat, P. and B. Nalebuff (1985), 'Exit', *Rand Journal of Economics*, 16, 184–94.

Hahn, F.H. (1962), 'The stability of the Cournot oligopoly solution', *Review of Economic Studies*, 29, 329–32.

Harrigan, K.R. (1980), *Strategies for Declining Businesses*, Lexington, MA., Lexington Books.

Huang, C.-F., and L. Li (1986), 'Continuous time stopping games', Working Paper, Sloan School of Management, MIT.

Lieberman, M.B. (1989), 'Divestment in declining industries: "shakeout" or "stakeout"?', Stanford University, mimeo.

Londregan, J. (1987), 'Exit and entry over the industry lifecycle', Carnegie Mellon University Working Paper.

Smith, J.M. (1974), 'The theory of games and the evolution of animals', *Journal of Theoretical Biology*, 47, 209–30.

Whinston, M. (1987), 'Exit with multiplant firms', H.I.E.R. Discussion Paper 1299, Harvard University, February.

(1988), 'Exit with multiplant firms', *Rand Journal of Economics*, 19, 568–88.

Chapter 5

Empirical evidence
Exit from declining industries: 'shakeout' or 'stakeout'?

Marvin B. Lieberman

1   Introduction

In a declining industry, who exits first: large firms or small? If capacity can be reduced incrementally, who makes the largest or most frequent cuts? Do firm sizes tend to converge or diverge, and does concentration rise or fall? Indeed can such generalizations be made, or does the pattern of divestment vary too greatly from one declining industry to another?

Several recent theoretical studies have addressed these issues of competition during decline. While they offer a number of predictions, verification has thus far been limited to interpretations drawn from a handful of industry case examples. This contribution evaluates the recent theories in the more rigorous context of a data sample covering 30 chemical products that have been declining for periods ranging from five to twenty-five years. The sample is large enough to allow statistical testing of hypotheses about the divestment process in declining commodity product industries.

The analysis is framed in terms of two contrasting sets of predictions. The first set of predictions is based on the observation that larger firms are often more efficient:

This article first appeared in the *Rand Journal of Economics*, 1990, Vol. 21, 4, winter, pp. 538–54. I thank Mark Williams for research assistance and SRI International for access to data. This article has benefited from comments by Richard Caves, Mary Deily, Murray Frank, Pankaj Ghemawat, Timothy Hannan, James Poterba, Stanley Reynolds, William Robinson, two anonymous referees, and seminar participants at Berkeley, NYU, Northwestern, and UCLA.

size may convey economies of scale or reflect a process of more rapid growth by superior firms. Such differences in efficiency would cause smaller producers to be 'shaken out' relatively early if prices fall during the decline phase. The second set of predictions is based on the Cournot–Nash result that in the absence of cost differences, smaller firms can remain profitable over a longer period as demand tapers off to zero. Given this superior ability of small firms to 'stake out' as the industry devolves, larger firms would rationally choose to exit early or to mimic their smaller rivals by drastically cutting capacity.

Firms can divest by cutting capacity incrementally or by exiting. Incremental reductions can be carried out by closing part of an on-going plant, or an entire plant in the case of a multi-plant firm. The chemical products sample collected for this study contains information on these various forms of divestment. The sample also tracks changes in producer concentration and the coefficient of variation in firm sizes. The 'shakeout' and 'stakeout' models offer diverse predictions with respect to these empirically observable factors.

The remainder of this chapter is organized as follows. Section 2 surveys the theoretical and empirical literature on divestment in declining industries. Section 3 describes the chemical products sample. Section 4 reports summary statistics on the capacity reduction process, measured at the firm level. More disaggregate tests are provided in section 5 in the form of a logit analysis of plant closures. Section 6 concludes the article and summarizes the main findings.

2　Prior theoretical and empirical findings on divestment in declining industries

Theoretical studies

Recent theoretical studies of competition in declining industries include Ghemawat and Nalebuff (1985, 1990), Londregan (1987), Reynolds (1988), and Whinston (1988). These studies use the logic of backward induction to predict the sequence of exits or capacity reductions when demand is perceived as ultimately diminishing to zero.[1] While the specific models differ slightly in their assumptions and results, all point out the potential strategic liability of large firm size.

Ghemawat and Nalebuff (1985) analyse the case in which producers have equal costs, demand is declining monotonically, and divestment is an all-or-nothing decision – firms either continue to operate at full capacity or exit the industry. Under these assumptions, Ghemawat and Nalebuff (hereafter G&N) prove the existence of a unique subgame-perfect Cournot–Nash equilibrium: the smaller of two equally efficient duopolists forces its larger rival to exit as soon as duopoly profits turn negative. The intuition behind this result is that the smaller producer, having lower

---

[1] Other theoretical studies, which model exit decisions in a more general context, include Jovanovic (1982), Fudenberg and Tirole (1986) and Frank (1988).

output, can operate as a profitable monopolist over a longer period of time as demand falls. Recognizing this fact, the larger firm exits first.

Generalized to the oligopoly case, the G&N (1985) model implies that exit occurs in decreasing order of firm size. Ghemawat and Nalebuff argue that this sequence is robust to the existence of small interfirm cost differences. Moreover, the basic conclusions hold under more general conditions in which industry re-entry is permitted (Londregan, 1987).

In a subsequent paper, G&N (1990) analyse the case in which firms can divest incrementally rather than on an all-or-nothing basis. Here the (capacity-constrained) Cournot–Nash equilibrium dictates that 'large firms reduce capacity first, and continue to do so until they shrink to the size of their formerly smaller rivals'. The intuition in this case is that larger firms have lower marginal revenue and hence greater incentives to cut capacity. Following the onset of industry decline, the largest firm reduces its capacity until it has shrunk to the size of the second largest firm: at this point both firms shrink together until their individual capacities equal that of the third largest firm; and so forth. Industry concentration diminishes over time, as firm sizes become more equal.

Other models, based on the more restrictive assumption that divestment must be undertaken in lumpy decrements, have reached more ambiguous conclusions. Reynolds (1988) obtains results similar to those of G&N (1990) under the assumption that all plants are of equal size. However, Whinston (1988) shows that when firms have different sized plants, multiple equilibria are possible – i.e., the largest firm will not necessarily be the first to exit or cut capacity.

In the absence of producer size differences, theoretical work confirms the intuitive prediction that the divestment sequence depends on relative cost. Reynolds (1988) demonstrates that high-cost plants will be closed before low-cost plants, and G&N (1985) show that high-cost firms will be first to exit. Fudenberg and Tirole (1986) show that in a duopoly environment with incomplete information the less-efficient firm will exit first, assuming that firms hold symmetric expectations.

Testable implications of the models

This study uses data on declining chemical products to test the predictions of the theoretical models. The fundamental question is the following: Is large firm size a strategic liability in a declining industry, and, if so, is this liability substantial enough to outweigh the cost advantage of achieving economies of scale? The liability of size could appear as higher exit rates for large firms (as implied by G&N (1985) and Londregan (1987)) or as higher rates of incremental capacity reduction (as implied by G&N, 1990 and Reynolds, 1988). If large and small size confer disadvantages of similar magnitude, the two liabilities might offset each other, so that comparable rates of divestment would be observed for both large and small firms.

The potential strategic liability of size is straightforward to detect if it appears as a higher rate of exit by larger firms. (Such a test is provided in section 4 below.) Less drastic forms of divestment are more difficult to assess, but I present several indicator measures in section 4. These include the rate of incremental capacity reduction, the rate of total divestment (exits and incremental reductions combined), and the change over time in the coefficient of variation in firm sizes.

The G&N (1990) findings imply that as demand declines, capacity would gradually be shed by the largest firms. Producers with large capacity shares would therefore exhibit higher rates of incremental capacity reduction. But large producers may also show higher rates of incremental cutback for the simple reason that they tend to operate multiple plants. (Note that a plant closure constitutes an exit when made by a single-plant firm but an incremental reduction when made by a multi-plant firm.) To determine whether the strategic liability of large firm size is substantial enough to offset cost advantages due to economies of scale, it is necessary to examine the distribution of total divestment. If the liability of large firm size outweighs the benefits of achieving economies of scale, then large-share firms would account for a disproportionate fraction of the total capacity shed from the industry.

Changes in the coefficient of variation in firm sizes (standard deviation divided by mean firm size) can also provide information on the interfirm distribution of divestment. This coefficient can be computed across all producers in the industry or across the cohort of firms that survive over the sample period. In the latter case, the number of firms included in the measure remains constant over time.

If computed across all firms in the industry the coefficient of variation provides only a weak basis for distinguishing among the models. Both of the G&N models predict that the coefficient would diminish over time as the largest producers either exit the industry or shrink in relative size. The coefficient would also diminish if smaller firms are 'shaken out' through a process of exit. Only if smaller firms shrink without exiting would the coefficient of variation increase over time. Thus a convergence in firm sizes would normally occur under both the 'shakeout' and 'stakeout' processes.

The coefficient of variation provides a stronger indicator if it is limited to the cohort of firms that survive over the sample period. The G&N (1985) model predicts no change in this coefficient, given that exiting firms are excluded. A 'shakeout' process would also leave this coefficient unaffected, assuming that small firms exit. (If small firms shrink without exiting, the coefficient would increase.) Only the G&N (1990) model predicts a diminishing coefficient, as large firms shrink to the size of their smaller rivals. Thus a reduction in the coefficient of variation in the size of surviving firms implies that within the cohort of survivors, large firms shrank proportionately more than small firms.

A more comprehensive set of tests, presented in section 5, involves the estimation of a logit model of plant closure. This model, which accounts for differences in both plant and firm size, allows the influences of plant-level scale economies and firm-level capacity share to be assessed independently.

Evidence from prior empirical studies

Empirical evidence on the pattern of capacity reduction in declining industries has been developed primarily from case studies. Many studies have found higher rates of closure for small firms and plants, but only limited evidence has been presented on the strategic liability of large firm size. G&N (1985, 1990) cite case studies of divestment in synthetic soda ash, steel castings, and basic steel. In all three of these industries, early capacity reductions were concentrated among the largest producers.[2]

Studies based on growing as well as declining industries have commonly found that smaller firms have higher exit probabilities. Mansfield (1962) uncovered this tendency in early work. Lieberman (1989) found that smaller entrants had significantly higher mortality rates in growing chemical markets. Evans (1987) and Dunne, Roberts, and Samuelson (1989b) confirmed this relation between exit and firm size using broad, cross-sectional data.

Similar findings have been obtained at the plant level. Deily (1988) and Tang (1989) noted that following the onset of industry decline, US steelmakers divested first from their smaller, high-cost plants. In petroleum refining, Londregan (1988) observed that small refineries were more likely to be closed. Dunne, Roberts, and Samuelson (1989a) found a similar pattern of plant closure in a range of industries.

Two studies have assessed divestment in declining sectors where cutbacks were coordinated through government-sanctioned cartels. These studies suggest that strong cartels often enforce a proportional divestment rule that overcomes the normal tendency for exits to be concentrated among small-share producers. Shaw and Shaw (1983) examined the European synthetic fibres industry during a period of decline in the late 1970s and early 1980s. They found that when an EEC-sponsored cartel was in place during the initial years of industry decline, firms cut capacity in proportion to their market shares. After the cartel was eliminated, smaller firms exited at disproportionately high rates. Peck, Levin, and Goto (1987) examined the behaviour of declining industry cartels in Japan. These cartels led producers in concentrated industries to cut back in proportion to their capacities, so that initial shares were preserved. In more fragmented industries where the cartels were less effective, rationalization proceeded more rapidly as many smaller firms exited.

3   Data sample

Table 5.1 summarizes basic features of the data sample used in this study. The sample includes 30 chemical products, each of which experienced chronic decline in US domestic output and capacity. Data were collected from the peak year of output or capacity (whichever occurred earlier) through the start of 1987.[3] On average, output declined by 42 per cent and capacity by 38 per cent from the historical peak. The magnitudes of capacity and output reduction were strongly (but far from perfectly)

---

[2] In his detailed study of the UK steel castings industry, Baden-Fuller (1989) found that the two largest producers accounted for about two-thirds of the capacity closed during the early years of decline. Nevertheless, these firms, which initially operated multiple plants, did not exit. Exits were concentrated among a group of diversified firms that were able to shift resources to other sectors at relatively low cost.

[3] For most products the output and capacity peaks roughly coincided. To be conservative, the analysis starts from the peak year of output or capacity, whichever occurred later.

Table 5.1 *Products included in declining industries sample (Per cent decline – Peak year to 1987)*

Product	Year of peak output	Year of peak capacity	Number of producers at peak capacity	Output	Capacity	Number of producers	Reasons of decline
Acetaldehyde	1969	1971	9	−61%	−68%	−78%	D,F
Acetone	1979	1981	16	−27%	−13%	−19%	G
Acetylene	1965	1965	13	−44%	−75%	−54%	F
Acrylic fibres	1980	1981	5	−21%	−22%	−20%	E
Adipic acid	1979	1979	4	−14%**	−12%	−25%	G
Calcium carbide	1964	1962	4	−81%	−64%	0%	E
Carbon black	1973	1975	8	−26%	−21%	13%	G
Carbon disulfide	1969	1971	4	−60%**	−20%	−25%	D,E
Cellophane	1960	1966	3	−68%§	−82%	−33%	B
Cellulose acetate fibres	1968	1968	4	−58%	−65%	−50%	B
Chloroacetic acid	N/A	1977	3	N/A	−18%	0%	G
Chlorobenzene (mono)	1969	1971	8	−58%	−46%	−63%	D
Cresylic acid	1976	1982	9	−44%	−39%	−56%	C,G
Ethyl chloride	1976	1976	6	−76%	−45%	−17%	D
Fumaric acid	1973	1972	6	−30%	−22%	−33%	B,C
Hydrofluoric acid	1974	1974	9	−2%	−49%	−56%	C,D
Isopropyl alcohol	1976	1981	4	−34%	−12%	0%	F,G
Lead alkyls	1970	1969	4	−62%§	−81%	−75%	A
Melamine	1974	1972	4	−23%*	−29%	−50%	C,G
Nitrile rubber	1974	1972	6	−34%	−2%	−33%	G
Phosphorus	1969	1969	8	−42%	−47%	−50%	D
Potassium sulfate	1977	1974	7	−61%	−65%	−14%	B,C,G
Rayon fibres	1968	1971	6	−62%	−57%	−33%	B
SBR rubber	1973	1972	11	−48%	−45%	−55%	B,G
Sodium	1973	1973	3	−60%**	−56%	−33%	D
Sodium bichromate	1974	1979	3	−29%**	−4%	−33%	B,C,G
Sodium phosphate	1970	1979	5	−48%	−12%	0%	A
Sodium sulfite	1967	1976	5	−51%	−41%	0%	A,B,C
Sodium tetraborate	N/A	1978	3	N/A	−6%	−33%	G
Sodium thiosulfate	1961	1973	4	−53%	−35%	−25%	B,G
Average			6	−42%	−38%	−32%	

Key to reasons for decline in demand:
A Chemical was found to be environmentally hazardous.
B Chemical was replaced by substitute product.
C US domestic production was replaced by imports.
D Downstream product was found to be environmentally hazardous.
E Downstream product was replaced by substitute.
F Change in manufacturing process for downstream product.
G Other factors leading to reduced demand for downstream product.
§ Data through 1981 only.
* Data through 1984 only.   ** Data through 1985 only.

correlated, with $r = 0.64$. The number of producers fell by an average of 32 per cent, nearly the same as industry capacity.

The data were obtained from chemical producer listings compiled by SRI International, supplemented by government and industry sources. The capacity data are from annual issues of the *Directory of Chemical Producers*, published by SRI International. This directory reports US production capacities by product, firm, and plant, observed at the start of each calendar year. Output data were collected from various sources.[4] Chemical trade journals were consulted to determine why products in the sample were in decline.

The sample products were selected as follows. The *Directory of Chemical Producers* includes annual capacity listings for approximately 240 products. Output data were collected on each of these products to identify those that were declining. The sample includes all products with published capacity data that were observed to be declining over a period of five years or more through to the end of 1986.[5] The sample is believed to be a fairly representative cross-section of commodity product industries in decline.[6]

The last column of table 5.1 summarizes the reasons why demand was falling for products in the sample. Decline often stemmed from a combination of factors. Three products had been found to be environmentally hazardous and were being restricted or phased out by regulatory agencies. Seven products served as inputs in the manufacture of downstream products that had been found hazardous. An additional seven products were being replaced by direct substitutes, and three products faced such replacement downstream. For three products, changes in downstream manufacturing processes reduced or eliminated demand for the product as an input. For seven products, competition from lower-priced imports was a factor contributing to the decline in US output.

No data are publicly available on cost differences among individual plants and firms in the sample. Nevertheless, engineering studies offer some rough generalizations regarding cost behaviour as a function of plant size. In the chemical industry, both capital and labour costs are typically subject to economies of scale. While capital costs

---

[4] Annual data on total US production of each product were obtained from *Synthetic Organic Chemicals, published by the US International Trade Commission, Current Industrial Reports*, published by the Census Bureau, and the *Chemical Economics Handbook*, published by SRI International. Output data are unavailable for two products: chloroacetic acid and sodium tetraborate. For several other products the available output data do not extend to 1986, the last full year of sample coverage.

[5] A few products were eliminated by the additional requirement that capacity as well as output be declining. Several others were excluded because they were produced primarily as by-products. Synthetic soda ash (discussed in G&N, 1985, 1990), and Harrigan, 1980) was excluded in light of the fact that total US demand for soda ash was increasing; only the fraction produced by synthetic means was in decline.

[6] One bias is that Directory of Chemical Products contains capacity listings only for chemicals with comparatively large markets. Hence, products in the sample typically have more producers than an average product listed in the Directory (but few producers compared with the number of firms observed in many manufacturing industries outside of the chemical sector). One would expect the stakeout models to be applicable only in reasonably concentrated industries, where marginal revenue differs significantly among producers.

can be ignored in a declining market given the existence of excess capacity, scale economies in the labour component of operating cost are often significant.[7]

Detailed engineering cost data for five products in the sample were obtained from the *Process Economics Program Handbook* published by SRI International (1976). Although a small subset, these five products are typical of the sample as a whole. The *Handbook* reports estimated capital and operating costs for plants whose 'capacities are representative of sizes of competitive US plants' built in the mid-1970s. The *Handbook* also reports costs for plants one half this size; these 'half-size' plants suffered operating cost penalties ranging from about 2 per cent to 9 per cent.[8] While these penalties appear minor as a percentage of total operating costs (including materials costs) they can account for a large proportion of value added. Moreover, many plants in the sample at the start of the decline phase were much smaller than the 'half-size' plants shown in the *Handbook* and hence suffered greater penalties in operating cost.

4   Empirical results at the firm level

Producer concentration and variation in firm sizes

Tables 5.2–5.7 give summary statistics on various characteristics of the capacity reduction process, measured at the firm level.

Table 5.2 describes changes in producer concentration over the sample period. For each product, the table gives the change in the Herfindahl concentration index (H), the number of producers (N), and the coefficient of variation in firm sizes (V).[9] The products in table 5.2 have been sorted in decreasing order of the percentage decline in total industry capacity. Given that a small amount of entry occurred over the coverage period,[10] two separate counts of the number of producers are provided for the terminal year: the total number of firms observed and the number of survivors remaining from the peak year. Similarly, two figures are reported for changes in the coefficient of variation: the first compares the size distribution of all producers in the peak year with the size distribution of all producers in the terminal year, whereas the second is computed over the subset of firms that survived from the peak year through the terminal year.

Table 5.2 reveals several strong tendencies. First, producer concentration increased for most products in the sample. Twenty-six products exhibited increases in the Herfindahl index, while four products exhibited slight decreases.

Given the identity relation, $H = (V^2 + 1)/N$, the observed increase in the Herfindahl index implies a reduction in the number of producers or an increase in the coefficient

---

[7] Scale economies in labour cost are obtained primarily through reductions in operating, maintenance, and overhead labour per unit of output.

[8] The cost penalties were as follows: isopropyl alcohol (2 per cent), acetone (2 per cent), acetaldehyde (4 per cent), acetylene (7 per cent), and adipic acid (9 per cent).

[9] These measures were computed from the capacity data. The Herfindahl index is $H = \sum s_i^2$ where s_i is the capacity share of firm i.

[10] Many of these entrants acquired the assets of exiting firms.

Table 5.2 *Change in Herfindahl index, number of firms and coefficient of variation in firm sizes*

Product	Per cent decline in capacity	Number of firms		
		N_{peak}	N_{87}*	N_{87}
Cellophane	−82%	3	2	2
Lead alkyls	−81%	4	1	1
Acetylene	−75%	13	5	6
Acetaldehyde	−68%	9	2	2
Cellulose acetate fibres	−65%	4	2	2
Potassium sulfate	−65%	6	3	6
Calcium carbide	−64%	4	4	4
Rayon fibres	−57%	6	2	4
Sodium	−56%	3	2	2
Hydrofluoric acid	−49%	9	4	4
Phosphorus	−47%	8	4	4
Chlorobenzene	−46%	8	3	3
Ethyl chloride	−45%	6	4	5
SBR rubber	−45%	11	4	5
Sodium sulfite	−41%	5	3	5
Cresylic acid	−39%	9	3	4
Sodium thiosulfate	−35%	4	2	3
Melamine	−29%	3	2	2
Acrylic fibres	−22%	5	4	4
Fumaric acid	−22%	6	3	4
Carbon black	−21%	8	5	9
Carbon disulfide	−20%	4	3	3
Chloroacetic acid	−18%	3	2	3
Acetone	−13%	16	13	13
Adipic acid	−12%	4	3	3
Isopropyl alcohol	−12%	4	4	4
Sodium phosphate	−12%	5	5	5
Sodium tetraborate	−6%	3	2	2
Sodium bichromate	−4%	3	2	2
Nitrile rubber	−2%	5	4	4

	Herfindahl index		Coefficient of variation in firm sizes		
	H_{peak}	$H_{87} - H_{peak}$	V_{peak}	$V_{87} - V_{peak}$	V_{87}* $- V_{peak}$*
Cellophane	0.466	0.034	0.631	−0.631	−0.683
Lead alkyls	0.352	0.648	0.639	−0.419[a]	−0.459[a]
Acetylene	0.169	0.112	1.096	−0.269	−0.064
Acetaldehyde	0.324	0.224	1.385	−1.074	−0.023
Cellulose acetate fibres	0.366	0.332	0.681	−0.051	0.329
Potassium sulfate	0.280	−0.035	0.824	−0.139	−0.014
Calcium carbide	0.425	−0.081	0.837	−0.224	−0.224
Rayon fibres	0.345	−0.040	1.033	−0.564	−0.545
Sodium	0.362	0.198	0.292	0.053	−0.006

Hydrofluoric acid	0.183	0.177	0.807	−0.142	−0.052
Phosphorus	0.205	0.068	0.799	−0.495	−0.099
Chlorobenzene	0.303	0.101	1.192	−0.735	0.105
Ethyl chloride	0.248	0.010	0.697	−0.160	−0.407
SBR rubber	0.149	0.107	0.796	−0.268	−0.006
Sodium sulfite	0.469	−0.009	1.159	−0.019	0.315
Cresylic acid	0.216	0.230	0.971	−0.086	0.000
Sodium thiosulfate	0.334	0.091	0.580	−0.054	−0.131
Melamine	0.370	0.130	0.333	−0.333	0.000
Acrylic fibres	0.294	0.034	0.684	−0.126	0.027
Fumaric acid	0.210	0.126	0.508	0.076	0.012
Carbon black	0.160	0.005	0.532	0.164	−0.061
Carbon disulfide	0.531	0.215	1.060	0.052	−0.112
Chloroacetic acid	0.482	−0.008	0.668	−0.019	0.050
Acetone	0.145	0.035	1.148	0.009	−0.003
Adipic acid	0.450	0.084	0.894	−0.118	0.033
Isopropyl alcohol	0.334	−0.009	0.580	−0.032	−0.032
Sodium phosphate	0.249	0.002	0.495	0.009	0.009
Sodium tetraborate	0.663	0.175	0.994	−0.172	0.108
Sodium bichromate	0.374	0.230	0.348	0.107	0.015
Nitrile rubber	0.306	0.084	0.727	0.020	0.160

Notes: * Survivor firms only. (Excludes firms that entered or exited between the peak year and 1987.)
[a] Based on last observation with two producers.

of variation of firm sizes (or both). Table 5.2 gives clear evidence of the former: all but three products had a reduction in the number of producers over the coverage period. There is, however, no evidence of increased variation in firm sizes. Indeed, table 5.2 documents a general pattern of firm size convergence; the coefficient of variation declined for more than three-fourths of the products in the sample. This size convergence could reflect one or more underlying processes: (1) disproportionate exit of large firms, (2) disproportionate exit of small firms, (3) disproportionate shrinkage of large firms, or (4) disproportionate growth of small firms.

The last column of table 5.2 offers evidence that size convergence was due, at least in part, to the disproportionate shrinkage of large producers. In this column, the change in the coefficient of variation is limited to the set of firms that survived from the peak year through the beginning of 1987. For the sample as a whole there was no strong tendency towards size convergence among surviving firms – only 17 of the 30 products exhibit such convergence. However, there is significant evidence of size convergence within the set of products that experienced the greatest decline. For example, of the 17 products with capacity reductions exceeding 35 per cent, 13 show convergence in the size of surviving firms.[11] These findings for the products in steepest decline are consistent with the predictions of G&N (1990).

[11] The null hypothesis of no convergence can be rejected at the 0.05 level, based on a binomial test.

Exit rates by size rank of producer

Table 5.3 gives information on the relative size of exiting firms. The table is in the form of a matrix in which the columns correspond to the number of producers at the start of the exit year and the rows correspond to the size rank of the firm (based on capacity at the start of the year). Within each column, exit rates have been normalized to sum to unity.

Table 5.3 shows that small firms had disproportionately high exit rates. Within each column of the table, the majority of exits lie below the mean rank. This propensity of smaller firms to exit is highly significant statistically.[12] Results are similar if marginal producers are excluded from the analysis,[13] or if firms are ranked on the basis of capacity in the peak year rather than the exit year.[14]

Thus the data sample offers no support for the G&N (1985) model, which predicts that the largest producers will be first to exit. Indeed, of the firms with largest capacity for each product in the peak year, only three of the 30 exited, as compared with 38 per cent of firms in the sample as a whole.

Incremental capacity reductions

While exit is the most dramatic form of divestment, capacity is more commonly eliminated through a process of incremental reduction (closure of part of an on-going plant, or of an entire plant in a multi-plant firm).[15] Table 5.4 focuses on such incremental cutbacks. It is in matrix form, similar to table 5.3.

Table 5.4 reports the relation between the frequency of capacity reduction and the relative size rank of firm. The table shows that firms above the mean rank (shaded region) accounted for the vast majority of incremental reductions. Thus large-share firms made incremental capacity reductions more frequently than small-share firms.[16]

The results in table 5.4 do not necessarily imply that large producers undertook

[12] Tests were based on a binomial model, assuming a null hypothesis of equal exit probabilities for small and large firms. Firms below the mean rank accounted for 77 per cent of all exits, which allows rejection of the null hypothesis at the 0.01 level. Results are similar when the sample is limited to products with high producer concentration or products in very steep decline.

[13] Fringe producers operating well below minimum efficient scale might account for a large fraction of the industry population measured in numbers but only a minuscule proportion of industry output and capacity. To avoid this bias, table 5.3 was recomputed after screening out firms whose peak-year capacity fell below 10 per cent of the largest producer. Eliminating such firms had little effect on the results.

[14] Producers with considerable peak-year capacity might divest incrementally and hold only very small market shares at the time of exit. To correct this possible bias, firms were classified according to their rank in the peak year. This reclassification led to only minor changes in table 5.4.

[15] Roughly half of the incremental capacity reductions included in table 5.4 were cutbacks at on-going plants and half were plant closures in multi-plant firms.

[16] Firms above median rank accounted for 67 per cent of the incremental capacity reductions shown in table 5.4. The null hypothesis that large- and small-share firms had equal probabilities of making such reductions can be rejected at the 0.01 level.

Table 5.3 *Frequency distribution of exits by number of producers and rank of firm*

Rank of firm (based on capacity at time of exit)	Number of producers at time of exit								
	2	3	4	5	6	7	8	9	10 or more
1	–	0.09	0.17	–	–	–	–	–	–
2	1.00	0.27	0.25	0.09	–	0.14	–	–	–
3		0.64	0.25	0.27	0.21	0.14	0.17	0.13	–
4			0.33	0.09	0.07	–	0.17	–	0.11
5				0.55	0.29	0.14	–	0.38	–
6					0.43	0.29	0.17	0.13	0.22
7						0.29	0.17	–	–
8							0.33	0.13	0.11
9								0.25	0.11
≥ 10									0.44
	1.00	1.00	1.00	1.00	1.00	1.00	1.00	1.00	1.00
Number of exits	1	11	12	11	14	7	6	8	9

Table 5.4 *Frequency of incremental capacity reductions by number of producers and rank of firm*

Rank of firm (based on capacity prior to reduction)	Number of producers								
	2	3	4	5	6	7	8	9	10 or more
1	0.64	0.48	0.48	0.24	0.41	0.24	0.36	0.33	0.14
2	0.37	0.33	0.20	0.24	0.12	0.26	0.14	0.33	0.19
3		0.19	0.16	0.28	0.24	0.09	0.07	–	0.05
4			0.16	0.14	0.06	0.12	0.07	–	0.10
5				0.10	0.12	0.09	–	0.17	0.10
6					0.06	0.15	0.14	–	0.5
7						0.06	0.14	–	0.14
8							0.7	–	0.10
9								0.17	0.05
≥ 10									0.10
	1.00	1.00	1.00	1.00	1.00	1.00	1.00	1.00	1.00
Number of capacity reductions	16	21	44	29	17	34	14	6	21

Table 5.5 *Average size or incremental capacity reductions (as fraction of firm's existing capacity)*

Rank of firm (based on capacity prior to reduction)	Number of producers								
	2	3	4	5	6	7	8	9	10 or more
1	−0.25	−0.29	−0.25	−0.24	−0.24	−0.12	−0.11	−0.11	−0.25
2	−0.36	−0.17	−0.25	−0.12	−0.33	−0.21	−0.19	−0.07	−0.12
3		−0.22	−0.16	−0.18	−0.19	−0.22	−0.14	−	−0.29
4			−0.28	−0.27	−0.48	−0.21	−0.08	−	−0.13
5				−0.27	−0.21	−0.24	−	−0.31	−0.22
6					−0.20	−0.31	−0.10	−	−0.20
7						−0.38	−0.25	−	−0.22
8							−0.13	−	−0.33
9								−0.07	−0.03
≥ 10									−0.41
	1.00	1.00	1.00	1.00	1.00	1.00	1.00	1.00	1.00
Average size of reductions	−0.29	−0.24	−0.24	−0.20	−0.25	−0.22	−0.14	−0.10	−0.22
Number of capacity reductions	16	21	44	29	17	34	14	6	21

more incremental divestment; this depends on the average magnitude of cutbacks as well as their frequency. Table 5.5 reports the fraction by which firms reduced their capacity, given that an incremental reduction was made. On average, firms cut capacity by a margin of about 20 per cent to 25 per cent. No strong pattern is evident with respect to firm size – large and small firms cut capacity by roughly the same percentage margin. This finding, combined with the results in table 5.4, implies that large firms undertook more incremental divestment than small firms.

The fact that industry demand was declining did not prevent some firms from expanding their facilities. Most of these expansions were the result of plant debottle-necking, a common practice in the chemical industry. Such expansions, which enable plants to achieve greater economies of scale, can often be implemented at trivial financial cost.[17] Table 5.6 gives the frequency of capacity increases as a function of the firm's rank. No strong pattern is apparent – large firms were about as likely to expand capacity as small firms.

---

[17] Debottlenecking is carried out by modifying equipment at points in the plant that are found to limit productive capacity.

Table 5.6 *Frequency of incremental capacity additions,* by number of producers and rank of firm*

Rank of firm (based on capacity prior to expansion)	Number of producers								
	2	3	4	5	6	7	8	9	10 or more
1		0.25	0.40	0.24	–	0.29	0.10	–	–	–
2		0.75	0.10	0.27	0.29	0.29	0.30	0.33	–	0.27
3			0.50	0.24	0.14	0.14	0.10	0.17	–	–
4				24	0.29	0.14	0.20	0.17	–	0.27
5					0.29	–	0.20	0.17	–	0.09
6						0.14	–	–	–	–
7							0.10	0.17	0.50	0.09
8									0.50	0.18
9										–
≥ 10										0.09
	1.00	1.00	1.00	1.00	1.00	1.00	1.00	1.00	1.00
Number of capacity additions	8	10	33	7	7	10	6	2	11

Note: * Excludes expansions smaller than 5 per cent of the firm's existing capacity.

Total divestment

The preceding analysis shows that small firms were more likely to exit, whereas large firms were more likely to cut capacity incrementally. Which group, on balance, accounted for the bulk of industry divestment? Table 5.7 addresses this question by aggregating the various forms of capacity change (exit, incremental divestment, and capacity addition) into a single summary measure. If all groups cut back by the same average proportion, the total net capacity reduction would be distributed evenly across size classes. However, if large (small) firms divested to a greater extent, then one would observe large (small) firms accounting for a disproportionate share of the total reduction in industry capacity.

To derive the results in table 5.7, a computer program was written to sort firms into the top, middle, and bottom thirds of the industry, based on peak-year capacity, and to keep track of subsequent capacity changes.[18] The allocation among size classes

[18] This program operated as follows. Producers were first arranged in decreasing order of peak-year capacity. Based on this ordering, the program identified whether the firm was in the top, middle or bottom third of the capacity distribution. Firms that straddled a cutoff point were assigned to two categories in proportion to the traction of their capacity falling in each category. All exits and incremental capacity changes between the peak year and 1987 were then allocated on the basis of these peak-year assignments. Finally, the total capacity change for each group was divided by the total capacity reduction observed for the product as a whole. Table 5.6 reports the simple average of these values across the 17 products with aggregate reductions greater than 35 per cent.

Table 5.7 *Distribution of total divestment by size class of firm* [a]

| | | Capacity percentile of firm in peak year | | |
	Total	Top third	Middle third	Bottom third
All firms	100%	33.3%	35.7%	31.0%
Exiting firms	60.6%	7.4%	21.5%	31.7%
Surviving firms	39.4%	25.9%	14.2%	(0.7%)[b]
Average number of plants per firm in peak year		2.8	1.8	1.3
Average plant scale in peak year (largest plant in operation = 1.0)		0.70	0.67	0.30

Notes: [a] Data are averages across the 17 products for which industry capacity declined by more than 35 per cent. (All products given equal weight.)
[b] Net increase in capacity by surviving firms.

becomes arbitrary for products where the aggregate reduction in industry capacity was small. To avoid this problem, the mean values reported in table 5.7 are limited to the 17 products for which the total net reduction in industry capacity exceeded 35 per cent. The figures in table 5.7 reveal a remarkably balanced pattern of capacity reduction. Very close to one-third of all divestment was undertaken by firms in each of the three size classes.

Despite the fact that incremental reductions were made at on-going plants, most divestments ultimately took the form of plant closures. On average across the 17 products included in table 5.7, capacity fell by 51 per cent between the peak year and late 1986. Plant closures by exiting firms eliminated 26 per cent of peak-year capacity; plant closures by surviving firms eliminated 23 per cent. Various other capacity changes occurred but were less important. Surviving firms expanded some of their remaining plants and cut capacity at others; on average, such expansions added 6 per cent to peak-year capacity while such cutbacks reduced capacity by 8 per cent. Plant sales by exiting firms accounted for 7 per cent of peak-year capacity; these plants were sold to surviving incumbents or new-entrant firms, although many of the plants were ultimately closed.

Summary of firm-level findings

In the declining products sample, small producers suffered disproportionately high mortality rates, whereas large-share firms made more frequent incremental reductions of capacity. Nearly all plant closures by 'bottom third' producers were exits, whereas 'top third' firms typically remained as producers despite closure of some plants. When exit and incremental divestment are combined, the total capacity reductions made by large and small firms were about equal. For survivor firms in the most steeply declining products there is evidence that firm sizes converged owing to more rapid divestment by the largest producers.

These findings at the firm level can be viewed as consistent with both the 'shakeout' model and G&N (1990). Many of the findings are also consistent with a more naive model of divestment. Assume that (1) large firms differ from small firms solely in the number of plants that they operate and (2) the probability of plant closure is uncorrelated with firm size. Under these conditions one would naturally observe more frequent exits by small producers, even though the rate of divestment, on average, is independent of firm size. The one finding inconsistent with this naive model is that of convergence within the cohort of surviving firms. A further basis for rejecting the naive model is provided by findings on plant-level divestment, reported in the next section.

5   Analysis of plant closures

Here I consider divestment at the plant level, using logit analysis to identify factors that influenced firms' decisions to close individual plants. The results show that small plants were more likely to be closed; but controlling for plant size, the probability of closure increased with the firm's capacity share, as predicted by the G&N (1990) model. Additional factors that might serve as 'exit barriers' along the lines proposed by Caves and Porter (1976) and Harrigan (1980) are also evaluated.

Multi-plant operation and average plant scale

The lower half of table 5.7 gives summary statistics on multi-plant operation and average plant scale by size class of producer in the peak year. Larger producers typically operated multiple plants. Firms in the 'top third' category operated an average of 2.8 plants in the peak year, as compared with 1.3 plants for 'bottom third' producers. For 12 of the 17 products included in table 5.7, the largest producer was a multi-plant firm.

Plant scale was measured relative to the capacity of the largest plant in the industry. For producers in the 'top third' category, an average plant had capacity equal to 70 per cent of the largest industry plant for that product. Plants operated by firms in the 'middle third' category were of nearly this size. However, firms in the 'bottom third' operated plants that were, on average, less than half as large. Hence, significant scale-related cost penalties were experienced by many 'bottom third' producers.

Logit analysis of plant closures

To further distinguish the effects of plant scale from those of firm size, a logit model of plant closures was estimated. The unit of observation in this analysis is an individual plant in a given year. The dependent variable equals one if the plant was closed during the year; zero if the plant remained open.

The probability of plant closure was related to the following explanatory variables:

> **Scale** = capacity of the plant, divided by the capacity of the largest plant in the industry, both observed at the start of the observation year.

Share = capacity share of the firm at the start of the observation year.

Multplant = one if the firm had multiple plants producing the product at the start of the observation year; zero if the firm operated only a single plant.

Specialist = one if the firm was undiversified, making only a single chemical product; otherwise zero.

Majorsite = one if the firm operated plants making other chemical products at the same geographic site as this plant; zero if the site was devoted to a single product.

Cu = total industry output of the product during the year preceding the observation year divided by total industry capacity at the start of the observation year.

SCALE and SHARE are included to provide tests for the 'shakeout' and 'stakeout' mechanisms, respectively. A significant negative coefficient for SCALE – indicating that larger plants were less likely to close – implies 'shakeout' of smaller plants. To distinguish between the G&N (1985) and (1990) models of 'stakeout' behaviour, SHARE is split into two separate terms depending on whether the firm operated a single plant or multiple plants at the start of the observation year.[19] The G&N (1985) model implies that the incentive for a single-plant firm to close its plant (i.e., exit) increases with the firm's market share. The G&N (1990) model implies that the incentive for a multi-plant firm to close one of its plants increases with market share. Hence, if both models apply one should observe significant positive SHARE coefficients for both single-plant and multi-plant firms.

The variables MULTPLANT, SPECIALIST, and MAJORSITE test for potential 'barriers to exit'. Controlling for divestment incentives related to plant scale and the firm's total capacity share, one might expect a single-plant firm to be more reluctant to shut its plant, given that such closure implies exit from the product market. Similarly, a firm that is specialized in the production of a single product might take greater steps to avoid plant closures given that exit normally implies dissolution of the firm. For diversified chemical producers a related argument can be made at the plant level: some plants are located within large diversified plant complexes that produce a variety of chemical products, whereas other stand-alone plants are geographically isolated. Firms may be reluctant to close isolated plants where the labour force would need to be laid off or relocated. These 'exit barrier' hypotheses imply positive logit coefficients for MULTPLANT and MAJORSITE and a negative coefficient for SPECIALIST.

One would also expect closure decisions to be influenced by the speed of demand decline and the gap between output and capacity, as reflected by CU. If closures are stimulated by low rates of utilization, a negative CU coefficient should be obtained.

---

[19] In table 5.8, the single-plant measure equals SHARE if the firm was a single-plant firm, and zero otherwise; the multi-plant measure equals SHARE if the firm was a multi-plant firm, and zero otherwise.

Logit results

Table 5.8 reports the logit results. The logit sample includes the 17 products that declined by more than 35 per cent over the sample period. The first two columns list the independent variables and their values at the sample mean. Logit equations 8.1 and 8.2 include all observations; equation 8.3 omits observations for which output data required to compute CU are unavailable. The coefficients in these equations are the partial derivatives of the logit probability of plant closure with respect to the independent variables, calculated at the sample mean.[20]

SCALE appears negative as expected and highly significant in table 5.8, confirming that larger plants were less likely to close. The coefficient of -0.183 in equation 8.1 implies that an increase of 0.1 in relative plant scale (e.g., from 46 per cent to 56 per cent of the capacity of the largest plant) would have reduced the probability of closure in a given year by 1.8 per cent (from 7.5 per cent to 5.7 per cent).

The SHARE coefficient appears positive and significant in equation 8.1, indicating that firms with larger shares of industry capacity were more likely to close plants, *ceteris paribus*. In equations 8.2 and 8.3 the SHARE coefficient is estimated separately for single-plant and multi-plant firms. The coefficient is positive and significant for multi-plant firms, in conformance with the predictions of G&N (1990). For single-plant firms the coefficient is insignificant: hence, there is no evidence that the probability of exit increased with share, as predicted be G&N (1985).[21]

The magnitude of the SCALE and SHARE coefficients offers further perspective on their counterbalancing effects. Consider the coefficients from equation 8.2, and assume for ease of interpretation that the probability derivatives remain constant for a doubling of SCALE and SHARE from their values at the sample mean. A doubling of plant scale (from 46 per cent to 92 per cent of the size of the largest plant) would have reduced the probability of closure in a given year by 7.8 per cent *ceteris paribus*. By comparison, a doubling of the firm's capacity share (from 24 per cent to 48 per cent) would have raised the probability of closure by 3.6 per cent for a multi-plant firm but only 1.3 per cent for a single-plant firm. For single-plant firms, changes in SCALE are always accompanied by the same proportionate changes in SHARE: for these firms the coefficients imply that relative scale was the dominant factor. For many multi-plant firms, however, the two effects may have roughly balanced each other, depending on the specific values of SCALE and SHARE.

The 'exit barrier' measures in table 5.8 give weak evidence of some of the hypothesized effects. MULTPLANT is not significant, indicating that firms exhibited

---

[20] If $\hat{\beta}$ is the vector of maximum likelihood estimates of the logit function, the partial derivative of the logit probability with respect to X_k is $\left(\exp\left[X'\hat{\beta} \right] \right) \left(1 + \exp\left[X'\hat{\beta} \right] \right)^{-2} \hat{\beta}_k$. It is the value of this partial derivative evaluated at the sample mean that appears in table 5.8.

[21] For single-plant firms there is strong correlation between SCALE and SHARE. (In the subsample of single-plant firms the simple correlation coefficient equals 0.88 versus 0.63 in the subsample of multi-plant firms.) This leads to a larger estimated standard error in the logit coefficient for SHARE.

Table 5.8 *Logit analysis of plant closures* [a]

Independent variable	Mean value	8.1	8.2	8.3
Constant	1.0	−1.36§ (0.17)	−0.131§ (0.019)	−0.093§ (0.031)
SCALE	0.46	−1.83§ (0.34)	−0.170§ (0.037)	−0.150§ (0.039)
SHARE	0.24	0.138§ (0.061)		
SHARE* (multi-plant firm)	0.35[b]		0.148§ (0.62)	0.140◆ (0.068)
SHARE* (single-plant firm)	0.16[c]		0.055 (0.120)	0.060 (0.153)
MULTPLANT	0.45	−0.17 (0.019)	−0.030 (0.025)	−0.035 (0.026)
SPECIALIST	0.10	−0.055◆ (0.32)	−0.054◆ (0.032)	−0.043 (0.033)
MAJORSITE	0.060	0.021 (0.016)	0.019 (0.016)	0.026 (0.015)
CU	0.54			−0.055 (0.040)
Number of observations		1,646	1,646	1,480
Number of closures		124	124	104
Probability of closure		7.5%	7.5%	7.0%
Log likelihood		−417.8	−417.4	−353.4

Notes: [a] Data cover 17 products with industry capacity reductions exceeding 35 per cent. (Equation 8.3 includes data for 15 products only.) Coefficients are derivatives of the logit probability evaluated at the sample mean. Numbers in parentheses are standard errors.
[b] Mean value of SHARE for subsample of multi-plant firms.
[c] Mean value of SHARE for subsample of single-plant firms.
§ Significant at the 0.01 level, one-tailed test.
◆ Significant at the 0.05 level, one-tailed test.

no particular reluctance to close their last plant. SPECIALIST is negative as expected and marginally significant in the first equation, suggesting that single-product companies may have been comparatively reluctant to shut their plants. The estimated coefficient implies that single-product companies had a probability of plant closure that was 5.5 percentage points lower than that of other firms. MAJORSITE appears with the expected positive sign, but the coefficient is not statistically significant.[22]

Table 5.8 shows that industry capacity utilization had little influence on the rate of

[22] Dummy variables were also defined for plants owned by major chemical companies and major petroleum companies to determine whether such firms of large absolute size might differ from others in their propensities to shut plants. No significant differences were detected.

plant closure. The CU coefficient in equation 8.3 appears negative as expected, but it is statistically insignificant.[23] Moreover, the coefficient is small; it implies that a ten percentage point drop in industry capacity utilization would have increased the probability of closure by only 0.5 per cent. This is roughly the same effect as a 3 per cent reduction in relative plant scale. Indeed, the low rates of utilization observed for most products in the sample (only 54 per cent on average for those covered in table 5.8) imply that redundant capacity was often maintained for long periods before finally being shut down. This contrasts with the strong and immediate link between increases in utilization and additions to capacity in growing chemical markets, as documented in Gilbert and Lieberman (1987) and Lieberman (1987).

In general, the plant-level results in table 5.8 confirm and extend the firm-level findings reported in section 4. Smaller plants had a higher probability of closure. Holding plant scale constant, multi-plant firms with large shares of industry capacity were more likely to close individual plants. Various other potential 'exit barriers' appear to have been less important in influencing divestment behaviour.

6   Conclusions

For the declining chemical products included in this study, exit behaviour appears to have been influenced by two frequently offsetting factors: (1) scale economies favouring the survival of large plants and firms and (2) the strategic liability of large firm size. For the products in steepest decline these two forces appear to have roughly balanced each other, as indicated by the fact that on average, aggregate divestment was distributed evenly across firm size classes.

The findings are consistent with multiple theories of divestment in declining industries. As predicted by the 'shakeout' theory, small-share firms exhibited high rates of exit, and small-scale plants were most likely to close. Other findings support the 'stakeout' models of G&N (1990) and Reynolds (1988). Controlling for plant size, the probability of plant closure increased with the firm's capacity share, assuming that the firm operated multiple plants. Within the cohort of surviving firms, large producers cut capacity by a greater percentage than small producers, leading to convergence of firm sizes. Despite this disproportionate shrinkage by large-share firms, there is no support for the more extreme prediction of G&N (1985) that large producers would be most likely to exit.

These findings imply that interfirm differences in both cost and marginal revenue can influence the order of divestment. Thus the 'shakeout' and 'stakeout' theories provide complementary explanations of exit behaviour. While both sets of influences appear to have been present in the sample, no simple divestment rule (or combination of rules) offers a high degree of predictive accuracy. The exit sequence was presumably affected by numerous factors in addition to the size-related determinants examined here.[24]

---

[23] Various measures of the rate of output decline were also tested and found insignificant.

[24] The absence of a strongly ordered exit sequence is also consistent with Whinston's (1988) theoretical observation that multiple equilibria can occur when plants are lumpy and differ in size.

Declining industries vary in the extent to which cost and marginal revenue differ among producers. Large differences in marginal revenue stem from asymmetric market shares combined with high producer concentration. Moreover, the evidence obtained here suggests that the strategic liability of large firm size arises only in steeply declining industries, where producers recognize that demand reductions are likely to be permanent. Plant-level economies of scale are responsible for significant cost differentials in chemicals manufacturing, but such economies may be less important in other industries, particularly those that are labour-intensive. Additional research is required to confirm that the basic conclusions of this study can be generalized to other types of declining industries.

Finally, to provide further perspective on the declining industry results, a sample of 30 growing chemical products was selected as a benchmark for comparison. Production capacity for these products expanded at rates ranging from 3 per cent to 25 per cent per annum from the late 1950s (or early 1960s) through 1973.[25] The two samples showed an almost identical tendency for exits to be concentrated among small firms. In the growing products sample, 76 per cent of exiting firms were in the bottom half of the size distribution based on rank in the year prior to exit; in the declining products sample the comparable figure was 77 per cent. The samples did, however, exhibit major contrasts in the shifting distribution of firm sizes. The declining products sample showed a strong trend towards size convergence, resulting from the exit of small firms and the shrinkage of large firms. In the growing products sample there was no significant trend toward either convergence or divergence: changes in the coefficient of variation in firm sizes were almost evenly split between increases and decreases.[26] For a typical product in this sample, small exiting firms were replaced by new entrants, large producers continued to expand, and the mean firm size gradually increased over time.

References

Baden-Fuller, C.W.F. (1989), 'Exit from declining industries and the case of steel castings', *Economic Journal*, 99, 949–61.
Caves, R.E. and M.E. Porter (1976), 'Barriers to exit', in R.T. Masson and P.D. Qualls (eds.), *Essays in Industrial Organization in Honor of Joe S. Bain*, Cambridge, MA, Ballinger.
Deily, M.E. (1988), 'Investment activity and the exit decision', *Review of Economics and Statistics*, 70, 595–602.
Dunne T., M.J. Roberts and L. Samuelson (1989a), 'The growth and failure of US manufacturing plants', *Quarterly Journal of Economics*, 104, 671–98.
(1989b), 'Patterns of firm entry and exit in US manufacturing industries', *Rand Journal of Economics*, 19, 495–515.

[25] The products are those with the highest rates of growth in the sample described in Lieberman (1987). The time series used for comparison run through 1973 only, as subsequent inflation in oil prices led to slower output growth for most products.
[26] The coefficient of variation computed across all producers in the initial year of coverage and again in 1973 increased for 17 products and decreased for 13.

Evans, D.J. (1987), 'The relationship between firm growth, size, and age: estimates for 100 manufacturing industries', *Journal of Industrial Economics*, 35, 567–82.

Frank, M.Z (1988), 'An intertemporal model of industrial exit', *Quarterly Journal of Economics*, 103, 333–44.

Fudenberg, D. and J. Tirole (1986), 'A theory of exit in duopoly', *Econometrica*, 54, 943–60.

Ghemawat, P. and B. Nalebuff (1985), 'Exit', *RAND Journal of Economics*, 16, 184–94.

(1990), 'The devolution of declining industries', *Quarterly Journal of Economics*, 105, 167–86.

Gilbert, R.J. and M.B. Lieberman (1987), 'Investment and coordination in oligopolistic industries', *RAND Journal of Economics*, 18, 17–33.

Harrigan, K.R (1980), *Strategies for Declining Businesses*, Lexington, MA, Lexington Books.

Jovanovic, B. (1982), 'Selection and the evolution of industry', *Econometrica*, 50, 649–70.

Lieberman, M.B. (1987), 'Postentry investment and market structure in the chemical processing industries', *RAND Journal of Economics*, 18, 533–49.

(1989), 'The learning curve, technology barriers to entry, and competitive survival in the chemical processing industries', *Strategic Management Journal*, 10, 431–47.

Londregan, J. (1988), 'Exit vs. survival in the petroleum refining industry', mimeo, Carnegie-Mellon University, January.

(1990), 'Entry and exit over the industry life cycle', *RAND Journal of Economics*, 21, 446–58.

Mansfield, E. (1962), 'Entry, Gibrat's law, innovation. and the growth of firms', *The American Economic Review*, 52, 1023–50.

Peck, M.J., R.C. Levin and A. Goto (1987), 'Picking losers: public policy toward declining industries in Japan', *Journal of Japanese Studies*, 13, 79–123.

Reynolds, S.S. (1988), 'Plant closings and exit behaviour in declining industries', *Economica*, 55, 493–503.

Shaw, R.W. and S.A. Shaw (1983), 'Excess capacity and rationalisation in the West European synthetic fibres industry', *Journal of Industrial Economics*, 32, 149–66.

SRI International (1976), *Process Economics Program Handbook*, SRI International, Menlo Park, CA.

Directory of Chemical Producers, SRI International, Menlo Park, CA, annual issues.

Tang, M. (1989), 'Industrial dynamics in the US steel industry', mimeo, University of Illinois at Urbana-Champaign.

Whinston, M.D. (1988), 'Exit with multiplant firms', *RAND Journal of Economics*, 19, 74–94.

Part II

INDUSTRIAL PRICING
AND PRICING SCHEMES

Chapter 6

Intertemporal pricing schemes
Experimental tests of consciously parallel behaviour in oligopoly

Ronald Harstad, Stephen Martin
and Hans-Theo Normann

1   Introduction

Economists' concern with the possibility that firm conduct might allow businesses to collect economic profit over the long run goes back at least to Smith's (1937, p. 128) oft-quoted observation that

People of the same trade seldom meet together, even for merriment and diversion, but the conversation ends in a conspiracy against the public, or in some contrivance to raise prices.

From that time forward, industrial economists have analysed structure–conduct–performance relationships and offered advice to policy makers on the kinds of rules for business behaviour that are conducive to good market performance. Consistent with this advice, competition policy for most market economies declines to enforce collusive agreements and prohibits a variety of types of conduct thought to facilitate collusive outcomes.[1]

Louis Phlips was offered the opportunity to assert co-authorship of this paper, which his contributions would have justified. We are grateful to the European University Institute for financial support, to Klaus Abbink and Abdolkarim Sadrieh for providing us with their RatImage computer program (Abbink and Sadrieh, 1995), to Professor Henning Bunzel, to the Department of Economics at the University of Aarhus, to Charles Holt, and to seminar participants at George Washington University, Michigan State University, and the University of Edinburgh. Responsibility for errors is our own.

[1] An older approach, which permitted collusion and sought to regulate its consequences, has generally fallen into disfavour. See Martin (1997).

Although the infusion of industrial economics by game theory has been marked by great technical advances, this precision is of limited use for the purpose of advising policy makers about rules for business behaviour. In the kind of imperfectly competitive market that characterizes major industries in modern economies, the best equilibrium market performance obtainable is that of the Nash equilibrium of a non-repeated game (henceforth, for conciseness, we will refer to this as the static Nash equilibrium). Game-theoretic models of markets as repeated games are plagued by a multiplicity of equilibria, many of which yield firms greater profit than they would earn in static Nash equilibrium. Indeed, the *Folk Theorem* states that in an infinitely repeated game non-cooperative behaviour can sustain *any* strategy yielding firms individual payoffs that exceed non-cooperative payoffs from the stage game, provided that the interest rate used to discount future profits is sufficiently low.[2] Theory alone cannot guide policy prescriptions.

The purpose of this study is to examine, in a laboratory situation, one type of firm conduct that is often alleged to worsen market performance. We consider a kind of signalling that has been the subject of policy concern in both the European Union and the United States: parallel pricing that emerges in an environment of public announcements of prices and price changes (Phlips, 1995, chapter 7). Such behaviour has been attacked in the United States as a violation of the Sherman Act Section 1 prohibition against contracts, combinations, and conspiracies in restraint of trade;[3] in the European Union as a violation of the Treaty of Rome Article 85 prohibition of agreements and concerted practices that distort competition within the common market.[4] In both jurisdictions, enforcement authorities' early inferences of collusion from parallel conduct by enforcement authorities were sustained by the courts, but later cases met the judicial objection that in imperfectly competitive markets outcomes that gave firms collusive payoffs might result from conduct that was not collusive in a legal sense:[5]

concertation is not the only plausible explanation for parallel conduct. To begin with, the system of price announcements may be regarded as constituting a rational response to the fact that the pulp market constituted a long term market and to the need felt by both buyers and sellers to limit commercial risks. Further, the similarity in the dates of the price announcements may be regarded as a direct result of the high degree of market transparency, which does not have to be described as artificial. Finally, **the parallelism of prices and the price trends may be satisfactorily explained by the oligopolistic tendencies of**

---

[2] Strategies yielding such payoffs may also be an equilibrium in finitely repeated games (Benoit and Krishna, 1985; Harrington, 1987; Basu, 1992).

[3] Leading cases are *Interstate Circuit, Inc. et al. v. US*, 306 US 208 (1938); *American Tobacco Co. et al. v. US*, 328 US 781 (1946); *Theater Enterprises, Inc. v. Paramount Film Distr. Corp. et al.*, US 537 (1953).

[4] See among other references *Dyestuffs* Commission Decision of 24 July 1969 JO L 195/11 [1969] CMLR D23 and Italian Flat Glass Commission Decision of 7 December 1988 OJ No. L33/44 4 April 1989.

[5] *Re Wood Pulp Cartel: A. Ahlström oy and others versus E.C. Commission* [1993] 4 CMLR 407 at 582-3; emphasis added. On the distinction between the legal and economic notions of collusion, see Baker (1993) and Martin (1993).

the market and by the specific circumstances prevailing in certain periods. **Accordingly, the parallel conduct established by the Commission does not constitute evidence of concertation.**

We seek to observe, in stylized experimental markets that capture the main structural characteristics of important oligopoly markets

> whether parallel pricing can emerge in a market that excludes explicit collusion by design;
> whether such pricing patterns, if they emerge, lead to market performance approaching that resulting from explicit collusion.

2   Conscious parallelism and the conscious parallelism game

Back-and-forth price announcements, sometimes implemented and sometimes not, are a hallmark of many industries. The US steel industry is one example. The experiment described here, which permits such behaviour, is patterned in a general way after MacLeod's (1985) formal model of consciously parallel price changes.[6]

The market is one in which each firm sells a single variety of a differentiated product. The model is one of a repeated game, in which each period has two stages. In the first stage, firms play an *announcement* game, announcing prices or price changes and reacting to the announcements of other firms. The announcement stage is followed by a second stage in which firms set actual prices.

2.1   The announcement stage

Let P be the vector of announced prices. MacLeod imposes three axioms on function $r_{ji}(P, \Delta P_i)$ that gives the response by firm j to a price change ΔP_i announced by firm i:

> r_{ji} is continuous and continuously differentiable;
> r_{ji} is independent of scale changes: $r_{ji}(\alpha P, \alpha \Delta P_i) = \alpha r_{ji}(P, \Delta P_i)$
> response functions are symmetric, in the sense that relabelling firms does not alter responses.

MacLeod (1985, proposition 3) shows that the unique response function satisfying these axioms is a matching function,

$$r_{ji}(P, \Delta P_i) = \Delta P_i \qquad (1)$$

a result that implies behaviour of the kind observed in conscious parallelism cases. He interprets this as a socially acceptable rule of thumb of the type that might be expected to emerge if profit functions are not common knowledge (1985, p. 32).

This price matching strategy is then embedded in an equilibrium strategy for the announcement game; this strategy specifies

---

[6] The discussion that follows is heuristic; for a comprehensive presentation, see MacLeod (1985).

a firm will match an announced price increase if it is individually profitable
to do so, assuming all other firms match the increase, and if all other firms
match the increase;
a firm will match an announced price decrease;
defection triggers reversion to the Nash equilibrium prices of the one-shot
game.

Informational requirements are minimal: each firm is able to observe the announcements of other firms, knows the Nash reversion prices, and knows whether or not the
increase, if matched by all firms would be profitable for itself. It does not know
whether or not the increase would be profitable for rivals.[7]

2.2   The price-setting stage

The announcement game is followed by a pricing game. The conscious parallelism
strategy requires firms to set the equilibrium prices from the announcement game. The
strategy is sustained by the threat that if any firm defects from announced prices, all
other firms will revert to the non-cooperative equilibrium prices of the underlying
stage game. The conscious parallelism equilibrium prices exceed these static Nash
prices by the same amount for all firms (this is a consequence of the matching rule
(1)), and are such that further matched increases will be unprofitable for at least one
firm.

3   The experimental market

MacLeod's analytical framework is quite general. Experimental implementation
required us to select specific functional forms for demand and cost functions. We
discuss the duopoly version here.[8]
    We assume linear demand curves

$$p_1 = a_1 - b(q_1 + \theta q_2) \tag{2}$$

$$p_2 = a_2 - b(\theta q_1 + q_2) \tag{3}$$

where $0 < \theta < 1$. Varieties are thus demand substitutes, and firms' choice variables,
prices, are strategic complements.
    We assume that fixed costs are zero and that marginal costs c_1 and c_2, respectively,
are constant. Without loss of generality, let

$$a_1 - c_1 \leq a_2 - c_2. \tag{4}$$

---

[7] One can conceive of a dual quantity-matching strategy, in which firms would announce and react
to announcements of output changes. For a discussion of quantity announcements in the US
automobile industry, see Doyle and Snyder (1996).
[8] Results generalize to the n-firm case, as shown in an appendix available on request from Stephen
Martin.

For simplicity and with some abuse of terminology we will refer to variety 2 as the higher-quality variety (strictly speaking this would require $a_2 > a_1$).

3.1   Static Nash equilibrium prices

If demand for both varieties is non-negative,[9] the quantity demanded of variety 1 satisfies

$$b(1 - \theta^2)q_1 = (a_1 - c_1) - \theta(a_2 - c_2) + \theta(p_2 - c_2) - (p_1 - c_1) \qquad (5)$$

with an analogous expression for variety 2. Firm 1's profit then satisfies

$$b(1 - \theta^2)\pi_1 = (p_1 - c_1)[(a_1 - c_1) - \theta(a_2 - c_2) + \theta(p_2 - c_2) - (p_1 - c_1)]. \qquad (6)$$

The first-order condition for maximizing π_1 with respect to p_1 gives the equation of firm 1's price reaction function

$$2(p_1 - c_1) = (a_1 - c_1) - \theta(a_2 - c_2) + \theta(p_2 - c_2). \qquad (7)$$

Solving the equations of the two reaction functions gives static Nash equilibrium prices, which satisfy

$$(4 - \theta^2)(p_1^N - c_1) = (2 + \theta - \theta^2)(a_1 - c_1) - \theta(a_2 - c_2), \qquad (8)$$

$$(4 - \theta^2)(p_2^N - c_2) = (2 + \theta - \theta^2)(a_2 - c_2) - \theta(a_1 - c_1). \qquad (9)$$

From these expressions it follows that the higher-quality variety has the greater static Nash equilibrium price–cost margin

$$p_2^N - c_2 \geq p_1^N - c_1. \qquad (10)$$

The equations of the reaction functions imply that the quantity demanded of each firm in static Nash equilibrium is proportional to its price–cost margin

$$b(1 - \theta^2)q_1^N = (p_1^N - c_1). \qquad (11)$$

Hence equilibrium profit is proportional to the square of the price-cost margin

$$b(1 - \theta^2)\pi_1^N = (p_1^N - c_1)^2 \qquad (12)$$

and in static Nash equilibrium the higher-quality variety has the greater payoff.

3.2   Conscious parallelism equilibrium prices

We now turn to a question that is critical for the conscious parallelism strategy of the MacLeod model, in which prices are raised until at least one firm is unwilling to

---

[9] In the n-firm case, if one firm prices so high that its sales are zero, the market becomes an $n - 1$-firm oligopoly among the remaining firms. Programming for the experiments included subroutines to deal with such events.

go along with additional increases. How high will prices rise if firms behave in this way?

From (5), if all prices are increased by Δp from the non-cooperative equilibrium level, the quantity demanded of variety 1 falls according to

$$q_1(p_1^N + \Delta p - c_1, p_2^N + \Delta p - c_2) = q_1^N - \frac{1}{1+\theta} \frac{\Delta p}{b}. \tag{13}$$

Player 1's profit, if all prices are increased by Δp from the non-cooperative equilibrium level, is

$$\pi_1 = \pi_1^N - \frac{1}{1-\theta} \left[\Delta p - \frac{\theta}{1-\theta} (p_1^N - c_1) \right] \frac{\Delta p}{b}. \tag{14}$$

This is quadratic in Δp and has a maximum at

$$\Delta p_1 = \frac{1}{2} \frac{\theta}{1-\theta} (p_1^N - c_1). \tag{15}$$

There is a similar expression for firm 2. These expressions give the price increase that firm i would prefer, assuming that the other firm matches the increase. By (10), it is the lowest quality variety that will have the smallest Nash equilibrium price–cost margin. The conscious parallelism strategy therefore implies that it will be the producer of the lowest-quality variety that calls a halt to price increases.

3.3   Joint-profit maximization

It is straightforward to show (and a standard result in this type of model) that joint-profit maximization requires each firm to set the price that it would set if it were a monopolist not faced with the competition of substitute varieties:

$$p_1^J - c_1 = \frac{1}{2}(a_1 - c_1). \tag{16}$$

3.4   Discussion

The conscious parallelism equilibrium is illustrated graphically in Figure 6.1. The non-cooperative equilibrium (point N) is to be found in the intersection of the reaction functions (R_1, R_2) of the two firms. The dotted CP line is a 45° line with N as the origin. It shows all possible conscious parallelism prices. The conscious parallelism prices preferred by firm 1 and firm 2 are found where isoprofit curves are tangent to the CP line: firm 1 prefers prices corresponding to CP^*, while firm 2 could still gain from a further price increase to CP' – given that this price would be matched by firm 1. Since firm 1 is worse off at point CP', it does not match this price increase and CP^* is the conscious parallelism equilibrium.

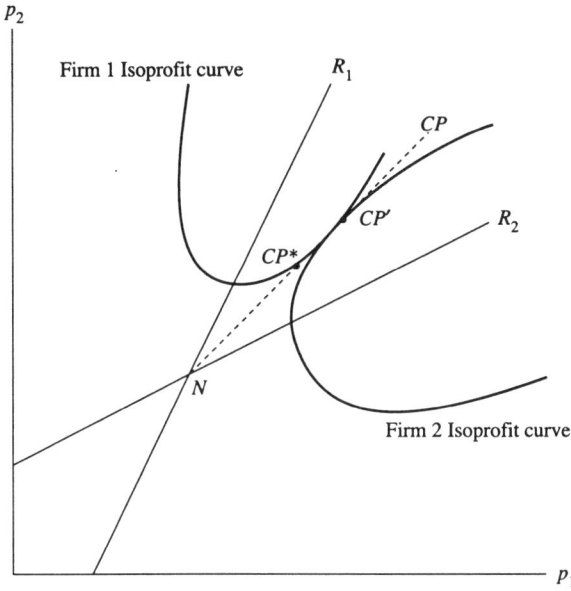

p_2

Firm 1 Isoprofit curve R_1

CP

CP′

R_2

*CP**

N

Firm 2 Isoprofit curve

p_1

Figure 6.1 The conscious parallelism equilibrium

4   Experimental Design

4.1   Treatments

Four treatments make up the overall experiment:

I A control treatment in which players act as independent price-setters.

In each period, each player selects a price; each player is informed of the prices chosen by the other players, of its own quantity sold and its own payoff; the experiment then proceeds to the next period. Subjects from this experiment do not participate in later experiments.

II A treatment to examine whether consciously parallel behaviour emerges spontaneously from oligopoly interactions.

Each period consists of two stages. In the first stage, players may announce prices. Any announcements are communicated to other players via the computer network. Firms may make multiple announcements, retract announced changes, and so on. When no announcement has been made for a specified interval (initially two minutes, reduced to 30 seconds after subjects have acquired experience with the mechanics of the procedure), the period moves to the second stage, in which firms select actual prices. Prices, own sales, and own payoffs are communicated as in the first session. The session then proceeds to the next period. Subjects from this experiment will not participate in later experiments.

III A treatment to examine the implications of consciously parallel behaviour for market performance.

As in treatment II, each period will consist of an announcement game and a pricing game. In the announcement game, players are constrained to match or to not match announced price changes. In other words, they are obliged to follow the MacLeod conscious parallelism strategy. The price-setting stage of the game is identical to that of treatment II.

IV A treatment to examine the impact of socialization on the sustainability of consciously parallel behaviour.

Subjects from treatment III participate in a follow-up session of treatment II. The hypothesis to be tested is that subjects who have had experience with price matching strategies in treatment III will tend to follow such strategies even when the experimental design does not force them to do so.

Treatment I is a posted-offer market with simulated demand. Treatment II is similar to the announcement games examined by Holt and Davis (1990) and Cason (1995), although we use a different market structure. Grether and Plott (1984) impose specific market practices (in their case, advance notice of price changes and most-favoured-nation clauses) on experimental markets, as we do in treatment III, and examine the consequences for market performance. Our focus on experience in comparing treatments III and IV is related to Benson and Faminow (1988), which uses a spatial differentiation model.

4.2   Parameter values/market characteristics

Each session involved four experimental subjects. Demand intercepts and marginal cost parameters were chosen so that

$$a_H - c_H = 32 \tag{17}$$

for two players and

$$a_L - c_L = 30 \tag{18}$$

for the other two players. Each player knew its own demand intercept and unit cost, and did not know those of the other players.

The product differentiation parameter θ was set equal to 2/3. This introduces enough differentiation to avoid substantial shifts in sales in response to small price changes, but means that different varieties are close enough substitutes so that there are substantial potential gains from coordinating behaviour.

As might be suspected from the discussion of duopoly (and as is shown in the appendix for the general case), it is only the differences $a - c$ that matter for incentives and payoffs. Adding/subtracting the same constant to/from all values of a and c in a session leaves the underlying game unchanged, although it does change equilibrium price levels. This aspect of the experimental market was used to vary the equilibrium

Table 6.1 *Comparative stage-game equilibrium values*

	Price–cost margins		Single-period payoffs	
	L	*H*	*L*	*H*
Static Nash	3.3125	4.4375	25.60	45.95
CP	13.250	14.375	58.52	101.22
JIIM	15.000	16.000	55.00	106.67

price levels of different sessions while maintaining comparability of margins across sessions. Subjects could therefore honestly be told that any information they might have received about price levels from subjects of previous sessions was not relevant for their session.

Table 6.1 compares price–cost margins and single-period payoffs in three alternative stage-game equilibria. It will be noted that the conscious parallelism margins and payoffs are very close to the joint-profit-maximizing values, and that both are substantially greater than the corresponding static Nash values. The potential reward to successful coordination is large.

Equilibrium payoffs for the *H* subjects are substantially greater than those for the *L* subjects. Differential exchange rates were used to convert the experimental currency unit (ECU) to Danish kroner (3 ECU/kroner for *L* subjects, 6 ECU/kroner for *H* subjects), so that potential cash payments to *H* and *L* subjects were essentially the same. These values were chosen so that experimental currency unit (ECU)–Danish kroner exchange rates could be used that would make mental conversions by subjects during the course of the session straightforward, while leading to payoffs within our budget constraint.

Subjects received a 60 kroner show-up fee as well as the kroner-equivalent of their experimental profits. The first period was a practice session that did not count toward the subject's payoff. Actual payments ranged from 180 to 540 Danish kroner (approximately $30 to $90) (before allowing for Danish income tax). Sessions lasted between 1.5 and 2 hours.

4.3   Organizational considerations

The experiments were carried out at the University of Aarhus. Subjects were mainly although not exclusively undergraduate economics majors.[10]

Each session lasted a minimum of 20 periods. We used a random stopping rule to determine the end of the session. At the end of period 20 and of each following period, a die was rolled in plain view of the experimental subjects. If the die came up 6, the experiment ended, otherwise it continued. The resulting ending probability makes the conscious parallelism strategy a non-cooperative equilibrium.

---

[10] The subject who earned the largest payoff was majoring in Japanese.

Table 6.2 *Aarhus conscious parallelism experiments: descriptive statistics*

Experiment	Session	Rounds
1	1	20
1	2	20
1	3	23
1	4	34
1	5	27
2	1	24
2	2	21
2	3	27
2	5	23 .
2	6	23
3	1	22
3	2	20
3	4	21
4	1	22
4	2	22
4	3	26
Total		375

The number of sessions for each treatment, and the number of rounds in each session, are reported in table 6.2.[11]

Experimental subjects were linked via a computer network. The programming language is Turbo-Pascal; we used the RatImage routines developed by Abbink and Sadrieh (1995), which were designed for computer-aided human behaviour experiments.

Instructions (reproduced in an appendix at the end of this chapter) were scrolled across the computer screen. Options available through the menu included a calculator and a history option that allowed a player to review previous prices of all firms as well as its own previous sales and profits. This is illustrated in figure 6.2, which shows a sample screen from treatment I.[12] In the event, experimental subjects consulted the price history for 1,130 of the 1,500 observations generated by the Aarhus sessions.

In treatment I, which involves price setting but no announcements, subjects saw a screen of the kind shown in figure 6.3 at the end of each period. This shows all four prices, as well as own quantity sold, own profit, and accumulated profit.

Figure 6.4 shows firm 1's screen appearance in treatment II, after firm 2 has announced a price change and other firms have had the opportunity to react to this announcement.

Figure 6.4 may be compared with figures 6.5 and 6.6. These show firm 1's screen in

---

[11] Session 4 of experiment 2 and session 3 of experiment 3 were terminated due to software problems.

[12] Additional screens from the various treatments are posted in the world wide web at url http:// www.ibt.dk/www/samf/oko/cie/screens.htm.

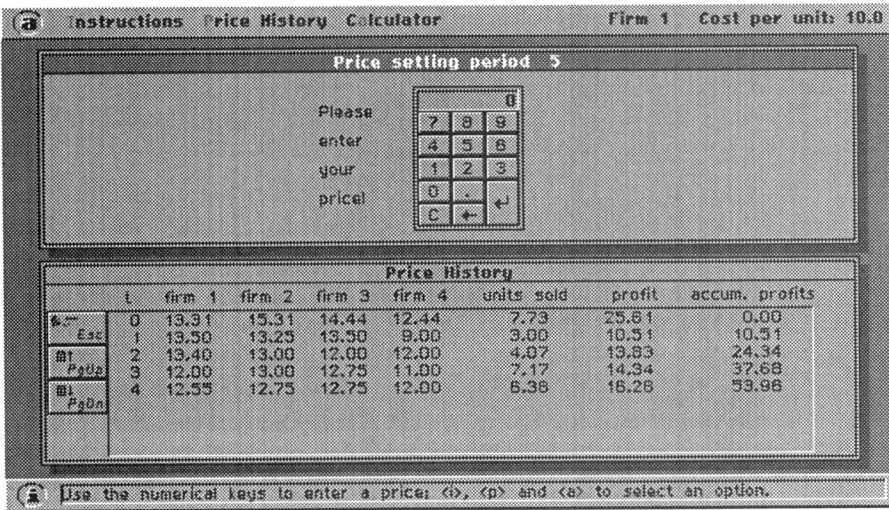

Figure 6.2 Price history screen image, treatment I (price setting only)

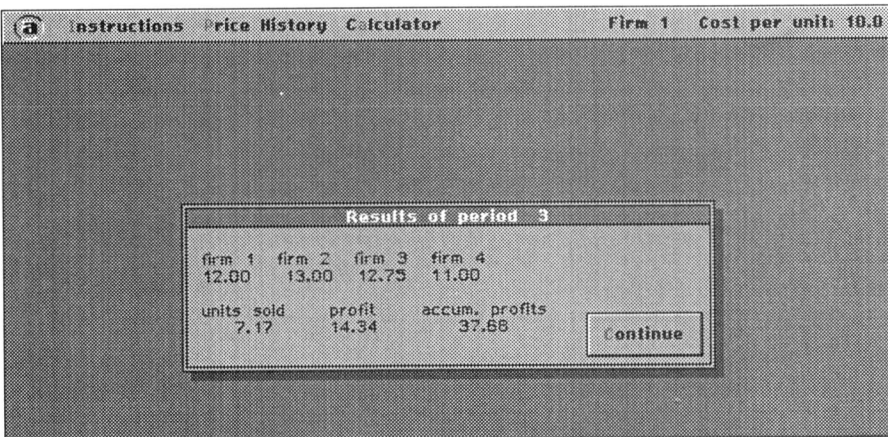

Figure 6.3 Results screen, treatment I (price setting only)

treatment III when a price change is announced (figure 6.5) and after players have been able to react to the announced change (figure 6.6). The information that is given to firm 1 in figure 6.5 is consistent with that required by MacLeod's formal model: under the conscious parallelism strategy, firms are to match announced price increases if it is profitable for them to do so and all other firms match the announced increase. Somewhat more broadly, we intended to give subjects information that would replicate the kind of information real-world firms might be expected to have if direct

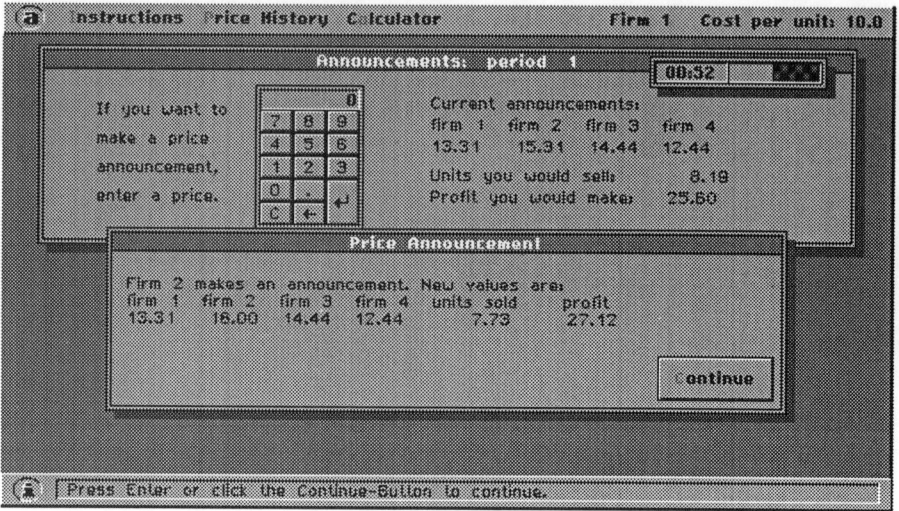

Figure 6.4 Treatment II, screen after an announcement is made

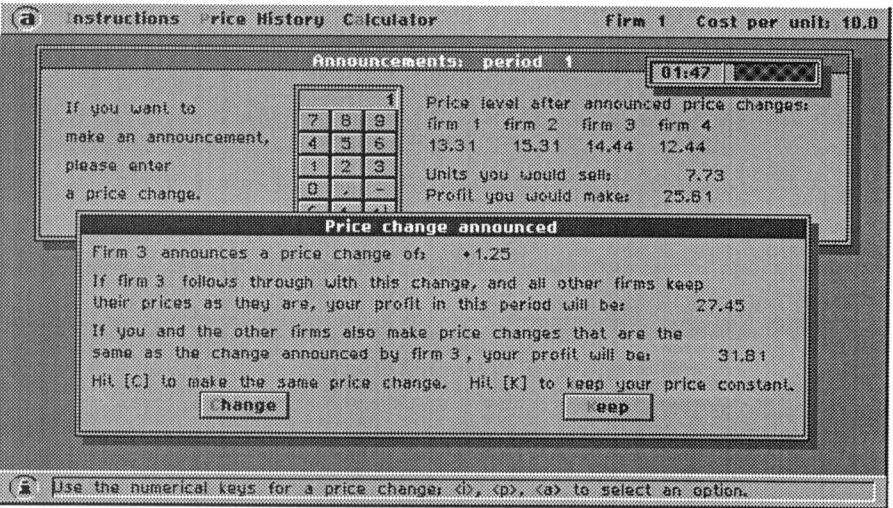

Figure 6.5 Treatment III, price change announced

communication among competitors is ruled out. This includes own cost and own and rivals' prices, as well as what realistically would be estimates of expected own sales and own profit.

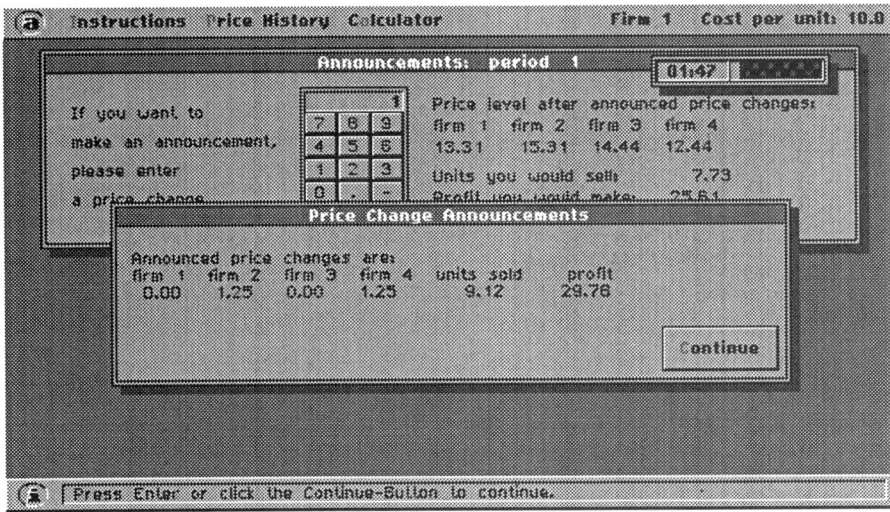

Figure 6.6 Treatment III, after all players have responded to an announced price change

5   Results

Table 6.3 gives a general description of the 16 sessions. Table 6.4 reports the average difference, subject by subject and session by session, between actual and static Nash price–cost margins. Negative values indicate that the subject set below-Nash prices, on average. The conscious parallelism values would be 9.9375 for L and H subjects; the joint-profit-maximizing values would be 11.6875 and 11.5625, for L and H subjects respectively.

5.1   Treatment I

Figure 6.7 shows the development of price–cost margins in the five sessions of treatment I (price-setting without announcements). What is shown in figure 6.7 are the arithmetic differences between the actual and the static-Nash price–cost margins, averaged over the four subjects in the session (two with low-quality, two with high-quality varieties).

In sessions I–1, I–2, and I–3 margins are below static-Nash levels early in the session. Margins in session I–1 rise steadily throughout the session. Margins in session I–2 fall quite low through period 5, rise sharply through period 12, then decline slightly thereafter. Margins in session I–3 rise above static-Nash levels through period 8, level off for about nine periods, then decline. The latter may appear to be endgame effects, which were evident in many of the sessions. Despite the continuation probability implied by the random stopping time, the first period in which the experiment might stop (period 20) seemed to be a focal point around which behaviour became more rivalrous.

Table 6.3 *Aarhus conscious parallelism experiments: qualitative descriptions*

Session	Comments	II/II^n (%)
I-1	3 firms progressively move to above-static Nash prices; firm 2 a maverick	83
I-2	all firms above Nash price in second half of the session	96
I-3	1 and 4 prices above Nash in middle periods; 2 and 3 Nash from period 7 on; endgame effects	90
I-4	3 Nash from period 5 on; other players persistently above Nash prices	135
I-5	above Nash throughout; apparent tacit collusion breaks down periods 16–22, then resumes 23–25	141
II-1	prices essentially always above Nash level; 2 and 3 usually near best response prices,1 and 4 above best response prices	130
II-2	1 and 4 persistently price above Nash, 3 slightly below Nash, 2 mostly above but with two episodes of low prices	101
II-3	1 and 4 persistently price above Nash, 2 and 3 price at Nash level throughout	104
II-5	signalling by 4, periods 11–17, all prices then above Nash; otherwise, prices at Nash level	124
II-6	prices at or above Nash levels, periods 8–14; player 2 never above Nash level; slow decline from period 15	107
III-1	prices rise sharply through period 6, decline slowly thereafter, above Nash levels throughout	151
III-2	prices fluctuate above Nash level first 10 periods, then rise sharply	121
III-4	prices above Nash throughout, substantially so periods 7–14, decline thereafter	145
IV-1	prices rise continuously through period 18, fall to Nash levels period 20, begin to rise again	181
IV-2	prices fluctuate substantially around an average above Nash levels	142
IV-3	prices rise through period 10, decline thereafter, end around Nash level	111

5.1.1   History matters

One aspect of the MacLeod conscious parallelism model is that the static Nash equilibrium is known at the start of the game (1985, p. 34). With this in mind, the instructions included a set of 'period 0' prices that were in fact the static Nash equilibrium prices. They were not described as such to the experimental subjects, who were told without editorial comment that the period 0 prices were based on previous experimental experience.

In treatment I, session 4, the period 0 prices were the joint-profit-maximizing prices (without identifying them as such). In treatment I, session 5, no period 0 prices were given. It is evident from table 6.4 that price–cost margins in sessions 4 and 5 were

Table 6.4 *Aarhus conscious parallelism experiments: average*
$(p - c) - (p - c)^N$, *by subject and session*

Session	L1	L2	H1	H2
1–1	−0.01	−1.52	−0.76	0.06
1–2	−0.32	−0.06	0.80	1.20
1–3	0.40	−0.34	−0.74	1.37
1–4	2.47	3.09	1.05	3.04
1–5	2.99	3.40	2.28	3.57
2–1	2.64	1.79	2.00	2.82
2–2	0.26	0.25	−0.13	0.24
2–3	0.44	−0.13	−0.13	1.07
2–5	1.49	2.00	2.15	3.73
2–6	0.49	−0.15	0.59	1.22
3–1	3.13	2.65	3.19	3.15
3–2	1.47	1.80	1.14	1.75
3–4	3.48	2.47	3.72	3.38
4–1	6.31	4.98	6.01	7.14
4–2	1.20	1.73	1.06	2.29
4–3	0.97	1.72	0.97	0.43

Notes: For treatments I, II, and II, L1 is player 1, L2 is player 2, H1 is player 3, H4 is player 4; for experiment IV, L1 is player 3, L2 is player 4;\ H1 is player 1, H2 is player 4; periods 16 and 17 omitted from sample for player 4, experiment 2, session 5 (see text).

consistently higher than in sessions 1 and 3. The final column of table 6.3 indicates that payoffs in these sessions were similarly higher than the other sessions of treatment I. In session 4, price–cost margins average 3.5 ECU above Nash levels in period 2 and declined slowly through 34 sessions to an average 1.1 ECU above the Nash level.

In treatment I, session 5 margins never fall below static Nash levels. There seem to be two relative breakdowns in coordination, once in period 12 and once over periods 19 through 23. The latter appears to be an endgame effect. When the game continues through several rolls of the die, prices rise again.

5.2   Treatment II

Treatment II allows players to communicate via cheap-talk announcements. Average excess price–cost margins for treatment II are shown in figure 6.8.[13]

Sessions 2, 3, and 6 fluctuate around and converge to roughly the static Nash level. Results for these sessions are consistent with those for related specifications that have been reported in the literature (for example, Holt and Davis, 1990).

Sessions II-1 and II-5 exhibit different types of behaviour. Average margins in session II-1 decline over the initial periods, but stay consistently above static Nash

---

[13] For session II-5, periods 16 and 17, the average margin is calculated for firms 1, 2, and 3 only.

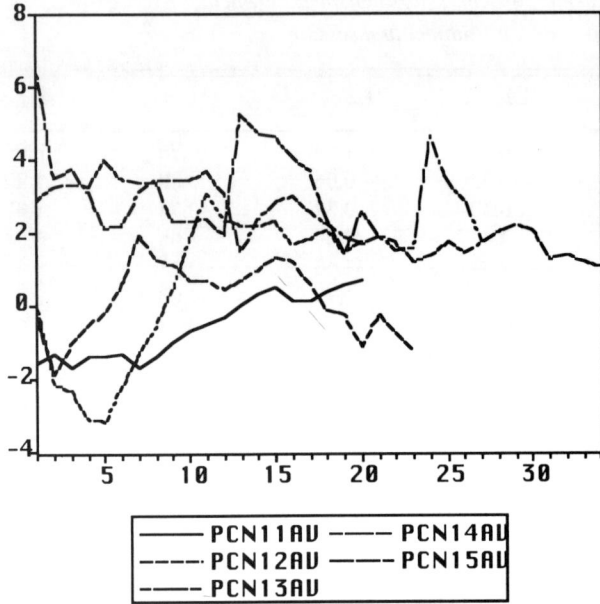

Figure 6.7 Treatment I, sessions 1–5, average $(p - c)$ – static Nash $(p - c)$, by session

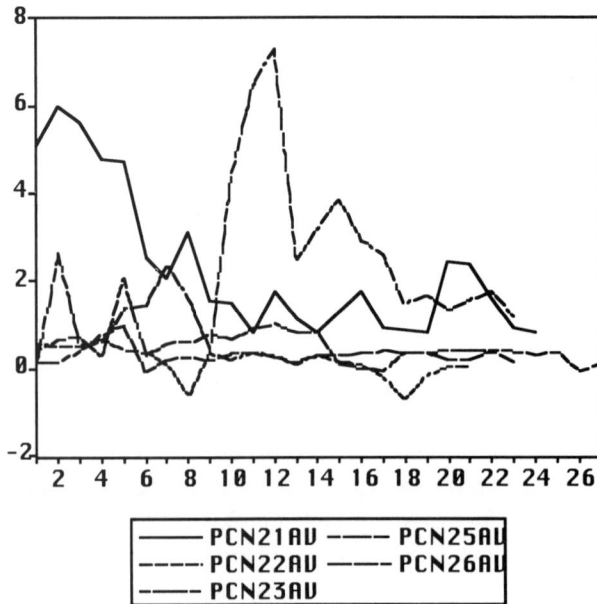

Figure 6.8 Average $(p - c)$ – static Nash $(p - c)$, treatment II, by session

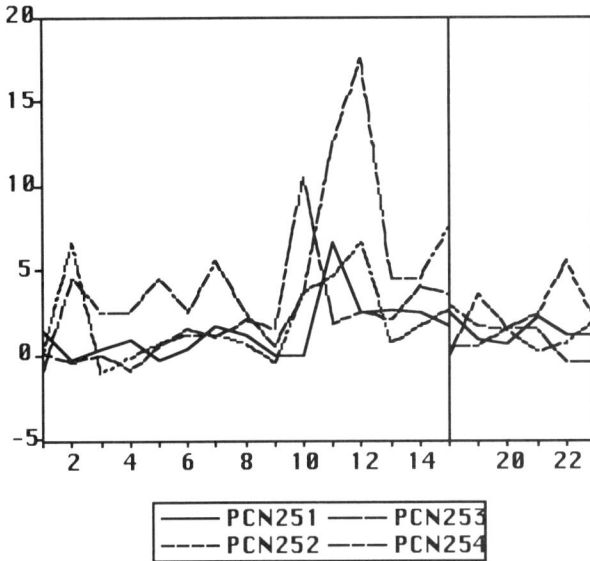

Figure 6.9 Treatment II, session 5, $(p-c)$ – static Nash $(p-c)$; periods 16 and 17 omitted

levels. The same is true for average margins in session II-5, which exhibit greater fluctuation. The effect of price announcements for these two sessions recall the results reported by Brown-Kruse, Cronshaw, and Schenk (1993) for location communications.

Treatment II, session 5 merits separate attention. Its time path of price–cost margins is shown in figure 6.9.

It will be noted that player 4 set very high prices in periods 11, 12, and 15. In periods 16 and 17, which are omitted from figure 6.9 for reasons of scale, player 4 set a price of 400. An interview after the session established that these high prices were an attempt to signal to other players and lead them to raise prices. This effort was abandoned in and after period 18, but the net result was relatively high margins and payoffs for the session as a whole.

5.3   Treatment III

In treatment III, players were able to make announcements, but they were obliged to follow the price-matching element of the conscious parallelism strategy. Margins and payoffs were high in all three sessions. The time paths of prices in the three sessions differed, however.

In treatment III, session 1, price–cost margins rose for the first six periods, then fell slowly for the rest of the session (figure 6.10). There is only one instance in which one player set a price below the Nash level, and this occurred in period 20. One might

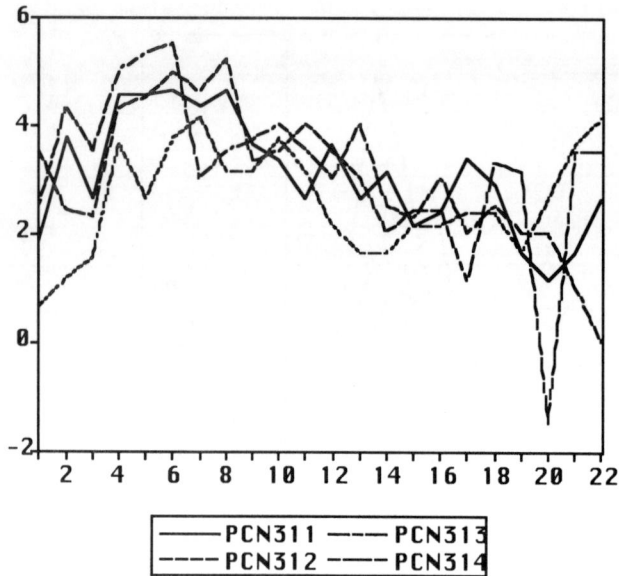

Figure 6.10 Treatment III, session 1, $(p - c)$ − static Nash $(p - c)$

interpret this as an early comprehension of the private benefits of refraining from vigorous competition, more or less sustained by the conscious parallelism announcement mechanism.

The sharp price increase in the session occurs in period 4, with further smaller increases in periods 5 and 6. These periods are marked by many announcements (ten in periods 4 and 5, 14 in period 6), mostly of small positive or negative changes.

In period 4, five of the 10 announced changes were matched by all players (table 6.5). All of these five announcements were increases. Two of the announcements in period 5 and two of the announcements in period 6 (all increases) were matched by all players.

In treatment III, session 2, on the other hand, price–cost margins fluctuated around Nash levels for more than half of the session (figure 6.11). In period 13, however, margins rose sharply, and they remained at this higher level for the rest of the session. In the announcement segment of period 13, player 1 announced a price increase of 2 ECU four times in a row (table 6.6). The first two times, all three of the other players matched the increase. The final two times, two of the other three players matched the increase. Actual prices that were set were somewhat below the announced levels, but substantially above the levels of previous periods.[14]

The path of price–cost margins in treatment III, session 4 (figure 6.12) resembles that of treatment III, session 1 in some ways. Prices start at and rise to a higher level

---

[14] That posted prices fell short of announced levels is generally characteristic of the announcement treatments. This is functionally equivalent to undertaking transactions at discounts from list price.

Table 6.5 *Session III-1, period 4: price change announcements*

Period 3 prices	16.00	16.90	16.80	16.00
3	**0.50**	**0.50**	**0.50**	**0.50**
3	0.00	−0.30	−0.30	−0.30
4	0.00	−0.50	0.00	−0.50
2	0.10	0.10	0.00	0.10
3	0.00	−0.30	−0.30	−0.30
4	0.00	−0.30	−0.30	−0.30
3	**0.20**	**0.20**	**0.20**	**0.20**
4	**0.50**	**0.50**	**0.50**	**0.50**
1	**1.00**	**1.00**	**1.00**	**1.00**
1	**1.00**	**1.00**	**1.00**	**1.00**
Period 4 prices	17.90	19.00	18.80	17.50

Note: First column identifies the player announcing a price change.

Table 6.6 *Session III-2, period 13: price change announcements*

Period 12 prices	13.50	16.50	15.44	13.50
1	**2.00**	**2.00**	**2.00**	**2.00**
1	**2.00**	**2.00**	**2.00**	**2.00**
1	2.00	2.00	2.00	0.00
1	2.00	2.00	0.00	2.00
Period 13 prices	17.00	20.00	17.44	19.000

Note: First column identifies the player announcing a price change.

in session 4 than in session 1. In session 4, the peak of prices comes in the middle of the session, not the beginning. In session 4, the sharp increase in prices occurs in period 7.

Six price change announcements were made in the announcement segment of period 7 (table 6.7). First player 3 announced an increase of 2 ECU; no other player matched this increase. Player 1 then successively announced three price increases of 1 ECU each. Each time, all three other players matched the announcement. Player 3 then announced an increase of 0.55 ECU, which was matched by players 2 and 4 but not by player 1. Then player 2 announced an increase of 1 ECU, which was matched by all other players.

5.4   Treatment IV

Treatment IV is identical in structure to treatment II: players may make and react to cheap-talk price change announcements in the first half of each period. They are not constrained to follow the conscious parallelism announcement strategy. All subjects in treatment IV had experience with treatment III.

The differing character of the three sessions is evident in figure 6.13. The

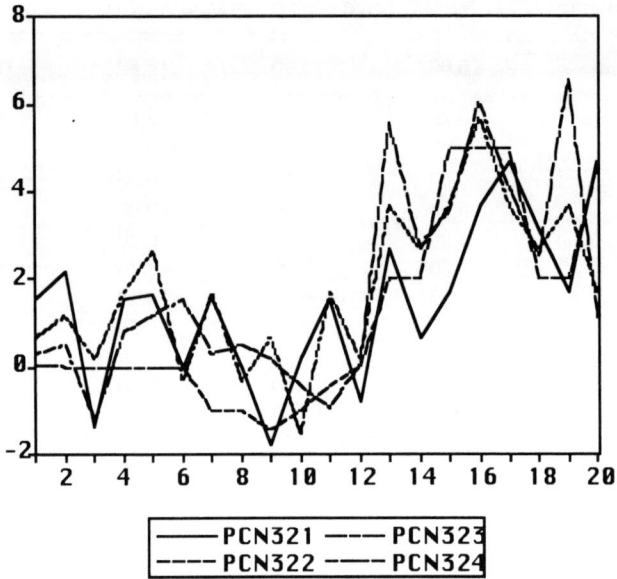

Figure 6.11 Treatment III, session 2, $(p - c)$ − static Nash $(p - c)$

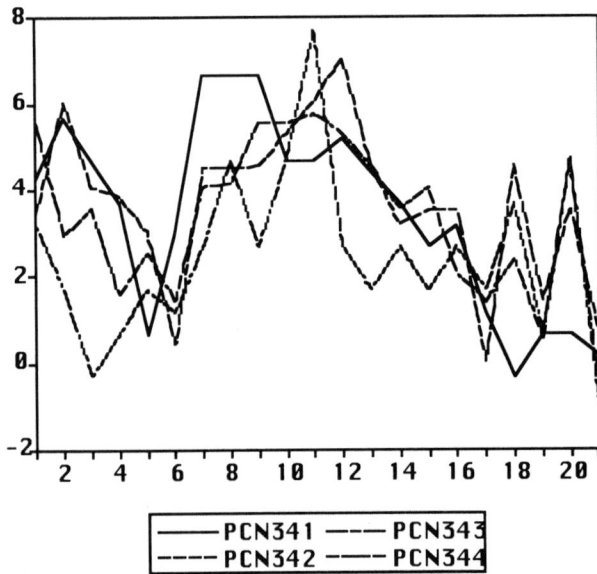

Figure 6.12 Treatment III, session 4, $(p - c)$ − static Nash $(p - c)$

Table 6.7 *Session III-4, period 7: price change announcements*

Period 6 prices	18.25	18.50	16.89	15.90
3	0.00	0.00	2.00	0.00
1	**1.00**	**1.00**	**1.00**	**1.00**
1	**1.00**	**1.00**	**1.00**	**1.00**
1	**1.00**	**1.00**	**1.00**	**1.00**
3	0.00	0.55	0.55	0.55
2	**1.00**	**1.00**	**1.00**	**1.00**
Period 7 prices	22.00	20.00	20.95	18.50

Note: First column identifies the player announcing a price change.

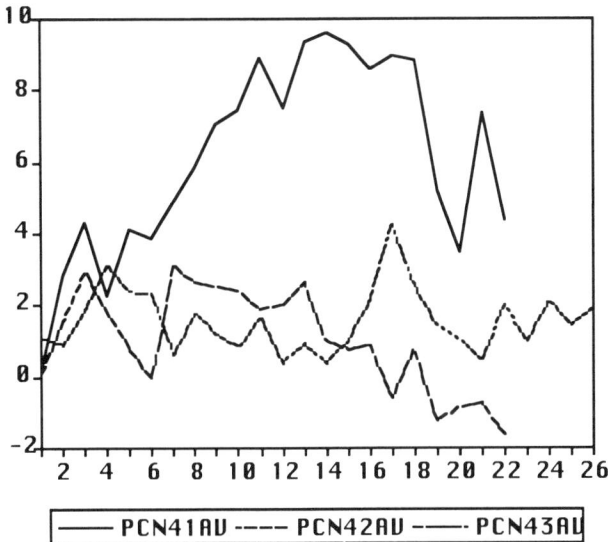

Figure 6.13 Average $(p - c)$ – static Nash $(p - c)$, treatment IV, by session

combination of experience and the possibility of making announcements yields very high margins in session IV-1 and comparatively high margins in session IV-2, but does not sustain margins above the static Nash level in session IV-3.[15]

Prices in treatment IV, session 1 rise steadily through period 14, level off for another four periods, and then fall in periods 19 and 20. This last may be interpreted as an endgame effect. Throughout this session, price–cost margins tended to move together.

In most of periods 1 through 14, many announcements were made. The general pattern was that announced prices were greater than prices that were actually set;

[15] The average margin in session IV–2 is 1.02 ECU above the static Nash level.

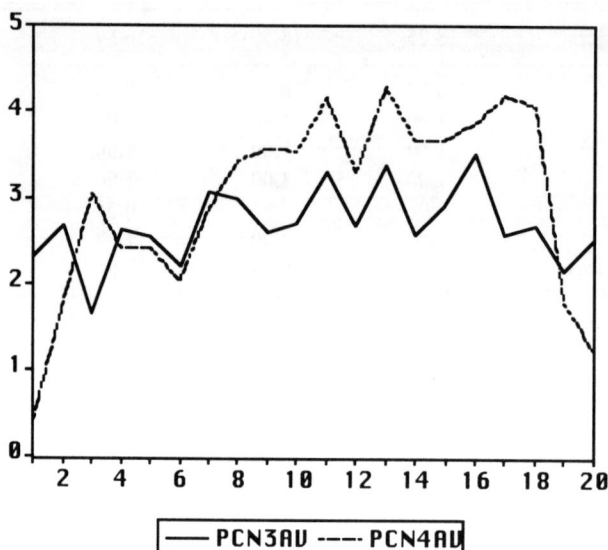

Figure 6.14 Average $(p - c)$ − static Nash $(p - c)$, period by period, treatments III and IV, periods 1–20

Cason (1995) reports similar behaviour. However, the trend in both announced and posted prices was upward through period 14.

The time-path of price–cost margins in treatment IV, session 2 is much more level. Prices rise through period 4, decline slowly and with much fluctuation for about ten periods, then rise somewhat.

In treatment IV, session 3, margins rise by period 3, fluctuate above Nash levels for 11 periods, then decline towards the end of the session.

5.5   Comparison of Treatments III and IV

It is instructive to compare treatments III and IV. Figure 6.14 shows the average price–cost margin, minus the static Nash margin, for the first 20 periods of all treatment III sessions and all treatment IV sessions. Each average is therefore taken over 12 experimental subjects, half with low-quality varieties and half with high-quality varieties. An average of zero means subjects are pricing at the static Nash level. The average of the conscious parallelism margins is 13.8125, of the joint-profit-maximizing margins 15.5 (table 6.1).

Subjects price above static Nash levels for both treatments III and IV, although they approach neither the conscious parallelism nor the joint-profit-maximizing level.[16] Margins are greater for treatment IV than for treatment III from period 9

---

[16] In this respect, our results are similar to those of Grether and Plott (1984).

Table 6.8 *Regression Results*

	(1)	(2)	(3)
C	1.1253	1.1343	−0.0907
	(4.5846)	(4.6315)	(0.3742)
D400	386.2814	378.2000	378.2000
	(1709.099)	(275.5513)	(275.3662)
F	−0.4572	−0.3971	−0.3253
	(1.3752)	(1.1960)	(1.0421)
H	0.2852	0.2624	0.2623
	(1.1446)	(1.0694)	(1.1653)
D24	−0.1294	−0.3156	0.9062
	(0.4762)	(1.2319)	(3.3491)
D3	1.3891	1.3887	2.6103
	(4.4520)	(4.4431)	(8.0897)
D4	1.7080	1.8938	1.8937
	(3.6185)	(4.0836)	(4.0798)
D14			2.3838
			(6.8418)
D15			2.6109
			(8.3719)
S251		2.0831	2.0863
		(4.009)	(4.0300)
S252		2.6026	2.6058
		(6.9875)	(7.0511)
S253		1.5186	1.5219
		(6.0682)	(6.2068)
S254		8.2815	8.2847
		(6.0405)	(6.0431)
R^2	0.9757	0.9771	0.9796

Dependent variable: $(p - c)$ – static Nash $(p - c)$; t-statistics in parentheses (based on Newey-West heteroskedasticity-consistent variance estimates).

through 18, at which point what should probably be interpreted as endgame effects kick in.

5.6 Statistical analysis

Table 6.8 reports the results of a regression analysis using the complete 1,500-element sample. The dependent variable is the deviation between observed and static Nash price–cost margins. The first 20 observations in this sample are for treatment I, session 1, subject 1; these are followed by 20 observations for treatment I, session 1, subject 2; and so on. The final 26 observations in the sample are for treatment IV, session 3, player 4.

In table 6.8, the coefficient of C is the constant term in the regression. F is a dummy variable that takes the value 1 for the first period in each session. This controls for the fact the subjects were told that they would not be paid for this period. H is a dummy variable that takes the value 1 for observations generated by subjects with high-quality varieties, and 0 otherwise. In static Nash equilibrium, high-quality varieties should exhibit larger margins. In conscious parallelism equilibrium, the excess of the margin over the static Nash level is the same for varieties of both types. The excess of the joint-profit-maximizing margin over the static Nash level is slightly greater for low-quality varieties than for high-quality varieties. In any event, neither F nor H have significant coefficients for any of the specifications reported in table 6.8.

$D24$ is a dummy variable that takes the value 1 for treatments II and IV, which have the same structure, and 0 otherwise. Similarly, $D3$ and $D4$ are dummy variables keyed on treatments III and IV respectively.

The residual category is therefore treatment I. The coefficient of $D24$ should indicate the impact on margins of allowing subjects to make announcements, relative to the price-setting only treatment. The coefficient of $D3$ should indicate the differential effect of constraining subjects to follow the conscious parallelism strategy, and the coefficient of $D4$ should indicate the impact of experience with the conscious parallelism strategy on margins, over and above any effect of the ability to make announcements pure and simple.

$D400$ is a dummy variable that takes the value 1 for the two observations from treatment II, session 5 in which subject 4 set a price of 400. Inclusion of this dummy variable does not affect the other coefficient estimates; it is responsible for the high R^2-square statistics in table 6.8.

Column 1 of table 6.8 distinguishes the impact of the different treatments on price–cost margins (relative to static Nash levels). The coefficient of $D24$ is not statistically significant – announcements as such do not generate increments in margins compared with treatment I – while $D3$ and $D4$ both have coefficients that are significant and large, relative to the static Nash margins given in table 6.1.

Column 2 in addition examines the impact of the signalling episode in treatment I, session 5. The variables $S251$, $S252$, $S253$, and $S254$ are dummy variables for each subject in this session that take the value 1 for periods in which player 4 appeared to follow a signalling strategy, and 0 otherwise. All four of these signalling variables have significant positive coefficients.

Column 3 of table 6.8 includes two additional dummy variables, one for treatment I, session 4 and one for treatment I, session 5. As noted above, session 1-4 gave subjects the joint-profit-maximizing prices as period 0 prices, while session 1-5 gave no period 0 prices. Both variables have significant positive coefficients.[17] In addition, when these variables that control for differences in initial conditions are included as explanatory variables, the coefficient of $D24$ becomes positive and statistically

[17] These results may be contrasted with those of Mason, Phillips, and Redington (1991), who test for and reject the hypotheses that experience with practice periods anchored behaviour in the session proper. Their treatments involved linear demand, two quantity-setting subjects (with constant but different unit costs), and a homogeneous good.

Table 6.9 *Margins and one-shot payoffs implied by table 6.8, column 3 specification*

	Price-cost margins		Single-period payoffs	
	L	H	L	H
Static Nash	3.3125	4.4375	25.60	45.95
Announcements + experience	6.0217	7.4090	38.86	59.07
CP	13.250	14.375	58.52	101.22

significant: controlling for other factors constant, the ability to make announcements has a moderate positive effect on price–cost margins.

The implications of the regression analysis for price–cost margins and payoffs are summarized in table 6.9.[18] In the experimental markets that we have examined, the possibility of making announcements increases margins, as does the use of the conscious parallelism mechanism and experience with announcements. Margins nearly double, and payoffs increase 30 per cent (*H* varieties) and 50 per cent (*L* varieties), compared with static Nash levels. While these are substantial increases, they remain below conscious parallelism and joint-profit-maximizing levels. Column 3 also indicates that either signalling or a history of high prices will sustain margins above those indicated in table 6.9.

6   Summary

We have described imperfectly competitive experimental markets designed to explore the impact of price announcements and consciously parallel behaviour on market performance.

We have observed behaviour under a single set of market conditions. As is traditional in experimental economics, focusing the design on research hypotheses has been assisted by the simplicities of linear demand and constant marginal costs. Also in accord with common practice, private information about demand intercepts and costs limited individual subjects to a proper subset of the minimal information for an explicit calculation of conscious parallelism or joint-profit-maximizing outcomes. All markets studied had each of four sellers produce a single variety of the commodity.[19] Perhaps the most important open question is the robustness of the results reported here to the degree of product differentiation (θ); this is the subject of on-going research.

Conditional on these elements of the specification, the ability to make announcements is here sufficient to sustain price–cost margins that are above static Nash levels.

---

[18] The payoff estimates in table 6.9 are from a separate regression, with dependent variable actual minus static Nash payoff and explanatory variables as in table 6.8, column 3.

[19] Most of the simplifications just listed are standard; empirical evidence of the robustness of observations with respect to these simplifications is rare. Holt (1995) indicates that four-seller markets have been seen to approximate behaviour of markets with five up to perhaps ten sellers.

Margins are higher still if subjects are constrained to match or not match announced price changes, although for such treatments margins do not reach levels of the conscious parallelism equilibrium. In such treatments, periods of sharp price increases are also periods of substantial price-matching behaviour.

Experience with the matching strategy also leads to greater margins, as do attempts to assume a price leadership role and a history of higher prices.

The results reported here suggest that imperfectly competitive markets often can yield prices above and efficiencies below the static Nash equilibrium standard.

The kinds of signalling mechanisms that appear in treatments II, III, and IV of this experiment are available in real-world markets, are not condemned by mainstream competition policies, and support returns above static Nash equilibrium levels.

7   Appendix Instructions

7.1   Experiment I

General description

Today we are going to set up an experimental market.

The market is supplied by four firms.

Each of you will take the part of one firm.

The profit or loss your firm makes in the market depends on the decisions you make and on the decisions made by the other firms, in a way that is explained below.

The profit or loss your firm makes in the market determines the amount you will be paid IN CASH at the end of the experiment.

The experiment will last at least 20 periods. The precise ending time of the experiment will be determined randomly.

You are firm number $== i ==$.

You do not know the firm numbers of the other participants in the experiment, and they do not know your firm number.

Description of the market

Each firm produces a product that is sold in competition with the products of other firms.

The amount your firm sells and the profit you make in each period depends on the price you set and the prices other firms set in that period.

Each unit of output that you sell costs you c to produce. You do not know the cost per unit of the other firms in the experiment and they do not know your cost per unit.

If your price is greater than your production cost, you will earn a profit on every unit of output that you sell.

If your price is less than your production cost, you will lose money on every unit of output that you sell.

The buyers in the market may consider products to be somewhat different. As a consequence of possible differences in demand and cost, differences in price may arise.

Information you will be given

Before the first period starts you will be given information from previous experimental experience in this market. You will get to know prices of all firms and the sales and the profit you would make if these prices were charged.

In every period, after all participants have entered a price for their firm you will be shown the prices of all firms and the sales and the profit you made in that period. You will also be given information about your accumulated profits.

You will be able to recall data from former periods (prices of all firms, sales and profit you made) by using the 'Price History' option.

PRESS ESCAPE TO LEAVE THE INSTRUCTIONS

7.2   Experiment II

General description
In addition to the instructions of experiment I

In every period there is an announcement phase and a price-setting phase. These two phases are explained below.

Description of the market
As in experiment I

Description of the announcement phase and the price-setting phase

During the announcement phase, firms indicate the prices they may charge. Afterwards, in the price setting phase, each firm will set the price that it will actually charge, and may choose a different price, higher or lower, than any price it announced.

Each firm may make as many announcements as it likes to make.

If no firm announces a price for two minutes, the announcement phase will be closed. Later in the experiment after you and the other participants have had some experience with the way the process works, the time period will be shortened to one minute and then to 30 seconds.

The experiment will then move to the price-setting phase, in which you decide the price you will actually charge in that period.

Information you will be given
In addition to the instructions of experiment II

Each firm will learn the announced prices of all firms. You will also be told how much sales and profits you would make if the announced prices were actually finalized.

PRESS ESCAPE TO LEAVE THE INSTRUCTIONS

7.3   Experiment III

General description

As in experiment II

Description of the market

As in experiments I and II

Description of the announcement phase and the price-setting phase

During the announcement phase, firms indicate price changes they may make. Afterwards, in the price-setting phase each firm will set the price that it will actually charge, and may choose a different price, higher or lower, than the price resulting from announced price changes.

Note that the announcements are price CHANGES, i.e., firms announce to increase or to decrease their price by a certain amount. In the price setting phase the ABSOLUTE prices which are charged in the market have to be set.

Each firm may announce as many price changes as it wishes to make. When one firm announces a price change, you will be given the opportunity to announce an identical price change.

If no firm announces a price change for two minutes, the announcement phase will be closed. Later in the experiment, after you and the other participants have had some experience in the way the process works, this time period will be shortened to one minute and then to 30 seconds.

The experiment will then move to the price-setting phase, in which you enter the price you will actually charge in that period.

Information you will be given

As in experiment II, with one change

Each firm will learn the announced price changes of all firms.

References

Abbink, K. and A. Sadrieh (1995), 'RatImage – research assistance toolbox for Computer-aided human behaviour experiments', *Discussion Paper no. B-325*, SFB 303, University of Bonn.

Baker, J.B. (1993), 'Two Sherman Act Section 1 dilemmas: parallel pricing, the oligopoly problem, and contemporary economic theory', *Antitrust Bulletin*, 38 (1, Spring), 143–219.

Basu, K. (1992), 'Collusion in finitely-repeated oligopolies', *International Journal of Industrial Organization*, 10 (4, December), 595–609.

Benoit, J-P. and V. Krishna (1985), 'Finitely repeated games', *Econometrica*, 53 (4, July), 905–22.

Benson, B.L. and M.D. Faminow (1988), 'The impact of experience on prices and profits in experimental duopoly markets', *Journal of Economic Behavior and Organization*, 9, 345–65.

Brown-Kruse, J., M.B. Cronshaw, and D.J. Schenk (1993), 'Theory and experiments on spatial competition', *Economic Inquiry*, 31, 139–65.

Cason, T.N. (1995), 'Cheap talk price signalling in laboratory experiments', *Information Economics and Policy*, 7 (2, June), 183–204.

Doyle, M.P. and C.M. Snyder (1996), 'Information sharing and competition in the motor vehicle industry', mimeo, George Washington University, December.

Edgeworth, F.Y. (1981), *Mathematical Psychics*, London. Kegan Paul.

Grether, D.M. and C.R. Plott (1984), 'The effects of market practices in oligopolistic markets: an experimental examination of the *Ethyl* case', *Economic Inquiry*, 24, 479–507.

Harrington, J.H. (1987), 'Collusion in multiproduct oligopoly games under a finite horizon', *International Economic Review*, 28 (1, February), 1–14.

Holt, C.A. (1995), 'Industrial organisation: a survey of laboratory research', in John H. Kagel and Alvin E. Roth (eds.) *The Handbook of Experimental Economics*, Princeton: Princeton University Press, pp. 349–443.

Holt, C. A. and D. Davis (1990), 'The effects of non-binding price announcements on posted-offer markets', *Economics Letters*, 34, 307–10.

Isaac, R.M., V. Ramey, and A. W. Williams (1984), 'The effects of market organization on conspiracies in restraint of trade', *Journal of Economic Behavior and Organization*, 5, 191–22.

MacLeod, W.B. (1985), 'A theory of conscious parallelism', *European Economic Review*, 27, 25–44.

Martin, S. (1993), 'On the divergence between the legal and the economic meanings of collusion', mimeo, European University Institute, Florence, Italy.

(1997), 'Competition policy: publicity vs. prohibition and punishment', Centre for Industrial Economics, University of Copenhagen, December.

Mason C., O. Phillips, and D. Redington (1991), 'On the role of gender in a noncooperative game', *Journal of Economic Behavior and Organization*, 15 (March), 215–35.

Phlips, L. (1995), *Competition Policy: A Game Theoretic Perspective*, Cambridge University Press.

Smith, A. (1937), *An Inquiry Into the Nature and Causes of the Wealth of Nations*, Edwin Cannon (ed.), New York, The Modern Library.

Chapter 7

Spatial pricing schemes
On the strategic choice of spatial price policy

Jacques-François Thisse and Xavier Vives

In any industry, current business practices are not only the result of an adaptation by firms to particular technological or institutional conditions but also reflect, or are the instruments of, a *strategic* positioning of firms in the markets. The specific price policies that firms follow are obviously one of the most important business practices in any market environment. Although their strategic importance is widely recognized in the business literature, perhaps somewhat surprisingly, the economics literature in general has not paid enough attention to the detail of specific pricing methods and, consequently, has not been able to provide convincing explanations of the incentive structure that lies behind certain price policies. In this chapter, we would like to present some very simple game-theoretic models which are naturally related to some pricing policies found in geographical or product differentiation contexts. Let us begin by describing some of these policies.

In a geographical context, examples of alternative pricing methods are: (i) the zone price system, under which a specific delivered price is charged to all buyers located in a given region, such as for plasterboard in the United Kingdom or cement in Belgium; (ii) the (single) basing point system, in which the delivered

This article first appeared in the *American Economic Review*, Vol. 78, 1988, pp. 122–37.
We are grateful to Jonathan Hamilton, Louis Phlips, Kriss Sjoblom, and an anonymous referee for helpful comments. The authors' research was supported respectively by the National Science Foundation grant no. SES-8502886 to the University of Pennsylvania and by the Research Fund, University of Pennsylvania.

price equals a base price plus the cost of shipping to the place of delivery from a given basing point that need not be where the seller is actually located, such as the Pittsburgh-plus system used in the steel industry in the United States until the mid 1920s or the Portland-plus system used for plywood in the United States until the 1970s; (iii) uniform free on board (FOB) prices, in which the delivered price equals the mill price – the same for all customers – plus the actual transport costs.[1]

In a product differentiation context, the choice of a price policy is, in a certain sense, closely related to the firm's variety offer. For example, car manufacturers may decide to provide a single standardized product to satisfy a hypothetical average consumer, as shown by the historical examples of the Ford T and the Volkswagen's 'Beetle'. Alternatively, they may offer a basic product with a series of options with different price tags such as most car manufacturers currently stock.[2] The first case corresponds to a uniform (FOB) price policy, in which the manufacturers leave the options to independent producers.[3] The second case, in which the options are under the manufacturers' control, typically involves discriminatory pricing.

A basic question, which interests both the analyst and the policymaker, is to determine what kind of price policy the government should encourage. In particular, is price discrimination necessarily evidence of lack of competition and harmful to the consumers?

In a geographical context, there is price discrimination when firms do not set uniform FOB prices, that is, when the difference between delivered prices at two distinct locations does not equal the transport cost between them. In a product differentiation context, we say that there is price discrimination if two varieties are sold at different base prices, that is, prices corrected by the cost of the corresponding options. Many countries have legislated against price discrimination defined as charging different prices to different buyers of the same goods. Obviously, the problem is to know whether the goods sold are the same since a given physical good is a different economic good depending on location, date of delivery, or service features, for example. In the United States, the Robinson–Patman Act prohibits charging different prices to different buyers of 'goods of like grade and quality' where the result 'may be substantially to lessen competition or then to create a monopoly in any line of commerce, or to injure, destroy, or prevent competition with any person who either grants or knowingly receives the benefit of such discrimination, or with customers of either of them' (see Scherer, 1980, p. 572). In the United Kingdom, the now abolished Price Commission has favoured uniform FOB pricing as shown, for example, by the

---

[1] See Scherer, 1980, chapter 11; Phlips, 1983, chapter 1, and Greenhut *et al.*, 1987, for a detailed description of spatial pricing policies. Actual pricing patterns are studied in Greenhut *et al.*, 1980, and Greenhut, 1981.

[2] The number of options may be very large indeed. The different makes of the Ford Escort, bumper-to-bumper, would cover the distance between Paris and Brussels, that is, 230 km (see Augier and Icikovics, 1982).

[3] Alfred P. Sloan, Jr., in the chapter about styling in his book *'My Years with General Motors'*, talks about the custom body shop of Don Lee of Los Angeles, CA, 'in which he built special bodies on both foreign and American chassis for Hollywood movie stars and wealthy people of California' (Sloan, 1972, p. 312).

series of reports published in 1978. In any case, it has been claimed that the motivation for these laws was more to limit than to promote competition (see, for example, Scherer, 1980, chapter 21) and that they may have perverse effects (see, for example, Schwartz, 1986).

The importance of price policies for the firms and the public authority is clear. Nevertheless, there exist very few models which rationalize in economic terms specific price policies, like the basing point system for example, or which explain the strategic incentives that firms may have to price discriminate. A great deal of attention has been paid to the issue of uniform versus discriminatory pricing in the general literature on *monopolistic price discrimination* (see, for example, Oi, 1971; Pigou, 1920; Robinson, 1933; Schmalensee, 1981) and in the theory of *spatial monopoly* (see Beckmann, 1976; Greenhut and Ohta, 1972; Holahan, 1975, for example). The general conclusion is that a monopolist can secure higher profits by price discriminating. On the other hand, there is no such clear-cut statement for the consumers. Very often (and this is true in the spatial monopoly case), they are partitioned under discriminatory pricing into those who pay a higher price and those who pay a lower price. However, as a whole, consumers often prefer uniform FOB pricing.

In contrast, much less attention has been devoted to the choice of a price policy in an oligopolistic environment in which strategic considerations are of primary importance.[4] The purpose of this chapter is to contribute to the analysis of this issue. More specifically, we want to examine (i) the incentives that arise in spatial competition for firms to price discriminate or price uniformly, and (ii) the consequences of the price policy choice for firms and consumers.

In this chapter, we consider a duopoly in which each firm is already located in some (geographical or characteristics) space and has to choose whether to price discriminate or not, taking the strategic effects of its choice into account. We deal, first, with the simultaneous choice of policy and price (section 2) and, second, with the case where firms may commit to a price policy first and then compete in prices contingent on the chosen policies (section 3).

When firms do not commit to a price policy, they compete with unrestricted price schedules, choosing a (delivered) price for every location. We are interested in knowing whether uniform (FOB) pricing can arise in equilibrium in such a situation. Under some circumstances, firms do commit themselves to a specific price policy. Such is the case, for example, in the basing point system. Suppose that there are two firms established at two different places and one basing point. The firm at the basing point is a price leader and announces a (uniform) base price. The other firm reacts optimally to the leader's choice by matching the full price (base price plus transport cost) wherever possible, that is, by price discriminating. In this situation, the leader prices uniformly and the follower price discriminates. In other words, the leader is

---

[4] Most contributions in spatial competition take the pricing policy as given. A notable exception is Greenhut and Greenhut (1975). However, these authors study spatial discrimination with quantity-setting firms. Here, we consider price-setting firms. A comparison of these two forms of spatial discrimination is contained in Hamilton *et al.* (1987).

committed to uniform FOB pricing. One question we want to answer is then: Can this system be rationalized in a context in which there is no scope for collusion, that is, in a two-stage game where, first, firms may commit to certain pricing policies and, then, compete in prices according to the selected policies?

In both the simultaneous no-commitment and the sequential commitment cases, *price discrimination* (by all firms in the market) *emerges as the unique equilibrium outcome*, even though it may well be that firms would make more profits by following a uniform price policy. This is so because spatial discriminatory pricing gives more flexibility to a firm to respond to its rival's actions. But then firms may get trapped in a Prisoner's Dilemma type situation and end up with lower profits due to the intense competition unleashed. Contrary to general belief, uniform (FOB) pricing is therefore not evidence of a more competitive environment.[5]

With simultaneous choice of policy and price the result is very general in terms of the characteristics space, density of demand, and transportation cost schedules which are allowable. With sequential choice much more restrictive assumptions are made in order to get existence and easy characterization of subgame-perfect equilibria (the assumptions are in any case usual in the literature). Section 1 presents the model, and our conclusions are given in section 4.

1   The model

We consider two firms $i = 1,2$ selling a homogeneous product. Firm i is located at point y_i of the n-dimensional space $\Re^n$ (when the model is interpreted in the geographical context, we have $n = 2$) and produces the product at a constant marginal cost c_i. It is supposed that firms are not located at the same point, that is, $y_1 \neq y_2$. Consumers are continuously distributed over a compact subset X of $\Re^n$. The density of demand for the product at $x \in X$ is given by a (measurable) function $f(p, x)$ of the full price p (that is, the price gross of transportation costs) paid by the consumers, and of the location x. The transportation cost of one unit of the product is given by a strictly increasing non-negative function $t_i(\|y_i - x\|)$ of the distance $\|y_i - x\|$, where $\|.\|$ is a norm defined on $\Re^n$ with $t_i(0) = 0$. In the geographical context typically, because of scale economies in transportation, t_i is a concave function of distance. Examples of norms that can be used are the Euclidean and the Manhattan norms.[6]

Two price policies are considered: uniform (U) and discriminatory (D). In the geographical context, uniform FOB pricing means that firm i charges the same mill price p_i to the consumers irrespective of their location. In this case, the full price of firm i at $x \in X$ is equal to the mill price plus the transportation cost, that is, $p_i(x) = p_i + t_i(\|y_i - x\|)$. This is so, for instance, because the transportation is under the control of the consumers who use the services of independent carriers charging

---

$t_i(\cdot)$ In the rest of the chapter, we refer to uniform FOB pricing as *uniform pricing*.[7] *Discriminatory pricing* occurs when firm i bears the transportation cost and chooses a price schedule $p_i(\cdot)$ which describes the delivered price $p_i(x)$ at which firm i is willing to supply consumers at location $x \in X$. The full price of firm i at x is now given by $p_i(x)$. The mill price effectively paid by the consumers, that is, $p_i(x) - t_i(\|y_i - x\|)$, generally changes with their location x. In other words, the firm discriminates among consumers on the basis of their location.

When the model is interpreted as a model of product differentiation, uniform pricing is equivalent to firm i's selling a *single* product located at y_i (in the characteristic space) and consumers paying a full price consisting of the price of the product plus the cost $t_i(\|y_i - x\|)$ incurred by the consumers in using the services of independent producers who adapt firm i's product to their requirements given by x. Now t_i is better viewed as a convex function of distance. In the discriminatory case, firm i bears the cost $t_i(\|y_i - x\|)$ of redesigning its basic product (y_i) and offers the whole *band* of varieties. As product design is under its control, the firm may discriminate among consumers on the basis of their requirements. We say that price discrimination occurs when the price difference between two varieties does not correspond to the difference in the respective costs of redesigning the basic product.

A slightly modified version of the celebrated Hotelling model is a good example to illustrate the above general model. Let us first consider the geographical interpretation. Two sellers of a homogeneous product are located at the endpoints of Main Street; geometrically, $y_1 = 0, y_2 = 1$, and X is the segment $[0,1]$. They have identical and constant marginal production costs. Customers are uniformly distributed along Main Street and have fixed and identical requirements for the product. Finally, transportation costs are linear in distance. If both sellers follow a uniform price policy (as in Hotelling), consumers pay the price at the firm's door where a consumer buys the product plus the transportation cost for delivery. On the other hand, when sellers deliver the product (as the pizzaman), they may discern between consumers and price discriminate with respect to locations by absorbing part of the transportation costs.

Let us now come to the characteristics interpretation. Following Hotelling, we suppose that the segment $[0,1]$ describes the sweetness of cider: $y_1 = 0$ means sour cider and $y_2 = 1$ sweet cider. Under uniform pricing, firms produce only the two extreme products, and consumers adapt these products to their most preferred level of sweetness at a cost corresponding to the transportation cost in the geographical approach (how to change the sweetness of cider is a technical detail that we leave to the imagination of the reader). On the contrary, under discriminatory pricing, the firms offer the whole spectrum of sweetness and price each variety.

---

[7] Let us emphasize the fact that what we call here uniform pricing is different from uniform delivered pricing as defined in postage stamp systems.

2   Simultaneous choice of policy and price

In this section we investigate whether discriminatory or uniform pricing arises in equilibrium when firms choose simultaneously pricing policy and price, that is, when firms compete in price schedules which are unrestricted. A strategy for firm i is then a *price schedule* $p_i(\cdot)$ that specifies the delivered price at which firm i is willing to supply consumers at location x in X. The delivered price at x must cover the total (production plus transport) marginal cost. If firm i were to price *below* total marginal cost it could do at least as well, for any given price of the rival, by pricing at marginal cost. Formally, we assume $p_i(\cdot)$ to be in the set

$\qquad P_i \equiv \{p_i(\cdot)$ a non-negative function defined on X, measurable and such that, for all $x \in X, p_i(x) \geq c_i + t_i(\|y_i - x\|)\}.$

The *potential market area* of firm i is the set of locations at which the firm faces a positive demand density when pricing at total marginal cost $m_i(x) \equiv c_i + t_i(\|y_i - x\|)$, that is, $A_i \equiv \{x \in X; f[m_i(x), x] > 0\}$.

The most interesting case occurs when the set of consumers who consider buying from either firm, that is, $A_1 \cap A_2$, is non-negligible (technically a non-zero measure set). Since the product is homogeneous, each consumer purchases from the firm with the lower delivered price. In the event of a price tie, we assume that consumers do the socially optimal thing and buy from the firm with the lower production and transportation cost. This may be rationalized noting that this firm can always price ε below its rival's total marginal cost. If, for some consumer location x, both firms have the same total marginal costs and charge the same delivered price, they split the local demand. Generically, the set of locations for which $m_i(x) = m_j(x)$ is negligible. To ease notation we will assume this to be the case.

Given the strategies $p_i(\cdot)$ and $p_j(\cdot)$ of the two firms, the *market area* of firm i, $M_i(p_i(\cdot), p_j(\cdot))$, is then the set of locations in the potential market area A_i for which, either firm i quotes the lower-delivered price or, if both firms quote the same price, firm i has the lower-total marginal cost. Firm i's *profits* are, therefore, equal to

$$\Pi_i(p_i(\cdot), p_j(\cdot)) = \int_{M_i(p_i(\cdot), p_j(\cdot))} [p_i(x) - m_i(x)] \times f[p_i(x), x] dx.$$

We thus have a well-defined game with strategy sets P_i and payoffs $\Pi_i, i = 1, 2$. To analyse the Nash equilibria of this game, we need some additional assumptions and definitions.

Let us assume that, for each location x in X, the demand density $f(p, x)$ is continuous and downward sloping in p, and that $pf(p, x)$ is bounded from above. This implies that there exists a monopoly price for every x in X which, for simplicity, we assume unique. Denote by $p_i^M(x)$ the monopoly price of firm i at location x, that is

$$p_i^M(x) = \arg\max_{p_i} \{(p_i - m_i(x))f(p_i, x)\}.$$

We say that firm i has a *monopoly position* at location x whenever its monopoly price at x does not exceed the total marginal cost of the rival firm, that is $p_i^M(x) \leq m_j(x), i \neq j$.

Suppose now that firm i does *not* have a monopoly position at x. We say that firm i has a *cost advantage* at location x if its total marginal cost is lower than that of its rival, that is, $m_i(x) < m_j(x)$. Let x be such a location and define $\bar{p}_i(x)$ as the profit-maximizing price at x when firm i cannot charge more than $m_j(x)$, that is

$$\bar{p}(x) \epsilon \arg\max_{p_i} \{(p_i - m_i(x))f(p_i, x); p_i \leq m_j(x)\}.$$

Without significant loss of generality, we may assume that $\bar{p}_i(x)$ is unique. Notice that when the profit $(p_i - m_i(x))f(p_i, x)$ is quasi-concave in p_i, $\bar{p}_i(x)$ takes its highest possible value, namely $\bar{p}_i(x) = m_j(x)$. Otherwise, the profit is not single peaked and there may be a local maximum at a price less than $m_j(x)$.

We claim that there exists an equilibrium for the above game in which firm i chooses a price schedule given by

$$p_i^*(x) = \begin{cases} p_i^M(x), & \text{if firm } i \text{ has a monopoly position at } x \\ \bar{p}_i(x), & \text{if firm } i \text{ does not have a monopoly position at } x \\ & \text{but has a cost advantage} \\ m_i(x), & \text{otherwise.} \end{cases}$$

The argument is as follows. Since the marginal production cost of firm i is constant and since the transportation cost to a point is unaffected by transportation to other points, it is sufficient to show that, given $p_j^*(x)$, firm i maximizes its profit density at (almost) every x in X by setting $p_i^*(x)$. We have

(i) If firm i enjoys a monopoly position at x, it will serve the local market and will reach its highest possible profits by monopoly pricing since $m_i(x) \leq p_i^M(x) \leq m_j(x)$.

(ii) If firm i does not have a monopoly position but has a cost advantage at x, then by pricing at $\bar{p}_i(x)$ it captures the local demand, since $\bar{p}_i(x) \leq m_j(x)$ and $m_i(x) < m_j(x)$ (recall that according to our convention if the two firms quote the same price consumers buy from the firm with lower total marginal cost) and maximizes its profits at x by definition of $\bar{p}_i(x)$.

(iii) If firm i has no cost advantage at x, that is, $m_i(x) \geq m_j(x)$, then for any price $p_i \geq m_i(x)$ the firm has no demand when $m_i(x) > m_j(x)$ since firm j can always undercut p_i, or it makes no profit when $m_i(x) = m_j(x)$. In any case, firm i earns zero profits and pricing at $m_i(x)$ is optimal.

Thus, as is often suggested in the marketing literature, $p_j^*(x)$ is set on the basis of either demand considerations, or a combination of demand and competition considerations, or finally, purely cost considerations; the dominant consideration being determined by the consumer location x.

The above-described equilibrium is the only one of the game. Intuitively, this is easy to understand. Indeed, for a given location x in which no firm has a monopoly position, Bertrand competition drives prices down to the level of the larger total marginal cost, $\max\{m_1(x), m_2(x)\}$, which then allows the firm with the cost advantage, say firm i, to charge $\bar{p}_i(x)$. If firm i has a monopoly position then $P_i^M(x)$ necessarily obtains; and similarly for firm j.[8]

The *equilibrium market price schedule* is then $p^*(x) = \min\{p_1^*(x), p_2^*(x)\}$ for all $x \in X$. That is, $p^*(x)$ equals the minimum of the monopoly prices, $p_i^M(x)$, the constrained prices, $\bar{p}_i(x)$ and the maximum of the total marginal costs, $\max\{m_1(x), m_2(x)\}$.

The equilibrium is illustrated in the following example.

The set X is a linear segment of length 1; firms 1 and 2 are located respectively at $y_1 = 0$ and $y_2 = 1$; consumers have linear demand functions $1 - p$; production costs are zero and transportation costs are given by tx. For $1/2 \le t \le 2$, it is then easy to verify that

$$P_1^*(x) = p_1^M(x) = \frac{1}{2} + \frac{t}{2}x \text{ for } 0 \le x \le (2t-1)/3t,$$

$$p_1^*(x) = m_2(x) = t(1-x) \text{ for } (2t-1)/3t \le x \le \frac{1}{2},$$

$$\text{and } p_1^*(x) = m_1(x) - tx \text{ for } \frac{1}{2} < x \le 1.$$

A similar argument can be developed for $p_2^*(\cdot)$. Figure 1 represents the resulting market price schedule.

Interestingly, we notice that, over a certain range of locations $(2t-1)/3t \le x \le 1/2$ (in figure 7.1), the equilibrium price schedule is *decreasing* in the distance to the firm. The reason is that a firm faces fiercer competition in remote places – and thus sets lower delivered prices – than it does at home, for it has to compete with another firm which is closer to these points. This seems to be confirmed by the observations made by Greenhut (1981) for whom negatively sloped delivered price schedules frequently characterize oligopolistic firms in Japan and West Germany.[9]

Proposition 1 states our result.

Proposition 1
Assume that the intersection of the potential market areas of the firms is a non-negligible set. If there is competition in price schedules, then the unique Nash equilibrium market price schedule is

---

[8] A more technical argument could be given following the lines of the proof of Theorem 1 in Lederer and Hurter (1986) (who consider the case of inelastic local demands).

[9] Greenhut reports that 'this type of pricing . . . was never found . . . in the United States. Instead, the American firms always charged higher prices to more distant buyers or at the limit followed uniform delivered prices over their market space. Quite conceivably it is the Robinson–Patman Act that causes the delivered price patterns of American firms to differ from those of firms in West Germany and Japan' (see Greenhut, 1981, p. 84). This suggests that the corresponding institutional constraint is binding for many American firms. For an illustration, see the simulation made by Hobbs (1986a), of a deregulated bulk power market in the United States.

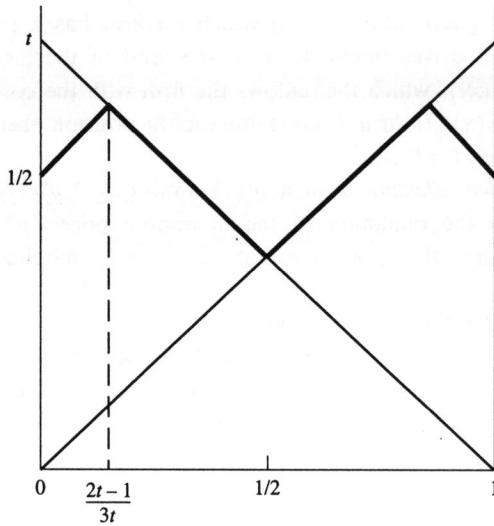

Figure 7.1
Note: the heavy line is the equilibrium market price schedule.

$$p^*(x) = \min\{p_i^*(x), p_2^*(x)\}.$$

Obviously, equilibrium prices involve price discrimination. In other words, *uniform pricing is never an equilibrium* when the potential market areas have a non-negligible intersection. If this intersection were to be negligible, then the two firms would become spatial monopolists. For one particular class of demand functions, negative exponential, discriminatory pricing boils down to uniform pricing.

3   Commitment to a price policy

In this section we consider two-stage games in which firms may commit to a particular price policy, uniform pricing (U), or may not commit at all and stay free to choose an unrestricted price schedule (D) at the market competition stage (this involves price discrimination in general).[10]

In order to make the analysis tractable, we will restrict ourselves to simple cases in which consumers are uniformly distributed over some space X (a segment or a circle) and each one of them has an *inelastic* demand for one unit of the good. Attention will be focused on subgame-perfect equilibria of the two-stage games in which firms anticipate the resulting Nash equilibria in prices at the second stage when choosing their price policies at the first stage. If one firm chooses uniform pricing and the other discriminatory pricing, there may not be a simultaneous move Nash equilibrium (in

---

[10] A model similar in spirit is developed by Singh and Vives (1984).

pure strategies) at the second stage. In what follows, we will assume that the firm which chooses to price uniformly will move first and be the price leader while the other firm will react optimally to the leader's price. This situation fits the single-basing point pricing (BPP) system in spatial price competition and we will see that it has a natural interpretation in the context of product differentiation. We deal first with spatial price competition and the equilibrium analysis of the BPP system, and second with product differentiation and the pricing of varieties.

3.1 Spatial price competition and basing point pricing

We suppose now that consumers are uniformly distributed with a unit density on the interval $X = [0,1]$, with firm 1 located at 0 and firm 2 at 1. Firms have constant marginal production costs and, without loss of generality, let them be 0 and $c \geq 0$ for firms 1 and 2, respectively. Transportation costs are linear with slope t $(t > 0)$.

Firms may commit to uniform pricing first and then compete on prices accordingly. Four possible cases may arise: (U, U), (U, D), (D, U), or (D, D). If both firms choose to price uniformly, (U, U), then a Nash equilibrium in (FOB) prices obtains at the second stage. If both firms choose to keep complete freedom of pricing, (D, D), then a Nash equilibrium in price schedules obtains at the second stage. If firm 1 chooses to price uniformly and firm 2 does not commit, (U, D), then firm 1 will be a price leader and firm 2 will react optimally to its price (figure 7.2 depicts the game tree).

This is a natural *competitive* view of the BPP system with a single-basing point (in which firm 1 is located at $y_1 - 0$). The leader announces a uniform base price, and the price the consumer pays is just the base price plus the transportation cost from 0 to the location of the consumer no matter what firm serves the consumer. Given the base price set by the leader, firm 2 then just undercuts the corresponding full price wherever possible. In other words, the market area of firm 2 is defined by the set of locations for which firm 1's full price is larger than the marginal production and transportation cost of firm 2. This is so because firm 1 is the first mover so that, for any posted price p_i, firm 2 can always capture the demand on $\{x \in X; P_1 + t|y_1 - x| > c + t|y_2 - x|\}$ by selling to consumers at $x - \varepsilon$ below firm 1's full price (see figure 7.3 where the market areas of firms 1 and 2 are given by $[0, \bar{x}]0$ and $[\bar{x}, 1]$, respectively, when c = 0).[11] Firm 1 is, therefore, a price leader that sets a uniform FOB price and firm 2 reacts optimally to the leader's base price by price discriminating. The case (D, U) is similar. We have thus that the mixed cases (U, D) and (D, U) represent single BPP equilibria with base points 0 and 1, respectively. Our approach results in separated market areas and, therefore, no cross-hauling occurs, that is, there is no location where two-way trade is observed.[12]

[11] Notice that the way demand is allocated between firms in the event of a price tie has been slightly modified with respect to the convention made in section 3 where it was assumed that customers were assigned to the firm with the cost advantage.
[12] In practice, however, market areas are not so clearly delineated as in our competitive interpretation of BPP and cross-hauling may occur. This observation already suggests that the

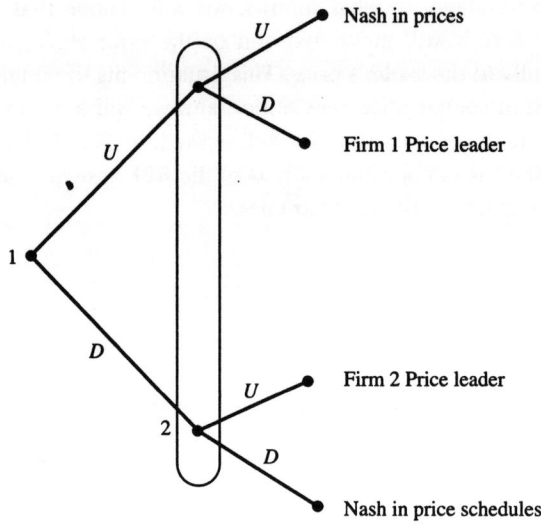

Figure 7.2 Game tree for the sequential game where firms may either commit to price uniformly (U) or keep their freedom of pricing (D)

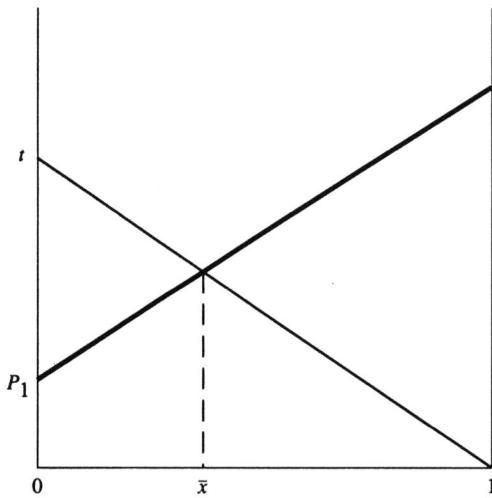

Figure 7.3 Single-basing point pricing with base at 0
Note: The heavy line is the full market price $p_1 + tx$. The intersection with the total marginal cost of firm 2 determines $\bar{x}$, the market share of the leader.

actual implementation of BPP may not be consistent with vigorous price competition since cross-hauling implies that firm 2 does not fully exploit its cost advantage with respect to the price set by firm 1.

We would like to examine the stability of basing point pricing in our competitive context. In particular, we would like to know whether BPP can emerge as an equilibrium of our two-stage game.

In order to find the subgame-perfect equilibria of our game we compute the firms' payoffs in each of the four possible situations. The cases (U, U) and (D, D) are standard and we will review them very briefly. We will assume that $t > c$ to ensure that firm 2 (the high-cost firm) is not priced out of the market.

(U, U): The market boundary for the two firms is given by the location $\bar{x}$ of the consumer who is indifferent between buying from either firm: $p_1 + t\bar{x} = p_2 + t(1 - \bar{x})$, from which it immediately follows that $\bar{x} = (p_2 - p_1 + t)/2t$. As consumers are distributed with a unit density, profits of firm 1 are given by $\pi_1 = p_1 \bar{x}$ and those of firm 2 by $\pi_2 = (p_2 - c)(1 - \bar{x})$. The unique pair of equilibrium prices is obtained from the first-order conditions as

$$\left(t + \frac{c}{3}, t + \frac{2c}{3}\right),$$

yielding market areas

$$\left(\frac{1}{2} + \frac{c}{6t}, \frac{1}{2} - \frac{c}{6t}\right)$$

and equilibrium profits

$$\left(\frac{1}{2t}\left(t + \frac{c}{3}\right)^2, \frac{1}{2t}\left(t - \frac{c}{3}\right)^2\right).$$

(D, D): If both firms compete on price schedules, the equilibrium price schedule $p^*(x)$ is $\max\{tx, c + t(1 - x)\}$ with $x \in [0,1]$, since localized Bertrand competition drives prices down to the higher total marginal cost (see proposition 1). The market boundary is given by $x^* = 1/2 + c/2t$, while equilibrium profits are

$$\pi_1 = \int_0^{x*} [c + t(1 - x) - tx]dx$$

$$= \frac{1}{4t}(c + t)^2 \text{ for firm 1, and}$$

$$\pi = \int_{x*}^1 [tx - (c + t(1 - x))]dx$$

$$= \frac{1}{4t}(t - c)^2 \text{ for firm 2.}$$

(U, D): Here the efficient firm is the leader and prices uniformly at p_1. The market boundary $\bar{x}$ is determined by $p_1 + t\bar{x} = c + t(1 - \bar{x})$, which yields $\bar{x} = (t + c - p_1)/2t$, since the optimal response of firm 2 is to match firm 1's full price $p_1 + tx$, whenever possible, that is when $p_1 + tx \geq c + t(1 - x)$. Profits of firm 1 are given by $\pi_1 = p_1 \bar{x}$

Table 7.1 *Summary of firms' payoffs*

1 \ 2	U	D
U	$\frac{1}{2t}\frac{(3t+c)^2}{9}, \frac{1}{2t}\frac{(3t-c)^2}{9}$	$\frac{1}{2t}\frac{(t+c)^2}{4}, \frac{1}{2t}\frac{(3t-c)^2}{8}$
D	$\frac{1}{2t}\frac{(3t+c)^2}{8}, \frac{1}{2t}\frac{(t-c)^2}{4}$	$\frac{1}{2t}\frac{(t+c)^2}{2}, \frac{1}{2t}\frac{(t-c)^2}{2}$

and the optimal price for firm 1 is $p_1^* = (t+c)/2$ with associated market boundary $x^* = t + c/4t$, yielding profits of $(t+c)^2/8t$. The equilibrium price schedule of firm 2 is $p_2^*(x) = \max\{p_1^* + tx, c + t(1-x)\}$ and the equilibrium profits are

$$\pi_2 = \int_{x^*}^{1}\left[\frac{t+c}{2} + tx - (c + t(1-x))\right]dx = \frac{(3t-c)^2}{16t}.$$

(D, U): We have now that the inefficient producer (firm 2) prices uniformly and is the price leader. A symmetric argument yields a market boundary $\bar{x} = p_2 + t/2t$, an optimal price for firm 2 equal to $t + c/2$ with associated equilibrium profits $(t-c)^2/8t$. Equilibrium profits for firm 1 are $(3t+c)^2/16t$. Table 7.1 summarizes the payoffs for the firms.

It is clear from the table that to keep pricing freedom and to price discriminate is a dominant strategy for any firm no matter what the difference in the production costs of the firms (provided that $c \leq t$). Committing to uniform pricing is, therefore, a dominated choice. Proposition 2 states the result.

Proposition 2

In the sequential commitment game, choosing the price discrimination policy is a dominant strategy for any firm and, consequently, (D, D) with resulting market price schedule $p^*(x) = \max\{tx, c + t(1-x)\}$ is the unique subgame-perfect equilibrium.

Proposition 2 says that no firm, not even the more efficient one, wants to be the price leader taking as basing point its location and, therefore, single BPP is not a stable configuration since it is not an equilibrium of our two-stage game. This suggests the hypothesis that BPP cannot be explained in the context of a non-cooperative model in which firms can choose their price policy and in which there is no repeated competition. Our analysis thus contrasts with the view (see, for example, Haddock, 1982) that BPP is fundamentally 'competitive' and suggests that theoretical explanations of BPP should consider its role as a coordinating and collusive device (see Scherer, 1980 and Stigler, 1949). Nevertheless, our hypothesis will obviously not hold when BPP coincides with the discriminatory solution. This would be the case, for example, when firm 1 has a second plant established next to firm 2 at location $y_2 = 1$ and both firms are equally efficient. Indeed, in the region where no firm has a cost advantage, competition would drive prices down to total marginal cost, while in the region in

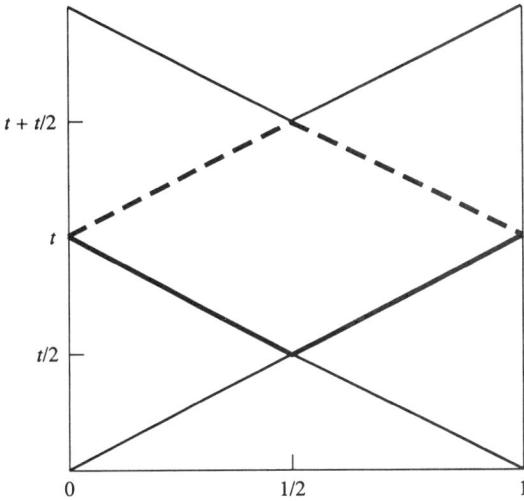

Figure 7.4
Note: The heavy line is the market equilibrium price schedule with discriminatory pricing,
$p^D(x) = \max\{tx, t(1-x)\}$. The dotted line corresponds to the uniform pricing case,
$p^U(x) = \min\{t(1+x), t(2-x)\}$.

which firm 1 has a cost advantage, the delivered price will be equal to the total
marginal cost of firm 2, that is, the equilibrium market price schedule would be given
by $t(1-x)$ for $0 \leq x \leq 1$. It is then clear that the above solution corresponds to BPP
with a single-basing point at $y_2 = 1$.

In the symmetric case where firms are of equal productive efficiency, $c = 0$, we have a
typical Prisoner's Dilemma situation since to price discriminate is a dominant strategy
but firms would make more profits by pricing uniformly.[13] In the (U, U) case each firm
earns $t/2$, whereas in the (D, D) case each firm earns $t/4$. Consumer surplus is larger in
this latter case since the full price at x is given by $p^D(x) = \max\{tx, t(1-x)\}$, whereas in
the (U, U) case the uniform price is t and, therefore, the full price at x is given by
$p^U(x) = \min\{t + tx, t + t(1-x)\}$ which is strictly larger than $p^D(x)$ for $0 < x < 1$:
each consumer in $]0,1[$ is, therefore, better off under discriminatory than uniform
pricing while consumers located at $x = 0$ and $x = 1$ are indifferent (see figure 7.4). Note
nevertheless that total surplus is equal in both cases; the pricing policy only affects the
distribution of surplus between firms and consumers. To check our claim suppose that
consumers have a (high enough) reservation price $v(v \geq 3t/2)$ and that the utility
provided by the consumption of one unit of the good equals v minus the full price paid
by the consumer. We have then that total surplus in the market is $v - t/2$ in both cases,
the differences between the reservation price and the transportation cost of the
consumer located in the middle of the segment.

[13] This result holds in various models: linear demand and endogenous location (Kats, 1987) and
product differentiation modelled by the logit (Anderson et al., 1987). Notice, however, that
discriminatory pricing may yield higher profits than uniform pricing when firms have monopoly
positions in some large enough segments of the market.

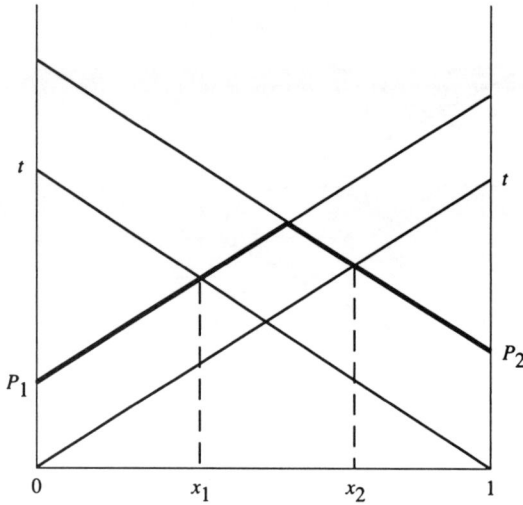

Figure 7.5 Multiple-basing point pricing with bases at 0 and 1
Note: The heavy line represents the delivered prices faced by consumers.

Imagining that location 0 corresponds to Pittsburgh and location 1 to Chicago, the case (U, D) would represent the Pittsburgh-plus system implemented until the mid 1920s in the US steel industry. After that period, several basing points were introduced involving, among others, both Pittsburgh and Chicago. Superficially, the (U, U) case could then be viewed as a very simplified version of the multiple-basing point system with two basing points at locations 0 and 1. Actually, this turns out not to be true as this system is always associated with the so-called 'alignment rule' (see Phlips, 1983, chapter 1, and Scherer, 1980, chapter 11). According to this rule, a firm will always accept to sell at the lower full price so that firms quote the same delivered price to everyone at each location (provided that this price is large enough for the firm to cover its marginal cost). Let us assume, for simplicity, that $c = 0$ so that both firms are equally efficient. Then, if firms 1 and 2 charge base prices p_1 and p_2, we can see in figure 7.5 that customers located in $[x_1, x_2]$ may pass orders to either firm since, by assumption, they both set the same delivered price at $x \in [x_1, x_2]$. As any assignment rule is *a priori* arbitrary at this stage of the analysis, we may follow Smithies (1942) and suppose that firms equally share the local market in the interval $[x_1, x_2]$. In this case, it is readily verified that, at the Nash equilibrium in base prices, both firms charge a base price that is just equal to the common equilibrium price arising in the (U, U) case, that is, $p_1^* = p_2^* = t$. However, because of the existence of cross-hauling over $[x_1, x_2]$, the corresponding equilibrium profits are lower and given by 3/8t. It is interesting to observe that these profits are still larger than those earned at the non-cooperative equilibrium of our two-stage game (D, D), *but* lower than those obtained at the 'cooperative' solution (U, U). What Smithies' approach leaves unexplained is the market sharing in the interval $[x_1, x_2]$ since,

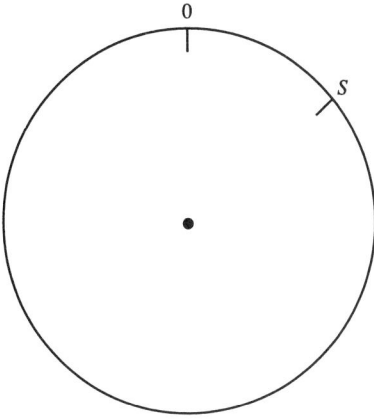

Figure 7.6
Note: Firm 1 is located at $x = 0$, Firm 2 at $x = s$

according to our results, firms have a strong incentive to price discriminate. Market sharing in the common area $[x_1, x_2]$ gives the multiple BPP a non-competitive flavour.[14]

3.2   Product differentiation and the pricing of varieties

Consider consumers distributed uniformly over the unit circle with firms 1 and 2 in arbitrary locations, the shortest arc distance between them being s (that is $s \leq 1/2$). In figure 7.6, firm 1 is located at $x = 0$ and firm 2 at $x = s$. Suppose that firms have no production costs and that transportation costs are quadratic with coefficient t and no linear term. (As explained in section 1, here transportation costs will be the costs associated with transforming a base product into a variety or specialized product.)

   In the situation we have in mind each firm produces a base product, corresponding to its location in product space (the circle), and at the first stage it has to decide whether to (potentially) offer the whole array of varieties and price discriminate or just to offer the base product and therefore to price uniformly. In the latter case the supply of specialized varieties is left to outside independent producers which, we will assume, price competitively at cost. In any case, we assume that the costs of redesigning the base product increase quadratically with the distance at which the variety chosen is located. The first-stage choice could also be interpreted as a decision as whether to integrate forward or not. The base product could be a base chemical or steel and the varieties the specialized chemicals or steels. Whatever the interpretation, if a firm chooses to produce only the base product, then it will choose a uniform price, and if it chooses to offer the array of varieties, it will choose a price schedule when the market stage comes. As before we assume that in the mixed cases (U, D) or (D, U) the

---

[14] However, Smithies is probably right when he claims that this system is far from complete agreement since profits are lower than in the second-best (U, U) case.

Table 7.2 *Firm 1's profits*

1 \ 2	U	D
U	$\frac{1}{2}s(1-s)t$	$\frac{1}{8}s(1-s)t$
D	$\frac{9}{16}s(1-s)t$	$\frac{1}{4}s(1-s)t$

firm that prices uniformly moves first and therefore figure 7.2 represents the game tree of our game. This may come about because this firm may need to advertise its price in order to get any sales (put advertisements in the newspapers, for example), whereas the price-discriminating firm may just announce that it will meet the competition (in any case to announce the whole price schedule in an intelligible way may be too complex and costly due to the large number of varieties).

It is a simple exercise to find the second-stage equilibria for the different cases. Note that since transportation costs are quadratic (with no linear term) an equilibrium in prices will always exist in the (U, U) case whatever the locations of the firms. In the appendix we provide the computations that lead to the profits of firm 1 in the four cases given in table 7.2 (profits of firm 2 have similar expressions).

As before, to choose the price-discriminating strategy is dominant for any firm in the circle model with quadratic costs. No firm wants to produce only the base product whatever the rival firm strategy is. It always pays to offer the whole array of varieties and let the market decide which ones will be effectively produced by each firm. As in the previous models, price discrimination gives more flexibility to a firm to respond to any potential strategy of the rival. A product proliferation strategy (in terms of horizontal differentiation) can thus be seen as an attempt by a firm to secure a flexible position for the ensuing price competition.

In fact we have checked that the same is true in a unit-segment model with quadratic transportation costs if the firms are symmetrically located. The payoffs to firm 1 are given dropping the common terms $s(1-s)t$ in table 7.2. If firms are asymmetrically located in the segment, then (D, D) is still the unique subgame-perfect equilibrium of the two-stage game but it is no longer necessarily a dominant strategy equilibrium. Going back to table 7.2, we observe that, as in the location model considered in section 3.1, the firms face a Prisoner's Dilemma-type situation with higher profits in the (U, U) case whereas the equilibrium dictates (D, D). Total surplus is equal in both situations and therefore, consumer surplus is higher with price discrimination and the two firms (potentially) offering the whole array of varieties.

4   Concluding remarks

We have examined the implications of letting firms choose their price policy in the context of a spatial competition model with given locations for firms. Either firms choose simultaneously price policy and actual prices, or firms may commit to a certain policy (uniform pricing) before the actual price competition takes place. The general conclusion is that *there is a robust tendency for a firm to choose the discriminatory policy* since it is more flexible and does better against any generic strategy of the rival, although, as we have seen in the models of section 3, firms may end up worse off than if they choose to price uniformly.

Furthermore, in those models, prices that consumers paid under uniform pricing were higher than under discriminatory pricing. This is not totally surprising: denying a firm the right to meet the price of a competitor on a discriminatory basis provides the latter with some protection against price attacks. The effect is then to weaken competition, contrary to the belief of the proponents of naive application of legislation prohibiting price discrimination like the Robinson–Patman Act in the United States, or similar recommendations of the Price Commission in the United Kingdom. Actually, as observed by Hoover:

The difference between market competition under FOB pricing (with strictly delineated market areas) and under discriminatory delivered pricing is something like the difference between trench warfare and guerrilla warfare. In the former case all the fighting takes place along a definite battle line; in the second case the opposing forces are intermingled over a broad area. (1948, p. 57)

Our results are short-run results since both the location and the number of firms are given. We know that the choice of a particular price policy leads to different long-run equilibrium patterns (see, for example, Greenhut *et al.*, 1987, part III). When policy and prices are chosen simultaneously, Proposition 1 (that can be generalized to the case of any number of firms) indicates that, at the long-run equilibrium, firms will choose to price discriminate in the absence of institutional constraints. Thus, at the long-run equilibrium, uniform pricing would not be observed. Lederer and Hurter (1986) have shown that, with perfectly inelastic demand, two price-discriminating firms will locate in order to minimize total transportation costs. In a free-entry context, the configuration of firms minimizing total production and transportation costs corresponds to a long-run equilibrium (see MacLeod *et al.*, 1985). Furthermore, in a free-entry, zero-profit equilibrium with linear demand, Hobbs (1986b) shows that welfare under discriminatory pricing is higher than under mill pricing for a wide range of fixed cost values.[15] These results, together with ours, point to the social desirability of price discrimination in spatial competitive markets. However, more work is called for before having robust policy-oriented recommendations.

Our analysis has also helped to clarify some issues related to standard business practices. With respect to geographical pricing policies, the tendency towards price discrimination makes in general the basing point system unstable since no firm, not even a very efficient one, would like to commit to uniform (FOB) pricing. Therefore, if the system is observed in practice, most probably it is because it serves as a coordinating or collusive device in a situation of repeated competition. With respect

---

[15] Like most models of spatial monopolistic competition, Hobbs assumes that firms are equally spaced. However, no justification is provided for that property.

to pricing in a product-differentiation context, the link between pricing policies and product strategies has been highlighted, noticing that for a firm to be able to price discriminate it must offer a band of varieties. Since it always pays to price discriminate, this may explain in part the observed change of firms' strategies from producing a single-standardized product to offering a whole spectrum of options.

Much work needs to be done to gain a solid understanding of current business pricing policies. Ours is only a first attempt and an illustration of how simple game-theoretic techniques may help to illuminate the issues involved.[16]

Appendix

Assume that locations (x) along the circle of unit length are measured in a trigonometric manner. Firm 1 is at $x = 0$ and firm 2 at $x = s$ with $0 < s \leq 1/2$.

(U, U): Consumers are indifferent between purchasing from either firm at points $\bar{x} = (p_2 - p_1 + ts^2)1/2ts$ and $\bar{y} = p_1 - p_2 + t(1 - s^2)/2t(1 - s)$. Consequently, profits of firm 1 are $\pi_1 = p_1(1 - \bar{y} + \bar{x})$ and profits of firm 2 are $\pi_2 = p_2(\bar{y} - \bar{x})$. The unique price equilibrium is given by $(ts(1 - s), ts(1 - s))$, yielding equilibrium profits $(ts(1 - s)/2, ts(1 - s)/2)$.

(D, D): If both firms price discriminate, it is readily verified that the equilibrium price schedule is given by

$$p^*(x) = \begin{cases} \max\{tx^2, t(x - s)^2\} & \text{for } 0 \leq x \leq 1/2 \\ \max\{t(1 - x)^2, t(x - s)^2\} & \text{for } 1/2 \leq x \leq 1/2 + s \\ \max\{t(1 - x)^2, t(1 - x + s)^2\} & \text{for } 1/2 + s \leq x \leq 1. \end{cases} \quad \text{(A1)}$$

The market boundaries are given by $\bar{x} = s/2$ and $\bar{y} = 1/2 + s + s/2$, whereas the equilibrium profits are

$$\pi_1 = \int_0^{s/2} \left[p^*(x) - tx^2\right]dx + \int_{1/2+s}^1 \left[p^*(x) - t(1 - x)^2\right]dx = \frac{ts(1 - s)}{4} \quad \text{(A2)}$$

similarly

$$\pi_2 = \frac{ts(1 - s)}{4}. \quad \text{(A3)}$$

(U, D): Firm 1 is the leader and prices uniformly at p_1. Given p_1, firm 2 sets a price at x which is equal to the maximum of firm 1's full price at x and firm 2's transportation cost to x. Accordingly, the market boundaries are as follows: (i) for $p_1 \leq ts^2$, we have

---

[16] Many other relevant issues have been left out. For example, we have considered complete information models (for models with informed and uninformed buyers, see for example, Salop and Stiglitz, 1977, and Katz, 1984) and we have ignored the possibility of non-linear pricing (see Spulber, 1981, for a study of nonlinear pricing in a spatial context).

$\bar{x} = (-p_1 + ts^2)/2ts$ and $\bar{y} = p_1 + t(1-s)^2/2t(1-s)$; (ii) for $ts^2 < p_1 \leq ts(1-s)$, we have $\bar{x} = (-p_1 + ts^2 + 2ts)/2ts$ and $\bar{\bar{y}} = \bar{y}$ (when $p_1 > ts(1-s)$ and all consumers buy from firm 2). Firm 1's profits are respectively defined by $\pi_1 = p_1(1 - \bar{y} + \bar{x})$ and $\pi_1 = p_1(\bar{\bar{x}} - \bar{y})$. As $\bar{\bar{x}} = \bar{x} + 1$, the expression of the profit function is uniquely determined and the profit-maximizing price of firm 1 is $p_1^* = ts(1-s)/2$. The corresponding demand is 1/4 and the equilibrium profits of firm 1 are $ts(1-s)/8$. For firm 2, the equilibrium price schedule is given by

$$p_2^*(x) = \begin{cases} \max\{p_1^* + tx^2, t(x-s)^2\}, & \text{for } 0 \leq x \leq 1/2 \\ \max\{p_1^* + t(1-x)^2, t(x-s)^2\}, & \text{for } 1/2 \leq x \leq 1/2 + s \\ \max\{p_1^* + t(1-x)^2, t(1-x+s)^2\}, & \text{for } 1/2 + s \leq x \leq 1 \end{cases} \quad (A4)$$

and the equilibrium profits are

$$\pi_2 = \int_0^{\bar{x}} \left[p_2^*(x) - tx^2 \right] dx + \int_{\bar{y}}^1 \left[p_2^*(x) - t(1-x)^2 \right] dx \quad (A5)$$

or

$$\pi_2 = \int_{\bar{y}}^{\bar{\bar{x}}} \left[p^*2(x) - t(1-x)^2 \right] dx,$$

which are both equal to

$$\frac{9}{16} ts(1-s).$$

(D, U): This is perfectly similar to the above one (up to a rotation of $1-s$ and a permutation of firms' names). Equilibrium profits are therefore

$$\pi_1 = \frac{9}{16} ts(1-s) \text{ and } \pi_2 = \frac{ts(1-s)}{8}.$$

References

Anderson, S. P., A. de Palma, and J.-F. Thisse (1987), 'Spatial price policies and duopoly', Université Catholique de Louvain, CORE Discussion Paper 8737.

Augier, L. and J.-P. Icikovics (1982), 'L'automobile 1982–1990', Science et Vie, Special Issue.

Beckmann, M.J. (1976), 'Spatial price policies revisited', Bell Journal of Economics, 7, 619–30.

Greenhut, J. and M.L. Greenhut (1975), 'Spatial price discrimination, competition and locational effects', Economica, 42, 401–19.

Greenhut, J., M.L. Greenhut, and S.Y. Li (1980), 'Spatial pricing patterns in the United States', Quarterly Journal of Economics, 94, 329–50.

Greenhut, M.L. (1981), 'Spatial pricing in the United States, West Germany and Japan', Economica, 48, 79–86.

Greenhut, M.L., G. Norman, and C.-S. Hung (1987), *The Economics of Imperfect Competition. A Spatial Approach*, Cambridge University Press.
Greenhut, M.L and H. Ohta (1972), 'Monopoly output under alternative spatial pricing techniques', *American Economic Review*, 62, 705–13.
Haddock, D.H. (1982), 'Basing-point pricing; competitive vs. collusive theories', *American Economic Review*, 72, 289–306.
Hamilton, J., J.-F. Thisse, and A. Weskamp (1987), 'Spatial discrimination: Bertrand vs. Cournot in a model of location choice', mimeo, Department of Economics, University of Florida.
Hobbs, B.F. (1986a), 'Network models of spatial oligopoly with an application to deregulation of electricity generation', *Operations Research*, 34, 395–409.
    (1986b), 'Mill pricing vs. spatial price discrimination under Bertrand and Cournot spatial competition', *Journal of Industrial Economics*, 35, 173–91.
Holahan, W.L. (1975), 'The welfare effects of spatial price discrimination', *American Economic Review*, 65, 498–503.
Hoover, E.M. (1948), *The Location of Economic Activity*, New York; McGraw-Hill.
Kats, A. (1987), 'Price discrimination in a spatial model of monopolistic competition with downward sloping demand', mimeo, Department of Economics, Virginia Polytechnic Institute and State University.
Katz, M.L. (1984), 'Price discrimination and monopolistic competition,' *Econometrica*, 52, 1453–71.
Lederer, P.J. and A.P. Hurter (1986), 'Competition of firms: discriminatory pricing and location', *Econometrica*, 54, 623–40.
Love, R.F. and J.G. Morris (1979), 'Mathematical models of road travel distances', *Management Science*, 25, 130–9.
MacLeod, W.B., G. Norman, and J.-F. Thisse (1985), 'Price discrimination and equilibrium in monopolistic competition', Université Catholique de Louvain, CORE Discussion Paper 8506.
Norman, G. (1983), 'Spatial pricing with differentiated products', *Quarterly Journal of Economics*, 97, 291–310.
Oi, W.Y. (1971), 'A Disneyland dilemma: two-part tariffs for a Mickey-Mouse monopoly', *Quarterly Journal of Economics*, 85, 77–96.
Phlips, L. (1983), *The Economics of Price Discrimination*, Cambridge University Press.
Pigou A.C. (1920), *The Economics of Welfare*, London: Macmillan.
Robinson, J. (1933), *The Economics of Imperfect Competition*, London: Macmillan.
Salop, S. and J. Stiglitz (1977), 'Bargains and ripoffs: a model of monopolistic competition with price dispersion', *Review of Economic Studies*, 44, 493–510.
Scherer, F.M. (1980), *Industrial Market Structure and Economic Performance*, Chicago: Rand McNally.
Schmalensee, R. (1981), 'Output and welfare implications of monopolistic third-degree price discrimination', *American Economic Review*, 71, 242–7.
Schwartz, M. (1986), 'The perverse effects of the Robinson–Patman Act', *Antitrust Bulletin*, 31, 733–57.
Singh, N. and X. Vives (1984), 'Price and quantity competition in a differentiated duopoly', *The Rand Journal of Economics*, 15, 546–54.
Sloan, A.P. Jr. (1972), 'My years with General Motors', in J. McDonald with C. Stevens (ed.), New York: Doubleday.
Smithies, A. (1941), 'Monopolistic price policy in a spatial market', *Econometrica*, 9, 63–73.
    (1942), 'Aspects of the basing-point system', *American Economic Review*, 32, 705–26.

Spulber, D.F. (1981), 'Spatial nonlinear pricing', *American Economic Review*, 71, 923–33.

Stigler, G.J. (1949), 'A theory of delivered price systems', *American Economic Review*, 39, 1143–59.

Ward, J.E. and R.A. Wendell (1985), 'Measuring distances via block norms with an application to facility location models', *Operations Research*, 33, 1074–90.

Price Commission (1978a), 'UG Glass Containers – price of glass containers', Price Commission Report 5, House of Commons 170, HMSO.

    (1978b) 'Metal Box Ltd – open top food and beverage and aerosol cans', Price Commission Report 3, House of Commons 135, HMSO.

    (1978c), 'Tate and Lyle Refineries Limited – sugar and syrup products', Price Commission Report 6, House of Commons 224, HMS0.

Chapter 8

Best-price policies
Facilitating practices: the effects of advance notice and best-price policies

Charles A. Holt and David T. Scheffman

1   Introduction

This chapter considers whether supracompetitive prices can result from the combination of public advance notification of list-price increases and the use of contractual provisions that ensure the buyer of obtaining the best available price. Under advance notification a list-price increase will typically be announced in the trade press several days before the advance notice deadline, which is usually 30 days before the effective date of the price increase. Then other firms' list-price announcements indicate whether they are willing to follow the increase. The resulting 'price signalling' may enable firms to collude tacitly on list prices.

'Best-price' provisions give buyers both meet-or-release and most-favoured-customer protection. A meet-or-release clause requires a seller to meet a lower offer to his customer or to release the customer from the contract; a most-favoured-customer clause guarantees that the buyer is receiving the lowest price offered to anyone by the seller. Best-price provisions may reduce incentives to offer discounts from list prices because discounts must be offered to all customers with most-favoured-customer protection and discounts offered to a competitor's customers are likely to be matched

This article first appeared in the *RAND Journal of Economics*, 1987, vol. 18, pp. 187–97.
This research was supported by the Federal Trade Commission, the Spanish Government Ministry of Science and Education, and the National Science Foundation (SES 82–19720). The opinions expressed are those of the authors, not those of the FTC. The chapter was substantially improved as a result of the extensive comments made by the referees and editor.

if contracts have meet-or-release clauses. Alternatively, the use of most-favoured-customer clauses may make a firm more vulnerable to discounting, because a firm with such clauses in its contracts has reduced incentives to match a discount offer. In this article we develop a model in which we can examine the effects of public advance notice and best-price policies.

We show that when firms choose *prices* non-cooperatively, but have best-price provisions in sales contracts, their effective strategies become analogous to Cournot strategies in which *quantities* are chosen. The intuition for this result is that the meet-or-release clause allows a discounter's rivals to maintain their sales by matching a discount, thereby making a Cournot assumption with respect to competitors' sales rational, and the most-favored-customer clause requires the discount to be offered to all existing customers. Salop (1985) presented some discrete-price duopoly examples that confirm the intuition that the use of both kinds of clauses can increase prices. Cooper (1986) considered a model with product differentiation and showed that the use of most-favoured-customer clauses can result in prices that exceed the Nash equilibrium prices. Very little is known, however, about the magnitude of the price increases that could result from the use of contracts with best-price provisions.

We consider a homogeneous-product model in which the use of advance notification can lead to supracompetitive list prices. We further show that there can be supracompetitive list prices that are not subject to non-selective (general) discounting when contracts contain best-price provisions, but that such list prices can be no greater than the 'Cournot price', i.e., the price that would result in a Nash equilibrium for a game in which firms' strategies are output levels. Finally, we consider the case in which discounts can be offered selectively to a subset of rivals' customers.

Our interest in this topic arose from the FTC *Ethyl* case in which the Commission found that the producers of lead-based gasoline additives had used public advance notification of list-price increases, uniform delivered pricing, and most-favoured-customer clauses in a manner that unreasonably restrained price competition.[1]

The use of public advance notification and meet-or-release clauses is common in producer-goods industries. Other producer-goods markets are as concentrated as the antiknock lead additives market, and, in some cases, environmentally based barriers to entry may be as significant as the EPA-mandated phase-out of lead-based antiknock additives. What is unusual about the antiknock lead additives industry is the use of most-favoured-customer clauses and uniform delivered pricing, and the fact that for some of the (four) producers discounts from the list price were very infrequent (Pautler, 1981).

We present the model in section 2 and analyse non-selective and selective discounting in sections 3 and 4, respectively. A discussion of the decisions to use best-

---

[1] The respondents' use of meet-or-release clauses was not litigated. The case was dismissed by the Second Circuit on appeal *(Ethyl Corp. et al.* 101FTC 423 (1983) (Docket No. D9128); *E. 1. DuPont DeNemours and Co.* v. FTC, 729F.2d 128 (2d Cir. 1984)). The *Ethyl* case is discussed in more detail in Holt and Scheffman (1985).

price provisions appears in section 5, and the concluding section summarizes our results and relates them to the experimental findings of Grether and Plott (1984).

2   The model

Consider a market for a homogeneous product that is sold by a fixed number, n, of producers with outputs $q_i, i = 1, ..., n$. Denote industry output by Q. There is an infinity of 'small', price-taking buyers, who are represented by a continuous distribution of reservation prices. This formulation is the limiting case of a model in which each buyer has a reservation price for one unit of the product, and the size of the unit decreases to zero as the number of buyers increases to infinity. The distribution function of reservation prices is denoted by $G(\cdot)$ so that $1 - G(p)$ is the *fraction* of buyers with reservation prices that are above a price p. Thus, the $G(\cdot)$ function determines the market demand function, denoted $D(p)$: $1 - G(p) = D(p)/D(0)$. The inverse of the market demand function is denoted $p = f(Q)$. The assumptions about demand and costs follow.

Assumption 1

The inverse demand function is twice continuously differentiable and strictly decreasing on $[0, \Phi], f(\Phi) = 0$ for some finite output A, and industry marginal revenue is downward sloping

$$f''(Q)Q/2 + f'(Q) \leq 0 \quad for \ Q \in (0, \Phi). \tag{1}$$

Assumption 2

Firms' variable cost functions, $c_i, (q_i), i = 1, ..., n$, are non-decreasing, convex, and twice continuously differentiable on $(0, \Phi)$, with $c_i'(0) < f(0)$. Fixed costs, denoted by F_i, are non-negative.

We shall introduce Assumptions 3 and 4, which pertain to buyer responses to price offers, in the next section.

We model the pricing process as a two-stage game. In the first stage the n firms select list prices, denoted $\bar{p}_i, i = 1, ..., n$, and in the second stage, the firms select discount prices, denoted $p_{di}, i = 1, ..., n$. Since the product is homogeneous and list-price reductions can be matched, we model the advance posting of list prices as an auction process in which the lowest preferred list price prevails. Thus, the result of public advance notification of list prices is a common list price, $\bar{p}$, determined by $\bar{p} = \min\{\bar{p}_i, ..., \bar{p}_n\}$.[2] The list price $\bar{p}$ is the common price that is in effect at the advance-notice deadline, and list-price sales contracts are signed at this time. We shall discuss the determination of list-price sales quantities in more detail later. Given the

---

[2] We are indebted to James Jordan for suggesting this method of modelling the situation in which there are no last-minute list-price reductions; i.e., a reduction announced at time $T - \varepsilon$ can be matched by others at time $T - \varepsilon/2$ for any $\in$. In this situation the prevailing list-price would be the lowest of the preferred list prices. This is also the approach taken by Kalai and Satterthwaite (1986).

common list price and the corresponding contract sales quantities determined in the first stage, each firm considers offering a discount in the second stage. The list-price contract provisions affect the rules of the game in the second stage. The most-favoured-customer provision requires that a discount offer to prospective buyers be granted to buyers who have already signed purchase contracts. The meet-or-release provision gives the seller an option to match a 'surprise' discount made by a rival seller. Subject to these constraints, the second stage is modelled as a very competitive form of interaction – Nash in prices.

We shall restrict our attention to subgame-perfect equilibria – equilibria in which the strategies constitute a Nash equilibrium for each subgame determined by a possible value of $\bar{p}$. In particular, we characterize conditions under which the list price will or will not be an equilibrium price in the sense that firms have no incentive to offer unilateral discounts from list price.

3   Non-selective discounting

We begin by analysing the second stage of the two-stage game, so that the common list price, $\bar{p}$, and the distribution of list-price sales are given. We first consider the incentive to discount when $\bar{p}$ is strictly greater than marginal cost for each firm; subsequently we consider the determination of equilibrium list prices and contract quantities. The analysis in this section concerns discounts that must be made non-selectively to all current and potential buyers in a market where all contracts contain best-price provisions. We discuss the incentives to use such contracts subsequently.

Incentives to discount non-selectively

Consider a firm's incentive to offer a discount price, p_d, if the list price $\bar{p}$ is greater than the marginal cost for each seller. If all producers use the meet-or-release clauses in their contracts to match a discount, then the firm offering a small non-selective discount will not divert existing sales from its competitors. The potential new sales at a price p_d (below $\bar{p}$) are $[D(p_d) - D(\bar{p})]$. We analyse the profitability of non-selective discounting under the following assumption.

Assumption 3
If contracts contain meet-or-release and most-favoured-customer provisions, a discounter offering a price p_d that exceeds other firms' marginal costs will anticipate new sales of $[D(p_d) - D(\bar{p})]$ units.

If a firm did not exercise its meet-or-release option to match a discount that exceeds its marginal cost, it would lose all sales because the discount is non-selective, so that it is reasonable to assume that discounting can only be motivated by the prospect of new sales. The assumption that the discounter expects to obtain all new sales *maximizes* the incentive to give a unilateral non-selective discount. If we show that with this assumption there are some supracompetitive prices at which no firm has a unilateral incentive to discount, this result also holds under more conservative assumptions about the expected gains to discounting.

Since firm i's sales contracts contain most-favoured-customer provisions, the firm must extend any discount offer to all of its existing customers. Let $\bar{q} = (\bar{q}_1, ..., \bar{q}_n)$ denote the vector of quantities that firms contract to sell at the common list price, $\bar{p}$. It follows that firm i's profit from offering a unilateral non-selective discount to price p_d which increases its sales by $[D(p_d) - D(\bar{p})]$, is

$$p_d[\bar{q}_i + D(p_d) - D(\bar{p})] - c_i(\bar{q}_i + D(p_d) - D(\bar{p})) - F_i. \tag{2}$$

Let x_d be the new sales for the discounter, $x_d = [D(p_d) - D(\bar{p})]$ and $p_d = f(\bar{Q} + x_d)$. Then we can write firm i's profit, if it discounts, as a function of x_d

$$f(\bar{Q} + x_d)[\bar{q}_i + x_d] - c_i(\bar{q}_i + x_d) - F_i. \tag{3}$$

Notice that using best-price clauses changes the usual Bertrand analysis of the profitability of discounting into a Cournot problem. The meet-or-release clauses permit firms to match a discount and thereby maintain their sales quantities, as in a Cournot analysis, and the most-favoured-customer clause forces the discounter to offer the discount to all of its existing customers.

We can determine firm i's profit-maximizing level of discounting from price $\bar{p}$ by maximizing (3) with respect to x_d, subject to the condition that $x_d \geq 0$ (which is equivalent to the condition that $p_d \leq \bar{p}$). The derivative of (3) with respect to x_d, evaluated at $x_d = 0$, is $f'(\bar{Q})\bar{q}_i + f(\bar{Q}) - c_i'(\bar{q}_i)$. Since it follows from the downward-sloping marginal revenue condition (1) that the second derivative of (3) with respect to x_d is negative, a sufficient condition for a non-selective discount from $\bar{p}$ by firm i to be profitable is that

$$f'(Q)q_i + f(Q) - c_i'(q_i) > 0 \tag{4}$$

when evaluated at $Q = \bar{Q}$, $q_i = \bar{q}_i$. Thus, the incentive to discount non-selectively is determined by the sign of the expression on the left side of (4), which is the partial derivative of the ith firm's profit with respect to its own output. We shall call this expression the firm's unilateral output expansion incentive and shall denote it by $I_i(Q, q_i)$.

We are now able to prove the following proposition.

Proposition 1

If contracts contain best-price provisions, then under assumptions 1–3: (a) any list price above the Cournot price gives some firm an incentive to discount non-selectively; and (b) at the Cournot price some firm has an incentive to discount non-selectively unless all firms are producing their Cournot equilibrium quantities.

Proof   We prove the result for (b) first. Consider a set of strictly positive Cournot outputs, $q_i^*, i = 1, ..., n$, defined by $I_i(Q^*, q_i^*) = 0$, and let $Q^* = \sum_i q_i^*$. If $q_i < q_i^*$ at the corresponding Cournot price $f(Q^*)$, then $I_i(Q^*, q_i)$ is positive because

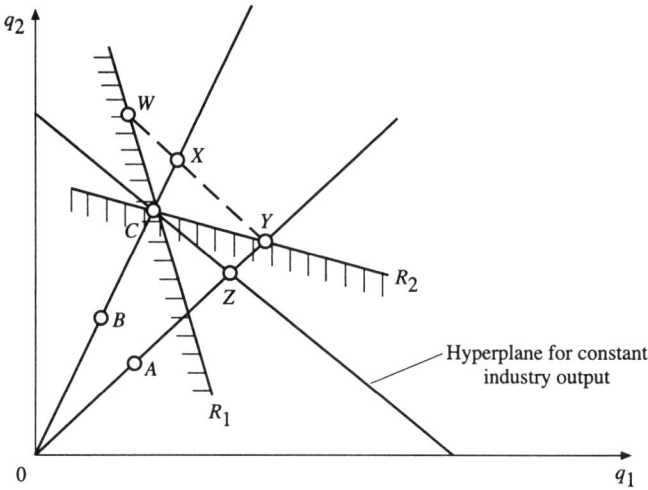

Figure 8.1 Incentives to offer non-selective discounts

the I_i function is decreasing in its second argument. Then, to prove part (a) we have by assumption that $\sum_i q_i < Q^*$. Multiply all firms' outputs by α and increase α from one to the level α^* for which $\sum_i \alpha^* q_i = Q^*$. We can easily see from the downward-sloping marginal revenue condition (1) that this will strictly decrease I_i for all i. By (b) some firm j will have a non-negative I_j at α^*, and hence $I_j > 0$ at the original outputs. ∎

The increase in the parameter α in the proof of Proposition 1 corresponds to a movement of the vector of firms' quantities out along a ray from the origin in output space, and such a movement reduces each firm's unilateral output expansion incentive. We illustrate this in figure 8.1, where the Cournot reaction functions, represented by R_1 and R_2, intersect at the Cournot equilibrium point, C. At least one firm has an incentive to discount nonselectively at any point to the left of either reaction function. Note that the proof of (b) shows that there can be only one Cournot equilibrium with positive outputs on any constant industry-output hyperplane in the space of firms' outputs; at least one firm has an incentive to expand output unilaterally at a point such as Z in figure 8.1. The proof of (a) shows that there cannot be another Cournot equilibrium at a higher price since the unilateral output expansion incentive is positive for at least one firm at the higher price. For example, firm 2, which has an incentive to expand output at point Z in figure 8.1, would have a stronger incentive to do so at point A.

The only use of assumption 3 in the proof of the proposition was to identify non-selective discounts with unilateral output expansions, so we have the following corollary about the uniqueness of the Cournot equilibrium.[3]

---

[3] Of course, a Cournot equilibrium may not exist. Novshek's (1985) theorem 3 implies that a Cournot equilibrium will exist for the model presented in this section if $f''(Q)Q + f'(Q) < 0$. This is a stronger condition than (1).

Corollary

Under assumptions 1 and 2 there is at most one Cournot equilibrium with strictly positive outputs for each firm.

At the Cournot price there is only one vector of sales quantities, the Cournot vector, that does not result in incentives to offer non-selective discounts. At any list price below the Cournot price, there is a range of firms' market shares for which such discounts are unprofitable. For example, the unilateral output expansion incentives are negative at a point such as X in figure 8.1 and at all points between W and Y on the constant-industry-output hyperplane through X. The incentive to offer a small non-selective discount decreases as one moves along any ray away from the origin. Hence, at an industry output higher than that at X, the range of market shares without such incentives to discount would include some market shares that are outside the range of market shares determined by points on the line WY. In this sense the common contract price $\bar{p}$ becomes more stable with respect to discounting as it falls from the Cournot price towards the competitive price.

The preceding analysis pertains to the unprofitability of discounting in the neighbourhood of the list price $\bar{p}$. Even if small discounts are unprofitable, large discounts may be profitable in the presence of significant cost asymmetries. For example, suppose that two firms' marginal costs differ, but that each is constant, and that each firm's sales quantity is equal to $\bar{Q}/2$ at the common list price $\bar{p}$. It will be profitable for the low-cost firm to offer a discount that is slightly below the other's marginal cost if the resulting profits for the low-cost firm at an output of $\bar{Q}$ exceed the firm's profits at price $\bar{p}$ and quantity $\bar{Q}/2$. It is easy to construct numerical examples in which the point $(\bar{Q}/2, \bar{Q}/2)$ is to the right of the firms' reaction functions in output space and a large discount is profitable. Such below-cost discounts are unprofitable when firms have identical cost functions.

Equilibrium

The remaining issue to be considered with respect to non-selective discounting is whether supracompetitive prices that are impervious to discounting can be established in an equilibrium of the two-stage game. A strategy for firm i in the two-stage game involves public advance notification of a list price, denoted $\bar{p}_i$, in the first stage and a discount price, $p_{di}(\bar{p})$, for the second stage that can depend on the prevailing list price, $\bar{p}$, at which contracts are signed. Since $\bar{p} \leq \bar{p}_i$, a complete specification of the ith firm's strategy requires only that $p_{di}(\bar{p})$ be defined for $\bar{p} \leq \bar{p}_i$. For example, the (two-stage) strategy $(\bar{p}_i, p_{di}(\bar{p}) = \bar{p}$ for $\bar{p} \leq \bar{p}_i)$ would involve setting the discount price equal to the prevailing list price. We shall refer to this strategy as a 'no-discount strategy'.

A firm will not refuse sales at the common list price if that price exceeds its marginal cost. But marginal costs will depend on the allocation of buyers at the common list price. We make the following assumption about demand allocation.

Assumption 4

When all firms charge the same list price, buyers randomly select sellers.

Recall that there is a continuum of buyers, so that this assumption implies that firms' market shares will be equal when the common list price exceeds firms' marginal costs at the resulting outputs. (As the number of balls goes to infinity, the fraction of balls in each of a fixed number, n, of urns goes to $1/n$.) Assumption 4 allows us to characterize equilibria for the symmetric-cost case.

Proposition 2

If assumptions 1–4 are satisfied and firms' cost functions are identical, then under best-price practices, any supracompetitive common list price, $\bar{p}$, that is less than or equal to the Cournot price constitutes a subgame-perfect equilibrium for no-discount strategies $p_{di}(\bar{p}) = \bar{p}_i = \bar{p}$.

Proof First, consider the second stage, in which the common list price $\bar{p}$ is at any level between the Cournot and competitive prices. Since costs are symmetric and list-price sales quantities are equal, any unilateral discount to a price that is above the competitive level will be to a price that exceeds other firms' marginal costs, and hence will be matched when these firms use their contractual option to meet a rival's price cut and thereby maintain their output quantities. Therefore, a unilateral discount in the second stage from any common list price below the Cournot price will be unprofitable.

In the proposed equilibrium all firms announce the same list price, $\bar{p}$, in the first stage, so that we now consider the profitability of a unilateral deviation from this list price. As noted in section 2, we have modelled the public advance notification process in the first stage as an auction in which firms select list prices $\bar{p}_i, i = 1, ..., n$, and the lowest preferred list price prevails: $\bar{p} = \min\{\bar{p}_i, ..., \bar{p}_n\}$. A unilateral increase in list price will not affect $\bar{p}$. A unilateral reduction in the list price by firm i would reduce the prevailing common list price by an equal amount. Under assumption 4 this reduction in the list price would not increase the firm's market share, s_i, which equals $1/n$, and it follows from the earlier analysis of the second stage that there would be no discounting in the subgame determined by this lower common list price. Hence, a unilateral reduction in $\bar{p}_i$ is unprofitable if $[f(Q)s_I Q_i - c_i(s_i Q)]$ is decreasing in Q, or equivalently, if

$$f'(Q)s_i Q + s_i f(Q) - s_i c_i'(s_i Q)] < 0.$$

Since firms' cost functions and market shares are identical, this inequality is satisfied when p is below the level that maximizes industry profit. It follows that no-discount strategies for $\bar{p}_i = \bar{p} = f(\bar{Q})$ will be subgame perfect. ∎

With symmetric costs, there is a continuum of common list prices that could occur in equilibrium. Within the set of subgame-perfect equilibria with no-discount strategies, each firm i will have a preferred (largest-profit) equilibrium, consisting of an equilibrium price, $\hat{p}_i$, between the Cournot and competitive levels, that is impervious to discounting. With symmetric costs $\hat{p}_i$ is the Cournot price. With cost asymmetries that are not excessive, there may also exist a range of common list prices for which *all* non-selective discounts are unprofitable, and cost asymmetries may cause $\hat{p}_i$ to differ from firm to firm. In any case the no-discount strategy with an announced list price of $\hat{p}_i$ weakly dominates any other no-discount strategy, because the prevailing list price is the minimum of the announced list prices, and the firm incurs no penalty for announcing a list price above that of its competitors. The common list price that results from the use of weakly dominant no-discount strategies would be the minimum of the $\hat{p}_j$, $j = 1, ..., n$, and this would exceed the competitive price.[4]

If there were no second stage, and hence no discounting, then in our model with symmetric costs a weakly dominant strategy for each firm would be to announce the perfectly collusive price in the first stage. This is precisely the result obtained by Kalai and Satterthwaite (1986), who consider a model like ours in which the lowest announced list price prevails, but in which there are no discounts from list price. We believe that discount possibilities are important in unregulated markets, and we do not believe that the advance-notice and best-price practices would result in perfect collusion. The experimental evidence discussed in the final section supports this belief.

4   Incentives to discount selectively

In this section we consider the situation in which sellers can offer discounts selectively to a particular group of competitors' buyers. Having the option of making a discount selective does not lower the unilateral incentive to discount. One reason for offering a selective discount would be to keep the offer secret from one's competitors. When contracts contain meet-or-release provisions, however, the firms' own customers will report discounts offered to them. Another reason to consider a selective discount is to avoid retaliation; a discount that is sufficiently large and selective may not be matched (since if the 'victim' matches, he must make the same offer on all his sales contracts with most-favored-customer clauses).

A selective discount that is matched will be no more profitable than an equal *non*-selective discount that is matched, since a matched non-selective discount will generate at least as many *new* (to the market) sales as a matched selective discount. Therefore, we shall restrict our consideration to selective discounts that are not matched.

In the analysis that follows, firm 1 is the 'discounter' and firm 2 is the 'victim' that considers a matching price cut. By assumption 4 each buyer with a reservation price above the initial list price $\bar{p}$ will purchase from one of the firms, and $\bar{q}_1 = \bar{q}_2 = D(\bar{p})/2$. At a price p_d that is below $\bar{p}$, new buyers, with reservation prices between p_d and $\bar{p}$,

---

[4] Liquor and beer are sometimes regulated in a manner that requires public advance notification and *strictly prohibits* discounting (Eckel and Goldberg, 1984). Our analysis of the first stage of our two-stage game is applicable to such situations. and it suggests that this type of regulation will result in supracompetitive prices.

increase market demand by $D(p_d) - D(\bar{p})$. In our model all new demand at lower prices originates with new buyers.

The discounter must select a discount price, p_d, and must decide on the degree of selectivity of the discount. If the discount offer is made to a fraction, λ, of the other firm's customers, and if this discount is not matched by the victim, the discounter diverts a quantity of sales, $\lambda\bar{q}_2$, from the victim. The total sales quantity for firm 1 that results from an unmatched discount to p_d will be denoted $\bar{q}_1 + \lambda\bar{q}_2 + \theta_d[D(p_d) - D(\bar{p})]$, where θ_d represents the fraction of new buyers that the discounter is able to reach. In the previous section's analysis of non-selective discounting we assumed that θ_d was one (assumption 3). In this section we allow θ_d to be less than or equal to one because it may not be possible for a discounter to contact all potential new buyers while offering the discount to only a fraction of the rival's current buyers. Since $\bar{q}_1 = \bar{q}_2 = \bar{Q}/2$, we can express that output for an unmatched selective discount, $q(p_d, \lambda)$, as

$$q(p_d, \lambda) = (.5 + .5\lambda - \theta_d)\bar{Q} + \theta_d D(p_d). \tag{5}$$

The profit for an unmatched selective discount characterized by (p_d, λ) will be denoted $\pi_1(p_d, \lambda)$. We calculate this profit in the usual way

$$\pi_1(p_d, \lambda) = p_d q(p_d, \lambda) - c_1(q(p_d, \lambda)) - F_1. \tag{6}$$

The first firm has an incentive to offer a small unmatched selective discount if $d\pi_1/dp_d < 0$ at $p_d = \bar{p}$ when λ is adjusted to prevent the discount from being matched. The incentive for the other firm to match depends on the fraction, θ_m, of the new sales, $D(p_d) - D(\bar{p})$, that it would obtain if it matched the discount p_d. Since θ_d pertains to the case in which the discount offer is not matched and θ_m pertains to the case in which the discount offer is matched so that new sales will be shared, we believe that $\theta_d \geq \theta_m$ is a reasonable condition. The main result of this section is the following proposition regarding the incentives to discount selectively.

Proposition 3

Under assumptions 1 and 2, even if sales contracts have best-price provisions, at least one firm will have an incentive to offer a selective discount from any common list price that is above each firm's marginal cost if an unmatched selective discount captures a greater fraction of new market sales than the fraction of such new sales obtained by a firm that matches another's discount, i.e., if $\theta_d \geq \theta_m$.

    Proof   See the appendix.   ∎

The main implication of this analysis is that competition is likely to be intensified when firms can make selective discounts. For example, in section 3 we showed that if the firms have symmetric costs and equal market shares, then the Cournot price p^* is impervious to non-selective discounting, even if the discounter gets *all* new business generated by the discount $(\theta_d - 1)$. But at least one firm will have an incentive to discount selectively, even if $\theta_d < 1$ as long as $(\theta_d - \theta_m) > 0$. Therefore, list prices and sales distributions that are impervious to non-selective discounting will often not be impervious to selective discounting.

5   Choice of practices

Each individual buyer may prefer to have a contract that preserves the option of obtaining the best available price. In particular, Salop (1985) notes that individual buyers in producer-goods markets may prefer contracts with best-price provisions to prevent competitors from gaining a cost advantage, even though the effect of the general use of these practices is to reduce sellers' incentives to discount. Buyers in our model are small, and no buyer's unilateral choice of contract provisions would have any effect on marketwide discounting activity. But a large, sophisticated buyer may realize that signing a contract with best-price provisions may reduce the sellers' incentives to discount. In particular, a buyer's most-favoured-customer clause reduces the incentive for the seller to offer a discount to some other buyer, and a buyer's meet-or-release clause reduces the incentive for some other seller to offer a non-selective discount.

Now consider firms' incentives to adopt best-price provisions. When discounts must be non-selective, it would be in firms' interests as a group to use best-price provisions, and collusion with respect to contractual practices, whether tacit or explicit, is easier to coordinate and to monitor than direct collusion on price. In addition, it may be in a firm's interest to adopt meet-or-release and most-favoured-customer provisions unilaterally. This incentive to adopt the practices is clearest in the case of meet-or-release clauses, because the exercise of the right to meet a rival's discount will reduce the profitability of such a discount. Also, the firm's *own* meet-or-release clause would not reduce the profit it would make by offering a discount. But, unlike the case of the meet-or-release clause, the most-favoured-customer clause can reduce the firm's flexibility, both in responding to a rival's selective discount and in initiating a discount, because a matching price reduction must be offered to all buyers with most-favoured-customer clauses in their contracts.[5]

6   Summary and discussion of experimental evidence

In this chapter we analysed the possible anticompetitive effects of some business practices that may enable firms to coordinate price increases and to resist the temptation to discount. We did not consider transactions efficiencies that may arise from the use of these practices. Our focus has been on coordination that is tacit, not overt, and therefore on whether the combination of practices we consider would arise

---

[5] Cooper (1986) showed that at least one firm would have a unilateral incentive to adopt most-favoured-customer clauses in his model with product differentiation. He also presented a numerical example in which both duopolists would use most-favoured-customer clauses in equilibrium.

in a market environment in which supracompetitive prices can be sustained *even if* firms would discount were such price-cutting perceived to be unilaterally profitable.

We show that public advance notification of list-price increases and the use of best-price policies can result in supracompetitive equilibrium list and transactions prices that are immune to discounting. Furthermore, there is a range of firms' sales quantities at common list prices above the competitive level for which small unilateral discounts are unprofitable if such discounts can only be given *non-selectively* to all buyers. If costs are symmetric and firms attain equal shares of contract sales at the common list price, then the range of common list prices impervious to discounting contains all prices up to the 'Cournot price', which would result in a Cournot equilibrium with output quantities being selected non-cooperatively.

If firms can give *selective* discounts (i.e., discounts offered to only a subset of a competitor's customers), then we show that the use of best-price clauses does not result in supracompetitive list prices that are immune to discounting as long as a firm making an unmatched discount offer obtains more sales than would a competitor who matches the offer. With most-favoured-customer clauses, however, selective discounting is not possible if each buyer purchases some units from each seller, so that buyer behaviour is an important determinant of the level of transactions prices in the presence of best-price clauses. In the *Ethyl* case, the evidence indicated that virtually all customers made purchases from the two largest producers.

The finding in the symmetric-cost case that list prices between the competitive and Cournot price are impervious to unilateral, non-selective discounting is consistent with the pricing behaviour observed in some experiments conducted by Grether and Plott (1984). In their experiments with advance notification and most-favoured-customer contracts, announced prices were continuously displayed to all buyers, and all transactions were required to take place at announced prices. Thus, a price cut would be public and effective immediately, and hence non-selective. All contracts were binding in these experiments, and the resulting 'no-release' condition is as strong a deterrent to non-selective discounting as the use of meet-or-release clauses. The experimentally induced demand and cost functions were discrete 'step functions', and therefore, did not satisfy assumptions 1 and 2. The market structure in the experiments was symmetric in the sense that the two large sellers that were not in the competitive fringe had identical cost functions. The net demand for these two firms was the market demand minus the supply of the fringe firms, as functions of price. Grether and Plott (1984) used this net demand to compute the Cournot price for the duopoly consisting of the two large firms that faced the net demand curve. Prices in the experiments were about halfway between the competitive and Cournot levels. The average price did not exceed the Cournot price in any period in any experiment. Under the control treatment with none of the practices, prices were above but very close to competitive levels.

Appendix

The proof of proposition 3 follows.

Proof of proposition 3   The largest quantity of sales the discounter (firm 1) can divert will be the amount that would leave the competitor (firm 2) indifferent to matching the discount offer of p_d. The 'no-matching condition' that determines this maximum quantity of diverted sales is

$$\bar{p}[(1 - \lambda)\bar{q}_2] - c_2((1 - \lambda)\bar{q}_2) = p_d[\bar{q}_2 + \theta_m[D(p_d) - D(\bar{p})]] \\ - c_2(\bar{q}_2 + \theta_m[D(p_d) - D(\bar{p})]) \quad (A1)$$

where the left side represents the firm's profit if it does not match and the right side represents its profit if it does match.

Equation (A1) implicitly defines a function $\lambda(p_d, \bar{p})$ that gives the maximum value of λ for an unmatched discount p_d from $\bar{p}$. Notice that $\lambda(\bar{p}, \bar{p}) = 0$, since a very small discount will be matched unless it is very selective. The function $\lambda(p_d, \bar{p})$ allows us to rewrite $q(p_d, \lambda)$ in (5) as $q(p_d, \lambda(p_d, \bar{p})) = q(p_d)$ and to rewrite $\pi_1(p_d, \lambda)$ in (6) as $\pi_1(p_d, \lambda(p_d, \bar{p})) = \pi_1(p_d)$ It will be profitable for the discounter to offer an unmatched selective discount from list price if the right-hand derivative $\pi'_d(\bar{p})$ is strictly negative.

To evaluate this derivative, it is first necessary to calculate $\partial\lambda/\partial p_d$. Using (A1) and the fact that $\lambda(p_d, \bar{p})$ is zero at $p_d = \bar{p}$, we can show that

$$d\lambda/dp_d|_{p_d=\bar{p}} = \frac{-\theta_m D'(p_d)}{\bar{q}_2} - \frac{1}{\bar{p} - c'_2(\bar{q}_2)}. \quad (A2)$$

Then, using (5), (6), and (A2), we can show that

$$\pi'_1(\bar{p}) = [(\theta_d - \theta_m)D'(\bar{p}) + \Delta][\bar{p} - c'_1(\bar{q}_1)] \quad (A3)$$

where

$$\Delta = .5\bar{Q}/[\bar{p} - c'_1(\bar{q}_1)] - .5\bar{Q}/[\bar{p} - c'_2(\bar{q}_2)]. \quad (A4)$$

The expressions in (A2)–(A4) that involve differences between price and marginal costs are non-negative because $\bar{p}$ exceeds the competitive level, and each firm can reject sales for which marginal cost exceeds price. Since $\bar{p}$ exceeds the competitive price, $\bar{p}$ will be strictly above marginal cost for at least one firm. We are free to number firms so that $\bar{p} - c'_1(\bar{q}_1) > \bar{p} - c'_2(\bar{q}_2)$ and Δ is negative. Since $\theta_d > \theta_m$ by assumption, the expression for $\pi'(\bar{p})$ in (A3) is negative.   ∎

References

Cooper, T.C. (1986), 'Most-favored customer pricing and tacit collusion', *Rand Journal of Economics*, 17, 377–88.

Eckel, C.C. and M.A. Goldberg (1984), 'Regulation and deregulation in the brewing industry: the British Columbia example', *Canadian Public Policy*, 10, 316–27.

Grether, D.M. and C.R. Plott (1984), 'The effects of market practices in oligopolistic markets: an experimental examination of the Ethyl case', *Economic Inquiry*, 22, 479–528.

Holt, C.A. and D.T. Scheffman (1985), 'The effects of advance notice and best-price policies theory, with applications *to Ethyl*, Thomas Jefferson Center Working Paper, University of Virginia.

Kalai, E. and M.A. Satterthwaite (1986), 'The kinked demand curve, facilitating practices, and oligopolistic competition', MEDS Discussion Paper no. 677, Northwestern University.

Novshek, W. (1985), 'On the existence of Cournot equilibrium', *Review of Economic Studies,* 52, 85–98.

Pautler, P. (1981), 'The *ethyl* case: facilitating practices in an oligopoly market', mimeo, Federal Trade Commission, Washington, DC.

Salop, S. (1985), 'Practices that (credibly) facilitate oligopoly coordination', in J. Stiglitz *et al.* (eds.), *New Developments in Market Structure,* Cambridge, MA: MIT Press.

Chapter 9

Vertical pricing schemes
Vertical restraints and producers' competition

Patrick Rey and Joseph Stiglitz

1   Introduction

Vertical relationships between producers and retailers or wholesalers often involve more or less complex contracting arrangements, broadly named vertical restraints. These arrangements can simply consist of non-linear tariffs, such as franchise fees, quantity forcing or pricing requirements (quotas, resale price maintenance), but they may also include the assignment of exclusive territories or exclusive dealing, tie-ins, etc.[1] This chapter is concerned with investigating the rationale for these restrictions and showing that there are important circumstances under which these restrictions have a significant anticompetitive effect, at the upper level as well as at the lower one.

The legal status of these restraints is not very clear, as it differs among countries and changes over time.[2] From the economic point of view, two main streams of ideas have emerged from the beginning: on the one hand, some produce the argument that,

This article first appeared in the *European Economic Review*, 1988, Vol. 32, pp. 561–8.

[1] See Blair and Kaserman (1983) and Caves (1994) for a general presentation of vertical restraints, as well as a comprehensive discussion of their economic incidence.

[2] For instance, RPM is generally considered as illegal; however, some States in the US had for a while adopted 'fair trade' laws, which partially authorized RPM. Thus, even looking only at the case of the US, RPM, which was originally viewed as per se violation of the Sherman Act, has then been accepted in some States until 1975; it is now once more illegal in all States. In the same way, assigning exclusive territories, after having been considered as per se illegal, is now subject to a rule of reason.

as markets are competitive and as these arrangements can be adopted only if joint profits are increased, there must necessarily be a gain in efficiency; on the other side, some emphasize the anticompetitive effects of these restraints at the lower (retailers' or wholesalers') level.

Recently, some efforts have been made in order to formalize the efficiency argument (see for example Mathewson and Winter, 1983, 1984). The vertical relationship is viewed as a principal-agent(s) one, and the emphasis is placed on *control problems:* a *monopolistic producer* deals with a set of more or less *competitive retailers,* whose actions (retail prices, selling efforts, etc.) affect the total profits; the problem for the producer is thus to design a contract in order to achieve the integrated solution, i.e., to make the retailers choose the right actions and to recover the profits generated. The main conclusion in this framework is that vertical restraints are always privately desirable, as they allow a better control of the retailers.[3] Moreover, as they help in correcting externalities associated with linear pricing rules, such as the double margin-alization problem (Spengler, 1950) or the free-rider problem (Telser, 1960), these vertical restraints are usually thought of as increasing social welfare.

This apologetical view has already been shaded by recent works, which emphasize for instance the divergence between the monopolists' and the consumers' evaluations of distributors' services (see Scherer, 1983; Comanor, 1985; Caillaud and Rey, 1987) or the role of distributors' private information in uncertain markets (see Rey and Tirole, 1986b). The general framework is however the same, and in particular interbrand competition (i.e., competition among producers) is neglected.

We will argue here that producers' competition is in fact a crucial element for the analysis of vertical arrangements. As we will show, when several producers are competing imperfectly at the upper level, then vertical restraints may serve to facilitate collusion. The contractual arrangement may indeed be efficient, in the sense that joint profits are higher, but the gains to the producers and distributors are at the expense of consumers. Vertical restraints may thus not be socially desirable.

We aim to emphasize the interaction between the internal (producer/retailer) contract designing and the external competitive situation at the upper level. The natural framework is provided by the multi-principal–multi-agents approach which, developed by Fershtman and Judd (1984, 1986), has recently been analysed by Bernheim and Whinston (1986), in the case of common agency, and by Katz (1987), in the case of rival agencies. This approach stresses in particular the role of internal principal–agents contracts as a commitment for sustaining collusion among principals; it also emphasizes the importance of the definition of *admissible contracts* and the role of each agent's information. This approach has already yielded new insights in the analysis of imperfect competition (see respectively Bernheim and Whinston (1985) and Bonanno and Vickers (1988) for applications in the context of common and rival

---

[3] For an introduction to the literature on vertical control, see Rey and Tirole (1986a). Indeed, one of the objectives of this literature is to define the 'minimal sets of sufficient tools', which lead to a perfect control of the distributors by the producer. (Exclusive territories plus franchise fees) generally constitutes an example of such a minimal set: it amounts in fact to 'sell the firm' (or, more exactly, the production technology) to distributors.

agencies). As we will see, it also constitutes a useful tool for the analysis of the rationale and the incidence of vertical restraints.

2   Exclusive territories as a device to reduce competition

We consider here a simple model, borrowed from Rey and Stiglitz (1985), which shows how exclusive territories, which obviously reduce competition at the lower level, may actually be a way of reducing competition also at the upper level. The basic idea is that when retailers enjoy some kind of monopolistic power, they may put higher markups in the retail price: this price distortion, in turn, induces some change to the cross sensitivity of this demand towards the prices of the manufacturers' competitors. The manufacturers may therefore perceive a less elastic demand than when they directly compete with each other or sell to competitive retailers. This effect in turn may induce both producers to assign exclusive territories to their retailers.

Let us describe this model. There are two manufacturers, each producing a simple good with a constant marginal cost c_i and distributing it via retailers who have no retail costs. The two products are imperfect substitutes. The final demand for good i, associated with retail prices q_1 and q_2, is given by $D_i(q_1, q_2)$. For simplicity, we assume symmetry: $c_1 = c_2$ and $\forall x, y \in \Re_+, D_1(x, y) = D_2(y, x)$. Consumers have no search costs and thus buy at the lowest possible price for each product. Lastly, we will suppose in the following that all profit functions are concave, admit a unique – and interior – maximum, and we will thus focus on first-order conditions.

We can define two useful benchmarks, corresponding respectively to *perfect collusion* and *direct competition* between producers:

the collusive outcome is defined by the maximization of the aggregate profits $(q_1 - c)D_1(q_1, q_2) + (q_2 - c)D_2(q_1, q_2)$, and leads to the monopolistic price q^m.

$$(q^m - c)/q^m = 1/(\varepsilon_1(q^m, q^m) + \varepsilon_2(q^m, q^m)) \qquad (1)$$

where ε_1 and ε_2 respectively denote the direct and cross-price elasticities of the final demands ($\varepsilon_i = -\partial \log D_1/\partial \log q_i$). The monopolistic markup is thus the higher, the lower is the sensitivity of the demand for a product with respect to its own price and the higher is the sensitivity of this demand to the price of the other product.[4]

The outcome associated with direct competition corresponds to the (Nash) equilibrium of the game defined by producer i's strategy q_i and payoff $(q_i - c)D_i(q_1, q_2)$. The 'competitive' price q^c is characterized (under standard assumptions on payoffs functions) by

$$(q^c - c)/q^c = 1/\varepsilon_1(q^c, q^c). \qquad (2)$$

Of course the 'competitive' profits are lower. When the two products are

---

[4] As the two goods are substitutes, one has $\varepsilon_2 \leq 0$.

substitutes, retail prices are also lower; the basic idea is that each producer, when he chooses his own price, does not take into account the fact that his rival's demand gains from an increase in his own price. Note that indeed, it would be in the interest of the producers to convince each other that they would follow up any price increase.

Let us now make the competitive framework precise. It is presumed that producers observe the quantity bought by the retailers and possibly whether or not the retailers distribute their products; they do not observe either the quantities sold by the retailers or their profits or the prices they charge. On the contrary, retailers have perfect information and observe the contracts signed by each producer; in particular, they can do arbitrage if a producer tries to discriminate between them. Finally, producers may assign exclusive territories to their retailers (in which case these territories are supposed to be symmetric and thus representative of the total market).[5] Given these informational assumptions, the *admissible contracts* between a producer and his retailers can only include, besides the assignment of exclusive territories, wholesale tariffs based on the quantity bought by the retailers. The possibility of arbitrage from the retailers rules out non-constant marginal prices; producers may however impose franchise fees on the retailers if they effectively observe who sells their products. We will consider both situations.

We formalize the competition framework as a two-stage game: in the first stage, given some vertical contracting arrangement, producers simultaneously choose their wholesale prices, p_1 and p_2 (and eventually the franchise fees); then, in the second stage, retailers observe all wholesale tariffs and simultaneously choose their retail prices. We will consider in the following the (subgame) perfect equilibria of this two-stage game, corresponding to two initial situations: in the first one, retailers are pure price competitors whereas in the second one, exclusive territories have been assigned to the retailers.

(1) In the absence of vertical arrangements, pure (intra-brand) price competition leads the retailers to charge zero markups in the second stage, and thus the retail prices are finally equal to the wholesale prices chosen in the first stage: $q_i = p_i$ (this in turn implies that franchise fees, even if they are available, must be equal to zero). The situation is therefore formally identical to the situation of 'direct' competition between producers that we already described. At the end of this subgame, the wholesale and retail prices are equal to the 'competitive' price q^c, retail profits are zero and producers get the 'competitive' profits.

---

[5] The following assumptions are more precisely presented and discussed in Rey and Stiglitz (1985). The two main assumptions are the asymmetry in information between retailers and producers about retail prices and sales, and the fact that all contracts are common knowledge. The first assumption may be justified in several ways, including moral hazard aspects on the retail side (see Rey and Tirole 1986b). The assumption that the retailers observe all producers' contracts allows producers, as we will see, to use these contracts in order to achieve better profits: they are therefore interested in making them common knowledge.

(2) Let us now suppose that producers have assigned exclusive territories to their retailers. These arrangements eliminate intra-brand competition and thus each retailer enjoys a monopolistic power over some fixed fraction of the final demand for his product. Given the producers' prices p_1 and p_2 at the second stage some retail price equilibrium will emerge, described by $(q_1^r(p_1,p_2), q_2^r(p_1,p_2))$: each retail price is a function of the two producers' prices; note that franchise fees, which should be viewed as fixed costs, can alter the retailers' decisions about whether or not to distribute a product, but do not change the price response functions. For simplicity, we will again assume symmetry: $\forall x, y \in \Re_+, q_1^r(x,y) = q_2^r(y,x)$.

(a) Suppose first that franchise fees are not available. At the first stage producer i chooses a price p_i to maximize

$$\pi_i = (p_i - c)D_i(q_1^r(p_1,p_2), q_2^r(p_1,p_2)) \tag{3}$$

which leads to wholesale and retail prices which satisfy $p_1 = p_2 = p^e$, $q_1 = q_2 = q^e \doteq q_i^r(p^e, p^e)$ and

$$(p^e - c)/p^e = 1/\left[\varepsilon_1(q^e, q^e)\rho_1(p^e, p^e) + \varepsilon_2(q^e, q^e)\rho_2(p^e, p^e)\right] \tag{4}$$

where ρ_1 and ρ_2 respectively denote the elasticities of a given retailer's price to his producer's (for ρ_1) and the rival's (for ρ_2) wholesale prices $(\rho_i = \partial \log q_1^r / \partial \log p_i)$.

(b) Suppose now that producers can charge franchise fees. Anticipating the retail price equilibrium (which, as already noted, is not modified when introducing franchise fees), the producer can recover the associated retail profits via the franchise fees. Thus producer i's profits are given by

$$\pi_i = (q_i^r(p_1,p_2) - c)D_i(q_1^r(p_1,p_2), q_2^r(p_1,p_2)). \tag{5}$$

The equilibrium condition becomes

$$(q^f - c)/q^f = 1/(\varepsilon_1(q^f, q^f) + \varepsilon_2(q^f, q^f)\rho_2(q^f, q^f)/\rho_1(q^f, q^f)). \tag{6}$$

Let us briefly comment on this analysis. If, as one might normally expect, competitive pressures result in ρ_1 being positive but less than one, and ρ_2 being positive but less than ρ_1,[6] then one obtains

$$q^e \geq p^e \geq p^c = q^c \quad \text{and} \quad q^m \geq q^f \geq q^c. \tag{7}$$

Thus, when exclusive territories are assigned, and whether or not franchise fees are required, the equilibrium retail prices are higher.

---

[6] Retailers that find that their wholesale prices have increased while their competitors' have not, do not simply pass on the cost increase with the usual markup, but rather absorb some of the cost increase themselves (i.e., $0 \leq \rho_1 \leq 1$). This in turn induces the competitors to increase their own retail prices ($\rho_2 \geq 0$); it seems, however, reasonable to suppose that the direct effect, measured by ρ_1, is higher than the indirect one: $\rho_2 \leq \rho_1$.

In the case where franchise fees are not allowed, wholesale prices are also higher when exclusive territories are assigned. This only comes from a change in the elasticity of the perceived demand; this change results from two causes: first, the reduction of demand is altered by the fact that the retail price of a product only partially responds to the corresponding wholesale price; secondly, the loss of sales is also decreased because the rivals' retailers, who then face higher retail prices, find it optimal to increase their own prices. This change of the sensitivity of demand leads to higher wholesale price response functions and, thus, to higher wholesale prices at equilibrium. If double marginalization problems are not too important, then producers' profits are also higher when exclusive territories are assigned to retailers.

In the case where franchise fees are allowed, then the above analysis shows that under reasonable assumptions, producers' profits are higher when exclusive territories are assigned. This does not come only from a decrease of the elasticity of perceived demand (note in particular that wholesale prices need not be higher), but also from the fact that, by assigning exclusive territories to their retailers, producers generate higher retail prices.[7]

3   Comments

In the model just analysed, the producers are presumably better off when exclusive territories are assigned to the distributors. It does not *a priori* imply that producers will indeed assign exclusive territories to their retailers (unless they can cooperatively agree to do so). A possible way of analysing the producers' choices of vertical arrangements consists of introducing a new stage at the beginning of the game, where each producer chooses between competition and exclusive territories for his retailers. Rey and Stiglitz (1985) provides an example where assigning exclusive territories and requiring franchise fees is actually a dominant strategy for each producer, although the corresponding outcome is Pareto dominated by the outcome associated with the situation where both producers commit themselves to assign exclusive territories and to require no franchise fees (there is thus a standard 'Prisoner's Dilemma'). This example highlights the potential role of vertical restraints for decreasing producers' competition and also emphasizes the divergence between collective and individual rationalities: two phenomena which were ignored in most of the previous analyses of vertical restraints.[8]

Indeed in this analysis, retailers can be considered as 'black boxes' or 'response

---

[7] Similar effects are present in the context analysed by Bonanno and Vickers (1988). Two situations are compared there: the first one corresponds to what we called 'direct competition' between producers; in the second one, each producer delegates the distribution of his good to a single agent. Formally, the first situation is similar to the situation where each product is distributed via perfectly competitive retailers, while the second situation (delegation) corresponds to exclusive territories in our framework.

[8] Telser (1960) and Posner (1977) suggested that RPM could help producers in sustaining collusion by reducing the interest of wholesale price cuts. It has also been suggested that exclusivity requirements (such as exclusive dealing) can serve to deter entry, as they compel the potential entrants to set up their own distribution networks.

machines'; by modifying the vertical arrangements proposed to his retailers, a producer simply commits himself to respond in a given way to any change of his rivals' attitudes. Of course if all possible 'response machines' were available, complete collusion would then be achievable (see Katz, 1987); the question therefore is to define the admissible 'black boxes'. In this respect, vertical restraints can be viewed as a natural tool for constructing more efficient response machines, i.e., response machines which enable the producers to decrease competition at their level. For instance, in the previous model, producers could modify the design of territories in order to decrease as much as possible the elasticity of the perceived demand; or they could give the right to sell their products to the same retailers (common agency), or distribute their products via wholesalers, who in turn could assign exclusive territories to retailers, etc. In other contexts, depending on observability and enforceability conditions, different vertical restraints might also be introduced to extend the set of available 'response machines'.

This analysis sheds new lights on the economic effect of the use of vertical restraints on market performance and social welfare. Until now, two extreme situations were mainly considered: the first one refers to perfectly competitive markets, where only efficiency arguments can explain the use of these restraints; the second situation corresponds to the case of a monopolistic producer and, although private and social interests may conflict, at least from the private point of view efficiency arguments may still, to some extent, be relevant. But if one considers a situation where there is imperfect competition at the upper level (which is generally true in most famous cases involving the use of vertical restraints), then a new motivation appears: vertical restraints may be used only to decrease competition between producers; this usually has a negative impact on social welfare, the gain in additional profits being overwhelmed by the loss of consumers' surplus. Of course the above analysis is very partial; it suggests, however, a new approach for the economic theory of vertical restraints.

References

Bernheim, B.D. and M.D. Whinston (1985), 'Common marketing agency as a device for facilitating collusion', *Rand Journal of Economics*, 16, 269–81.
    (1986), 'Common agency', *Econometrica*, 54, 923–42.
Blair, R. and D. Kaserman (1983), *Law and Economics of Vertical Integration and Control*, New York, Academic Press.
Bonanno, G. and J. Vickers (1988), 'Vertical separation', *Journal of Industrial Economics*, 36, 257–65.
Caillaud, B. and P. Rey (1987), 'A note on vertical restraints with provision of distribution services, INSEE Discussion Paper 8702.
Caves, R. (1984), 'Vertical restraints in manufacturer distributor relations: incidence and economic effects', mimeo, Harvard University.
Comanor, W.S. (1985), 'Vertical price fixing and market restrictions and the new antitrust policy', *Harvard Law Review*, 98, 983–1002.
Fershtman, C. and K.L. Judd (1984), 'Incentives equilibrium in oligopoly', CSMEMS Working Paper 642, Northwestern University.

(1986), 'Strategic incentive manipulation in rivalrous agency', mimeo.

Katz, M. (1987), 'Game-playing agents: contracts as precommitments', Princeton University Discussion Paper.

Mathewson, G.F. and R. Winter (1983), 'The economics of vertical restraints in distribution', in J.E. Stiglitz and G.F. Mathewson (eds.), *New Developments in the Analysis of Market Structure*, New York, Macmillan.

(1984), 'An economic theory of vertical restraints', *Rand Journal of Economics*, 15, 27–38.

Posner, R. (1977), 'The rule of reason and the economic approach: reflections on the Sylvania decision', *University of Chicago Law Review*, 45, 1–20.

Rey, P. and J. Stiglitz (1985), 'The role of exclusive territories on producers' competition', mimeo, revised version July 1987.

Rey, P. and J. Tirole (1986a), 'Vertical restraints from a principal-agent viewpoint', in L. Pellegrini and S.K. Reddy (eds.), *Marketing Channels*, Lexington MA, Lexington Books, pp. 3–30.

(1986b), 'The logic of vertical restraints', *American Economic Review*, 76, 921–39.

Scherer, F.M. (1983), 'The economics of vertical restraints', *Antitrust Law Journal*, 52, 687–707.

Spengler, J. (1950), 'Vertical integration and anti-trust policy', *Journal of Political Economy*, 58, 347–52.

Telser, L. (1960), 'Why should manufacturers want fair trade?', *Journal of Law and Economics*, 3, 86–105.

Chapter 10

Price discrimination in a common market
International price discrimination in
the European car market

Frank Verboven

1   Introduction

Large differences in car prices across countries have been a persistent phenomenon in
Europe. A series of studies by the European Bureau of Consumers Unions, BEUC
(1981, 1986, 1989, 1992), shows that pretax prices for identical car models may vary
by over 90 per cent across countries. Mertens and Ginsburgh (1985) construct a
quality-adjusted price index for the whole industry and find that the general pretax
price level in Belgium, France, Germany, Italy, and the United Kingdom varies by up
to 30 per cent. Although the price differences have somewhat diminished during the
past decade (Ginsburgh and Vanhamme, 1989; Mertens, 1990), they remain quite
large, and they are not likely to disappear in the near future. Flam (1992) reports that
current pretax price differences of 90 per cent for identical car models are still no
exception. The question arises why profit-maximizing firms find such large price
differences desirable. Do car producers face different costs of operating in the various

This article first appeared in the *RAND Journal of Economics*, 1996, vol. 27, pp. 240–68.
An earlier version of this article was part of my Ph.D. dissertation at the University of Toronto. I am
grateful to Mel Fuss, Nancy Gallini, Yahuda Kotowitz, and Angelo Melino from the University of
Toronto, to Steve Berry, Victor Ginsburgh, Penny Goldberg, Shane Greenstein, Arie Kapteyn, and
Jim Levinsohn, and to participants at various seminars. Further thanks go to FEBIAC (Brussels) and
CCFA (Paris) for allowing access to their libraries, and to Patrick Van Cayseele and the Centrum
voor Economische Studiën at the K.U. Leuven for providing research facilities during the summer of
1993. The current version benefited from the careful and detailed comments of an editor and two
referees.

markets? Or, alternatively, do firms charge different markups in different countries and engage in international price discrimination?

To address these questions, I construct and estimate an oligopoly model that captures the essential determinants of pricing behaviour in the European car market. I consider multi-product price-setting firms, selling differentiated products in geographically segmented markets with import quota constraints. The resulting equilibrium pricing equations reveal that the price of each car model in each market equals its marginal cost plus a markup over marginal cost. Price differences across countries may follow either from cost differences or from differences in markups. Markups depend on three factors: the price elasticities implied by the demand model of product differentiation, the possible presence of an import quota against the selling firm, and the possible presence of collusive behaviour. These three determinants of markups are at the same time, then, three possible sources for international price discrimination.

I have estimated the model with product-level data using an econometrically tractable method recently proposed by Berry (1994). Several modifications of Berry's method were required to take into account the specific characteristics of the European car market.[1] The data include the prices, sales, and physical characteristics of (almost) all car models sold in 1990 in five European countries: Belgium, France, Germany, Italy, and the United Kingdom. The data reveal that international price discrimination accounts for an important part of the observed price differences in the European car market. First of all, the estimated price elasticities imply that there are substantial cross-country differences in domestic market power. The domestic firms in France, Germany, the United Kingdom, and especially in Italy tend to face much lower price elasticities than the foreign firms. Furthermore, the import quota constraints on Japanese cars are binding in France and Italy. Finally, the possibility of collusion in Germany and the United Kingdom cannot be rejected.

Although the presence of large pretax price differences across countries in the European car market has become well documented, there have been virtually no formal attempts to systematically explain these differences. In their conclusion, Mertens and Ginsburgh (1985) and Flam and Nordstrom (1994) informally conjecture that differences in domestic market power are important, based on their observation of significant cross-country differences in concentration. In reduced-form models, de Melo and Messerlin (1988), Gual (1993), and Flam and Nordstrom (1994) find that import quota constraints influence price differences.[2] Kirman and Schueller (1990) emphasize the role of cost differences in explaining the observed price differences. All these potential explanations are here systematically incorporated in a structural oligopoly model of pricing behaviour. The estimated structural parameters make it

---

[1] Berry (1994) considered single-product firms in a simpler model of product differentiation without import quota constraints. Potentially more realistic, but computationally burdensome, models of product differentiation have been developed by Feenstra and Levinsohn (1995) and Berry, Levinsohn, and Pakes (1995).

[2] Gual (1993) and Flam and Nordstrom (1994) also show the importance of tariffs to explain price differences. In the present article, I consider only countries in which tariffs are absent.

possible to quantify the importance of international price discrimination through the computation of the implied markups.

In section 2, I analyse the presence of car price differences across countries in 1990, and discuss some essential structural characteristics that may influence pricing in the European car market. Section 3 develops the formal oligopoly model to be taken to the data. Section 4 discusses the econometric methods and the data. Section 5 provides and interprets the empirical results. Conclusions and suggested extensions follow in section 6.

2   A first look at the European car market

In 1990, the total number of new car registrations in the 12 countries of the European Community (now European Union) was approximately 12.1 million, compared with 9.2 million in the United States and 5.1 million in Japan. The number of car registrations in the five countries studied in this article, Belgium, France, Germany, Italy, and the United Kingdom, was 10.2 million, covering about 84 per cent of all new car registrations in the EC.

Price differences across national markets

The presence of car price differences across the various countries in the EC has become well documented since the early 1980s. One of the first studies was done by BEUC (1981), the European Bureau of Consumers Unions. BEUC showed that prices of identical car models may vary by over 90 per cent across countries. These findings were confirmed in subsequent studies: BEUC (1986, 1989, 1992), Monopolies and Mergers Commission (1992), and Commission of the European Communities (1992). For each car model available in the five studied European countries, figure 10.1 plots the average pretax price over the five countries (in ECUs) against the maximum percentage price difference and the standard deviation of the price differences. This plot illustrates the presence of large price differences for identical models across countries in 1990. To analyse whether there are also systematic price differences across markets, a 'hedonic' price index may be constructed. This is a price index that adjusts for 'quality' differences as measured by the observed physical characteristics. Griliches (1971), for example, constructed such an index to study quality-adjusted price changes over time in the American car market. More related to the present study, Mertens and Ginsburgh (1985), Ginsburgh and Vanhamme (1989) and Mertens (1990) have constructed hedonic price indices to compare the quality adjusted car price level across several European countries.

To construct a hedonic price index, assume that the price of a car j in market m, p_{jm} is a function of its observed physical characteristics, a vector w_{jm}. Conforming to previous studies, assume the following functional form:

$$p_{jm}/(1 + t_m) = \exp(w_{jm}\gamma + \omega_m + \omega_{jm}) \tag{1}$$

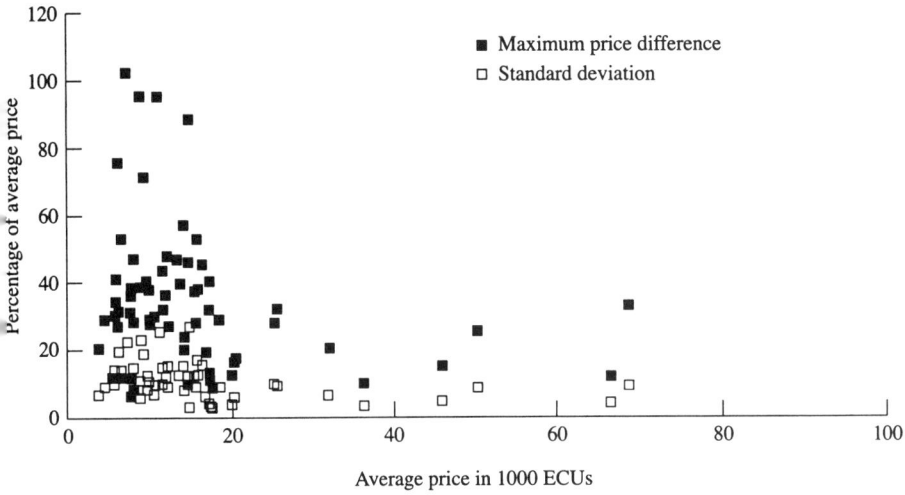

Figure 10.1 Cross-country price differences

where ω_{jm} is an econometric error term. The term ω_m is a fixed effect capturing the market-specific part of car prices that cannot be attributed to the observed physical characteristics, w_{jm}. Equation (1) is estimated as a simple ordinary least-squares regression. The price $p_{jm}/(1 + t_m)$ of car j in market m is the consumer list price before taxes, converted into ECUs. The vector of physical characteristics, w_{jm}, consists of the technical characteristics: horsepower, weight, width and height, and a set of country-of-origin dummy variables identifying French, German, Italian, UK, US, and Japanese cars from 'other' (mainly East European) cars. The variables are discussed in more detail in the data section below.

The market-specific fixed effects, the ω_m, are estimated using dummy variables with Belgium as the reference country. The ω_m are then used to construct the hedonic price index, where the index number for market m, p_m, is given by the formula, $p_m = \exp(\omega_m)$. The obtained hedonic price index is presented in table 10.1. It shows that pretax prices in 1990 for cars with identical physical characteristics differ systematically across countries. They are significantly higher in Germany, and especially so in Italy and the United Kingdom, than in Belgium and France. This ranking is roughly consistent with the previous hedonic studies mentioned above. Note that the ranking does not seriously change if dealer discounts are taken into account. Including maximum discounts, as given in table 10.1, reduces the estimate of the fixed effect for the United Kingdom by 4 per cent, and increases the fixed effects of the other countries by 1 per cent to 3 per cent, relative to Belgium. The robustness with respect to discounts is consistent with the studies by BEUC, the Monopolies and Mergers Commission, and the EC Commission.

Table 10.1 *Characteristics of the European car market in 1990*

	Belgium	France	Germany	Italy	United Kingdom
Pretax hedonic list price index	100	105	110	116	120
Value-added taxes (in %)[a]	25	25	14	19	24.6
One-year exchange rate change (in %)[b]	1.7	1.0	0.3	-1.3	-6.2
Five-year exchange rate change (in %)[b]	6.3	-1.4	8.9	-4.6	-17.3
Maximum dealer discounts (in %)[c]	11	8	10	10	15
Average dealer margin (range in %)[d]	12–16	N/A	16–19	14–17	16–18
Dealer margin, Opel Astra (in %)[e]	14	14.5	16	16	17
Total sales (in 1,000 units)	473.5	2,309.1	3,040.8	2,348.2	2,008.9
Parallel imports (range in 1,000 units)[f]	N/A	30–40	25–35	70–80	1–2.5
C1-concentration ratio (in %)	15.9	33.1	25.6	52.4	25/3
C4-concentration ratio (in %)	53.0	76.1	61.1	77.9	64.5
C7-concentration ratio (in %)	72.9	90.0	76.7	91.8	79.0
Domestic market share (in %)		60.8	67.7	52.4	55.9
Japanese market share, actual (in %)	20.0	3.3	15.9	1.9	11.5
Japanese market share, quota (in %)[g]		3.0	15.0	1.1	11.0

Notes: [a] In Belgium, 33% for cars over 3000cc. In Italy, 38% for cars over 2000cc. UK figure includes 17.5% value-added tax plus a car tax equal to 10% of 5/6 of the factory price. French tax applies since September 1989; before it was 28%.
[b] Relative to the ECU (European currency unit).
[c] Based on interviews by BEUC (1989), estimates for 1989. Roughly consistent with Monopolies and Mergers Commission (1992).
[d] Based on unpublished interviews in 1991 by CECRA, the European Committee for Motor Trades and Repairs (Brussels). Sales weighted minimum and maximum dealer margins on PSA, Fiat, Ford, GM, Rover, and VW cars.
[e] Monopolies and Mergers Commission (1992).
[f] Based on industry sources, collected by BEUC (1989), estimates for 1989. Belgian parallel imports reported to be 'small' (mainly some German luxury cars).
[g] Based on Commission of the European Communities (1992). France, Germany, and the United Kingdom: 'voluntary' percentage import constraint. Italy: absolute quota constraint under 1%. Belgium: no import quota.

Geographical market segmentation

The observed cross-country price differences may follow either from systematic differences in the marginal cost of operating in the various markets or from systematic differences in markups, i.e., international price discrimination. A necessary condition for the presence of international price discrimination is the presence of arbitrage costs leading to geographical market segmentation. In the absence of arbitrage costs, consumers would exploit all cross-country differences in markups and buy cars in one country to resell them in another. Several factors do, in fact, contribute to substantial arbitrage costs associated with crossborder trade, leading to geographical market segmentation.

The distribution of cars in the EC falls under Regulation 123/85, which is a block exemption from Article 85(1) of the Treaty of Rome. This regulation was in force from 1985 to 1995 and has recently been extended for another ten years. It authorizes a selective and exclusive distribution system for new cars sold within the EC. This system aims to restrict sales of new cars in the EC to dealers chosen by the manufacturers. As a result, it becomes very difficult for independent wholesalers to buy cars in bulk in one country and resell them in another.[3] Although Regulation 123/85 only authorizes the selective and exclusive distribution of cars on the condition that there are no 'excessive' price differences across the markets,[4] this condition has never been enforced in practice. Furthermore, while final consumers in principle have the freedom to purchase their own cars abroad, they encounter considerable legal, administrative, and other obstacles in cross-border purchases. One such obstacle is the requirement of national approval of the imported model. Differences in national standards for safety and environmental reasons often make costly modifications or certification fees necessary.[5] Another obstacle, for the United Kingdom, is the need for right-hand-drive cars. A detailed discussion of various other (administrative) consumer obstacles is provided by BEUC (1992). This discussion then indicates that there are indeed various cross-border arbitrage costs, leading to geographical market segmentation.

The degree of geographical market segmentation is illustrated in table 10.1 by the level of parallel imports, i.e., the goods imported by unauthorized resellers (as defined by Malueg and Schwartz, 1994). Table 10.1 shows that the level of parallel imports is usually small, relative to the total number of new car registrations in the various markets. The highest level of parallel imports is in Italy, but even here parallel imports are only about 3 per cent of the total number of new car registrations. The low level of parallel imports, despite the high cross-country price differences established above, may be viewed as evidence reinforcing the theoretical arguments given for the presence of geographical market segmentation. International price discrimination cannot then

---

[3] Since the release of a Communication by the EC Commission in 1991, independent wholesalers can engage in cross-border purchases. However, they remain subject to quantitative and other restrictions. See BEUC (1992) for details.

[4] For unspecified reasons, an original specification that price differences should not be more than 12 per cent was later removed. See BEUC (1992) or Davidson *et al.* (1989).

[5] Since 1993, the European Commission has agreed upon a uniform set of technical requirements.

be ruled out as a potential explanation for the observed price differences in the EC car market.

Concentration and international penetration

A relatively large number of firms are present in the European car market, suggesting a relatively competitive environment. However, given the high degree of geographical market segmentation, it is more appropriate to consider the number of large firms per country separately. This reveals a rather different picture. In most countries only a few large firms are present. This is illustrated in table 10.1 by the Cl, C4, and C7 concentration ratios, measuring the market shares of the single largest, the four largest, and the seven largest firms. Compared with Belgium, these concentration ratios are high for Germany and the United Kingdom and especially high for France and Italy.

Furthermore, different firms are present in different markets. Except for Belgium, all countries have large domestic producers: Italy has Fiat (owning Fiat, Alfa Romeo, and Lancia); France has PSA (owning Peugeot and Citroen) and Renault; Germany has VW (owning Volkswagen and Audi), GM (owning Opel), Ford, Mercedes, and BMW; and the United Kingdom has Rover (owning Austin and Rover), Ford, and GM (owning Vauxhall).[6] Table 10.1 reveals correspondingly large domestic market shares in these countries.

Finally, the non-European firms, consisting mainly of Japanese firms (Honda, Mazda, Mitsubishi, Nissan, Toyota), are present to different degrees in the various countries. The Japanese firms have a large market share in Belgium, a significant market share in Germany and the United Kingdom, and a small market share in France and Italy. The Japanese firms' market share is related to the market share implied by the import quotas. In France and Italy, with very strict import quotas, the Japanese firms' market share significantly exceeds the import quota levels, which is probably due to parallel imports. In Germany and the United Kingdom, with milder 'voluntary' export restraints, the Japanese firms' market share only slightly exceeds the quotas.[7]

It is tempting to relate these structural properties of the various national markets to the observed systematic cross-country price differences, as measured by the hedonic (pretax) price index. In Belgium, the low concentration and high international penetration suggest intense competition and low markups. Correspondingly, the price level is relatively low. The other markets, Germany, the United Kingdom, and especially France and Italy, are substantially more concentrated, and they experience less competition from foreign European and non-European producers. This is reflected in a higher price index for France, Germany,· Italy, and the United Kingdom. The

---

[6] The definition of domestic firms includes the transplants of multi-nationals, i.e., Ford and GM in Germany and the United Kingdom.

[7] Note that there is actual disagreement about whether import quota constraints exist in Germany. Commission of the European Communities (1992) states that the 15 per cent voluntary export restraint in Germany is fiercely denied by the German industry.

relatively low price level in France, despite its concentrated and protected market structure, is puzzling. A more important puzzle is the very high price level in the United Kingdom, compared with France and Germany with a similar market structure, and compared with Italy with a more concentrated and protected market structure.

Perhaps cost-side elements should be taken into account to understand the price differences more completely. Tax differences are already incorporated. In some countries firms may face an unobserved extra marginal cost, for example due to the obligated use of catalytic converters and the included roadside assistance in Germany or the United Kingdom. In addition, in some countries the price level (measured in ECUs) may reflect the incomplete pass-through of past exchange rate fluctuations.[8] However, given the depreciation of the pound over the last few years, incomplete exchange rate pass-through would imply a reduction of the ECU price level in the United Kingdom.[9]

Finally, in some countries firms may pay out higher dealer markups, which are usually calculated as a percentage on the pretax consumer list price. Complete data on the dealer markups are not available. There is, however, a common industry wisdom (present in most studies cited above) that dealer markups are especially high in the United Kingdom. This is illustrated in table 10.1 by the average minimum and maximum dealer markups of a selected set of firms, and by the dealer markup of the Astra, a car model from GM that has a significant market share in most countries. Another indicator of differences in dealer markups across countries is the maximum discount on the consumer list price allowed by the dealers (table 10.1). All other things being equal, high maximum discounts indicate that manufacturers set high consumer list prices allowing for (artificially) high percentage dealer markups.[10]

Mertens and Ginsburgh (1985) also make attempts to relate the observed price differences, as measured by the hedonic price index, to the structural characteristics of the European car market. However, they conclude their article with the following warning (p. 165):

Clearly a careful study of the various price elasticities in these countries would help in interpreting the results, as would a deeper analysis of product differentiation. The paper does not examine whether price differentials originate in deliberate international producer discrimination policies, or whether this situation is the consequence of collusion among local dealers.

What is needed to more fully understand the observed price differences in the EC is a systematic model that explicitly considers the pricing decisions of the car manufacturers.

---

[8] Incomplete exchange-rate pass-through, or local currency price stability, may follow from the presence of imperfect competition (price elasticities) or, in a dynamic setting, adjustment costs (see, e.g., Knetter (1993) and the references therein).

[9] The hedonic study by Ginsburgh and Vanhamme (1989) indicates that this is indeed the case. Hence, before 1990 prices in the United Kingdom were even higher.

[10] This practice may be the case in the United Kingdom, and could follow from the fact that the country has a high proportion of fleet sales, about 34 per cent of total sales, according to Monopolies and Mergers Commission (1992).

3   An oligopoly model for the EC car market

Rosen (1974) considers a perfectly competitive model with price-taking firms, showing that the hedonic pricing equation (1) may be interpreted as a marginal cost function. According to this competitive interpretation, the estimated fixed effects (the ω_m) would indicate that the marginal costs of operating were the lowest in Belgium and France, and significantly higher in Germany and especially in Italy and the United Kingdom. Kirman and Schueller (1990) argue that substantial cost differences between countries do indeed exist. However, an explanation that is based solely on cost differences is at least suspect. The above description of the EC car market, with its geographical market segmentation and cross-country differences in concentration and international penetration, suggests that firms may be charging different markups in the various countries, engaging in international price discrimination. To system-atically investigate this possibility, I use the above information on the EC car market to develop a realistic yet econometrically tractable oligopoly model, covering the competitive interpretation of the hedonic pricing equation as a special case. The oligopoly model allows one to empirically investigate whether the data support a pure cost-side interpretation of the observed car price differences in the EC, or whether in addition international price discrimination is present. The model distinguishes three possible sources of international price discrimination: cross-country differences in price elasticities, import quota restrictions, and collusive behaviour.

Pricing

There are F multi-product firms operating in M national markets. In each market m a firm f sells a subset, F_{fm} of the J_m car models sold in the market m. The sales of a typical car j in market m, $q_{jm}(p_m)$ are a function of the consumer price vector in market m, $p_m = (p_{1m}, ..., p_{j_m m})$ and not of the price vectors in the other markets.[11] This is based on the assumption of prohibitive arbitrage costs to consumers. Prices are in a common currency, e.g., the ECU. Because a single cross section (for the year 1990) is used, it is not possible to take into account exchange rate fluctuations over time and their possible incomplete pass-through to consumers, as in, e.g., Knetter (1993). The total cost of producing a typical car j, $C_j = (q_{j1}(p_1), ..., q_{jm}(p_m))$, is a function of the sales of car j in the M markets. Firm f's profit is

$$\Pi_f = \sum_{m=1}^{M} \sum_{j \in F_{fm}} p_{jm}^w q_{jm}(p_m) - \sum_{j \in F_{fm}} C_j(q_{j1}(p_1), ..., q_{jM}(p_M)) \tag{2}$$

where p_{jm}^w is the wholesale price of a car j in market m received by the firm. The firm's wholesale price, p_{jm}^w, may differ from the consumer price, p_{jm}, because of value-added taxes imposed by the governments or because of dealer markups. The specific relation-

---

[11] A related model of multi-market oligopoly with geographical market segmentation is by Bulow, Geanakoplos, and Klemperer (1985).

ship between p_{jm}^w and p_{jm} is modelled as an exogenous relationship. The possible strategic interdependence between firms, dealers, and governments is thus ignored, conforming to most previous empirical studies.[12] The focus is instead on the interdependence among firms themselves.

Firms set the prices of their differentiated products to maximize profit. The assumption of price-setting behaviour in the car market is common and consistent with industry wisdom, see, e.g., the discussion of pricing practices by the UK Monopolies and Mergers Commission Report (1992).[13] Some firms are not subject to an import quota while other firms are. A firm that is not subject to an import quota simply chooses a wholesale price, p_{jm}^w, for every car it markets to maximize its profit, given the prices set by its competitors. A firm that is subject to an import quota solves a constrained profit-maximization problem. In some markets (e.g., in Italy) the constraint specifies that the firm's demand cannot exceed a certain absolute level D_{fm}, i.e., $D_{fm} \geq \sum_{j \in F_{jm}} q_{jm}(p_m)$. In other markets (e.g., in France, Germany and the United Kingdom) the constraint specifies that the firm's demand cannot exceed a certain percentage of total market demand d_{fm}, i.e., $d_{fm} \geq \sum_{j \in F_{jm}} q_{jm}(p_m) / \sum_{j=1}^{J_m} q_{jm}(p_m)$. Solving the firms' profit-maximization problem generates the following first-order condition for a car j in market m, owned by firm f:

$$\sum_{k \in F_{jm}} \left(p_{km}^w - \frac{\partial C_k}{\partial q_{km}} - \lambda_{fm}^a \right) \frac{\partial q_{km}}{\partial p_{jm}^w} + q_{jm} = 0 \tag{3a}$$

and

$$\sum_{k \in F_{jm}} \left(p_{km}^w - \frac{\partial C_k}{\partial q_{km}} - \frac{\lambda_{fm}^r}{Q_m} \right) \frac{\partial q_{km}}{\partial p_{jm}^w} + \frac{\lambda_{fm}^r}{Q_m} \frac{Q_{fm}}{Q_m} \sum_{k=1}^{J_m} \frac{\partial q_{km}}{\partial p_{jm}^w} + q_{jm} = 0 \tag{3b}$$

where $Q_m \equiv \sum_{j=1}^{J_m} q_{jm}$, and $Q_{fm} \equiv \sum_{j \in F_{jm}} q_{jm}$. Equation (3a) represents markets with an absolute import quota, and (3b) represents markets with a percentage import quota. In choosing an optimal price for car j in market m, firm f takes into account its effect not only on the sales of the car j itself, through $\partial q_{jm}/\partial p_{jm}^w$, but also on the sales of the other cars it owns in market m, through the $\partial q_{km}/\partial p_{jm}^w$. If firm f is subject to an import quota, it also takes this into account: the λ_{fm}^a and λ_{fm}^r are defined as firm-specific variables equal to zero if the firm is not subject to a quota and equal to the respective Lagrange multipliers if the firm is subject to an absolute or a percentage import quota. The larger the Lagrange multiplier, the more binding is the import quota for the firm subject to the quota.

Taken together, there are $J = \sum_{m=1}^{J_m} J_m$ first-order conditions, constituting a Bertrand–Nash equilibrium. Caplin and Nalebuff (1991) have shown the existence of a pure-strategy Nash equilibrium in a fairly general demand model, assuming single-

---

[12] One exception is the study by Bresnahan and Reiss (1985), who develop and estimate a successive monopoly model.

[13] See Feenstra and Levinsohn (1995) for an empirical approach in which Cournot behaviour is also allowed for.

product firms and ignoring import quota constraints. Results from Anderson and de Palma (1992) indicate that for the specific demand model to be developed below, the existence result probably generalizes to multi-product firms. It is not so clear whether the existence result also generalizes to markets with import quota constraints. Krishna (1989) develops a model with import quotas in which a pure-strategy equilibrium fails to exist due to a discontinuity in the reaction functions. I will here follow the approach taken in Goldberg (1995) and simply assume that a pure-strategy Nash equilibrium exists.

The J first-order conditions (3a) and (3b) can be transformed to obtain J pricing equations, decomposing the price of a car j in market m into its marginal cost and a markup over marginal cost. To see this, define, for each market m, a J_m-by-J_m matrix, $\mathbf{\Delta}_m$ with a typical element $\Delta_{jkm} = -\partial q_{km}/\partial p_{jm}^w$ if k and j are produced by the same firm, and $\Delta_{jkm} = 0$ otherwise. Similarly, define $\mathbf{q}_m$ as a J_m-by-1 vector with typical element q_{jm}, and $\mathbf{q}_m^r$ as a J_m-by-1 vector with typical element $q_{jm} + (\lambda_{fm}^r/Q_m)(Q_{fm}/Q_m)$ $\sum_{k=1}^{J_m} \partial q_{km}/\partial p_{jm}^w$. It is then possible, for each market m, to write the system of j_m first-order conditions in vector notation and rearrange by pre-multiplying by the J_m-by-J_m matrix, $\mathbf{\Delta}_m^{-1}$ the inverse of $\mathbf{\Delta}_m$. This yields the following for each car j in market m:

$$p_{jm}^w = \frac{\partial C_j}{\partial q_{jm}} + \mathbf{\Delta}_{jm}^{-1}\mathbf{q}_m + \lambda_{fm}^a \tag{4a}$$

and

$$p_{jm}^w = \frac{\partial C_j}{\partial q_{jm}} + \mathbf{\Delta}_{jm}^{-1}\mathbf{q}_m^r + \frac{\lambda_{fm}^r}{Q_m} \tag{4b}$$

where $\mathbf{\Delta}_{jm}^{-1}$ is the jth 1-by-J row of $\mathbf{\Delta}_m^{-1}$. Equation (4a) represents markets with an absolute import quota, and (4b) represents markets with a percentage import quota.

The pricing equations (4a) and (4b) reveal that the equilibrium price of each car j in market m is separable into two components: its marginal cost and a markup over marginal cost. Both cost differences and markup differences may in principle be responsible for price differences across car models and across markets. To the extent that price differences across markets come from differences in markups, there is international price discrimination. The markups reveal that there are at least two sources of international price discrimination. First, there may be cross-country differences in price elasticities. Markups are inversely related to the firms' perceived price elasticities of demand, entering through the set of own- and cross-demand derivatives in $\mathbf{\Delta}_{jm}^{-1}$.[14] Second, there may be differences in import quota constraints, entering through the Lagrange multipliers λ_{fm}^a and λ_{fm}^r. A third source for international price discrimination can easily be incorporated in the developed framework: differences in collusive behaviour. Collusion may be modelled as the joint-profit maximization of a coalition of firms. The set F_{fm} determining which cross-demand

---

[14] In the standard single-product firm case, a car's relative markup simply equals the inverse of its own price elasticity of demand. In the case of multi-product firms, a car's relative markup equals the inverse of some measure of the firm's perceived price elasticity of demand.

derivatives enter in Δ_{jm}^{-1}, may accordingly be reinterpreted as the set of cars involved in a collusive coalition f in market m. It is then possible to model different coalitions in different markets by appropriately defining the sets F_{fm}.

Functional forms

I discuss the functional form of both components of the pricing equation, marginal cost and markup, in turn. An introductory remark applies. I restrict most parameters to be the same across markets, except for the 'fixed effects' that allow the constants to vary across markets. These cross-market restrictions make it possible to pool the data, and they facilitate the estimation.

The functional form of the marginal cost in equation (4) is

$$\frac{\partial C_j}{\partial q_{jm}} = \exp(w_{jm}\gamma_w + \gamma_q \ln Q_j + \omega_m + \omega_{jm}) \tag{5}$$

where w_{jm} is a vector of physical characteristics of car j in market m. The variable $Q_j = \sum_{m+1}^{M} q_{jm}$ the total (world) sales of a car j in all M markets, indicates whether marginal costs are increasing, constant, or decreasing in outputs.[15] The error term, ω_{jm} has the economic interpretation of capturing unobserved (to the econometrician) car characteristics that influence the marginal cost of car j in market m. Similarly, the fixed effect ω_m captures unobserved characteristics that systematically influence the marginal cost of all cars operating in market m. This may follow from, for example, unobserved national differences in cost-increasing regulations, such as the required use of catalytic converters in Germany. Note that when markups approach zero due to perfect competition, and when $\gamma_q = 0$, the pricing equation reduces to the simple hedonic specification (1).

The specific relationship between the firm's wholesale price, p_{jm}^w and the consumer (list) price, p_{jm}, takes the following functional form:

$$p_{jm}^w = p_{jm}/[(1 + t_m)(1 + \tau_m)] \tag{6}$$

i.e., the firm's wholesale price, p_{jm}^w is a fraction of the consumer (list) price, p_{jm}. The variable t_m captures the observable percentage deviations of p_{jm}^w from p_{jm}, such as value-added taxes.[16] The variable τ_m is a fixed effect capturing the unobservable (to the econometrician), market-average percentage deviations of p_{jm}^w from p_{jm}, in particular dealer markups.[17] The interpretation of τ_m as unobserved market-specific

---

[15] There is a theoretical problem in formulating a functional form that captures decreasing/increasing marginal cost as a function of world output. A typical car model has different specifications in different markets. World output should influence only the marginal cost of the 'base model', i.e., the minimum specification of the model in all markets. For simplicity, I ignored this problem and simply assumed specification (5), as it would be if a car model has the same specification in all markets.

[16] This specification is for notational simplicity. In the actual estimation I allow taxes to differ across cars in the same market, i.e., t_{jm} which is the case for a few models in Belgium and Italy.

[17] This specification would easily generalize to allow for firm-specific effects, i.e., τ_{fm}. However, estimation would then use up too many degrees of freedom.

dealer markups will often be used below. It is consistent with a standard practice by the car manufacturers in the EC. Indeed, as discussed in Monopolies and Mergers Commission (1992), the dealer markups are usually calculated as a percentage on the pretax consumer list price $p_{jm}/(1 + t_m)$.

The functional forms of the own-demand derivatives $\partial q_{jm}/\partial p_{jm}$ and the cross-demand derivatives $\partial q_{km}/\partial p_{jm}$ appearing in the pricing equation through Δ_{jm}^{-1} are derived from a version of the nested logit model. This model of product differentiation aims to capture the essential characteristics of the demand side of the European car market, while remaining econometrically tractable. There are L_m potential consumers located in market m, with prohibitive arbitrage costs of travelling to another market. These consumers either buy one of the J_m car models available in market m, or they buy an 'outside good'. The set of car models available in a market m is partitioned into $G_m + 1$ groups, $g = 0, ..., G_m$ where group 0 is reserved for the outside good. Each group $g = 1, ..., G_m$ is further partitioned in H_{gm} subgroups, $h = 1, ..., H_{gm}$. The cars belonging to the same group have in common one discretely measured characteristic, such as 'class'. The cars belonging to the same subgroup have in common a second discretely measured characteristic, such as country of origin. The nested logit model allows an individual's preferences for a car j in market m to be correlated with other cars from the same subgroup or group. This generates aggregate demand functions with relatively plausible and still econometrically tractable substitution patterns, allowing for the possibility of localized competition between cars from the same subgroup or group. Berry (1994) develops a simplified version of the nested logit model in an oligopoly context. Berry, Levinsohn, and Pakes (1995) develop a more sophisticated but computationally burdensome model. They essentially allow an individual's preferences for a car j in a market m to be correlated with other cars having similar continuously measured characteristics, rather than with other cars sharing the same discretely measured characteristics. Goldberg (1995) adopts a version of the nested logit model using micro-data (at the household level). This also generates some extra flexibility on the demand functions. Nevertheless, as shown below, the nested logit model in the present article is already flexible enough to capture the presence of international price discrimination based on cross-country differences in price elasticities.

As derived in more detail in the appendix, the specific functional form of the aggregate demand for a car j in market m, belonging to a subgroup h of a group g, is given by

$$q_{jm} = \frac{e^{\delta_{jm}/(1-\sigma_1)}}{e^{I_{hgm}/(1-\sigma_1)}} \frac{e^{I_{hgm}/(1-\sigma_2)}}{e^{I_{gm}/(1-\sigma_2)}} \frac{e^{I_{gm}}}{\sum\limits_{g=1}^{G_m} e^{I_{gm}}} L_m \tag{7}$$

where L_m is the number of potential consumers located in market m, I_{hgm} and I_{gm} are 'inclusive values' defined as

$$I_{hgm} \equiv (1 - \sigma_1)\ln \sum\limits_{l \in V_{ghm}} e^{\delta_{lm}/(1-\sigma_1)}, \qquad I_{gm} \equiv (1 - \sigma_1)\ln \sum\limits_{h \in V_{gm}} e^{I_{hgm}/(1-\sigma_2)} \tag{8}$$

and where V_{hgm} is the set of cars in subgroup h of group g in market m, and V_{gm} is the set of subgroups in group g of market m. The variable δ_{jm} measures the 'mean utility' from consuming car j in market m, i.e., the part of utility that is common to all individuals. Let δ_{jm} be a function of a vector of physical characteristics, x_{jm} and price p_{jm} as follows

$$\delta_{jm} = x_{jm}\beta - \alpha \frac{(p_{jm})^{\mu} - 1}{\mu} + \xi_m + \xi_{jm} \qquad (9)$$

where ξ_m is a market-specific fixed effect, and ξ_{jm} is an error term capturing unobserved characteristics influencing δ_{jm}. Using the demand equation (7), the demand derivatives for each car j in market m can now be calculated (see the appendix) and substituted into pricing equation (4).

The nested logit model generates several testable hypotheses that may be taken to the data. As shown by McFadden (1978), the nested logit model is consistent with random-utility maximization for $0 \leq \sigma_2 \leq \sigma_1 \leq 1$. If both σ_1 and σ_2 are zero, an individual's preferences are uncorrelated across all cars sold in market m, resulting in the simple logit model with symmetric (non-localized) competition across cars in market m. If only σ_1 is positive and σ_2 is zero, individual preferences are only correlated across cars from the same subgroup, resulting in localized competition between cars from the same subgroup. If in σ_2 addition is positive, individual preferences are also correlated across cars from a different subgroup within the same group. If σ_2 approaches σ_1, preferences are equally correlated across all cars belonging to the same group.[18] Anticipating the results below, the data will favour a specification in which groups are defined by class (mini and small, medium, large, executive, luxury, and sports), and subgroups are defined by country of origin (domestic versus foreign cars) within a given class. The estimates will reveal a particularly strong correlation of preferences for cars from the same country of origin within a given class. The resulting strong localized competition will be reflected in the presence of strong domestic market power.

4   Econometric considerations and data

The model to be estimated consists of pricing equation (4) and demand equation (7), with the appropriate substitutions using (5), (6), (8), and (9). I estimated the model using the non-linear three-stage least-squares estimator (NL3SLS) of Gallant and Jorgenson (1979). This is an estimator for a system of simultaneous, non-linear, implicit equations. In particular, the NL3SLS estimator allows the error terms, ω_{jm} and ξ_{jm} to be correlated. Such a correlation may be expected given that unobserved physical characteristics may influence both marginal cost and demand. Furthermore, the NL3SLS estimator takes into account the possible endogeneity of variables such as sales and prices, q_{jm} and p_{jm}, through appropriately chosen instrumental variables.

---

[18] Furthermore, if σ_1 approaches one, cars in the same subgroup become perfect substitutes. If the addition σ_2 approaches one, cars in the same group become perfect substitutes.

Details of the NL3SLS estimator, and of the quasi-likelihood ratio test used for hypothesis testing, are found in Gallant and Jorgenson (1979).

Before the NL3SLS estimator can be used, a computational problem must be resolved. The error terms, ω_{jm} and ξ_{jm} enter non-linearly in the pricing equation (4) and the demand equation (7). To avoid the need for computationally burdensome simulation methods, the demand and pricing equations are therefore first transformed in such a way that the error terms enter linearly. This idea was proposed by Berry (1994), in a more simple version of the nested logit model and with single-product firms. The transformations are given in the appendix. For simplicity, it is assumed that the multi-product firms only take into account the cross-demand derivatives of the cars they own in the same subgroup.[19] This yields the following model, first for demand, then for pricing, that is taken to the data

$$\ln(q_j/L_m) = \ln[1 = Q_m/L_m] + \sigma_1 \ln(q_j/Q_{hgm}) + \sigma_2 \ln(Q_{hgm}/Q_{gm})$$

$$+ x_{jm}\beta - \alpha \frac{(p_{jm})^\mu - 1}{\mu} + \xi_m + \xi_{jm} \tag{10}$$

and

$$\ln p_{jm} + \ln(1 - m_{jm}) = w_{jm}\gamma + \gamma_q Q_j + \ln(1 + t_m) + \tau_m + \omega_m + \omega_{jm} \tag{11}$$

where m_{jm}, to be interpreted below, is given by

$$m_{jm} \equiv \frac{p_{jm}^{-\mu}}{\alpha} \frac{1 - (1 - \sigma_1) \sum\limits_{k \in F_{jm} \cap V_{ghm}} \left[1 - \left(\frac{p_{km}}{p_{jm}} \right)^{1-\mu} \right] q_{km} r_{ghm}}{\dfrac{1}{1-\sigma_1} - \sum\limits_{k \in F_{jm} \cap V_{hgm}} q_{km} r_{hgm}}$$

$$+ (1 + t_m)(1 + \tau_m)\lambda_{jm} p_{jm}^{-1} \tag{12}$$

and

$$r_{hgm} \equiv \left(\frac{1}{1-\sigma_1} - \frac{1}{1-\sigma_2} \right) \frac{1}{Q_{hgm}} + \frac{\sigma_2}{1-\sigma_2} \frac{1}{Q_{gm}} - \frac{1}{L_m} \tag{13}$$

where $Q_{hgm} \equiv \sum_{j \in V_{hgm}} q_j, Q_{gm} \equiv \sum_{h \in V_{gm}} Q_{hgm}$, and where $\lambda_{jm} \equiv \lambda_{jm}^a$ in markets with absolute import quotas and $\lambda_{jm} \equiv (\lambda_{jm}^r/Q_m)(1 - Q_{jm}/L_m + Q_{jm}/Q_M)$ in markets with relative import quotas. The error terms ω_{jm} and ξ_{jm} indeed enter linearly in these transformed equations. Note, however, that several parameters enter non-linearly. To obtain good initial values of the parameters, I first estimated a simplified version of the model with $\mu = 0$ and with $-m_{jm}$ as an approximation for $\ln(1 - m_{jm})$.

---

[19] Firms typically do not own cars from different subgroups (country or origin) within the same group. Furthermore, the cross-demand derivatives with respect to cars from different subgroups or groups were found to be extremely small. In a previous version of the article, Verboven (1994), I experimented with the cross-demand derivatives with respect to cars from different subgroups or groups, and showed that they hardly made any difference.

To estimate a specification with collusion, the set of cars belonging to the same joint-profit-maximizing coalition should be specified. I specify a coalition as the set of all cars belonging to the same subgroup. The specification to be estimated is then the straightforward analog to (11). Because cars within a subgroup turn out to be relatively close substitutes, in contrast to cars from different subgroups, this specification seems to capture most of the potential collusion fairly well. To formally test for the presence of collusion, a general specification was estimated, nesting specifications (11)–(13) and the analogous collusive specification as two special cases. Details for the test are found in the appendix.

Identification problems

The pricing equations (11)–(13) reveal some identification problems. It is not possible to separately identify the market-specific fixed effects ω_m or the multipliers λ^a_{fm} or λ^r_{fm} from τ_m. The market-specific fixed effects, which are estimated using market-specific dummy variables, should therefore be interpreted with care. They reflect both cross-country differences in the marginal cost of operating in the various countries (ω_m) and cross-country differences in percentage deviations of the wholesale price from the consumer price τ_m. Similarly, the Lagrange multipliers should be interpreted with care. They are identified only up to a factor $(1 + \tau_m)$. A high estimate of the multipliers may therefore partly reflect a high τ_m. The inability to obtain a separate identification for τ_m makes it impossible to accurately compute the absolute wholesale markups received by the firms, i.e., $p^w_{jm} - \partial C_j/\partial q_{jm}$. Fortunately the relative wholesale markups can easily be computed from the estimates, despite the identification problems. Indeed, it may be verified that the relative markup for a car j in market m equals

$$\frac{p^w_{jm} - \partial C_j/\partial q_{jm}}{p^w_{jm}} = m_{jm} \tag{14}$$

where m_{jm} is defined by (12) and can easily be computed from the estimates. The estimates of the relative wholesale markups can then be used to quantify the presence of international price discrimination.

To estimate the Lagrange multipliers (multiplied by $(1 + \tau_m)$), I assume that $\lambda^a_{fm} = \lambda^a_m$ and $\lambda^r_{fm} = \lambda^r_m$ for all Japanese firms subject to the import quota in market m.[20] The Lagrange multipliers are then estimated using dummy variables identifying the Japanese cars operating in market m. There is a potential identification problem because these dummy variables may also capture some unobserved marginal costs that are specific to firms of Japanese origin.[21] To have an idea of the importance of this identification problem, I also estimated a Lagrange multiplier for Japanese firms selling in Belgium, even though there is no import quota against Japanese cars in that

---

[20] Following Goldberg (1995), one may interpret this as an assumption that the Japanese government allocates the quotas such that the shadow price of the constraint is equalized across firms.
[21] Goldberg (1995) could reduce this identification problem, because some of the Japanese firms sell

country. I will interpret an insignificant estimate of the Lagrange multiplier for Belgium as evidence that the estimated Lagrange multipliers for the other countries capture the effect of the quota constraint rather well.

The choice of appropriate instrumental variables

I assume that the vectors of physical characteristics w_{jm} and x_{jm} are exogenous and consequently orthogonal to the error-terms w_{jm} and ξ_{jm}. This exogeneity assumption is the main identification assumption for estimation of the pricing and the demand equations. The assumption seems reasonable in the short run, because firms cannot quickly adjust the characteristics of their cars marketed. In the long run, when firms can choose the characteristics of their cars, this assumption may be more problematic.

Prices and market shares are endogenous and correlated with the error terms ω_{jm} and ξ_{jm} even in the short run. This is because they are simultaneously determined in the Bertrand–Nash equilibrium. In homogeneous-goods models of supply and demand, instruments are readily available: there are generally enough exogenous variables that affect marginal cost and not demand, and exogenous variables that affect demand but not marginal cost. In the present model with product differentiation, most exogenous variables, the observed physical characteristics, affect both marginal cost and demand. Indeed, it is even possible that $w_{jm} = x_{jm}$, in which case no traditional instruments can be used. Fortunately, there are other instruments available. Because the pricing equation holds for all cars simultaneously, constituting a Nash equilibrium, the physical characteristics of each car's competitors are correlated with its own price and demand. Consequently (functions of) these variables may be used as instruments. Pakes (forthcoming) and Berry, Levinsohn, and Pakes (1995) discuss the general question of how to obtain efficient instruments when any functions of the competitors' characteristics are potential candidates. I use their results to include the following instruments: the elements of the vectors of exogenous variables x_{jm} and w_{jm}, the average of the elements of x_{jm} and w_{jm} across other cars owned by the same firm, and the average of the elements of x_{jm} and w_{jm} across other cars not owned by the same firm. The precise elements of the vectors x_{jm} and w_{jm} are discussed in detail in the data discussion below. I added the following instrument to the list just mentioned: the number of dealers per firm in each country. This variable may be viewed as exogenous at the pricing stage, and at the same time highly correlated with prices and sales.

The data

The data consist of almost all available base car models in five European countries: Belgium, France, Germany, Italy, and the United Kingdom. Only models with

cars that are both subject and not subject to quotas. Note that in my model the identification problem is slightly reduced under relative import quotas, because in this case the Lagrange multipliers are interacted with the variables Q_{fm} and Q_m.

extremely low market shares are omitted. This gives a sample of 512 observations in 1990. All data are from publicly available sources.[22]

The vectors of physical characteristics, w_{jm} and x_{jm}, affecting the marginal cost and demand, contain the same elements and may be summarized in two categories. The first category consists of the technical characteristics horsepower, weight, width, and height. Horsepower, weight, and height (measuring aerodynamics) jointly determine the performance variables 'speed' and 'acceleration'. Both width and weight capture 'safety'. Width and height capture 'size' or 'comfort'. The technical characteristics enter x_{jm} logarithmically, so that their coefficients may be interpreted as elasticities. The second category of physical characteristics in w_{jm} and x_{jm} consists of country-of-origin dummy variables. The coefficients of French, German, Italian, UK, US, and Japanese cars are to be interpreted relative to the 'other' cars, mainly East European. An interaction dummy reflects a systematic disadvantage to foreign firms. The country-of-origin variables in the vector w_{jm} capture unobserved differences in the marginal cost of producing cars of a given origin, e.g., due to differences in productivity across countries. The country-of-origin variables in the vector x_{jm} capture unobserved differences in tastes for cars of a given origin. In addition, the country-of-origin variables in both w_{jm} and x_{jm} may capture differences in cost-increasing and demand-reducing trade restrictions imposed against cars from certain countries. The coefficients of the dummy variables cannot identify whether cost/taste differences or differences in trade restrictions are important. Nevertheless, the inclusion of these dummy variables is necessary to avoid biased estimates of the other coefficients.

The nested logit model divides the set of cars into groups and subgroups. I define groups according to their class and subgroups according to their country of origin, although a model with the reverse definition was also estimated. There are seven classes: mini, small, medium, large, executive, luxury, and sports. This classification is based on common industry and marketing classifications in Europe.[23] To evaluate this classification, I checked whether the classes may be interpreted as discrete variables capturing the cars' continuous physical characteristics. I compared the cars' physical characteristics horsepower, weight, width, and height across the various classes. It turned out that the range of characteristics of cars from one class did not generally overlap with that of cars from other classes. The only exception were the classes mini and small. I therefore treated these as one single class, so that a total of six separate classes remains. The classes defined this way may then be viewed as a first proxy for the underlying continuous physical characteristics mentioned above. Groups are split

---

[22] These sources are: *l'Argus de l'Automobile et des Locomotions, Autogids, Auto Moto Revue, Journal de l'Automobile, Katalog der Automobil Revue, MVRIS, Nieuwe tot het Verkeer Toegelaten Voertuigen, Notiziario Statistica, Tatsachen und Zahlen aus der Kraftsverkehrswirtschaft, World Motor Vehicle Data.* I consulted these sources at the libraries of FEBIAC (Brussels) and CCFA (Paris).

[23] These classifications can be found in, for example, *l'Argus de l'Automobile et des Locomotions,* and in the EC Commission car price differential report. The classification in Goldberg (1995) for the American car market seems to be similar, although the labels of the classes differ somewhat: subcompacts, compacts, intermediate, standard, luxury, and sports.

into two subgroups according to country of origin: domestic cars and foreign cars. A domestic car is defined as a car that is produced domestically. According to this definition GM and Ford are domestic cars in Germany and the United Kingdom. Japanese cars are generally treated as foreign cars in all European countries. The exception is the Nissan Primera/Bluebird. Because Nissan started with the production of these cars in the United Kingdom in the 1980s, I treated them as UK cars in the United Kingdom but as Japanese cars elsewhere.[24] The other domestic firms were described in detail in section 2.

All prices are list prices, converted into ECUs using period average market rates. Recall that the wholesale prices appearing in the pricing equation are treated as a (partly unobserved) fraction of the list prices through (6). Ideally, the consumer prices appearing in the demand equation and in the demand derivatives of the pricing equation should be transaction prices instead of list prices. I considered a specification with maximum dealer discounts, given in table 10.1, as a proxy for transaction prices, but this hardly affected the results.

Sales are the annual number of new car registrations. To consider whether marginal cost is increasing, constant, or decreasing in total output, EC production data by car model are available. Unfortunately, these figures are of little help for the production levels of the Japanese car models, which are mainly produced outside of Europe. For consistency I therefore use an alternative measure of total production per car model. For each car model j owned by firm f, I multiply the share of car j's sales in firm f's sales, using the data on the five markets, i.e., $\sum_{m=1}^{5} q_{jm} / \sum_{m=1}^{5} Q_{fm}$ by the total (world) production of firm f, for which data are available. This measure of total world production per car model (drastically) assumes that the share of a car j's sales in firm f's sales using the data in the five markets is representative for the whole world. I experimented with alternative measures of world production, such as the total sales of cars in the five markets under study. The estimate of the parameter γ_q and most other parameters was robust with respect to both measures, although some of the country of origin dummy variables (especially the Japanese) were affected.

The number of potential consumers in each market m, L_m may in principle be estimated, as in Greenstein (1994), using market-level data that determine L_m, such as population, income, or the total demand for cars – a durable good – in previous periods.[25] Because only five markets are considered, I choose to keep L_m as a known variable. I follow Berry, Levinsohn, and Pakes (1995) and set equal to the total number of households in the economy, assuming that each household is a potential buyer of a new car in every year. I also considered an alternative specification in which L_m equals only 25 per cent of the households. This alternative specification assumes that only 25 per cent of the households are potential buyers of a new car; the other households only consider buying a car on the second-hand market (in which they are likely to repurchase

---

[24] This is because it is impossible to trace down the origin of the Nissan, United Kingdom or Japan, in the other countries.

[25] In a more sophisticated model, dynamic aspects of durable good competition may be explicitly incorporated.

their own car). It turned out that the empirical results were robust to alternative specifications of L_m, due to a low estimate of substitution towards the outside good.

5   Empirical results

Groups are defined according to their class (with one of the groups being the outside good), and subgroups according to their country of origin, foreign or domestic. I used the quasi-likelihood ratio test of Gallant and Jorgenson (1979) to test for several alternative specifications of the nested logit model, all of which were rejected at traditional 5 per cent significance levels, as discussed in detail in Verboven (1994). First, the data rejected the special cases of both the competitive, hedonic pricing model with zero markups, and the simple logit model with non-localized competition ($\sigma_1 = \sigma_2 = 0$). Second, the data rejected a more sophisticated version of the nested logit model, with an extra nest indicating whether to buy a car from a 'high' category (collecting the three highest classes) or a 'low' category (collecting the three lowest classes). Third, the data rejected a version of the nested logit model with an extra nest (at the top of the tree) indicating whether to buy the outside good or a car from one of the other classes.[26] Fourth, the data rejected an alternative ordering of the nesting structure, in which groups are defined according to country of origin and subgroups according to class. This specification led to an estimate of σ_1 significantly below σ_2, an undesirable result in terms of McFadden's random utility maximization. These various rejections are roughly consistent with Goldberg (1995), who uses micro-level data on the US car market. I also estimated a specification in which cars belonging to the same subgroup behave as a collusive coalition. This specification was rejected by the data at a 10 per cent significance level.

The estimates

Table 10.2 presents the estimates of the pricing and the demand equation for the unrejected specification of the nested logit in which groups correspond to class and subgroups to country of origin (domestic or foreign). Consider first the estimated coefficients appearing only in the demand equation and not in the pricing equation. Recall that the coefficients on the technical characteristics may be interpreted as elasticities. The elasticity of both horsepower and width have the expected sign and are estimated precisely. Demand is especially elastic with respect to width. Weight and height enter demand insignificantly. This may be explained by the fact that weight and height have an ambiguous impact on their underlying performance variables: weight increases safety but reduces speed/acceleration; height increases size/comfort but

---

[26] In the specification with the extra nest for the outside good there is one new substitution parameter σ_3 (in addition to σ_2 and σ_3). This parameter allows for a larger substitutability towards a different class than towards the outside good. In the specification without the extra nest for the outside good, the parameter σ_3 is equal to zero: the outside good is just like another class because of the same substitutability. Estimation of the more general specification showed that σ_3 is in fact not significantly different from zero.

Table 10.2 *NL3SLS estimates of nested logit (512 observations)*

	μ	α	σ_1	σ_2
	-02.78	71.812	0.522	-0.081
	(.036)	(27.994)	(.062)	(.162)

	Other Parameters			
	Demand Equation		Pricing Equation	
	Estimate	Standard error	Estimate	Standard error
Fixed effects				
France	0.463^a	0.172	-0.008^b	0.029
Germany	0.359^a	0.207	0.060^b	0.028
Italy	0.673^a	0.172	0.020^b	0.030
United Kingdom	1.408^a	0.207	0.116^b	0.029
Constant	152.084	65.768	7.503	0.272
Foreign firm disadvantage	-1.122	0.146	0.081	0.022
Returns to scale			-0.116	0.011
Technical characteristics				
HP	2.148	0.441	0.075	0.005
Weight	0.411	0.535	0.119	0.094
Width	13.846	1.548	1.711	0.165
Height	-0.187	1.163	-0.447	0.126
Country of Origin				
France	1.033	0.183	0.171	0.027
Germany	1.805	0.220	0.322	0.028
Italy	0.495	0.0150	0.056	0.027
United Kingdom	0.647	0.188	0.052	0.034
United States	1.187	0.186	0.231	0.030
Other country	0.401	0.137	0.105	0.029
Country-specific quotas in Japanese firms				
France			826.5	248.3
Germany			-176.9	248.1
Italy			1,820.8	293.1
United Kingdom			214.3	244.1

Notes: Estimates of equations (10)–(11), after substituting (12) and (13). Standard errors are in parentheses. For France, Germany, and the United Kingdom, the estimate of λ_m is divided by Q_m to generate the same order of magnitude as for Italy.
[a] ξ_m (relative to Belgium).
[b] ω_m (relative to Belgium).

decreases speed/acceleration. The significant variables horsepower and width do not have such an ambiguous impact. Country of origin seems to be an important differentiating physical characteristic. Interpreting the country-of-origin variables as capturing differences in taste, consumers have a high preference for German cars, a lower preference for French and European-built US cars, and the lowest preference for UK, Italian, Japanese, and other (mainly East European) cars. To compare the 'net country-of-origin' effect in a given country, one has to add the foreign firm disadvantage effect where appropriate. In France, for example, it may be verified that consumers tend to prefer French cars to German cars once the foreign firm disadvantage effect is taken into account. Of course, as argued in the discussion of the data, the country-of-origin variables may capture not only direct taste differences, but also systematic demand-reducing trade restrictions against certain countries.

Now consider the estimated cost coefficients. The coefficient on production, $\gamma_q = -0.11$, reveals that marginal cost is decreasing in total output, indicating the presence of returns to scale. Increasing production of a car by 10 per cent increases total variable cost by only $(10 - 1.1) = 8.9$ per cent. The estimate of this coefficient was robust with respect to alternative measures of total world output. Notice that the estimate of γ_q is much below (in absolute value) Berry, Levinsohn, and Pakes' (1995) estimate for the US market, which they found implausibly high. Consistent with previous hedonic studies (based on a competitive interpretation), the technical characteristics entering the marginal-cost equation all significantly contribute to marginal cost in the expected direction. The country-of-origin dummies all have positive coefficients relative to 'other' (mainly East European) countries. German cars have the highest estimated coefficient. Whether the country-of-origin differences are due to differences in productivity across the various countries or to cost-increasing trade restrictions cannot be discerned from the available data. The foreign firm disadvantage effect on cost is significantly positive and large. This indicates that foreign firms operate at a systematically higher cost, possibly due to an unobserved trade barrier. The fixed effects are estimated jointly significantly different from zero. As explained above, in the present model significant estimates of the fixed effects may follow either from systematic differences in the marginal cost of operating in the various markets (i.e., ω_m) or from systematic differences in percentage deviations of p_{jm}^w from p_{jm} (i.e., τ_m), in particular due to dealer markups. A more detailed interpretation of the significant estimates of the fixed effects is given below.

Now consider the coefficients that enter both the demand equation and the pricing equation through the demand derivatives: $\alpha, \sigma_1.\sigma_2$, and μ. They are all consistent with the restrictions of the nested logit model, stating that $\alpha > 0, 0 \le \sigma_2 \le \sigma_1 \le 1$, although σ_2 is actually estimated slightly negative with a high standard error.[27] The estimates of these parameters are responsible for a relatively plausible pattern of own- and cross-price elasticities, in contrast to the elasticities implied by some of the rejected models, such as the simple logit model and the nested logit model with the

---

[27] The imprecise estimate of σ_2 may be due to the choice of instruments. Without the instrumental variables method, σ_2 was estimated significantly positive.

reverse nesting structure. The own-price elasticities (not shown here) vary between 5 and 15, roughly consistent with estimates for the US car market by Bresnahan (1981), Feenstra and Levinsohn (1995), Goldberg (1995), and Berry, Levinsohn, and Pakes (1995). Domestic cars usually have the smallest own-price elasticity. Intuitively, domestic cars operate in an uncrowded subgroup with little competition, and competition between the domestic cars from the uncrowded subgroups and the foreign cars from the crowded subgroups is relatively weak (because of the significant difference between σ_1 and σ_2). This may be due to genuine consumer preferences for domestic products or to a better-established dealer network by domestic firms. Note also that inexpensive cars from low classes tend to have higher own-price elasticities than do expensive cars from high classes. This is due both to the fact that lower classes are more 'crowded' with competitors than high classes and to the significantly negative estimate of μ. The pattern of cross-price elasticities is also intuitive. A percentage decrease in the price of a car has a relatively high impact on the demand for cars from the same country of origin (domestic or foreign) within a class, a smaller impact on the demand for cars from a different country of origin within the same class, and the smallest impact on the demand for cars from different classes. This pattern of cross-price elasticities follows partly from the formulae implied by the nested logit model and partly from the data that favoured one specific version of the nested logit model. First, the nested logit formulae for the price elasticities, given by (A4) in the appendix, show that a percentage price decrease has a higher impact on the demand for cars belonging to the same subgroup than for cars belonging to different subgroups or groups. Second, the data favoured one specific version of the nested logit model, with groups defined according to class and subgroups according to country of origin within a given class, yielding the above-described intuitive pattern of elasticities. The data rejected other versions of the nested logit model (e.g., with the reverse ordering of the nesting structure), as well as the simple logit model, which would have yielded a counterintuitive pattern of cross-price elasticities.

Finally, consider the Lagrange multipliers. Although they are, as discussed above, only identified up to a factor $(1 + \tau_m)$, interpret them for simplicity in the narrow sense of Lagrange multipliers. A specification (not shown) was estimated with a Lagrange multiplier for Belgium, in which there is no import quota. The estimate of the Belgian Lagrange multiplier was insignificantly different from zero, and did not affect the estimates of the other parameters by very much. As noted above, this fact may be viewed as evidence that the multipliers capture the quota constraints fairly well, rather than other elements systematically influencing the marginal cost of Japanese firms. The Lagrange multipliers are significantly positive for France and Italy, indicating that the tight import quota constraints are indeed binding in these countries.[28] The Lagrange multipliers for the United Kingdom and Germany, with less tight import quotas, are insignificant.

---

[28] The estimates of the Lagrange multipliers in markets where there is a percentage quota constraint were divided by Q_{fm}. This gave numbers of the same order of magnitude as the multipliers in markets with absolute quota constraints, so that comparison is easier.

The presence of international price discrimination

Do the estimates of the price elasticities and the import quota constraints reveal something about the presence of international price discrimination? To answer this question I have computed the relative wholesale markups of the various cars in the various markets, as given by (14). Table 10.3 presents the estimates of the relative markups for selected cars based on the estimates in table 10.2. These cars were selected because they represent all product classes and the countries of origin. The first striking finding is the firms' ability to charge substantially higher markups on their cars sold domestically than on their cars sold abroad. In this sense, domestic firms can be said to price discriminate against the consumers of their home market. As extreme examples, compare the high markups of the Fiat Uno, Tipo, and Croma in Italy to the much lower markups of Fiat elsewhere. Similarly, contrast the markups of the Renault 5 and 19 in France with the markups in other countries. Formally, the high significance of σ_1, in interaction with the sales variables q_{jm}/Q_{hgm}, is responsible for this result. Intuitively, there is strong domestic market power as implied by the estimated price elasticities. Domestic firms operate in uncrowded subgroups, segmented from the more crowded subgroups consisting of the foreign firms. Moreover, the domestic firms often own several (in the case of Fiat, all) car models in the already uncrowded subgroups. As mentioned above, the significant segmentation between the domestic and foreign subgroups may be due to genuine consumer preferences for domestic products or to better-established dealer networks by domestic firms. Whatever the underlying reason, the resulting smaller price elasticities for domestic firms are exploited by charging higher markups.

The second important finding in table 10.3 is the high relative markups of Japanese cars in countries where the quota constraints are binding. In these countries, the Japanese firms obtain a quota rent: they choose to set higher prices than they would in the absence of the constraint. Note that this does not necessarily mean that the Japanese firms are better off due to the quota constraints. The increase in the Japanese firms' unit profits due to the quota may be offset by the reduction in the total number of cars sold.

As a final remark regarding table 10.3, note that the relative markups do not only vary across countries, but also across classes. The high-class cars tend to charge the highest markups. Reading from top to bottom, and ignoring the domestic or Japanese cars, the relative markups roughly increase. The most notable exception is the Fiat Croma, which can charge a high markup only in Italy.

Much of the discussion on the empirical results with regard to international price discrimination may be summarized by one summary statistic: the Lerner index. This index has been commonly used in traditional industry case studies. The Lerner index is defined as the sales-weighted average of relative markups in an industry, or in a 'segment' of the industry. In traditional industry case studies, the markups required to calculate the index are taken directly from (unreliable) accounting data. In the present study, the markups are inferred from observed pricing behaviour. I present the estimated Lerner indices for the various countries in table 10.4. I computed Lerner

220   F. Verboven

Table 10.3 *Relative markups of selected cars (in %)*

Model	Belgium	France	Germany	Italy	United Kingdom
Fiat Uno	7.6	8.7	9.8	21.7	8.7
Ford Fiesta	8.0	8.9	10.5	9.5	11.7
Nissan Micra	8.1	23.1	8.9	36.1	12.5
Renault 5	8.0	10.4	8.4	8.8	8.4
Fiat Tipo	8.4	9.2	9.0	20.8	9.1
Ford Escort	8.5	9.5	8.9	8.9	11.5
Renault 19	8.9	13.0	9.2	9.5	9.0
Toyota Corolla	9.7	19.6	13.0	24.2	13.6
VW Golf	9.3	10.3	12.2	11.0	10.0
Lancia Dedra	9.1	9.9	9.2	21.8	9.8
Mazda 626	9.8	19.3	13.0	21.7	13.3
Opel Vectra	9.3	9.5	10.7	9.2	11.8
Peugeot 405	9.9	13.4	10.2	9.9	11.6
Audi 80	10.8	11.3	14.3	12.6	10.9
Opel Omega	10.2	10.0	11.6	10.2	12.2
Citroen XM	11.1	14.1	12.4	12.0	11.3
Fiat Croma	9.0	9.6	9.7	21.2	9.8
Mercedes 190	14.3	14.4	17.2	15.6	12.3
BMW 5–series	12.5	12.4	12.3	12.7	13.0
Mercedes 200	15.1	15.2	17.9	16.8	–
Honda Prelude	15.1	19.6	17.9	20.6	17.1
BMW 7–series	15.7	15.7	14.7	19.0	21.5

Note: Based on equation (14) using estimates in table 10.2.

Table 10.4 *Lerner indices, per segment (in %)*

Segment	Belgium	France	Germany	Italy	United Kingdom
Mini and small	8.1	10.4	9.5	16.4	10.2
Medium	9.2	11.5	11.3	16.1	11.0
Large	9.8	12.1	12.2	15.6	11.8
Executive	10.4	13.2	11.4	14.6	12.5
Luxury	13.4	13.4	15.9	18.8	14.2
Sports	14.4	15.3	15.2	17.5	19.9
Whole industry	9.4	11.4	11.9	16.3	11.4

Note: Sales-weighted average of relative markups, as calculated on table 10.3.

indices both for the whole market and for different segments of the market, as defined by their class.

Consider first the market-average Lerner indices. These differ substantially across countries. Belgium, with no domestic producer and no import quota constraint, has the lowest Lerner index. France, Germany, and the United Kingdom have an index up to 3 per cent higher. Italy has by far the largest Lerner index: as was clear from table 10.3 on selected car models, this is the consequence of both domestic market power, as implied by the estimated price elasticities, and the import quota restrictions. In Italy the domestic firm Fiat is almost a monopoly, as it is the single manufacturer in its subgroup. Furthermore, in Italy the Japanese firms are subject to a tight, and binding, quota constraint of 1 per cent.

The Lerner indices by class give some interesting further insights. Note first that the Lerner indices are higher for higher classes, with the exception of Italy, where markups follow a perverse pattern. Generally speaking, price discrimination is present in all classes and follows the same pattern as the market-average Lerner index, with the highest markups in Italy and the lowest markups in Belgium. However, the degree of price discrimination turns out to be different in different classes. Price discrimination is more pronounced in the low classes and less pronounced in the high classes. This follows from two factors. First, domestic firms are more able to exploit their domestic market power (low price elasticities) in the low-class segments than in the high-class segments. In Italy, Fiat is very strong in the low- and medium-class segments, but not in the high-class segments. In France, PSA and Renault are stronger in the low- and medium-class segments than in the large-class segments. The exception is Germany, where the domestic producers Mercedes, BMW, and VW (Audi) are strong in the high-class segments. Correspondingly, in Germany markups are especially high in the high-class segments. Second, a binding import quota constraint on a Japanese firm has a stronger effect on the price of its small and inexpensive cars than on its large and expensive cars, as can be seen from the formula for the relative markups (14) using (12). Intuitively, this follows from the fact that the import quota restricts the number of imported cars and not the value of imports. As a result, a Japanese firm attempts to shift its demand from its small to its large and expensive products. In future research, it would be interesting to explore the role of a third possible factor responsible for the more pronounced price discrimination in the low classes: the specific role of cross-border arbitrage costs. It may be expected that cross-border arbitrage is relatively less costly for cars from high-class segments than for cars from low-class segments.

Unexplained price differences

The above results established the presence of international price discrimination as measured by cross-country differences in relative wholesale markups. Price differences that do not follow from differences in markups are captured by the market-specific fixed effects, to be interpreted relative to Belgium. Note that these fixed effects are substantially smaller than the fixed effects of the hedonic specification (as implied by the hedonic price index in table 10.1 and the formula for each index number, i.e., $p_m = \exp(\omega_m)$. The interpretation of the drops in the fixed effects, relative to Belgium, is intuitive and illuminating. Recall that the hedonic specification may be interpreted as the special case of perfect competition with zero markups. The fixed effects in the hedonic specification then took over the effect of an 'omitted' markup variable: as shown above, the estimated markups are relatively high in all countries, as compared with Belgium.

Despite their drop, the estimates of the fixed effects for Germany and especially the United Kingdom remain quite large, relative to Belgium. The data reject the restricted model without further effects in the pricing equation at a high significance level. Although the fixed effects have a broad economic interpretation of capturing both systematic differences in the marginal cost of operating in the various countries (through ω_m) and systematic differences in percentage deviations of the wholesale price, p_{jm}^w from the consumer list price, p_{jm} (through τ_m) I find them quite substantial; they deserve a more detailed analysis.

A first potential explanation for the significant estimates of the fixed effects may be the imperfect specification of the price elasticities as implied by the nested logit model. As explained above, the price elasticities are an important explanation of cross-country price differences through their effect on markups. If these elasticities are badly specified, they may not explain the cross-country price differences very well, so that the fixed effects may (partly) take over their role. This was especially the case for the (rejected) hedonic specification with its perfect competition interpretation, for the (rejected) simple logit specification with its non-localized competition, and for the (rejected) version of the nested logit model with the reverse nesting structure. Similarly, a more sophisticated model than the present nested logit model, perhaps Berry, Levinsohn, and Pakes' (1995) or Feenstra and Levinsohn's (1995) model of product differentiation, could capture the price elasticities even better and generate less-significant estimates of the fixed effects.

A second potential explanation for the significant estimates of the fixed effects may be a bad specification of the firms' actual behaviour. In some countries firms may set prices collusively. Recall that a specification in which collusion is present in all countries was rejected by the data. (It also yielded more significant fixed effects.) I also estimated a specification in which collusion is present in some countries and absent in others. The presence of collusive pricing could not be rejected for Germany and the United Kingdom.[29] The fixed effects may then be interpreted as taking over behavioural differences between the countries. According to this interpretation, there may be a third source for international price discrimination. In addition to cross-country differences in price elasticities and import quota constraints, there may be differences in the degree of collusive behaviour. A more detailed analysis as to why there would be differences in behaviour across countries is still desirable.

[29] These results should be interpreted with care. It was not possible to allow for the possibility of collusion in all countries simultaneously. I therefore restricted the specification in Belgium to non-collusive behaviour. A further analysis, with a larger data sample, is called for.

A third explanation for the large and significant fixed effects in Germany and the United Kingdom is that there are indeed several factors in these countries that contribute to large marginal costs, or to large deviations of the list price, p_{jm}, from the wholesale price, p_{jm}^w. Taxes have already been included and therefore cannot be an explanation of the fixed effects. Transportation costs are probably no explanation either. None of the five countries considered is located extremely far from the others. Furthermore, in a reduced-form model, Gual (1993) found that transportation costs could not explain price differences. Incomplete exchange rate pass-through may in principle explain part of the fixed effects. In a country with past exchange rate appreciations, prices (expressed in a common currency such as the ECU) will increase relative to the prices in the other countries, if foreign producers incompletely pass through the appreciation into local prices. Incomplete pass-through might explain the relatively high fixed effect in Germany, given the appreciation of the deutsche mark over five years. However, as already mentioned in section 2, incomplete pass-through certainly cannot explain the very high fixed effect in the United Kingdom, given the past depreciations of the pound. The high estimate of the fixed effect in both Germany and the United Kingdom may follow from the obligated use of catalytic converters and from the inclusion of warranties and roadside assistance. These cost determinants were not taken into account as characteristics in the marginal cost specification. Though they are difficult to measure, the Commission of the European Communities (1992) estimates that these elements may account for up to an extra 1–15 per cent of the price of a car in Germany and the United Kingdom. The high estimate of the fixed effect in the United Kingdom might also follow from the cost-increasing right-hand drive regulation. However, the same study indicates that this accounts only for about 1 per cent of the extra cost.[30] Moreover, this extra cost is likely to enter fixed (development) costs rather than marginal costs.[31]

The high estimate of the fixed effect in the United Kingdom may finally follow from the presence of systematically higher dealer markups in that country. These are calculated as percentages on the pretax list prices. As explained in section 2, there is a common industry wisdom that dealer markups are especially high in the United Kingdom. Unfortunately, complete data on dealer markups are not available. A direct proxy is given in table 10.1 by the market-average dealer markups and the Opel Astra dealer markup. These figures suggest that dealer markups are indeed higher in the United Kingdom. An indirect proxy for dealer markups is the maximum discount on the list price allowed by the dealer.[32] All other things being equal, high maximum discounts may indicate that manufacturers set high list prices, allowing for (artificially) high percentage dealer markups. According to this reasoning, the high maximum

---

[30] Commission of the European Communities (1992) has calculated that the extra cost for right-hand drive equals roughly 100 ECU per car. For a representative car of 10,000 ECU, this is only 1 per cent of the price.

[31] The right-hand-drive regulation may of course still have an indirect effect through an increase in arbitrage costs.

[32] These data were available from two independent sources: BEUC (1989) and Monopolies and Mergers Commission (1992).

discounts in the United Kingdom seen in table 10.1 may reflect high dealer markups on the list price allowed by the manufacturers.[33] I used the alternative proxies for systematic differences in dealer markups to re-estimate the model. The resulting estimate of the fixed effect for the United Kingdom indeed becomes less significant.

To obtain a more complete understanding of the role of the fixed effects, it would be desirable to collect data over a larger time horizon in future research. If the fixed effects really capture systematic cross-country differences in marginal costs and in deviations of p_{jm}^w from p_{jm} then one might expect them to be not too volatile over time.

6   Conclusions and extensions

The observed price differences in the European car market have been puzzling to many economists and policy makers. In this article I have used an oligopoly model to analyse to what extent the presence of international price discrimination, as measured by cross-country differences in relative wholesale markups, can explain the puzzle. Three sources for international price discrimination are considered: cross-country differences in price elasticities, differences in quota regimes, and differences in the degree of collusive behaviour. My empirical results establish the presence of international price discrimination. Large differences in price elasticities are estimated, indicating the presence of domestic market power. The domestic firms in France, Germany, the United Kingdom, and especially Italy tend to face much lower own-price elasticities than the foreign firms. Significantly binding quota constraints on Japanese firms are found in France and Italy. The possible presence of collusive behaviour cannot be rejected for Germany and the United Kingdom. The empirical results are encouraging and suggest two specific topics for further research on price differences in the European car market.[34]

More detailed data

The collection of additional data could generate additional insights in our understanding of the price differences. Collecting detailed data on country-specific dealer margins and dealer discounts and on country-specific demographics is a first important way to proceed. In addition, it would be desirable to collect data over a longer time horizon, say the period 1970–95. Several facts indicate that this period has been far from stable. A detailed analysis would provide a good test for the robustness of the empirical results. The descriptive studies mentioned in the Introduction suggest a gradual increase in the cross-country price differences during the 1970s and early 1980s, followed by a decrease (Mertens, 1990). During the same period there have been large

[33] Of course, the reason for such a practice should be further explored. One explanation that is frequently mentioned is the significant presence of 'fleet sales' in the United Kingdom (about 34 per cent of the 1990 market).

[34] General topics for further research, recognized in the large literature on the US car market, are the problems associated with the exogeneity assumptions of the physical characteristics of the cars, the modelling of the cost side (excluding plant-level factors prices), and the durability of cars.

exchange-rate fluctuations, which producers may or may not have passed through to consumers. A detailed analysis of the exchange-rate–pass-through relationship would be desirable to better understand some of the short-term price differences across countries. See Knetter (1993) for some first results on exchange rate pass-through in the car market. Furthermore, there has been a continuous decline of the domestic market shares in several European countries (see, e.g., de Melo and Messerlin, 1988). This suggests a gradual decline in domestic market power (as implied by the price elasticities). Moreover, the import quota constraints were introduced in the late 1970s and will only be removed at the end of the century. Finally, the European Commission has taken several measures to better integrate the EC car market and lower cross-border arbitrage costs. Though the deadline for integration was 1992, many of these measures took effect afterward, e.g., the tax harmonization and the uniform set of technical requirements in 1993. The selective and exclusive distribution system, limiting cross-border arbitrage, is an arrangement for the period 1985–95, but it has been renewed for another ten years, with some additional specifications to facilitate cross-border trade.

Policy analysis

The empirical results may be used in policy analysis to analyse the welfare effects of future policy changes. For example, in a theoretical model of the European car market, Davidson *et al.* (1989) have stressed the ambiguous effects of antidiscrimination regulation on total welfare. Less ambiguous conclusions may be obtained in my theoretical model, augmented with model simulations using the data and the estimates. Similarly, the effects of other policy measures may be analysed, such as a reduction (or elimination) of the consumer cross-border arbitrage costs, the removal of the import quota constraints, or the harmonization of taxes in 1993.

Appendix

The nested logit model and the transfer and demand and pricing equations

I specify the version of the nested logit model in more detail, and show how the demand and the pricing equations are transformed such that the error terms ξ_{jm} and ω_{jm} enter linearly.

In each market m there are L_m potential consumers, with the total number of consumers being $L = \sum_{m-1}^{M} L_m$. Each consumer either buys one car j in market m at price p_{jm} or buys an outside good at a price p_{0m}. The outside good guarantees that the total demand for cars is not perfectly inelastic. Indirect utility of consumer i from buying car j in market m is

$$u_{jm}^{i} = \delta_{jm} + v_{jm}^{i}. \tag{A1}$$

Indirect utility thus consists of two parts: a mean-utility part equal for all consumers, δ_{jm}, and an individual specific part, v^i_{jm}. Normalize the mean-utility for the outside good in market m to zero, i.e., $\delta_{0m} = 0$, and specify the mean-utility for a car j in market m, δ_{jm} as (9) in the text.[35] Specify the individual-specific part of utility for car j in market m, v^i_{jm}, as

$$v^i_{jm} = \varepsilon^i_m + \varepsilon^i_{gm} + (1 - \sigma_2)\varepsilon^i_{hgm} + (1 - \sigma_1)\varepsilon^i_{jm} \tag{A2}$$

where h refers to a subgroup h and g to a group g as given in the text. The distribution of ε^i_m takes an extremely simple form: $\varepsilon^i_m = 0$ if consumer i is one of the L_m consumers located in market m, and $\varepsilon^i_m = -\infty$ if consumer i is not one of the L_m consumers located in market m, i.e., there are prohibitive arbitrage costs of travelling to another market. The distributions of ε^i_{gm}, ε^i_{hgm}, and ε^i_{jm} are standard to the nested logit model: they have the unique distribution such that ε^i_{gm}, $(1 - \sigma_2)\varepsilon^i_{hgm} + (1 - \sigma_1)\varepsilon^i_{jm}$ and $\varepsilon^i_{gm} + (1 - \sigma_2)\varepsilon^i_{hgm} + (1 - \sigma_1)\varepsilon^i_{jm}$ have the extreme value distribution. Each consumer i chooses the car that yields the highest utility, u^i_{jm}. Aggregating these choices over all consumers, the distributional assumptions on ε^i_{gm}, ε^i_{hgm} and ε^i_{jm} generate the well-known nested logit formulae for the conditional choice probabilities, or approximately market shares, $s_{j/hgm}$, $s_{h/gm}$ and $s_{g/m}$ as provided by, e.g., McFadden (1978), Ben-Akiva and Lehrman (1985), and in a representative consumer framework, Verboven (1996). The distributional assumption on ε^i_m, guaranteeing no arbitrage, generates a simple formula for the share of market m in the total market, s_m, i.e., $s + m = L_m/L$. These formulae can then be substituted in

$$q_{jm} = s_{j/hgm} \cdot s_{h/gm} \cdot s_{g/m} \cdot s_m \cdot L \tag{A3}$$

to obtain the functional form for demand (7) as provided in the text.

Note that q_{jm} does not depend on the prices of cars sold in markets other than market m, due to the distributional assumption for ε^i_m, guaranteeing no arbitrage. I can therefore drop the subscript m without risk of confusion. The derivation of the appropriate transformation of the demand equation such that the error term ξ_j enters linearly is a rather tedious generalization of Berry (1994). The same is true for the calculation of the own- and cross-demand derivatives and their implied elasticities. I therefore refer to Berry (1994) or Verboven (1994) for these calculations. The resulting transformed demand equation is given by (10) in the text. The own- and cross-price elasticities for a typical car j are

$$e_{jj} \equiv -\frac{\partial q_j}{\partial p_j}\frac{p_j}{q_j} = ap^\mu_j \left[\frac{1}{1 - \sigma_1} - \left(\frac{1}{1 - \sigma_1} - \frac{1}{1 - \sigma_2} \right) \frac{q_j}{Q_{hg}} - \frac{\sigma_2}{1 - \sigma_2}\frac{q_j}{Q_g} - \frac{q_j}{L} \right] \tag{A4a}$$

---

[35] One may want to check whether this utility specification is consistent with a consumer utility-maximization problem subject to a budget constraint. However, this is not a simple task when goods (cars) are durable. Quoting Goldberg (1995, p. 12), 'The expected future income rather than present income, and the life cost of the vehicle instead of the current price should enter the budget constraint.' Because of a lack of a satisfying theory of durable goods in an oligopoly context with product differentiation, the flexible specification of price in utility is a useful alternative approach.

$$e_{jk} \equiv \frac{\partial q_k}{\partial p_j} \frac{p_j}{q_k} = a p_j^{\mu} \left[\left(\frac{1}{1-\sigma_1} - \frac{1}{1-\sigma_2} \right) \frac{q_j}{Q_{hg}} + \frac{\sigma_2}{1-\sigma_2} \frac{q_j}{Q_g} + \frac{q_j}{L} \right] \qquad (A4b)$$

$$e_{jk'} \equiv \frac{\partial q_{k'}}{\partial p_j} \frac{p_j}{q_{k'}} = a p_j^{\mu} \left[\frac{\sigma_2}{1-\sigma_2} \frac{q_j}{Q_g} + \frac{q_j}{L} \right] \qquad (A4c)$$

$$e_{jk''} \equiv \frac{\partial q_{k''}}{\partial p_j} \frac{p_j}{q_{k''}} = a p_j^{\mu} \frac{q_j}{L} \qquad (A4d)$$

where k, k', and k'' index cars that respectively belong to the same subgroup, to a different subgroup within the same group, and to a different group.

I now derive an appropriate transformation of the first-order conditions, such that the error term ω_{jm} enters linearly. To simplify, first ignore the λ_f, capturing import quota constraints. Notice that the multi-product firms typically do not own cars from a different subgroup (i.e., country of origin) within the same group. Assume furthermore that the multi-product firm ignores the cross derivatives of demand for cars sold in different groups: these are typically very small, so this does not affect the results very much. (A previous version of the article experimented with a pricing equation including these cross derivatives, and found that they indeed hardly made any difference.) Maximizing profits (2) using (6), the first-order condition for a car j then is

$$\sum_{k \in F_{jm} \cap V_{hg}} (1+t)(1+\tau) \left(p_k^w - \frac{\partial C_k}{\partial q_k} \right) \frac{\partial C_k}{\partial p_j} + q_j = 0 \qquad (A5)$$

where $\partial q_j / \partial p_j$ takes the form implied by (A4a) and the all take the $\partial q_k / \partial p_j, k \neq j$ form implied by (A4b). After substituting these demand derivatives, it remains impossible to estimate the first-order condition because there are several marginal cost terms, one for each car k produced by the firm, and hence several error terms. To solve this problem, the first-order condition is transformed. (This is equivalent to solving the inverted matrix in (4).) Substitute the demand derivatives implied by (A4a) and (A4b), rearrange slightly, and divide by $a p_j^{\mu-1} q_j$ to obtain

$$(1+t)(1+\tau) \left(p_j^w - \frac{\partial C_j}{\partial p_j} \right) \frac{1}{1-\sigma_1} - \frac{1}{\alpha} p_j^{1-\mu}$$

$$= \sum_{k \in F_j \cap V_{hg}} (1+t)(1+\tau) \left(p_k^w \frac{\partial C_k}{\partial q_k} \right) q_k r_{hg} \qquad (A6)$$

where

$$r_{hg} \equiv \left(\frac{1}{1-\sigma_1} - \frac{1}{1-\sigma_2} \right) \frac{1}{Q_{hg}} + \frac{\sigma_2}{1-\sigma_2} \frac{1}{Q_g} + \frac{1}{L}. \qquad (A7)$$

Because the right-hand side is the same for any car sold by the same firm, this implies that

$$(1+t)(1+\tau)\left[p_j^w - \frac{\partial C_j}{\partial q_j}\right]\frac{1}{1-\sigma_1} - \frac{1}{\alpha}p_j^{1-\mu}$$

$$= (1+t)(1+\tau)\left[p_k^w - \frac{\partial C_k}{\partial q_k}\right]\frac{1}{1-\sigma_1} - \frac{1}{\alpha}p_k^{1-\mu} \tag{A8}$$

for any car sold by the same firm, so that

$$p_k^w - \frac{\partial C_k}{\partial q_k} = \left(p_j^w - \frac{\partial C_j}{\partial q_j}\right) + \frac{1}{(1+t)(1+\tau)}\frac{1-\sigma_1}{\alpha}(p_k^{1-\mu} - p_j^{1-\mu}). \tag{A9}$$

Substituting this into (A6) for all $k \in F_f \cap V_{hg}$ allows us to substitute out all $\partial C_k/\partial q_k$ terms, so that only $\partial C_j/\partial q_j$ remains, with its corresponding error term ω_j. Substituting and rearranging gives

$$p_j^w = \frac{\partial C_j}{\partial q_j} + \frac{1}{\alpha}p_j^{1-\mu}\frac{1}{(1+t)(1+\tau)}\frac{1-(1-\sigma_1)\sum_{k\in F_f\cap V_{hg}}\left[1 - \left(\frac{p_k}{p_j}\right)^{1-\mu}\right]q_k r_{hg}}{\frac{1}{1-\sigma_1} - \sum_{k\in F_f\cap V_{hg}}q_k r_{hg}}. \tag{A10}$$

The second term is effectively the solution to $\Delta_j^{-1}\mathbf{q}$ in (4). Equation (A10) can be rewritten such that only $\partial C_j/\partial q_j$ appears on the right-hand side. Then one can substitute the functional form of $\partial C_j/\partial q_j$ from (5), and the functional form of p_j^w from (6), and log-linearize both sides so that ω_{jm} appears linearly, using the approximation $\ln(1+\tau) = \tau$, to obtain (11) without import quotas.

Now consider the first-order condition of firms subject to an import quota. The case of an absolute import quota is straightforward, because λ_j^a just adds up to $\partial C_j/\partial q_j$ in pricing equation (4). In the case of a relative quota, a term λ_j^r/Q must be added up to $\partial C_j/\partial q_j$. However, there is an additional term, $(\lambda_{fm}^r/Q_m)(Q_{fm}/Q_m)(\sum_{k=1}^J \partial q_{km}/\partial p_{jm})$, that must be added up to $q_{jm}(p_m)$. It can be verified that $\sum_{k=1}^J \partial q_{km}/\partial p_{km}^w = -(1_t)(1+\tau)ap_j^{\mu-1}q_j(1 - Q?L)$. Steps similar to those for the case without quotas then show that a term $\lambda_j^r/Q(1 - Q_f/L + Q_f/Q)$ must effectively be added up to $\partial C_j/\partial p_j$ to obtain the pricing equation in the case of relative quota.

Finally, consider the case in which firms can collude. Assume that collusive coalitions consist of subgroups. This eliminates most of the competition, as car models from different subgroups are not very close substitutes. A previous version of the article followed a conjectural variation approach. This approach assumes that a firm expects a decrease of its rivals' prices by ϕ units, when decreasing its own price by one unit. Unfortunately, the conjectural variation approach – with price-setting firms – does not have the convenient property that it nests both the Bertrand and the collusive outcomes as special cases, an observation similar to Gasmi, Laffont, and Vuong (1992). I therefore consider an alternative approach to nest both models (which *de facto* turns out to be not too different from the conjectural variations approach anyway). To test whether a firm is maximizing its joint profit (i.e., colluding) with all cars in its subgroup, rather than only with the cars it owns in the subgroup, I estimate the following specification of the pricing equation nesting the two special cases (ignoring quotas):

$$p_j^w = \frac{\partial C_j}{\partial q_j} + \frac{1}{\alpha} p_j^{1-\mu} \frac{1}{(1+t)(1+\tau)} \times$$

$$\frac{1 - (1+\sigma_1) \left[(1-\phi) \sum_{k \in F_f \cap V_{hg}} \left(1 - \left(\frac{p_k}{p_j} \right)^{1-\mu} \right) q_k r_{hg} + \phi \sum_{k \in V_{hg}} \left(1 - \left(\frac{p_k}{p_j} \right)^{1-\mu} \right) q_k r_{hg} \right]}{\frac{1}{1-\sigma_1} - (1-\phi) \sum_{k \in F_f V_{hg}} q_k r_{hg} - \phi \sum_{V_{hg}} q_k r_{hg}} \quad (A11)$$

If $\phi = 0$, a firm considers the effect only on the profits of its own cars in its subgroup. If $\phi = 1$, a firm considers the effect only on the profits of its own cars in its subgroup. Using a parameter ϕ equal for all markets, one may test whether there is collusion in all markets; using market-specific parameters ϕ_m, one may test whether there is market-specific collusion.

References

Anderson, S.P. and A. de Palma (1992), 'Multiproduct firms: a nested logit approach', *Journal of Industrial Economics*, 40, 261–76.

Ben-Akiva, M. and S. Lehrman (1985), *Discrete choice analysis: theory and application to predict travel demand*, Cambridge, MA, MIT Press.

Berry, S.T. (1994), 'Estimating discrete-choice models of oligopoly product differentiation', *RAND Journal of Economics*, 25, 242–62.

Berry, S. T., J. Levinsohn, and A. Pakes (1995), 'Automobile prices in market equilibrium', *Econometrica*, 63, 841–90.

BEUC (1981), 'Report on car prices in the EEC countries', Brussels: European Bureau of Consumers Unions, BEUC/71/81.

(1986), 'Car prices in the EEC countries', Brussels: European Bureau of Consumers Unions, BEUC/121/86.

(1989), 'Car prices and progress towards 1992', Brussels: European Bureau of Consumers Unions, BEUC/10/89.

(1992), 'Parallel imports for cars in the EC', Brussels: European Bureau of Consumers Unions, BEUC/222/92.

Bresnahan, T.F. (1981), 'Departures from marginal-cost pricing in the American automobile industry', *Journal of Econometrics*, 17, 201–27.

Bresnahan, T.F. and P.C. Reiss (1985), 'Dealer and manufacturer margins', *RAND Journal of Economics*, 16, 253–68.

Bulow, J. J. Geanakoplos, and P.D. Klemperer (1985), 'Multimarket oligopoly: strategic substitutes and complements', *Journal of Political Economy*, 93, 488–511.

Caplin, A. and B. Nalebuff (1991), 'Aggregation and imperfect competition: On the existence of equilibrium', *Econometrica*, 59, 25–59.

Commission of the European Communities (1992), 'Intra-EC car price differential report', Brussels: IV/4043/92.

Davidson, R., M. Dewatripont, V. Ginsburgh, and M. Labbe (1989), 'On the welfare effects of antidiscrimination regulations in the EC car market', *International Journal of Industrial Organization*, 7, 205–30.

De Melo, J. and P.A. Messerlin (1988), 'Price, quality and welfare effects of European VERs on Japanese autos', *European Economic Review*, 32, 1527–46.

Feenstra, R.C. and J.A. Levinsohn (1995), 'Estimating markups and market conduct with multidimensional product attributes', *Review of Economic Studies*, 62, 19–52.

Flam, H. (1992), 'Product markets and 1992: Full integration, large gains?' *Journal of Economic Perspectives*, 6, 7–30.

Flam, H. and H. Nordstrom (1994), 'The single market for cars in Europe', mimeo, Institute for International Economic Studies, Stockholm University.

Gallant, A.R. and D.W. Jorgenson (1979), 'Statistical inference for a system of simultaneous, non-linear, implicit equations in the context of instrumental variable estimation', *Journal of Econometrics*, 11, 275–302.

Gasmi, F., J.-J. Laffont, and Q. Vuong (1992), 'Econometric analysis of collusive behaviour in a soft-drink market', *Journal of Economics and Management Strategy*, 1, 277–311.

Ginsburgh, V. and G. Vanhamme (1989), 'Price differences in the EC car market', *Annales d'Economie et de Statistique*, 15/16, 137–49.

Goldberg, P. (1995), 'Product differentiation and oligopoly in international markets: The case of the US automobile industry', *Econometrica*, 63, 891–951.

Greenstein, S. (1994), 'From super-Minis to super-computers: Estimating surplus in the computing market', NBER Working Paper no. 4899.

Griliches, Z. (1971), 'Hedonic price indexes for automobiles: An econometric analysis of quality change', in Z. Griliches (ed.), *Price Indices and Quality Change*, Cambridge, MA, Harvard University Press.

Gual, J. (1993), 'An econometric analysis of price differentials in the EEC automobile market', *Applied Economics*, 25, 599–607.

Kirman, A.P. and N. Schueller (1990), 'Price leadership and discrimination in the European car market', *Journal of Industrial Economics*, 39, 69–91.

Knetter, M.M. (1993), 'International comparisons of pricing-to-market behaviour', *American Economic Review*, 83, 473–86.

Krishna, K. (1989), 'Trade restrictions as facilitating practices', *Journal of Industrial Economics*, 26, 251–70.

Malueg, D.A. and M. Schwartz (1994), 'Parallel imports, demand dispersion, and international price discrimination', *Journal of International Economics*, 37, 167–95.

McFadden, D. (1978), 'Modelling the choice of residential location', in A. Karlqvist *et al.* (eds.), *Spatial Interaction Theory and Planning Models*, New York, North-Holland.

Mertens, Y. (1990), 'Modelling price behaviour in the European car market', mimeo, Department of Economics, London School of Economics.

Mertens, Y. and V. Ginsburgh (1985), 'Product differentiation and price discrimination in the European Community: the case of automobiles', *Journal of Industrial Economics*, 34, 151–65.

Monopolies and Mergers Commission (1992), *New Motor Cars*, London, HMSO.

Pakes, A. (forthcoming), 'Dynamic structural models: problems and prospects. Mixed continuous discrete controls and market interactions', in J.-J. Laffont and C. Sims (eds.), *Advances in Econometrics*, New York, Cambridge University Press.

Rosen, S. (1974), 'Hedonic prices and implicit markets: Product differentiation in pure competition', *Journal of Political Economy*, 82, 34–55.

Schmalensee, R. (1985), 'Econometric diagnosis of competitive localization', *International Journal of Industrial Organization*, 3, 57–70.

Verboven, F. (1994), 'International price discrimination in the European car market',
    CENTER Discussion Paper no. 9451.
    (1996), 'The nested logit model and representative consumer theory', *Economics Letters*,
    50, 57–63.

Chapter 11

Tacit collusion (1)
Interfirm rivalry in a repeated game: an empirical test of tacit collusion

Margaret E. Slade

1   Introduction

This chapter uses a unique data set to test for the degree and to discriminate among models of tacit collusion. The market investigated is the Vancouver, British Columbia retail gasoline market. The players are service stations who meet daily to compete. Station operators choose price, and the quantity of gasoline sold at each station each day depends on the prices chosen by all.

Oligopolistic interaction is modelled as a repeated game. In an earlier paper (Slade, 1989) I derive a method of producing price wars in price-setting supergames. The method is illustrated with two examples: one where firms use discontinuous strategies in the spirit of Friedman (1971) and the other where strategies are continuous as in Kalai and Stanford (1985).

The present chapter attempts to distinguish between these two supergame price-war models. The object of the chapter is to examine the behaviour of firms during wars. Because many punishment strategies can support the same collusive outcome, it is of

This article first appeared in *The Journal of Industrial Economics*, 1987, Vol. 35, pp. 499–516.

This research was supported by a grant from the Canadian Social Sciences and Humanities research Council. I would like to thank the ten oil-company regional marketing managers and the thirteen service-station operators that were involved in the data collection. Without their cooperation, this study would not have been possible. I would also like to thank Charles Blackorby, Timothy Bresnahan, Paul Geroski, Jonathan Hamilton, Louis Phlips, and Richard Schmalensee for thoughtful and constructive comments on an earlier draft.

interest to determine what strategies firms actually use in a particular situation. To anticipate results, weak support is given to the continuous-reply model, where small deviations lead to small punishments, over its discontinuous alternative.

The exercise is very different from the Porter (1983b) empirical work, where tests are made for the occurrence and timing of price wars. In this market, it is obvious to all customers, dealers, and observers when a war is occurring. Cooperative periods in the industry are characterized by identical prices for all firms which are constant over time. Such data are therefore useless for empirical purposes. For this reason, my data do not include stable periods.

The data set, which I collected, pertains solely to a price-war period. It consists of daily price, sales volume, and cost figures for three types of gasoline sold at 13 service stations in a submarket of Vancouver. The data are therefore extremely rich, making it possible to estimate demand, cost, and reaction functions at a very micro level. These estimated functions are then used to calculate various solutions to the game – non-cooperative and cooperative solutions to the one-shot game and the actual outcome of the repeated game. By comparing solutions, it is possible to see if firms in fact do better through repeated play than they would if they played the game only once. In addition, it is possible to test the explanatory power of various price-war models.

2   The Model

2.1   Background

The game that is described in this section is non-cooperative. Overt collusion is ruled out because, at least in North America, binding agreements on price or output are illegal. Nevertheless, when a game is repeated many times, solutions that have a collusive flavour can emerge.

In a companion paper (Slade, 1989) I derive a method of generating price wars in supergame models. The market considered is one where oligopolists produce a differentiated product and use price as a strategic variable. Prices are posted and can be observed by all. In addition, rival sales can be monitored. There is thus little uncertainty or scope for secret price cutting.[1] Nevertheless, price wars occur. Many real-world markets which are plagued by price wars fit this description – retail gasoline and airline-seat sales are just two examples.

In the Slade model, price wars are information-gathering devices. Demand is subject to periodic but infrequent random shifts. After a demand shift has occurred, unless firms change prices they cannot know the new demand conditions. Incentives are such that considerable price cutting and undercutting occurs before the market settles down to the new equilibrium.

The method of generating price wars is illustrated with two examples. Example 1

---

[1] Price-war models such as that of Green and Porter (1984) and Porter (1983a) rely on unobservability of choice variables and inability to detect cheating to produce wars.

involves discontinuous or 'grim' strategies in the spirit of Friedman (1971). With a grim strategy, punishment for any deviation from the collusive outcome involves reversion to Nash behaviour for the one-shot game. Example 2 uses continuous strategies as in Kalai and Stanford (1985). With a continuous strategy, small defections trigger small punishments and large defections trigger large punishments. The price-war dynamics inherent in the two examples have much in common. There are, however, testable differences as described below.

2.2   The constituent game

Suppose that N firms in a market produce a differentiated product. Suppose additionally that the N firms can be partitioned into M strategic subgroups, where all members of a group face similar demand conditions and exhibit similar responses to rival actions. All members of a group are then considered to be identical and the players in the game are the strategic groups.

This does not mean that players within groups collude to choose their strategies. What it means is that, because all members of a group are identical and because each member chooses its actions optimally, the actions chosen will be the same for like players.

To identify the groups, the set of integers from 1 to N is partitioned into M subsets, where the ith member of this partition indexes the firms in strategic group i. Denote the ith set by N_i, which has M_i members.

Assume that M demand equations are known, one for each group, where the quantity sold by a given firm depends on the prices posted by all firms. Let these demand equations be approximated by linear functions

$$q^i = a_i + b_i p^i + c_i \sum_{\substack{j \in N_i \\ j \neq i}} w_j^{ii} p^j + \sum_{\substack{h=1 \\ h \neq i}}^{M} d_{hi} \sum_{k \in N_h} w_k^{ih} p^k + g_i(z), \quad i = a, \dots, M \quad (1)$$

where

q^i is the quantity sold by a firm from group i,
p^i is the price charged by this firm,
p^j is a price charged by another firm from group i,
p^k is a price charged by a firm from a different group,
w^{ih} is a vector of weights of unit norm, $h = 1, \dots, M$, and
z is a vector of exogenous variables that shift demand.

Note that, even though in equilibrium the prices charged by firms in the same group will be equal, in this specification of the demand equations, each price is allowed to move independently. Equation (1) will be estimated to obtain the demand parameters $a_i, \dots, d_i, i = 1, \dots, M$.

Strategies for the constituent game consist of the choice of prices, p^i, one for each group. The payoff for each firm is its profit, $\pi^i(p)$, where p is a vector of M prices. If marginal cost is constant, then the profit for a firm from group i can be written as

$$\pi^i(p) = \left(p^i - mc^i\right)q^i(p) \tag{2}$$

where

π^i is the profit earned by a representative firm from group i, and mc^i is that firm's marginal cost.

Each firm's objective is to choose price so as to maximize profit,

$$\max_{p^i} \pi^i(p) \tag{3}$$

First-order conditions for this maximization are

$$d\pi^i/dp^i = \left(p^i - mc^i\right)dq^i/dp^i + q^i = 0, \quad i = 1, \ldots, M. \tag{4}$$

Different assumptions about the way in which firms respond to each other determine dq^i/dp^i. And, when expressions for dq^i/dp^i are substituted into the first-order conditions, they determine different solutions to the constituent game.

For example, suppose that each firm plays Bertrand–Nash. Then dq^j/dp^i is zero for j not equal i and $dq^i/dp^i = b_i$. When b_i is substituted for dq^i/dp^i in (4), we have M linear equations in M unknown prices, which can be solved for the unique vector of Nash prices p_n. Corresponding quantities and profits, q_n, and π_n, can then be obtained from equations (1) and (2).

More generally, suppose that players have linear reaction functions with slopes $dp^j/dp^i = R^{ji}, R^{ji} \in I_R = [-1, 1]$. Then dq^i/dp^i is

$$dq^i/dp^i = b_i + c_i R^{ii} + \sum_{\substack{h=1 \\ h \neq i}}^{M} d_{hi} R^{hi} \tag{5}$$

and the first-order conditions (4) become

$$d\pi^i/dp^i = \left(p^i - mc^i\right)\left[b_i + c_i R^{ii} + \sum_{\substack{h=1 \\ h \neq i}}^{M} d_{hi} R^{hi} \right] + a_i + b_i p^i$$

$$+ c_i \sum_{\substack{j \in N_i \\ j \neq i}} w_j^{ii} p^j + \sum_{\substack{h=1 \\ h \neq i}}^{M} d_{hi} \sum_{k \in N_h} w_k^{hi} p^k + g_i(z) = 0, \quad i = 1, \ldots, M. \tag{6}$$

Given any matrix of reactions R, if we assume that prices are the same for firms in the same group, the system of M linear equations (6) can be solved for the unique vector of M prices, P_R, corresponding to R. It is easy to show that many sets of prices, including all those between Bertrand and monopoly, can be obtained through appropriate choices of R.

Bertrand–Nash behaviour corresponds to a particular choice of R, R_n identically equal to zero. We wish to consider another special matrix R_b corresponding to the single-period best replies. Consider equation (6), firm i's first-order condition.

Suppose that firm j in group i initiates a price change. Because optimal behaviour satisfies the first-order conditions, firm i's best response, $R_b^{ii} = dp^i/dp^j$ for j in N_i, is the one that restores the first-order condition to zero. Differentiating (6) with respect to p^j results in

$$\pi_{ji}^i = d^2\pi i/dp^j dp^i = R^{ii}\left[b_i + c_i R^{ii}\sum_{\substack{h=1\\h\neq i}}^M d_{hi}R^{hi}\right] + b_i R^{ii}$$

$$+ c_i\left[w_j^{ii} + \sum_{\substack{l\in N_i\\l\neq i\\l\neq j}} w_j^{ii}R^{ii}\right] + \sum_{\substack{h=1\\h\neq i}}^M d_{hi}R^{hi} = 0. \qquad (7)$$

Using the same technique, all M^2 equations of the form of $\pi_{jk}^k = 0, k, j = 1,\ldots,M$, can be obtained. The result is M^2 quadratic equations in M^2 unknowns R^{jk}, which can be solved for the best-reply matrix R_b. When R_b is substituted into equation (6), best-reply prices p_b are found. Corresponding quantities and profits, q_b and , can then be calculated from equations (1) and (2).

Finally, we wish to consider a cooperative solution to the constituent game. Suppose that instead of each firm maximizing its own profit, given rival reactions, the firms in the market collude to maximize joint profit.[2] Joint profit can be expressed as

$$\Pi(p) = \sum_{h=1}^M M_h\left(p^h - mc^h\right)q^h(p). \qquad (8)$$

A vector of prices p^h, $h = 1,\ldots, M$, is chosen to maximize (8) subject to the demand constraints (1).[3] First-order conditions for this maximization are

$$\partial\Pi/\partial p^i = M_i\left(p^i - mc^i\right)\partial q^i/\partial p^i + M_i q^i + \sum_{\substack{h=1\\h\neq i}}^M M_h\left(p^h - mc^h\right)\partial q^h/\partial p^i = 0,$$

$$i = 1,\ldots, M. \qquad (9)$$

Differentiating the demand equation to obtain $\partial q^j/\partial p^i$, substituting into (9) and rearranging, we have

$$M_i\left\{(2p^i - mc^i)(b_i + c_i) + a_i + g_i(z)\right\} + \sum_{\substack{h=1\\h\neq i}}^M M_h M_i\left\{(d_{hi} + d_{ih})p^h - d_{ih}mc^h\right\} = 0$$

$$i = 1,\ldots, M. \qquad (10)$$

---

[2] Because firms are asymmetric and because there are no sidepayments, joint-profit maximization is not the expected outcome of successful collusion. This calculation is performed in order to get a reasonable upper bound for prices.

[3] Additional constraints that all profits be non-negative or that the solution be individually rational can also be imposed.

The M linear equations of the form of (10) can be solved for the unique joint-profit-maximizing price vector p_m. Corresponding quantities and profits, q_m and π_m can be found in the obvious fashion. p_m is a cooperative solution to the constituent game. It is, however, not a non-cooperative equilibrium. The problem is that when $M-1$ groups play cooperatively, the Mth group can unilaterally improve its profit by cutting price. When all deviate, however, all are worse off. As discussed in the next section, p_m and many reaction-function price vectors p_R can be stationary non-cooperative equilibria for the repeated game.

2.3   The repeated game

The repeated game consists of playing the constituent game an infinite number of times. A strategy for the ith player in the repeated game is a choice of price to play in every period $(p_0^i, p_1^i, \ldots)$, where p_t^i can depend on the history of play. Payoffs in the repeated game take the form

$$\Gamma^i = \sum_{t=0}^{\infty} \delta^t \pi^i (p_t), \quad i = 1, \ldots, M, \quad 0 < \delta < 1 \tag{11}$$

where

> Γ^i is the payoff to a firm from group i in the repeated game, and
> $\delta = 1/(1 + \rho)$ is the discount factor (ρ is the discount rate).

In the Slade (1985) model, demand shocks trigger the punishment strategies which support the collusive outcomes that are observed during stable periods. With example one, during wars firms aim at the expected values of their Bertrand–Nash prices, p_n^i for the new (post demand-shock) one-shot game. Expectations about the new demand conditions are updated in each period as new price–quantity combinations are observed. Behaviour during wars is thus described by

$$\Delta p_t^i = \Delta E (p_n^i | \Omega_t) + \eta_t^i, \quad i = 1, \ldots, M \tag{12}$$

where

> Δ denotes a first difference,
> E is the expectation operator,
> Ω_t is the information available at time t, and
> η is a random disturbance.

If demand and cost conditions are similar for firms in different groups, contemporaneous price changes will be correlated as players use the same information to update their expectations. Players may thus appear to be moving in tandem. However, they will not react to rival previous-period price changes.

With example two, in contrast, firms follow their intertemporal reaction functions during wars. Their behaviour is thus described by

$$\Delta p_t^i = \sum_{h=1}^{M} R^{ih} \left(\sum_{\substack{k \in N_h \\ k \neq i}} w_k^{ih} \Delta p_{t-1}^k \right) + \eta_t^i, \quad i = 1, \dots, N. \tag{13}$$

With this example, R^{ih} is the response of a player in group i to previous-period price changes initiated by players from group h. The Rs are thus slopes of intertemporal reaction functions.

Given any reaction matrix $R = (R^{ih})$ there is a unique fixed point for the mappings (12) which is a stationary Nash equilibrium for the supergame with payoffs given by (11).[4] This vector, which we denote p_R, will be observed during stable periods. During price wars, however, prices will be below p_R. In these periods, firms move along their reaction functions.

This situation is illustrated in figure 11.1 for the case of two players. In the figure, $\bar{p}_w^i$ is the average price charged by player i during a war and p_R^i the price that the same firm will charge when the war is over.

An equation for price changes that nests these two examples can be written as

$$\Delta p_t^i = \sum_{h=1}^{M} \left\{ \alpha_{ih} R^{ih} \sum_{\substack{k \in N_h \\ k \neq i}} w_k^{ih} \Delta p_t^k + (1 - \alpha_{ih}) R^{ih} \sum_{\substack{k \in N_h \\ k \neq i}} w_k^{ih} \Delta p_{t-1}^k \right\} + \eta_t^i,$$

$$i = 1, \dots, N, \quad 0 \leq \alpha_{ih} \leq 1. \tag{14}$$

The R's have different interpretations, depending on the example. With example one, R is a matrix of contemporaneous price-change correlations whereas, with example 2, it is a matrix of slopes of intertemporal reaction functions.

A test for example one is $\alpha_{ih} = 1$. Here, the R matrix may or may not be zero. A test for example two, in contrast, is $R^{ih} > 0$ and $\alpha_{ih} = 0$.

These hypotheses can be assessed statistically if demand and price-change equations have been estimated. In addition, Bertrand–Nash, best-reply, and monopoly prices, p_n, p_b, and p_m can be calculated and compared to the prices observed both during and after the price war. Finally, equilibrium reaction-function prices p_R can be compared with the stable prices that were observed when the war was over. In this way, it can be seen if the estimated reaction-function strategies are capable of supporting the prices that were the outcome of the war.

3   The Vancouver retail gasoline market

Prior to 1981, the retail gasoline market in Canada was very stable. Prices and sales rose in a steady and orderly fashion, price dispersion was almost non-existent, and

---

[4] Slade (1989) demonstrates this for the case of symmetric duopolists.

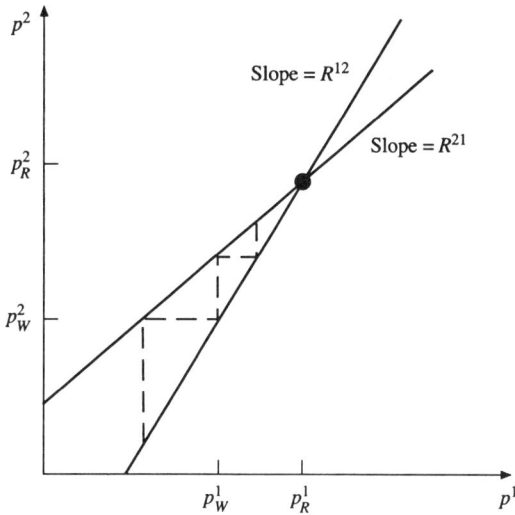

Figure 11.1 Intertemporal reaction functions

discounts for type of service (self-service or cash transactions, for example) were small.[5]

Recently, a combination of excess refining capacity and softening world-wide petroleum markets have led to radical changes in Canadian gasoline-marketing practices. The last several years have been characterized by some degree of price instability in all urban centers of Canada. One key change that occurred in the early 1980s was the reversal of the Canadian–American relative price. Traditionally, the Canadian price was lower. It continued to rise, however, at the time when the US price began to fall and eventually gasoline became cheaper in the US. Because many Canadians live within easy driving distance of the American border, buying gasoline in the US became a regular activity. This shift in demand seems to have been largely unanticipated and has left the industry with unwanted excess capacity. The result has been instability and price wars.

With the exception of periodic demand shifts, there is little uncertainty in this market. Prices are posted and posted prices are the same as transactions prices. In addition, rival sales can be monitored by counting rival customers. This market, therefore, seems to conform closely to the theoretical model of Slade (1989).

The specific marketing area studied is a heavily travelled five-mile strip that is known as the Kingsway region of Vancouver. Stations along the Kingsway strip are well connected but are only loosely connected to other regions of the city. The area

[5] Between 1972 and 1979, despite price increases, Canadian consumption of gasoline grew at a steady rate of 4 per cent per year. In 1980, consumption levelled off. Then in 1981, it dropped by 4 per cent, to be followed by a 10 per cent decline in 1982.

contains stations owned by most of the major and independent oil companies active in British Columbia as well as stations owned by the government. Ten companies and 13 retail outlets are involved.

The product sold, gasoline, is relatively homogeneous. Differentiation exists, however, for two reasons. First, stations are differentiated by type of ownership and service offered, the characteristics that determine the strategic groups. And, second, stations are differentiated by location, the characteristic that determines the weights used to average prices within groups.

The strategic groups remain to be specified. Service stations are characterized by type of ownership – major, independent, or government; type of service offered – self or full serve; and by extent of horizontal and vertical integration. Not all of these characteristics, however, are important determinants of producer and consumer behaviour (that is, of the demand facing the station and of the station's reactions to rival price changes).

A priori, one might expect to find three distinct groups of stations: those owned by major integrated firms, those owned by small independent marketers, and those owned by the government. In an earlier study (Slade, 1986), however, only two distinct groups were identified: majors and independents.[6] The behaviour of the government firm was seen to be indistinguishable from that of a private firm.

The government firm, Petro-Canada, owns two types of stations in the area. Some stations market under the name Petro-Canada and display the characteristic red maple leaf. The behaviour of these stations was seen to be indistinguishable from the behaviour of the integrated privately owned majors.

Petro-Canada has acquired most of its assets through purchase rather than through construction. When it purchases independent retail outlets, it may decide not to rebrand these outlets. Instead it may operate the stations as second or 'fighting' brands, a practice that is common for the majors as well. Second-brand stations maintain their independent 'personalities'.[7] The behaviour of the government second brand, PayNSave, was seen to be indistinguishable from that of the independents.

For these reasons, the Petro-Canada stations were included with the majors whereas PayNSave stations were included with the independents.

4   Data construction and estimation technique

4.1   The data

The data set used in this study was collected by the author in the summer of 1983. It consists of observations on price, variable cost, and sales volume for three types of

---

[6] A third class of station was identified in Slade (1986). These were denoted mid-tier. Unfortunately, there is only one mid-tier station in the sample, Husky. To avoid publishing numbers that can be identified with a particular station, therefore, Husky was dropped from the sample.

[7] A representative of Petro-Canada, in describing the decision to rebrand or not, stated that it depends on many factors. The stations that are operated as second brands tend to be older, have outdated equipment, and/or be run by operators with 'independent' personalities.

gasoline at each of the 13 service stations in the Kingsway region. Data were collected over a three-month price-war period.

Prices are posted at each station and are therefore public knowledge. In order to collect sales and cost data, however, it was necessary to obtain the cooperation of the ten regional-marketing managers and the 13 station operators. All were very accommodating in releasing this information. The one stipulation that they made was that when results were presented, stations be identified by number and not by name or brand.

For each station there are three variables to specify, p^i, q^i, and mc^i, as well as the weights, w^{ih}. The variable p^i is constructed as a Divisia price index for the three types of gasoline sold. q^i is then constructed as the implicit Divisia quantity index corresponding to p^i. Price is measured in cents per litre and quantity in 100 litres.

The construction of marginal cost requires several assumptions. It is clear that capital is fixed in the short run. It is additionally assumed that labour is fixed. At least one person must be employed to sell gasoline and, for many modern stations, only one person is required. Even when more than one person is employed or when a single employee spends only a fraction of his time selling gasoline, the number of people at a given station varies little with the quantity sold. Marginal cost is therefore assumed to be the cost of purchasing wholesale gasoline, which is also measured in cents per litre.

The weights w^{ih}_k used to average prices charged by stations within a group are inversely proportional to distance. That is, if d_{ik} is the distance between station i and station k, where $k \in N_h$, then w^{ih}_k is proportional to $1/d_{ik}$.

Finally, the exogenous demand-shift variables are chosen to be six dummy variables that distinguish the days of the week plus two dummies for the two holidays that occurred during the period of data collection.

4.2   Estimation

When additive disturbance terms have been appended to the N demand equations of the form of (1), they are estimated as a simultaneous seemingly unrelated system using iterative three-stage least squares. Correction for autocorrelation is performed when indicated. Coefficient restrictions are imposed so that parameters for stations in the same group will be equal.

The R matrix must also be assessed. This is accomplished by estimating N equations of the form of (14) as a simultaneous system. For the estimation, prices are calculated net of marginal cost so that price changes include only those not due to cost changes.[8] Again, iterative three-stage least squares is used, correction for autocorrelated errors is performed when appropriate, and coefficient restrictions are imposed so that stations in the same group will have the same parameters. The estimated response matrix is denoted R_a.

---

[8] Many of the cost changes during the year were due to tax changes or to the introduction or removal of dealer supports as described in Slade (1986). For this reason, it seems reasonable to assume that players know rival costs.

With both sets of equations, p_t^i and q_t^i are endogenous variables. The instruments used in the estimation of (1) and (14) are the station and firm characteristics discussed in Slade (1986), the demand-shift variables, and lagged values of the endogenous variables.

A problem arises in interpreting the estimated α's and therefore in discriminating between the two examples. The period of data collection does not necessarily correspond to the response period. In practice, reaction times are very short in this market. Obtaining an α close to one, therefore, may not be evidence against example two, the reaction-function example. A large value of α may just mean that stations change prices more often than once a day. Obtaining a value of $1 - \alpha$ that is significantly non-zero, in contrast, is evidence against example one, the discontinuous-strategy example. With short reaction times, it is highly unlikely that contemporaneous price changes occur a day apart.

5   Empirical results

5.1   The demand equations

There are only two groups N_i and N_m with M_i and M_m members respectively. Let v^m be a price charged by an independent and let v^m be a price charged by a major. Define

$$\bar{p}(i) = \sum_{\substack{j \in N_i \\ j \neq i}}^{N} w_j^{ii} p^j \tag{15}$$

and

$$\bar{p}(m) = \sum_{j \in N_i} w_j^{im} p^j. \tag{16}$$

For independent station i, $\bar{p}(i)$ is the inverse-distance-weighted average of rival independent prices, and for major station $m, \bar{p}(m)$ is the inverse-distance-weighted average of rival independent prices. $\bar{v}(m)$ and $\bar{v}(i)$ are defined similarly.

Using this notation, the demand equations are

$$q_t^i = a_1 + b_1 p_t^i + c_1 \bar{p}(i)_t + d_1 \bar{v}(i)_t + g_1(z_t) + \varepsilon_t^i \tag{17}$$

and

$$q_t^m = a_2 + b_2 v_t^m + c_2 \bar{v}(m)_t + d_2 \bar{p}(m)_t + g_2(z_t) + \varepsilon_t^m \quad i \in N_i, \quad m \in N_m \tag{18}$$

where g_1 and g_2 are linear functions of the demand-shift dummy variables.

Equations (17) and (18) were estimated by the method described in the previous section. Table 11.1 shows the estimated demand parameters. In the table, t-statistics are shown under the corresponding estimated coefficients.

An inspection of table 11.1 shows that own-price effects are negative and significant. Rival-price effects are positive, both for members of the same group and for members

Table 11.1 *Empirical estimates, estimated demand equations*

	Coefficients			
Group	a_1	b_1	c_1	d_1
Independents	73.55	-12.96	0.67	11.86
		$(-4.9)^*$	(0.23)	$(4.9)^*$
	a_2	b_2	c_2	d_2
Majors	149.10	-12.44	9.75	0.80
		$(-8.3)^*$	$(3.7)^*$	(0.40)

ESTIMATED RESPONSE MATRICES
Coefficients

Group	R_a^{ii}	α^{ii}	R_a^{im}	α^{im}
Independents	0.81	0.80	0.55	0.56
	$(11.0)^*$	$(17.6)^*$	$(11.9)^*$	$(13.0)^*$
	R_a^{mm}	α^{mm}	R_a^{mi}	α^{mi}
Majors	0.56	0.71	0.73	0.61
	$(12.2)^*$	$(17.3)^*$	$(5.6)^*$	$(7.8)^*$

Note: * Denotes significance at the 99 per cent level of confidence.

of the opposite group. What is surprising is that pricing by the independents, other than an independent's own price, has little effect on demand. Both c_1 and d_2 are small and statistically insignificant.

In the middle of the period of data collection, there was a temporary lull in pricing activity. It is therefore possible that what we have is two price wars occurring back to back. To test this hypothesis, the sample was divided into two subperiods and separate demand equations were estimated for each.[9] Quasi-likelihood-ratio tests (Gallant and Jorgenson, 1979) were then calculated to see if demand was stable over the entire period or whether there were two distinct demand regimes. The quasi-likelihood ratio (QLR) is distributed asymptotically χ_r^2, where r equals the number of independent restrictions.

Calculated QLRs are 7.3 for the independent demand equations and 1.2 for the major demand equations. Stability of demand over the entire period therefore cannot be rejected at any reasonable level of confidence. The test thus gives support to the idea of a single price war.

---

[9] The first subperiod consists of observations 1 through 40 whereas the second consists of observations 41 through 92.

5.2   The estimated response matrices

To estimate the response matrices used in the repeated game, prices are calculated net of marginal cost. Net prices are denoted by capital letters. That is, $P^i = p^i - mc^i$ is a net price for an independent firm $V^m = v^m - mc^m$ and is a net price for a major. $\bar{P}(i)$ and $\bar{P}(m)$ are then defined as in equations (15) and (16) with p^j replaced by P^j. $\bar{V}(m)$ and $\bar{V}(i)$ are defined similarly.

Using this notation, equation (14) becomes

$$\Delta P_t^i = \alpha_{ii} R_a^{ii} \Delta \bar{P}(i)_t + (1 - \alpha_{ii}) R_a^{ii} \Delta \bar{P}(i)_{t-1}$$
$$+ \alpha_{im} R_a^{im} \Delta \bar{V}(i)_t + (1 - \alpha_{im}) R_a^{im} \Delta \bar{V}(i)_{t-1} + \eta_t^i \qquad (19)$$

$$\Delta V_t^m = \alpha_{mm} R_a^{mm} \Delta \bar{V}(m)_t + (1 - \alpha_{mm}) R_a^{mm} \Delta \bar{V}(m)_{t-1}$$
$$+ \alpha_{mi} R_a^{mi} \Delta \bar{P}(m)_t + (1 - \alpha_{mi}) R_a^{mi} \Delta \bar{P}(m)_{t-1} + \eta_t^m. \qquad (20)$$

If the estimated αs do not equal one, the matrix $\hat{R}_a$ is an estimate of the intertemporal responses for the repeated game. This response is distributed over two periods. In contrast, if the estimated αs equal one, $\hat{R}_a$ is an estimate of contemporaneous price-change correlations.

The second half of table 11.1 shows the estimated Rs and αs. Asymptotic t-statistics are shown under each estimated coefficient.[10]

5.3   Solutions to the game

Given the demand and cost parameters, calculation of the various outcomes for the constituent game requires numerical solution of systems of equations. For example, calculation of the best-reply matrix R_b, is accomplished by solving the M^2 quadratic equations of the form of (7) for the M^2 unknowns R_b^{kj}.

Responses R^{kj}, where k and j take on the values i for independent and m for major, are shown in the first half of table 11.2. Three response matrices appear: Nash, best-reply, and actual (or econometrically estimated). Under the actual replies the parameters α_{kj} are listed. The α's distinguish between same-day and previous-day price-change correlations as discussed earlier.

The table also shows t-statistics that test the hypotheses $R_a^{kj} = R_n^{kj}$ and $R_a^{kj} = R_b^{kj}$. It can be seen that both uncorrelated Bertrand–Nash and one-shot best-reply behaviour are resoundingly rejected.

The t-statistics that test the hypotheses $(1 - \alpha_{kj}) = 0$ are also shown. These hypotheses are also rejected, which can be interpreted as evidence against the discontinuous-strategy example and in favour of the continuous-strategy alternative.

---

[10] Equations (19) and (20) are non-linear in the structural parameters. The asymptotic t-statistics are therefore really the square root of a chi-squared variable with one degree of freedom. The distribution of that statistic, however, is almost the same as a two-tailed t-statistic for large samples.

Table 11.2 *Solutions to the game*

		Responses			
		ii	*mi*	*im*	*mm*
Nash	R_n	0.0	0.0	0.0	0.0
Best replies	R_b	0.03	0.02	0.14	0.13
Actual	R_a	0.81	0.73	0.55	0.56
	α	0.80	0.61	0.56	0.71
Test for			*t*-statistics		
$R_a = R_n$		1.0*	5.6*	11.9*	12.2*
$R_a = R_b$		10.6*	5.4*	8.9*	9.4*
$(1 - \alpha) = 0$		4.4*	5.0*	10.2*	7.1*

	Prices and profits		
	Independent Price, p	Major price, v	Industry Profit, Π
Model			
$p_n \Pi_n$	44.6	45.1	277 628
$p_b \Pi_b$	44.9	45.6	303 011
$p_R \Pi_a$	50.0	48.8	419 948
$p_m \Pi_m$	55.1	64.9	1 032 010
Observed			
Price war	44.7	45.2	282 369
Stable outcome	50.0	50.0	428 678

Note: * Denotes rejection at the 99 per cent level of confidence.

Unfortunately, given the data, it is not possible to test the continuous-reaction-function example directly. Indirect tests, however, are discussed below.

Table 11.2 shows certain empirical regularities. Consider the best replies for the constituent game. Reactions to price changes initiated by independents (R_b^{ii} and R_b^{mi}) are very small. This is not very surprising, given that analysis of the estimated demand equations revealed that prices charged by independent rivals are not significant determinants of sales. In contrast, reactions to price changes initiated by majors are moderate but not large.

The actual responses R_a are very different from R_b and from R_n. It is in general true that

$$R_a > R_b > R_n. \tag{21}$$

Repeated play is thus associated with more 'punishment' in the form of price-matching behaviour than is associated with single-period solutions. In addition, actual responses to price changes initiated by independents are larger than actual responses to major-price changes. It seems that the independents are being punished more than the majors.

There is a possible explanation for this behaviour. Price uniformity appears to be a goal of the majors.[11] When interviewed, marketing managers spoke of not 'allowing' independents to charge lower prices than the majors charge. In equilibrium, the price that a firm chooses is inversely related to its own price elasticity of demand and directly related to rival responses to price changes that it initiates. The independents face more elastic demand than the majors (Slade, 1986).[12] Price uniformity therefore requires that responses to their price changes be larger.

The second half of table 11.2 shows price and profit combinations for various solutions to the game. The first four rows show estimated single-period prices and profits for various solution concepts. The monopoly solution shown was calculated subject to a constraint of individual rationality. That is, joint profits were maximized subject to the constraint that each group do as well as in the single-period Bertrand–Nash equilibrium.[13]

The calculation of prices and profits corresponding to the intertemporal reaction functions with slopes R_a involves the discount factor δ. For the solution shown, δ was set equal to one and equation (7) was used.[14] Given the speed of reaction in this market, the approximation should be reasonable.

It can be seen that

$$\Pi_m > \Pi_a > \Pi_b > \Pi_n. \tag{22}$$

Through repeated play, therefore, stations do better than they would if they played the non-cooperative game only once. Profit, however, is far short of the monopoly profit.

Finally, table 11.2 shows average prices observed during the price war and the stable prices that prevailed when the war was over.[15] These correspond to $\bar{p}_w$ and p_R in figure 11.1. Two features of these prices are of interest. First, average prices observed during the price war are indistinguishable from Nash prices. If one had only aggregate data on prices and quantities, therefore, it would be difficult to reject Nash behaviour during the war. When we observe how stations respond to one another, however, one-shot Nash behaviour is easily rejected.

Second, during stable periods prices do not change. It is therefore impossible to estimate response matrices for these periods. We can, however, perform a weaker test. It is possible to check if the equilibrium prices p_{Ra} corresponding to the estimated response matrix R_a are close to the prices observed when the war was over, as example

---

[11] It is not clear why the majors desire uniformity but it is clear that uniformity is a goal.

[12] Demand elasticities can be calculated from table 11.1 as $\varepsilon_j = -\hat{b}_j \bar{p}_j / \bar{q}_j$, where $j = i, m$ and a bar over a variable denotes its mean. The two $\hat{b}$'s and $\bar{p}$'s are nearly equal. $\bar{q}_m > \bar{q}_i$, therefore implies that $\varepsilon_i > \varepsilon_m$.

[13] In the unconstrained monopoly solution, some firms earn negative profits.

[14] When $\delta = 0$, response is immediate and therefore the value of α is irrelevant.

[15] After the price war, the period of price stability lasted for nearly a year until the summer of 1984.

two would predict. A glance at table 11.2 reveals that these two price vectors are very close, a fact that gives further credence to the continuous-reaction-function example.

A final test of the reaction-function example is performed – the stability of the estimated response matrix is investigated. With example two, these functions are institutional regularities that determine the equilibrium price vector. Lack of stability of this matrix would therefore be evidence against the example.

As with the demand equations, the sample was divided into two subperiods and separate response matrices estimated for each. Likelihood ratios that test for stability are as follows

Response	R^{ii}	R^{mi}	R^{im}	R^{mm}
QLR	5.6	3.4	9.56*	2.6

In general, the responses are stable. Only the stability of the response of independents to major-price changes is rejected at the 95 per cent level of confidence. With this response, there is a trend over time. In the first subperiod, the response is 0.46 whereas in the second, the response increases to 0.69. The average over the entire period is 0.55.

It is also possible that near the end of each subperiod, when prices are approaching stability, reactions change. For each response and each subperiod, an additional test was performed to assess if the last ten observations in the period belong to a different regime. With this test, stability of responses was never rejected.

6   Summary and conclusions

The existence of a very large number of solutions to a repeated game leads one naturally to an empirical assessment of the outcome that in fact results in a given game. This is one object of the present chapter. It is possible, using data on service stations in the Vancouver retail gasoline market, to calculate and compare cooperative and non-cooperative solutions to the constituent game and the actual outcome of the repeated game.

The actual outcome turns out to be substantially less lucrative than the cooperative solution to the one-shot game. It is, however, more profitable for all players than non-cooperative single-period solutions. The possibility of punishing undesirable behaviour that arises through repeated play is therefore a threat that enables firms to move in the direction of the cooperative outcome.

A second object of the chapter is to model the price-war dynamics in such a way that tests of alternative supergame strategies are possible. In particular, discontinuous punishment strategies are assessed versus the alternative of continuous reaction-function strategies. With reaction-function strategies, firm price changes are related to previous-period rival-price changes. With discontinuous strategies, in contrast, price wars are periods of reversion to Nash behaviour.

With example one, in each period firms charge prices close to the expected value of their Bertrand–Nash prices for the one-shot game. If demand and cost conditions are not too different across firms, therefore, Nash prices may be similar and contemporaneous price changes may appear to be correlated as players update their expectations. With example two, in contrast, firms react to rival previous-period price changes.

Definitive tests that distinguish between the two examples are not possible. The problem arises because the period of data collection is longer than the response time. Nevertheless, the evidence seems to point to the reaction-function example as the most appropriate for this market.

After the price war came to an end, prices were stable for nearly a year. Without any price variation, it is impossible to estimate response matrices. A weaker test of the reaction-function model, however, was performed. The equilibrium prices associated with the response matrix that was estimated from the price-war data were calculated and compared with the stable prices that were observed at the end of the war. These two price vectors were seen to be almost equal.

Stability of the reaction functions was not rejected by most of the tests performed. There is some evidence, however, of a trend in the response parameters for the independents. This raises the possibility of allowing firms to update their expectations about rival responses to the changes that they initiate. Such investigations will be pursued in the future.

References

Friedman, J. (1971), 'Noncooperative equilibria for supergames', *Review of Economic Studies*, 38, 1–12.
Gallant, R. and D.W. Jorgenson (1979), 'Statistical inference for a system of simultaneous equations in the context of instrumental-variable estimation', *Journal of Econometrics*, 11, 275–302.
Green, E.J. and R.H. Porter (1984), 'Noncooperative collusion under imperfect price information', *Econometrica*, 52, 87–100.
Kalai, E. and W. Stanford (1985), 'Conjectural variations in accelerated Cournot games', *International Journal of Industrial Organization*, 3, 133–52.
Porter, R.H. (1983a), 'Optimal trigger-price strategies', *Journal of Economic Theory*, 29, 313–38.
    (1983b), 'A study of cartel stability: the Joint Executive Committee, 1880–1886', *The Bell Journal of Economics*, 14, 301–14.
Slade, M.E. (1986), 'Conjectures, firm characteristics, and market structure', *International Journal of Industrial Organization*, 4, 347–369.
    (1989), 'Price wars in price-setting supergames', *Economica*, 56, 295–310.

Chapter 12

Tacit collusion (2)
Collusive equilibrium in the great salt duopoly

Ray Rees

This chapter sets out to test two interesting lines of recent development in oligopoly theory. The first, arising out of the analysis of infinitely repeated games, suggests conditions under which collusive outcomes can be supported as non-cooperative equilibria by appropriate threat strategies. The second considers the nature of equilibrium in a homogeneous duopoly in which firms set prices subject to fixed capacity constraints. Both these bodies of theory are discussed more fully in the next section.

The data used for the tests are given in a report on the UK Monopolies and Merger Commission (MMC) inquiry into price behaviour in the UK market for white salt.[1] In this market two firms produce an essentially homogeneous commodity with blockaded entry and fixed capacities. The report provides detailed data on prices, outputs, and

This article first appeared in *The Economic Journal*, 103, pp. 833–48.

Earlier versions of this paper have been presented at seminars at the Universities of Birmingham, Bristol, East Anglia, and Swansea, the European University Institute, Florence, the Institute of Economics and Statistics, University of Oxford, and Northwestern University, Evanston, Ill. I am grateful to participants in those seminars for many helpful comments, as well as to James Friedman, Rolf Färe, Shawna Grosskopf, Dan Kovenock, Val Lambson, Venk Sadanand, Mike Waterson and two referees. None of these of course bears responsibility for the final version.

[1] 'White salt: a report on the supply of white salt in the United Kingdom by producers of such salt', HMSO London 1986. This is subsequently referred to as MMC (1986). Though the present author was at the time a member of the MMC he was not involved in this particular inquiry, and all the information used in this chapter was derived solely from the published report.

(marginal) costs as well as a great deal of more qualitative information which is valuable in interpreting these data. The information in the report is derived directly from the working of a real-world oligopoly. Its main drawback is that it relates only to five years, and does not allow standard econometric methods to be applied, in particular to the estimation of a demand function.

Nevertheless, this chapter hopes to demonstrate that some quite strong conclusions can still be drawn, in particular on the extent to which the various possible equilibrium concepts proposed by the theoretical literature can explain the apparent nature of the equilibrium in this case. The wealth of detail given in the report seems too good to ignore, even if it cannot support a standard econometric investigation.

There is a correspondence between the two types of model with which this paper is concerned and the positions taken by the MMC and the firms that were the subject of the inquiry. The theory of price-setting duopoly under capacity constraints assumes that firms act non-cooperatively, making no attempt, whether tacit or explicit, to agree upon their choice of prices. The firms in the MMC inquiry claimed that they had in fact not colluded, and that the market outcome was fully consistent with 'competitive' behaviour. By examining whether the predictions of the price-setting model match what happened in this market, we have simultaneously a test of the model and also of whether the firms' claims can be accepted.

While skating carefully around the word 'collusion', the MMC concluded that the firms had 'severely restrained price competition'.[2] The basis for this judgement appears to have been some evidence on communication between the firms, the fact that over a long period prices had been virtually identical and changed more or less simultaneously, and finally a view of what the outcome should have been had the firms in fact competed. This view was not based on the predictions of the models considered here, and it is indeed questionable that it could be supported by any generally accepted positive model of the market, but later in this chapter we argue that the MMC's judgement was essentially correct.

Given then that the behaviour of the firms can be taken to be collusive, the question arises of whether this can be explained by recent developments in the analysis of repeated games. In the next section we present brief outlines of the relevant theories and identify the sense in which they will be tested in this chapter.

1   Theoretical background

Consider a market with two firms producing homogeneous outputs in a single time period, and independently choosing prices subject to equal, constant marginal costs and exogenously given capacity constraints. Edgeworth (1897) showed that if each firm's capacity is less than market demand at a price equal to the given marginal cost, the Bertrand result that equilibrium price equals marginal cost no longer holds. If the market situation is repeated over a sequence of periods, price will vary cyclically between well-defined upper and lower limits, p_h and p_l. The upper limit p_h is the price

---

[2] Para. 9–10, MMC (1986).

which maximizes a firm's profit given that it is undercut by its competitor. The firm with the lower price produces at capacity, the higher-priced firm is then faced with a residual demand with respect to which it finds the most profitable price p_h. The lower limit p_l is the price which yields a firm the same profit π^* when it is the lower-priced firm and produces to capacity, as when it is the higher-priced firm and sets p_h. In general p_l exceeds marginal cost. If, however, we insist that the analysis must relate to only one time period, i.e., to a 'one-shot game', then Edgeworth essentially shows that no equilibrium price exists in this model.

Shubik (1959) gave this result a game-theoretic reinterpretation: in this game there is no equilibrium in pure price strategies, but there is an equilibrium in mixed strategies. Beckman (1965) and Levitan and Shubik (1972) derived these equilibrium mixed strategies for specific examples of the model, the main difference between them being in the assumptions made about the rationing process. When the firms set different prices, some assumption must be made as to how the residual demand facing the higher-priced firm is determined, or equivalently, how buyers wishing to be supplied by the lower-priced firm are rationed. Beckman assumed a form of random rationing. Levitan and Shubik assumed *efficient rationing:* the lower-priced firm supplies those buyers with higher willingness to pay.[3] For concreteness, we focus here on this latter case. Then the equilibrium outcome in this type of market is predicted to be as follows: there is a given interval of prices which is defined by the Edgeworth upper and lower bounds p_h and p_l. Firms choose prices randomly from this interval, and the equilibrium probability distributions regulating these choices are such that each firm has the same expected profit π^* whatever the price pair chosen. It follows that there is a zero probability that the firms will choose equal prices, and that if the market situation is repeated after a period, each firm's price changes randomly (within the given interval) over time.[4]

An interesting extension of these results with particular relevance to the market studied in this chapter has recently been made by Deneckere and Kovenock (1992). They allow the (still exogenously given) capacity levels of the firms, as well as their (constant) marginal costs, to differ, and consider the question of the endogenous non-cooperative determination of the identity of a price leader in this model. That is, firms engage in a game of timing of price announcements, and the equilibrium of the game determines which firm is the price leader and which the follower. Their result is that

---

[3] For a thorough discussion of the economics of these rationing schemes see Dixon (1987).

[4] Capacity is here taken to be exogenous. Kreps and Scheinkman (1983) allow capacity levels to be chosen endogenously, in a two-stage game. At the second stage firms play a price-setting game with fixed capacities. At the first stage they choose capacities in the light of their effects on the equilibrium at the second stage. The interesting result is that capacities are chosen to be such that outputs and price are precisely those given by the Cournot equilibrium of the model. This result is further generalized by Osborne and Pitchik (1986). Unfortunately, as Davidson and Deneckere (1986) show, this striking reconciliation of the results of quantity-setting and price-setting duopoly models is not robust to relaxation of the 'efficient-rationing' assumption. Moreover, as we show below, its prediction that both firms will produce at capacity is not confirmed in the market being considered. However, this is probably not a fair test of the theory, since capacity in this market is best taken as exogenous over the period to which the observations relate.

the firm with larger capacity will be the price leader, while the smaller firm will follow with a price just below that of the leader, and will produce at full capacity. Thus the price set by the leader is p_h, the upper bound of the Edgeworth interval, and it earns the same profit π^* as in the mixed strategy equilibrium. On the other hand, the smaller firm earns higher profit under price leadership than under simultaneous choice of (mixed strategy) prices, since it is producing to capacity at a price greater than p_l.

The theories then give quite definite testable predictions about the kind of price behaviour we should observe in this type of market. It is argued in the next section that the market for white salt is the type of market for which these models can apply, and therefore can be used to test these theories.

The models just discussed are essentially 'one-shot games': they are concerned with deriving a Nash equilibrium in a single play of the price-setting game. However, if we move to the empirically more relevant view of the market as an infinitely repeated game, then it is well known that repeated plays of the one-shot Nash equilibrium also represent a Nash equilibrium of the repeated game. However, the important point is that other Nash equilibria are possible, and in particular those that yield the firms more profitable outcomes than those in the one-shot non-cooperative equilibrium. The basic idea underlying the work of Friedman (1971), Abreu (1986, 1988) and Fudenberg and Maskin (1986) among others is that these more profitable outcomes in the one-shot game may be sustained as non-cooperative Nash equilibria of the repeated game by threats of appropriate punishments for deviation. The intuition is clear. If a firm deviates from an agreement to collude in one period, it could be punished in later periods, and the threat of this *ex ante* may be enough to sustain collusion. However, going beyond intuition, a number of issues have to be considered. What form can or should punishment take and will it be sufficient in fact to offset these gains since it causes future losses which have to be discounted to be comparable with immediate gains from deviating? Moreover, since punishment will often hurt the punishers, for example a punitive price war reduces profits to all firms, will threats to carry out such punishment in fact be credible?

A formal answer to these questions is given by Abreu's theory of 'simple penal codes', which has been applied to the case of price-setting capacity-constrained oligopoly by Lambson (1987, 1991). Suppose that firms agree, tacitly or explicitly, on a particular price and allocation of outputs for each period. They also agree on a time path of prices that will be applied as a punishment for a deviation from the agreed price by a firm, where this punishment path may depend on exactly which firm deviates. A punishment path is credible if it is in each firm's interest not to deviate from it in the event that it has to be imposed. An agreed price and output allocation is sustainable if it would not pay any firm to deviate from it given the credible punishment path that would then be imposed. An interesting aspect of the punishment path is its 'stick and carrot' nature. In the first stage of punishment, price is cut to inflict loss of profit, but this is followed by a second stage of reversion to the more profitable price and output allocation. It then pays a firm that has just deviated to accept its punishment, since failure to do so leads to reimposition of the punitive phase of the punishment path and postponement of the return to the more profitable cooperative phase. If a firm that did not deviate originally refused to participate in punishing the firm that did, then it itself would become a deviant and have the appropriate punishment path inflicted on it. In this theory the requirement of credibility is formally embodied in the concept of subgame-perfect equilibrium. The strategy of adhering to the agreed price and output allocation as long as no firm deviates, and adhering to the prescribed punishment path immediately following any deviation, is shown to induce a Nash equilibrium for every possible subgame of the infinitely repeated game. Of course, if the cooperative agreement *is* sustainable, we would not actually observe implementation of the punishment strategies – the observed market equilibrium would be the agreed price and output allocation.

Any particular price and output allocation may or may not be sustainable by Abreu's punishment strategies or simple penal code. This depends on the firms' discount factors and the structure of the market – the demand and cost functions the firms face. Those determine the extent of the gains from deviation, the losses of profit that can be inflicted through punishment, and the present value of future losses relative to immediate gains from deviation. For our present purposes, we are interested in the question: if we were to accept that firms in the white salt market behaved collusively, whether tacitly or explicitly, is this consistent with the models of Abreu and Lambson? We would conclude that it was, if the actual allocation turned out to be sustainable by Abreu-type punishment strategies, while if the actual allocation turned out to be not sustainable (at reasonable discount rates), we would have to reject the theory and look for some alternative explanation of collusion. Note that this is a one-sided test of the theory. It would also be interesting to find a market in which collusion did not take place, and to examine whether more profitable allocations than the actual one would be sustainable, in which case we could again reject the theory.[5] This will however have to be left for further work.

2   The market for white salt

This section sets out briefly some salient facts about the salt market.[6]

Production

Salt production in the United Kingdom consists essentially of the extraction and processing of a non-renewable natural resource. However, reserves are so large

---

[5] To put this more precisely, consider the set of all markets, and the subsets of markets (a) which satisfy Abreu's conditions for the sustainability of an agreed allocation by credible threats and (b) in which collusion is observed. I interpret Abreu's theory to say that these subsets are equal. All that this chapter can do, in considering just one market, is to show that their intersection is not empty, if Abreu's conditions are satisfied; or that the sets are not equal, if the conditions are not satisfied. In this latter case the set in (a) could still be a subset of that in (b), in which case Abreu's conditions would be sufficient but not necessary for collusion.

[6] A fuller description, together with a complete set of the data on which the later discussion is based, is given in Rees (1991).

relative to consumption that the resource rent is effectively zero and we can regard salt as a manufactured commodity. Water is pumped down into salt strata lying underground, this dissolves the salt to form brine, which is then pumped to the surface and transported through a pipeline to, initially, a purification plant. Here chemicals are added to remove unwanted minerals, then the purified brine is pumped to an evaporation plant. Six large boilers, known as effects, are arranged in sequence, brine is pumped into the first, the water is boiled off and the salt precipitated, and the waste steam is passed into the second effect where it is used to heat more brine, and so on. After the evaporation process 'undried salt' is produced, with the consistency of wet sand. Part of this output is shipped immediately to chemical plants, mainly for use in production of caustic soda and chlorine. The remainder is dried, and then shipped, in bulk or in bags, again to chemical plants for use in production of sodium and chloride, but also to food manufacturing and animal feed preparation plants, and tanning and dyeing works. Less than 10 per cent of total salt output is sold for cooking or table use.

Concentration

There are effectively just two producers: British Salt (BS), a self-contained but wholly owned subsidiary of an industrial engineering and contracting group, Stavely Industries; and ICI Weston Point (WP), a small part of the Mond division of the large chemicals conglomerate ICI. Fortunately for this study WP is a self-contained accounting unit selling less than 5 per cent of its output to other ICI plants. Imports and a number of very small salt works account for around 3 per cent of the market and so in the rest of this study will be ignored. We treat BS and WP as single-plant profit-maximizing firms. BS takes on average about 55 per cent of the UK market and WP the remainder.

Capacity

Each firm is subject to a maximum capacity constraint, which is 824 kilotonnes (kte) pa for BS and 1095 kte pa for WP. Over the years 1980–4 there was considerable excess capacity: BS averaged less than 75 per cent capacity utilization, while WP's UK sales alone amounted only to 45 per cent of capacity, on average, though its export sales, made at a much lower profit, brought its capacity utilization rate up to around 65 per cent. The degree of excess capacity appears to have been caused by an unanticipated decline in demand since the capacity was first installed in the early 1970s.

Entry

Though salt strata suitable for extraction are common in the United Kingdom, a combination of planning controls and high transport costs seems to rule out production outside the Cheshire area in which both BS and ICI's plants are located.

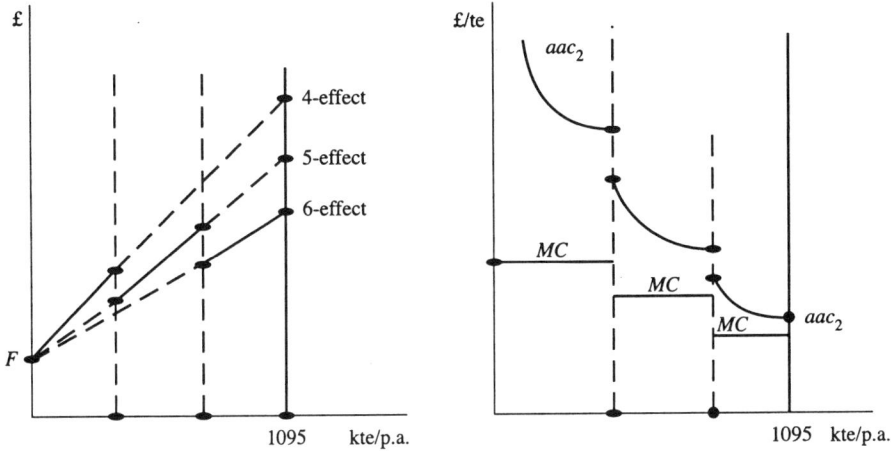

Figure 12.1 Cost structure for WP

The main users are located quite closely to the salt plants, while at the prevailing prices imports were not regarded as a threat because of the high cost of transport and transshipment relative to value. The major salt strata in Cheshire are owned by the incumbent firms. Moreover, there are significant economies of scale and as we have just seen significant excess capacity in the market. In the rest of this study therefore we assume that the market behaviour of the incumbents has been influenced by the threat of new entry only to the extent that the possibility of imports places an upper bound on the price that can be set.

Costs

The MMC report suggested that variations in output by BS can be achieved without significantly affecting energy usage per unit of output (para 4.10, MMC, 1986) and, since this is the main variable input, we translate this into the assumption that over the relevant range of outputs average variable cost of production *(avc)* is constant as output varies and so equals marginal production cost. WP, which has a somewhat different technology than BS, has a more complex cost structure. Reductions in output below capacity are most efficiently coped with by reducing the number of effects in operation, and this raises *avc* in a stepwise way[7] (see figure 12.1). The MMC report gives an indication of the heights of these steps but does not give the precise

---

[7] As Figure 12.1 shows, fixed production costs are assumed not to depend on the number of effects in operation. The total cost function jumps discontinuously at an output level (here 400 kte pa and 800 kte pa are chosen for purposes of illustration) at which it becomes efficient to change the number of effects in operation. Essentially, however, we are interested only in the middle step, which corresponds to the actual operations, and costs in the neighbourhood of WP's capacity output.

Table 12.1 *Firms' Marginal and Average Avoidable Costs*

		1980	1981	1982	(£/te) 1983	1984
				Year		
avc	*BS*	6.30	8.07	8.12	9.21	9.07
	WP	6.02	7.39	9.49	10.82	11.47
mc	*BS*	9.81	12.11	12.03	13.67	13.36
	WP	12.77	14.22	14.74	16.77	16.14
$\overline{aac}$	*BS*	12.61	15.07	14.72	17.07	17.01
	WP	14.46	15.68	16.28	18.49	17.72

Source: MMC (1986).

output levels at which the steps occur. In the period under study WP operated along the middle step.

In addition to production cost, the other component of variable cost is distribution cost, consisting mainly of transport costs. We assume these are constant per unit of output. Marginal cost *MC* is then the sum of *avc* and average distribution cost. Finally, we define as average avoidable cost *(aac)* a firm's *MC* plus 'fixed production costs' per unit of output. The latter, consisting mainly of labour, management, and maintenance costs, do not vary with output, but are incurred if and only if the plant is operating: *aac is* therefore zero if output is zero and the plant is shut down. $\overline{aac}_1$ denotes BS's *aac* at its capacity output, and similarly $\overline{aac}_2$ is WP's capacity *aac* and takes into account WP's lower average variable production cost at capacity, due to six-effect operation. Since all these costs play an important role in what follows, it is useful to summarize the full range of information in table 12.1.

The data in table 12.1, interpreted here as the actual values of marginal and average avoidable costs firms would have used in their decision taking, are one of the most valuable contributions of the MMC report, given the concerns of this chapter. We should at this point therefore enter a qualification. We shall throughout conduct the analysis as if there is only one output. However, there are at least three: undried and dried salt sold in bulk, and dried salt sold in bags. The last two outputs must be somewhat costlier to produce because of the additional drying and/or bagging costs. It is impossible to disaggregate the cost data among these three outputs (for example no separate figures are given on bulk and bagged dried salt sales). However, for each firm the proportions of total output accounted for by each type of salt remained fairly stable over this period. For WP, undried salt varied apparently randomly between 35 per cent and 41 per cent of total output and for BS between 30 per cent and 37 per cent. Thus we assume that no significant systematic bias results from treating output as homogeneous. This is helped by the fact that, as we see below, the two firms made identical percentage increases in the prices of all types of salt over this period.

Prices

In a fascinating section of the report (paras. 5.25–5.41 in MMC, 1986), the MMC lists the dates and amounts of the 17 changes to list prices made by the two firms between January 1974 and January 1984. The increases are always either exactly or virtually identical. From 1980 each firm made the same percentage increases across all grades of salt, prior to this increases varied across grades. In each case one firm announced its price increases and the second firm followed within a month and usually within two weeks. Of the 13 price increases announced from 1974–80, BS led eight times and WP led five times. In each of the years 1981–4, WP was the leader. Typically the leader would inform the follower of its planned price increase a month before it came into effect, and the latter would then inform the leader of its proposed (identical) price change within that period (table 5.8 of MMC, 1986).

In their evidence to the MMC on this matter, the firms denied collusion[8] and the exchange of any information other than of proposed price changes[9] (paras. 8.8–8.17, 8.56–8.74, MMC, 1986). They made the point that in a competitive market prices would be identical and would move closely together. They also argued that it is not enough to consider only list prices, since there is widespread discounting to buyers and so actual prices paid could well have moved differently. To test this latter point the MMC examined the discount structure of each seller. Until 1980 the rebate scales of the firms had been identical. Furthermore, for the majority of buyers discounts have been insignificant, amounting to less than 1 per cent of the list price. For a few very large buyers, BS's discount structure after 1980 implied a price per tonne of roughly 0.25 per cent below that of WP. Moreover, the MMC sampled a group of buyers to identify the values of differences in prices they had been quoted by the two sellers. These differences average about 0.5 per cent of the price, with the highest at 2.2 per cent and the modal value close to zero (table 5.14, MMC, 1986). The proposition that buyers perceived price uniformity is supported by the fact that around 78 per cent of buyers had not changed their sources of supply over the five years previous to the enquiry (para. 5.13, MMC, 1986).

Profits

The accounting rates of return on capital employed (ROC), net of depreciation, and at historic cost, are shown for the two firms in table 12.2, which also gives some other

---

[8] Prior to the Restrictive Practices Act, 1956, a formal agreement to set common ex works and delivered prices for producers and common resale prices for merchants had been in force for more than 20 years. There was also an aggregated rebate scheme under which buyers received a discount based on aggregate purchases from all sellers. The Act required such agreements to be registered with the Registrar of Restrictive Practices, following which they could be challenged in the Restrictive Practices Court. The salt agreement was discontinued and not registered.

[9] The firms explained that this was done because each bought salt from the other and it was usual to notify buyers in advance of price increases.

Table 12.2 *Capacity utilization, market share, prices and profits*

	Year				
	1980	1981	1982	1983	1984
I Capacity utilization (%)					
BS	85	71	79	69	67
WP (UK output/capacity)	54	47	43	40	41
WP (total output/capacity)	75	60	65	59	64
II Shares of UK market (%)	54	53	58	57	55
BS	46	47	42	43	45
WP	46	45	53	52	53
III ROC (%)	33	32	30	24	24
BS	19.4	7.5	14	8	5
WP	BS	WP	WP	WP	WP
IV Rate of price increase (%)					
Firm initiating					

Source: MMC (1986).

important market information. Over the same period, the comparable rate of return for all large quoted companies varied between 9 per cent and 13 per cent, and of companies in the chemicals and man-made fibres industries between 7 per cent and 16 per cent. However, in the remainder of this chapter we consider only profits defined as revenues less variable and fixed production and distribution costs. The reason is of course that the capital costs were essentially sunk and did not vary either with the level of output or the shutdown decision. Profits are the short-run quasi-rents which the firms are assumed to maximize.

3   Competition, price leadership, collusion and joint-profit maximization

The data on costs, capacities and prices given by the report we take to be 'hard data'. Though they are subject to interpretation, the numbers themselves are those the firms themselves would have had to work with. We can give reasonably firm answers, on the basis only of these data and, in some cases, general assumptions on demand, to the three questions with which we are concerned. Did the firms behave non-cooperatively as in the Edgeworth–Levitan–Shubik (ELS) or Deneckere–Kovenock models? If not, does an Abreu–Lambson type of explanation of collusion hold? Did they maximize joint profits? We consider these in turn.

From the results summarized in section 1, we know that the one-shot non-cooperative equilibrium involves firms operating at below capacity and choosing mixed strategies in prices.[10] Clearly, both firms were producing at less than capacity.

[10] In fact, there are two other equilibrium possibilities, each of which can be ruled out in the salt market. Where firms' capacities are sufficiently large, we would have the Bertrand equilibrium with

If they had been choosing prices according to mixed strategies, then the probability that every time they chose prices those prices would be identical, is zero. Yet on each of the 17 times prices were set in the period 1974–84 prices were in fact identical. Thus we could reject the ELS model, even if we had no knowledge of the extent to which the firms actually exchanged information on proposed price changes, and thus could be said to be correlating strategies.

A somewhat stronger case could be made for the Deneckere-Kovenock theory of price leadership. The theory predicts that the larger firm would be the price leader. This was true in each year 1981–4. In the seven years previous to that, leadership varied between the two firms, but we have cost data only for 1980–4. In the Deneckere–Kovenock model, the smaller firm could be price leader if its marginal cost is sufficiently higher than that of the larger firm, and only in 1980 can we certainly say that this was not true, so that BS's price leadership in that year contradicts the theory. The theory also predicts that the follower will price 'just below' the leader, and, though this is not consistent with the data on list prices, the evidence on discounts given by the MMC could perhaps be interpreted as just consistent with this. However, the crucial mismatch is in respect of capacity utilization. In the Deneckere–Kovenock price leadership equilibrium, the follower sells at full capacity. This was clearly not the case in the white salt market.

Thus, in this market at least, the predictions of the ELS and Deneckere–Kovenock theories are not confirmed. The main reason, we would claim, is that they are derived from one-shot non-cooperative equilibria.

In its evidence to the MMC, BS stated that 'if it raised prices by a lesser amount than [WP], and [WP] failed to lower its own price to the same level, there would be an immediate transfer of business to itself . . . This would lead to a long-term retaliation by [WP] who would seek to take customers from British Salt' (MMC, 1986, para. 28.11). This statement shows that the firms clearly share the intuition underlying the idea of collusive equilibrium supported by the threat of retaliation, which is hardly surprising, simple as it is.

We now have to see if the outcome in this market is consistent with the more formal theory. We assume that the actual prices and profits in each of the years 1980–4 correspond to collusive allocations, and we wish to test whether these can be sustained by credible threats. Following Lambson (1987), we have the criteria for:

(i) Sustainability: Let π_i^c denote the one-period profit firm $I = 1, 2$ earns under the agreement, π_i^R the maximum profit it can earn by reneging on this agreement, τ_i a punishment path of prices that will be imposed in the period following a violation of the agreement by firm i, $V_i(\tau_i)$ the present value at the date punishment begins of

---

price equal to marginal cost. This was clearly not the case here. Alternatively, if each firm's capacity is less than or equal to its Cournot output in this market each would produce at capacity or price would clear the market. Since both firms produced below capacity we can also rule out this as a possible equilibrium.

profits to firm i along this path, $r > 0$ the per-period interest rate, and $\delta = (1 = r)^{-1}$ the discount factor. Then the agreed allocation is sustainable if at each time t

$$\pi_i^R - \pi_i^C \leq \pi_i^C / r - \delta V_i(\tau_i) \quad i = 1, 2. \tag{1}$$

This says that the one-period gain from deviating at time t is less than the present value at t of the future loss of profit from having the punishment path inflicted next period rather than enjoying the collusive profit forever. Provided the punishment path is credible, satisfaction of (1) ensures that the threat of future punishment will deter a one-shot violation of the agreement.[11]

(ii) Credibility: Let π_i^P denote the profit in some given period t that firm i will make on a prescribed punishment path,[12] π_i^{RP} the maximum profit it could make at t if it reneged on the punishment path in that period, and V_i^L the present value at $t + 1$ of profit the firm would earn from adhering to that prescribed punishment path from $t + 1$ onward. Then that punishment path is credible if

$$\pi_i^{RR} - \pi_i^P \leq \delta \left[V_i^L - V_i(\tau_i) \right] \quad i = 1, 2. \tag{2}$$

The right-hand side of (2) gives the present value at t of the difference in profits between continuing along the prescribed punishment path from $t + 1$ on, and having a punishment path for a deviation imposed at $t + 1$ from its beginning. The left-hand side gives the one-shot gain from deviating from the prescribed punishment path. If this inequality is satisfied, it does not pay firm i to deviate from the prescribed punishment path and so the threat of imposing that path is credible.[13]

To test whether these conditions can be satisfied in the market under study we first need to specify a time period and associated interest rate. We take three months and 10 per cent respectively as reasonable assumptions.[14] Next we need to specify the exact nature of the punishment price paths. In general, a path which can satisfy (1) and (2) for some set of interest rates is not unique, but the following specification has some intuitive appeal:

---

[11] Abreu (1988) shows that if deviation is unprofitable for one period it will never be profitable.

[12] Strictly we should write π_{iij}^P, $t = 1, \ldots, j = 1, 2$ since profits may well vary along a punishment path, and the path may depend on which firm deviated, but no confusion should result from keeping the notation uncluttered here.

[13] Simply rearranging the condition as $\pi_i^{RP} + \delta V_i(\tau_i) \leq \pi_i^P + \delta V_i^L$ shows that we could equivalently interpret the condition as saying it is better to continue along the given punishment path than to deviate this period and have punishment begin anew next period.

[14] The longer the time period, the more profitable does reneging become, since the longer the period for which additional profit is earned and the further into the future retaliation takes place. Assuming a period of one year does not change the conclusion that for reasonable interest rates the cooperative allocations in this market were sustainable by credible threats, though to assume that one firm would take an entire year to react to open price-cutting by the other is extreme. A quarterly interest rate of 10 per cent is equivalent to an annual rate of 46 per cent, which again seems to be a reasonable upper bound.

If either firm deviates, in the following three periods both firms set price at aac_2 and then they revert to the initial allocation.

Since on this (symmetric) punishment path price falls to WP's actual aac, it makes no profit in the punishment phase, while BS makes a small profit because its aac is somewhat lower. The punishment strategy corresponds to a 'price war' in which prices are slashed to the break-even level (at actual output) for the highest cost firm.

To quantify the effects of punishment on the firms' profits as well as the gains from one-shot deviations from the punishment path we require some assumption about market demand. As a first approximation, we assume zero elasticity of demand at any prices below the agreed price. Since, if this were true at prices above the agreed price, the latter could not be profit maximizing, we are implicitly assuming a kink in demand at the actual price, possibly due to the threat of imports.

Finally, we need to assume how total market demand will be shared between the firms along a punishment path. Since they set the same prices, it seems reasonable to assume that their market shares are as in the actual allocation. Thus, effectively we assume that along a punishment path the firms would produce the same outputs as those they actually produced, but at much lower prices and profits. For each of the years 1980–4, we then calculate the values of the quantities entering into conditions (1) and (2), given the punishment strategies just described. The results[15] are given in table 12.3, and show that the specified punishment path was credible in each year, and could sustain the actual allocation.

Thus for example if in the first quarter of 1984 BS (WP) had undercut the agreed price slightly,[16] it would have gained just over £1.6m. (£3.63m.) in additional profit in that quarter, but would have lost just over £6m. (£3.65m.) in present value of profit from the ensuing three quarter long price war, relative to the agreed allocation.[17] On the credibility of the punishment path, if BS reneged on the first quarter's punishment, by setting price slightly below the agreed level of WP's ^{aac} and producing to capacity, then it would have made a net gain of close to £1/2m., but would have lost over £1.8m. in present value of profit from postponing the time of reversion to the agreed allocation by one period. In WP's case, in 1980 and 1982 it was more profitable to renege on the punishment path by setting price at the actual level and allowing itself to be undercut by BS. Market demand in those years was sufficiently high that its residual output was large enough to give it more profit than if it undercut the punishment price slightly and produced at capacity. In the other years market demand was so low that the latter was the better means of reneging. In no year however did it pay WP to renege on punishment. The figures in brackets are the quarterly interest rates at which condition (2) for WP is just satisfied as an equality. Condition (2) for

---

[15] Space limitations preclude presentation of the detailed calculations here. An appendix presenting these was supplied to the referees and is available from the author upon request.

[16] The numerical calculations assume a price cut resulting in a 1 per cent fall in 'net sales value', i.e., revenue minus distribution cost per unit.

[17] In fact a punishment phase lasting only one quarter would have been sufficient to deter BS from reneging on the agreed allocation. However this would not have been sufficient to deter BS from reneging on the first period of a punishment path following a deviation by WP.

Table 12.3 *Gains and losses from deviation and punishment (£000)*

	$\pi_i^R - \pi_i^C$		$(n_i^C/r) - \delta V_i$		$\pi_i^{RP} - \pi_i^P$		$\delta(V_i^L - V_i)$		
	BS	WP	BS	WP	BS	WP	BS	WP	
1980	367	2,015	3,347	3,759	256	1,068	1,012	1,136	(17%)
1981	964	2,901	4,172	4,148	376	636	1,260	1,254	(116%)
1982	800	3,340	5,143	4,006	276	735	1,554	1,211	(80%)
1983	1,377	3,397	5,041	3,621	494	948	1,524	1,094	(26%)
1984	1,631	3,633	6,035	3,645	468	819	1,824	1,101	(49%)

BS (as well as condition (1)) could be satisfied at far higher interest rates even than these. Thus we conclude that on our assumptions conditions (1) and (2) were satisfied and cooperation in this market was consistent with the Abreu–Lambson theory.

This then raises the question of how to explain the collusive allocation. The solution most usually considered in the literature is that of joint-profit maximization. On the face of it, this would immediately be rejected as an explanation of the actual equilibrium in this market, since we would expect it to imply that the firm with the lower marginal cost, in this case BS, would produce to capacity, leaving the higher marginal cost firm to meet residual demand. The fact that both firms produced well below capacity is then not consistent with this. However, some care must be taken in drawing this conclusion in the present instance, because two important non-convexities in the cost functions complicate the analysis. First, as figure 12.1 showed, at low levels of output WP has to switch to four-effect operation, resulting in a significant increase in unit production cost (MMC(1986) para. 4.37). It may actually minimize total production costs to keep WP's output high enough for it to maintain five–effect working, therefore. Secondly, for each firm there is a large fixed production cost which is avoidable if the plant shuts down. In order to identify the output allocation which minimizes total avoidable costs, therefore, we consider four sets of costs:

(A) the variable and fixed production costs actually incurred in producing total market output;

(B) the cost resulting when BS produces to capacity in each year, with WP meeting residual demand, on the assumption that five–effect working could be maintained and WP operates at the corresponding (actual) marginal cost;

(C) the costs resulting when BS produces to capacity and WP meets residual demand with four–effect working;

(D) the costs resulting when WP produces to capacity and BS meets residual demand[18] at its actual marginal cost.

[18] Only in 1980 was total market output significantly greater than WP's capacity of 1095 kte pa. In 1983 and 1984 total output was less than this, and in 1981 and 1982 was greater by 4 kte and 30 kte respectively. In neither of these two latter cases would it have been worth incurring the fixed production cost to open up the BS plant.

Table 12.4 *Total cost comparisons*

	Output (kte)	A	B	(£000) C	D
1980	1,294	19,455	19,095 (-1.9)	19,884 (+2.2)	20,103 (+3.3)
1981	1,099	19,479	18,399 (-5.5)	19,546 (+0.3)	17.170 (-11.8)^a
1982	1,125	20,074	19,598 (-2.4)	20,393 (+1.6)	17,827 (-11.2)^b
1983	1,007	21,352	20,567 (-3.7)	21,117 (-1.1)	18,730 (-12.3)
1984	1,003	21,031	20,281 (-3.6)	20,852 (-0.8)	18,054 (-14.2)

a The market would have been undersupplied by 4 kte.
b The market would have been undersupplied by 30 kte.
Figures in parentheses are per cent deviation of cost of B, C, and D from A, A, B, C, and D are defined above in the text.

Table 12.4 gives the results. The figures in brackets show the percentage deviation of the given cost figure from the actual cost figure for that year.

Thus we see that total costs could have been around 2 per cent to 5 per cent lower if BS had always produced to capacity, but only if WP would have been able to maintain five–effect working. If this had not been the case then overall there would have been no cost advantage in doing this. The interesting result however is that in every year except 1980, because market output was close to or below WP's capacity, the cost-minimizing policy was clearly to close BS's plant and meet market demand only from WP. Although, even at full capacity (six–effect) working WP's marginal cost was above that of BS, the latter's capacity was too small to meet market demand, and the saving in fixed production costs from shutting down BS more than offsets the higher variable production costs from switching production to WP. Thus we can conclude that the actual production allocation between BS and WP did not minimize total costs, and therefore did not maximize joint profit. An explanation for the non-maximization of joint profit is of course that side-payments would have been required, and these would have been clear evidence of collusion.

4   Conclusions

The first conclusion of this chapter is that the type of market behaviour predicted by the non-cooperative one-shot game models of Edgeworth, Levitan, and Shubik, and Deneckere and Kovenock was not observed in the white salt market. The predictions of these models call into question the standard defence of oligopolists (also used by the salt producers) that identical prices which change (virtually) simultaneously by identical amounts is evidence of 'competitive' behaviour. Of course we cannot expect 'perfectly competitive' outcomes in these markets, and the only feasible requirement for 'competitive' behaviour is that it be non-cooperative. But in a market for which these models are appropriate, namely a homogeneous, price-setting duopoly with exogenous capacity constraints, non-cooperative behaviour does not result in identical prices.[19] For this reason, we would support the MMC's conclusion that the salt duopolists 'acted to restrain competition'.

The second conclusion is that the intuitive idea, apparently shared by the firms, that deviation from the (possibly tacitly) agreed prices could not pay, is fully borne out by application of the more formal analysis of Abreu and Lambson. Taking a time period and interest rate which err on the side of favouring deviation, we show that the gains from deviating from the actual prices were easily outweighed by the losses from credible, relatively short-lived punishments. Because of its lower degree of capacity utilization, the higher-cost firm WP had the greater incentive to deviate, but a short price war in which price was cut to its average avoidable cost was a credible deterrent to this deviation. On the one hand, this tells us that it is not difficult to explain collusion in this market, and on the other that behaviour in the market was consistent with the theory of Abreu and its extension by Lambson.

Finally, we conclude that the actual allocation did not correspond to joint profit maximization, because the output allocation did not minimize the (avoidable) production costs of total output. The apparent cost-minimizing allocation would have BS, the firm with lower marginal cost, producing to capacity. However, given the fairly small residual output, this may well have caused a jump in WP's marginal production cost and, our calculations show, total cost may not have been lower as a result. In fact, given that aggregate output was about or below WP's capacity, the cost-minimizing allocation would involve shutting down BS, thus saving its fixed production costs, and meeting total output requirements from WP. The general point is that the non-convexities in the cost structures of the two firms make marginal cost-based comparisons potentially misleading.

If side-payments between the firms are ruled out then there is no compelling reason to expect the agreed allocation to be joint profit maximizing. This is reinforced in the present case by the extreme nature of the joint-profit-maximizing solution. This still leaves open the question of how to explain the observed prices and outputs in this market. That appears to be a fruitful subject for further study.

References

Abreu, D. (1986), 'Extremal equilibria of oligopolistic supergames', *Journal of Economic Theory*, 39, 191–225.

(1988), 'On the theory of infinitely repeated games with discounting', *Econometrica*, 56, 383–96.

Beckman, M.J. (1965), 'Edgeworth–Bertrand duopoly revisited', in R. Henn (ed.), *Operations Research-Verfahren*, *III*, Meisenheim am Glan, Hain.

Davidson C., and R. Deneckere (1986), 'Long-run competition in capacity, short-run competition in price and the Cournot model', *Rand Journal of Economics*, 17, 404–15.

---

[19] This is not to say that there are no non-cooperative duopoly models which predict identical prices – homogeneous quantity-setting duopoly is obviously one. The point is rather that non-cooperative behaviour may well not result in identical prices.

Deneckere R., and D. Kovenock (1992), 'Price leadership', *Review of Economic Studies*, 59, 143–62.

Dixon, H. (1987), 'The general theory of household and market contingent demand', *The Manchester School*, 55, 287–304.

Edgeworth, F.Y. (1897), 'La teoria pura del monopolio', *Giorn. Econ. Ser.*, 15, 13–31, 307–320, 4054–14. (English translation 'The pure theory of monopoly', in *Papers Relating to Political Economy*, (ed. F. Y. Edgeworth), 1, 11–142. London, Macmillan.)

Friedman, J.W. (1971), 'A non-cooperative equilibrium for supergames', *Review of Economic Studies*, 38, 1–12.

Fudenberg, D. and E. Maskin (1986), 'The folk theorem in repeated games with discounting or with incomplete information', *Econometrica*, 54, 533–54.

Kreps, D.M. and J.A. Scheinkman (1983), 'Quantity precommitment and Bertrand competition yield Cournot outcomes', *Bell Journal of Economics*, 14, 326–37.

Lambson, V. (1987), 'Optimal penal codes in price-setting supergames with capacity constraints', *Review of Economic Studies*, 54, 385–98.

(1991), 'Optimal penal codes in asymmetric Bertrand supergames', *Brigham Young University Working Paper* 91–03.

Levitan, R. and M. Shubik (1972), 'Price duopoly and capacity constraints', *International Economic Review*, 13, 11–122.

Osborne, M.J. and C. Pitchik (1986), 'Price competition in a capacity-constrained duopoly', *Journal of Economic Theory*, 38, 238–60.

Rees, R. (1991), 'Collusive equilibrium in the great salt duopoly', *University of Guelph Discussion Paper* 1991–15.

Shubik, M. (1959), *Strategy and Market Structure*, New York, Wiley.

Part III

COMPETITION POLICY

Chapter 13

Collusion and predation
On the detection of collusion and predation

Louis Phlips

1   Introduction

Let me start with a quotation from the Bible: '*And Moses went down from the mount unto the people, and sanctified the people; and they washed their clothes. And he said unto the people, "Be ready against the third day: come not at your wives"*'.

This quotation seems appropriate, not because this congress is lasting three days, but because – like Moses – I shall come down from the mountain and bring you the tablets with the commandments. This will be my gift to those of you who are or will be involved in the implementation of competition policy at the European or national level. If those working for the defence, the so-called expert witnesses, obey the ten commandments, they will make the detection of collusion even more difficult than it is today. Yet, if the antitrust authorities know the ten rules of the game the defence is playing, they will react better than they currently do and increase their chances of detecting collusion.

In plain words, my topic is about how game theory can help collusion detection and especially about how game theory can help in making collusion detection difficult. Indeed, since we, the economic experts, are more often than not paid to testify for the defence, I shall pay special attention to the arguments they need to make their case.

Presidential address to the 10th Congress of the European Economic Association in Prague. First published in the Papers and Proceedings of that congress in the *European Economic Review*, 1994, Vol. 40, pp. 495–510.

It should be clear, therefore, that I shall disappoint those of you who expected me to enumerate all the weaknesses of the current use or misuse of game theory in industrial economics, as well as those of you who thought I would give my views on how competition policy ought to be conceived in the light of current developments of micro-economic theory. I shall resist the first temptation, because I am too young to get involved in methodological issues. I shall resist the second temptation, because as a fully trained lawyer I must take the legal framework within which competition policy is operating in Europe as given. This view may seem old-fashioned in view of the current legal doctrine, but I am too old to change my legal instincts.

So let me start by briefly reminding you of this legal framework as formulated in Article 85 and Article 86 of the Treaty of Rome and in most national legislations (which are, today, directly inspired by these articles).

First of all, cartels, price agreements and market separating agreements are illegal and therefore not enforceable. I call these examples of *explicit collusion*.

Second, *tacit collusion* is also illegal. Tacit collusion refers to collusive outcomes that are sustained as equilibria of a non-cooperative repeated game. Article 85 calls these 'concerted practices', that is, collusive outcomes based on a 'concordance of wills' in the absence of explicit agreements. There may have been pre-play communication, but certainly no communication during the play. This, I understand, distinguishes European competition policy from US antitrust law.

Third, according to Article 86, the *abuse of a dominant position*, not the dominant position as such, is illegal. The abuse can take any form.

A few general comments seem to be in order at this point. In this legal framework, antitrust authorities are not social planners. The objective of European competition policy cannot be construed as getting price down to marginal cost or maximizing social welfare. So the theorems of welfare economics are not to be applied per se. (Please interpret this as a statement of fact rather than a methodological statement.)

Also note that I defined tacit collusion in terms of market outcomes rather than conduct. I suspect that antitrust lawyers may have difficulties with this, given that they are used to trying to give proof of anticompetitive *behaviour*. Their hesitations may also be due to the fact that economics, and especially game theory, comes in when one has to define and measure market outcomes.

Finally, let me mention that cartel laws, such as the ones just described, are good not only for consumers but also for business, as Selten (1984) has shown. The intuition behind this result is that collusive profits are likely to attract new entry. When collusion is effectively prevented by cartel laws, there are fewer competitors around. More precisely, the maximal number of entrants compatible with non-negative non-collusive Cournot profits is smaller than the number of entrants in a collusive game. As a consequence, the expected sum of all profits in an industry and the expected profit per producer is larger when cartel laws are enforced.

A natural way to proceed is to discuss first the enforcement of Article 85, with special emphasis on the detection of tacit collusion since that is the main problem antitrust authorities are facing today, and then to consider the detection of abuses of dominant positions.

2   Enforcement of Article 85

2.1   Explicit collusion

In the early days, some 30 years ago, the first task of DG IV, the Directorate General of the Commission in charge of competition policy, was to detect explicit collusion. In those days, it was said that one should watch markets in which competitors are 'few'. The reason was a simple one – and a wrong one: the more competitors there are, the more difficult it is to agree. In addition, nobody knew what 'few' meant. Today we know how many 'few' are. Selten (1973) gave the answer, an amazingly precise one: '4 are few and 6 are many'. If there are four or less competitors, the probability of finding a cartel is 1. If there are five, the probability that all five will collude is 0.221. If there are more than five, this probability is 1 per cent or less.

Why is this? Because if there are less than five competitors in a market, they will all find it profitable to collude. If there are more than five, it becomes more advantageous to stay out of a cartel formed by others, that is, the position of an outsider becomes relatively more attractive as the number of competitors increases.

The argument hinges on the number of firms that find it profitable to stay out of a collusive agreement. Let k be this number and let n be the number of competitors in a market. Let these n players play a 3-stage game in which they decide to participate in a collusive agreement or not in the first stage. In the second stage, those who decided to participate agree on a quota cartel, and, finally, all decide how much to supply in a third Cournot subgame.

Up to $n = 4$, for *all* of them to participate, or $k = 0$, is a subgame-perfect equilibrium. When there are more than four firms, cartel equilibria with less than n firms participating can be found. However, if the number of non-participants is $k \geq (n-1)/2$, then every player receives the unrestricted Cournot–Nash equilibrium profit. In other words, it then does not make sense to set up a cartel because the participators will behave like the non-participators. So, for a cartel to be effective, we must have $k < (n-1)/2$. This means that in a market with five or six competitors, an effective cartel has four members. With seven or eight competitors, the cartel will have five members, and so on.

How general is this result? I think it is quite general. The assumptions made, such as linearity and symmetry, are simplifying assumptions and are not really restrictive. The only potential problem is that, in Selten's game, the players have complete information. Is it still true that '4 is few and 6 are many' when firms have private information about their costs and are not symmetric? The surprising answer is: yes! Truthful cost reporting, that is, incentive compatibility, combined with efficiency is enforceable only up to $n = 4$. This is the important result obtained by Cramton and Palfrey (1990).

2.2   Tacit Collusion

When the legal advisors of cartel members discovered that Article 85 had to be taken seriously, they had their clients throw their agreements in the waste basket. Simultaneously, the attention of DG IV shifted to the detection of tacit collusion, on the assumption that explicit collusion was being replaced by tacit collusion. Inevitably, DG IV began to discover the ubiquity of oligopolistic situations, characterized by strategic interdependence, and the irrelevance of the pure competition model.

A theory of oligopoly was needed. However, in the absence of a well-developed game-theoretic approach in the sixties, all micro-economic theory had to offer was what I would call the Stigler approach. George Stigler's 1964 paper on 'A theory of oligopoly' indeed provided the dominant frame of reference, in Europe as well as in the United States. In today's game-theoretic jargon, it appears as a model in which oligopolists play a 'one-shot game' with two strategies: either cooperate to fix prices or deviate by cheating. In Jonathan Baker's (1993, p. 151) words:

Indeed, the unilateral incentive to deviate on a cooperative arrangement to fix price, highlighted by Stigler, is the very market force by which competition insures low prices and high output to the benefit of consumers and the economy.

To put it sharply, cheating became synonymous with competitive behaviour. Anything that makes it difficult for an individual firm to cheat, such as information sharing or actual punishments, was used as proof of tacit collusion. In fact, antitrust authorities spent a lot of time trying to collect evidence of direct communication between competitors, threats of punishment, or actual punishments of deviators.

The difficulty with this approach is that, when no cheating and therefore no punishment is observed, there is no way to distinguish tacit collusion from strategic interdependence. The concept of a non-cooperative Nash equilibrium, from which nobody wishes to deviate, but in which a collusive as well as a non-collusive outcome can be sustained, was missing. To construe the absence of cheating as evidence of tacit collusion is no longer acceptable.

Today's insights derived from the theory of repeated games, initiated by Jim Friedman in 1971 and further developed as different versions of the so-called Folk Theorem, underpin a new approach to the detection of tacit collusion. Experts for the defence are likely to find strong arguments in what I am going to say and will force the antitrust authorities to rethink their approach. While many game theorists find the Folk Theorem deceptive, because it shows that many more or less collusive equilibria can result from repeated non-cooperative play when deviations can be punished in a credible way, I find the theorem very useful from the point of view of competition enforcers. Indeed, it should make them understand that: (a) collusive outcomes are possible without there being anticompetitive conduct, (b) to that extent, there may be no need for firms to even try to make secret agreements, whether written or oral, (c) it may be a waste of time to look for evidence on attempts to collude or attempts to punish cheaters, and (d) when the Folk Theorem is in operation, antitrust proceedings will have to concentrate more and more on assessments of market outcomes, that is, the more or less collusive or non-collusive nature of non-cooperative equilibria. In one word, industry behaviour can no longer be understood as emerging from the one-shot game proposed by Stigler but has to be seen as emerging from a repeated game (Baker, 1993, p. 153).

This reasoning leads me to a stylized description of future antitrust proceedings in the following terms. On the one hand, the economic expert speaking for the defence (in a case where firms are accused of concerted practices) has to be able to argue (and will be paid exactly to this effect) that the observed prices, sales, and profits are typical for a non-collusive equilibrium sustained in a non-cooperative repeated game. In the absence of direct evidence of collusion (no written agreements were discovered, there are no tapes recording secret conversations), the antitrust authority, on the other hand, has to put forward (and to pay) an economic expert that contradicts the expert for the defence and is trying to show that the prices, sales, and profits observed are collusive equilibria sustained in a non-cooperative repeated game.

A natural starting point for these experts is to postulate the existence of demand and cost functions and to start talking about the parameters of these functions. This, then, raises the question to what extent these parameters are known and by whom. At this point, it seems to me that the economists working for the antitrust authority are in a more difficult position than the economists working for the defence. They are at an informational disadvantage, for the simple reason that they have to get the relevant numbers from the firms that are under attack.

Given this informational disadvantage – which I think is very real – I wish to argue that the defence can make proof of collusion very difficult, to the extent that it can make the collusive outcome of the game indistinguishable from the non-collusive one. I am referring here to joint work with Ronald Harstad (1994). We call this immodestly our 'indistinguishability theorem'.

The simplest way to explain it is to do the following numerical exercise. Let there be a market with n competitors selling a homogeneous product. The antitrust authority knows that they all produce at the same marginal cost c and the numerical value of c, which was truthfully reported. The authority also knows that their market demand is linear and that its intercept shifts from season to season. However, the authority does not know the numerical value of these intercepts. But it observes the time path of the price per season, since this is reported in the specialized press. The problem is to figure out whether the observed price, p_s, for season s, is the result of a Cournot–Nash equilibrium – in which case there is no collusion – or the result of, say, joint-profit maximization. I suppose joint-profit maximization to simplify the presentation, it being understood that the repeated game could have many other collusive outcomes with profits below the monopoly level.

In a Cournot–Nash equilibrium the price is

$$p_s^c = \frac{a_s + nc}{(n+1)} \tag{1}$$

where a_s is the unknown demand intercept for season s. With

$$n = 3$$
$$c = 10$$
$$a_s = 14$$

we obtain

$$p_s^c = \frac{14 + 3(10)}{4} = \frac{44}{4} = 11.$$

In a collusive outcome with joint-profit maximization, the price in season s is

$$p_s^M = \frac{a_s + c}{2} \qquad (2)$$

or, using the same parameter values

$$p_s^M = \frac{14 + 10}{2} = \frac{24}{2} = 12.$$

Suppose that the observed price is actually 12, and that these three firms were tacitly colluding. What should the economic expert for the defence do? He or she should convince the authority that 12 is a Cournot–Nash equilibrium price. That is easy enough. Put (1) equal to (2) and solve for $\hat{a}_s$, the false intercept to report

$$\frac{\hat{a}_s + nc}{(n+1)} = \frac{a_s + c}{2}$$

or

$$\hat{a}_s = \frac{1}{2}[a_s(n+1) - c(n-1)]$$
$$= \frac{1}{2}[14(4) - 10(2)] = \frac{1}{2}(56 - 20) = \underline{18}.$$

Overemphasizing the level of market demand does the trick: pretend that a_s is 18 rather than 14. Indeed, using $\hat{a}_s = 18$ in the Cournot–Nash solution (1) gives

$$\frac{18 + 3(10)}{4} = \frac{48}{4} = 12.$$

The observed price appears as competitive. In this sense, the two games cannot be distinguished.

Note that demand shocks, that is, changes in a_s, should be exaggerated also: always emphasize seasonalities! Needless to say, the same exercise can be done when the authority lacks information about other parameters, say marginal cost. Then the defence should exaggerate the level of costs but *under*-report cost changes.

The intuition behind the indistinguishability theorem should be clear. It goes back to Bentley MacLeod's remark in his 1985 *European Economic Review* paper on 'conscious parallelism': as long as the profit functions are not known, there are no systematic differences between the size of price responses to exogenous shocks at the non-collusive and collusive equilibria. Clearly, this basic wisdom was ignored in the famous *Wood Pulp* decision. On 19 December 1984, the Commission decided that several North American, Finnish, and Swedish producers who imported wood pulp into Europe (to be used by the paper industry) had to pay fines ranging between 50,000 and 500,000 ECU, because they had announced and enforced parallel seasonal price changes. In 1993, the European Court of Justice annulled the decision and most of the fines for lack of proof. Indeed, the Commission had looked only for evidence of direct communication and used the absence of deviations from the parallel time path as evidence of collusion. Before the Court, the concept of a Cournot–Nash equilibrium was mentioned by the Advocate-General. But it was not used in the reasoning of the Court, nor was the concept of a repeated game. At any rate, I am very pleased with this judgement.

The indistinguishability theorem can also be illustrated in terms of *price strategies* instead of quantity strategies (see Böhnlein, 1994). Consider the ICI-Solvay decision of 1990. ICI was selling soda ash, a raw material used in the glass manufacturing industry, in the UK and Ireland. Solvay, the largest producer of soda ash, was selling in continental Europe. Several cartel agreements dating back to the last century had assigned continental Europe to Solvay while ICI had agreed to restrict its activity to the British Commonwealth. In 1972, the last of these explicit agreements was terminated. Yet, both firms continued to serve their former markets. During the eighties, UK prices rose by about 15–20 per cent above those of continental Europe, more than the cost of shipping soda ash across the Channel. The Commission used the fact that neither ICI nor Solvay invaded each other's market during this decennium as proof of tacit collusion.

Again, the absence of market penetration can be rationalized as a feature of the non-collusive Nash equilibrium of a stage game in a repeated game. Suppose each producer sets a national limit price equal to the marginal cost of serving customers in the home market plus shipping costs across the Channel: market penetration is not profitable. Then equate this competitive price with the monopoly price in each producer's national market, equal to the national demand intercept + marginal cost divided by 2. Now the expert for the defence has three parameters with which to play in order to make the absence of market penetration appear as a competitive equilibrium. He or she should obviously exaggerate the intercept of the national demand curve or the level of the firm-specific production costs, as in the previous example with Cournot strategies. However, I recommend an exaggeration of the transportation costs, especially the shipping costs across the Channel, since these are subject to considerable economies of scale so that they depend on the market share that could be captured in the foreign market. Since both firms do not actually enter the foreign market, there is no available data on the entrant's potential market share.

Note that the expert for the prosecution was in a somewhat stronger position in the ICI-Solvay case than in the Wood Pulp case. He or she could have convincingly argued that the price gap between the UK and the Continent was collusive by proving that the two competitors had the same production costs, the same delivery costs, and the same shipping costs over the Channel. Then the limit prices would have been the same in the two markets and any price difference would have been proof of collusion. An additional argument was to show that the intercepts of the market demand curves differed a lot while the costs did not since these intercepts show up in the monopoly prices only. To my knowledge, none of these questions were seriously discussed before the Commission reached its conclusion.

These two examples indicate that the indistinguishability I am talking about is not to be interpreted as a classic identification problem, as encountered in econometrics. The industrial economists among you know how identification can be obtained in the measurement of market power, as exemplified by the work of Bresnahan (1989). However, the problem there is to measure departures from perfectly competitive behaviour. Here the problem is to distinguish two different equilibria. A correct econometric approach can be found in Margaret Slade's (1987) well-known work on tacit collusion among gasoline stations in Vancouver. She was able to estimate demand, cost and reaction functions and thus to compare collusive and non-collusive outcomes of the stage game with the actual observed outcome of the repeated game. Note, however, that she benefited from most favourable circumstances, which are not likely to be present in an antitrust proceeding. First, a price war was actually going on, with price changes occurring often within a day, so that the data displayed an exceptional variability. Second, the variable cost of a gasoline station is simply the wholesale price of gasoline, which was also highly variable. Third, Slade was able to collect prices, costs, and sales on the spot, day by day, until the price war stopped. Finally, the price war was typically an information-gathering device about the new level of demand after a demand shock had occurred. A comparable variability and reliability of the data is not likely to be available in antitrust proceedings.

It would therefore be nice if a simple test, involving a back-of-the-envelope calculation on indisputable data and based on a theoretically solid analysis, was available. I am glad to report that such a test can indeed be derived from the Bertrand–Edgeworth price-setting duopoly game with given capacities as formalized by Kreps and Scheinkman (1983). The test itself is due to Osborne and Pitchik (1987). Let one duopolist have a larger capacity than the other and let these capacities be determined noncooperatively in a first stage. In a second stage of the game, the duopolists collude. (This is a case of so-called 'semicollusion'.) If the cost of capacity is below some limit, the collusive equilibrium implies excess capacity in the industry, in the sense that the sum of the two capacities exceeds the total sales that yield the unconstrained monopoly profit. The duopolists plan their capacities in such a way that part of their capacities is *not* going to be used for production. In such an equilibrium, the profits are not proportional to the capacities, so that the profits per unit of capacity differ between the two competitors. In fact, Osborne and Pitchik show that: (a) it is the firm with the smaller capacity that makes the higher profit per unit of capacity and (b) this profit increases relative to that of the large firm when their joint capacity increases relative to market demand. In the absence of collusion, however, the corresponding Kreps–Scheinkman equilibria imply unit profits that are the same.

In his recent paper on the great salt duopoly, Ray Rees (1993) tried to show that the two British producers of white salt replaced their explicit price agreement, that was discontinued in 1956 after the passing of the Restrictive Practices Act in the UK, by tacit collusion. He used a version of the Folk Theorem to show that none of the duopolists had an interest in deviating from parallel pricing, given a particular type of punishment.[1] The immediate objection is that this is not really proof of collusion: if parallel pricing is an implication of a non-collusive Nash equilibrium, there is no incentive to deviate either. The Osborne-Pitchik detector, to the contrary, derives from a direct comparison between a collusive and a non-collusive Nash equilibrium. Throughout the period under investigation (1980–84), both British Salt (BS) and ICI Weston Point (WP) had excess capacity. BS had a given capacity of 824 kilotonnes, WP had a given capacity of 1095 kilotonnes. All I had to do was to divide the yearly profits by the capacities and to divide the sum of the capacities by total sales, to find the numbers given in table 13.1.

Not only was BS's profit per unit of capacity larger than WP's: it also increased relative to WP's as their joint capacity increased relative to market demand. None of these numbers is disputable (except for errors in my divisions). This test beats the indistinguishability theorem: I wish more such tests were available.

3   Enforcement of Article 86

I now turn to the enforcement of Article 86, which condemns abuses of a dominant position. Note that market dominance, or more generally market power as such, are not under attack. I wish to concentrate on the detection of one form of abuse, namely predatory pricing. Strangely enough, predatory pricing is not on the list of examples given by the Treaty of Rome (which refers to unfair prices, restriction of production, discrimination, and tying) and was not part of the vocabulary of DG IV until the defence in the AKZO case argued that its client, AKZO, was not guilty of predation – something DG IV had never claimed it was guilty of!

We know, since the publication of Selten's Chainstore Paradox, in 1978, how difficult it is to explain the occurrence of predation theoretically. We also know, since Isaac and Smith's (1985) experiment, how difficult it is to see it happen in the laboratory: we had to wait until the experiment by Jung, Kagel, and Levin (1994) where incomplete information about the incumbent's type was introduced in a form that is compatible with the Kreps–Wilson (1982) model.

My concern, today, is with the detection of predation in practice. As with tacit collusion, I wish to argue that a good detector requires good game-theoretic model-ling. My approach is to define predation as a pricing policy that turns a profitable entry opportunity for an entrant into an unprofitable one. To discover whether such an opportunity exists, that is, whether there is room for an additional firm in a market, it is necessary to find out whether the entrant would make a profit in a non-cooperative post-entry Nash equilibrium. It is only if the entrant could have made profits that predation can be claimed. Typical for my approach is the focus on the *entrant*'s profits, to check whether these could be positive in the circumstances under investigation. This seems to be a new idea, to the extent that the conventional

---

[1] In the unpublished 1991 version of his paper, Rees postulates mutual minimaxing as in Fudenberg and Maskin (1986). In the published 1993 version, the duopolists are supposed to use the simple penal code defined by Lambson (1987).

Table 13.1 *The great salt duopoly*

	1980	1981	1982	1983	1984
BS profit	7,065	7,622	10,489	10,150	10,882
WP profit	7,273	7,527	6,841	6,297	6,204
BS profit per unit of capacity	8.6	9.3	12.7	12.3	13.2
WP profit per unit of capacity	6.6	6.9	6.3	5.8	5.7
industry capacity/total UK sales	1.5	1.7	1.7	1.9	1.9

approach in antitrust proceedings concentrates attention on whether the incumbent is pricing below cost. (Antitrust authorities are used to taking a close look at the incumbent's costs, not at the entrant's!) Once it is established that the entrant could have made profits in equilibrium, it remains to show, needless to say, that the losses incurred result from being preyed upon and not from the entrant's mistakes or his aggressive behaviour in establishing leadership, that is, Stackelberg warfare.

To illustrate, let me first take the example of the 'bus wars' in the UK. In 1986, local bus services were deregulated, so that local bus operators were free to operate commercial services on any route in town, including routes served by municipally owned public bus companies which operated traditional double-deckers. In many towns, private firms came in with frequent minibus services on the main routes through the city centres. The local incumbents reacted by reducing their fares and drastically increasing the bus miles operated.

In Inverness, a town in the Scottish Highlands, an entrant started eight minibus routes in May 1988. In August it expanded with a further seven minibus routes. In March 1989 it went bankrupt and was taken over. In September 1991, the local incumbent, HSO (Highland Scottish Omnibuses) withdrew from the town. The UK Office of Fair Trading referred the case to the Monopolies and Mergers Commission on the grounds that the incumbent (HSO) had restricted the entrant's ability to compete, since it, the incumbent, had not earned enough revenue to cover total costs. The Monopolies and Mergers Commission (1990, p. 1) agreed with this reasoning and concluded that HSO 'went too far: its provision of new services and duplicates was grossly excessive, incurring losses that were unjustified. . .'.

In an impressive paper published in 1993 in the *Journal of Transport Economics and Policy*, Dodgson, Katsoulacos, and Newton made a careful analysis of the case and compared the actual losses of the incumbent and the entrant with their Nash equilibrium profits. The situation one month after entry is depicted in figure 13.1. Point A represents the losses made by both firms. Point E represents the positive Nash equilibrium profits, indicating that there was room in the market for two firms. Figure 13.2 shows that the same was true a year later but that the Nash equilibrium had become more asymmetric. This is consistent with there being predation.

However, these losses were avoidable. Look at the reaction curves in figure 13.3, where the numbers on the axes represent 10,000 bus miles. The curves intersect at the

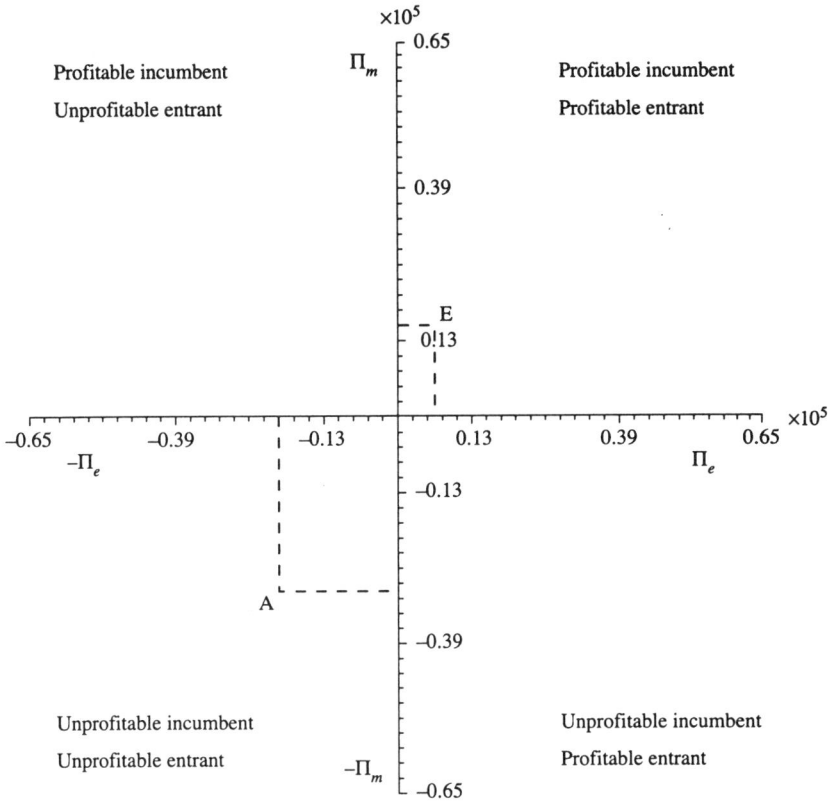

Figure 13.1 Actual and Nash equilibrium profits in Inverness one month after entry
Source: Dodgson *et al.* (1993, figure 2).

point where the incumbent operates 25,000 bus miles and the entrant 7,000 miles. In fact, they operated 72,000 and 48,000 bus miles respectively, as shown by point A. This point lies above the line BB', at which the incumbent makes zero profit ($\Pi_m = 0$).

The entrant entered with a level of output which was not only excessive but so high as to deny the incumbent the possibility of a profitable response. During subsequent periods, both firms continued to increase their bus miles: this is clearly a case of Stackelberg warfare, both fighters trying to secure a leadership position in the future.

This fascinating episode has shown that a competitive battle can be (and is easily) misinterpreted as predation. The time has come to draw the lesson: a plaintiff (the entrant) in a case of alleged predation can easily make a fight by the incumbent price leader appear as predatory behaviour. Conversely, the defence (the incumbent) can make predatory prices appear as non-cooperative Cournot–Nash outcomes that are not objectionable. Is this the Harstad–Phlips indistinguishability (1994) theorem again? Yes, it is.

In such a case of alleged predation, the incumbent is in the defence. So one

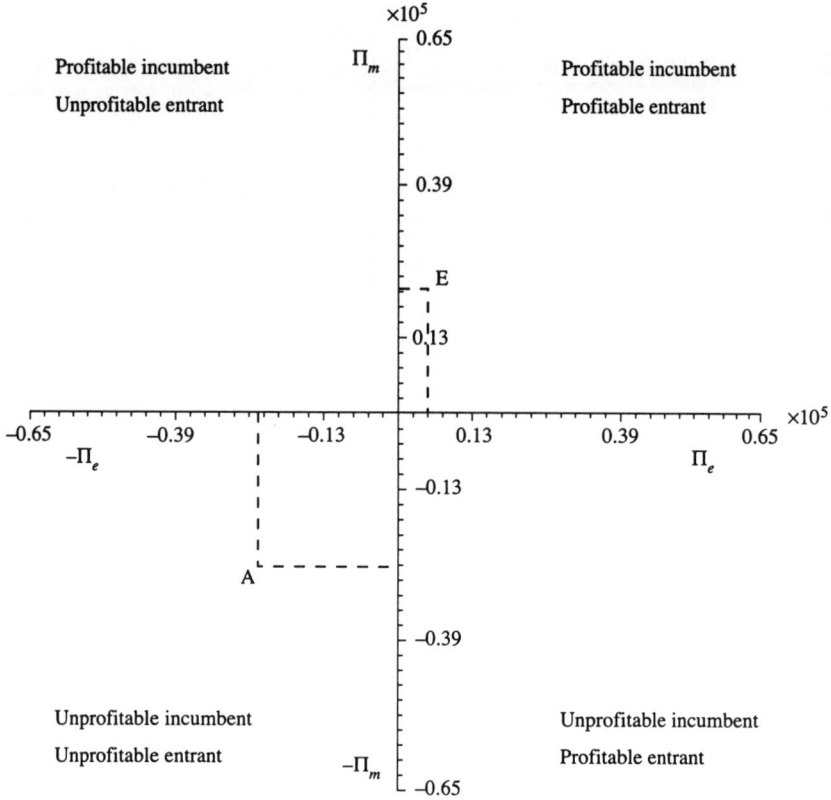

Figure 13.2 Actual and Nash equilibrium profits in Inverness one year after entry
Source: Dodgson et al. (1993, figure 3).

possibility for the defense is to argue that the observed prices and quantities result from a Cournot–Nash equilibrium of the stage game rather than from predatory behaviour. To see what sort of advice to give, the expert for the defence could do the following exercise (see Normann, 1994). First compute the usual first-order conditions for a Cournot–Nash equilibrium. Then compute the first-order conditions describing predatory behaviour, on the assumption (for example) that a predator would sell a quantity such that the entrant makes at best zero profit. Equating the equilibrium quantities, it is clear that the incumbent can justify his larger sales and low prices by underreporting its marginal cost or the level and slope of the market demand curve (which implies telling lies in a direction opposite to what the defence should do in the case of tacit collusion).

In real-life cases, the situation is more subtle, however. As we saw in the Inverness bus war, it is often the entrant that engages in warfare to make the incumbent withdraw from its leadership position. In my opinion, this also happened in the famous AKZO case. In December 1985, the Commission imposed a fine of 10 million ECU on the Dutch chemical concern AKZO Chemie for abuse of its dominant

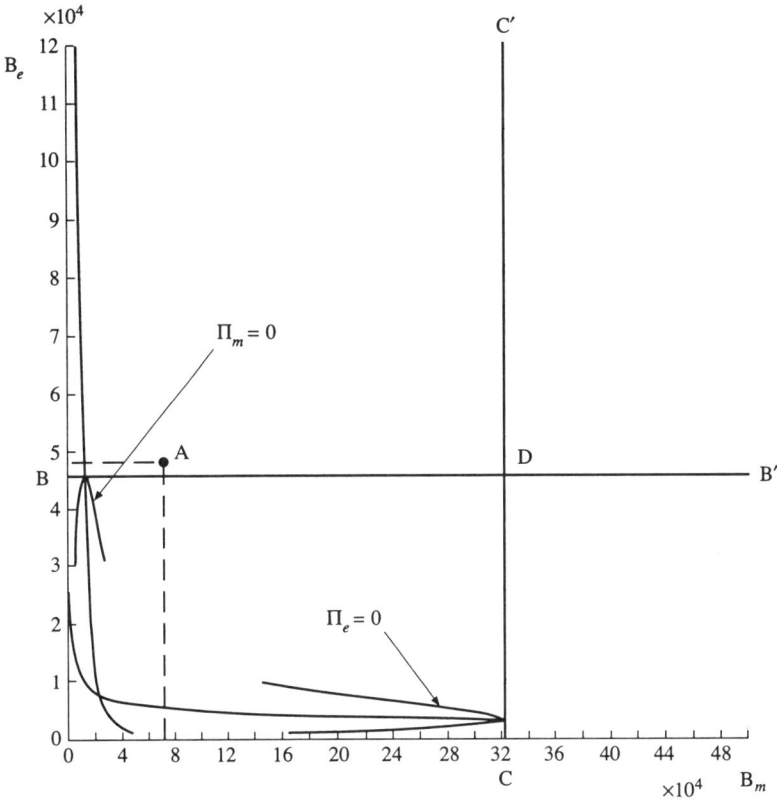

Figure 13.3 Bus miles reaction curves in Inverness one month after entry
Source: Dodgson *et al.* (1993, figure 4).

position in the local UK market for flour additives sold to bakeries. Allegedly, AKZO had damaged the business of a small British producer called Engineering and Chemical Supplies Ltd. (ECS) by starting a price war in the UK market for flour additives, to punish ECS for entering both the UK and the German market for plastics. The situation is typical for predation: there is entry in one market and the entrant is punished in another market. Again, game theory tells us which questions should have been asked and which answers given.

First, the Commission used as evidence the fact that the managers of AKZO had formulated threats that, unless ECS withdrew from the plastics market, retaliation from AKZO would follow in the market for flour additives. One AKZO manager mentioned not only overall price reductions but also selective price cuts aimed at particular customers of ECS. The problem is whether such threats are credible, knowing that both firms had a long history of friendly collaboration and were perfectly informed about each other. During the proceedings, this question of credibility was not even raised.

Second, shortly after the threats had been formulated, AKZO made a binding commitment to eliminate predation from its action set, thus indicating that it was willing to collaborate. Since ECS had been a price follower for a decade, AKZO could expect ECS to continue to follow. Yet, when AKZO announced the usual price increase in the following year, ECS did *not* follow and made offers to AKZO's customers at the old price. The Commission did not interpret this as an attack. But when AKZO did counter-attack, in late 1980, that was interpreted as an abuse of a dominant position.

Third, when ECS argued that it had lost business, the Commission looked at AKZO's costs of production, *not* at those of ECS! AKZO appealed before the European Court of Justice, where the Advocate-General suggested that the Court should have a look at the entrant's cost of entry and cost of production. Amazingly, the Court decided, in 1991, that an analysis of ECS's cost structure is irrelevant. All it wanted to find out was whether AKZO had priced below cost.

Fourth, and last, suppose the Court had accepted to look into ECS's cost structure. What should its economic expert have done? The indistinguishability theorem suggests again that he or she should have urged ECS to overstate its costs of production as well as its cost of entry.

On the third day, Moses went up the mountain again: 'there were thunders and lightnings, and a thick cloud upon the mount, and the voice of the trumpet exceedingly loud. . .'. When he came down, he was carrying the tablets with the ten commandments. Let me follow this illustrious example and bring you the ten commandments which summarize the advice I'd like to give the economic experts for the defence:

THE TEN COMMANDMENTS

  1 Thou shalt have no other gods before competition
  2 Thou shalt exaggerate the level of demand
  3 Thou shalt exaggerate demand shocks
  4 Thou shalt exaggerate the inelasticity of demand
  5 Thou shalt exaggerate the level of costs
  6 Thou shalt under-report cost shocks
  7 Thou shalt exaggerate asymmetries between firms
  8 Thou shalt exaggerate asymmetries between markets
  9 Thou shalt exaggerate costs of transportation
10 Thou shalt otherwise tell the truth.

References

Baker, J.B. (1993), 'Two Sherman Act section 1 dilemmas: parallel pricing, the oligopoly problem, and contemporary economic theory', *Antitrust Bulletin*, Spring, 143–219.
Böhnlein, B. (1994), 'The soda-ash market in Europe: multi-market contact with collusive and competitive equilibria', EUI Working Paper Eco no. 94/42, Florence.
Bresnahan, T.F. (1989), 'Empirical studies of industries with market power', in

Schmalensee R. and R. Willig (eds.), *Handbook of Industrial Organization*, vol. II, Amsterdam, North-Holland, chapter 17.

Cramton, P.C. and T.R. Palfrey (1990), 'Cartel enforcement with uncertainty about costs', *International Economic Review*, 31, 17–47.

Dodgson, J.S., Y. Katsoulacos and C.R. Newton (1993), 'An application of the economic modelling approach to the investigation of predation', *Journal of Transport Economics and Policy*, 153–70.

Friedman, J.W. (1971), 'A non-cooperative equilibrium for supergames', *Review of Economic Studies*, 38, 1–12.

Fudenberg, D. and E. Maskin (1986), 'The folk theorem in repeated games with discounting or with incomplete information', *Econometrica*, 54, 533–54.

Harstad, R.M. and L. Phlips (1994), 'Informational requirements of collusion detection: simple seasonal markets', mimeo, European University Institute, Florence. Reproduced in Phlips (1995, ch. 8).

Isaac, R.M. and V.L. Smith (1985), 'In search of predatory pricing', *Journal of Political Economy*, 93, 320–45.

Jung, Y.J., J.H. Kagel, and D. Levin (1994), 'On the existence of predatory pricing: an experimental study of reputation and entry deterrence in the chain-store game', *The Rand Journal of Economics*, 25, 72–93.

Kreps, D.M. and J.A. Scheinkman (1983), 'Quantity precommitment and Bertrand competition yield Cournot outcomes', *Bell Journal of Economics*, 14, 326–37.

Kreps, D.M. and R. Wilson (1982), 'Reputation and imperfect information', *Journal of Economic Theory*, 27, 253–79.

Lambson, V.E. (1987), 'Optimal penal codes in price-setting supergames with capacity constraints', *Review of Economic Studies*, 54, 385–97.

MacLeod, B. (1985), 'A theory of conscious parallelism', *European Economic Review*, 27, 25–44.

Normann, H.-T. (1994), 'Informational requirements of predation detection', EUI, Department of Economics, Florence, mimeo, reproduced in Phlips (1995, ch. 13).

Osborne, M.J. and C. Pitchik (1987), 'Cartels, profits and excess capacity', *International Economic Review*, 28, 413–28.

Phlips, L. (1995), *Competition Policy: A Game-Theoretic Perspective*, Cambridge University Press.

Rees, R. (1991), 'Collusive equilibrium in the great salt duopoly', mimeo.
    (1993), 'Collusive equilibrium in the great salt duopoly', *Economic Journal*, 103, 833–48.

Selten, R. (1973), 'A simple model of imperfect competition where four are few and six are many', *International Journal of Game Theory*, 2, 141–201, reprinted in R. Selten, *Models of Strategic Rationality*, Kluwer Academic Publishers, 1988, 95–155.
    (1978), 'The chain store paradox', *Theory and Decision*, 9, 127–59.
    (1984), 'Are cartel laws bad for business?', in Hauptman *et al.* (eds.), *Operations Research and Economic Theory*, Springer Verlag, reprinted in R. Selten, *Models of Strategic Rationality*, Kluwer Academic Publishers, 1988, 183–215.

Slade, M.E. (1987), 'Interfirm rivalry in a repeated game: an empirical test of tacit collusion', *Journal of Industrial Economics*, 35, 499–516.

Stigler, G.J. (1964), 'A theory of oligopoly', *Journal of Political Economy*, 72, 44–61.

Chapter 14

Vertical restraints
Vertical restraints in European competition policy

J. A. Kay

1   The meaning of vertical restraints

A vertical restraint is a restriction imposed by manufacturers or wholesalers on those
to whom they sell their products. We are subject to such restraints more often than we
think. The publishers of most books sold in the UK attempt to impose three vertical
restraints. One is a requirement that 'no part of this publication may be reproduced or
transmitted, in any form or by any means, without permission'. It limits the use which
the owner may make of the book he has purchased: he may not reproduce or transmit
it in any form or by any means.

Another is that the book is sold subject to the standard conditions of the Net Book
Agreement. The most important of these conditions prohibits a retailer from selling
the book at a price other than that fixed by the publisher. Books are one of the small
number of commodities which may legally be subject to this resale price maintenance,
as a result of a ruling in 1962 that the net book agreement – an agreement registered
under the Restrictive Practices Act – was in the public interest.[1]

A third restraint prohibits the purchaser from rebinding the paperback edition in
hard covers. The price difference between the paperback and hardback editions
exceeds the cost of binding. In producing two versions of the same book, the publisher
hopes to segment the library market – in which he believes demand is inelastic – from

This article first appeared in the *European Economic Review*, 1990, Vol. 34, pp. 551–61.
[1] The case is described in Andrews (1962).

sales to individuals. The restriction is designed to limit arbitrage between these two markets.

Each of these vertical restraints is patently anticompetitive in its intention and effects. The first is designed to prevent other publishers from producing the same book at a lower price – it aims to establish a barrier to entry. The second seeks to limit competition between retailers. The third is intended to support the segmentation of the market and associated price discrimination by the publisher. These objectives – entry prevention, limitation of retail competition, and market segmentation – are typical of vertical restraints.

Yet it is apparent that a case can be made that each of these restrictions is of public benefit. If other publishers and readers were free to Xerox books at will, sales would be reduced and publishers would find it difficult to recover the fixed costs of typesetting and royalties to authors which their competitors would not have to incur. Resale price maintenance is harder to defend, but representatives of the Publishers Association succeeded in persuading a sceptical court of senior judges that it was in the public interest. Price discrimination permits books to be published, and made available in student editions, which might otherwise never see the light of day, or otherwise be available only to very few readers. Defer judgement on the merits of these arguments for the moment: note only that they can be made. It is the possibility that vertical restraints can be both restrictive of competition and of general benefit, that has made policy towards them such a difficult issue.

2   Attitudes to vertical restraints

Competition policy has tended to view vertical restraints with considerable suspicion. Several of the landmark cases in the evolution of the antitrust policy of the European Community have been concerned with vertical restraints – such as the incentives offered by Michelin Tyres to its distributors, the aggregated rebate scheme used by Hoffman la Roche to sell its vitamins, territorial restrictions on the sale of Grundig appliances, and the control by United Brands of the European banana market. However, a number of important classes of restraint have secured the block exemption available under Article 85(3) from the provisions of the Treaty.

In the US too, vertical restraints have been a principal concern of the competition authorities. In the last fifteen years, however, the interpretation of American antitrust law has undergone major changes and in no area has this change been as radical as in the judicial approach to vertical restraints. Broadly, the Justice Department will now not normally challenge a vertical restraint and a private plaintiff is unlikely to be able to do so with much hope of success. William Baxter – an assistant Attorney General in charge of antitrust policy in the Reagan administration, who both symbolized and was partly responsible for this shift in stance – has been quoted as saying 'In my view, there is no such thing as a vertical "problem" . . ... The only possible adverse competitive consequences of vertical arrangements are in their horizontal effects' (Howard, 1983).

This shift in opinion is the result partly of a general change in intellectual climate.

However, a group associated with the University of Chicago[2] has been particularly influential, both through articles and books, and as a result of testimony in particular cases. Their approach begins by noting that the principal interest which the manufacturer of a product has in the conditions under which it is sold is that they should be such as to maximize his sales. This is not often achieved by limiting retail competition. It follows that although vertical restraints may often be anticompetitive in appearance, in some more fundamental sense they facilitate the operation of the competitive process.

Thus if – to take an extreme case – I am a wholesaler or manufacturer of perfume, the environment in which my product is sold is a matter of prime importance. I am selling magic, not simply smells, and magic is not available in discount stores or at cut prices. I therefore insist that my perfume is sold only by attractive sales assistants in luxurious surroundings and if I facilitate its sale at reduced prices at all, it is only in airport shops where the customer believes (erroneously) that the low price is the result of reduced taxes rather than reduced margins.

Now this view may be mistaken. Purchasers of perfume may be as hard-nosed as purchasers of potatoes and base their choices on a careful assessment of value for money. In that case my strategy will be less profitable than one which does not include vertical restraints. But that is a matter for my commercial judgement and it is no more sensible or reasonable for the competition authorities to insist that I sell my perfume through Woolworths than it is appropriate for them to prescribe the ingredients from which it should be manufactured or the way in which it should be packaged or advertised.

It would seem to follow from this view that vertical restraints are matters of public concern if, and only if, competition is already restricted in one or other of the markets which are linked by the vertical relationship. If I am the only supplier of perfume, then my power to withhold supply may affect not only my own trade but the whole structure of retailing. Vertical restraints may be a means of extending monopoly or market dominance in one market into another. Privatization has drawn attention to the importance of this issue, since state industries are often vertically integrated (or may see the freedom given by privatization as an opportunity to become vertically integrated). Monopoly or near monopoly is inescapable in one area. Public policy may seek to promote competition, but the privatized industry may have other ideas (note, for example, British Telecom's acquisition of its supplier Mitel or the vertically integrated operations of British Gas) (MMC, 1986, 1988).

Similarly, vertical restraints may be anticompetitive if competition is limited at the retail level. Resale price maintenance may, for example, be a means by which a cartel of retailers is supported in circumstances where direct agreement between retailers to fix prices would be illegal or difficult to achieve. It is necessary to go on to explain why manufacturers would be willing participants in such arrangements, since a retailing cartel would normally be adverse to their interests as well as those of consumers but,

---

[2] See, particularly, Posner (1981), Bork (1978).

for example, the (possibly implicit) threat of a collective boycott by retailers might do the trick. This sounds strained but it is not easy to see other reasons why (to take one celebrated and controversial case before the abolition of resale price maintenance in Britain) the manufacturers of instant coffee thought it was in their own interests to fix a minimum retail price at which their product could be sold. It makes sense to talk of magic as a characteristic of perfume sales, but when the commodity in question is instant coffee?

In both these types of case – where the vertical restraint reflects the absence of sufficient competition at either wholesale or retail level – the restraint may compound the adverse effects of that lack of competition. It would often be better for public policy to confront the lack of competition directly, but if it cannot do so, then imposing restrictions on the kinds of vertical relationship which are permitted may be the next best solution. If telephone networks were a truly competitive business, then BT's acquisition of Mitel, would raise no issues of public policy. But telephone network services are subject to only very limited competition and this is a state of affairs which is likely to remain for the foreseeable future. Hence the BT-Mitel relationship must be regulated. This was the conclusion which the MMC reached and it is one which would probably be followed both by the Chicago School and by the US Justice Department and Courts. Indeed, even under the 'new learning', it was the vertical relationships surrounding AT&T which were central to the settlement reached in that case (Temin, 1987).

The American position, then, is that a vertical restraint will not normally be treated as anticompetitive unless it is imposed by wholesalers or manufacturers who themselves enjoy considerable market power, and appears to be related to the exercise or maintenance of that power: or unless retail competition has been considerably eroded. In little more than a decade, the US has moved from being – generally – more critical of vertical restraints than Europe to being – generally – more indulgent. Should we follow?

3   The purposes of vertical restraints

Vertical restraints are imposed by firms in pursuit of a variety of objectives. Here I review the principal ones.

3.1   Influencing the quantity or quality of resources in retailing

The volume of sales will often depend on the way in which a good is treated at the retail level. A perfume manufacturer is concerned that his goods should be sold by attractive women in a luxurious ambience. A whisky distiller will wish his distributors to promote sales of his brand. A producer of cigarettes is anxious that many outlets should stock his product. Some of these can be made the subject of express contract provision: others have to be achieved by means of the incentive structure offered to retailers. This creates potential issues of downstream moral hazard.

3.2   Discouraging opportunism

A vertical relationship often requires specific expenditures by both parties. A franchisee of McDonald's receives advice and training, which has an opportunity cost to both franchiser and franchisee. These costs are irrecoverable if the franchise agreement ends. These sunk costs give scope for opportunistic behaviour by either side.

3.3   Biasing retailers

I would like my retailers to put my cornflakes at the front of the store. An insurance company hopes that brokers will recommend its products. An airline is keen that reservation agents should draw attention to its flights. This may be because I produce the nicest cornflakes, the best insurance policies and the most convenient flights. Or it may be the consequence of the incentive structures offered to distributors.

3.4   Supporting market segmentation

Producers frequently engage in price discrimination with the product differentiated geographically or by other means (such as hardback and paperback books). Such practices need to be supported by restrictions on arbitrage which frequently involve vertical restraints.

3.5   Raising switching or search costs

If, for example, only one brand of beer is available in any bar, that increases both the costs to consumers of switching between brands and of obtaining information about relative prices of different brands. Both factors increase the market power of the supplier.

3.6   Discouraging entry

Vertical restraints discourage entry, in general, by raising the sunk costs associated with new entry. If an entrant has to build his own chain of pubs or petrol stations (because all existing outlets are owned by established producers) sunk costs are greater than if he can lease the services of outlets. Aggregated rebates or tie-in sales may force an entrant to compete across a wide product range if he is to compete at all.

3.7   Extending monopoly

Vertical restraints may be used to extend monopoly power into a previously competitive industry. This may be done by distorting the transfer price between the monopoly and competitive industries. (Regulation of access charges to the natural monopoly of the local network is critical to competition in telecommunications.) Or the monopoly may allow the firm to obtain information which disadvantages competitors. (The fact that alternative suppliers would need to use the transmission network of British Gas served to alert the company to any potential competitive supply: banks can provide information identifying suitable customers to their financial services associates.) In all these cases, there may be genuine offsetting economies of scope in the combined activity.

4   Types of vertical restraint

4.1   Specifying contract terms

The simplest form of vertical restraint defines the conditions under which the product may be sold. Most franchise contracts prescribe this in considerable detail. Or the specification may be implicit: a manufacturer of food may choose to supply only to outlets which meet appropriate standards of hygiene.

4.2   Resale price maintenance

Producers will rarely be directly interested in the retail price of the goods they manufacture (although they might if the price signals the quality of the product, as for perfume). RPM will therefore mostly be used for its indirect effect – particularly on the quantity of retail resources.

4.3   Exclusive dealing

This prohibits the retailer from stocking competing products. Wholesalers of petrol, beer, and cars, for example, normally seek to establish exclusive dealing relationships with their retailers.

4.4   Non-linear price schedules

Incentive structures often suggest the use of non-linear prices. Insurance agents are generally offered override commissions – remuneration increasing more than proportionately with the total amount of business done with a particular company. Travel agents receive similar incentives, which may also be related to the increase in business over a base period. Aggregated rebates relate to the totality of business done with a supplier – thus Hoffman la Roche offered discounts based on the customer's purchases of all vitamins from the company.

4.5   Territorial exclusivity

Territorial exclusivity arises where a manufacturer agrees to supply to only one agent in a particular locality (common in franchise agreements, for example) or where he permits the agent only to supply to customers within that particular locality (as, for example, in support of price discrimination for Scotch whisky or bananas).

4.6   Raising sunk costs and taking hostages

Producers may raise the sunk costs of the retailer by requiring expenditures specialized to that product. Examples include trademarked equipment for cooking hamburgers, poles displaying the BMW logo. Hostages are bonds posted which may be forfeited for opportunistic behaviour. Many franchise agreements require that the franchiser be given a head lease on the premises, for example.

4.7   Refusal to supply

Selective distribution is a mechanism for influencing the quality and quantity of resources devoted to retailing, either directly or by care in the choice of those who are authorized dealers. It may also aid market segmentation and, by limiting availability of comparative products, raise search and switching costs.

4.8   Restrictions on resale

These may cover the geographical distribution of the product (as in 4.5) but may also include measures to support market segmentation by product.

4.9   Payments for exclusivity or bias

Brewers commonly make loans to retailers in return for exclusive or favourable promotion of their beers. Airlines provide travel agents with computerized reservation systems biased in their favour at prices below cost.

5   The relationships between targets and instruments

The simplest mechanism for influencing the *quantity and quality of retailing resources* is to specify contractually the conditions under which the product is to be sold. This is often not enough, however: no Court will adjudicate on the attractiveness or helpfulness of sales assistants; no individual retailer has control over the total number of retail outlets. *Resale price maintenance, territorial exclusivity*, and *selective distribution* can all be used to give incentives to increase the resources devoted to retailing a particular product.

Opportunism is made possible by the existence of asset specificity and sunk costs on one side of the relationship and is discouraged by increasing them on the other. *Exclusive dealing relationships* and *territorial exclusivity* are both means of increasing the commitment of the two parties to the relationship. Raising the other party's sunk costs has the same effect.

One way of securing *bias* is to build it into the terms and conditions of supply – a stockist of my washing machines may be required to devote a certain amount of space to their display. Bias is intrinsic to an exclusive dealing arrangement. The most valuable bias, however, is that provided by a retailer who appears to be independent. Override commissions to travel agents or insurance brokers may achieve this. So may direct payment for promotion of the product. (These are more usually made indirectly through the provision of cheap loans or equipment.)

Market segmentation may be defended by contractual prohibitions on arbitrage, while resale price maintenance may make arbitrage unprofitable. *Exclusive dealing* arrangements increase search and switching costs for consumers, and may also raise switching costs for retailers, since they tend to increase the extent to which assets are specific to a particular manufacturer. *Non-linear price schedules* make alternative sourcing on a small scale expensive. *Increasing sunk costs* which are specific to a particular producer directly increases the costs to retailers of switching supplier. All these devices also have the effect of creating *obstacles to new entry*.

Vertical restraints can most effectively be used to extend monopoly through a form of exclusive dealing: purchase of the monopoly product is conditional on buying the competitive products from the same supplier. Alternatively, the competitive and monopoly products are often combined in a single bundle.

The matrix of relationships between targets and instruments is shown in table 14.1. The lists are not exhaustive: nor are the entries in the cells of the matrix complete. But the structure illustrates why vertical restraints pose a general problem for competition policy. Some of the objectives of vertical restraints are essentially benign. In respect of the manufacturer's interest in the absolute conditions of product sale, for example, it is difficult to detect any divergence between the interests of consumers and producers. The situation is, however, very different when measures to discourage entry are concerned. But the difficulty is that there is no one to one mapping between targets and instruments. The same mechanism may serve both innocuous and anticompetitive ends.

It follows from this that rules which are based on the form of a particular restraint are likely to be inadequate. Nor is it possible, or sensible, to look at intent: since there are several purposes to any particular action, there is no reason why even a frank respondent should be clear about the relative contributions of his different motives. That requires that public policy should undertake a cost–benefit analysis of the consequences of any particular restraint: but is it realistic to expect that the antitrust authorities will make an assessment of a rule such as McDonald's hamburgers must be sold under golden arches?

6   The legality of vertical restraints

The basic legal principle is that the Courts will enforce a valid contract. It follows that if the conditions of sale include a vertical restraint, then that restraint binds the purchaser. Exceptionally, the law may make certain restraints ineffective by express provision. This is common, for example, where the manufacturer seeks to escape liability to purchasers of defective products. A seller may also require the purchaser to impose conditions on subsequent purchasers – as is true of the restriction on rebinding

Table 14.1

	1 Retail quantity	2 Retail quality	3 Opport- unity	4 Bias	5 Segment- ation	6 Switching costs	7 Entry prevention	8 Monopoly extension
1 Contract terms	x	x		x	x			
2 RPM	x	x			x			
3 Exclusive dealing			x			x		
4 Non-linear prices				x		x		
5 Territorial exclusivity	x	x	x				x	
6 Raising sunk costs			x			x	x	
7 Refusal to supply	x	x			x	x		x
8 Resale restrictions					x			
9 Fixed fees			x					

books. Transfers of land may often be subject to irrelevant or onerous conditions which were imposed for the first time in transactions which occurred many centuries ago.

Vertical restraints imposed within the European Community fall under the scope of Articles 85 and 86 of the Treaty of Rome. Article 85 prohibits an agreement between undertakings which restricts or distorts competition and has an effect on trade between member states. Article 85(3) provides, however, for the exemption of agreements which are of economic benefit. This provision has been used by the Commission to grant block exemption for certain important categories of vertical restraint, particularly the selective distribution agreements between motor manufacturers and their franchisees and the exclusive dealing arrangements between the suppliers of beer and petrol and their retailers.

A vertical restraint may also be an abuse of a dominant position in terms of Article 86. There is no equivalent provision for exemption from Article 86, and Article 86 has been applied against a range of vertical restrictions, including territorial exclusivity (Grundig), incentive schemes for dealers (Michelin Tyres) and aggregated rebates (Hoffman la Roche).

Some Community states also have domestic legislation which bears on – at least some – kinds of vertical restraint. In the UK, resale price maintenance is generally illegal. Policy towards other forms of restriction broadly follows the European model. A vertical restraint is likely to be an anticompetitive practice in terms of the 1980 Competition Act, which means that if it is found, after investigation by the

Monopolies and Mergers Commission, to be against the public interest, it can be prohibited. Raleigh's refusal to supply bicycles other than through specialist retailers fell under these provisions. If they are undertaken by a firm or groups of firms who occupy a monopoly position, vertical restraints may be the subject of specific recommendation following an investigation by the MMC of the industry as a whole. This was the basis of the recent recommendations made (but not substantially implemented) for loosening the ties between breweries and public houses. The German position is similar. Section 15 of the Restraint of Competition Act (GWB) imposes a general prohibition of resale price maintenance. There are no per se rules about other vertical restraints, but section 18 allows the Cartel Office to declare specific practices illegal.

7   Conclusions

It should be apparent from the preceding discussion that few general rules are appropriate in dealing with vertical restraints. The Chicago approach correctly recognizes that vertical restraints may often serve wholly legitimate commercial purposes: but it underestimates the extent to which vertical restraints may be motivated by strategic objectives designed to change the structure of the industry, or to resist changes in the structure of the industry. It is difficult to escape a sense that, at least in the European environment, many vertical restraints have been imposed by producers with a view to maintaining the existing pattern of distribution, whatever that pattern might be, without any careful analysis of whether that pattern served their interests. The defence of resale price maintenance in many sectors, Raleigh's unsuccessful attempts to confine distribution of their bicycles to specialist retailers, and the brewers' adherence to the tied house system, may all be explicable in these terms.

But since the same restraints may be, in different circumstances, beneficial or adverse in their impact, *ad hoc* assessment is inescapable. Moreover, since there is considerable opportunity to substitute one kind of restraint for another, policy in this area has difficulty in becoming effective. The best conclusion is that we should look principally at the consequences, rather than the form or first-order effects of the restraints. We are concerned about restraints if, and generally only if, prices are high and entry is inhibited. If these things are indeed true, then it is appropriate to attack vertical restraints in the industry and to go on attacking them until these adverse consequences are reduced. If prices are reasonable and entry frequently occurs, then the decision to impose a vertical restraint can be treated as a valid exercise of commercial judgement. It is in this sense that Europe can indeed learn from the US emphasis on the horizontal effect of a vertical restraint.

References

Andrews, P. (1962), 'A commentary on the economic aspects', in R.E. Barker and G.R. Davies (eds.), *Books are Different: An Account of the Defence of the Net Book Agreement Before the Restrictive Practices Court*, 1962, London, Macmillan.

Bork, R. (1978), *The Anti-Trust Paradox*, New York, Basic Books.

Howard, M. (1983), *Anti-Trust and Trade Regulation: Selected Issues and Case Studies*, Englewood Cliffs, NJ, Prentice Hall.

Monopolies and Mergers Commission (1981), *Bicycles: A Report on T.I. Raleigh Industries* (1981/2), HC 67.

(1986), 'British tele-communications plc and Mitel Corporation: a report on the proposed merger', Cmnd 9715.

(1988), 'Report on Gas' (1988/9), CM500.

Office of Fair Trading (1982), T.I. Raleigh Industries Ltd. (an investigation under Section 3 of the Competition Act, 1980).

Posner, R. (1981), 'The next step in the antitrust treatment of restricted distribution – per se legality', *University of Chicago Law Review*, 48, 6–26.

Temin, P. (1987), *The Fall of the Bell System*, Cambridge University Press.

Chapter 15

Franchising agreements
Economic assessment of competition law
provisions applicable to franchising

OECD

1   Territorial restrictions

Broadly speaking, territorial restrictions are often (but not always) acceptable under
the competition policies of Member countries and the EC,[1] although such provisions
tend to reduce intra-brand competition when part of a franchise agreement. There are
several differences, however: in the extent to which competition authorities are
concerned with intra-brand competition between franchisees, and with the degree of
market competition between brands and retailers carrying various brands, and also in
the strictness of the territorial restrictions that are allowed.

The general acceptance of territorial restrictions is illustrated by the position of the
Australian TPC, which stressed that although Coca-Cola granted each franchisee a
monopoly position in each territory, the franchise agreement had pro-competitive
effects as well. It is interesting to note that the TPC insisted that territorial exclusivity
must be limited to a 'reasonable' period, generally not exceeding five years. Among
the evidence cited by the Commission was the lack of complaints by competitors. As a
general observation, such evidence should be interpreted with caution, since territorial
restrictions could be used to decrease interbrand competition with other suppliers as
well as intra-brand competition within the franchise system.

This is taken from Chapter 5 of *Competition Policy and Vertical Restraints: Franchising Agreements*,
OECD, 1994.

[1] That is, member countries of the OECD and the European Communities.

In the United States, the Supreme Court's reasoning in *Continental TV v. GTE Sylvania* explicitly applied not only to territorial restrictions but more generally to non-price vertical restrictions. The Court stressed the efficiency justifications for and the pro-competitive effects of territorial restrictions in particular and non-price vertical restrictions in general. Since vertical non-price restrictions could not be presumed to have anticompetitive effects, the Court found that they should be judged under the rule of reason, rather than be *per se* illegal as in the earlier *Schwinn* case.[2] The Supreme Court also stressed the adverse effects that a *per se* rule may have on small and independent business.

First, the language of the decision indicates that restrictions on intra-brand competition are justified because they may result in increased interbrand competition. Vertical restraints certainly often can lead to increased competition between suppliers of different brands. It is not true, however, that vertical restrictions that reduce intra-brand competition can be justified on efficiency grounds only if entry is encouraged and interbrand competition thereby increased.[3] Even without encouraging entry, vertical restraints can promote economic efficiency and benefit consumers by improving the efficiency with which existing competitors supply their products or services, particularly if overall market conditions ensure that interbrand competition remains robust. Since it is difficult to say in such situations that interbrand competition has been increased in any measurable fashion, evidence of actual or likely increases in interbrand competition should not be considered necessary to prove the efficiency benefits of vertical restraints.

Second, the *GTE Sylvania* decision gives considerable prominence to the free-rider effect as an efficiency justification for non-price vertical restrictions. There is less attention, however, to the particular circumstances in which free riding provides an efficiency justification for vertical restrictions. This is understandable in context; the Court was not itself conducting or evaluating a rule of reason analysis, but was determining whether a rule of reason approach, rather than *per se* illegality, was appropriate. To support its decision, the Court only needed to show that non-price vertical restrictions need not be anticompetitive.[4] For other courts applying the rule of reason, and the general analysis of *GTE Sylvania*, however, it is important to recall what conditions are necessary for free riding to pose a substantial threat to efficiency.

A concurring opinion by Justice White in *Sylvania*, although it differs at several points from the main opinion by Justice Powell, raises two issues of general importance: the role of interbrand competition and market structure, and the effect of more or less strict territorial restrictions on intra-brand competition. Each issue, Justice White argued, provided grounds for distinguishing the *GTE Sylvania* case

---

[2] Territorial restrictions were not generally considered *per se* illegal prior to the Schwinn ruling. In a 1963 case, *United States v. White Motor Co.*, 372 US 253 (1963), the Supreme Court had declined to find territorial allocations illegal *per se*. See, e.g. Neale and Goyder (1980, p. 284).

[3] This point about the *GTE Sylvania* decision is made in Mathewson and Winter (1986, p. 218).

[4] For a discussion of the issue before the Court, see ABA Antitrust Section (2nd edn., 1984, pp. 67–70).

from *Schwinn*.[5] First, Justice White pointed to differences in market share: 'Sylvania, unlike Schwinn, had an insignificant market share at the time it adopted its challenged distribution practice and enjoyed no consumer preference that would allow its retailers to charge a premium over the other brands'.[6] Schwinn was 'the leading bicycle producer in the Nation', with a national market share of 22.5 per cent,[7] whereas Sylvania was a 'faltering, if not failing' producer of television sets, with a relatively insignificant (1 per cent to 2 per cent) share of the national market in which the dominant manufacturer had a 60 per cent to 70 per cent share.[8]

The underlying general point about the significance of market competition between brands is important and well taken, and certainly should be relevant to a rule of reason determination. However, the evaluation of this interbrand competition, and of the effect of territorial restrictions on interbrand competition, should go well beyond simple consideration of market share. One such additional consideration, changes in market structure over time, undermines a claim that lack of interbrand, market competition supported a finding that the Schwinn agreement was anticompetitive. A source of much criticism of the *Schwinn* decision was that while Schwinn's market share was 22.5 per cent in 1951, its share had fallen to 12.8 per cent by 1961.[9]

Justice White also argued that a distinction should be drawn between *Schwinn* and *Sylvania* because of differences in the strictness of the territorial restrictions involved.[10] He recalled that under Schwinn's customer restrictions, the franchised dealers were not allowed to sell to discounters or other non-franchised dealers. Sylvania's location restrictions, on the other hand, though they 'inhibited to some degree the freedom of the retailers to dispose of the purchased products by requiring the retailer to sell from one particular place of business (they left the retailer) still free to sell to any type of customer – including discounters and other non-franchised dealers – from any area'.[11] Therefore, the restrictions employed by Sylvania were supposed to reduce intra-brand competition less than those employed by Schwinn.

This argument is only in part convincing. A provision not to sell to customers in other territories does have a bigger impact on intra-brand competition than a simple location restriction. The argument about the possibility of selling to non-franchised dealers is dubious however. In fact, even if reselling is allowed, there may well be an implicit general understanding that franchisees should not engage in such a practice (e.g., such as selling to discounters who are present in another franchise's territory),

---

[5] The main opinion disagreed. The Ninth Circuit had distinguished *Schwinn* and *Sylvania*, but the main opinion overruled the Ninth Circuit, finding the two cases indistinguishable, and instead replaced *Schwinn*'s *per se* treatment of territorial restrictions by the rule of reason approach. See the discussion in ABA Antitrust Section (2nd edn., 1984, p. 69).

[6] *Continental TV Inc. v. GTE Sylvania*, 433 US (1977) at 2562.

[7] 388 US (1967), at 368, 374 and 87 S. Ct. at 1860, 1863.

[8] *Continental TV Inc. v. GTE Sylvania*, 433 US at 2551, 2562 n. 29.

[9] Neale and Goyder (1980, p. 285).

[10] While Justice White urged that a distinction based on the strictness of territorial restrictions was important, the main opinion of the Court in *Sylvania* did not agree that it was appropriate to consider strict territorial restrictions *per se* illegal.

[11] 433 US (1977), at 2563.

since this would result in indirect competition and would eventually decrease every franchise's profits. (Justice White actually did not mention whether there was substantial competitive pressure for Sylvania products from discounters, integrated outlets or other types of non-franchised dealers.)

More important are two closely related general issues. First, to what extent do efficiency effects justify competition policy distinctions between more and less strict territorial restrictions? Second, to what extent and in what circumstances should competition policy be concerned specifically with preserving intra-brand retail competition as well as with the competitiveness of upstream and downstream markets, which may include suppliers and retailers of several brands? This second issue is central to evaluating not only territorial restrictions, but also other vertical restraints that limit intra-brand competition.

The distinction between 'absolute' and 'limited' or 'passive' exclusive territories suggested by Justice White's opinion (but not by the main Court opinion) is a central part of the competition policy of the EC towards territorial restrictions (a franchisee is allowed to sell 'passively' if he is allowed to accept orders from outside his territory). In its *Pronuptia* exemption decision, for example, the Commission stressed that the location restriction it was exempting did not prevent customers from choosing where to buy the goods (it also mentioned that the franchisees were free to sell to each other).[12] This distinction between 'absolute' and 'limited' territorial protection has been recalled in all successive franchise cases (*Yves Rocher, Computerland, Service-Master, Charles Jourdan, . . .*) and constitutes one of the building blocks of the franchise exemption regulation. The reasons given for limited territorial restrictions being acceptable and for strict territorial restrictions being unacceptable, however, are not completely convincing in justifying the distinction from the standpoint of economic efficiency.

The Commission lists a number of reasons why limited location provisions were important – indeed 'indispensable' – for franchise distribution, which means of distribution in turn offered substantial benefits. These reasons included the need to give some assurance to franchisees that their initial investments could be recovered, and to give them incentives to exert important efforts. These reasons, however, also would justify stronger provisions that protected franchisees more completely from intra-brand competition.[13]

The Commission, however, argues that stricter territorial restrictions would not qualify for exemption under Article 85(3), in part because they would more completely eliminate intra-brand competition. The preliminary considerations of the franchise block exemption regulation state in particular that, 'To guarantee that competition cannot be eliminated for a substantial part of the goods which are the subject of the franchise, it is necessary that parallel imports remain possible . . .',[14] and Article 5–g

---

[12] Decision (87/17/EEC) OJ L13, 15 January 1987, p. 38 at para. 37.
[13] To justify stronger restrictions, Article 85(3) would require finding that they were also indispensable.
[14] Commission Regulation No. 4087/88, preamble para. 12.

asserts that agreements cannot be exempted under which 'the franchisees are obliged not to supply within the Common Market the goods or services which are the subject-matter of the franchise to end users because of their place of residence'. Therefore, although the Commission recognizes that reducing intra-brand competition may in some contexts increase interbrand competition, it nevertheless insists on maintaining a 'substantial amount of intra-brand competition'. This calls for three remarks.

First, there may be some circumstances where there is relatively little difference in the extent to which 'absolute' and 'limited' territorial protection reduce intra-brand competition. The franchise exemption regulation allows the franchiser to commit himself not to compete with his franchisees, either directly or indirectly,[15] and it also allows him to require that his franchisees should not compete 'actively' in other franchisees' territories.[16] Since there are no limitations imposed on the size of the territories, a franchiser may indeed use such provisions to grant his franchisees a quite high level of intra-brand protection. This also suggests that the level of intra-brand competition preserved by having only limited territorial protection will vary considerably from one franchise to another.

Second, as stressed above, there is no obvious reason in terms of economic efficiency for establishing an 'automatic', *per se*-like borderline. Higher degrees of protection from intra-brand competition may be desirable in periods of transition when a franchisor seeks to enter a new market, whereas even limited protection should be ruled out when it is used by long-established, dominant firms in order to facilitate collusion. Even if this limited exemption rule is the best compromise to be found among possible *per se* rules, it is not clear that such an automatic rule should be favoured over a more contingent one, based on pre-specified characteristics of the market. In particular, designing or allowing more permissive rules for small firms may decrease the delays and the costs associated with administrative or judicial procedures – both being especially important for small firms.

Third, the importance of allowing only limited territorial restrictions in order to maintain some intra-brand competition is expressed in terms of one of the conditions that must be met for an exemption under Article 85(3): to guarantee that competition is not eliminated for a substantial part of the products in question.[17] The extent to which intra-brand competition must be preserved to satisfy this condition turns on the interpretation of a phrase and the objective of the condition. First, what are the products in question? If the products in question are those of the particular franchise system, then by definition eliminating intra-brand competition eliminates competition between the products in question. Another approach, however, is to ask, what is the objective that underlies the concern that competition not be eliminated? To the extent that concern is economic efficiency, then what matters is competition in the relevant product and geographic markets for competition policy analysis. The products in question – that is, the products relevant for evaluating whether efficiency will be

---

[15] Commission Regulation No. 4087/88, Article 2–a.
[16] Commission Regulation No. 4087/88, Article 2–d.
[17] See Regulation No. 4087/88, preamble para. 12.

harmed by the elimination of some or all intra-brand competition – are not necessarily only the products of the particular franchise system, but what often will be the broader set of products or brands in the relevant market. On this interpretation it is the preservation of overall competition in the relevant market, and not specifically of intra-brand competition, that would be necessary to satisfy this condition of Article 85(3).

These comments consider only the immediate impact on economic efficiency of more or less strict territorial restrictions. It seems likely, however, that the distinction by the Commission is based at least in part on considerations and objectives other than direct effects on economic efficiency. In particular, one should recall that one of the main aims of the Treaty of Rome was to improve internal trade and business among Member countries of the Community, which helps explain why any exclusive practice which might restrict trade between states has been treated with suspicion. This issue is discussed in the last section of this chapter.

2   Exclusive dealing arrangements

Exclusive dealing can be socially as well as privately beneficial when it serves to ensure a minimum level of services at the franchisees' level or when it protects the franchisor's rights in a specific investment in a form of know-how which has to be transmitted to the franchisees for the good operation of the franchise business. On the other hand it can reduce market competition with other brands or retailers when a franchiser uses exclusive contracts to foreclose his market, or to pre-empt interesting outlet locations or prominent franchisees. This latter feature is likely to be most harmful when used by well-established franchisers, and when there is a shortage, at least a transitory one, of possible franchisees – because of the lack of space, for example, or of the absence of skilled franchisees. It is thus particularly relevant here to distinguish the situation of experienced franchisers long established in a market from the situation of new franchisers or the situation of franchisers attempting to enter new markets. Moreover, since other means exist to ensure a provision of services by the franchisees without risking market foreclosure that raises entry barriers, arguments in favour of exclusive dealing should concentrate on the protection of the franchisor's specific investment.

Several Member countries do aim at distinguishing between whether franchisers are well-established in their markets ('major suppliers') or are new entrants, and apparently are succeeding in doing so. In Canada, the *Bombardier* case is particularly interesting. Article 77.4.a of the Competition Act allows the competition authorities to exempt exclusive dealing provisions, for a reasonable period, when these provisions mainly serve to facilitate the entry of a new firm or of a new product. In its *Bombardier* decision the Restrictive Trade Practices Commission clarified the application of this article of the Competition Act and developed an interesting analytical framework for the evaluation of the relative importance of Bombardier in its market (including Bombardier's market share, financial strength and record of innovation, the evolution of relative market shares, the availability of other distributors for competing manufacturers, the choice offered to consumers in remote locations . . .).

In the United States, the decision of the Supreme Court in *Tampa Electric v.*

Nashville Coal pointed towards evaluating the internal efficiency and market effects of exclusivity provisions, rather than looking more mechanically only at market shares. The decision, however, provided little guidance about how this analysis should be carried out (recall that the Court simply asserted that affecting 0.77 per cent of the coal market was not significant enough to be considered as a violation of competition regulations). Subsequent decisions have applied such an approach. In the *Beltone Electronics* case, the Federal Trade Commission applied a general analysis of the economic effects in finding acceptable the exclusive dealing provisions of a manufacturer with a 7–8 per cent market share. The Commission reached a decision on the grounds that this manufacturer's sales were declining (so that the exclusive dealing arrangement could be interpreted as a way of placing the firm in a good position for a new start), that other distributors were available to competing manufacturers, and that the arrangement aimed to stimulate the distributors' efforts to promote Beltone's products. The Commission, however, did not discuss the possibility that exclusive dealing protected the franchisor's investments except for citing the franchisor's need to protect its 'investments' in clients that it referred to its franchisees.

The standards set in the later 7th Circuit decision in *Roland Machinery Co. v. Dresser Industries, Inc.,* 749 F.2d. 380, 384 (7th Cir. 1984), for determining whether exclusive dealing is anticompetitive also suggest a willingness to use economic reasoning to analyse the competitive effect of exclusive dealing. Judge Posner said that a plaintiff in an exclusive dealing case must prove that the exclusion is 'likely to keep at least one significant competitor of the defendant from doing business in a relevant market' and that 'the probable (not certain) effect of the exclusion will be to raise prices above (and therefore reduce output below) the competitive level or otherwise injure competition'. The second condition, determining whether exclusive dealing is likely to affect prices, involves looking directly at whether exclusive dealing allows increased exercise of market power. The first condition, determining whether a competitor is kept from doing business, is more problematic. Keeping a competitor from doing business is one means by which exclusive dealing might harm competition, particularly if 'competitor' is interpreted to include potential entrants as well as firms that have supplied or are supplying the market. Exclusive dealing, however, also could harm competition without preventing either existing suppliers or entrants from doing business; if exclusive dealing provisions raise the costs of some rival suppliers or entrants they may be unable to prevent the increased exercise of market power even though they continue to do business.

The European Economic Community case is slightly more complex. The franchise block exemption regulation allows exclusive dealing provisions, but only in some situations. First, the Commission draws a distinction between those products which are at the core of the franchise agreement, and more secondary products such as accessories or spare parts; exclusive agreements cannot be employed for these secondary products. The Commission also allows exclusivity requirements for other goods or services purchased by the franchisee, provided certain conditions are satisfied; in particular, the exclusivity clause must be necessary for the protection of the franchisor's rights, and it must be impossible to achieve similar goals in different ways, such as by specifying objective quality standards. The exemption regulation therefore does not apply when the franchisee can buy from other suppliers items which could meet reasonable and explicit quality requirements (except, of course, if the goal of the franchise consists exactly in distributing the franchisor's products). In the same spirit, even if the aim of the franchise is the distribution of the franchisor's products, the franchiser cannot prevent his franchisees from buying the franchisor's products from other franchisees or retail outlets (cf. the previous discussion on territorial restrictions).

The European Commission's emphasis in its list of acceptable franchise provisions on the necessity of the exclusive arrangement for the protection of the franchisor's rights is significant. The difference between core products and secondary ones is interesting; in many cases quality and other efficiency arguments will be stronger for products that are the subject matter of the franchise. It is less clear how consistently this distinction will draw a line between exclusivity arrangements that do and do not increase efficiency.[18] In particular, where there is little prospect of any effect on market power, exclusivity arrangements could be allowed for a broader range of products without much risk of harming economic efficiency. Similarly, the exclusivity requirements for spare parts or accessories could be interpreted as a tie-in, and could be analysed and accepted as such in some circumstances rather than being automatically ruled out.[19] Also, the effect on economic efficiency of another limitation in the block exemption restriction – the prohibition on preventing a franchisee from buying the franchisor's products from other franchisees – is not clear. For example, this prohibition could be used by the franchiser to sustain a non-linear tariff – such as progressive rebates for large quantities – in order to give franchisees incentives to promote the franchisor's products, a purpose that could be completely consistent with economic efficiency. It could also be used to improve protection of the franchisor's rights. On the other hand, allowing franchisees to buy from each other does not seem to create substantial risks of reduced interbrand competition or market foreclosure.

3   Price restrictions

Price restrictions succeed in generating a broad consensus among the different countries, although particular countries' practices do differ somewhat. All countries are very suspicious of restrictions that aim to limit the franchisees' freedom to choose their own price, and it is difficult to find another topic where there is such unanimity.

---

[18] It should be noted, however, that while such obligations are stated in Article 3 of the franchise block exemption to be acceptable only 'in so far as they are necessary to protect the franchisor's industrial or intellectual property rights or to maintain the common identity and reputation of the franchised network', the non-opposition procedure specified in Article 6 may allow such obligations to be included in acceptable agreements even if they do not meet these conditions, so long as the obligations are not expressly prohibited by Article 5.

[19] More generally, obligations covered by these provisions of the franchise block exemption might be analysed as tying arrangements under US law. See the comments below on the relationship between current US treatment of tying and the EC block exemption regulation.

Resale price maintenance is virtually always unlawful.[20] Only more limited restrictions – such as the use of recommended prices – are tolerated and even then sometimes only in exceptional circumstances such as promotional campaigns for the introduction of new products.

The French position is one example of a strong stand against restrictions aimed at controlling prices. It is based in part on a desire to assure the liberty of prices at the retail level following the elimination of price controls in 1986, as well as a desire to ensure the freedom of legally independent enterprises to set their own prices and to pass on any cost savings they might generate. Further, there is the desire to eliminate the possibility of collusive conduct by upstream firms, based on concern that cartel conduct, widespread in the past, remains a significant problem. Nonetheless, the French authorities permit recommended prices, recognizing their role in communicating to consumers and downstream firms the level of price and associated 'image' of the product or service.

The Canadian position is another example of a tough position. The Canadian Competition Act proscribes not only resale price maintenance, but also any attempt or intention to fix resale prices. This prohibition of course applies to direct tools of price control, but also to indirect tools, such as financial or non-financial incentive schemes, refusals to deal with price-cutters, etc. 'Attempt' or 'intention' to control resale prices is to be understood broadly, so that franchisers have to be cautious about any related provision, like recommended prices. Other countries are more permissive towards recommended prices, or apply different treatment to the use of price floors and price ceilings.

Here these policies are analysed in terms of the effect of vertical price restrictions on economic efficiency. The focus is on three issues: first, the sharp distinction frequently drawn by competition policy between price and non-price vertical restraints and the use of *per se* rules of illegality for resale price maintenance; second, distinctions between minimum and maximum price restrictions; and, third, policy towards recommended prices. It is important to re-emphasize, however, that while the analysis of this report focuses on issues of economic efficiency, rules against vertical price restrictions may be justified by other policy goals or by consideration of the enforcement costs of alternative policies.

4   Price versus non-price vertical restraints

What is most striking from the economic point of view is that the strong contrast between the unanimity against vertical price restraints and the more or less sympathetic attitude towards non-price vertical restrictions (such as exclusive territories) is not matched by a corresponding contrast in the effects of price and non-price vertical restraints on economic efficiency. It is difficult to find a marked contrast between the

---

[20] In New Zealand, however, under the Commerce Amendment Act 1990, resale price maintenance may be authorized by the Commerce Commission in cases where benefits can be shown to outweigh anticompetitive effects.

economic effects of 'necessarily bad' price restrictions and those of 'possibly good' non-price restrictions. Either type of restriction may either improve or harm economic efficiency. Indeed price and non-price vertical restrictions often are alternative ways for the franchise to achieve the same objective and, in particular, either may be used to allow increases in retail prices and services (that may or may not benefit consumers on balance). Many arguments used in recent American cases in which non-price vertical restrictions were finally allowed could be used equally well in support of price restrictions. To develop the point, this report follows the arguments of the US Supreme Court in *GTE Sylvania* and subsequent cases in support of the proposition that non-price vertical restraints can be beneficial and should be judged by the rule of reason, while vertical price restraints should continue to be *per se* illegal.

The Court has focused on three ways in which vertical restraints can affect economic efficiency: (a) non-price vertical restraints prevent externalities that reduce the efficiency with which products or services are supplied; (b) non-price vertical restraints promote interbrand competition; and (c) vertical price restraints are much more likely to reduce interbrand competition. In each area the economic effects of resale price maintenance (concentrating on minimum price restrictions) and of non-price vertical restraints (concentrating on exclusive territories) will be briefly reviewed and compared.

5   Efficiency of supply

Arguments that non-price vertical restraints can improve the efficiency with which products and services are supplied have often been based on the possibility of free riding. For services not definable in the contract and whose benefits are non-appropriable, free riding may lead to their underprovision, not only from the firms' points of view, but also from that of total economic welfare. Then both private and social objectives agree that practices that reduce or eliminate the problem should be encouraged. This clearly applies to the use of exclusive territories since they prevent the franchisees, at least partially,[21] from free riding on each other's efforts. The argument also applies to resale price maintenance, specially to the imposition of minimum resale prices. By eliminating intra-brand price competition and guaranteeing a minimum markup to franchisees, the franchiser can promote intra-brand non-price competition and induce a higher provision of services on behalf of the franchisees.[22]

---

[21] Free riding is ruled out if exclusive territories are understood in their strongest meaning, i.e., if one franchisee is not allowed to deal with customers located in other franchisees' territories. If exclusive territories are understood in a weaker sense, i.e., if only 'active' selling activities are forbidden outside one's own territory, then free riding may not be totally prevented, but nonetheless it is more difficult and will have less effect on incentives to provide services.

[22] As Klein and Murphy (1988) note, however, this argument is not complete, since franchisees still would have more incentive in engaging in non-price competition to increase the supply of services whose benefits were appropriable than those whose benefits were inappropriable. As a result, to promote the desired supply of services whose benefits were non-appropriable, minimum price restrictions might be packaged with other provisions, for example direct specification that certain services be provided.

The Supreme Court of the United States summarized the argument to support its *Sylvania* decision that non-price vertical restrictions, in particular exclusive territories, should be evaluated under a rule of reason:

Established manufacturers can use (vertical restrictions) to induce retailers to engage in promotional activities or to provide service and repair facilities necessary to the efficient marketing of their products. The availability and quality of such services affect a manufacturer's goodwill and the competitiveness of his product. Because of market imperfections such as the so-called 'free-rider' effect, these services might not be provided by retailers in a purely competitive situation, despite the fact that each retailer's benefit would be greater if all provided the services than if none did.[23]

From the discussion above, one can see that these arguments could be used, with the very same words, to show that resale price maintenance also can be beneficial.

Free riding is not the only reason that franchises might use either price or non-price vertical restraints to reduce intra-brand competition. Vertical restraints could also be used to allow greater control of the supply of retail services or pricing. Either price or non-price restrictions could be used by a franchiser to reduce intra-brand competition, however, and either might improve efficiency, but also might raise profits at the expense of consumer surplus and total welfare.

Another argument involving the efficiency of supply is sometimes made against price restrictions. It is argued that resale price maintenance imposed by the manufacturer, or franchiser, necessarily will lead to inefficiencies because it will prevent differences in the retail costs of various distributors from being passed on as differences in retail prices. Retail prices that do not reflect differences in retail cost are a source of inefficiency, but there are several observations that can be made about this argument. First, it assumes that the franchiser imposes a uniform resale price. In principle the franchiser could recognize differences in retail costs and set different prices for franchisees with different levels of costs.[24] Second, the franchiser in general will want retail prices to vary when retail costs vary in order to maximize profits. If retail costs do vary significantly, the franchisor will have an incentive to set different retail prices. If this is not possible, the franchiser will have a reason to use a vertical restraint other than resale price maintenance that does not force uniform retail prices with the resulting loss of such profits. Third, one may question to what extent retail costs will vary among franchisees in a business format franchise; the uniformity of the business format should go a long way towards reducing such variations.

Fourth, retail price maintenance could also cause inefficiencies by preventing retail prices from reflecting retail cost differences due not to differences in the costs of doing business efficiently at different locations, but to differences in the efficiency with which various retailers operate. Franchise systems, however, have a profit incentive to avoid using retail price maintenance provisions if they prevent the franchise's retail opera-

---

[23] *Continental TV In. v. GTE Sylvania*, 433 US at 55 (1977). Also quoted by the Supreme Court in its decision in *Business Electronics Corporation v. Sharp Electronics Corporation*, 485 US 717 at 724–5 (1988).

[24] In the absence of competition, however, differences in retail cost would only be passed on in part.

tions from being efficient; retail inefficiencies reduce the joint profitability of the franchise system as well as reducing economic efficiency. Rather than rely on price competition to enforce such efficiency, however, the franchise may choose to use other tools, such as direct control of franchisee operations and requiring the franchisee to use the standard business methods. Indeed, the uniform retail business methods that often form a large part of a franchise system may go far to establish the efficiency of its retail operations.

Finally while resale price maintenance will have some efficiency costs if it prevents retail prices from varying with retail costs, non-price vertical restraints can have analogous efficiency costs. Exclusive territories may be made larger than would be most efficient in order to reduce intra-brand competition; such an efficiency cost is likely to be greater if only passive territorial restrictions are allowed. Thus while this argument does identify a possible efficiency cost of vertical price restrictions, it is not clear either that the loss will be substantial, or that such considerations provide a basis for distinguishing between price and non-price vertical restrictions.

6   Promotion of interbrand competition

In arguing that non-price vertical restrictions may be beneficial, the Supreme Court in *Sylvania* also stressed their potential for promoting entry and increased interbrand competition in the long run:

Vertical restrictions reduce intra-brand competition by limiting the number of sellers of a particular product competing for the business of a given group of buyers . . . .

Vertical restrictions promote interbrand competition by allowing the manufacturer to achieve certain efficiencies in the distribution of his products. These 'redeeming virtues' are implicit in every decision sustaining vertical restrictions under the rule of reason. Economists have identified a number of ways in which manufacturers can use such restrictions to compete more effectively against other manufacturers. For example, new manufacturers and manufacturing entering new markets can use the kind of investment of capital and labour that is often required in the distribution of products unknown to the consumers.[25]

The Supreme Court clearly recognizes that vertical restrictions (location restrictions, in that particular case) may have negative effects on intra-brand competition, and yet advocates a rule of reason because of the possible 'redeeming virtues' of these restrictions on interbrand competition.

Economic analysis does support the proposition that non-price vertical restraints can encourage entry and promote interbrand competition. Such pro-competitive arguments partly rely on the fact that, by allowing greater efficiency to be achieved or even by merely facilitating rising profits in the short run, franchise arrangements can attract more entrants, particularly when important investments need to be made to enter the market. The arguments, however, should not be limited to non-price vertical

---

[25] 433 US at 54–5 (1977).

restrictions. Price restrictions also can promote entry and interbrand competition by increasing the profitability, and perhaps also the efficiency, of the franchise.

7   Restriction of interbrand competition

The Supreme Court has recognized that non-price vertical restraints will have an effect on price, which comes close to acknowledging that price and non-price vertical restraints can have very similar economic effects. In *Monsanto* v. *Spray Rite,* the Court noted:

It is precisely in cases in which the manufacturer attempts to further a particular marketing strategy by means of agreements on often costly non-price restrictions that it will have the most interest in the distributors' resale prices. The manufacturer often will want to ensure that its distributors earn sufficient profit to pay for programs such as hiring and training additional salesmen or demonstrating the technical features of the products, and will want to see that 'free-riders' do not interfere.[26]

Because price and non-price vertical restraints both can have similar effects on price (albeit one directly and the other indirectly), distinguishing the two can be difficult. In *Business Electronics Corp. v. Sharp Electronics Corp.,* 485 US 717 (1988) the Court grappled with the difficulties of drawing a line between *per se* illegal price vertical restraints and non-price vertical restraints to be judged under the rule of reason, given that both affected retail prices:

The District Court's rule on the scope of *per se* illegality for vertical restraints would threaten to dismantle the doctrine of *GTE Sylvania.* Any agreement between a manufacturer and a dealer to terminate another dealer who happens to have charged lower prices can be alleged to have been directed against the terminated dealer for 'price cutting.' In the vast majority of cases it will be extremely difficult to convince a jury that its motivation was to ensure adequate services, since price cutting and some measure of service cutting usually go hand in hand . . . . Moreover, even vertical restraints that do not result in dealer termination, such as the initial granting of an exclusive territory or the requirement that certain services be provided, can be attacked as designed to allow existing dealers to charge higher prices . . . . We cannot avoid this difficulty by invalidating as illegal *per se* only those agreements imposing vertical restraints that contain the word 'price', or that affect the 'prices' charged by dealers . . . . All vertical restraints, including the exclusive territory agreement held not to be *per se* illegal in *GTE Sylvania,* have the potential to allow dealers to increase 'prices' and can be characterised as intended to achieve just that.[27]

While the Court recognized that upstream producers using non-price restrictions will be concerned with retail prices, and non-price restrictions often will have the effect of increasing retail prices, the Court was anxious both to protect the doctrine of *GTE Sylvania* that non-price restrictions be judged under the rule of reason and to retain the rule of *per se* illegality for vertical price restrictions. Thus it was necessary to establish what was a vertical price restriction that was *per se* illegal, and what was a vertical non-price restriction (that perhaps affected prices) to be judged under the rule

---

[26] 465 US 752 at 762–3 (1984).   [27] 485 US 717 at 727–728 (1988).

of reason. The *Monsanto* and *Sharp* decisions both addressed this question; the *per se* rule applies only if there is clear evidence of agreement between manufacturer and distributor which 'tends to exclude the possibility of independent action' by·the two (*Monsanto*),[28] and there is agreement about the price or price levels (*Sharp*), and not only an agreement (e.g., on a non-price restriction) that might affect price but did not establish that price.

In retaining the rule of *per se* illegality for vertical price restraints, the Court insisted there is a substantial distinction to be drawn. In *Business Electronics Corp. v. Sharp Electronics Corp.*, 485 US 717 (1988), the Court reviewed *GTE Sylvania* and reiterated that price and non-price restraints should be distinguished:

Our opinion in *GTE Sylvania* noted a significant distinction between vertical non-price and vertical price restraints. That is, there was support for the proposition that vertical price restraints reduce interbrand price competition because they 'facilitate cartelizing' . . . . The authorities cited by the Court suggested how vertical price agreements might assist horizontal price fixing at the manufacturer level (by reducing the manufacturer's incentive to cheat on a cartel, since its retailers could not pass on lower prices to consumers) or might be used to organise cartels at the retailer level. Similar support for the cartel-facilitating effect of vertical non-price restraints was and remains lacking.[29]

With this claim in mind, it is possible to review the analysis on the potential for price and non-price restraints to reduce market competition. The review will begin with possible effects on the ability of existing suppliers to collude.

Resale price maintenance or the fixing of minimum prices in a franchise agreement clearly may reduce competition and efficiency if the provisions serve merely to sustain a downstream cartel arrangement among franchisees (and perhaps other retail dealers) selling substitutable products or services that are designed to maintain high prices, limit output and divide markets. Two remarks are in order. First, such 'fake' franchise agreements could also use the assignment of exclusive territories to achieve similar negative effects. Second, such horizontal cartel agreements are more generally undesirable as such, and clearly deserve specific treatment.

The Court (in the passage quoted above) cites the argument that 'vertical price agreements' can facilitate collusion by reducing the incentive of a franchiser to cheat on a cartel by lowering wholesale price.[30] This argument is made in the economics literature.[31] The argument, however, has not been formalized and still lacks convincing empirical evidence. The argument implicitly relies on the assumption that the franchiser can undertake not to modify the retail price set by the franchisee – that, for example, franchise contract terms make it impossible to renegotiate the retail price, or that retail prices are made more difficult or costly to renegotiate or reset than wholesale prices. If this were not the case, a franchiser could 'cheat' on the cartel

---

[28] 465 US 752 at 768 (1984).   [29] 485 US 717 at 725–6 (1988).

[30] In the earlier Supreme Court decision in *White Motor Co. v. United States*, Mr. Justice Brennan asserted that 'resale price maintenance is not only designed to, but almost invariably does in fact, reduce price competition not only among sellers of the affected product, but quite as much between that product and competing brands'; 372 US, 253 at 268 (1963).

[31] The Court cited Posner (1975).

agreement, despite resale price maintenance, by modifying both the retail price and the wholesale price at the same time. Furthermore, even if one accepts the argument as given, resale price maintenance is not claimed to do more than facilitate collusion; collusion still could be effective and persist only under familiar, identifiable conditions, which include the existence of barriers to entry, high market concentration, and so forth.

The economic literature, however, also outlines ways in which vertical non-price restrictions may reduce interbrand competition between upstream producers. One possibility is that franchisers in a concentrated market may be able to reduce the strength of competition by delegating retail pricing responsibility to franchisees while reducing intra-brand competition with territorial restrictions. By delegating retail pricing and reducing intra-brand competition, the franchisers reduce their incentives to lower wholesale prices because franchisees, in the absence of vigorous retail competition, will pass on only part of any reduction in the wholesale price.

Other arguments in the literature outline how vertical non-price restraints may limit market competition between brands by deterring otherwise efficient entry. Exclusive dealing provisions could raise entry barriers. Territorial restrictions might help deter entry by allowing retail franchisees with pricing freedom to make credible threats that they would respond to geographically limited entry with price wars. Provisions establishing resale price maintenance would not affect pricing behaviour incentives in the same way. If nonetheless franchisers used price restrictions to set low retail prices that forced exit of an efficient rival or prevented entry by efficient suppliers, competition policy rules could be enforced against the pricing itself (rather than against the pricing provisions).

In sum, it is hard to support the Supreme Court's claim that a clear distinction can be made on the danger to interbrand competition posed by price and non-price competition. In particular, it is hard to support the Court's assertion that 'similar support for the cartel-facilitating effect of vertical non-price restraints was and remains lacking'; there certainly does exist support in the analytical literature for the proposition that non-price vertical restraints also may restrict interbrand competition.

8   *Per se illegality versus a rule of reason*

This review does not argue for a sharp distinction in the legal treatment of price versus non-price restrictions based on their effect on economic efficiency. If the emphasis is placed on the possibility of undesirable effects, both should be *per se* unlawful. Both may be used to reduce market competition in some circumstances. If, on the contrary, attention is paid to the possibility of intra-brand efficiency-enhancing effects or of desirable long-run effects on interbrand competition, then a rule of reason could be applied to both. Vertical price restrictions, as well as vertical non-price restrictions may promote economic efficiency, although neither necessarily will do so. However, a *per se* rule also could be chosen to reduce enforcement costs or to serve objectives other than economic efficiency as discussed later in this chapter.

9   The difference between minimum and maximum prices

There does appear to be a difference in the economic impact of price floors or minimum resale prices, and the effects of price ceilings or maximum resale prices. Here, however, the contrast in economic effects sometimes is greater than the contrast in competition policy towards the two practices.

The effects on economic efficiency of price ceilings, on the one hand, and those of minimum resale price maintenance, on the other hand, are quite different. Price ceilings can be used to eliminate double markup problems, which increases economic efficiency, while price floors cannot. Price ceilings cannot be used to limit intra-brand competition, while price floors can. Price ceilings are unlikely to facilitate collusion, while price floors might in some circumstances be used to sustain a cartel arrangement, at least at the retail level. The primary way in which they might reduce competition would be if franchisers set maximum prices at low levels to force the exit of efficient rivals or to prevent efficient entry; to deal with such cases competition policy could enforce rules against price ceilings being set at 'predatory' levels, rather than against provisions allowing maximum prices to be set at all. Price ceilings also could reduce economic efficiency if, in the absence of strong competition from other brands and retailers, the franchise system used this tool to indirectly limit the level of retail services and the most profitable level of services was lower than the most efficient level.[32] Of course, with a different pattern of consumer preferences for services, price floors may reduce economic efficiency in the same way; price floors may be used to encourage an increased supply of retail services which is profitable, but greater than what would be most efficient.

There is thus a considerable difference between the economic effects of imposing minimum and maximum prices. A number of countries, however, treat maximum price-fixing schemes like any other kind of price restriction. In *United States v. Socony-Vacuum Oil Co.,* for example, the Supreme Court of the United States recalled that 'under the Sherman Act a combination formed for the purpose and with the effect of raising, depressing, fixing, pegging, or stabilizing the price of a commodity in interstate or foreign commerce is illegal *per se*',[33] Other cases in which price ceilings were treated as *per se* illegal in the United States are *Kiefer-Stewart Co. v. Joseph E. Seagram & Sons, Inc.,*[34] *Albrecht v. Herald Co.,*[35] and *Arizona v. Maricopa County Medical Society.*[36]

The arguments given to sustain this position are sometimes dubious. Consider the

---

[32] The franchise structure with market power would choose an inefficiently low level of retail services if inframarginal consumers value the services more than marginal consumers (assuming the absence of horizontal externalities and free riding).

[33] *United States v. Socony-Vacuum Oil Co.*, 310 US 150, at 223 (1940).

[34] *Kiefer-Stewart Co. v. Joseph E. Seagram & Sons, Inc.,* 340 US at 211, 213 (1951); there was in that case an additional horizontal component since the agreement was between two suppliers that had agreed to sell liquor only to wholesalers adhering to maximum prices above which the wholesalers could not resell.

[35] *Albrecht v. Herald Co.*, 390 US at 145 and 152–3 (1968).

[36] *Arizona v. Maricopa County Medical Society*, 457 US at 332 (1982).

decision of the US Supreme Court in *Albrecht v. Herald Co.*, 390 US 145 (1968). First, the Court points to the possibility that maximum prices may limit the supply of services:

Maximum prices may be fixed too low for the dealer to furnish services essential to the value which goods have for the consumer or to furnish services and conveniences which consumers desire and for which they are willing to pay.[37]

Maximum prices might be used to limit the supply of services, but the Court's argument is incomplete since it fails to explain why the upstream supplier (the franchiser in this case) would wish to limit the supply of services that 'are essential to the value which goods have for the consumer . . . and for which they are willing to pay'. Limiting the supply of services for which consumers are willing to pay would not in general be profitable; it is profitable only when (a) the suppliers have some market power, and (b) consumers willing to pay the additional cost will purchase even if the additional services are not provided (although they suffer a loss of consumer surplus), while other consumers, who would not be willing to pay the cost of additional services will stop buying (or reduce their purchases) if the services are supplied.

The Court also supports finding maximum price agreements illegal by arguing that maximum prices may harm competition and increase prices in the market. In *Albrecht v. Herald Co.* the Court argues that:

schemes to fix maximum prices, by substituting the perhaps erroneous judgement of a seller for the forces of the competitive market, may severely intrude upon the ability of buyers to compete and survive in that market.[38]

It is doubtful that a franchiser and his franchisees would agree on a price-fixing scheme, however, if it were to lead to such inefficiencies; both are interested in the franchisees being able to survive in the market place. Also, in the same decision, the Supreme Court quite wrongly asserted that:

if the actual price charged under a maximum price scheme is nearly always the maximum price, which is increasingly likely as the maximum price approaches the actual cost of a dealer, the scheme tends to acquire all the attributes of an arrangement fixing minimum prices.[39]

Although maximum price-fixing schemes potentially can 'fix' prices, the impact on efficiency is the opposite of that of minimum price-fixing agreements (excepting the imposition of predatory prices). The situation the Court identified as that in which maximum prices are most likely to be the price set in the market – the situation in which the maximum price just covers the cost of the dealer – would be a situation in which the 'agreed' price would be the same as the price set by dealers in a competitive retail market.

Some countries, however, have adopted a more permissive position towards the use of maximum prices. For example, Australia generally allows a supplier to stipulate

---

[37] 390 US 145, at 152–3 (1968).
[38] 390 US 145, at 152 (1968).   [39] 390 US 145, at 152 (1968).

maximum prices. In Canada, competition law only prohibits restrictions that prevent reductions in prices or influence prices upward. In the United Kingdom, the Resale Prices Act makes it unlawful for suppliers of goods to impose minimum resale prices on dealers, but does not prohibit the setting of maximum resale prices. In New Zealand, the showing that the benefits of a price restriction outweigh anticompetitive costs, which is required under the Commerce Amendment Act 1990 for authorization, may prove easier for maximum than minimum price restrictions. Also, in a recent decision, *USA Petroleum Co. v. Atlantic Richfield Co.,* the United States Court of Appeal for the Ninth Circuit recognized that: 'Maximum and minimum price fixing may have different consequences in many situations'.[40] While the Supreme Court in this case reaffirmed the *per se* illegality of such agreements, it also asserted that 'actions *per se* unlawful may nonetheless have some procompetitive effects'[41] and found that the plaintiff, a competitor, did not have standing because he had not shown any antitrust injury.

10   Suggested prices

Lastly, a *per se* rule against price restrictions may lead firms to find alternative, but related, ways to formally circumvent this rule, such as the use of strongly 'suggested' or 'recommended' prices. Moreover, it can lead unconvinced Courts or other antitrust authorities to 'close their eyes' to such practices even in circumstances in which recommended prices do become the prevailing retail price, and thus have economic effects nearly indistinguishable from minimum price restrictions. In general it will be difficult to distinguish recommended prices from imposed price restrictions so that the resulting groups of practices have clearly different economic effects. Doing so would depend on difficult determinations of the extent to which recommended prices are followed, and in fact result in prices different from what they would be in the absence of the practice.

Some of these difficult problems are illustrated in the US case, *Business Electronics Corp. v. Sharp Electronics Corp.,* 485 US 717 (1988). Business Electronics (BE in the following) and another retailer, Hartwell, were authorized by Sharp to sell its electronics calculators in a given area. In response to Hartwell's complaints about BE's prices, Sharp terminated BE's dealership. Although there was some non-negligible indirect evidence suggesting the existence of a 'price conspiracy' between the respondent and the other retailer,[42] the United States Court of Appeal for the Fifth Circuit and later the Supreme Court refused to apply the *per se* rule because of the lack of agreement on specific prices or price levels, and argued in part that despite the recommended price and the apparent effort to enforce adherence, it could not be

[40] *USA Petroleum Co. v. Atlantic Richfield Co.,* 859 F. 2d 687 (9th Cir, 1988).
[41] *USA Petroleum Co. v. Atlantic Richfield Co.,* 1105. Ct. 1884 (1990).
[42] Among other things, BE's retail prices were often below the prices suggested by Sharp. Hartwell complained to Sharp on a number of occasions about BE's prices, and BE was terminated no more than one month after Hartwell's ultimatum that it would terminate its own dealership unless Sharp ended its relationship with BE within 30 days.

presumed that retail prices would be controlled as they would be by a direct agreement.[43]

Finally, recall that in some countries, such as France, suggested prices are acceptable on the grounds that such price recommendations can communicate information to consumers and franchisees about the general price level of the product or services and its associated 'image'.

11   Tie-ins

Like all other vertical restraints, tie-ins may be either harmful or beneficial, depending on context. This is reflected in the laws of the various countries, which generally apply a flexible rule of reason. The United States has been one exception, with tying arrangements being considered *per se* illegal. This is somewhat misleading, however, because a number of conditions must be satisfied before the *per se* rule is applied, and under the current standard these conditions involve considerable market analysis. We begin with the definition of a tying arrangement, then comment on the application of the rule of reason.

12   The definition of the tying product

Since tying arrangements require two products, an important legal question, particularly in the United States, has been whether two products were involved in an agreement. This question became particularly important following several decisions, notably *Susser v. Carvel* and *Siegel v. Chicken Delight,* suggesting that the franchisor's brand or trade mark could be a separate tying product. That in turn potentially made any obligation to purchase a product or service from the franchiser a 'tied' product. Under some decisions, the selling of an 'XYZ' shoe might have been found to be a tying arrangement, since it required buying simultaneously the shoe and its 'XYZ' trademark.

The United States courts struggled with this issue for some years. The Supreme Court's decision in *Jefferson Parish,* however, has provided a new test for separate products, the two-market test, that has been widely followed. A considerable virtue of the *Jefferson Parish* approach is that it focuses on tests involving the market consequences of agreements, rather than on drawing distinctions using criteria that may have no close relationship to market outcomes. This test does seem to prevent a finding of separate products and tying arrangements in many situations in which the alleged tie clearly could have no adverse effect on market competition. Under *Jefferson Parish* a product and its trademark could not be two products. On the other hand, the two-market test would seem to make it possible to find that a franchisor's trade name or brand was a product separate from a product or service that could be used by the franchisee without changing the basic nature of the product or service sold

---

[43] For the Court of Appeal decision, see 480 F. 2d 1212.

under the trademark, a circumstance in which it might be possible for a tying arrangement to reduce competition by raising entry barriers.

In the case of a business-format franchise, the 'way-of-doing-business' can be identified as a distinct product. The Court of Appeal in *Principle v. McDonald's Corp.*, was correct to observe that 'McDonald's offers its franchisees a complete method of doing business from the design of the menu board to the amount of ketchup on the hamburgers'. This 'complete method' identifies a product that is both demanded and offered: potential franchisees are interested in acquiring the rights to operate any of several 'fast food' franchises, and there are a variety of suppliers including both some bigger competitors (Burger King, etc.) and a competitive fringe. This does not mean, however, that all 'ingredients' should necessarily be considered intrinsic parts of the 'product'. Some products sold by a franchisee, such as soft drinks and hamburgers, may be in separate product markets; if so, requiring a franchisee, for example, to distribute only some specific brand of drinks – putting aside quality considerations – clearly looks like a tying arrangement.

Finally, it is interesting that the *Jefferson Parish* two-market test brings US jurisprudence on tying closer to the position of the EC franchise block exemption regulation on the types of products that franchisees may be obligated to purchase from the franchiser. Under the EC regulation, an obligation is permissible that prevents the franchisee from buying elsewhere products or services that compete with those of the franchiser and are the subject matter of the franchise.[44] Such a product or service and the franchisor's trademark would be unlikely to pass the two-market test. The EC block exemption is much more restrictive about requiring franchisees to buy other goods or services, which in some instances at least would also be more likely to be found separate from the franchise trademark under the two-market test.

13   Evaluating the effects of a tying arrangement

One of the main arguments against tie-ins involves the possibility that the franchiser has 'sufficient economic power with respect to the tying product to appreciably restrain free competition in the market for the tied product'.[45] Tying can indeed leverage market power and be harmful when: (i) the franchiser has some market power in the market of the tying product; and (ii) the franchiser forecloses a non-negligible share of the market for the tied product thereby making entry more difficult.

The first condition on the franchisor's market power for the tying product has been interpreted in various ways, sometimes with a very loose standard. In the United States, a variety of standards were used to determine if there was sufficient economic power over the tying product; some decisions were willing to accept use of a brand name as sufficient evidence of economic power. These standards properly have been replaced, especially in Jefferson Parish, with standards based on the franchisor's

---

[44] Regulation No. 4087/88, Article 2–3.

[45] *Northern Pacific Railway Co. v. United States*, 356 US 1 at p. 6 (1958).

market power in the market for the tying product, rather than on only the less well-defined concept of economic power. The threshold level of market power seems however to have been relatively high. In *Jefferson Parish,* for example, the Supreme Court considered that a 30 per cent market share was 'insufficient as a basis to infer market power', even though it recognized at the same time that there existed 'market imperfections' that allowed the hospital to charge non-competitive prices; it is immediately added in the decision of the Court that 'while these factors may generate "market power" in some abstract sense, they do not generate the kind of market power that justifies condemnation of tying'.[46]

The second condition, which relates to the structure of the market for the tied product, is often missing in the application of the rule of reason to tie-ins. It is very significant, however, for the economic impact of a tying arrangement. Even if the franchiser succeeds in using a significant market power in one market to force his franchisees to buy other goods as well, this may have little impact on competition in the other markets if his franchisees represent only a negligible share of the customers of the other products. Chicken Delight's requirement to buy packing items, for example, may have had only negligible consequences on the competition in the packing industry. In the US, application of the *per se* rule against tying does require showing that a 'not insubstantial' amount of commerce is foreclosed in the market for the tied product. Courts, however, often have found the necessary showing satisfied by evidence on the total dollar amount of commerce foreclosed to competitors by the tie, rather than by evidence on the proportion of the market for the tied product or on the economic effect the tie has in the market for the tied product. Several circuits, however, have also required a showing that tying resulted in the actual foreclosure of competition in the market for the tied product, or that there was a substantial danger that the tie would allow the seller to acquire market power in the tied product market.[47]

In addition, tie-ins can have efficiency-enhancing effects. One way a tie can enhance efficiency is by preventing inefficient input substitution. This argument, however, does not seem to be much accepted in competition policy jurisprudence as·a basis for allowing use of tying provisions.

In the United States, *Siegel v. Chicken Delight, Inc.* provides for another possible efficiency enhancing use of tie-ins. Rather than requiring any franchise fee or royalties, Chicken Delight used the packing items needed in the franchised business operation as a 'counting device' to recover a return proportional to the volume of sales. This counting device worked well for the franchisee: it was simple and avoided requiring franchisees to report sales accurately. The Court of Appeal, however, rejected this argument and, although Chicken Delight's franchisees represented a relatively small

---

[46] *Jefferson Parish Hospital District No. 2 et al. v. Hyde,* 466 US 2 (1984).
[47] The 9th Circuit Court, citing *Jefferson Parish,* found that this last requirement was satisfied by showing a substantial volume of commerce was foreclosed, suggesting a more market-based approach to the latter requirement. For citations to cases see ABA Antitrust Section (2nd edn. 1984, pp. 88–9, and 1988, pp. 1–82–4), on which the discussion of US jurisprudence in this paragraph is based.

share of customers for similar packing, condemned the tying requirement; without franchise fees and royalties, the franchiser did not survive very long after the decision.

Other possible efficiency enhancing uses of arrangements involve preservation of the franchisor's goodwill and quality reputation. There has been some willingness to consider such uses of ties in both the United States and the EC. In the US in *Mozart v. Mercedes Benz,* a tying arrangement involving parts was found legal, largely on the grounds that it was justified by the benefits of quality control. The EC franchise block exemption allows franchisers to obligate franchisees to purchase from specified sources where necessary to protect the identity and reputation of the network (but only if quality standards cannot be specified).

Whether a tying agreement is in fact necessary to protect quality or otherwise enhance efficiency should be checked carefully in circumstances in which competition might be threatened. The distinction drawn by the Canadian Restrictive Trade Practices Commission between efficiency effects in the joint production of the tying and tied products, on the one hand, and quality arguments used to justify tying arrangements for inputs, on the other hand, seems particularly relevant. It should also be checked that alternative methods do not exist with similar efficiency-enhancing effects, if the market circumstances described above indicate a risk of harm to competition. The EC block exemption allows the designation of suppliers to protect quality only if it is 'impracticable' to set objective quality specifications.[48] In another US case, *Metrix v. Daimler Benz,* the same tying arrangement for parts considered in *Mozart* (but applied to a different distributor) was not allowed on the grounds that there were alternative methods available to ensure quality.

14   Refusal to deal

In most cases would-be franchisees must meet certain skills or ability requirements, or must have a minimal financial strength for the success of the franchise. As long as these requirements can be precisely formulated and are clearly necessary, franchisers must certainly be allowed to refuse any candidate who would fail to meet these requirements – and franchisers are actually allowed to do so.

The case is less clear when relevant requirements cannot be made explicit or are based on features difficult to verify. It should be stressed, however, that the right to refuse a potential franchisee is a necessary counterpart to most of the other restrictions discussed above. Suppose for example that a franchiser decides to grant his franchisees exclusive territories. This is possible only if he can guarantee a franchisee that no other franchised outlet will appear in the given territory, which in turn implicitly requires the ability to refuse to deal with any potential franchisee in this territory.

It is difficult to define a relevant jurisprudence for refusals to deal independently from the positions adopted in favour of or against other types of restrictions. When a high initial fee is involved, however, a distinction could be drawn between a refusal to deal with a would-be franchisee and the unilateral termination of an existing franchise

---

[48] Regulation No, 4087/88, Articles 3–1-a and 3–1-b.

agreement. A similar distinction may be relevant when the franchise operation requires important specific investments on the franchisees' side.

15   Non-competition provisions

Franchise contracts often include a provision preventing the franchisee from engaging in direct or indirect competition with the franchiser, either during the duration of the contract, or for some period after its termination, or both. When it applies to the period covered by the contract, such a restriction usually constitutes a corollary to other restrictions, such as territorial restraints or exclusive dealing arrangements, and must be judged along the same line as the restriction of which it is the counterpart.

On the other hand, limits on the franchisee's right to compete after the franchise agreement is terminated have their own justifications. The most convincing involves the protection of the franchisor's specific investment in the franchise business, particularly when the franchiser transfers some know-how and technical skills to his franchisees. Such post-termination restrictions, however, also may have non-negligible consequences for interbrand competition and for the franchisor's rights – which in turn affects competition in the long run. The beneficial effect of encouraging efficient investments therefore has to be appropriately weighed against possible *ex post* negative effects. Many countries have decided to allow such a post-termination restriction for a period of at most one year, which seems a reasonable compromise.

References

American Bar Association Antitrust Section (1984), Antitrust Law Developments, 2nd edn., ABA Press.
Klein, B. and K.M. Murphy (1988), 'Vertical restraints as contract enforcement mechanisms' *Journal of Law and Economics*, 31, 265–97.
Mathewson, G.F. and R.A. Winter (1986), 'The economics of vertical restraints in distribution', in Joseph E. Stiglitz and G.F. Mathewson (eds.), *New Developments in the Analysis of Market Structure*, Cambridge, MA, The MIT Press, pp. 211–36.
Mendelsohn, M. (1985), *The Guide to Franchising,* 4th ed., Pergamon Press.
Neale, A.D. and D.G. Goyder (1980), *The Antitrust Laws of the United States of America*, 3rd edn., Cambridge University Press.
OECD (1989), *Competition Policy and Intellectual Property Rights*, Paris.
Overstreet, Th. Jr. (1983), 'Resale price maintenance: economic theories and empirical evidence', Bureau of Economics Staff Report to the Federal Trade Commission.
Picot, A. (1991), 'Resale price maintenance: what do economists know and when did they know it? Comment', *Journal of Institution and Theoretical Economics*, 147.
Posner, R. (1975), 'Antitrust policy and the Supreme Court: an analysis of the restricted distribution, horizontal merger and potential competition decisions', *Columbia Law Review*, 75, 282.

Chapter 16

Joint R&D ventures
Cooperative and non-cooperative R&D in duopoly with spillovers

C. d'Aspremont and A. Jacquemin

Contrary to the usual assumption made in most oligopoly models, relations among firms are seldom of a wholly cooperative or non-cooperative type: in many situations, they compete in some fields, while they cooperate in others. An important example is the case of cooperative research efforts bringing fierce competitors together.

Two types of agreement are observed. First R&D cooperation can take place at the so-called 'precompetitive stage': companies share basic information and efforts in the R&D stage but remain rivals in the market-place.[1]

A second type of agreement involves an extended collusion between partners, creating common policies at the product level. The usual justifications of this extension are the difficulties of protecting intellectual property. The idea is then to allow partners who have achieved inventions together, to also control together the processes and products which embody the results of their collaboration, in order to recuperate jointly their R&D investments.[2]

This article first appeared in the *American Economic Review*, 1988, vol. 78, pp. 1133–7.
We are grateful to Jean Gabszewicz for his comments. Also the first author acknowledges support from the CIM, Belgium, and the hospitality of the Graduate School of Business, Stanford University.

[1] A well-known example is the European Strategic Program for R&D in Information Technologies (ESPRIT). The Microelectronics and Computer Technology Corporation (MCC) in the United States, and the Very Large-Scale Integration Program (VLSI) in Japan are other examples.
[2] An illustration is given by the EUREKA project intended to undertake common European research with concrete objectives and leading to the joint exploitation of the results.

What could be expected from these types of agreement is a reduction in R&D expenditures, because of less wasteful duplication, and a reduction of total production, because of more monopoly power. Using a two-stage approach, this chapter provides an example that does not fulfil these expectations and that allows a social welfare comparison between the corresponding games. An important factor in this analysis consists in the externalities or spillovers in R&D from one firm to another.

1   The example

Consider an industry with two firms facing an inverse demand function $D^{-1}(Q)$, where $Q = q_1 + q_2$ is the total quantity produced. Each firm has a cost of production $C_i(q_i, x_i, x_j)$ which is a function of its own production, q_i, of the amount of research x_i that it undertakes and the amount of research x_j that its rival undertakes. Both D^{-1} and C are assumed linear, so that

$$D^{-1} = a - bQ \text{ with } a, b > 0, \text{ and}$$

$$C_i(q_i, x_i, x_j) = \left[A - x_i - \beta x_j\right] q_i, \quad i = 1, 2, i \neq j$$

with $0 < A < a, 0 < \beta < 1$; $x_i + \beta x_j \leq A$; $Q \leq a/b$.

The R&D externalities or spillovers imply that some benefits of each firm's R&D flow without payment to other firms. In our specification the external effect of firm j's R&D is to lower firm i's unit production cost.[3] The cost of R&D is assumed to be quadratic, reflecting the existence of diminishing returns to R&D expenditures.[4]

Firms' strategies consist of a level of research and a subsequent production strategy based on their R&D choice. We shall now analyse three different games.

1 In the first one, firms act non-cooperatively in both output and R&D. Consider the profit of firm i at the second stage, conditional on x_1 and x_2

$$\pi_i = [a - bQ] q_i - \left[A - x_i - \beta x_j\right] q_i - \gamma \frac{x_i^2}{2}, \quad j \neq i, i = 1, 2.$$

The Nash–Cournot equilibrium can be computed to be[5]

$$q_1 = \frac{(a - A) + (2 - \beta) x_i + (2\beta - 1) x_j}{3b}.$$

---

[3] One interpretation is that successful inventions of rivals can be imitated at less cost to firm i than if it were to invent the new processes itself. See Hartwick (1984) who presents a static Cournot model with free entry and concludes that with R&D spillovers one cannot conclude that the corresponding equilibrium is associated with excessive duplication as Dasgupta and Stiglitz (1980).

[4] A valuable justification of this assumption is that 'the technological possibilities linking R&D inputs and innovative outputs do not display any economies of scale with respect to the size of the firm in which R&D is undertaken' (Dasgupta, 1986, p. 523).

[5] Notice that $q_1 + q_2 \leq \frac{1}{3b}[2(a - A) + 2A] \leq \frac{a}{b}$.

At the preceding stage, in which firms choose R&D levels, profits can be written as

$$\pi_i^* = \frac{1}{9b}\left[(a - A) + (2 - \beta)x_i + (2\beta - 1)x_j\right]^2 - \gamma\frac{x_i^2}{2} \quad j \neq i, i = 1, 2.$$

This integrates a triple influence of the R&D levels: via the outputs, the unit production cost, and the R&D costs themselves.

There exists a unique (and symmetric) solution[6] satisfying $\partial\pi_i^*/\partial x_i = 0$, for which

$$x_i^* = \frac{(a - A)(2 - \beta)}{4.5b\gamma - (2 - \beta)(1 + \beta)} \quad i = 1, 2.$$

$$Q^* = q_i^* + q_j^* = \frac{2(a - A)}{3b} + \frac{2(\beta + 1)}{3b}x_i^*$$

$$= \frac{2(a - A)}{3b}\left[\frac{4.5b\gamma}{4.5b\gamma - (2 - \beta)(1 + \beta)}\right].$$

2 In the second game, we introduce cooperation in R&D, the second stage remaining non-cooperative. At the first stage the firms maximize the joint profits, as a function of x_1 and x_2:

$$\hat{\pi} = \pi_1^* + \pi_2^* = \frac{1}{9b}\sum_{i=1}^{2}\left\{\left[(a - A) + (2 - \beta)x_i + (2\beta - 1)x_j\right]^2 - \gamma\frac{x_i^2}{2}\right\}, \quad j \neq i.$$

Considering the symmetric solution $x_i = x_2 = \hat{x}$, we obtain[7] the following unique solution for the equilibrium with cooperation in R&D:

$$\hat{x} = \frac{(\beta + 1)(a - A)}{4.5b\gamma - (\beta + 1)^2}; \hat{Q} = \frac{2(a - A)}{3b} + \frac{2(\beta + 1)}{3b}.\hat{x} = \frac{2(a - A)}{3b}\left[\frac{4.5b\gamma}{4.5b\gamma - (1 + \beta)^2}\right].$$

These solutions correspond to an internalization of the R&D external effects through joint decision on the levels of R&D expenditures. Contrary to what could have been expected from possible reduction in the duplication of R&D, especially in the case of large spillovers, a comparison between $\hat{x}$ and x^* clearly indicates that for large spillovers, that is,[8] $\beta > 0.5$, the level of R&D increases when firms cooperate in R&D, that is, $\hat{x} > x^*$. In the same perspective, as shown by the respective values of $\hat{Q}$

---

[6] Second-order conditions require that

$$\frac{2(2 - \beta)^2}{9b} - \gamma < 0$$

or $\frac{2}{9}(2 - \beta)^2 < b\gamma$.

[7] Second-order conditions require $\frac{2}{9}(1 + \beta)^2 < b\gamma$.

[8] Indeed, if $\beta + 1 > 2 - \beta, x^* < \hat{x}$

and Q^*, the amount of production is also higher with cooperation in R&D, than in the non-cooperative situation, that is, $\hat{Q} > Q^*$.

To the extent that profits are higher in the case of cooperative research than in the non-cooperative game[9] private incentives, independently of any public policy such as subsidies, can be sufficient to lead to such a cooperation.

3 The third case deals with monopoly: firms cooperate in both stages of the game. At the second stage, the joint profit conditional on x_1 and x_2 is given by

$$\pi = [a - bQ]Q - AQ + (x_1 + \beta x_2)q_1 + (x_2 + \beta x_1)q_2 - \gamma \sum_{i=1}^{2} \frac{x_i^2}{2}.$$

For $x_2 = x_1 = x$, the symmetric solution $\tilde{q}_1 = \tilde{q}_2$ leads to[10]

$$Q = q_1 + q_2 = \left[(a - A) + (1 + \beta)x\right]/2b.$$

At the preceding stage, the joint profit becomes

$$\tilde{\pi} = \frac{1}{b}\left[\frac{a - A + (1 + \beta)x}{2}\right]^2 - \gamma x^2.$$

The symmetric cooperative equilibrium in R&D and in production corresponds to the following unique solution[11]

$$\tilde{x} = \frac{(a - A)(1 + \beta)}{4b\gamma - (1 + \beta)^2}; \tilde{Q} = \frac{(a - A)}{2b} + \frac{(1 + \beta)}{2b}.\tilde{x} = \frac{a - A}{2b}\left[\frac{4b\gamma}{4b\gamma - (1 + \beta)^2}\right].$$

Here as expected, the collusive output, for a given level of R&D, is smaller than the non-cooperative one, but it is not necessarily so when the optimal amount of R&D is incorporated.[12] Similarly, the collusive amount of R&D varies with the value of β and is, for reasonably large spillovers, higher than in the fully non-cooperative

---

[9] Indeed the non-cooperative choice could always be adopted by cooperating firms, if more profitable.

[10] Notice that $\tilde{Q} \leq \frac{1}{2b}[2(1 - A) + 2A] = \frac{a}{b}$.

[11] According to the second-order conditions, $\partial^2\tilde{\pi}/\partial\tilde{x}^2 = (1 + \beta)^2/2 - 2\gamma < 0$ or $(1 + \beta)^2/4 < b\gamma$. Also we consider here only the *symmetric* cooperative equilibrium. The producers could reach higher joint profits by having different R&D expenditures and only one firm producing (the one with the lower unit cost). However, to consider this asymmetric cooperative solution would not affect our qualitative results.

[12] We have $\tilde{Q} < Q^*$ iff $5\beta^2 + 4\beta - 1 < 3\beta\gamma$. For $\beta = 1, \tilde{Q} < Q^*$ would require that $\beta\gamma > \frac{8}{3}$, which is more restrictive than second-order conditions.

equilibrium.[13] Furthermore the amount of R&D in the case of collusion in both output and R&D is higher than in the case of pure R&D cooperation. This stems from the fact that less competition in the product market allows the firms to capture more of the surplus created by their research and induce more R&D expenditures. But despite this larger amount of R&D, the quantity produced at the fully cooperative equilibrium is less than with a cooperation limited to the R&D stage.[14]

2   Welfare conclusions

Given this set of results, it is not a priori clear that, from a social welfare point of view, one type of behaviour is more efficient than another. Indeed more cooperation could lead to higher profits but lower consumer surplus. Less production could be compensated by more R&D. And a higher level of research could correspond to a wasteful duplication that ignores R&D externalities. In order to classify the solution obtained in the different situations, we need an efficiency standard. Let us define social welfare $W(Q)$ as the sum of the consumer's surplus $V(Q)$ and the producer's surplus (assuming $x_1 = x_2 = x$)

$$W(Q) = V(Q) - AQ + (1 + \beta)xQ - \gamma x^2.$$

Given x, the efficient output is the following

$$Q = \frac{1}{b}[a - A + (1 + \beta)x].$$

At the first stage social welfare is

$$W^{**} = V(Q) - AQ + (1 + \beta)xQ - \gamma x^2.$$

The efficient level of R&D satisfying the first-order conditions[15] is

$$x^{**} = \frac{(a - A)(1 + \beta)}{2b\gamma - (\beta + 1)^2}.$$

And, finally, the socially efficient amount of production incorporating the efficient level of research can be written as

$$Q^{**} = \frac{a - A}{b} + \frac{1 + \beta}{b}.x^{**} = \frac{a - A}{b}\left[\frac{2b\gamma}{2b\gamma - (1 + \beta)^2}\right].$$

[13] It appears that $\bar{x} > x^*$
iff

$$\frac{(1 + \beta)}{4b\gamma - (1 + \beta)^2} > \frac{(2 - \beta)}{4.5b\gamma - (2 - \beta)(1 + \beta)}, \text{ or}$$

$$\beta > 0.41.$$

[14] Indeed $\bar{Q} < \hat{Q}$ whenever $b\gamma > (1 + \beta)^2/3$, a less restrictive condition than some of our second-order conditions.
[15] The second-order condition requires that $[(1 + \beta)/2]^2 < b\gamma$.

Therefore the solution obtained by maximizing social welfare requires not only more production but also a higher level of R&D than what is obtained with any of the previous non-cooperative and cooperative equilibria.

Indeed, $x^{**} > x^*$, since

$$\frac{1+\beta}{2b\gamma - (1+\beta)^2} > \frac{2-\beta}{4.5b\gamma - (2-\beta)(1+\beta)}$$

and $Q^{**} > Q^*$.

Similarly $x^{**} > \tilde{x} > \hat{x}$ and $Q^{**} > \hat{Q} > \tilde{Q}$.

This provides us with a convenient social efficiency standard to classify our various results.

The clearest conclusion is that cooperation in R&D (but not in production) increases both expenditures in R&D and quantities of production, with respect to the non-cooperative solution, that is, $\hat{x} > x^*$ and $\hat{Q} > Q^*$, whenever the spillover effect is large enough; otherwise it is the reverse.

Further, considering separately production and R&D aspects, the cases of large and small spillovers should also be distinguished. For large spillovers, such that $\beta > 0.5$, the amount of research which is the closest to the social optimum is the one achieved by firms' cooperating in both output and research; and the most distant, the one obtained by non-cooperative behaviour. The complete classification is the following

$$x^{**} > \tilde{x} > \hat{x} > x^*.$$

Concerning the quantity of production, the closest to the social optimum is what is produced by firms cooperating at the 'precompetitive stage', that is, in research. The classification is then

$$Q^{**} > \hat{Q} > Q^* > \tilde{Q}.$$

For small spillovers, such that $\beta \leq 0.4$, the classifications are different and the 'second-best' for R&D is obtained by a non-cooperative behaviour in both stages.[16]

To conclude, our example has shown that cooperative behaviour can play a positive role in industries having a few firms and characterized by R&D activities generating spillover effects. This is in line with the permissive American and European antitrust regulations allowing cooperative research whereby member firms agree to share the costs and the results of a research project.[17]

However, in order to compute explicitly and to classify our various types of subgame-perfect solutions, our analysis has been very partial and based on a model ignoring many crucial aspects of R&D activities.[18]

---

[16] The classifications are then $x^{**} > x^* \geq \tilde{x} > \hat{x}; Q^{**} > Q^* > \hat{Q} > \tilde{Q}$.

[17] Policy questions are analysed in Jacquemin (1987, 1988).

[18] For a broader analysis, see Katz (1986). An overview of the main aspects of R&D activities and innovations is to be found in Davies (1979) and Spence (1986). Multi-national aspects are considered in De Bondt et al. (1988).

References

Davies, S. (1979), *The Diffusion of Process Innovations,* Cambridge University Press.

Dasgupta, P. and J. Stiglitz (1980), 'Industrial structure and the nature of innovative activity', *Economic Journal,* 90, 266–93.

(1986), 'The theory of technological competition', in J. Stiglitz and F. Mathewson (eds.), *New Developments in the Analysis of Market Structure,* Cambridge, MA, MIT Press.

De Bondt, R., L. Sleuwaegen, and R. Veugelers (1988), 'Innovative strategic groups in multinational industries', *European Economic Review,* 32, 905–26.

Hartwick, J. (1984), 'Optimal R&D levels when firm *j* benefits from firm *i*'s inventive activity', *Economics Letters,* 16, 165–70.

Jacquemin, A. (1987), *The New Industrial Organization,* Cambridge, MA, MIT Press, chapter 6.

Jacquemin, A (1988), 'Cooperative agreements in R&D and European antitrust policy', *European Economics Review,* 32, 551–60.

Katz, M. (1986), 'An analysis of cooperative research and development', *Rand Journal of Economics,* 17, 527–43.

Spence, M. (1986), 'Cost reduction, competition and industry performance', in J. Stiglitz and F. Mathewson (eds.) *New Developments in the Analysis of Market Structure,* Cambridge, MA, MIT Press.

Part IV

MERGERS AND MERGER CONTROL

Chapter 17

Unprofitable exogenous mergers
Losses from horizontal merger: the effects of an exogenous change in industry structure on Cournot–Nash equilibrium

S. W. Salant, S. Switzer and R. J. Reynolds

I   Introduction

In the Cournot (1838) solution to the oligopoly problem, each firm's output choice is profit maximizing given the outputs of the other firms. The Cournot approach is conventionally extended to industries with merged firms and cartels by treating each merged entity as a collection of plants under the control of a particular player in a non-cooperative game. The payoff to each coalition is the sum of the profits that accrue to each of its members. For each exogenous specification of market structure (partition of plants into coalitions), outputs, profits, and market prices are endogenously determined.

The purpose of this article is to explore and evaluate an unnoticed comparative-static implication of such Cournot models: some exogenous mergers *may reduce* the endogenous joint profits of the firms that are assumed to collude. Similar results arise using other solution concepts (Cave, 1980). In the Cournot case losses from horizontal merger may seem surprising, since the merged firm always has the option of producing exactly as its components did in the pre-merger equilibrium. But such a situation is not an equilibrium following the merger, since – *given* unchanged outputs of the other players – the merged firm would then have an incentive to alter its production (i.e., to reduce it).

This article first appeared in *The Quarterly Journal of Economics*, 1983, Vol. 98, pp. 185–99.

In the next section we raise the possibility diagramatically that some exogenous mergers may be unprofitable. Section 3 then establishes that this outcome can in fact arise by examining Cournot's original example where identical firms with constant unit costs of production sell a homogeneous product to consumers with a linear demand curve. The section also establishes a number of other bizarre comparative-static results for this example. At the conclusion of the section, the example is modified to show that exogenous mergers can still cause losses even when the merger creates such large efficiency gains through scale economies that it would be socially advantageous.

We wish to emphasize at the outset that Cournot's example is chosen merely as the simplest in which to display various puzzling phenomena. In particular, the loss-from-merger result *can also arise* in more complex Nash equilibrium models – with differentiated products, dynamics, increasing marginal costs, and so forth. Indeed, we first observed losses from merger in a dynamic oil model where each Cournot player chooses a time-dated vector of extraction (subject to capacity and exhaustion constraints) and incurs marginal costs that are increasing functions of the rate of extraction. The parameters used in this computerized model (Salant, 1981 and 1982) were not intended to generate peculiar behaviour, but rather to approximate the current world oil market. Nor does the loss-from-merger result arise because of the partial-equilibrium nature of the analysis. In an independent analysis using a general-equilibrium framework, Okuno *et al.* (1980, p. 29) display an example with the same characteristic.

Section 4 discusses the significance of our paradoxical comparative-static results for attempts to build a theory of horizontal mergers. Should the Cournot–Nash equilibrium concept – and indeed any solution concept where an exogenous merger can cause a loss – be discarded? Few solution concepts would survive such a test. Or should the decision to merge be endogenized as a move in a larger game? This latter approach is exciting because it would permit *predictions* about which mergers are contained in the set of equilibria and which mergers will never occur. Antitrust authorities need not concern themselves with blocking mergers outside the equilibrium set, since market forces would prevent their occurrence; for the same reason, the government could not cause such mergers to occur (without using supplementary incentives) even if they would be socially desirable. Finally, such models may ultimately help us understand the evolution of industry structure over time as coalitions form and regroup.

To illustrate how the decision to merge can be endogenized as a move in a larger game, a simple model is outlined with a single stage of coalition formation. In this model all of the mergers in the equilibrium set are profitable, thus eliminating the paradoxes that arise when mergers are treated as exogenous. Furthermore, among the equilibria are not only merger to monopoly but also less complete mergers. Such a characteristic seems important in a model of horizontal mergers; otherwise, its predictions will conflict with the structure of every industry in existence that is not a complete monopoly. The simple model outlined in section 4 is provided only as an illustration of a promising approach. A more complex but realistic model using this same approach is under construction.

2   The potential loss from horizontal mergers

Consider a Cournot equilibrium in which each firm in an industry operates independently. This can be compared with the Cournot equilibrium in which a subset of the firms merge, while the other firms remain independent. Such a comparison can be used to examine those cases in which the joint profits of the merged firms would be *smaller* than the sum of their profits prior to merger. It is convenient to refer to the subset of firms that will participate in the proposed merger as 'insiders' and those firms that will continue to behave independently after the merger as 'outsiders'. We shall make use of figures 17.1 and 17.2. To simplify the figures, we have drawn the functions in each as linear; however, no result depends on the linearity of our drawing. Denote by $R_0(Q)$ the total amount that non-cooperating outsiders would produce for any given aggregate production (Q) by insiders. $R_0(Q)$ can easily be computed by deducting the given aggregate production by insiders (Q) from the consumer demand curve, computing the Nash equilibrium among the non-cooperating outsiders relative to this residual demand curve, and adding up the equilibrium production at each outsider firm. Denote by $R_I^{NC}(q)$ the total amount that the non-cooperating insiders would produce (prior to merger) for any given aggregate production (q) by outsiders. $R_I^{NC}(q)$ can easily be computed by deducting from the consumer demand curve the given aggregate production by the outsiders (q), computing the Nash equilibrium among the non-cooperating insiders relative to this residual demand curve, and adding up the equilibrium production at each insider firm. We can then use these curves to determine outputs prior to the merger. In figure 17.1, a Nash equilibrium occurs at A, where the reaction functions of the outsiders (R_0) and the non-colluding insiders (R_I^{NC}) intersect. Outsiders produce the horizontal component of $A(q_{NC})$ in aggregate and insiders produce the vertical component (Q_{NC}). An exogenous merger will displace the equilibrium. Graphically, it will cause some of these curves to shift. Since the response of the non-colluding outsiders to the aggregate supply of the insiders does not depend on whether that supply was produced by a merged firm or a set of non-colluding firms, R_0 does not shift. In contrast, the reaction function of the insiders will shift when the insiders merge. Denote by $R_1^C(q)$ the production of the insiders after the merger, given outsider production q. Then, $R_C1(q) < R_I^{NC}(q)$. For any given output by outsiders, insiders will contract their aggregate output when they merge because they will then internalize the inframarginal losses that they impart to each other.

We conclude, therefore, that a merger causes the equilibrium output of the insiders to contract and the output of the outsiders to expand. To determine its effects on profits, we examine figure 17.2. Denote the sum of the profits of the insiders prior to and following the merger, respectively, as $\pi_I^{NC}(q)$ and $\pi_I^C(q)$. For any given level of production by outsiders, the aggregate profits of the insiders can only increase (since they can always run their plants so as to mimic the pre-merger equilibrium). Hence π_C1 lies above π_I^{NC}. But as the outputs of the outsiders increase, the profits of the insiders decrease. Hence the *possibility* arises that the increase in production by outsiders following the merger will reduce insider profits by more than the increase in

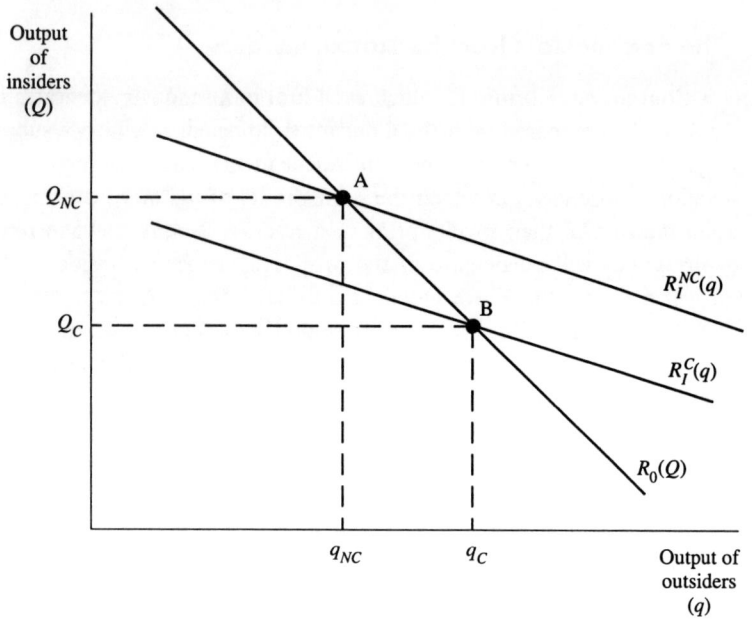

Figure 17.1 Production responses from merger

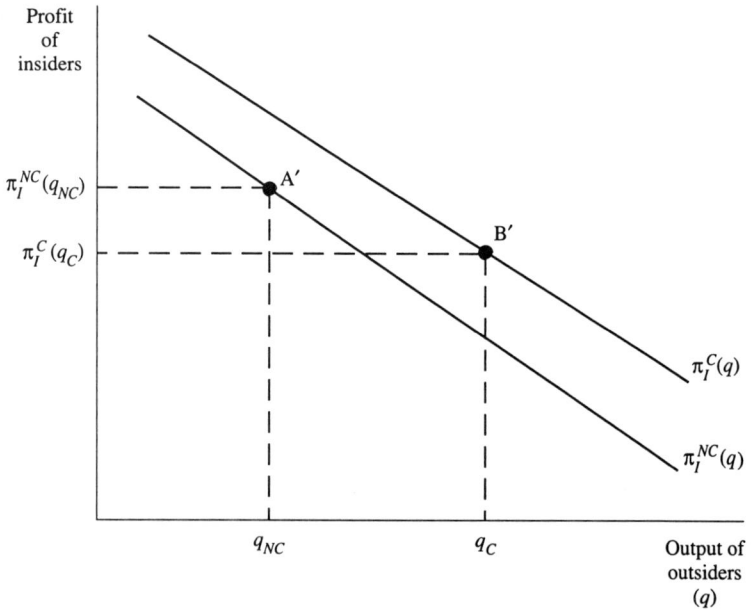

Figure 17.2 Profit consequences of merger

profits that would have occurred had outsider production remained constant. This possibility is illustrated in figure 17.2, where the profits following the merger (the vertical component of B') are smaller than the profits prior to the merger (the vertical component of A'). Thus, it is the output expansion of the outsider firms that can in principle cause a reduction in profits for the merging firms.[1]

Of course, the model has more structure than we have considered. Hence, conceivably the possibility illustrated in figure 17.2 can never occur. To demonstrate that the possibility can indeed arise, we need look no further than Cournot's classic example.

3   Cournot's example

In the previous section we showed how the profits of a designated group of insiders depended on whether they were colluding or not. The profits of this group also depend on its composition. As a simplifying assumption, suppose that there are n identical firms in an industry. Then we can specify the composition of the insider group merely by describing the number of firms it contains. Suppose that there are $m + 1$ insiders (for m an integer between 0 and $n - 1$).

Denote by $\pi^{NC}(n, m)$ the joint profits to insiders prior to the merger if the insider group contains $m + 1$ non-colluding firms (and the outsider group the residual). Denote by $\pi^C(n, m)$ the joint profits to the insiders subsequent to the merger if the insider group contains $M + 1$ colluding firms (and the outsider group the residual).

Denote by $g(n, m)$ the increase in joint profits that results if $m + 1$ insiders in an industry of n firms collude.

Then, by definition

$$g(n, m) = \pi^{NC}(n, m).$$

To simplify further, we assume that marginal costs are constant. Then if each firm in an x-firm equilibrium earned $\pi(x)$

$$\pi^{NC}(n, m) + (m + 1)\pi(n); \tag{1}$$

$$\pi^C(n, m) = \pi(n - m); \tag{2}$$

and

$$g(n, m) = \pi(n - m) - (m + 1)\pi(n). \tag{3}$$

Equation (1) follows from the assumption that all firms are identical. Hence prior to the merger, the $m + 1$ insiders earn jointly $m + 1$ times as much as the typical firm in the n-firm equilibrium. Equation (2) depends, in addition, on the assumption of

---

[1] It should be noted, however, that industry profits will always increase in response to the merger. If the merger is unprofitable, the profits of the non-colluding firms will have increased by more than the loss in the profits of the insiders.

constant marginal costs. Because of this assumption the insiders – once they have merged – behave exactly like any of the other firms in an $n-m$ firm symmetric equilibrium. Equation (3) follows by substitution.

In Cournot's example with constant marginal costs (α) and linear[2] demand $\left(P = \beta - \sum_{i=1}^{n} Q_i\right)$, it is straightforward to calculate $\pi(n)$

$$\pi(n) = ([\beta - \alpha]/[n + 1])^2. \tag{4}$$

To verify this, we first deduce the output of each firm in an n-firm symmetric Cournot equilibrium and then calculate the resulting profit per firm as a function of n. Firm j maximizes profits by setting Q_j to solve

$$\max_{q_j \geq 0} Q_j \left[B - Q_j \sum_{i \neq j} Q_i - \alpha \right].$$

If optimal production by firm j is positive, then $p - \sum_{i \neq j} Q_i - \alpha - 2Q_j = 0$. In a symmetric Nash equilibrium, the output of each firm in the industry will be identical so that $Q_i = Q - j = Q$. Therefore, $Q = [\beta - \alpha]/[n + 1]$. Since $\pi(n) = (P - \alpha)Q$, we can substitute the equilibrium output per firm and verify equation (4)

$$\pi(n) = (\beta - nQ - \alpha)Q$$
$$= ([\beta - \alpha]/[n + 1])^2.$$

The change in insider profits due to merger (equation (3)) can, therefore, be re-expressed as

$$g(n, m) = \left(\frac{\beta - \alpha}{n - m + 1} \right) - (m + 1)\left(\frac{\beta - \alpha}{n + 1} \right)^2$$
$$= (\beta - \alpha)^2 \{(n - m + 1)^{-2} - (m + 1)(n + 1)^{-2}\}. \tag{3'}$$

For any specified number of firms (n) in the pre-merger equilibrium, equation (3′) can be used to determine whether collusion by $m + 1$ insiders would be profitable. Losses from merger occur if and only if $g < 0$. In figure 17.3 we plot $\pi_C(n, m)$, $\pi^{NC}(n, m)$ and $g(n,m)$ against m (for a fixed n). The $g(n,m)$ function can be used to deduce several noteworthy properties of this example (for $n \geq 2$).

A. If there is no merger, there will be neither gain nor loss. Trivially, if a single insider is joined by no others in a merger, then its profits will be unchanged $g(n, 0) = 0$, for $n = 2, 3, \dots$. The profit of the firm will be $\Pi(n)$ both before and after this degenerate merger.

---

[2] Since any linear demand curve can be expressed in this form if the output units are defined appropriately, the assumption of a unitary slope is unrestrictive.

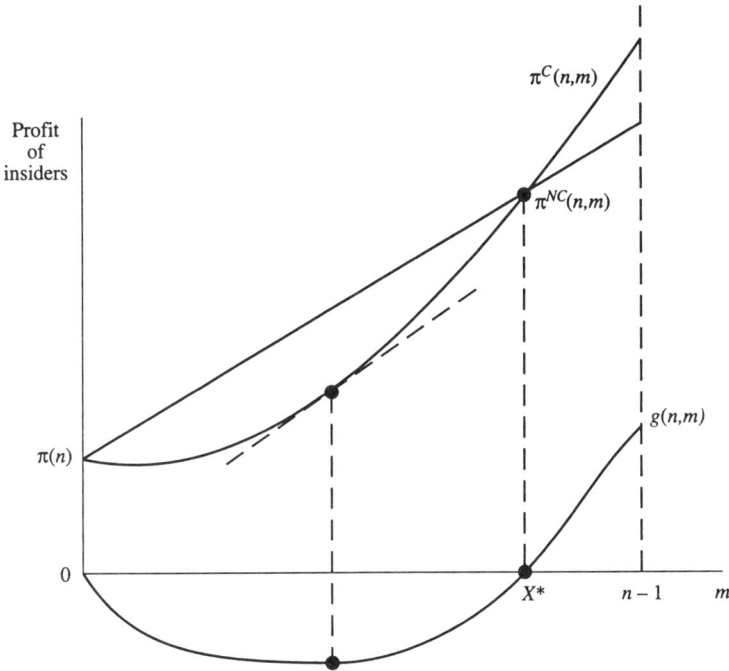

Figure 17.3 Unprofitable merger

B. Merger by a larger number of firms *may* cause a loss to the colluding firms. This result follows,[3] since

$$\frac{\partial g(n,m)}{\partial m}\Big|_{m=0} < 0.$$

Indeed, over a range of m, losses from merger are *larger* the greater the number of firms in the coalition. For example, if $n = 12$, a merger by seven firms ($m = 6$) generates even larger losses than a merger by any smaller number of firms.[4]

C. Merger to monopoly is always profitable. When all the firms in an n-firm equilibrium collude, so that there are no outsiders, profits must increase, since joint profits will then be maximized. Formally, $g(n, n - 1) > 0$, for $n = 2, 3, \dots$.

D. For any given number of firms in the pre-merger equilibrium, if a merger by a specified number of firms causes losses (respectively, gains), a merger by a smaller (larger) number of firms will cause losses (gains). We have noted that

[3] $\dfrac{\partial g(n,m)}{\partial m} = (B - \alpha)^2 [2(1 + n - m)^3 - (1 - n)^{-2}].$

[4] To illustrate, when there are 12 firms in the pre-merger equilibrium ($n = 12$), a merger by seven firms ($m = 6$) will generate larger losses to the insiders than the losses that would be incurred by three merging firms. For $m = 6$, while for $m = 6$, $g(n, m)/(B - \alpha)^2 = -0.021$, while for $m = 2$, $g(n, m)/(B - \alpha)^2 = -0.010$. Indeed, the loss is more than twice as large.

$g(n, 0) = 0, \partial g(n, 0)/\partial m < 0$ and $g(n, n1) > 0$, from properties A, B, and C, respectively. Since $g(\cdot, \cdot)$ is continuous in its second argument, there must exist at least one root $x^* > 0$ such that $g(n, x^*) = 0$. Furthermore, since $g(n, x)$ is strictly convex[5] in its second argument, $g(n, x) < 0$ for $x^* > x > 0$. Similarly, $g(n, x) > 0$ for $x > x^*$.

E. For *any* n, it is sufficient for a merger to be unprofitable that less than 80 per cent of the firms collude. Consider the gain-from-merger function $g(n, m)$ defined above. Let $x^*(n) + 1$ be the (unique) number of firms in the coalition that will lead to neither gains nor losses for an industry with n firms in the pre-merger equilibrium. Let $a + (m + 1)/n$ be the number of insiders as a proportion of all the firms in the industry. Then a merger causes neither losses nor gains if $\hat{a} = [x^*(n) + 1]/n$. This break-even fraction $\hat{a}$ reaches its minimum value of 0.8 when $n = 5$. In other words, the break-even value for all other industry sizes *exceeds* 80 per cent.[6] The result, therefore, follows from property D. To illustrate, note that if $n = 3$, a merger by a pair of firms is unprofitable; and if $n = 4$, a merger by either two or three firms is unprofitable.

F. If any given fraction $\alpha(< 1)$ of an industry is assumed to merge, there is an industry size (n) large enough for this merger to cause losses. Let R be the ratio of the post-merger profits of the insiders to their pre-merger profits. That is, $R = \pi^C(n, m)/\pi^{NC}(n, m) = \pi^C(n, \alpha n - 1)/\pi^{NC}(n, \alpha n - 1)$, where $\alpha = (m + 1)/n$. If $R < 1$ for a merger by a proportion α of an industry of size n, then such a merger would be unprofitable. The proposition follows by noting that (for any $\alpha < 1)R \to 0$ as $n \to \infty$.[7] For example, even when 98 per cent of the firms in an industry merge, there exists an industry size large enough for this 'virtual' monopolization to cause a loss.

5 $\dfrac{\partial^2 g(n, m)}{\partial m^2} = (B - \alpha)^2 [6(1 + n - m)^{-4}] > 0.$

6 $g(n, \alpha n - 1) = (\beta - \alpha)^2 \left[\dfrac{(1 + n)^2 - \alpha n(2 + n - \alpha n)^2}{(2 + n - \alpha n)^2(1 + n)^2} \right]$, where $g(n, \alpha n - 1) = 0$ when the numerator

(N) of the bracketed term equals zero: $N = (1 + n)^2 - \alpha n(2 + n - \alpha n)^2 = 0$. This equation is a cubic in α and has three roots:

$\alpha_1 = 1/n, \quad \alpha_2 = \dfrac{(2n + 3) - \sqrt{4n + 5}}{2n}$, and $\alpha_3 = \dfrac{(2n + 3) + \sqrt{4n + 5}}{2n}.$

The third root exceeds unity and is inadmissible; the first is the root associated with the degenerate merger. The second is the root of interest – that is, $\hat{\alpha} = \alpha_2$ – and is itself a function of n:

$\dfrac{d\hat{\alpha}}{dn} = \dfrac{(2n + 5)(4n + 5)^{1/2} - 3(4n + 5)}{2n^2(4n + 5)};$

$\dfrac{d^2\hat{\alpha}}{dn^2} = \dfrac{6(4n + 5) - (2n + 10)(4n + 5)^{1/2} - (4n^2 + 10n)(4n + 5)^{-1/2}}{2n^3(4n + 5)}$

Thus, $\hat{\alpha}(n)$ reaches a relative minimum at $n = 5$ and a relative maximum at $n = -1$. Hence for $n \geq 1, \hat{\alpha}(n) \geq \hat{\alpha}(5) = 0.8$.

7 $R = \dfrac{(n + 1)^2}{(m + 1)(n - m + 1)^2} = \dfrac{(n + 1)^2}{\alpha n(n - \alpha n + 2)^2}.$

For any $\alpha < 1$, $\lim\limits_{n \to \infty} R = 0$.

G. Mergers that create efficiency gains through scale economies can still cause losses. Suppose, in our example, that a merger of two firms resulted in a loss of L. If instead each firm had positive fixed costs but the same constant marginal costs as before, the post-merger equilibrium would be unchanged, but the entire output of the merged firm would be produced by a single plant – the plant with the lower fixed cost. As long as the fixed cost of each plant was less than L, the fixed cost saved by shutting down the highest cost plant would be too small to make the exogenous merger profitable.

H. A merger that provides efficiency gains may be socially beneficial even if it is privately injurious to the merging parties. Consider a merger that results in a loss to insiders. Since the merger results in a price increase, it also injures consumers. Nonetheless, in some cases, those producers not party to the merger gain so much that these other losses are outweighed. We define any situation where the sum of consumer and producer surpluses increases as an improvement in social welfare. To see how such a case can be constructed, consider again the Cournot example. In the absence of fixed costs, the gain to the merging firms is $g(n,m)$, defined in equation (3'). It was shown that $g(n,m)$ is zero for $m = 0$, is a strictly convex function of m, and initially decreases in m. Similarly, we can write the gain in *social* welfare when $m + 1$ firms out of n firms merge as $S(n,m)$, where

$$S(n,m) = (B-\alpha)^2 \left\{ \frac{n-m}{1+n-m} - \frac{n}{1+n} - \frac{1}{2}\left(\frac{n-m}{1+n-m}\right)^2 + \frac{1}{2}\left(\frac{n}{1+n}\right)^2 \right\}.$$

It can be verified that $S(n,m)$ is zero for $m = 0$, is a strictly concave function of m, and initially decreases in m – but at a *slower* rate than $g(n,m)$. It follows, therefore, that for small m the social loss is smaller than the loss to the merging parties. Now, if each firm has a fixed cost of F, the social gain from a merger by $m + 1$ firms is $\hat{S}(n,m)$ where $\hat{S}(n,m) = S(n,m) + mF$. Similarly, the gain to the merging firms is $\hat{g}(n,m)$ where $\hat{g}(n,m) = g(n,m) + mF$. That is, both the merging parties and society benefit by the same amount when the m plants are shut down following the merger. Since the social loss was smaller than the loss to these firms, it is possible to select F so that $\hat{S}(n,m) > 0 > \hat{g}(n,m)$. We illustrate this in Figure 17.4, where $S(n,m)$, $g(n,m)$, $\hat{S}(n,m)$, and $\hat{g}(n,m)$ are plotted against m (holding n fixed). Denote the merger size that results in zero social gain (respectively, zero private gain to the merging parties) as l (as k). For $m > 1$, mergers cause private gains ($\hat{g} > 0$ but social losses $\hat{S} < 0$). Such mergers are presumably ones antitrust authorities should discourage. For $k < m < l$, mergers create both private and social gains. For $m < k$, however, mergers would create social benefits but would injure the merging parties. Such mergers are presumably ones antitrust authorities would like to occur.

4   Significance of the results

Since the results of this chapter seem counterintuitive, it is important to ponder their significance. Our analysis has ruled out one possibility – that firms can act like

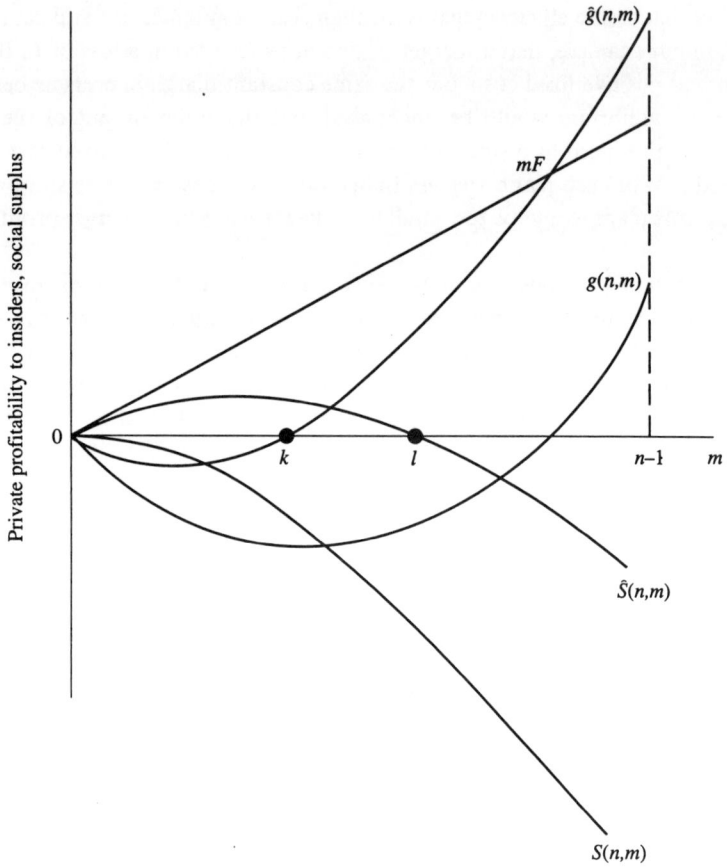

Figure 17.4 Unprofitable merger may be socially desirable

Cournot players in deciding how much to produce, can merge with anyone, and can always benefit from merger.[8] In this section we consider the three remaining logical alternatives: (1) Firms produce like Cournot players, and some horizontal mergers may cause losses; (2) firms do not always act like Cournot players in deciding how much to produce; and (3) firms do produce like Cournot players, and some specifiable mergers never occur.

The first of these alternatives treats our analysis not as showing that received theory is in need of revision but as deducing a testable proposition about the real world.

---

[8] The assertion in the text is true if the interaction among the firms occurs in a single period. It might be possible, however, that exogenous mergers will always be profitable if the interaction among firms has no definite horizon. For it seems possible that each outsider firm would be reluctant to expand output in a period by so much that the merger would be unprofitable for fear the merger would be dissolved, leaving each outsider firm with less profits in every period thereafter. We wish to thank the referee for pointing out the possible implications of this repeated game.

After all, if mergers never cause losses, the evidence of profitable mergers should be overwhelming. In fact, as Scherer (1980, p. 546) notes, 'the weight of the post-merger profitability evidence for an assortment of nations suggests that on average the private gains from mergers were either negative or insignificantly different from zero'.

Economists who give little weight to such evidence must logically espouse the second or third alternative. The second questions the appropriateness of the Cournot solution concept. Some economists feel the Cournot solution is never appropriate, while others believe that firms sophisticated enough to merge will not subsequently be naive enough to play Cournot even if they behaved that way prior to the merger.[9] Now the Cournot solution concept (as generalized by Nash, 1951) underlies most of non-cooperative game theory. Before dispensing with so serviceable a concept, it seems reasonable to contemplate possible replacements and to ask on what foundation, if not the Nash–Cournot solution, is a theory of mergers to be based? In response to our earlier draft, Cave (1980) has shown that exogenous mergers may cause losses under a large variety of cooperative and non-cooperative solution concepts including Nash non-cooperative equilibrium, Nash (trembling hand) perfect equilibrium, strong equilibrium, Nash–Harsanyi bargaining with either fixed or variable threats, and the Shapley value. Moreover, Aumann (1973) discovered that mergers may be disadvantageous using the core solution.[10] If every solution concept which implies that exogenous mergers may cause losses is to be shunned, there remain few candidates on which to base a theory of mergers, and these seem inappropriate on other grounds. Under such circumstances – *and without the necessary empirical information to choose among solution concepts* – it seems imprudent to reject any solution concept simply because it predicts that exogenous mergers can generate losses.

Instead, it may be more useful to extend the existing Cournot theory so as to *endogenize* the merger decision. The new theory should then *predict* that specific mergers – being disadvantageous – would not occur in equilibrium. This underlies the third alternative mentioned above.

To illustrate, we sketch a simple model where firms decide whether or not to merge and how much to produce. The model uses the Nash–Cournot solution concept and treats the merger decision as a move in an enlarged non-cooperative game.[11] In equilibrium, no merger causes a loss.

The players in our illustrative game are the n independent firms. Each player's strategy consists of a partition of the firms in the industry into coalitions and an output proposal for each firm in the coalition to which the particular player belongs. Each player's payoff depends on the strategies of the n players. If players pick

[9] If this latter view is correct, it would have an important implication. The behaviour of a multi-plant player in an oligopolistic industry could not be predicted without knowing the historical circumstances under which the many plants came to be operated by that player.

[10] Okuno, Postlewaite, and Roberts (1980) have independently shown that exogenous mergers may cause losses, using a Nash non-cooperative solution to a Shapley–Shubik exchange game with a continuum of traders. Their article provides a useful review of the literature on disadvantageous coalitions, which grew out of Aumann's work.

[11] For a related approach see Selten (1973).

different partitions, the unmerged 'status-quo' profits result. If all players pick the same partition, each firm shares equally in the profits of the coalition to which he belongs. The profits result from each firm producing the mean of what is proposed for him by all participants in his coalition.[12]

It should be evident that no Nash equilibrium in this game can be disadvantageous, since any player can always propose a different partition than the other players and thereby obtain the status quo profit. This makes valid our intuition that (in equilibrium) firms cannot do worse than they did prior to merger, since they can always replicate what they did earlier. In addition, every advantageous merger in the game where industry structure is exogenous can be supported as a Nash equilibrium in the extended game. This follows, since each firm perceives itself to control the outputs of every member of its own coalition and gets a given fraction of the coalition profits; it therefore will make the same choices as the multi-plant Cournot player in the game with the market structure exogenous. Finally, no extraneous equilibria have been introduced by enlarging the game, since any equilibrium in the extended game must also be an equilibrium in the game with exogenous market structure. An analysis of this as well as more realistic but complex games where mergers are endogenized is reported in Cave and Salant (1981).

We conclude by noting the implications for policy by recognizing that the merger decision is endogenous. In any model with endogenous mergers, the only mergers the private market will let stand are those in the equilibrium set.[13] Socially injurious mergers that are not in the set of equilibria need not be guarded against, since they are disadvantageous and will not occur. Socially beneficial mergers that, although they

---

[12] An alternative specification may seem more plausible and will generate the identical set of equilibria. Suppose that a strategy for each player consists of a description of whom he would like to collude with and the proposed total output of that coalition. That is, the player specifies nothing about mergers to which he is not a party, nor does he propose how the total output is to be produced within his own coalition. Given the strategies of the players, the payoffs are determined as follows. If any player proposes a coalition whose other members do not propose that same coalition, no mergers occur, and the status quo profits result. If there is agreement about coalitions, each player gets an equal share of the profits of the coalition to which he belongs. Profits of any particular coalition depend on market price (a decreasing function of the sum of average joint output proposals of each coalition), and on the average proposed output of the particular coalition, and on the cost of producing the average proposed output in the cheapest way. In equilibrium, given the proposals of the other players none of the n firms has any incentive to alter the average proposed output of his own coalition although he perceives himself able to do so by altering his own proposal for its total output.

[13] The reader should note that the decision to spin-off from a parent corporation or to defect from a cartel is simply the reverse of the merger decision. Hence our analysis has implications for these issues. Consider, for example, the question of cartel stability. All cartels contain at least one destabilizing force, since each member can benefit from cheating given an unchanged price or unchanged outputs of other producers. But if the other cartel members should be injured by the defection, they may make attempts to deter it. Such attempts, if successful, impart stability to the cartel. In contrast, if circumstances prevail where a merger would be disadvantageous, the defection may be beneficial to every member of the cartel. In that case, the cartel is unstable, and the defection is assured.

create efficiency gains,[14] are not in the set of equilibria cannot be achieved (without using supplementary incentives) for the same reason.

References

Aumann, R. (1973), 'Disadvantageous monopolies', *Journal of Economic Theory,* 6, 1–11.
Cave, J. (1980), 'Losses due to merger', Federal Trade Commission Working Paper.
Cave, J. and S. Salant (1981), 'Towards a theory of mergers', mimeo.
Cournot, A. (1838), *Researches into the Mathematical Principles of Wealth,* translated by N. T. Bacon, New York, Macmillan, 1897.
Nash, J. (1951), 'Non-cooperative games', *Annals of Mathematics,* 54, 286–96.
Okuno, M., A. Postlewaite, and J. Roberts (1980), 'Oligopoly and competition in large markets', *American Economic Review,* 70, 22–31.
Salant, S.W. (1981), *Imperfect Competition in the World Oil Market,* Lexington, MA, Lexington Books.
  (1982), 'Imperfect competition in the international energy market: a computerized Nash–Cournot model', *Operations Research,* 30, 252–80.
Scherer, F.M. (1980), *Industrial Market Structure and Economic Performance,* 2nd edn, Chicago, Rand McNally.
Selten, R. (1973), 'A simple model of imperfect competition where 4 are few and 6 are many', *International Journal of Game Theory,* 2, 141–201.

---

[14] See the end of section 3.

Chapter 18

Profitable horizontal mergers and welfare
Horizontal mergers: an equilibrium analysis

Joseph Farrell and Carl Shapiro

Mergers between large firms in the same industry have long been a public policy concern. In the United States, section 7 of the Clayton Act (as amended by the Celler–Kefauver Act) prohibits mergers that 'substantially decrease . . . competition or tend . . . to create a monopoly'. Under the Hart–Scott–Rodino Act, large firms must report any proposed substantial merger to the Department of Justice and the Federal Trade Commission, which evaluate the merger's likely effect on competition and can choose to permit or to oppose it.

In evaluating proposed mergers, federal antitrust officials generally apply rules summarized in the Department of Justice's Merger Guidelines (1984).[1] An important part of merger analysis under these guidelines involves estimating the effect of a

This article first appeared in the *American Economic Review*, 1990, Vol. 80, pp. 107–26.
Some of the results in this chapter were in Farrell and Shapiro (1988), which has been split into the current paper and Farrell and Shapiro (1990). We thank Peter Bronsteen, Avinash Dixit, Gene Grossman, Michael Katz, Louis Kaplow, F. William McElroy, Rob Porter, Stephen Salant, Marius Schwartz, John Vickers, Robert Willig, and seminar participants at the Antitrust Division, Department of Justice, the Federal Trade Commission, UC at Berkeley, UC at San Diego, Maryland, Northwestern Princeton, Columbia, Harvard, and Stanford for their comments. We especially thank Steve Salop for valuable suggestions. Both authors acknowledge the financial support of the National Science Foundation, Farrell under grant IRI 87–12238, and Shapiro under grant no. SES–8606336. Farrell also thanks the Hoover Institution and Shapiro the John M. Olin Foundation.
[1] For a discussion of these guidelines, see the symposium in the *Journal of Economic Perspectives*, Fall 1987.

proposed merger on market concentration. In particular, the analyst is instructed to pay careful attention to the initial *level* of concentration in the industry and the predicted *change* in concentration due to the merger. Roughly speaking, the guidelines permit mergers that will not increase concentration by very much or that will leave it low even after the merger. This reflects a view that anticompetitive harm is an increasing function of concentration, which is measured using the Herfindahl–Hirschman index, H, defined as the sum of the squares of the firms' market shares.

The Merger Guidelines, while surely more sophisticated than what they replaced, are not based on explicit analysis of how a merger will affect equilibrium output and welfare. This theoretical shortcoming leads to two basic problems with the guidelines' use of concentration measures.

The first such problem is the curious rule that the guidelines use to estimate the effect of a merger on H. This rule takes the initial market shares of the merging firms, s_1 and s_2, and assumes that the new entity's market share will be $s_1 + s_2$, so that the merger will increase H by $(s_1 + s_2)^2 - (s_1^2 + s_2^2) = 2s_1 s_2$. But if indeed all firms maintain their pre-merger outputs, then the merger will affect neither consumers nor non-participant firms, so it will be socially desirable if and only if it is privately profitable. If, as is more likely, outputs change in response to the merger, then the $2s_1 s_2$ formula is wrong. Equilibrium analysis, such as we provide below, is necessary to compute the change in H in a logically consistent manner.

The second problem is deeper and more serious. Implicitly, the guidelines assume a reliable (inverse) relationship between market concentration and market performance. In particular, the entire approach presumes that a *structural* change, such as a merger, that increases the equilibrium value of H also systematically reduces equilibrium welfare, W, defined as the sum of consumer and producer surplus or equivalently the difference between gross consumer benefits and production costs.

Is there in fact such a reliable relationship between changes in market concentration and changes in economic welfare? In some very special circumstances, there is. For example, if n equally efficient firms with constant unit cost compete as Cournot oligopolists, then W is increasing in n and $H = 1/n$, so there is a rigid (inverse) relationship between H and W as n varies.[2] But if the competing firms are not equally efficient, or if there are economies of scale, there is no reason to expect that concentration and welfare will move in opposite directions in response to a merger.[3]

The dangers of identifying changes in H with changes in W are suggested by the fact that, starting at a Cournot equilibrium, welfare rises with a small change in firms' outputs if and only if

$$\frac{dX}{X} + \frac{1}{2}\frac{dH}{H} > 0 \tag{1}$$

---

[2] In this model, aggregate output, X, is also a sufficient statistic for welfare, as it is more generally if total production costs depend only on aggregate output, and not on the distribution of output across firms.

[3] For further discussion of the relationship between changes in H and changes in W, see Farrell and Shapiro (1990).

where X is aggregate output. (See the appendix for a derivation of this condition.) Of course, increases in output ($dX > 0$) tend to raise welfare, since price exceeds marginal cost in equilibrium. But if a firm with a large market share increases its output, then H, X, and W will all rise. And condition (1) shows that for any given (percentage) change in X, welfare is more likely to rise if H *increases;* it is even possible to have $dX < 0$, $dH > 0$, and yet $dW > 0$.[4]

How can increases in the concentration be associated with increases in welfare? In Cournot equilibrium, larger firms have lower marginal costs, so welfare is enhanced if a fixed total output X is shifted towards them and away from smaller, less-efficient firms. But such shifts will increase concentration.

This observation is not a theoretical curiosity. Critics of US antitrust policy have long argued that large firms may be large because they° are efficient. If so, then economic welfare may be enhanced if these efficient firms acquire more of the industry's productive capital and thus increase their market share.[5] One means to do this is by buying the assets of smaller, less-efficient rivals. Any useful theory of oligopoly and horizontal mergers should account for the role that mergers may play in this process.

Given the complex relationship between concentration, output, and welfare, a careful analysis of the welfare effects of mergers is badly needed. The few existing theoretical analyses of the effects of horizontal mergers have used very special models, and their insights of course re-emerge below.[6] But our goal is more ambitious: we use Cournot oligopoly theory, with quite general cost and demand functions, to study the output and welfare effects of mergers. At a theoretical level, we develop some techniques for analysing welfare changes in Cournot markets; these techniques apply not only to mergers but more generally. At a policy level, we find surprisingly general sufficient conditions for when a merger should be approved or prohibited.

Our policy analysis is in two parts. First, we study a merger's effect on price. This inquiry will be most telling for those antitrust practitioners who see consumer welfare as the sole objective of antitrust policy. We provide a necessary and sufficient condition for a merger to raise price (proposition 1) and show in general that mergers in Cournot oligopoly raise price if they generate no synergies between the merging firms (propositions 2 and 3). We also show that firms with large market shares must achieve impressive synergies or scale economies if their merger is to reduce price.

Second, we study a merger's effect on welfare, W. Here we emphasize the *external* effects on consumers and on non-participant firms. In this, our work is squarely in the tradition of mainstream economic analysis, whose presumption has always been that a

---

[4] For example, consider a Cournot duopoly in which firm 1 has low marginal cost and hence a large market share, and firm 2 has high marginal cost and is small. Closing down firm 2 will scarcely reduce welfare (since its marginal cost is close to the price). And if firm 1 expands at the same time, the net welfare effect will be favourable, since firm 1's marginal cost is distinctly less than the price. Such an output shift would lower X, raise H, and yet raise W.

[5] For an influential statement of this view, see for instance Demsetz (1973, 1974).

[6] Salant, Switzer, and Reynolds (1983), Deneckere and Davidson (1985), and Perry and Porter (1985) are the most prominent papers.

debate about intervention should focus on externalities.[7] Write $\Delta\pi^I$ for the change in joint profits of the merging firms (the 'insiders'), and ΔW for the change in total welfare associated with a merger. We analyse the next external effect of the merger on rival firms ('outsiders') and on consumers, $\Delta W - \Delta\pi^I \equiv \Delta\pi^0 + \Delta CS$. Since any proposed merger is presumably privately profitable, it will also raise welfare if it has a positive external effect – a condition that is, perhaps surprisingly, quite often satisfied. We thus find sufficient conditions for profitable mergers to raise welfare (proposition 5).

Our emphasis on the external effect also has a great practical advantage. To assess the externality turns out to require much less information than to assess the overall welfare effect, since the effect on insiders' profits depends on internal cost savings. Such cost savings are often hard to observe, and as a result are given little weight in the Merger Guidelines and in many practitioners' thinking, even though, as Williamson (1968) stressed, they may well be very important in a merger's overall welfare effect. Thus, White (1987, p. 18) wrote:

Efficiencies are easy to promise, yet may be difficult to deliver. All merger proposals will promise theoretical savings in overhead expense, inventory costs, and so on; they will tout 'synergies'.

Fisher (1987, p. 36) concurred:

The burden of proof as to cost savings or other offsetting efficiencies, however, should rest squarely on the proponents of a merger, and here I would require a very high standard [of proof]. Such claims are easily made and, I think, often too easily believed.

This emphasis on the externality is our first innovation in merger policy analysis, and it also leads us onto our second. Although the externality is easier to work with than the total welfare effect, directly signing the externality is mathematically difficult even in the simplest cases, and completely intractable in general. To overcome this, we introduce differential techniques. The external effect of a merger involving a change ΔX_I in the merging firms' joint output can be calculated as the integrated external effect of *small* changes dX_I. We call such a small change an 'infinitesimal merger'. It turns out to be easy to sign the external effect of an infinitesimal merger (proposition 4), and in fairly general circumstances we can sign the external effect of a merger (proposition 5).

Our chapter is organized as follows. In section 1, we recall some results from standard Cournot oligopoly theory. In section 2, we analyse the output and price effects of a merger among Cournot oligopolists, and find broad sufficient conditions for a merger to raise the equilibrium price. In section 3, we calculate the external effect of an infinitesimal merger, and show that it depends only on the merging firms' joint market share and on the output responsiveness and market shares of non-participant

---

[7] Of course, mergers typically do not generate externalities in the usual sense of the term. With imperfectly competitive markets, however, a change in the behaviour of merging firms does affect the welfare of consumers and other firms. Throughout the chapter we take 'externality' to mean $\Delta W - \Delta\pi^I$.

firms. We then give conditions under which privately profitable mergers raise total welfare. Finally, in section 4, we use our methods to provide welfare analyses of two other oligopoly problems: commitment in Cournot competition and the optimal level of an import quota. A conclusion follows.

1   Cournot oligopoly

We use the traditional model of Cournot oligopoly with homogeneous goods. Demand is given by $p(X)$, where p is price, X is industry output, and $p'(X) < 0$; we write for the absolute value of the elasticity of demand, $\varepsilon(X) \equiv -p(X)/Xp'(X)$. The number of firms, n, is exogenous (although of course it changes with a merger), reflecting some important barriers to entry.[8] We denote firm i's cost function by $c^i(x_i)$, where x_i is firm i's output. For notational ease, we write $c^i \equiv c^i(x_i)$ for firm i's total cost and $c_x^i \equiv c_x^i(x_i)$ for firm i's marginal cost. Importantly, we permit the firms to differ in efficiency.

In the Cournot equilibrium, each firm i picks its output x_i to maximize its profits, given its rivals' outputs. Writing $y_i \equiv \sum_{j \neq i} x_j = X - x_i$ for aggregate output of all firms other than firm i, firm i's profits are $\pi^i(x_i, y_i) \equiv p(x_i + y_i)x_i - c^i(x_i)$. Firm i's first-order condition, $\partial \pi^i/\partial x_i = 0$, is

$$p(X) + x_i p'(X) - c_x^i(x_i) = 0, \quad i = 1, \dots, n. \tag{2}$$

A Cournot equilibrium is a vector $(x_1, \dots, x_n)$ such that equation (2) holds for all n firms. We denote firm i's market share by $s_i \equiv x_i/X$.

Comparing two firms i and j, the Cournot equilibrium conditions, (2), tell us that $x_i > x_j$ if and only if $c_x^i < c_x^j$. In equilibrium, larger firms have lower marginal costs. In any Cournot equilibrium in which different firms produce different quantities, marginal costs differ across firms, so that costs are not minimized given the aggregate output level, and consequently aggregate output, X, is *not* in general a sufficient statistic for welfare.

Throughout the chapter, we make two weak assumptions on the Cournot equilibrium; we require both to hold throughout a relevant range, as will become clear below. First, we assume that each firm's reaction curve slopes downward. Equivalently, an increase in rivals' output, y_i, lowers firm i's marginal revenue

$$p'(X) + x_i p''(X) < 0, \quad i = 1, \dots, n. \tag{3}$$

Inequality (3) is a very weak assumption and is standard in Cournot analysis; see Dixit (1986) and Shapiro (1989). It holds if the industry demand curve satisfies $p'(X) + Xp''(X) < 0$.[9]

---

[8] Our analysis can easily accommodate entry by, or the existence of, price-taking fringe firms, if we reinterpret the demand curve $p(X)$ as the residual demand curve facing the oligopolists that we model. What we are ruling out is entry by additional large firms that behave oligopolistically.

[9] If $p'' \leq 0$, then (3) surely holds. If $p'' > 0$, then $p' + Xp'' > p' + x_i p''$.

Second, we assume that each firm's residual demand curve, $p(. + y_i)$, intersects its marginal cost curve from above. This is equivalent to

$$c^i_{xx}(x_i) > p'(X), \quad i = 1, \ldots, n. \tag{4}$$

Condition (4) is surely met if marginal cost is non-decreasing, i.e., if $c^i_{xx} \geq 0$. It is among the weaker known stability conditions for Cournot equilibrium (Dixit, 1986).

We now note some comparative-statics properties of Cournot equilibria that will be important below. Consider the effect of a change in rivals' aggregate output, y_i, on firm i's output. From equation (2), the slope of firm i's reaction schedule is given by

$$\frac{dx_i}{dy_i} \equiv R_i = \frac{p' + x_i p''}{2p' + x_i p'' - c^i_{xx}}.$$

From condition (3) and firm i's second-order conditions $R_i < 0$; with (4) we also have $-1 < R_i < 0$. That is, if its rivals jointly expand production, firm i contracts, but by less than its rivals' expansion. From $dx_i = R_i dy_i$ we have $dx_i(1 + R_i) = R_i(dx_i + dy_i) = R_i dX$, or

$$dx_i = -\lambda_i dX \tag{5}$$

where

$$\lambda_i \equiv \frac{R_i}{1 + R_i} = -\frac{p'(X) + x_i p''(X)}{c^i_{xx}(x_i) - p'(X)}.$$

Below, it will prove easier to work with λ_i instead of R_i. Under conditions (3) and (4), $\lambda_i > 0$. The λ_i's are important below, so we pause here to show how they can be expressed in terms of more familiar elasticities. Write $E \equiv -Xp''(X)/p'(X)$ for the elasticity of the slope of the inverse demand curve, and $\mu_i \equiv x_i c^i_{xx}/c_{ix}$ for the elasticity of firm i's marginal cost, c^i_x, with respect to its output, x_i. Then[10]

$$\lambda_i = \frac{s_i - s_i^2 E}{s_i + \mu_i(\varepsilon - s_i)}. \tag{6}$$

With constant elasticity of demand ε, $E = 1 + 1/\varepsilon$, so λ_i can be expressed solely in terms of s_i, μ_i, and ε. With linear demand and constant marginal costs, $E = 0 = \mu_i$, so $\lambda_i = 1$.

Finally, we prove in the appendix and record here a fact[11] about the response of all other firms to an output change by one firm:

Lemma

Consider an exogenous change in firm 1's output, and let the other firms' outputs adjust to re-establish a Cournot equilibrium among themselves. If firms' reaction curves slope

---

[10] Note that λ_i is the inverse of the elasticity of firm i's competitive supply curve.

[11] Dixit (1986) notes this property of Cournot equilibrium.

downward (condition (3)), and if the stability condition (4) holds, then aggregate output moves in the same direction as firm 1's output, but by less.

Note that for the lemma to hold it is *not* necessary that firm 1 behave as a Cournot oligopolist.

2   Price effects of horizontal mergers

We model a merger as a complete combination of the assets and of the control of the merging firms, whom we call the 'insiders'. After the merger, a new Cournot equilibrium is established between the merged entity M and the non-participant firms, whom we call the 'outsiders'. In this section, we examine the effect of a merger on aggregate output, X. This is, of course, the central question if merger analysis is concerned only with consumer welfare (ignoring consumers' ownership of profits). As we shall see in section 3, it is also an essential component of an analysis of overall economic welfare, W.

Mergers differ enormously in the extent to which productive assets can usefully be recombined, and in the extent to which output decisions can usefully, or anticompetitively, be coordinated. At one extreme, consider a production technology in which all firms have constant and equal marginal costs, and the merged entity has the same costs. In this special case, mergers are purely anticompetitive: there is no other motive. For a slightly rosier view, recall that by equation (2), firms' marginal costs typically differ in Cournot equilibrium, so that a merger may offer an opportunity to *rationalize production* – that is, without changing total output, to shift output to the facility with lower marginal cost. A still sunnier view is that mergers may create synergies. For example, two firms that own complementary patents may combine and produce much more efficiently than either could alone (without a licensing agreement).

For a theory of horizontal mergers to be useful for policy purposes, it should be general enough to allow for all these possibilities, which can be captured in assumptions about the relationship between the merged entity's cost function, $c^M(\cdot)$, and those of the insiders. Our theory is very general in this regard, as we make no a priori assumptions on $c^M(\cdot)$ beyond those implied by conditions (3) and (4). Our first proposition gives a necessary and sufficient condition on $c^M(\cdot)$ for equilibrium output to fall with the merger.

Proposition 1
A merger of a group of firms in Cournot oligopoly raises price if and only if M's markup would be less than the sum of the pre-merger markups at its constituent firms, were M to produce just as much as its constituent firms together did before the merger.

Proof See the appendix.

In the typical situation where two firms (1 and 2) are merging, price will fall if and only if $p - c_x^M > (p - c_x^1) + (p - c_x^2)$, where p is the pre-merger price, c_x^1 and c_x^2 are measured at pre-merger output levels, $\bar{x}_1$ and $\bar{x}_2$, and c_x^M is measured at output $\bar{X}_M \equiv \bar{x}_1 + \bar{x}_2$. Equivalently, price will fall if and only if

$$c_x^2 - c_x^M > p - c_x^1. \tag{7}$$

By condition (7), M must enjoy *substantially* lower marginal costs than did its constituent firms, if price is to fall. Furthermore, the required reduction in marginal costs is larger, the larger were the pre-merger markups of the merging firms; and those markups were, by (2), proportional to pre-merger market shares.

Using equation (2), we can express (7) in terms of pre-merger variables that are relatively easy to observe

$$c_x^M < p \left(1 - \frac{s_1 + s_2}{\varepsilon}\right).$$

This version shows how much less than current prices the merged firm's marginal costs must be, if price is to fall. We now present some illustrative calculations to draw out some of the implications of condition (7) and proposition 1.

2.1   Mergers with no synergies

In many mergers, the insiders (firms $i \in I$) cannot recombine assets to improve their *joint* production *capabilities*. After the merger, the combined entity M can perhaps better allocate outputs across facilities ('rationalization'), but M's production *possibilities* are no different from those of the insiders (jointly) before the merger. In this case we say that the merger 'generates no synergies'. Formally, with no synergies

$$c^M(x) \equiv \min\left\{\sum_{i \in I} c^i(x_i') \,\Big|\, \sum_{i \in I} x_i' = x\right\}. \tag{8}$$

This holds, for instance, in the constant average cost model of Salant, Switzer, and Reynolds (1983) and in the quadratic cost model of Perry and Porter (1985).

Proposition 2
If a merger generates no synergies, then it causes price to rise.

Proof See the appendix.

When will our no-synergies condition, (8), apply? For illustration, write firm i's cost function as $c^i(x_i) = \theta_i \phi(x_i, k_i)$, where $\phi(\cdot, \cdot)$ is a short-run variable cost function, k_i measures the amount of a possibly fungible capital good employed at firm i, and θ_i inversely measures 'knowledge' at firm I.

With this form of the cost function we can distinguish three types of cost savings from a merger. (1) Participants may rationalize output across their facilities (recall that pre-merger marginal costs are typically unequal); this consists of changing the x_i's but not the k_i's or the θ_i's. (2) They may shift capital across their facilities, changing the distribution of the k_i's (but not the total capital stock available). (3)

They may learn from each other, that is, share techniques, patents, or management skills; learning will change the θ_i's.

Proposition 2 tells us that efficiencies of the first kind, while of course desirable, cannot suffice to make output rise instead of fall.[12] Efficiencies of the second kind apply only in the 'short run' – that is, when capital cannot be brought in from the outside. These efficiencies are further limited by the observation that equation (8) holds even with mobile capital, if the firms produce according to the same long-run cost function (i.e., they have the same level of knowledge) and if this common technology exhibits constant returns to scale. In that case, even if capital can be moved, there is no point in doing so: equivalent results can be achieved by reallocating output across facilities. This proves:

Proposition 3
Suppose that a merger involves no learning. Then, in the long run, the merger will raise price. In the short run, it will raise price (1) if capital is immobile across facilities, or (2) if all merging firms are equally efficient and their long-run production function exhibits constant returns to scale.

Thus, a merger can raise output and make consumers better off only if it permits the merging firms to exploit economies of scale or if the participants learn from it. In the next two subsections, we illustrate how large these effects must be for a merger to lower price.

2.2   Mergers with economies of scale

Consider the possibility that some form of 'capital' may be best recombined after merger. In particular, suppose that it pays – and is possible – to bring together all the new entity's capital rather than leaving it divided among its plants (formerly, firms) in its pre-merger configuration. This will always be desirable if there are economies of scale; whether capital is mobile is of course a technical question. How much economies of scale are needed for a merger to increase output and reduce price?

Consider for illustration a merger between two *ex ante* identical firms each with a pre-merger market share of s. There is a common variable cost function $c(x, k)$, and each firm owns an amount k of capital prior to the merger. The merger permits the firms to combine their capital as well as reallocate outputs; and, with economies of scale, M will do so. The one combined facility will then produce with the variable cost function $c(\cdot, 2k)$.

We show in the appendix that the merger will lower price if and only if

$$c_x(2x, 2k) \le \left[1 - \frac{s}{\varepsilon - s}\right] c_x(x, k). \tag{9}$$

To illustrate (again, see the appendix for details), let $c(x, k)$ be dual to the

---

[12] After our paper was revised, we became aware of the work of William McElroy (1988), who proves a result similar to our proposition 2.

production function $f(L,k) = k^a L^a$. If $s = 0.2$ and $\varepsilon = 1$, then (9) requires $a \geq 1/\log_2 3$: twice the inputs must produce at least $2^{2/\log_2 3} \approx 2.4$ times the output.

2.3   Mergers with learning

A merger may enhance efficiency at some or all of the merging facilities: one facility may learn from its partner's patents, management expertise, etc. How much such learning is needed for a merger to increase output and reduce price?

Suppose that firms 1 and 2 merge. Suppose for simplicity that capital cannot be reallocated across firms,[13] so we can write firm i's cost function as $\theta_i \varphi(x_i)$; suppose further that marginal costs are non-decreasing. In the appendix we show that, for price to fall, the merger must either reduce θ_1 by at least a factor $s_2/(\varepsilon - s_1)$ or reduce θ_2 by at least a factor $s_2/(\varepsilon - s_2)$. In the symmetric case with $s_1 = s_2 = 0.2$ and $\varepsilon = 1$, this means that at least one plant must achieve a reduction in θ of at least 25 per cent as a result of merger if price is to fall.

2.4   Policy implications

Propositions 1 to 3, and our illustrative calculations in subsections 2.2 and 2.3, support the presumption that an oligopolistic merger will reduce aggregate industry output, and point to the nature and degree of synergies or scale economies that are required to overturn this presumption. If the merger changes the behavioural mode in the industry – from Cournot behaviour to something more collusive – then the presumption is even stronger that price will rise.

We have identified the factors that determine a merger's effect on price in Cournot equilibrium. In particular, the larger are the market shares of the participating firms, or the smaller is the industry elasticity of demand, the greater must be the learning effects or scale economies in order for price to fall. It is perhaps encouraging that these are exactly the factors that the Merger Guidelines instruct antitrust offficials to consider.

Some antitrust scholars and practitioners, including the National Association of Attorneys General, argue that the objective of antitrust policy is to maximize consumers' surplus.[14] Under this view, mergers should be blocked if and only if they are expected to raise price. Propositions 1, 2, and 3, and our illustrative calculations point to the relevant factors in making such an assessment.[15] We find that rather

---

[13] Equivalently, consider the long run, in which case capital does not appear in the cost function at all.

[14] For example, in *Proctor & Gamble* the Supreme Court stated that 'Possible economies cannot be used as a defense to illegality. Congress was aware that some mergers which lessen competition may also result in economies, but it struck the balance in favor of protecting competition.' See the discussion in Williamson (1968), for instance.

[15] Note that under this view of antitrust policy, rival firms should not have standing to sue to block a proposed merger, since their interests are diametrically opposed to consumers'. Indeed, when rival firms contest a proposed merger, arguing (ostensibly with commendable unselfishness) that the proposed merger would reduce output and should be forbidden, we should perhaps infer that they

impressive synergies – learning, or economies of scale – are typically necessary for a merger to reduce price.

But few economists would accept that antitrust policy should aim to maximize consumer surplus alone, with no weight given to profits. Although direct stock ownership is concentrated among the relatively rich, many people are indirect shareholders, for instance through pension funds, so it seems inappropriate to ignore profits entirely. In a conventional economic view, the proper goal of antitrust policy is to maximize overall market efficiency or welfare, and in this case further analysis is required.

3   Welfare effects of horizontal mergers

We will now analyse the welfare effects of horizontal mergers. Unfortunately, it is hard to compare pre- and post-merger allocations directly, even in the simplest special cases. But we will show that a merger's effect on the welfare of non-participating firms and consumers, although generally unavailable in closed form, can be expressed as the integral of a relatively simple integrand, namely the external effect of what we will call an 'infinitesimal merger'. We obtain some powerful results by examining that integrand.

A merger generally changes all firms' outputs in equilibrium. But consumers care only about the net effect on aggregate output, ΔX, and (in Cournot equilibrium) rivals care only about the change in equilibrium output by the merging ('insider') firms, ΔX_I, not about what caused that change. Therefore, in examining the external effects of a merger, once we know the equilibrium change ΔX_I we need no information about what went into that change: we can simply ask how outsider firms respond and what is the effect on their profits and on consumer surplus, and in doing so we can treat ΔX_I as exogenous.

Moreover, the effect of ΔX_I can be decomposed into the integral of the effects of infinitesimal changes dX_I that make up ΔX_I. We call such a small change in insiders' output, dX_I, an 'infinitesimal merger' if it has the same sign as the change in X_I consequent on the merger among the insiders. For mathematical convenience, we can think of a merger as the composite of many such infinitesimal mergers.[16]

3.1   External welfare effects of mergers

Consider an infinitesimal merger, dX_I. Because the marginal gross benefits of output are measured by the market price p, we have

---

believe the opposite, and that the merger would probably benefit consumers! Sometimes rivals adopt a theory of 'incipient predation', arguing that the merged entity will increase output, but only as a form of predation against them. This too is unconvincing since predation can be directly, and profitably, fought under the treble-damages provisions of the antitrust laws.

[16] An infinitesimal merger may correspond to an economic event, such as the transfer of a small amount of capital from one firm to another or the purchase by one firm of a small ownership stake in another firm. In Farrell and Shapiro (1990) we explore these changes in the ownership of assets in oligopoly. But here we use infinitesimal mergers strictly as a mathematical construct.

$$dW = pdX_I - dc^I + \sum_{i \in O} [p - c_x^i] dx_i \qquad (10)$$

where c^I is the insiders' total cost and O is the set of outsider firms. These outsiders' output responses are given by (5), $dx_i = -\lambda_i dX$, and their markups are given by (2), $p - c_x^i = -x_i p'(X)$. Adding and subtracting $X_I dp$, and making these substitutions, we can rewrite (10) as

$$dW = (pdX_I + X_I dp - dc^I) - X_I p'(X) dX + \sum_{i \in O} p'(X) \lambda_i x_i dX. \qquad (11)$$

In (11), the first three terms constitute the change in the insiders' joint profits, $d\pi^I$. Clearly, $d\pi^I$ involves the cost term dc^I, which is very hard for antitrust enforcement officials to observe, and any attempt to put numbers or signs to equation (11) is consequently difficult. But this troublesome term drops out when we examine the *external* welfare effect. From (11)

$$dW - d\pi^I = -X_I p'(X) dX + \sum_{i \in O} p'(X) \lambda_i x_i dX$$

or

$$dW - d\pi^I = \left[\sum_{i \in O} \lambda_i x_i - X_I \right] p'(X) dX.$$

Defining

$$\eta \equiv \sum_{i \in O} \lambda_i x_i - X_I \qquad (13)$$

the net externality from an infinitesimal merger that induces an overall output change dX is $\eta p'(X) dX$, which has the sign of η if $dX < 0$. Converting η into market shares, we have:

Proposition 4
Consider any change in behaviour by a subset of firms, 'insiders', in an oligopolistic industry. The net external effect of this change on other firms, 'outsiders', who are Cournot oligopolists, and on consumers depends only on the equilibrium change in the insiders' output, X_I. A small reduction in X_I has a net positive welfare effect on outsiders and consumers if and only if $\sum_{i \in O} \lambda_i s_i > s_I$.

Proposition 4 underlines the importance of non-participant firms' responses to the change in X_I.[17] If they did not respond, that is, if $\lambda_i = 0$ for $i \in 0$, then every output reduction would be bad for rivals and consumers jointly: rivals would benefit, but

---

[17] Salant, Switzer, and Reynolds (1983) emphasize this effect in their very special model, although they do not explicitly discuss the externality. We will return to their case below.

consumers would lose by more. This often seems to be implicitly assumed in merger policy. But in fact, as proposition 4 shows for small arbitrary changes and proposition 5 will show for mergers, many output-reducing changes benefit rivals more than they hurt consumers.

We now use proposition 4 to establish our central result: a sufficient condition for a privately profitable merger to be socially beneficial. Evidently, this suggests a 'safe harbor' provision for merger policy: if Cournot behaviour is thought to be a good description of industry behaviour and if the conditions of proposition 5 hold, then any proposed merger should be permitted.

If a merger, or other discrete change, causes the insiders' equilibrium output to change from $X_I^{initial}$ to X_I^{final}, we have

$$\Delta W - \Delta \pi^I = \int_{X_I^{initial}}^{X_I^{final}} \left(\frac{dW}{dX_I} - \frac{d\pi^I}{dX_I} \right) dx_I \tag{14}$$

where for each X_I, the integrand is evaluated assuming a Cournot equilibrium among outsiders given X_I. For expositional simplicity, and as suggested by propositions 1–3, we focus on output-reducing mergers, for which $\Delta X_I < 0$. With X_I falling, we rewrite (14) as

$$\Delta W - \Delta \pi^I = \int_{X_I^{final}}^{X_I^{initial}} \left(\frac{dW}{dX_I} - \frac{d\pi^I}{dX_I} \right) dx_I. \tag{15}$$

Using (12) and (13), we can rewrite (15) as

$$\Delta W - \Delta \pi^I = \int_{X_I^{final}}^{X_I^{initial}} \eta(X)[-p'(X)] \frac{dX}{dX_I} dX_I. \tag{16}$$

This shows that the net externality is a weighted integral of η along a path from $X_I^{initial}$ to X_I^{final}. Consequently, if we can sign η throughout such a path, then we can sign the total external effect, $\Delta W - \Delta \pi^I$.

In proposition 5, we give conditions sufficient for η to increase as X_I falls. When those conditions hold, it follows that if $\eta \geq 0$ before a merger, and if the merger will involve a reduction in insiders' output, then the total externality $\Delta W - \Delta \pi^I$ is surely positive.[18]

Proposition 5

Consider a proposed merger among firms $i \in I$, and suppose that their initial (joint) market share s_I does not exceed $\sum_{i \in O} \lambda_i s_i$. Suppose further that p'', p''', and c_{xx}^i are all non-negative and c_{xxx}^i is non-positive in the relevant ranges and for all non-participant firms i. Then, if the merger is profitable and would raise the market price, it would also raise welfare.

---

[18] Moreover, under the conditions of proposition 5, if $\eta < 0$ *after* the merger, that is, at $X_I = X_I^{final}$, then we know that consumers and rival firms jointly are harmed by the merger.

Proof See the appendix.

We pause now to discuss the conditions of proposition 5. The requirement that $p'' \leq 0$ is met, for example, by all constant elasticity demand curves and of course by linear demand. The condition that marginal costs not decrease, $c_{xx} \geq 0$, is also quite widely met. For moderate sized mergers (those involving modest changes in X_I), these second-order terms will dominate the calculations, so the conclusion of proposition 5 is likely to hold even if p''' may be negative or c^i_{xxx} may be positive. For a large merger, we need conditions on third derivatives in order to sign its external effect. This is not surprising. For example, if the outsiders face capacity constraints, so $c^i_{xxx} > 0$, their ability to increase output will be limited and the λ_i's must fall as the merger proceeds and their output rises. Likewise, if $p''' < 0 X_I$ then outsiders' responses to decreases in X_I may diminish as X_I does. Because these third-order effects inevitably appear, and because a merger is inherently a lumpy, non-marginal change, we believe that proposition 5 may be the strongest 'clean' result available for general cost and demand functions.

3.2   Implications for antitrust policy

As we remarked in the introduction, most economists believe that interventions in the economy should be based on analysis of externalities. We might therefore hope that our explicit analysis of the externalities from a merger in Cournot oligopoly will help us discuss proper policy towards mergers.

Privately unprofitable mergers will not be proposed, so proposed mergers should be permitted unless their external effects are 'sufficiently' bad to outweigh their private profitability. In particular, if a proposed merger would have a *beneficial* external effect, then it should be allowed.[19] We might be able to identify such cases using equations (15) or (16). In particular, if $\eta > 0$ at pre-merger equilibrium then there is some reason to expect the net externality $\Delta W - \Delta \pi^I$ to be positive, unless we have reason to expect η to change sign over the course of the merger (regarded as a gradual sequence of fictitious infinitesimal mergers). More rigorously, proposition 5 gives sufficient – but far from necessary – conditions for this inference to be valid. Thus, when the conditions of proposition 5 hold, any privately profitable merger should be permitted.

But a policy that allows only mergers with positive net external effects will be too restrictive to maximize overall economic surplus. Many profitable mergers that involve a negative 'wedge' ($\Delta W - \Delta \pi^I < 0$) will nevertheless increase total surplus ($\Delta W > 0$). Although we have no formal results for this case, we hope that our externality technique may nevertheless be useful in informing merger policy, as the following diagrammatic framework may illustrate.[20] In figure 18.1, a merger is

[19] Note that, since non-participant firms' and consumers' interests concerning insiders' output are strictly opposed, a merger will never generate a Pareto improvement; we are aggregating non-participants' and consumers' surplus into a single measure.

[20] We are especially indebted to Steven Salop for suggesting this treatment.

represented by a point whose horizontal component is the net wedge, $\Delta W - \Delta \eta^I$, that it would generate, and whose vertical component is the private profitability, $\Delta \pi^I$. Ideally, we would like to find a policy that would permit exactly those mergers 'northeast' of the negatively sloped 45° line through the origin – that is, those in regions A, B, and C; those are the 'socially beneficial' mergers (those with $\Delta W > 0$).

In figure 18.1, we can see why a policy of allowing only mergers with positive net wedges is too restrictive. For if such a policy were implemented, then only mergers in the northeast quadrant (region B) of figure 18.1 will take place (be proposed and approved). It seems worth considering, therefore, whether there is a policy that might allow more of the desirable mergers without also permitting others that are profitable but socially undesirable. Evidently, no policy that does not involve compulsion or subsidies to merger – both of which would be enormous changes from our antitrust policy – can hope to get mergers in region A implemented. We focus, therefore, on whether a policy might be found that would permit us to distinguish proposed mergers in regions B and C (profitable and socially beneficial) from those in region D (profitable but socially harmful).

Our analysis suggests the following two-part procedure for evaluating a proposed merger. First, using (16), estimate the net wedge, $\Delta W - \Delta \pi^I$. Second, if the net wedge appears to be negative, estimate the profit effect, $\Delta \pi^I$. This might be done by observing how the aggregate stock market valuation of the participants changes with the news of the proposed merger. These estimates of the net wedge and of the profit effect can then be plotted on figure 18.1, and the merger should be approved if and only if the point so plotted lies in the northeast half-plane in figure 18.1.

We stress, however, that such a procedure would involve a number of problems, some severe. Estimating the net wedge involves estimating structural parameters such as the λ_i's, and how they will change in equilibrium with changes in X_I. The estimate of the private profitability $\Delta \pi^I$, which is needed only if the net wedge appears to be negative, is also problematic. Using the stock market response to the announcement of the proposal assumes that no significant insider trading predates the announcement and that the stock market can accurately value the proposed change. More fundamentally, this rule would seem to create a multiple-equilibrium problem for proposed mergers that in fact lie in region C. If the market believes that the merger will be approved, then the increase in stock market value will so impress the regulators that they will indeed approve it. If, however, the market expects regulatory opposition, then the value will rise by little, and the regulators will indeed oppose the merger!

3.3   Linear demand and constant costs

In this subsection and the next, we illustrate proposition 5 by recalling the cases analysed by Salant *et al.* (1983) and by Perry and Porter (1985) and McAfee and Williams (1988).

Salant *et al.* assume symmetric Cournot competition among *n* firms, which have identical constant marginal cost *c* and face a linear demand curve. They consider the

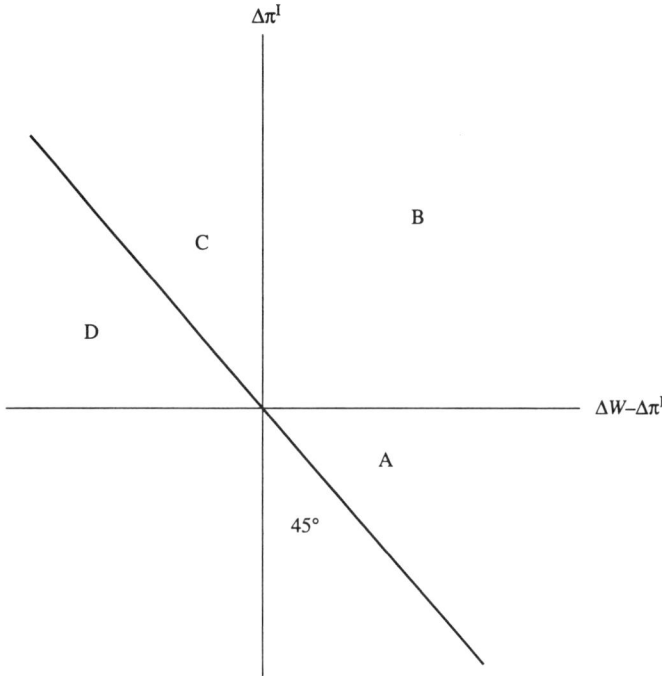

Figure 18.1

private and social benefits of a merger of $m + 1$ of those firms – that is, a shift from Cournot to collusive behaviour within the group.

For constant marginal costs and linear demand, $\lambda_i = 1$ for all i, and $\eta = X_O - X_I$. Hence, a merger among $m + 1$ out of the n firms will have $\eta \geq 0$ all along the path from $X_I^{initial}$ to X_I^{final} if the *pre-merger* outputs satisfy $X_O - X_I \geq 0$, that is, if $n - m - 1 \geq m + 1$, or $m + 1 \leq n/2$. In this model, then, any profitable merger involving at most half the industry is socially desirable.

This may seem puzzling, since, with constant unit costs, welfare declines with any merger. Salant *et al.* resolve this puzzle by pointing out that outsiders' responses may make the merger unprofitable, especially when m/n is small.[21] They also emphasize, however, that internalized savings (for example, fixed costs, which are perfectly consistent with constant marginal costs) may reverse that unprofitability – and hence also reverse the welfare undesirability.

Similarly, the net external effect of a merger among $m + 1$ firms is surely negative if the *post-merger* outputs satisfy $X_I \geq X_O$, that is, when $1 \geq n - m - 1$, or when the number of merging firms is at least $n - 1$ (merger to duopoly). This does not

---

[21] Gaudet and Salant (1988) study how large a group of firms must be for coordinated output reductions by the group to be profitable, despite the increased output by rivals that such reductions will induce.

necessarily mean that no such merger should ever be approved, but there is certainly a case to answer.

Observe that in this model it does not matter for the externality how X_O is divided amongst the outsiders, for λ_i is independent of firm i's output or market share. In our next example we shall see that this is not generally the case.

3.4   Linear demand and quadratic costs

For our second illustration, consider the quadratic cost and linear demand functions used by Perry and Porter (1985), and by McAfee and Williams (1988). Demand is given by $p(X) = A - X$, and costs are given by $c(x,k) = \frac{1}{2}x^2/k$ at all firms.[22] This variable cost function, which is dual to the Cobb-Douglas production function $x = \sqrt{Lk}$, exhibits constant returns to scale (it is homogeneous of degree one in capital and output). Hence, by proposition 3, every merger reduces output. Proposition 5 applies, and simple calculations show that $\lambda_i = x_i/p = s_i/\varepsilon$. Consequently, a merger surely has a positive externality if

$$s_I < \frac{1}{\varepsilon}\sum_{i \in O} s_i^2 \qquad (17)$$

where these are pre-merger market shares. Thus a merger is more likely to help rivals and consumers jointly if s_I is small – this conforms with standard merger analysis – and if the rest of the industry is *more* concentrated!

The reason for this surprising conclusion is that, in this model, λ_i is larger for larger firms $i(\lambda_i = x_i/p)$. In economic terms, if there are large outsiders, then any reduction in X_I will induce an especially large output response by them – which is just where increases in output are socially most valuable. Concentration among outsiders therefore makes their output response more socially beneficial. If λ_i were smaller at larger firms, as can easily happen,[23] then the outsiders' output response might either be weakened or less socially beneficial in a more concentrated market. The Salant–Switzer–Reynolds model is a borderline case: $\lambda_i = 1$ for all i, so that the distribution of market shares among non-participants does not matter there.

Another interesting feature of condition (17) is that a merger is *more* likely to have a negative external effect, and hence to require careful antitrust scrutiny, when demand is *more* elastic. The reason is that with elastic demand outsiders' markups are small, so little welfare benefit is to be had from their increased output (while consumers still suffer from any price increase caused by the merger).

In the linear-quadrant model, unlike the constant marginal cost model, mergers may increase welfare even absent fixed-cost savings. In a previous version of this chapter, we showed, by viewing infinitesimal mergers as transfers of small amounts of capital, that welfare rises ($\Delta W > 0$) if the merging firms are small and the rest of the

---

[22] The analysis would be identical in a model with $p = A - bX$ and $c(x,k) = cx + ex^2/2k$, but the parameters b, c, and e would clutter our formulas.

[23] For example, if firm i has constant unit cost c_i and if $p'' > 0$, then λ_i will be inversely related to x_i.

industry is highly concentrated.[24] This is so even though there are no synergies, output falls, and concentration increases! Small merging firms have small price–cost margins, so a reduction in their output has little social cost, whereas large non-participant firms increase their output and this is socially valuable. In terms of condition (1), the increase in concentration dH/H, outweighs the reduction in output, dX/X, yielding an *increase* in welfare. Thus, as hinted in the introduction, structural changes such as mergers can lead to changes in H and in W that have the same sign, even without synergies. That this can happen more generally, with or without synergies, is shown by proposition 5.

3.5   Constant-elasticity demand and constant costs

For constant marginal costs and constant elasticity demand, $\lambda_i = 1 - s_i(1 + 1/\varepsilon)$. The net externality from an infinitesimal merger that raises price is positive if and only if

$$2(s_1 + s_2) < 1 - \left(1 + \frac{1}{\varepsilon}\right) \sum_{i \in 0} s_i^2.$$

In this example, although the $p''' \geq 0$ condition of proposition 5 does not hold, we can nonetheless show directly that any merger for which the above inequality holds at pre-merger shares generates a positive net externality. To establish this result, it is sufficient to show that the above inequality continues to hold as x falls. Differentiating totally, this is equivalent to $\sum_{i \in 0} \lambda_i ds_i \geq 0$. Since all the λ_i are positive, it is enough to show that s_i increases as X falls. But firm i's first-order condition requires that $s_i = \varepsilon(1 - c_x^i/p)$; since ε and c_x^i are constants, s_i must rise with p.

We therefore have derived, in an important special case, a sufficient condition in terms of the pre-merger market shares and the elasticity of demand, for every profitable merger to improve welfare. This result illustrates that the sufficient conditions of proposition 5 are not necessary.

3.6   Extending beyond Cournot

We have used the Cournot assumption in this section in two ways: (a) to measure outsiders' markups, $p - c_x^i$, by $-x_i p'(X)$, and (b) to compute outsiders' responses as measured by the λ_i's.[25] But within the class of homogeneous-goods models, our qualitative results extend well beyond Cournot behaviour. Whatever the behaviour of the non-participating firms, there are two external effects of a change in X_I. First, the price changes, causing a loss of $X_I dp$ to consumers.[26] Second, outsider firms are

---

[24] McAfee and Williams (1988) also construct examples of welfare-improving mergers in this model, using computer simulation.

[25] We also have used price to measure marginal gross benefits. This procedure is valid provided only that the good is homogeneous and buyers have no market power.

[26] The price effect on outsider firms' output, $X - X_I$, is merely a transfer from consumers to outsiders.

induced to change their outputs by some amounts, say $\psi_i dX_I$, and the social value of this is $\sum_{i \in O} [p - c_x^i] \psi_i dX_i$. Consequently, the externality is positive if and only if

$$\sum_{i \in O} [p - c_x^i] \psi_i dX_I - X_I dp > 0. \qquad (18)$$

Equation (11) and proposition 4 are a special case of equation (18). More generally, the ψ_i must be recalculated for each oligopoly theory, but the basic equation (18) persists.

To illustrate, we sketch here how our results would differ with non-zero conjectural variations. Suppose that firm i believes that its rivals will respond to its output changes with $dy_i/dx_i = \nu_i$.[27] Then firm i's equilibrium markup is $p - c_x^i = x_i p'(X)(1 + \nu_i)$ and its equilibrium responsiveness is

$$\hat{\lambda}_i = -\frac{p' + x_i p''(1 + \nu_i)}{c_{xx}^i - p'(1 + \nu_i)}.$$

The condition in proposition 4 for a positive externality becomes

$$\sum_{i \in O} \hat{\lambda}_i s_i (1 + \nu_i) > s_I.$$

We now ask how $\hat{\lambda}_i(1 + \nu_i)$ varies with ν_i. This will tell us how the external effect of a small reduction in output by (say) firms 1 and 2 in an industry with a given vector of market shares $(s_1, s_2, \ldots, s_n)$, varies with the industry's competitiveness. In other words, *given* the observed market shares, how will the external effect of the merger depend upon the behaviour that led to the observed pre-merger equilibrium? This is the relevant question for policy: it determines whether high or low perceived ν_i's would make a proposed merger more socially acceptable, given the observed market shares.

Straightforward calculations show that $\hat{\lambda}_i(1 + \nu_i)$ is increasing in ν_i if and only if

$$(1 + \nu_i)^2 x p' p'' - (p' + 2(1 + \nu_i)x p'')c_{xx} > 0.$$

This condition certainly holds if demand is linear and $c_{xx} \geq 0$: in that case, more collusive behaviour (an increase in ν_i) raises $\hat{\lambda}(1 + \nu_i)$, so an output reduction by firms 1 and 2 becomes more attractive to the rest of society, given all the firms' market shares. Perhaps surprisingly, the more tacit collusion that exists in pre-merger equilibrium and would exist after the merger (we assume the two are the same), the more likely it is that a privately profitable merger is socially desirable.

---

[27] The parameter ν_i is called firm i's 'conjectural variation'. Although the conjectural variation model is logically flawed, it is a useful way of parameterizing the degree of competition among oligopolists. Such behaviour might, for example, arise as the equilibrium of an (unmodelled) dynamic oligopolistic game.

4   Other applications of the externality technique

The externality formula of proposition 4 has applications that extend well beyond horizontal merger policy. We sketch two such applications here: (1) investment or commitment by an oligopolist and (2) an import quota in an industry with a domestic oligopoly.

4.1   Investment or commitment in oligopoly

What is the welfare effect of a small, observable, unilateral change by an oligopolist that shifts outwards its reaction function? In particular, what external effects on consumers and other firms result from an oligopolist's decision to invest in new capital, or from an increase in its ability to commit to a high output level, for example, through long-term contracts? As above, we can analyse these external effects in terms of an infinitesimal (but in this case a positive) change in X_I, where the subset I of 'insiders' consists of the investing firm alone.[28] Applying proposition 4 gives

Proposition 6
The external effect of a small outward shift in firm 1's reaction function has the sign of

$$s_I - \sum_{i=2}^{n} \lambda_i s_i. \tag{19}$$

Expression (19) is most likely to be negative if firm 1's rivals have large market shares and therefore high price–cost margins, and if their equilibrium outputs are sensitive to expansion by firm 1. In such a market, firm 1 'steals' a great deal of valuable business from its rivals when it invests. This negative externality imposed on rivals must be compared against the transfer to consumers of the price change on firm 1's output.[29] Clearly, if firm 1 is sufficiently small, (19) is negative. Thus, although investment by a small firm lowers price and benefits consumers, it harms rival firms by more.

The impact on rivals and on consumers of allowing one firm in a Cournot oligopoly some power of pre-commitment is given also by proposition 6. If we move from a regime of less commitment power to one of more, we have $dX_I > 0$. Consequently, the external welfare effects of allowing more output commitment by one firm are beneficial if and only if that firm has a sufficiently large market share. And it is certainly profitable for the firm with the commitment power. Hence, if one firm has a market share in Cournot oligopoly that exceeds the 'weighted sum of all others', then it is socially desirable to give that firm some Stackelberg power. And if the conditions of proposition 5 hold, it follows that it is desirable to go all the way to give the firm complete Stackelberg power.

As an illustration, take the simplest possible model. There are two firms, each with

---

[28] Additional applications of proposition 4 to investment are presented in our (1990) paper.
[29] The price effect on other firms' outputs is merely a transfer from rivals to consumers. Marius Schwartz (1989) discusses some similar examples in a special model.

zero marginal costs, and $p(X) = 1 - X$. Recall that $\lambda_i = 1$ with this specification, so that, in the (symmetric) Cournot equilibrium, $s_I = \frac{1}{2} = \lambda_2 s_2$. In Cournot equilibrium, each firm produces output 1/3, and makes profits of 1/9, while consumer surplus is 2/9. But if firm 1 is Stackelberg leader, then $x_I = 1/2$ and $x_2 = 1/4$, giving firm 2 profits of 1/16 and consumers surplus of 9/32. Since $(9/32 + 1/16) > (2/9 + 1/9)$, firm 2 and consumers jointly benefit from the shift to Stackelberg behaviour, as proposition 5 predicted. Of course, firm 1 also gained.

4   Import quotas in oligopolistic industries

We now show how propositions 4 and 5 illuminate the domestic welfare consequences of quotas when the domestic industry consists of a Cournot oligopoly (plus perhaps a competitive fringe). Thinking of foreign suppliers as the 'insiders', we can view a tightening of a quota as a reduction in X_I. Moreover, the welfare of outsiders (domestic firms) and consumers is simply domestic welfare. Proposition 4 therefore gives us:

Proposition 7
Consider the effect of an import quota in an industry where domestic firms are Cournot oligopolists, perhaps including a competitive fringe. Slightly tightening the quota raises domestic welfare if and only if the share of imports is less than the λ-weighted sum of domestic producers' shares.

Proposition 5 – when its assumptions hold – implies that a small enough import sector should be excluded altogether![30] Although this would hurt consumers, it would help domestic producers by more. For instance, in the constant-cost, linear-demand case, proposition 5 states that if imports have no more than half the market in Cournot equilibrium, domestic welfare would be greater if imports were completely excluded! To illustrate, take the same model as in the previous subsection: demand is $p = 1 - X$ and there are two firms (one now foreign), each with zero marginal costs. Domestic welfare in Cournot equilibrium is $2/9 + 1/9 = 1/3$. Excluding the foreign firm creates a domestic monopoly, which will produce output of 1/2, yielding (domestic) welfare of $(1/8 + 1/4) = 3/8 > 1/3$.

5   Conclusions

We have studied the output and welfare effects of mergers in Cournot oligopoly, using cost and demand functions restricted only by standard stability assumptions.

   We found that mergers do indeed, typically, raise price. In particular, any merger that generates no synergies, in the sense of equation (8), raises price. And for a merger to lower price requires considerable economies of scale or learning. This result is only strengthened if the merger causes behaviour in the industry to shift from Cournot to

[30] Janusz Ordover and Robert Willig (1986) obtain a similar result in a model with linear demand and constant unit costs.

something less competitive. Furthermore, and consistent with the approach taken by the merger guidelines, we found that the economies of scale or learning effects necessary for a merger to lower price are greater, the larger are the merging firms' market shares and the less elastic is industry demand.

In our policy analysis, we focused on the external effects of a merger rather than trying directly to sign its overall welfare effect. This approach, as well as being consistent with market-oriented policy analysis in general, has a great practical advantage: the information required is much more readily available. Looking at the external effect would also allow antitrust authorities to make use of the fact that only privately profitable mergers are proposed, and it would permit them to give cost savings a larger role in merger policy (as Williamson's (1968) calculations suggest they deserve) without demanding either information or credulity about alleged synergies.

The information that is needed in our analytical scheme is in two separable parts. First, to test whether a merger will indeed reduce output requires information only on participants' (pre-merger) marginal-cost functions and on that of the merged entity. Although this information may be hard to obtain, our observation does indicate exactly what the relevant information is. Information about market demand and other firms' costs is not relevant for determining whether price will rise or fall, so long as Cournot behaviour applies both before and after the merger. Second, to sign the external effect of an output-reducing merger – whether it benefits or harms rival firms and consumers jointly – requires information only on market shares and the output responsiveness parameters (the λ_i) of non-participants.

Inevitably, for general results one requires information not only at the pre-merger equilibrium, but along a path from pre-merger to post-merger equilibrium. But proposition 5 gives conditions – general enough to cover the special cases previously studied and many more – under which no such global inquiry is required: one need merely compare the participants' pre-merger joint market share with the λ-weighted sum of their rivals'. We can thus give surprisingly general (sufficient) conditions under which all privately profitable mergers raise welfare, and presumably all proposed mergers should be approved.

Our techniques have a wide range of applications in oligopoly theory, as propositions 6 and 7 show. Quite generally, our results imply that many output-reducing changes should not be grudgingly tolerated, but should be positively welcomed by the rest of society. The counterintuitive, almost paradoxical, fact is that, in Cournot and similar theories of oligopoly with homogeneous goods, the presence of small firms with little market power is not desirable. Their output, produced at a marginal cost that almost consumes its gross social benefit, also displaces or discourages output at (larger) firms with lower marginal costs (this displacement effect is, of course, absent in perfect competition). Consequently, it often enhances economic welfare – defined in the usual way – to close down small or inefficient firms, or, failing that, to encourage them to merge so that they produce less output. This observation may call for some rethinking of our views on policy towards competition, including horizontal merger policy. We believe that our chapter provides useful tools and insights for horizontal merger policy. But our analysis is limited in two major ways, both of which are inherent in the standard Cournot model (and its conjectural-variations extensions). First, we analyse a homogeneous-goods industry; our results may not apply well to markets in which product differentiation is substantial. Applying techniques such as those presented here to differentiated-product industries is an important topic for future research. Second, by assuming that the firms behave as Cournot competitors, both before and after the merger, we ignore any effect of a merger on the probability or nature of explicit collusion. We believe that the Cournot model captures the notion of *tacit* collusion fairly well, but we are well aware that many antitrust practitioners are more concerned with the possibility of *explicit* collusion than with the nature of tacit collusion. Unfortunately there is no fully satisfactory model of the probability of successful explicit collusion in oligopoly. Such a model could be used to estimate a merger's effect on the probability of collusion.

Appendix

The Herfindahl index in Cournot oligopoly   Consider a Cournot oligopoly in which firm i ($i = 1, \ldots, n$) produces output x_i at cost $c_i(x_i)$. Total output is $X \equiv \sum_{i=1}^{n} x_i$, and the market price, $p \equiv p(X)$, measures the marginal gross benefit of output. For an arbitrary change $\{dx_i\}$ in firms' outputs

$$dW = \sum_{i=1}^{n} (p - c_x^i) dx_i.$$

In Cournot equilibrium, firm i's first-order condition gives $p - c_x^i = -p'(X)x_i$. Hence

$$dW = -p'(X) \sum_{i=1}^{n} s_i dx_i.$$

Now this change in welfare is related to the Herfindahl index, H, since

$$\sum_{i=1}^{n} x_i dx_i = \frac{1}{2} d \left[\sum_{i=1}^{n} x_i^2 \right] = \frac{1}{2} d[X^2 H] = XH dX + \frac{1}{2} X^2 dH.$$

Thus we have $dW = -X^2 h_{p'}(X) \left\{ \dfrac{dx}{x} + \dfrac{1}{2} \dfrac{dH}{H} \right\}$.

With downward-sloping demand, $p'(X) < 0$, so dW has the sign of

$$\frac{dX}{X} + \frac{1}{2} \frac{dH}{H}.$$

See Cowling and Waterson (1976) or Dansby and Willig (1979) for related calculations showing the welfare significance of the Herfindahl index in Cournot oligopoly.

Proof of lemma   Write Δx_1 and ΔX for the changes in firm 1's output and in aggregate output. It is enough to prove the lemma for an infinitesimal change dx_1, since $0 < dX/dx_1 < 1$ implies $0 < \Delta X/\Delta x_1 < 1$. For any firm $i \neq 1$, $dx_i = -\lambda_i dX$.

Adding up for $i \neq 1$ we have $dy_i = \sum_{i \neq 1} \lambda_i dX$. Adding dx_1 to this equation gives $dX = -\sum_{i \neq 1} \lambda_i dX + dx_1$, or $dX(1 + \sum_{i \neq 1} \lambda_i) = dx_1$. With conditions (3) and (4), each λ_i is positive, so dX has the same sign as dx_1 but is smaller in magnitude.

Proof of proposition 1   By our lemma, we need only sign the effect on the insiders' total output. And in order to do that, we need only find whether the new firm M would increase or decrease its output if the non-participant firms held their outputs constant at pre-merger levels.

Denote pre-merger outputs by $\bar{x}_i$ and $\bar{X}$, and call the insiders' aggregate pre-merger output $\bar{X}_M$. At pre-merger output levels, M's marginal revenue is $p(\bar{X}) + \bar{X}_M p'(\bar{X})$. So M will reduce its output if and only if $c_x^M(\bar{X}_M) \geq p(\bar{X}) + \bar{X}_M p'(\bar{X})$, or $p(\bar{X}) - c_x^M(\bar{X}_M) < -\bar{X}_M p'(\bar{X})$. Thus it is enough to show that $-\bar{X}_M p'(\bar{X})$ is equal to the sum of the merging firms' pre-merger markups. But, for each firm $i \in I$, $c_x^i(\bar{x}_i) = p(\bar{X}) + \bar{x}_i p'(\bar{X})$ or $p(\bar{X}) - c_x^i(\bar{x}_i) = -\bar{x}_i p'(\bar{X})$. Adding this up over $i \epsilon I$ we find that

$$\sum_{i \in I} [p(\bar{X}) - c_x^i(\bar{x}_i)] = -\bar{X}_M p'(\bar{X})$$

as required.

Proof of proposition 2   We give the proof for a two-firm merger, but it extends to multi-firm mergers. The proof proceeds in four steps.

Step 1. First, by the lemma, the change in total output has the same sign as the change in the insiders' output. Therefore, it is enough for us to show that the insiders will want to reduce their aggregate output, if the outsiders' output is held constant at $\bar{X}_O$. For notational simplicity, since the outsiders' output is fixed, we shall write $p(x_1 + x_2)$ instead of $p(x_1 + x_2 + \bar{X}_O)$.

Step 2 Next, we show by a revealed-preference argument that both firms' outputs cannot rise when the two firms maximize joint profits rather than their own profits (as in Cournot equilibrium).

Denote by $\bar{x}_i$ firm i's output in pre-merger Cournot equilibrium, and by x_i its output when the two firms maximize joint profits. We will show that it is impossible to have $x_i > \bar{x}_i$ for $i = 1, 2$. By revealed preference

$$(x_1 + x_2)p(x_1 + x_2) - c^1(x_1) - c^2(x_2) \geq (\bar{x}_1 + \bar{x}_2)p(\bar{x}_1 + \bar{x}_2) - c^1(\bar{x}_1) - c^2(\bar{x}_2) \quad (20)$$

and

$$\bar{x}_1 p(\bar{x}_1 + \bar{x}_2) - c^1(\bar{x}_1) \geq x_1 p(x_1 + \bar{x}_2) - c^1(x_1), \quad (21)$$

$$\bar{x}_2 p(\bar{x}_1 + \bar{x}_2) - c^2(\bar{x}_2) \geq x_2 p(\bar{x}_1 + x_2) - c^2(x_2). \quad (22)$$

Adding equations (21) and (22), and comparing to (20), yields

$$(x_1 + x_2)p(x_1 + x_2) \geq x_1 p(x_1 + \bar{x}_2) + x_2 p(\bar{x}_1 + x_2) \tag{23}$$

which is inconsistent with both $x_1 \geq \bar{x}_1$ and $x_2 \geq \bar{x}_2$ unless both hold with equality. Without loss of generality, suppose that the output at facility 2 does not rise after the merger: $x_2 \leq \bar{x}_2$.

Step 3 Let x_1' be the output that maximizes π_1 given outputs x_2 and $\bar{X}_O$. Since $x_2 \leq \bar{x}_2$, the lemma tells us that $x_1' \geq \bar{x}_1$ and $x_1' + x_2 \leq \bar{x}_1 + \bar{x}_2$.

Step 4 Finally, if $x_2 > 0$, when firm 1 is maximizing joint profits, it will produce strictly less (given firm 2's output) than if it were maximizing only its own, since increases in x_1 reduce the profits earned at facility 2. That is, $x_1 < x_1'$. Using step 3, we thus have $x_1 + x_2 < \bar{x}_1 + \bar{x}_2$ as was required. If $x_2 = 0$ then $x_1 = x_1'$ and the result follows directly from the lemma.

Economies of scale

For equilibrium output to increase, proposition 1 requires that marginal cost at twice the pre-merger capital and output levels must be less than pre-merger marginal cost, by an amount equal to the pre-merger markup. That is

$$c_x(2x, 2k) \leq c_x(x, k) - [p - c_x(x, k)]$$

where p is the pre-merger price and x is each firm's pre-merger output. Now the pre-merger markup $p - c_x(x, k)$ is equal, by the pre-merger first-order condition, (2), to $s/(\varepsilon - s)$ times pre-merger marginal cost $c_x(x, k)$. So output falls unless

$$c_x(2x, 2k) \leq \left[1 - \frac{2}{\varepsilon - s}\right] c_x(x, k).$$

If $c(x, k)$ is dual to the generalized Cobb–Douglas production function $f(L, k) = k^a L^b$, then $c_x(x, k) \equiv w/bx^{1/b-1}k^{-a/b}$, where w is the price of the variable input L, so that

$$\frac{c_x(2x, 2k)}{c_x(x, k)} = 2^{1/b-1-a/b}.$$

Hence, (9) states that

$$a + b \geq 1 + b \log_2(\varepsilon - s) - b \log_2(\varepsilon - 2s).$$

If $s = 0.2$ and $\varepsilon = 1$, and if $a = b$, this requires $a \geq 1/\log_2 3$.

Learning

Suppose that firms 1 and 2 merge, capital is immobile and marginal costs are nondecreasing. We prove here that for price to fall, the merger must either reduce θ_1 by at least a factor $s_2/(\varepsilon - s_1)$ or reduce θ_2 by at least a factor $s_1/(\varepsilon - s_2)$.

At least one of the insiders, call it firm 1, must at least maintain its pre-merger output level if price is not to rise. And, by the envelope theorem, M's marginal cost will equal firm 1's marginal cost at its post-merger level of output. But, by equation (7), for output to rise we must have $c_x^1 - c_x^M > p - c_x^2$, so firm 1's marginal costs must fall by at least firm 2's markup. However, with $c_{xxx}^1 \geq 0$ and firm 1 expanding, firm 1's marginal costs could fall only due to synergies. If price is to fall, therefore, synergies must reduce firm 1's marginal costs by at least the extent of firm 2's markup.

Just how strong a synergistic cost reduction is needed for this condition to be met and thus reverse the presumption that aggregate output will fall with the merger? In the pre-merger equilibrium, we have $(p - c_x^i(x)i))/p = -x_i p'/p = s_i/\varepsilon$. Hence, $(p - c_x^2)/p = s_2/\varepsilon$ and $p/c_x^1 = \varepsilon/(\varepsilon - s_1)$.

The reduction in firm I's marginal costs required for price to fall is $c_x^1 - c_x^M > p - c_x^2$. In percentage terms, this requires

$$\frac{c_x^1 - c_x^M}{c_x^1} > \frac{p - c_x^2}{p} \frac{p}{c_x^1}.$$

Substituting for the two factors on the right-hand side, we must have

$$\frac{c_x^1 - c_x^M}{c_x^1} > \frac{s_2}{\varepsilon} \frac{\varepsilon}{\varepsilon - s_1} = \frac{s_2}{\varepsilon - s_1} = \frac{p}{c_x^1}.$$

Learning must reduce firm I's marginal costs by at least $s_2/(\varepsilon - s_1)$ for price to fall.

Proof of proposition 5   We will show that the conditions given imply that $d[\lambda_i x_i]/dX \leq 0$ for $i \in O$. Since an output-reducing merger involves a reduction in X_I, an infinitesimal merger's effect on $\eta \equiv \sum_{i \in O} \lambda_i x_i - X_I$ is therefore unambiguously positive. So, after doing an infinitesimal merger that benefits non-participants, we will find that a further infinitesimal merger benefits them by even more, and so on until the merger is complete. Evidently, this implies (it is much stronger than) proposition 5.

Recall that we are considering an exogenous change dX_I, which induces changes dx_i by outside firms i, and hence induces a change dX in aggregate output and changes $d\lambda_i$ in the λ's. Since $d[\lambda_i, x_i] = \lambda_i dx_i + x_i d\lambda_i$, and since $dx_i = -\lambda_i dX$, we have

$$d[\lambda_i, x_i] = -\lambda_i^2 dX + x_i d\lambda_i.$$

Now think of $\lambda_i \equiv -p'(X) + x_i p''(X)/c_x^i(x_i) - p'(X)$ as a function of two variables, X and x_i. Thus we have

$$\frac{d[\lambda_i x_i]}{dX} = -\lambda_i^2 + x_i \left(\frac{\partial \lambda_i}{\partial X} - \lambda_i \frac{\partial \lambda_i}{\partial x_i} \right).$$

Substituting in for λ_i, and its partial derivatives, we get

$$(c_{xx} - p')^2 \frac{d[\lambda_i x_i]}{dX} = -(p' + x_i p'')^2 - x_i^2 p'''(c_{xx} - p')$$

$$+ x_i c_{xxx} \frac{(p' + x_i p'')^2}{c_{xx} - p'} - x_i p''[c_{xx} + p' + 2x_i p''].$$

(24)

For quadratic $p(\cdot)$ and $c(\cdot)$ functions, we can ignore the terms in c_{xxx} and in p''', and then $d[\lambda_i x_i]/dX$ has the sign of

$$-x_i p''[c_{xx} + p' + 2x_i p''] - (p' + x_i p'')^2 = -x_i p'' c_{xx}$$

$$- \left(p' + \frac{3}{2} x_i p''\right)^2 - \frac{3}{4} x_i^2 (p'')^2$$

which is negative provided that p'' and c_{xx} are non-negative (actually, provided that their product is non-negative). The proposition follows by inspection of equation (24), since p''' and c_{xxx} enter with unambiguous signs.

References

Cowling, K. and M. Waterson (1976), 'Price-cost margins and market structure', *Economica,* 43, 267–74.

Dansby, R.E. and R.D. Willig (1979), 'Industry performance gradient indexes', *American Economic Review*, 69, 249–60.

Demsetz, H. (1973), 'Industry structure, market rivalry, and public policy', *Journal of Law and Economics,* 16, 1–10.

  (1974), 'Two systems of belief about monopoly', in H. Goldschmid *et al.* (eds.), *Industrial Concentration: The New Learning,* Boston, MA, Little Brown, pp. 164–84.

Deneckere, R. and C. Davidson (1985), 'Incentives to form coalitions with Bertrand competition', *Rand Journal of Economics,* 16, 473–86.

Dixit, A. (1986), 'Comparative statics for oligopoly', *International Economic Review*, 27, 107–22.

Farrell, J. and C. Shapiro (1988), 'Horizontal mergers: an equilibrium analysis', John M. Olin Program for the Study of Economic Organization and Public Policy, Discussion Paper no. 17, Princeton University.

  (1990), 'Asset ownership and market structure in oligopoly', *Rand Journal of Economics,* 21, 275–92.

Fisher, F.M. (1987), 'Horizontal mergers: triage and treatment', *Journal of Economic Perspectives,* 1, 23–40.

Gaudet, G. and S. Salant (1988), 'The profitability of exogenous output contractions in Cournot equilibrium: implications for strikes, mergers and export subsidies', mimeo, University of Michigan.

McAfee, R.P. and M.A. Williams (1988), 'Horizontal mergers and antitrust policy', unpublished manuscript, US Department of Justice.

McElroy, F.W. (1988), 'Price and welfare effects of oligopolistic mergers and partial acquisitions', unpublished manuscript, Georgetown University.

Ordover, J.A. and R.D. Willig (1986), 'Perspectives on mergers and world competition', in R. Grieson (ed.), *Antitrust and Regulation,* Lexington, MA, Lexington Books, DC Heath, 201–18.

Perry, M.K. and R.H. Porter (1985), 'Oligopoly and the incentive for horizontal merger', *American Economic Review,* 75, 219–27.

Salant, S., S. Switzer and R. Reynolds (1983), 'Losses due to merger: the effects of an exogenous change in industry structure on Cournot–Nash equilibrium', *Quarterly Journal of Economics*, 98, 185–99.

Schwartz, M. (1989), 'Investments in oligopoly: welfare effects and tests for predation', *Oxford Economic Papers*, 41, 698–719.

Shapiro, C. (1989), 'Theories of oligopoly behavior', in R. Schmalensee and R. Willig (eds.), *The Handbook of Industrial Organization,* New York, Elsevier North-Holland.

US Department of Justice (1984), 'Merger Guidelines', 2 Trade Reg. Rep. (CCH), 4491–5.

White, L.J. (1987), 'Antitrust and merger policy: a review and critique', *Journal of Economic Perspectives*, 1, 13–22.

Williamson, O.E. (1968), 'Economies as an antitrust defense: the welfare tradeoffs', *American Economic Review*, 58, 18–36.

Chapter 19

Using the Herfindahl–Hirschman index
Horizontal mergers: comment

Gregory J. Werden

Joseph Farrell and Carl Shapiro (1990a) present an interesting and elegant analysis of horizontal mergers in the context of a Cournot model under quite general demand and cost conditions. One section of their paper deals with the effects of mergers on price or consumer welfare. In it they show that, in a Cournot model, mergers that do not lower costs always raise price and that mergers that lower costs still raise price unless they lower costs quite a lot. These results are much more general than anything in the prior literature. Another section of the paper deals with the effects of mergers on non-merging firms and consumers, which Farrell and Shapiro term 'external'. With some minor additional assumptions, they show that a merger is externally welfare-enhancing if (but not only if)

$$\sum_{i \in I} s_i \equiv s_I < \sum_{i \in O} \lambda_i s_i \tag{1}$$

where s_i is firm i's share of total output, λ_i is a measure of its output response to changes in industry output, I is the set of merging firms, and O is the set of non-merging firms.

Several portions of the paper are devoted to antitrust policy towards mergers. In one, Farrell and Shapiro (1990a, pp. 116–17, 122–3) make the largely unqualified

This article first appeared in *American Economic Review*, 1991, Vol. 81, pp. 1002–6.
Antitrust Division, US Department of Justice. I thank Mary Fitzpatrick, Paul Joskow, David Malueg, Bobby Willig, and two referees for helpful comments. The views expressed herein are not purported to be those of the US Department of Justice.

suggestion that current enforcement policy be replaced with an analysis based on the external effects of mergers.[1] In others, they offer a series of criticisms of the *Merger Guidelines* (US Department of Justice, 1984) use of two structural indicators: the post-merger *Herfindahl–Hirschman index* (HHI) and the change in the HHI. The post-merger HHI is an HHI constructed by treating the merging firms as one. It contrasts with the pre-merger HHI, which treats the merging firms as separate. The change in the HHI is the post-merger HHI minus the pre-merger HHI, or, with two merging firms, twice the product of their market shares.

Farrell and Shapiro (1990a, pp. 107–8) first criticize the *Merger Guidelines'* use of the post-merger HHI and the change in the HHI on the grounds that both measures erroneously assume that the market share of the merged firm will equal the sum of the shares of the merging firms. They argue that outputs will readjust after the mergers so pre-merger outputs are not indicative of post-merger outputs. That argument is correct, but the *Merger Guidelines* do not assume otherwise. The post-merger HHI is used merely as a concentration index to help gauge the effects of a merger, and it is not purported to be a prediction of post-merger concentration. Moreover, in homogeneous goods industries – the only ones considered by Farrell and Shapiro (1990a) – the *Merger Guidelines* (section 2.4) prefer that market shares be based on the capacities of the firms in the market, rather than on their outputs. At least in the short run, capacities normally do not adjust after a merger.

Farrell and Shapiro (1990a, p. 108) next argue that increases in the HHI are not necessarily associated with a lessening of economic welfare. That too is correct. In asymmetric Cournot equilibria: (a) production is inefficiently allocated among firms, with the smaller firms overproducing relative to the larger ones; (b) firms below a certain relative size actually produce more than they would under competition; and (c) because of (a) and (b) it is possible for a merger to enhance welfare even though it results in an output restriction. Farrell and Shapiro (1990a, p. 108), however, erroneously assert that this Cournot result is theoretical support for Harold Demsetz's (1973) argument that larger firms became larger because, for reasons unrelated to initial size, their managements were more insightful or just luckier than those of rivals. The potential welfare gain from increased concentration in the Cournot models considered by Farrell and Shapiro (1990a) stems entirely from exogenous size

---

[1] Farrell and Shapiro (1990a, pp. 116–17) argue: 'Privately unprofitable mergers will not be proposed, so proposed mergers should be permitted unless their external effects are "sufficiently" bad to outweigh their private profitability. In particular, if a proposed merger would have *beneficial* external effects, then it should be allowed.' While this policy prescription has merit, it also has three significant qualifications that were overlooked by Farrell and Shapiro. First, privately unprofitable mergers may indeed be proposed if managers are motivated by objectives other than profit. Second, mergers may be privately profitable as the result of tax savings or other forms of redistribution, which entail an external welfare loss on the part of taxpayers or some other group that also must be considered. Third, many mergers involve firms operating in several markets and may be motivated by cost savings in markets totally unrelated to the markets in which the merger threatens competition. Even if externally welfare-enhancing, such mergers should not be permitted if they could be restructured in such a way that the efficiencies can be realized without the competitive harm. Elsewhere (Werden, 1990 pp. 2–3), I elaborate these and related points.

differences among otherwise identical firms. Thus, the Cournot result is unrelated to Demsetz's argument.

Finally, Farrell and Shapiro note that, in the case of linear demand and quadratic cost, equation (1) reduces to

$$\sum_{i\in I} s_i \equiv s_I < \varepsilon^{-1} \sum_{i\in O} s_i^2 \tag{2}$$

where ε is the elasticity of demand. From this condition they (1990a, p. 119) conclude that 'more concentration' among the non-merging firms makes it *more* likely that the merger will be externally welfare enhancing. This conclusion certainly is the strongest criticism they make regarding the use of the HHI as an indicator of the welfare effects of mergers, and it is a misinterpretation of inequality (2). Moreover, in the linear-demand, quadratic-cost case, the HHI and change in the HHI are reasonably good indicators of the effects of mergers on price.

Before considering these two propositions, it is helpful to introduce a partial ordering of distributions of capital called 'unambiguously more concentrated' (UMC) and denoted, $>_{umc}$. If the distribution of capital among firms in a market is denoted $\{k_i\}$, then $\{k_i\}_t >_{umc} \{k_i\}_s$ if and only if $\{k_i\}_t$ can be derived from $\{k_i\}_s$ through a series of small reallocations of capital from smaller firms to larger firms. Conventional axioms for concentration indexes require that $\{k_i\}_t$ be assigned a greater value than $\{k_i\}_s$, if $\{k_i\}t >_{umc} \{k_i\}_s$ and the pre-merger HHI based on capital satisfies such axioms. However, like other conventional concentration indexes, the HHI is a complete ordering of distributions. Thus, the HHI ranks distributions that cannot be compared using the UMC partial ordering.

Return now to the linear-demand quadratic-cost case considered by Farrell and Shapiro (1990a) and others.[2] Let x_i be firm i's output, and let k_i be its capital stock. Define

$$X = \sum x_i \tag{3a}$$
$$\kappa_i = k_i/(1+k_i) \tag{3b}$$
$$\kappa_{i+j} = (k_i+k_j)/(1+k_i+k_j) \tag{3c}$$
$$\kappa = \sum \kappa_i \tag{3d}$$
$$\kappa = \sum k_i \tag{3e}$$

and assume

[2] This is the model considered by McAfee and Williams (1989, 1990) and by Perry and Porter (1985). It also is the most interesting special case considered by Farrell and Shapiro (1990a). The other two special cases they consider are not very interesting because they involve constant marginal cost without capacity constraints. In such models, mergers are the same as exits (see Perry and Porter, 1985, pp. 219–20). If the merging firms have the same costs, then the merged firm is identical to both of them. If one of the merging firms has lower costs than the other, then the merged firm is identical to the lower-cost firm. Moreover, this is the only special case considered by Farrell and Shapiro (1990a) from which they derive conclusions significantly at variance with the implications of the *Merger Guidelines*.

$$p(X) = a - X \tag{4a}$$
$$C_i(x_i) = x^2/2k_i. \tag{4b}$$

It is easy to show that, in equilibrium,

$$x_i = p\kappa_i \tag{5a}$$
$$X = p\kappa \tag{5b}$$
$$p = a/(1 + \kappa) \tag{5c}$$
$$\varepsilon^{-1} = \kappa \tag{5d}$$
$$s_I - \kappa_I/\kappa \tag{5e}$$

(see, e.g., Farrell and Shapiro, 1990b).

Equations (5d) and (5e) imply that a reallocation of capital among the non-merging firms that unambiguously increases concentration affects not just $\sum_O s_i^2$ but also each of the other terms in inequality (2). (The effect of a capital reallocation on κ is shown in equation (12) below.) Furthermore, it is possible for $\sum_O s_i^2$ to *decrease* as the distribution of capital among the non-merging firms becomes more concentrated, because $\sum_O s_i^2$ decreases.[3] These facts combine to make a comparative-static interpretation of inequality (2) very difficult.

A more manageable version of inequality (2) can be derived by multiplying both sides by κ and expressing both only in terms of parameters:

$$\sum_{i \in I} \kappa_i < \sum_{i \in O} \kappa_i^2. \tag{6}$$

The left-hand side of inequality (6) does not vary with a change in the concentration of capital among the non-merging firms, so one need only examine the right-hand side. Consider a small reallocation of capital from firm j to firm i. Totally differentiate $\sum_O \kappa_i^2$, substitute in $dk_j = -dk_i$, and simplify to

$$d\sum_{i \in O} k_i^2 = \left[\frac{2k_i}{(1 + k_i)^3} - \frac{2k_j}{(1 + k_j)^3} \right] dk_i. \tag{7}$$

For $k_i, k_j > 1/2$, $2k(1 + k)^3$ is decreasing in k, so the term in brackets is negative if $k_i > k_j$. Thus, unambiguous increases in the concentration of capital among the non-merging firms actually make it *less* likely that a merger will be externally welfare-enhancing, provided that the k_i's are sufficiently large.[4] Of course, not all distributions can be compared using the UMC partial ordering, and a distribution of capital among

[3] Consider two distributions of capital among four firms. In the first, each firm has two units of capital. In the second, two firms have two units, one has three, and one has one. In both cases, suppose that firms with two units of capital are merging. The second distribution is unambiguously more concentrated than the first, both overall and with respect to just the non-merging firms. However, it works out that $\sum_O s_i^2$ equals 0.125 for the first distribution and about 0.122 for the second.

[4] It should he noted that the k_i's cannot be scaled arbitrarily. The equilibrium is not uniquely determined by the k_i/k's.

the non-merging firms with a higher HHI based on capital need not be associated with a lower $\sum_O \kappa_i^2$.

Further illustration can be provided by a numerical example. Consider an industry consisting of six firms, each with one unit of capital, and in which two of the firms propose to merge. A bit of arithmetic indicates that both sides of inequality (6) equal 1. Now consider an unambiguously more concentrated industry consisting of five firms, four with one unit of capital and one with two units and in which two of the one-unit firms propose to merge. A bit of arithmetic indicates that inequality (6) is still not satisfied. The left-hand side still equals 1, but the right-hand side now is only 0.94. Expressed in terms of inequality (2), s_I is 0.33 in the former case, and 0.38 in the latter; $\varepsilon^{-1} \sum_O s_i^2$ is 0.33 in the former case, and 0.35 in the latter.[5]

It is also possible to show that the HHI and the change in the HHI are reasonably good predictors of the effects of mergers on price. The effect of a merger on price is indicated by its effect on κ, and the effect on κ of the merger of firms i and j is

$$\Delta\kappa = \kappa_{1+j} - (\kappa_i + \kappa_j). \tag{8}$$

By substituting definitions (3b) and (3c) into equation (8) and simplifying, it can be seen that $\Delta\kappa < 0$. Since $p = a/(1 + \kappa)$ and $\Delta\kappa < 0$, all mergers raise price.

The proportionate increase in price from the merger of firms i and j can be written

$$-\Delta\kappa/(1 + \kappa + \Delta\kappa) \tag{9}$$

where κ is its pre-merger value. Expression (9) is strictly decreasing in $\Delta\kappa$ for all positive values of κ and $\Delta\kappa$, so a smaller (more negative) value of $\Delta\kappa$ is associated with a larger proportionate effect on price. Consider any given allocation of capital, and consider the effect of replacing merging firm i with a larger firm. This does not affect the pre-merger κ, and its qualitative effect on $\Delta\kappa$ is given by

$$\frac{d\Delta\kappa}{dk_i} = \frac{1}{(1 + k_i + k_j)^2} - \frac{1}{(1 + k_1)^2} < 0. \tag{10}$$

Thus, increasing the share of capital of either merging firm, holding κ constant, increases the proportionate price increase from the merger.

Now consider replacing both merging firms with another pair from the same distribution that has the same $k_i + k_j$. This does not affect the pre-merger κ, and the qualitative effect on $\Delta\kappa$ can be determined by considering a small reallocation of capital from firm j to firm I. Totally differentiate $\Delta\kappa$, substitute in $dk_j = dk_i$, and simplify to yield

---

[5] Calculating the welfare effects of the two mergers is tedious, but it works out that both mergers are externally welfare-enhancing (which is possible because the Farrell and Shapiro (1990a) condition is not necessary). External welfare increases more from the merger in the less concentrated industry than from the merger in the more-concentrated industry. In addition, both mergers lessen total welfare, and the merger in the more-concentrated industry lessens welfare more than the merger in the less-concentrated industry.

$$d\Delta\kappa = \left[\frac{1}{(1+k_j)^2} - \frac{1}{(1+k_1)^2}\right]dk_i. \tag{11}$$

The term in square brackets is negative if $k_j > k_i$ (positive if $k_j < k_i$), so decreasing (increasing) the disparity between the shares of the merging firms decreases (increases) $\Delta\kappa$ and, holding κ constant, increases (decreases) the proportionate price increase from the merger.

If market shares are measured in terms of capital,[6] the change in the HHI increases as the share of capital of either merging firm increases and as the disparity of shares between the merging firms decreases, holding their aggregate share constant. Thus, for any given initial distribution of capital market shares, the greater the change in the HHI from the merger of two firms, the greater is the proportionate increase in price from that merger.

Holding $\Delta\kappa$ constant, one can consider how unambiguous increases in the concentration of capital among the non-merging firms affect the proportionate price increase from the merger. Consider a small reallocation of capital from firm j to firm i. Totally differentiate κ, substitute in $dk_j = -dk_i$ simplify to yield

$$d\kappa = \left[\frac{1}{(1+k_i)^2} - \frac{1}{(1+k_j)^2}\right]dk_i. \tag{12}$$

The term in brackets is negative if $k_i > k_j$, so unambiguous increases in the concentration of capital of the non-merging firms decrease κ and, holding $\Delta\kappa$ constant, increase the proportionate price increase from the merger. It has already been shown that the proportionate increase in price from the merger will be greater the greater is the change in the HHI. Thus, the post-merger HHI based on capital is a reasonably good indicator of the effects of mergers on price.[7]

Farrell and Shapiro have derived some interesting and powerful results relating to the effects of mergers in Cournot models. Their theoretical work is an important contribution to the literature. Their policy conclusions, however, are largely unwarranted and partly incorrect. Their criticisms of the use of conventional structural

[6] Capital in this model is the proper index of capacity. For the purposes of measuring market shares, a firm's capacity should be defined as the quantity it can produce at a marginal cost at or below the prevailing price or a slightly higher price. From equation (5a), that quantity for firm i is pk_i. Thus, k_i is a scaled measure of firm i's capacity, and its share of total capacity, k_i/k, is unaffected by the scaling and is independent of price.

[7] If one adds the rather artificial assumption that the output determined by the linear-demand, quadratic-cost Cournot model actually is produced efficiently (i.e., $x_i = Xk_i/k$), then total welfare moves in the opposite direction of price, and the HHI and the change in the HHI also are reasonably good predictors of welfare (see Werden, 1990, p. 7). While this model may not be inherently interesting, its equilibrium can be achieved through contracts that require firms to sell only the outputs they would select given access only to their own individual production facilities but that also allow firms to produce for others. Moreover, this equilibrium is Pareto-superior to that in the Cournot model without the assumption of efficient production, so with perfect information and no transaction costs it would dominate the equilibrium in the model without the assumption of efficient production.

indicators are based on misconceptions about those indicators and misinterpretations of their own results.

References

Demsetz, H. (1973), 'Industry structure, market rivalry, and public policy', *Journal of Law and Economics*, 16, 1–10.

Farrell, J. and C. Shapiro (1990a), 'Horizontal mergers: an equilibrium analysis', *American Economic Review*, 80, 107–26.

(1990b), 'Asset ownership and market structure in oligopoly', *Rand Journal of Economics*, 21, 275–92.

McAfee, R.P. and M.A. Williams (1989), 'The Department of Justice Merger Guidelines: a critique and a proposed improvement,' *Pepperdine Law Review*, 16, 1069–81.

(1990), 'Horizontal mergers and antitrust policy,' unpublished manuscript, University of Texas.

Perry, M.K. and R.H. Porter (1985), 'Oligopoly and the incentive for horizontal merger,' *American Economic Review*, 75, 219–27.

Werden, G.J. (1990), 'Antitrust policy toward horizontal mergers: a comment on Farrell and Shapiro', Antitrust Division, US Department of Justice, Economic Analysis Group Discussion Paper 90–4, 15.

US Department of Justice (1984), *Merger Guidelines*, reprinted in *Trade Regulation Reporter*, 13, 104, Chicago: Commerce Clearing House.

Chapter 20

Cournot and merger control
Horizontal mergers: reply

Joseph Farrell and Carl Shapiro

The comment by Gregory J. Werden (1991) on our paper, 'Horizontal mergers: an equilibrium analysis (Farrell and Shapiro, 1990a) is largely based on a misunderstanding. We first address some general issues that he raises and then turn to the technical point that occupies most of his comment.

1   Policy and externalities

Werden writes that we 'make the largely unqualified suggestion that current enforcement policy be replaced with an analysis based on the external effects of mergers' (p. 368–9). We are not sure what he means by 'largely unqualified', but we do indeed believe, on general grounds, that an externality-based policy, if feasible, would be desirable.

The very basis of a market economy is to restrict government intervention to the minimum necessary. While economists differ considerably in what they believe to be necessary intervention, almost all would agree that externalities should constitute the main basis for intervention other than income-distribution concerns. Moreover, antitrust (including merger) policy that is *not* based on the analysis of externalities may prevent efficiency gains that may often outweigh the anticompetitive inefficiencies prevented by the antitrust policy (see Oliver Williamson, 1968). In our view, a serious

This article first appeared in *American Economic Review*, 1991, Vol. 81, pp. 1007–11.

obstacle facing current merger policy is that the regulators must try to evaluate, from the outside, the likely internal efficiencies resulting from a proposed merger. Because these hard-to-evaluate internal effects must be weighed against other, separately estimated effects, the regulators are obliged to be quite skeptical of claims that efficiencies will result.

We think it would be desirable to be able to identify mergers that do not harm non-participants in the aggregate, so that such mergers (like other activities that are on the whole victimless) could be freed from further scrutiny. Perhaps surprisingly, our analysis revealed relatively simple conditions in the Cournot model for a merger to qualify for approval on this basis.

Werden also attacks the working assumption that a proposed merger will be privately beneficial (profitable), by noting some reasons to doubt that firms' behaviour is always motivated by profit maximization. While this is surely true, he gives no reason to believe that profit maximization is a worse model in merger policy than in any other context in which we use it for policy guidance, nor does he suggest a workable alternative. Certainly, current merger policy relies heavily on the assumption that the merging partners are motivated to maximize their joint profits; we see this assumption as both reasonable and indispensable for policy purposes.

2   Limits of the Cournot model

We now discuss the question of what relevance our model might have for actual merger policy. Obviously the possible relevance of any simple model is limited. In particular, we are well aware of the limitation of any analysis based on Cournot equilibrium, and we were careful to articulate these limitations in our paper. Nevertheless, we believe our analysis yields several insights that are useful for policy purposes, and we discuss those insights in our paper. In particular, a thorough welfare analysis of a merger should account not only for synergies and for changes in industry output, but also for any redistributions of output among firms with unequal marginal costs.

We see three limitations of our analysis as most significant. First, there is of course nothing to guarantee that firms behave as Cournot competitors. We regard Cournot equilibrium, with its smooth relationship between market concentration and price-cost margins (which seems to mimic the empirical evidence, although this is not entirely clear: see, e.g., Richard Schmalensee, 1989), as a useful simple model of non-cooperative oligopolistic rivalry, but clearly competition in practice is not static. Whether or not the Cournot model is helpful for merger policy is very hard to know *ex ante:* clearly the assumptions are false, but it is much less clear whether they are false in such important ways that the conclusions are misleading. For what it is worth, we remind the reader that our analysis extends readily to conjectural-variations models (Farrell and Shapiro, 1990a, p. 120).

Second, our welfare analysis relies heavily on the assumption of homogeneous products. Even if static quantity-setting behaviour is thought to be a good model of oligopolistic rivalry in a differentiated products industry, a different welfare analysis will be necessary. With differentiated products, typically some consumers will be on the margin of buying one versus another industry product, as well as on the margin of simple quantity-adjustment; moreover, when a consumer switches brands, the quality of the match between consumers and brands is affected.

Third, and most important for policy purposes, the Cournot model ignores the possibility of explicit collusion. As we emphasize in the conclusion to our paper, concern that a merger might facilitate explicit collusion has historically been the driving force behind antitrust policy towards horizontal mergers. Nonetheless, tacit collusion and the danger that a more concentrated market structure will, even without explicit collusion, lead to higher prices are also key concerns in formulating merger policy.

Our goal in analysing horizontal mergers with Cournot oligopoly was to improve the understanding of the effect of mergers on oligopolistic rivalry and tacit collusion. It would shock and dismay us, as well as others, if the Department of Justice and the Federal Trade Commission were to decree that, henceforth, proposed mergers should be analysed solely using the Farrell–Shapiro model. In a number of ways, our model is more general, and our welfare and policy analysis is more sophisticated, than the pre-existing formal literature on mergers and merger policy, which has surely had some effect on actual merger policy. As such, we think that our paper may be a useful practical as well as academic contribution. We never thought of it as a last word.

While on the subject of the Cournot model, let us address a relatively minor point: whether our model captures elements of Harold Demsetz's (1973) view of concentration. Werden (1991, p. 1003) claims that welfare gains from mergers in our model stem 'entirely from exogenous size differences among otherwise identical firms' and that therefore 'the Cournot result is unrelated to Demsetz's argument'. This is quite untrue. We assumed that firms differ in their costs and derived endogenous differences in firm sizes on account of these costs. In particular, we allowed for the possibility that an especially efficient firm (which is large in the pre-merger Cournot equilibrium as a result of its superior efficiency) may acquire a less efficient rival and thereby grow by using the capital goods of the acquired firm and by spreading superior efficiency through the operations of it. This seems to us to follow quite closely the ideas urged by Demsetz, contrary to Werden's suggestion.

3   Discussions of an inequality

The bulk of Werden's comment concerns a key condition from our paper

$$s_I < \sum_{i \in O} \lambda_i s_i. \tag{1}$$

Here s_i is firm i's market share of total output, λ_i is a measure of firm i's output response to changes in total industry output, O is the set of non-merging firms, I is the set of merging firms, and $s_i \equiv \sum_{i \in I} s_i$ is the combined pre-merger share of the merging parties.

We showed in proposition 5 of our paper that inequality (1), along with some other conditions on demand and cost functions, is sufficient for a price-increasing horizontal merger in Cournot oligopoly to generate positive external benefits (i.e., to benefit consumers and rival firms in the aggregate measured by total economic surplus). Assuming that the merging firms profit from their proposed combination, any merger generating positive external benefits actually raises welfare.

Werden considers only the special example of linear demand and quadratic costs, in which case inequality (1) becomes

$$s_I < \frac{H_o}{\varepsilon}. \tag{2}$$

Here ε is the absolute value of the price elasticity of demand at the pre-merger equilibrium, and $H_o \equiv \sum_{i \in O} s_i^2$ is the 'outsider Herfindahl index', a modified version of the conventional Herfindahl index of market concentration. Inequality (2) has the attractive property of involving only terms that are relatively amenable to direct measurement.

We noted in our paper that, given the share of the market controlled by the merging parties (s_I), greater concentration of output among non-merging parties (a larger value of H_o) would make it easier to satisfy (2) (in the sense that more values of ε satisfy it) and thus to conclude that the merger enhances welfare. This inference is simply a matter of translating (2) back into words. Yet Werden calls this conclusion 'a misinterpretation' of inequality (2). How can this be? The answer is that Werden is conducting a different 'comparative-static' exercise than we did. We will try to clarify this fact and will argue that ours is the appropriate exercise.

Our point was simply that, under the assumptions of Cournot behaviour (both before and after the merger), linear demand, and quadratic costs, *measuring* the elasticity of demand near the pre-merger equilibrium and *measuring* the firms' market shares allows one to determine whether (2) is satisfied and thus whether a privately profitable merger necessarily raises welfare. If merger policy were to be based on the Cournot model and the added assumptions of the special case under discussion, then the rule should count higher H_o as a factor favourable to a proposed merger, not (as the current *Merger Guidelines* (US Department of Justice, 1984) do) as an unfavourable factor. One might well be wary of such a conclusion, based as it is on many special assumptions, but for what it is worth, that is what the model says.

Werden's calculation concerns a different and, we think, a rather artificial exercise: reallocating a fixed amount of capital among the non-merging firms. He notes that increasing the concentration of capital among those firms (prior to Cournot competition) will affect the equilibrium value of ε as well as H_o and will therefore not necessarily make (2) easier to satisfy. This observation may have some useful implications. For example, it suggests (within this example) that the completion of one merger does *not* tend to make another proposed merger more likely to be externally beneficial. That is a worthwhile observation, especially in the light of our finding that the consummation of one merger *does* make another merger more profitable in this special model (proposition 6 in Farrell and Shapiro, 1990b, p. 285), but it is hardly surprising; nor does Werden's observation contradict anything we wrote.

Indeed, Werden's result follows simply from some properties of the example under discussion that we reported in our paper and in Farrell and Shapiro (1990b). In this example, increasing the concentration of capital (among any group of firms) always causes the Cournot equilibrium price to rise (Farrell and Shapiro, 1990b, p. 282). Along a linear demand curve, a price increase always increases the elasticity of demand in absolute value. With the higher elasticity of demand, (2) is more difficult to satisfy (in the sense that fewer values of s_I satisfy it). The only part of Werden's argument that is not clear at this level of abstraction is that this elasticity effect can outweigh the direct effect of increasing H_o that follows from increasing the concentration of capital among non-merging firms. Werden shows that it can; but what possible implications can this have for policy?

Suppose for a moment that a class of markets were well described by the linear/quadratic model with the *same* demand curve and the *same* total quantity of capital and that these markets differed only in the distribution of that capital. In that case, it is true that the elasticity of demand would vary across markets in a way systematically linked with the variations in concentration. Were this the case, then identical results would be obtained by applying the rule that we think is suggested by (2), in which lower measured elasticity of demand and higher measured concentration among non-participants both favour a proposed merger, and by applying the rule (seemingly more congenial to Werden) that elasticity need not be measured (since it is causally linked to concentration) and that higher concentration among non-participants argues *against* a proposed merger. Yet even in this very special and quite artificial setting in which Werden's rule makes sense, it is equivalent to ours, not superior, and it involves measuring firms' capital stocks or cost functions, which arguably is more difficult than measuring their market shares and the market elasticity of demand.

Even if we restrict attention to the very special linear/quadratic Cournot model, we should surely allow for the possibility that markets differ in the intercepts or slopes of their (linear) demand curves or in the total quantity of productive capital. With this extension, the two rules are no longer equivalent, and the rule we suggest, based on measuring all the quantities in condition (2), is unambiguously superior.

4   Predicting the price effects of mergers

Werden (1991, p. 1003) argues in the special example that the Herfindahl–Hirschman index (HHI) and the non-equilibrium 'change in the HHI' (i.e., $2s_1 s_2$, where s_1 and s_2 are the merging firms' pre-merger market shares) are 'reasonably good indicators of the effects of mergers on price' in the sense that they have some of the same qualitative properties as price, when viewed as functions of firms' market shares. What is the value of this observation?

If it were a rule of thumb for predicting when a merger would raise price, this might be useful; but in the example under discussion, all mergers raise price (Farrell and Shapiro, 1990a, p. 118). Moreover, we have provided a far more general necessary and sufficient condition for mergers to raise price in Cournot oligopoly (propositions 1 and 2 in Farrell and Shapiro (1990a, p. 112)), and our condition has little to do with the HHI.

Another possible point might be to estimate the *size* of the increase in price following from a merger. However, the appeal of any such rule of thumb depends on its being simple to use, and it seems that this rule requires us to use market-share numbers based not on sales but on 'capital', which of course is much harder to observe or even to interpret in a more general model. Moreover, Werden's analysis toward this end is highly incomplete. In particular, the assumption that the total industry output produced in Cournot equilibrium is produced efficiently is 'rather artificial', as Werden admits in his footnote 7. In fact, unless all firms have identical market shares, their marginal costs also differ in Cournot equilibrium, so output is not efficiently produced, and this fact is an important ingredient of our analysis. Finally, Werden's analysis seems superseded by the recent work of Robert Willig (1991), which studies more precisely how the net price effect of a merger depends on the degree of market concentration among non-participants, via the slope of their joint reaction function.

Finally, one might be interested in whether changes or levels of the HHI predict changes in welfare due to a merger or other change. We have separately provided a general necessary and sufficient condition (under Cournot oligopoly) for *equilibrium* increases in the HHI to go along with decreases in welfare (proposition 7 in Farrell and Shapiro, 1990b, p. 289). There, we showed that, starting from a Cournot equilibrium, an arbitrary change in all firms' outputs, $\{dx_i\}$ for all i, causes welfare and the Herfindahl index (H) to move in opposite directions if and only if

$$0 \leq \frac{\sum_{i=1}^{n} s_i dx_i}{dX} \leq H.$$

While we did not study the relationship between changes in welfare and the non-equilibrium 'change in the HHI' (i.e., $2s_1 s_2$), we have yet to be persuaded that this is an interesting question.

References

Demsetz, H. (1973), 'Industry structure, market rivalry, and public policy', *Journal of Law and Economics,* 16, 1–10.
Farrell, J. and C. Shapiro (1990a) 'Horizontal mergers: an equilibrium analysis', *American Economic Review,* 80, 107–26.
  (1990b), 'Asset ownership and market structure in oligopoly', *Rand Journal of Economics,* 21, 275–92.
Schmalensee R. (1989), 'Inter-industry studies of structure and performance', in R. Schmalensee and R.D. Willig (eds.), *The Handbook of Industrial Organization,* vol. II, Amsterdam, North-Holland, chapter 16.
US Department of Justice (1984), *Merger Guidelines,* reprinted in *Trade Regulation Reporter* 13, 104, Chicago, Commerce Clearing House.

Werden,G.J. (1991), 'Antitrust policy toward horizontal mergers: comment', *American Economic Review,* 81, 1002–6.

Williamson, O.E. (1968), 'Economies as an antitrust defense: the welfare tradeoffs', *American Economic Review,* 58, 18–36.

Willig, R.D. (1991), 'Notes on IO theory and merger analysis' *Brookings Papers on Economic Activity: Microeconomics,* 281–312.

Chapter 21

Vertical mergers
Vertical mergers in multi-product industries and Edgeworth's paradox of taxation

Michael A. Salinger

1 Introduction

The fundamental difference between comparative statics for single- and multi-product monopolists is a point that seems to have been largely forgotten; and its implication for the effects of vertical mergers have been completely overlooked. In 1897, Edgeworth (1925) showed that a tax on one of two substitute goods sold by a monopolist can result in the reduction of both prices. This result is known as Edgeworth's paradox of taxation. Seligman (1910) dismissed the result as an example of how mathematical analysis could produce absurd propositions, which prompted Edgeworth's (1899) reply.[1]

Although the result seems no longer to be widely known, Seligman's comment has prompted several of the giants of economics to address this issue. Edgeworth (1910) himself returned to the question of whether the paradox is likely to occur more than a decade after the initial exchange with Seligman. He conceded that '(t)he improbability

This article first appeared in *The Journal of Industrial Economics*, 1991, Vol. 34, pp. 545–56.
I have received helpful comments from Stanley Besen, Severin Borenstein, Alan Fisher, Elizabeth Jensen, Peter Reiss, John Vickers, two anonymous referees, and participants in seminars at Columbia and NERA.

[1] The responses appear anachronous. Edgeworth's paper was published originally in 1897 but was in Italian. The 1925 date is for the English translation in a collection of Edgeworth's papers. The 1910 date on Seligman's is for the third edition of *Shifting and Incidence*, which is the earliest one I could find. Edgeworth's comments were on the second edition, published in 1899.

of the event . . . is considerable' (p. 299), but cited the relative ease of constructing examples in which it arises, as evidence that 'it (i.e., the improbability) is not enormous. . . .' (p. 299). Hotelling (1932) made the most compelling argument to date that the paradox might occur in practice. He produced a quite plausible discrete example concerning different classes of railway service in which the paradox arises. Coase (1946) provided an excellent graphical presentation of why the paradox can arise.

Vertical mergers provide an application in which the neglect of joint demand is crucial. In current antitrust enforcement, there is a general presumption that vertical mergers are not anticompetitive. The successive monopoly model, frequently accredited to Spengler (1950) but originally due to Cournot (1838), is a major intellectual impetus for that policy. It says that a merger of successive monopolists results in a reduction of the final good price by eliminating the double marginalization. Formally, the model is equivalent to the point that a single-product monopolist reduces its price in response to a cost increase.

In non-technical discussions of vertical mergers, one finds concerns that remaining unintegrated rivals might be foreclosed. In the Brown Shoe decision,[2] for example, the Supreme Court argued that Kinney outlets would no longer sell shoes manufactured by Brown's competitors. Regardless of the merits of the argument in that particular case, there are several more recent examples in which similar issues arise.

In the mid 1980s, both Coke and Pepsi acquired some of their major bottlers. A Coke or Pepsi franchise contract forbids the bottler from distributing other brands of colas, but allows it to sell non-colas produced by other companies. Most Coke and Pepsi franchise bottlers distribute a number of 'allied brands', such as Seven Up and Dr Pepper. Did these mergers create an incentive for Coke or Pepsi to raise the price of the allied brands to increase the sales of their own brands? Indeed, could they use their control over their bottlers to reduce competition from the allied brands so much that they would find it profitable to raise the prices of their own brands?

The cable television industry provides still another current example of this issue. Time Warner both operates cable franchises and owns two major pay cable services, Home Box Office and Cinemax. Similarly, another cable franchise operator, Viacom, owns both Showtime and The Movie Channel. Do Time Warner and Viacom have an incentive either to raise the price of the pay services they do not own or simply not to offer some services in order to increase demand for the services they do own? If so, does their ability to disadvantage competing services give them an opportunity to charge more for their own services than an unaffiliated franchise would?

The successive monopoly model provides essentially no insight into these issues because it does not take account of unintegrated firms. To address the validity of the concerns, one must assume that the downstream firm (the bottler or the cable franchise) sells at least two products. One can then analyse the effect of a merger

[2] *Brown Shoe Co. v. United States*, 370 US 294, 1962.

between the downstream monopolist and one of its suppliers. Given Edgeworth's paradox and the formal equivalence of the successive monopoly model to the analysis of a cost decrease, it is not surprising that the qualitative result of the successive monopoly model does not extend to the multi-product case.

The next section of this chapter briefly presents Edgeworth's paradox and derives the welfare implications of it. Section 3 discusses the application of the paradox to vertical mergers and presents a numerical example in which the paradox still holds despite a price reduction by the remaining unintegrated upstream firm. Section 4 contains some concluding comments.

2   Edgeworth's paradox

Consider a monopolist that sells two substitute goods. The demand for the two goods is given by

$$q_i = q_i(P_1, P_2) \frac{\partial q_i}{\partial P_i} < 0, \quad \frac{\partial q_i}{\partial P_j} > 0 \quad i = 1, 2 \quad j = 2, 1 \tag{1}$$

where P_i and Q_i represent the price and quantity of good i, respectively. Assume that the monopolist has constant per-unit costs w_1 and w_2, which may differ from the true social costs, c_1 and c_2, either because of taxes or market power upstream.

Assuming constant returns to scale, the monopolist's profits are given by

$$\Pi = (P_1 - w_1)q_1(P_1, P_2) + (P_2 - w_2)q_2(P_1, P_2) \equiv f(P_1, P_2; w_1, w_2). \tag{2}$$

The first-order conditions for profit maximization are

$$\frac{\partial f}{\partial P_i} = q_i + (P_1 - w_1)\frac{\partial q_1}{\partial P_i} + (P_2 - w_2)\frac{\partial q_2}{\partial P_i} = 0 \quad i = 1, 2. \tag{3}$$

The second-order conditions for a maximum are

$$\frac{\partial^2 f}{\partial P_1^2} < 0 \tag{4}$$

$$\frac{\partial^2 f}{\partial P_1^2} \frac{\partial^2 f}{\partial P_2^2} - \left(\frac{\partial^2 f}{\partial P_1 \partial P_2}\right)^2 > 0. \tag{5}$$

To find the effect of a change in w_1, totally differentiate (3) and solve for

$$\frac{\partial P_1}{\partial w_1} = \frac{1}{D_1}\left[\frac{\partial^2 f}{\partial P_2^2}\frac{\partial q_1}{\partial P_1} - \frac{\partial^2 f}{\partial P_1 \partial P_2}\frac{\partial q_1}{\partial P_2}\right] \tag{6}$$

$$\frac{\partial P_2}{\partial w_2} = \frac{1}{D_1}\left[\frac{\partial^2 f}{\partial P_1^2}\frac{\partial q_1}{\partial P_2} - \frac{\partial^2 f}{\partial P_1 \partial P_2}\frac{\partial q_1}{\partial P_1}\right] \tag{7}$$

where

$$D_1 = \frac{\partial^f}{\partial P_1^2} \frac{\partial^2 f}{\partial P_2^2} - \left(\frac{\partial^2 f}{\partial P_1 \partial P_2}\right)^2.$$

The paradox is that the second-order conditions do not imply a definite sign for either (6) or (7). The one case that can be ruled out is the combination of $\partial P_1/\partial w_1 < 0$ and $\partial P_2/\partial w_1 > 0$. Salinger (1987) contains a proof.

Figure 21.1 shows a case in which an increase in w_1 causes both prices to drop.[3] The lines represent first-order conditions with respect to prices. The solid lines are for a lower value of w_1. An increase in w_1 causes the first-order conditions with respect to P_1 to shift to the right, indicating that a higher P_1 maximizes profits for any given value of P_2. This shift corresponds to the result that a single-product monopolist increases its price in response to a cost increase. The increase in w_1 also causes the first-order condition with respect to P_2 to shift down. Given any P_1, the increase in w_1 gives the monopolist an incentive to lower P_2 to induce customers to purchase good 2 instead of good 1. Figure 21.1 makes it clear that the new profit-maximizing prices must lie to the right of the old $\partial f/\partial P_1$ schedule and below the old schedule. Regardless of the shape of the first order conditions, that region cannot contain any point 'northwest' of the original profit-maximizing point.[4]

The intuition that an increase in w_1 must cause an increase in P_1 fails because it is based on the result for a single-product monopolist, in which all other prices are held constant. In this model, another price changes. Specifically, the price of good 2, which is a substitute for good 1, can go down. If $\partial^2 f/\partial P_1 \partial P_2 > 0$, a reduction in the price of good 2 induces a reduction in the price of good 1, all else equal. This effect can, in principle, dominate.

As Edgeworth showed in his initial exposition of the paradox, an increase in w_1 causes Q_1 to drop even when it lowers P_1. Viewed in this light, the paradox is somewhat less puzzling. Moreover, given that a tax causes the output of at least one of the goods to drop, it is not as obvious as it might have initially appeared that welfare improves when both prices drop.

To address this question, assume that the economy consists of a single representative consumer who owns all firms in the economy and receives all tax receipts as a lump-sum transfer. For simplicity, assume that there is perfect competition and constant returns upstream. These assumptions insure that upstream profits are 0 and therefore allow us to ignore them. Let t_1 and t_2 be taxes on the inputs for each good and let $T = t_1 Q_1 + t_2 Q_2$ be total tax receipts. The consumer's indirect utility function, which is a measure of welfare, is given by $V = V(P_1, P_2, \Pi, T)$. The effect of a change in w_1 on utility is given by

---

[3] Coase (1946) contains a similar diagram.
[4] In figure 21.1, it is assumed that $\partial^2 f/\partial P_1 \partial P_2 > 0$. It is possible for the cross-partial of the profit function to be negative. If so, then $\partial P_1/\partial w_1 > 0$ and $\partial P_2/\partial w_1 < 0$. Note that the sign of the cross-partial does not determine whether the goods are strategic substitutes or strategic complements. (See Bulow, Geanakoplos, and Klemperer, 1985). Strategic substitutability and complementarity turns on the slope of best-response functions. The lines in figure 21.1 are first-order conditions.

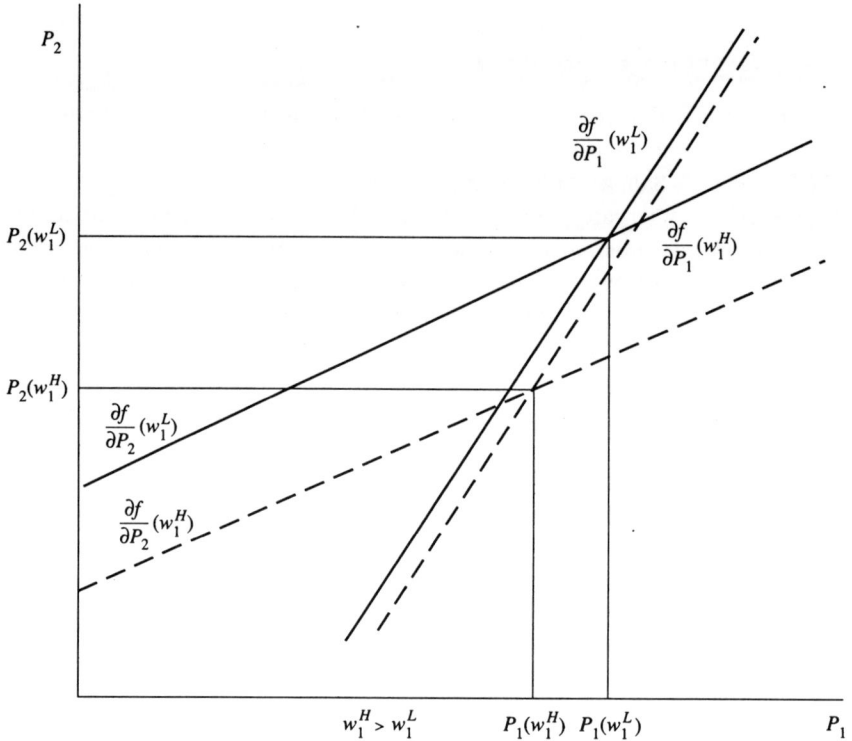

Figure 21.1 Edgeworth's paradox

$$\frac{dV}{dt_1} = \frac{\partial V}{\partial P_1}\frac{\partial P_1}{\partial w_1} + \frac{\partial V}{\partial P_2}\frac{\partial P_2}{\partial w_1} + \frac{\partial v}{\partial \Pi}\frac{\partial \Pi}{\partial_1} + \frac{\partial V}{\partial T}Q_1 + \frac{\partial V}{\partial T}t_1\frac{\partial Q_1}{\partial w_1} + \frac{\partial V}{\partial T}t_2\frac{\partial Q_2}{\partial w_1}. \quad (8)$$

The third term reflects the change in the profits of the downstream monopolist.[5] The fourth and fifth terms reflect the change in tax receipts from good 1 while the sixth term captures the change in tax receipts from good 2. Let γ represent the marginal utility of income. Imposing Roy's identity on the first two terms and the envelope theorem on the third reduces (8) to:[6]

$$\frac{\partial V}{\partial t_1} = \gamma\left[-Q_1\frac{\partial P_1}{\partial w_1} - Q_2\frac{\partial P_2}{\partial w_1} + t_1\frac{\partial Q_1}{\partial w_1} + t_2\frac{\partial Q_2}{\partial w_1}\right]. \quad (9)$$

In assessing (9), begin by letting $t_1 = 0$ and $t_2 = 0$. That is, examine the welfare implications of a small increase in t_1 when there are no initial distortions upstream. If $\partial P_1/\partial w_1$ and $\partial P_2/\partial w_1$ are both negative, such an increase improves welfare. This result can be compared with the competitive case, in which a small increase in w_1

---

[5] Because of perfect competition and constant returns upstream, $dw_1/dt_1 = 1$.
[6] $\partial Q_i/\partial w_1$ can be found as $(\partial Q_i/\partial P_1)(\partial P_1/\partial w_1) + (\partial Q_i/\partial P_2)(\partial P_2/\partial w_1)$.

induces no welfare loss,[7] and the single-product monopoly case, in which a small increase in w_1 lowers welfare. Note also that an increase in w_1 can improve welfare even if $\partial P_1/\partial w_1$ is positive, provided that it is not too large and $\partial P_2/\partial w_1$ is sufficiently negative.

When t_1 and t_2 differ from 0, then two additional terms enter the welfare calculations. As Edgeworth showed, $\partial Q_2/\partial w_1$ can be negative. When it is, (9) implies that $\partial V/\partial w_1$ is also negative. This result confirms the intuition that if the outputs of both goods go up, welfare also increases. If $\partial Q_2/\partial w_1$ is positive, the welfare consequences of a change in w_1 are harder to ascertain. Because the sign of (9) depends on the upstream margins, one cannot say anything about it without being specific about the initial distortions.

3   Application to vertical mergers

To adapt the above model to vertical mergers, equation (3) should be interpreted as the profit function for a downstream firm that has a monopoly over two products.[8] At least some of the inputs for each product come from different firms. The upstream prices of those inputs, w_1 and w_2, exceed c_1 and c_2 because the inputs are not supplied competitively and because contracts in which the marginal price equals marginal cost cannot be written and enforced.[9] If the monopolist merges with the supplier of the inputs for one of the goods (good 1, let us say), it can subsequently get those inputs at

---

[7] See Atkinson and Stiglitz (1980), p. 368, who in turn attribute the point to Samuelson (1964). The 'competitive case' means here that there is perfect competition both upstream and downstream. With perfect competition downstream, the third term of (10) would equal $-\gamma Q_1(1 - \partial P_1/\partial w_1)$.

[8] The downstream monopolist has to be a monopolist in the sense that it is the sole seller of the two particular brands in question. Other upstream brands and downstream firms can exist, provided that the 'monopolist' has an exclusive contract to handle the two upstream brands that are being modelled explicitly. If so, (1) and (2) represent the demand curves perceived by the monopolist and can be embedded within a model of downstream oligopoly. In general, one would expect any oligopolist equilibrium downstream to reinforce any cases of Edgeworth's paradox. That is, suppose that an input price decrease induced the monopolist to raise its prices downstream, holding constant the prices of its competitors. If the reaction functions are all upward sloping (i.e., if the downstream goods are all strategic substitutes), then the 'initial' set of price increases would induce the downstream rivals to raise their prices as well.

[9] Indeed, a relatively simple contract would seem to reproduce vertical integration. As Bernheim and Whinston (1985) show, both upstream firms charging a two-part tariff with a unit-price equal to marginal cost is a Nash equilibrium in a model like this one. Under such circumstances, a vertical merger would have no effect, except possibly to alter the initial fee. As they point out, however, and as Rey and Tirole (1986) emphasize, such a contract places all risk on the downstream firm. If the downstream firm is a relatively inefficient bearer of risk, as is arguably the case in soft drinks, it might be desirable to shift some of the risk upstream even if doing so creates a double marginalization. Also, the effects of vertical integration can be achieved contractually in their model because optimal behaviour has to be elicited from only the downstream firm. In many cases, however, behaviour at both stages is an issue. In soft drinks, for example, the upstream firms advertise. In cable television, the service providers choose program quality. Typically, a contract is made incentive compatible by giving an agent all of the marginal benefits of his actions. It is not practical, however to write a contract that gives both the upstream and the downstream firms the marginal benefits of increased sales.

marginal cost. If the monopolist did not sell a second good or, alternatively, if demand for the two goods were independent the merger would simply result in a reduction in the price of good 1. That is the successive monopoly model. When the goods are substitutes for each other, however, the preceding analysis suggests that the elimination of the double marginalization can have one of three effects. Both prices can fall, both can rise, or the price of good 1 can fall and the price of good 2 can go up.

The elimination of the double marginalization is not, however, the only effect of a vertical merger. The remaining unintegrated firm will typically have an incentive to respond. When a reduction in w_1 causes the downstream firm to purchase less of the input for good 2, one might expect firm 2 to want to lower w_2. It can be shown that when $\partial P_2/\partial w_1$ is negative, $\partial P_1/\partial w_2$ and $\partial P_2/\partial w_2$ must both be positive. A reduction in w_2 would therefore have the opposite effect of and possibly dominate the reduction in w_1.[10]

Addressing the effect of a change in w_2 in response to a vertical merger raises complicated issues that frequently arise in the analysis of vertical relationships.[11] If the number of firms involved is small, bargaining is likely to occur. In addition, contracts can be complicated.[12] While a more general analysis of these issues would be of interest, we can use a special case to demonstrate that a vertical merger can cause both prices to increase even if the remaining unintegrated upstream firm lowers its price. The three special assumptions that are made here are (i) linear demand, (ii) price-taking by the downstream firm, and (iii) Nash-in-price competition by the upstream firms.

With linear demand curves, the analysis is simpler if we work with the inverse demand curves.[13] Thus let

$$P_i = \alpha_i - \beta_{ii}Q_i - \beta_{ij}Q_j \quad i = 1,2 \quad j = 2,1. \tag{10}$$

Substituting (10) into (3) and solving for Q_1 and Q_2 yields the downstream firm's profit-maximizing quantities

$$q_i = \frac{1}{D_2}[2\beta_{jj}(\alpha_i - w_i) - (\beta_{ij} + \beta_{ji})(\alpha_j - w_j)] \quad i = 1,2 \quad j = 2,1 \tag{11}$$

where

[10] For linear demand curves for the final goods, the optimal response of the unintegrated firm is to lower its price. For non-linear demand curves, however the optimal response might be a price increase, which would cause the final prices to go up even further. See Salinger (1988a).

[11] The only post-merger response that I consider is a price reduction. For models that allow for more general post-merger responses by other firms, see Ordover, Saloner, and Salop (1990) and Hart and Tirole (1990).

[12] For a model of vertical mergers when more complicated contracts are allowed, see Hart and Tirole (1990).

[13] In working with linear demand curves, it is important to check that the quantities and prices are all positive. In the following discussion, I will assume that the necessary parameter restrictions hold. For a more general discussion, see Salinger (1988a).

$$D_2 = 4\beta_{11}\beta_{22} - (\beta_{12} + \beta_{21})^2.$$

Substituting (11) into (10) gives the downstream prices as a function of w_1 and w_2

$$P_i = \alpha_i - \frac{1}{D_2}\{[2\beta_{ii}\beta_{jj} - \beta_{ij}(\beta_{ij} + \beta_{ji})](\alpha_i - w_i) + \beta_{ii}(\beta_{ij} - \beta_{ji})(\alpha_j - w_j)\}$$
$$i = 1,2 \quad j = 2,1. \tag{12}$$

Equation (12) is linear in w_1 and w_2, so the derivatives of the downstream prices with respect to the prices of inputs can be seen from the coefficients. In particular, the condition for Edgeworth's paradox to hold (for good 1, say) is

$$2\beta_{11}\beta_{22} - \beta_{12}(\beta_{12} + \beta_{21}) < 0. \tag{13}$$

Before solving the upstream equilibrium, note that (13) can hold only if $\beta_{12} > \beta_{21}$. To see why this must be the case, note from (12) that this condition is necessary for $\partial P_2/\partial w_1$ to be negative. As was mentioned above, $\partial P_2/\partial w_1$ is necessary (but not sufficient) for $\partial P_1/\partial w_1$ to hold. Global welfare analysis requires $\beta_{ij} = \beta_{ji}$, which is the integrability condition. Thus, linear demand curves cannot be the basis of a global welfare analysis of Edgeworth's paradox.[14]

Equation (11) represents the derived demand curves faced by the two upstream firms. Taking the other upstream price as given, the profit-maximizing condition for an upstream firm is

$$\frac{\partial \Pi_i}{\partial w_i} = \frac{1}{D_2}[2\beta_{jj}\alpha_i - (\beta_{ij} + \beta_{ji})\alpha_j + 2\beta_{jj}c_i - 4\beta_{jj}w_i + (\beta_{ij} + \beta_{ji})w_j] = 0$$
$$i = 1,2 \quad j = 2,1. \tag{14}$$

Solving (14) yields the Nash-in-price equilibrium prices (w_i^N)

$$w_i^N = \alpha_i - \frac{1}{2D_3}\left[(\alpha_i - c_i) + \frac{\beta_{ij} + \beta_{ji}}{4\beta_{jj}}(\alpha_j - c_j)\right] \tag{15}$$

where

$$D_3 = 1 - \frac{(\beta_{ij} + \beta_{ji})^2}{16\beta_{ii}\beta_{jj}}.$$

There are two natural options for modelling the post-merger equilibrium. The first is to assume that the unintegrated firm sets w_2, after which the merged entity sets the final prices, P_1 and P_2. This sequence entails the implicit assumption that the merged entity transfers the upstream version of good 1 at marginal cost. One might suspect that there would be a strategic advantage to setting a still lower transfer price in order to reduce the downstream division's demand for the upstream version of good 2,

---

[14] With non-linear demand curves, Edgeworth's paradox can arise when the integrability conditions hold. See Hotelling (1932).

which would in turn cause the unintegrated firm to lower its price. To try to formalize this notion, one can assume that in the first stage of the game, the merged entity sets w_1 at the same time as the unintegrated firm sets w_2. The downstream division is then told to maximize its stand-alone profits taking w_1 (as well as w_2) as given. As it turns out, the optimal w_1 under these assumptions is c_1. An intuitive explanation is that if w_1 and w_2 are set simultaneously, then the monopolist is taking w_3 as given. Since its choice of w_1 does not affect w_2, the transfer price has no strategic role. One could, of course, introduce a strategic role for the transfer price by assuming that the monopolist sets w_1, then the unintegrated firm sets w_2, and then the monopolist sets P_1 and P_2. There does not seem to be any rationale, though, for why the monopolist would have such a first-mover advantage.

Because the monopolist uses c_1 as the transfer price, the post-merger price of good 2 (w_2^P is the solution to (14) with $w_1 = c_1$. It is given by

$$w_2^P = \frac{\alpha_2 + c_2}{2} - \frac{(\beta_{12} + \beta_{21})(\alpha_1 - c_1)}{4\beta_{11}}. \tag{16}$$

To find P_1 before the merger, substitute (15) into (12). To find P_1 after the merger let w_1 equal c_1 and use equation (19) to substitute for w_2 in (15). The difference in those prices is

$$\Delta P_1 = \frac{1}{D_2}\left[2\beta_{11}\beta_{22} - \frac{3}{4}\beta_{12}^2 - \beta_{12}\beta_{21} - \frac{1}{4}\beta_{21}^2\right](c_1 - w_1). \tag{17}$$

It is easy to construct examples for which (17) is positive. One such example is

$$P_1 = 3 - 4Q_1 - 3Q_2 \tag{18}$$

$$P_2 = 2 - \frac{1}{2}Q_1 - Q_2 \tag{19}$$

and $c_1 = c_2 = 1$. The pre-merger upstream prices are $w_1^N = 11/9$ and $w_2^N = 10/9$. The pre-merger final good prices are $P_1 = 49/27$ and $P_2 = 46/27$. After the merger, $w_2^B = 17/16$. Note that the remaining upstream producer nearly halves its price–cost margin. Nevertheless the post-merger prices are $P_1 = 11/6$ and $P_2 = 85/48$, which are higher than the pre-merger prices.

In general, mergers in oligopolistic industries can be unprofitable. For example, Salant, Switzer, and Reynolds (1983) showed that a merger by two Cournot oligopolists lowers their joint profits. It is easy to check that joint profits go up in the above example, but there is no reason to restrict our attention to this case. Vertical mergers are almost universally profitable in this model. Mergers can be unprofitable in models of oligopoly because of the reactions they induce in other firms. In Salant, Switzer, and Reynolds, the merging firms reduce their own output. The reduction would be profitable if other firms kept their output constant, but turns out to be unprofitable because the other firms respond by expanding output. In this model, the only firm that can respond to the merger is the remaining upstream producer. If it does not change its price (i.e., if $w_2^N = w_2^P$), then the merging firm can earn the same profits it earned prior to the merger by choosing the pre-merger downstream prices. Any change it makes in its prices must increase its profits. If the unintegrated firm responds by lowering its price, then the merger is still more profitable; monopolists benefit from reductions in input costs. Thus, the only way that a merger could be unprofitable in this model would be if it induced an increase in the upstream price.[15]

4   Conclusion

Until relatively recently, the thrust of the economics literature on vertical integration was that as a matter of pure theory, it could not be anticompetitive. The possibility of price increases due to vertical integration in the variable proportions case has been understood for some time, but it is hard to imagine that model as a serious basis for any public policy concern with vertical mergers. The implication of this chapter as well as Ordover, Saloner, and Salop (1990), Hart and Tirole (1990), and Salinger (1988b) is that the effects of vertical mergers are an empirical question.

From the standpoint of both theory and the history of economic thought, the most interesting aspect of the model in this chapter is the possibility that a vertical merger can cause both prices to rise. There is a danger, though, that people will consider the paradox merely a theoretical curiosity, somewhat like Giffen goods, and in turn judge the model to provide no new insight into appropriate antitrust policy towards vertical mergers. That would be a mistake. In this model, both prices do not have to rise for a vertical merger to lower welfare. When one price goes down and the other goes up, the latter effect might dominate. The policy dilemma in such circumstances is how to evaluate the trade-off. Of course, that question is not an easy one to answer.

---

[15] One issue that has been important in the Chicago School critique of foreclosure theories and has been addressed explicitly by Ordover, Saloner, and Salop (1990) and Hart and Tirole (1990) is the possibility that unintegrated firms will respond to vertical mergers by undertaking vertical mergers of their own. In this model, a merger between the merged firm and the remaining unintegrated firm would increase profits (or, at least, would not lower them). The subsequent merger would, however, be horizontal and might therefore violate the antitrust laws. Such a concern would be particularly serious in a case like the soft drink industry. Consider, for example a merger between Coke and single Coke/Dr Pepper bottler. Suppose that the merger would raise prices in that area but that a three-way merger between Coke, Dr Pepper, and the bottler would lower prices. Presumably it would not make sense to let Coke and Dr Pepper merge (assuming that such a merger would lower competition in the other areas where they both sell soft drinks) even if the merger, in combination with the merger with the bottler, lowered prices in one area. In addition, none of the results of the model require that $w_2 > c_2$. If the inputs for the second good are supplied competitively, then a merger with a seller of the inputs for good 2 will not offset any detrimental effects of a merger between the downstream monopolist and the seller of the input for good 1.

References

Atkinson, A.B. and J.E. Stiglitz (1980), *Lectures on Public Economics*, New York, McGraw Hill.

Bernheim, B. and M.D. Whinston (1985), 'Common marketing agency as a device for facilitating collusion', *The Rand Journal of Economics*, 16, 269–81.

Bulow, J.I., J.D. Geanakoplos, and P.D. Klemperer (1985), 'Multimarket oligopoly: strategic substitutes and complements', *Journal of Political Economy*, 93, 488–511.

Coase, R.H. (1946), 'Monopoly pricing with interrelated costs and demands', *Economica*, 13, 278–94.

Cournot, A. (1838), *Recherches sur les Principes Mathématiques de la Théorie des Richesses*, Paris, Hachette.

Edgeworth, F.Y. (1899), 'Professor Seligman on the mathematical method in political economy', *Economic Journal*, 9, 286–315.

(1910), 'Applications of probabilities to economics', *Economic Journal*, 20, 284–304.

Edgeworth, F.Y. (1925), 'The pure theory of monopoly', in *Papers Relating to Political Economy*, vol. I, New York, Burt Franklin.

Hart, O. and J. Tirole (1990), 'Vertical mergers and market foreclosure', *Brookings Papers on Economic Activity - Microeconomics*, 205–76.

Hotelling, H.H. (1932), 'Edgeworth's paradox of taxation and the nature of supply and demand functions', *Journal of Political Economy*, 40, 577–615.

Ordover, J.A., G. Saloner, and S. C. Salop (1990), 'Equilibrium vertical foreclosure', *American Economic Review*, 80, 127–142.

Rey, P. and J. Tirole (1986), 'The logic of vertical restraints', *American Economic Review*, 76, 921–39.

Salant, S.W., S. Switzer, and R.J. Reynold (1983), 'Losses from horizontal merger: the effects of an exogenous change in industry structure on Cournot–Nash equilibrium', *Quarterly Journal of Economics*, 98, 185–99.

Salinger, M.A. (1987), 'Vertical mergers and market foreclosure with differentiated products', First Boston Working Paper Series FB-86–29R.

(1988a), 'Edgeworth's paradox of taxation and vertical mergers', mimeo, Boston University.

(1988b), 'Vertical mergers and market foreclosure', *Quarterly Journal of Economics*, 103, 345–56.

(1989), 'The meaning of upstream and downstream and the implications for modeling vertical mergers', *Journal of Industrial Economics*, 37, 373–88.

Samuelson, P.A. (1964), 'Discussion', *American Economic Review*, Papers and Proceedings, 54, 93–96.

Seligman, E.R.A. (1910), *The Shifting and Incidence of Taxation*, Third Edition, New York, Columbia University Press.

Spengler, J.J. (1950), 'Vertical integration and antitrust policy', *Journal of Political Economy*, 58, 347–52.

Chapter 22

Enforcement of the US merger guidelines
Empirical evidence on FTC enforcement of the merger guidelines

Malcolm B. Coate and Fred S. McChesney

1 Introduction

The 1982/4 'merger guidelines' adopted by the Antitrust Division of the Department of Justice (DOJ) and followed by the Federal Trade Commission (FTC) marked important antitrust policy changes by the Reagan administration. The Herfindahl index replaced the four-firm ratios used in the old (1968) guidelines as the measure of concentration. Other non-concentration factors (barriers to entry, ease of collusion) were elevated in importance. In the 1984 revision of the 1982 guidelines, efficiency considerations were for the first time generally included as a relevant factor.

However, commentators who applauded the newer guidelines have complained subsequently that the Reagan administration did not apply them. The objections of two veteran academic anti-trusters, Krattenmaker and Pitofsky (1988, p. 232), are typical:

This article first appeared in *Economic Inquiry*, 1992, Vol. 30, pp. 277–93.
Richard Higgins helped shape several points analysed here while co-authoring an earlier paper with us (Coate *et al.* 1990). He, George Bittlingmayer, Thomas DiLorenzo, David Haddock, James Langenfeld, William Shughart, and Robert Tollison provided helpful comments. This article is based on nonpublic data obtained from Federal Trade Commission internal files. The Commission's General Counsel has authorized publication of such data in aggregated form under commission Rule 5.12(c), 16 C.F.R. 5.12(c). The analysis and conclusions presented herein are those of the authors and do not purport to represent the view of the Commission, or of any individual commissioner or the official position of any commission bureau.

Certainly, in many respects, the announced merger guidelines are a substantial accomplishment. This accomplishment, however, has been almost completely undercut by the Administration's behaviour in ignoring those guidelines in practice and instead enforcing, without any public explanation, a merger policy that was not only exceptionally lenient but substantially at odds with professed standards.

In an earlier paper (Coate *et al*, 1990), we, along with co-author Richard Higgins, tested one hypothesis why merger policy (at least at the FTC in 1982–6) has departed from mere enforcement of the guidelines: politics. We showed how external pressures imposed on the Commission by Congress to block mergers, independent of the factors identified in the guidelines as meriting a merger challenge, are a statistically significant factor in the FTC's decision whether to challenge a merger.

In the present contribution, we use the same data – 70 horizontal mergers from 1982 to 1986 – to examine in greater detail the charges that the FTC has not followed the guidelines, plus several related issues not considered in our earlier article. These include the extent to which various guidelines factors are either necessary or sufficient for the Commission to vote to challenge a merger, and the role of the new efficiency criterion in merger evaluation. An econometric model is presented as one approach to determine how the FTC balances the various guidelines factors. This allows an estimate of the relative importance and influence of lawyers and economists in the evaluation process. Finally, the data also permit an appraisal of the extent to which a structuralist or Chicago approach to competition issues dominated merger votes at the FTC during the relevant period.

Section 2 discusses briefly the factors identified in the merger guidelines and the process by which the Commission determines whether to oppose a proposed merger. That section also identifies several testable hypotheses concerning the Commission's reliance on the guidelines variables. Section 3 then explains the data to be used for testing. Section 4, the bulk of the paper, presents empirical evidence concerning the FTC's use of the guidelines and related issues.

2   Evaluating mergers at the Federal Trade Commission

The merger guidelines

The Federal Trade Commission enforces (along with the Justice Department) the federal antitrust laws, including those applicable to mergers. The Commission takes formal action through a majority vote of the sitting (ordinarily five) commissioners. Commissioners vote whether to challenge a merger on the basis of formal staff memoranda that the lawyers of the Bureau of Competition (BC) and the economists of the Bureau of Economics (BE) prepare and submit separately. The memoranda are based in turn on data submitted to the Commission by would-be merging partners as required by the Hart–Scott–Rodino Act, and on information developed independently by FTC staff lawyers and economists. Mergers that raise greater anticompetitive concerns usually elicit a supplemental FTC demand for more information, known as a Hart–Scott–Rodino 'second request'. The parties to the merger also may present their own analyses to the staff, and thus may influence either the Bureau of Competition or Bureau of Economics evaluation.

In analysing a prospective merger, the FTC claims that its own process follows the Department of Justice merger guidelines.[1] The current guidelines were promulgated in June 1982 (and fine-tuned somewhat in 1984), replacing the guidelines issued in 1968. They focus on preventing a price increase from enhanced market power due to a merger, particularly when no countervailing efficiencies are present. To determine whether such a price increase is likely, the guidelines call for examination of several factors: concentration (including definition of relevant markets), entry barriers, ease of collusion, efficiency, and failing-firm status.[2]

Concentration analysis, based on the Herfindahl–Hirschman index (HHI), is probably the guidelines' best-known aspect. The 1984 version establishes three index classifications:

1 Where the post-merger Herfindahl index is under 1000, the merger will be challenged only 'in extraordinary circumstances'. Thus, a Herfindahl index of 1000 is a safe harbour; mergers falling below that level will rarely be challenged.

2 If the post-merger Herfindahl index is between 1000 and 1800 and the merger increases the Herfindahl by 100 points, the government is 'likely' to challenge these transactions unless other factors suggest 'the merger is not likely substantially to lessen competition'.

3 Finally, for a post-merger index value over 1800, a challenge is 'likely' if the merger increases the index by over 50 points, unless other factors suggest 'the merger is not likely substantially to lessen competition'. However, there will be a challenge in all but 'extraordinary circumstances' if the merger raises the Herfindahl index by over 100 points to a level substantially above 1800.

The remaining (non-concentration) factors in the guidelines influence the decision within each Herfindahl index class. Ease of entry will prevent current rivals from raising price for any extended period, and so lowers the likelihood of a merger challenge. Entry is considered easy if a new firm can break into the market within two years of a merger, and difficult if entry would take longer. The guidelines note that likelihood of entry is a function of sunk assets, industry growth rate, economies of scale, and the specific capital needed to compete. But no quantitative measures of these entry determinants are provided, leaving one with the practical two-year standard.

---

[1] The FTC's 'Statement concerning horizontal mergers' of 14 June 1982 noted that the 1982 guidelines had been a joint effort of the DOJ and the Commission staffs, and that the guidelines 'will be given considerable weight' in FTC merger evaluations.

[2] Of course, antitrust lawyers and economists differ considerably about the relevance, measure, and even definition of such things as concentration, efficiency, and entry barriers. See, for example, Demsetz (1982). In this article, we take as given the definitions and measures provided in the merger guidelines and the relevance of the variables included therein. Our interest is solely in the positive issue whether the guidelines are followed in government merger enforcement.

The guidelines analyse ease of collusion or dominant-firm pricing (for reasons other than entry barriers) through proxies: product homogeneity, spatial similarities of merging firms, information available in the market, ease of fringe expansion, market conduct, and past performance. No weights for those proxies are given. Although consideration of collusion would appear necessary in all cases to tell an economically plausible anticompetitive story, the guidelines state that the collusion factors will be most important when the merger decision is a close call. (For simplicity, we refer to these other factors under the heading 'collusion' although they may sometimes refer to dominant-firm behaviour.)

Greater efficiency (scale economies or lower transportation costs, for example) was generally excluded from consideration in the 1968 guidelines. But the 1984 guidelines listed efficiency gains as a factor that may save a merger that otherwise would be challenged. Efficiencies must be shown by 'clear and convincing' evidence, a higher standard than that for anticompetitive factors (high concentration, entry barriers, and ease of collusion).[3]

The final guidelines factor discussed is merger with a failing firm. If one merging firm will soon exit the market anyway, fewer competitive concerns arise. Since the Supreme Court has accepted this argument as a legal defence, antitrust regulators are unlikely to challenge a merger with a failing firm.

Empirical issues

The merger guidelines are supposed to structure merger regulation to make enforcement decisions consistent, increasing predictability and lowering private transaction costs. Subsequent application of the guidelines, however, has resulted in two general types of complaint.

Failure to follow stated guidelines

Many commentators complain that antitrust enforcers do not follow their own guidelines. Some, such as Leddy (1986) and White (1987), claim that the Justice Department and the FTC have ignored mergers in the concentration ranges that the guidelines label as likely to elicit challenge and have targeted only those with greater Herfindahl index numbers.[4] Similarly, Krattenmaker and Pitofsky state (1988, p. 226), 'What is clear, but is very difficult to document by people who lack access to the confidential H–S–R (Hart–Scott–Rodino) reports and DOJ and FTC internal memor-

[3] This higher standard may betray an institutional bias against case-by-case efficiencies. Policy makers argue, however, that the other guidelines factors are themselves designed to tolerate some chance of anticompetitive effects in mergers, to insure that efficiency-enhancing mergers are allowed without the need to prove efficiencies explicitly. If efficiencies are already incorporated in other factors, one would expect the case-specific efficiency defence would succeed less often.

[4] Just the opposite complaint was raised about enforcement under the 1968 guidelines. Rogowsky (1984), for example, finds empirically that prior to 1982 the Justice Department brought many cases involving such small levels of concentration that under the applicable (1968) guidelines the mergers should have been allowed to proceed.

anda, is that the agencies have . . . not enforced the guidelines. As described below, access to the documents Krattenmaker and Pitofsky refer to permits us to evaluate their claims.'

Likewise, questions have been raised about whether some finding of important barriers to entry is required before a merger will be challenged. Almost all economists would deem the existence of significant entry barriers a necessary condition for mergers to reduce welfare appreciably. But the guidelines leave it unclear whether barriers are necessary for a merger challenge, stating that '(t)he more difficult entry into the market is, the more likely the Department is to challenge the merger'. Indeed, because the guidelines state that significant mergers in concentrated markets will be challenged in all but extraordinary circumstances, enforcers presumably believe entry to be almost impossible in those cases.

The role of the other (non-entry) collusion factors also merits attention. The guidelines state that these factors 'are most likely to be important where the Department's decision to challenge a merger is otherwise close'. This suggests that these factors would affect the occasional case, but would not be a systematic consideration in decisions to challenge mergers. The role of both entry barriers and perceived ease of collusion can both be evaluated using the internal FTC data at our disposal.

Use of the new efficiency criterion has also drawn criticism. Some (e.g., Lande, 1988) claim that efficiency has been elevated to a favoured position in merger analysis, dominating the more traditional concentration and non-concentration criteria. The data permit an evaluation of this claim as well.

The relative importance of different factors

A second set of questions concerns the trade-offs among the different guideline factors. The guidelines leave to the discretion of antitrust enforcers how to weigh the different concentration and non-concentration factors. This is another feature that has been criticized: 'Where everything is relevant, nothing is determinative' (Krattenmaker and Pitofsky, 1988, p. 220). If one factor (high concentration, for example) is a necessary but not sufficient condition for a merger challenge, how are high Herfindahl numbers traded off against other factors, such as entry barriers and perceived ease of collusion?

A related issue concerns the different agency roles of lawyers and economists. One feature frequently noted about antitrust in the Reagan years was that 'staff economists at the Commission and the DOJ have gained considerable influence' (Salop, 1987, p. 3). Their antitrust assessments are said to differ from those of lawyers, particularly because lawyers have greater incentives to litigate in order to increase their human capital for subsequent careers in private practice (Posner, 1969, p. 86; Clarkson and Muris, 1981, p. 300). If so, the ultimate trade-off made by the Commission among guideline factors would depend on the differing evaluations by the two groups and their relative influence on Commission votes. Both issues can be examined with the available FTC data.

A final issue concerning FTC application of the different guidelines factors can be addressed with the data. The intellectual battles in antitrust for the past generation have pitted more traditional structuralists against partisans of the Chicago school of antitrust. In some areas of antitrust law, Chicago-school learning has gained ascendancy among academicians and even in the courts. It is not clear, however, to what extent antitrust enforcers themselves have adopted a Chicago-style approach. The differences between the two models, however, are registered largely in terms of the relative importance of the variables (concentration, entry barriers, collusion) identified by the guidelines, meaning that our data can be used to determine which model better predicts Commission decisions.

3   Data

To explore the empirical issues noted above, we used a data set of 70 merger investigations at the FTC from 14 June 1982 (the date of the new merger guidelines) to 1 January 1987. The sample includes every important horizontal merger that came to the FTC at that time, as indicated by the fact that it merited a 'second request' for data under the Hart–Scott–Rodino Act.[5] In 43 of the cases, the Commission allowed the merger, while in 27 the Commission voted to challenge the merger.[6]

For each proposed merger in the sample, we reviewed the separate lawyers' and economists' memorandum-evaluations of the different guidelines factors. Markets were defined and concentration data were available in all proposed mergers, and we noted the various estimates of the Herfindahl index and the change in the index for both the lawyers in the Bureau of Competition and the economists in the Bureau of Economics. Entry barrier data were available in most of the memos, with 54 observations for the Bureau of Economics and 66 for the Bureau of Competition. We follow the general interpretation of the guidelines, treating evidence that entry would require at least two years as indicating that important barriers exist, and evidence that entry could occur within two years as evidence that entry was easy. Evidence on the perceived ease of collusion was sparser. We found analysis of an anticompetitive effect in 37 of the Bureau of Economics memos and in a somewhat different group of 37 Bureau of Competition memos; information was obtained from at least one bureau in

---

[5] The 70-case sample includes all the 109 second requests made by the FTC during the relevant period, except those for vertical mergers (ten cases), joint ventures (four cases), and cases where the post-merger Herfindahl index was below 1,000 (five cases). (The FTC blocked no mergers with Herfindahls under 1,000.) Also excluded are cases where the FTC files contained insufficient information for our evaluation, such as when the attempted merger was abandoned when the second request was issued (eight cases), the merger was given early approval following the second request (nine cases), or the case was closed prior to completion of the Hart–Scott–Rodino filing (three cases).

[6] There is a growing literature (e.g., Priest and Klein, 1984; Cooter and Rubinfeld, 1989) modelling disputants' decisions to settle or litigate. One prediction of the basic model is that, under certain plausible assumptions, plaintiffs would win about half the cases litigated. In that respect, it is of interest that the FTC, as plaintiff in challenging mergers, won all 27 of the challenges it brought. (Three victories in litigation are still on appeal or undergoing other review.) Thus the FTC's litigation record is surprising.

46 cases. We required the memo explicitly to explain how the collusion-based factors did or did not produce an anticompetitive effect before counting the analysis as information sent to the Commission. Efficiency and failing-firm factors were even more rarely considered or discussed. The Bureau of Economics addressed efficiencies in 28 memos and the Bureau of Competition in 23. Finally, the Bureau of Competition raised the failing firm defence in four of the reports.

Before these data are used to answer the questions about FTC merger enforcement presented above, one issue must be addressed. Guidelines factors could conceivably not be evaluated on their merits, but might instead be manipulated to push a result that the FTC staff has decided (for whatever reason) it wishes the Commission to take. If so, the guidelines themselves would afford no predictability in evaluating mergers. It is important to determine, therefore, whether the individual guidelines factors are analysed on their own merits.

One way to check is to look at the correlations between each pair of guidelines factors. If the factors are not independently evaluated, there should be high correlation among them.[7] We calculated the simple correlations among the concentration, entry barriers, and ease of collusion variables, and found no significant correlation between any pair of variables, as they were evaluated by either lawyers or economists. Apparently, then, variables are evaluated independently and pressure to make or close a case does not generally lead to 'cooking' the data.[8]

4   Empirical evidence

Role of individual guidelines factors

Concentration

The internal FTC evidence allows one to determine if the Commission is actually following the guidelines with respect to concentration. Table 22.1 presents a classification for the Bureau of Competition estimates of the Herfindahl indices and changes in index values for the 70 cases. (The Bureau of Economics data are distributed similarly.) As the table shows, in 22 of the 27 cases filed, the Herfindahl index was over 1,800; 12 had index numbers over 3,000. There were no complaints when the Herfindahl index increased less than 100 points, and only five when it increased less than 200. In 11 complaints, the increase exceeded 500 points. There is, however, a surprisingly similar pattern for the 43 closed cases. Twenty-nine cases were not brought even when the Herfindahl index exceeded 1,800; in 11 of those cases, the index increased by more than 500 points.

Thus, the FTC's practice from 1982–6 does not corroborate the guidelines' claim

---

[7] It might be argued that if one wanted to manipulate a result, one would do so for the single variable most likely to be believed. But as shown below, a merger is unlikely to be challenged if only a single guideline variable is thought worrisome.

[8] In a similar vein, we tested (Coate *et al.* 1990, p. 478) for political influence on Bureau of Competition staff in making recommendations to the Commission about particular mergers. While the commission itself is demonstrably influenced by politics in its votes, the evidence indicates that Bureau of Competition staff recommendations to the Commission do not reflect political pressure.

that a challenge will be made in all but the most 'extraordinary circumstances' when the post-merger Herfindahl index is over 1,800 and the change is greater than 100. There were eight cases in which the merger was abandoned when the second request was issued (and thus could not be included in the sample here). Even if all eight involved high concentration and would have resulted in merger challenges, this would mean 30 merger challenges and 27 closed cases in highly concentrated industries with changes of over 100 points. It is hard to believe that truly 'extraordinary circumstances' could exist in almost half the cases.[9] Thus, it would appear that the guidelines have been implicitly revised, with the term 'challenge' replaced by 'investigate'.

By comparison, the data indicate that the Commission has not implicitly raised the lower bound for an investigation from the Herfindahl index level of 1,000 stated in the guidelines. Five complaints were filed when the Herfindahl index did not exceed 1,800. Fourteen cases with index numbers below 1,800 were investigated, although closed upon further analysis. Of these, five involved Herfindahls under 1,400; five had changes in the index of less than 200 points.

By itself, the table suggests that levels and changes in the Herfindahl numbers may not matter in the FTC vote. Cases were brought in all the Herfindahl classifications, from between 1,000 and 1,400 to over 3,000. Moreover, cases were closed in all these classifications. The relatively small number of cases in most of the cells of table 22.1 makes statistical testing difficult. However, index data can be aggregated into three cells (under 1,800, 1,800–3,000, over 3,000) and separated into complaints and closings. In a test of the hypothesis that the decision on a merger is independent of the Herfindahl level, the chi-square statistic is 2.14, well below the critical level necessary to reject the hypothesis of independence. The same test for Herfindahl change yields the same inference, with a chi-square of 1.97. These results should be interpreted with care, given the aggregation necessary to run the test.

The data are also useful for evaluating the guidelines' assertion that the government is 'more likely than not' to challenge a merger when the Herfindahl index is under 1,800 but 'other factors' support issuance of a complaint. If the other factors are taken to mean both entry barriers and ease of collusion, there were six cases (using the Bureau of Competition's evaluations) in which a challenge should have been 'more likely than not'. In fact, the Commission challenged four of those mergers.

Barriers to entry
The evidence suggests that entry barriers are virtually a necessary condition for a merger challenge. In the Commission's 27 complaints, the Bureau of Competition claimed barriers would block entry for at least two years in 26 cases and the Bureau of

[9] We interpret the 'extraordinary circumstances' language as applying to the set of mergers reviewed by the enforcement agencies. Firms would attempt mergers in highly concentrated industries when they believed (1) they could substantiate a broad market so the Herfindahls would be low; (2) the competitive concern would be only a small part of the transaction and hence subject to a divestiture (as happened in 11 of our 27 complaints); or (3) extraordinary circumstances existed. Thus we believe that the data should reflect the extraordinary nature of closing a high-concentration merger if the language was actually enforced.

Table 22.1 *Herfindahl indices and change in Herfindahls for FTC decisions to challenge/ not challenge merger (Bureau of Competition Evaluations)*

Post-merger Herfindahl	Change in Herfindahl					
	0–99	100–199	200–499	500–999	1,000	TOTAL
1,000–1,400	0/0	1/3	0/2	0/0	0/0	1/5
1,401–1,800	0/1	1/1	3/7	0/0	0/0	4/9
1,801–2,400	0/0	1/2	4/4	2/2	0/0	7/8
2,401–3,000	0/1	2/2	1/4	0/1	0/0	3/8
3,001+	0/1	0/1	3/3	3/1	6/7	12/13
TOTAL	0/3	5/9	11/20	5/4	6/7	27/43

Note: Figures refer to mergers challenged/not challenged by the FTC following a Hart–Scott–Rodino second-request filing.

Economics agreed in 22 of them. The evidence also suggests, however, that entry barriers were not a sufficient condition. There were 16 cases in which the Bureau of Competition found both low Herfindahl index numbers and difficult entry. The Commission issued complaints in only five of these cases. Moreover, in the 43 cases where the FTC voted not to challenge, the Bureau of Competition noted high barriers for 31 mergers; the Bureau of Economics claimed barriers were high for 20. Evidently, the FTC has required evidence beyond entry barriers to vote a complaint. Nor does the Herfindahl statistic interact predictably with entry barriers to generate a complaint. The Bureau of Competition reported entry barriers for 20 of the 28 (71 per cent) closed cases with Herfindahls over 1,800 and changes of over 50, and for 11 of the 15 (73 per cent) closed cases where the Herfindahl index was below 1,800 (or change was less than 50). Figures for Bureau of Economics findings of high barriers were also similar: eleven of 21 (52 per cent) for high-Herfindahl closed cases and nine of 22 (41 per cent) for low-Herfindahl mergers.

Ease of collusion
The guidelines indicate that ease of collusion will be particularly important in marginal cases. In marginal cases, difficulty of collusion should result in case closings, and ease of collusion should cause complaints to be filed. To evaluate this assertion, one must define marginal cases. For example, a marginal case could be a merger with an Herfindahl index under 1,800 or a change in the index of under 200.

The evidence indicates that collusion has not played the role indicated in the guidelines. For marginal cases resulting in complaints, the Bureau of Competition presented evidence of feasible collusion in five of eight mergers. The Bureau of Economics staff found collusion plausible in just two of ten marginal cases ending as complaints; the Bureau of Economics even thought collusion difficult in three of the ten. In the marginal cases ultimately closed, the Bureau of Competition found collusion difficult in only four of 19 cases, but collusion easy in five. The Bureau of

Economics found collusion difficult in ten of 21 marginal cases that closed, and collusion allegedly easy in only two.

The evidence thus contradicts the claim that perceived ease of collusion is a tiebreaker in marginal cases. For the Bureau of Competition, collusion seems to explain some complaints, but it cannot explain the numerous closings of marginal cases. Conversely, the Bureau of Economics collusion evaluations help explain closings but not complaints. Overall, no predictive pattern emerges from the data on collusion.

Efficiency

The internal FTC data also permit evaluation of the claim that the new efficiency criterion has come to dominate other considerations in merger policy. If efficiency considerations have really affected merger policy, one would expect to see otherwise anti-competitive transactions excused because of expected resource savings. In particular, one would expect in numerous closed cases to find efficiency explanations and evidence suggesting complaints would be favoured but for the efficiency argument.

The Bureau of Economics and Bureau of Competition claims of efficiencies can be contrasted with the Commission's final decision on the merger. Perhaps surprisingly, efficiency claims were made more frequently in challenged cases, with the Bureau of Economics claiming efficiencies existed in 33 per cent of the complaints filed and the Bureau of Competition in 26 per cent. But the Bureau of Economics found efficiencies in only 21 per cent and the Bureau of Competition in 7 per cent of the closed cases. Obviously, this evidence suggests that the legal and economic staffs' efficiency defences are not generally successful.[10]

One can further explore the efficiency issue by comparing the number of factors (Herfindahl index, barriers, or collusion) either favouring or disfavouring complaints in the closed cases where efficiencies were found to those where no efficiencies were claimed. For the Bureau of Economics, in the nine closed cases where efficiencies were claimed, the staff found an average of 1.44 factors indicating the merger would otherwise not have an anticompetitive effect. This is not significantly different ($t = 0.25$) from the average number of 1.38 factors deemed not anticompetitive by the Bureau of Economics in the other closed cases. Thus, a Bureau of Economics efficient claim apparently did not substitute for other guidelines factors that the Bureau of Economics said supported letting a merger proceed, when the Commission decided to close the case. For the Bureau of Competition, the inference is the same. In the three closed cases for which the lawyers claimed efficiencies existed, they found an average of 1.33 other factors suggesting a problem could exist, as compared with the average of 1.68 factors thought to be at anticompetitive levels for the other cases. This difference is also insignificant ($t = 0.76$). Again, at the margin the efficiency factor seems unimportant in explaining FTC merger challenges.

---

[10] This result is compatible with the hypothesis that merger partners present efficiency defences for troublesome mergers.

Multivariate analysis

Analysing the role of a single guidelines factor without controlling for other factors is potentially misleading. Multivariate techniques may be more appropriate. Multivariate analysis is also useful for investigating two issues in merger enforcement of interest to many: the relative importance of the different guidelines factors, and the differences between lawyers and economists in influencing Commission votes.

Weights of different guidelines factors

Using the internal FTC data, we defined a probit model for the Commission's decisions on merger challenges (Coate *et al.*, 1990). The dependent variable (*VOTE*) equalled 1 if the Commission approved a complaint (including cases in which the parties negotiated a settlement) and 0 if the investigation was closed with no action. We explained the merger vote as a function of both the Bureau of Competition and Bureau of Economics analysis of the Herfindahl, barriers to entry, and ease of collusion. To avoid extreme multicollinearity problems, we transformed the Bureau of Competition and Bureau of Economics concentration estimates into two dummy variables.[11] For the Bureau of Competition, the concentration variable (*BCHERFHI*) takes on the value of 1 if the Herfindahl is over 1,800 and the change is more than 50, and a value of 0 otherwise. The Bureau of Economics dummy variable (*BEHERFLO*) was defined as a mirror image of the Bureau of Competition variable, with a value of 1 if the Herfindahl was below 1800 or the change was less than 50 and 0 in all other cases.[12]

For the first non-concentration factor, entry barriers, we constructed two dummy variables, the first (*BCBARHI*) with the value 1 if the Bureau of Competition evaluated barriers to entry as high, and the other (*BEBARLO*) equalling 1 if the Bureau of Economics thought serious barriers did not exist. For the next non-concentration factor, ease of collusion, again we constructed two variables, one (*BCCOLHI*) with the value 1 when the Bureau of Competition found collusion likely and the other (*BECOLLO*) with the value 1 when Bureau of Economics found collusion was unlikely. Finally, the legal failing-firm defence was included by a variable (*FAILFIRM*) equal to 1 in those four cases in which the Bureau of Competition claimed the defence applied.

Two political pressure variables are also included. The first (*CITES*) is the number of *Wall Street Journal* articles about the merger prior to the FTC's decision and is

---

[11] The correlation coefficient between the continuous measures of the Bureau of Competition and Bureau of Economics Herfindahl index is 0.95. For the binary variables used here (BCHERFHI and BEHERFLO), the coefficient is -0.67.

[12] Reversing the coding on the Bureau of Competition and Bureau of Economics variables is done for ease of interpreting coefficients. It reflects the fact (explained further below) that in more than half the second-request cases lawyers support a merger challenge, while economists oppose a challenge in most cases. In the typical case, the regression analysis here shows, the Bureau of Competition evaluated the guidelines factors in such a way as to increase the likelihood of a merger challenge, while the typical Bureau of Economics analysis decreased that likelihood. The coding of course has no effect on the significance of the results or inferences therefrom, other than to change the intercept term.

Table 22.2 *Parameter estimates for the probit model (absolute value of* t-*statistics in parentheses)*

	1 Base model	2 Efficiency model	3 Recoded model	4 Continuous model
BCHERFHI	1.11* (1.53)	1.11* (1.52)	1.12* (1.55)	0.144 (1.21)
BCBARHI	1.84** (1.85)	1.84** (1.84)	1.79** (1.78)	1.50* (1.64)
BCCOLHI	1.65*** (3.16)	1.65*** (3.11)	1.16*** (2.47)	1.60*** (3.26)
BEHERFLO	−0.962* (1.65)	−0.962* (1.63)	0.857* (1.53)	−0.556 (1.29)
BEBARLO	−0.880* (1.58)	−0.880* (1.58)	5.86 (1.13)	−0.777* (1.39)
BECOLLO	−0.880** (1.83)	−0.880** (1.81)	1.08* (1.31)	−0.635* (1.39)
FAILFIRM	−4.33 (0.01)	−4.33 (0.01)	−3.04 (0.03)	−4.43 (0.002)
CITES	0.169** (1.82)	0.169** (1.82)	0.190** (2.19)	0.159** (1.84)
HEARINGS	0.151** (1.71)	0.151** (1.70)	1.81** (2.00)	0.098 (1.29)
EFFCY	—	−0.0002 (0.0005)	—	—
Constant	−4.01 (2.47)	−4.01 (2.47)	−5.89 (3.38)	−3.04 (2.38)
Adj.R2	0.493	0.493	0.458	0.467
Likelihood	46.3	46.3	43.1	43.9

Note: * significant at 0.10 level.
** significant at 0.05 level.
*** significant at 0.01 level.

designed to measure the pressure to block high-profile transactions. The second (*HEARINGS*) is a 12-month moving average of the number of times Congress summoned FTC commissioners or politically appointed staff to hearings to defend their antitrust records.

The probit parameter estimates are shown as regression 1 ('base model') in table 22.2. As expected, Bureau of Competition analysis that concentration, entry barriers and collusion possibilities are at worrisome levels significantly enhances the probability of a complaint; Bureau of Economics evaluation that none of the guidelines factors are worrisome significantly lowers the likelihood of a challenge. The political, the Bureau of Competition and the Bureau of Economics variables all pass independent chi-square tests, indicating that each type of variable affects the Commission's decision making.

As a test of the role of efficiencies, a variable not included in the first model, we now insert a dummy variable (*EFFCY*) equal to 1 for any case in which either the Bureau of Competition or Bureau of Economics claimed that efficiencies were present. As shown in regression 2 ('efficiency model') of table 22.2, efficiencies themselves are an insignificant factor in FTC votes, and their inclusion in the model has only trivial effects on the size and significance of the other variables. With other guidelines factors controlled for, staff efficiency claims have no apparent influence on a Commission merger decision.

The model is robust with respect to other specifications. One important issue concerns the missing values for the independent variables. As noted above, for example, out of the 70 total cases, the Bureau of Competition discussed collusion in only 37 and the Bureau of Economics in a somewhat different set of 37 mergers. Regressions 1 and 2 are based on a default coding of zero for the Bureau of Competition and Bureau of Economics independent variables when the bureau failed to mention a particular factor. But the results are not sensitive to this coding option, as regression 3 ('recoded model') in table 22.2 indicates. Reversing the coding of the Bureau of Economics variables to match the Bureau of Competition variables, so the missing values would be treated identically, results in only minor differences from the prior estimates. Finally, if the concentration dummies for the Bureau of Competition and Bureau of Economics are multiplied by the Herfindahl index estimated by each bureau so as to create a truncated continuous variable, the estimated coefficients are insignificant, as shown in regression 4 of table 22.2. This may suggest that the FTC responds less to continuous Herfindahl changes than to discrete changes in classification (e.g., a post-merger HHI above 1,800).[13]

Using the first probit equation (regression 1) and holding the political variables constant at their means, one can investigate the relative importance of the merger guidelines factors in a Commission decision to challenge a merger. If lawyers and economists agree that the Herfindahl index, entry barriers, and ease of collusion are all at levels deemed worrisome under the guidelines, the probability of a merger challenge is 97 per cent. Suppose, next, that both the Bureau of Competition and Bureau of Economics agree that one of the factors is not a concern. If both bureaus find that the Herfindahl level is low, the probability of an FTC challenge falls from 97 to 43 per cent, a statistically significant decline. Since every merger in the 1982–6 FTC sample had an Herfindahl index above 1,000 and all but three increased the index by at least 100 points, it is interesting that the Commission would challenge only 43 per cent of those mergers, even when both entry barriers and an ability to collude allegedly were present.

The Herfindahl index was apparently of less importance to the Commission during

---

[13] We also tested whether Commission decisions respond to cost or benefit variables similar to those included in models of private litigation decisions (see note 7). None of the variables proved significant. For example, larger firms might more easily bear the fixed costs of litigating to achieve a merger, meaning that the FTC would itself have to expect higher litigation costs if it voted to challenge. However, firm size (measured by sales) was not a significant determinant of the FTC decision whether to litigate, *ceteris paribus*.

this time than other guideline measures. Although there is still a 43 per cent chance the Commission will challenge a merger when lawyers and economists agree that the Herfindahl is low (and the two other factors are high), bureaucratic agreement that either of the other guideline factors is low reduces the probability of a merger challenge even more. When both bureaus agree that the Herfindahl is high and collusion likely, but also that entry barriers are low, there is only a 21 per cent probability of a merger challenge. Likewise, when concentration and barriers are judged high, but collusion is thought unlikely, the probability of a complaint is only 27 per cent. *Ceteris paribus*, satisfying the FTC staff that the Herfindahl is under 1,800 (or its change is less than 50) appears less likely to shield a merger from challenge than a bureaucratic finding that entry barriers or the likelihood of collusion are low. (Of course, the best way to prevent a merger challenge under the guidelines is to show that the Herfindahl index is below 1,000.)

These results are consistent with the conclusion above that, despite the guidelines, the Commission was not 'likely to challenge' but rather 'likely to investigate' mergers pushing the Herfindahl index over 1,800. Even if the Herfindahl is assumed to be high, the decision whether the merger will be challenged depends heavily on the evaluation of the other guidelines factors. Indeed, the regression model shows, if concentration alone were judged high but barriers judged low and collusion difficult, a complaint would have no measurable chance of success.

Bureau of Competition and Bureau of Economics Agreement on Guidelines Factors

Table 22.3 notes the positions taken by both the Bureau of Economics and Bureau of Competition with respect to the Herfindahl index, barriers, ease of collusion, and efficiencies. There was considerable agreement among lawyers and economists concerning the facts presented to the Commission, ranging from 83 per cent on the Herfindahl index to 61 per cent on the ease of collusion. Disagreements occurred almost exclusively when the Bureau of Competition thought a variable indicated anticompetitive problems, but the Bureau of Economics did not.

However, the data mask some disagreements, such as differences in market definition or market share. Only 59 per cent of the Herfindahl statistics were absolutely identical. Moreover, missing values indicated large potential for further disagreement between the Bureau of Economics and Bureau of Competition. Counting as disagreements any situation where one bureau ventured an opinion and the other did not lowers the agreement rate to 73 per cent for barriers, 37 per cent for ease of collusion, and 52 per cent for efficiencies.

The table indicates that when presented with the same facts, attorneys are more likely than economists to claim that a merger raises issues of antitrust concern. This finding is consistent with the hypothesis that different career incentives induce lawyers to support cases more often than economists. This hypothesis can be tested directly. The internal files reveal that the Bureau of Competition staff supported a complaint in 54.3 per cent of the sample cases, while the Bureau of Economics staff supported a complaint in only 30 per cent. This difference is statistically significant at the 1 per cent level.

Table 22.3 *Evaluation of guideline variables by bureaus of competition and economics*

Number of cases in which BE claims the variable is:	Number of cases in which BC claims the variable is:	
	HIGH	LOW
HIGH		
HHI	39	1
Barriers	40	0
Collusion	12	0
Efficiencies	9	0
(i.e., no efficiencies present)		
LOW		
HHI	11	19
Barriers	15	9
Collusion	11	5
Efficiencies	4	7
(i.e., no efficiencies present)		

The effects of bureaucratic disagreement tend to indicate that lawyers have greater influence over the ultimate Commission vote. Table 22.4 (estimated from regression model 1 of table 22.2 with political variables held constant at their means) presents the effects of bureau disagreements over the Herfindahl index, entry barriers and ease of collusion under alternative assumptions concerning evaluation of each of these factors. Suppose hypothetically that both groups at first agree that one variable – the Herfindahl, barriers to entry, or likelihood of collusion – is low while the other two are high. Then let the lawyers change their opinion and also evaluate the first variable as high. As shown in line 1 of table 22.4, the probability of a challenge rises by 40 to 64 per cent, depending on the variable. Suppose alternatively that both the Bureau of Competition and Bureau of Economics initially find that all merger guidelines factors are high, but that the economists then re-evaluate one of these factors as low. Line 2 of table 22.4 indicates that the probability of a challenge falls by 12 to 14 per cent.[14]

In short, under our econometric model of Commission decision making the lawyers' evaluation of the merger guidelines variables apparently have had a greater impact than those made by economists. Moreover, all the predicted probability

---

[14] The hypothetical cases used here reflect the fact that the Bureau of Competition is more likely to support cases than the Bureau of Economics. Thus, the most likely scenarios involve either the Bureau of Competition changing their evaluations of a particular guidelines factor from low to high while the Bureau of Economics continues to evaluate the factor as low or the Bureau of Economics changing from high to low while the Bureau of Competition continues to evaluate the factor as high. These are the two cases presented in table 22.4.

Table 22.4 *Impact of bureau disagreement on probability of merger challenge*

	HHI	Barriers	Collusion
BC changes from LOW to HIGH (BE remains LOW)	+40**	+64*	+58*
BE changes from HIGH to LOW (BC remains HIGH)	−14	−12	−12

Note: * significant at the 0.05 level.
** significant at the 0.10 level.
The change in probabilities of an FTC merger challenge accompanying a change by one bureau in its evaluation of the factor stated is based on the assumption that the other two factors are already evaluated as being high.

changes for lawyers are statistically significant at the 0.05 and 0.10 levels. The estimated effects for economists are not significant.[15]

Structuralist vs. Chicago approaches at the FTC

The probability models above use econometric techniques to determine the simultaneous impact of particular variables on FTC merger decisions. That approach is usually the only one available, because economic theory itself does not specify a priori the exact relationship between the dependent and explanatory variables. In this case, theory suggests two deterministic models that can be constructed with data on Herfindahls, entry barriers, and ease of collusion to model FTC merger decisions.

Economists differ on those conditions necessary for a merger to be anticompetitive, although entry barriers would probably be given by all as a necessary condition. If barriers are present, evaluation of a merger hinges on how easily one believes firms could coordinate their actions. So-called 'Chicago school' economists typically maintain that something other than mere concentration is necessary for successful, long-term collusion. 'Structuralists', on the other hand, tend to hold that once entry barriers have been shown, high concentration can substitute for evidence of the ease of collusion as a sufficient predictor of anticompetitive effect.

The debate is a long-running one. It is interesting, therefore, to use the FTC data on merger challenges to see whether the Chicago-school or structuralist model better predicts FTC merger challenges. We used two definitions that fit the competing theories. A Chicago-school approach would require evidence of all three of the principal guidelines factors: high Herfindahl index, entry barriers and ease of collusion. If any of these factors was missing, a Chicagoan would likely infer that the merger could not be anticompetitive. But a structuralist approach would deem a

---

[15] Our model fails to capture any influence that the Bureau of Economics has on the Bureau of Competition's factual analysis, and therefore may understate the influence of economists at the FTC.

merger anticompetitive if, in addition to entry barriers, either the Herfindahl index was high or collusion was perceived to be easy. Neither of these approaches is the same as the probit model set out in the regressions above. On that third model, the bureaucracy's evaluation of mergers under its own guidelines is treated as making no one factor either necessary or sufficient; external pressure variables are included as significant predictors as well.[16]

The issue thus is which model better predicts Commission decisions, the Chicago or structuralist model. We used each model to predict the anticompetitive effect of a merger for both the Bureau of Competition and Bureau of Economics data.[17] Under the Chicago model, a challenge would be predicted whenever (under the Bureau of Competition and Bureau of Economics data, alternatively) all three factors were deemed worrisome: concentration, entry barriers and ease of collusion. Under the structuralist model, a challenge is predicted when barriers and either high concentration or ease of collusion is posited.

It is useful to separate the sample into three periods. The first, from the announcement of the 1982 merger guidelines to the 1984 revision, contains 16 cases. The second period (with 27 cases) runs from the revision to the resignation of FTC Chairman James C. Miller III. A question naturally of interest to economists is whether the FTC evaluated mergers differently during the tenure of Miller, the only professional economist ever to chair the Commission. The third period (also 27 cases) runs from Miller's resignation to the end of the sample.

Table 22.5 compares, for all three subperiods, the predictive success of each model. The structuralist model with the Bureau of Competition data predicts Commission merger decisions 67 per cent of the time, while the Chicago model is correct 74 per cent of the time. Similar results are found by using the Bureau of Economics data with either model. Thus, the deterministic models of Commission decision making do not show that lawyers have more influence than economists on enforcement decisions.

Among the three subperiods,[18] one finds that the Chicago model seemingly outperformed the structuralist model while the 1982 guidelines were in effect, but again there was no significant difference. When the 1982 guidelines were revised, the Chicago model's predictive success fell for both the Bureau of Competition and Bureau of Economics data, with the Bureau of Economics decline being statistically significant ($t = 1.90$). However, the opposite result occurred following Chairman Miller's departure, with the increase in the Bureau of Economics predictive ability again significant ($t = 3.53$).[19] The predictions of the Chicago and structuralist models

---

[16] Both the Chicago-school and structuralist models treat antitrust as a 'public interest' form of regulation, and thus would treat political variables as irrelevant. See McChesney (1991).

[17] The predictions were adjusted for the few failing-firm defences in the sample.

[18] For the subperiods, there is a risk of bias if the results of one cell are driven by the type of case (closing or complaint) considered disproportionately during the period. To check for this problem we used the sample weights of 38.5 per cent complaints and 61.5 per cent closings to weight the predictions of complaints and closings to determine the sample prediction rates. The results were comparable to those in table 22.5, indicating no bias problem.

[19] Table 22.5's Bureau of Economics figures do not depend critically on the Bureau of Economics' position on collusion in those cases when the economists did not mention collusion explicitly in

Table 22.5 *Success of dtructuralist and Chicago models in predicting FTC merger challenges*

	Time period			
	June 1982– May 1984	June 1984– Aug. 1985	Aug. 1985– Dec. 1986	TOTAL
1 Using BC evaluation of guidelines factors				
Structuralist model	63	63	74	67
Chicago model	81	74	70	74
2 Using BE evaluation of guidelines factors				
Structuralist model	69	64	78	70
Chicago model	81	55	93	76

can be compared with the results obtained from the bureaucratic-political probit model (regression 1 of table 22.2). Assuming a fitted probability from the regression of over (under) 50 per cent predicts a complaint (closing), the probit model correctly forecasted the Commission's decision with 84 per cent accuracy. Figures for the three subperiods are 88, 81, and 85 per cent, respectively. The probit model generally outperforms the Chicago and structuralist models, not a surprising result since the probit model incorporates significant political variables.

Conclusion

As the merger wave of the 1980s rolled on, commentators alleged that antitrust agencies had tacitly revised the merger guidelines, challenging only extreme increases in concentration. Also, efficiencies supposedly had been elevated above the other guidelines factors. Moreover, there were rumours that economists were actually taking part in antitrust enforcement decisions.

It is useful to look back and separate fact from fiction. Our data on Federal Trade Commission merger challenges from the mid 1980s provide evidence that for the most part the merger guidelines have not been applied as written. The use of concentration measures is perhaps the best example. However, the data do not reveal an increase in the critical Herfindahl levels. Instead, the evidence suggests simply that concentration has not been used to establish a presumption of guilt. Rather, it has served to

their memoranda. As noted above, we treated failure to mention collusion as indicating that economists believed it plausible. If the opposite inference is drawn, the predictability of the Chicago model using Bureau of Economics data declines from 93 per cent in the post-Miller years to 74 per cent. However, treating failure to discuss collusion as an indication that economists thought it unlikely increases the predictive power of the Chicago model for the Miller years, and so has little impact on the model's power overall.

determine which cases should be investigated. The cases appear to be examined on their merits and some proof of anticompetitive effect – beyond mere concentration numbers – is often required before a complaint is issued. In that respect, the FTC's approach thus has been consistent with economic theory: concentration has been a necessary but not a sufficient condition for a merger challenge.

As for non-concentration factors, there is considerable evidence that a finding of barriers to entry was a necessary but not sufficient condition for a merger challenge. On the other hand, there is no evidence (despite critics' claims to the contrary) that explicit inclusion of efficiencies in the guidelines has made any difference. Closed cases where efficiencies were allegedly present in 1982–6 presented competitive concerns similar to those in which no efficiency claims were made.

Moreover, both economist and attorney evaluations of guidelines factors appear to have an impact. At the margin, attorneys seem to have more influence at the Commission if one accepts the econometric model. Finally, both the structuralist and Chicago models predict the Commission's decisions reasonably well over the sample period. But both are inferior to the probability model, shown to be rather robust here, that includes political variables as predictors of FTC merger decisions.

References

Clarkson, K.W. and T. J. Muris (1981), 'Commission performance, incentives, and behaviour', in K.W. Clarkson and T.J. Muris (eds.), *The Federal Trade Commission Since 1970: Economic Regulation and Bureaucratic Behavior*, Cambridge University Press, pp. 280–306.

Coate, M.B., R.S. Higgins, and F.S. McChesney (1990), 'Bureaucracy and politics in FTC merger enforcement', *Journal of Law and Economics*, 33, 463–82.

Cooter, R.D. and D.L. Rubinfeld (1989), 'Economic analysis of legal disputes and their resolution', *Journal of Economic Literature*, 27, 1067–97.

Demsetz, H. (1982), 'Barriers to entry', *American Economic Review*, 72, 47–57.

Krattenmaker, T.G. and R. Pitofsky (1988), 'Antitrust merger policy and the Reagan Administration', *Antitrust Bulletin*, 33, 211–32.

Lande, R.H. (1988), 'The rise and (coming) fall of efficiency as the ruler of antitrust', *Antitrust Bulletin*, 33, 429–65.

Leddy, M. (1986), 'Recent merger cases reflect revolution in antitrust policy', *Legal Times*, 3 November, p. 2.

McChesney, F.S. (1991), 'Be true to your school: conflicting Chicago approaches to antitrust and regulation', *Cato Journal*, 775–98.

Posner, R.A. (1969), 'The Federal Trade Commission', *University of Chicago Law Review*, 37(1), 47–89.

Priest, G.L. and B. Klein (1984), 'The selection of disputes for litigation', *Journal of Legal Studies*, 13, 1–55.

Rogowsky, R.A. (1984), 'The Justice Departments merger guidelines: a study in the application of the rule', *Research in Law and Economics*, 6, 135–66.

Salop, S.C. (1987), 'Symposium on mergers and antitrust', *Journal of Economic Perspectives*, 1, 3–12.

US Department of Justice (1986), 'Merger guidelines', (1968, 1982 and 1984 versions), in

Horizontal Mergers: Law and Policy, Section of Antitrust Law, American Bar Association, 264–336.

White, L.J. (1987), 'Antitrust and merger policy: a review and critique', *Journal of Economic Perspectives*, 1, 13–22.

Chapter 23

Enforcement of the European merger regulation
The merger decisions of the European Commission

Damien Neven, Robin Nuttall and Paul Seabright

1   Introduction

In this chapter we present an analysis and assessment of the reasoning presented by the European Commission in justification of its decisions under the Merger Regulation since September 1990. The purpose of doing so is not primarily to see whether the Commission's decisions were in fact the right ones to make in the circumstances. Too much of the information that would be needed to make that assessment reliably is not available to us, for unavoidable reasons (such as business confidentiality) as well as some avoidable ones. Instead, the purpose of this chapter is to infer from the Commission's published reasoning what in fact have been the procedures and criteria it has used in the assessment of merger proposals, and to evaluate these. To make this inference will require substantial examination of the detailed reasoning in a large number of cases[1], partly because a general tendency in the Commission's procedures cannot be revealed in single cases, and partly because (as will be seen) there has not

---

This chapter is an abbreviated version of *Merger in Daylight: The Economics and Politics of European Merger Control*, CEPR, 1993, chapter 3. References to other chapters of that book were deleted.

[1] We nevertheless cite in the text only a minority of the decisions taken, since most decisions do not raise issues of particular significance. However, we have reviewed all cases published by 21 September 1992, as well as important decisions up until mid March 1993. We have drawn also on widely available sources like industry studies, official publications by Eurostat, the OECD, national antitrust authorities and the financial press, as well as on interviews with officials of the Merger Task Force and national antitrust authorities, lawyers, and financial commentators.

always been consistency between the reasoning deployed in different cases. Nonetheless, even bearing in mind the limitations of this kind of inference, we conclude that the Commission's procedures are open to a number of criticisms:

1 The definition of concentrative joint ventures is open to considerable manipulation, in that changes in the form of transactions may be encouraged by the desire of firms to have their proposals reviewed under the Regulation instead of under procedures elsewhere.

2 The procedures used for market definition are frequently inconsistent; in particular supply substitution is sometimes taken into account at the market definition stage and sometimes at the stage of assessing dominance, with usually no clear rationale for the difference in treatment. Supply substitution is also sometimes counted twice. The failure to take supply substitution into account will probably tend on average to result in excessively narrow market definitions. Although it is not possible to point with confidence to particular cases in which this bias has made a difference to the market definition adopted, we indicate one or two instances where it could have been significant.

3 Both market definitions and some of the factors relevant to the assessment of dominance rely unnecessarily on qualitative assertions and hunches even when more quantitative evidence could have been made available. While we appreciate the limitations on the availability of quantitative evidence, we suggest a number of ways these limitations can be overcome consistently with maintaining a reasonably streamlined procedure.

4 Examination of cases confirms our conjecture that the Commission uses a sequential rather than a simultaneous procedure for product and geographic market definition, which will tend on average to lead to a further bias in favour of narrow markets.

5 The assessment of dominance has also displayed an unnecessarily unsystematic and arbitrary character, especially in estimating the strength of remaining competitors, potential entrants, and countervailing buyer power.

6 Claims about efficiencies have been treated inconsistently, in one case as a potential (if practically negligible) defence, and in others as a potential source of dominance.

7 Conditions ('remedies') attached to decisions have often done little to meet competition concerns, since they have relied on excessive optimism about the future development of competitive forces. They have also, and to an increasing degree, relied upon undertakings from the parties whose credibility may be in some doubt.

Overall, we conclude that the unnecessarily unsystematic character of the procedures as they appear from the cases reviewed makes it particularly difficult to judge whether the Commission's judgement in individual cases has been sound. This raises issues of transparency. We also, if more tentatively, conjecture that the character of the procedures, especially with regard to remedies, is suggestive not so much of random variations as of the outcome of a process of negotiation in which firms and the Commission bargain over the outcome of a particular case.

2   Definition of a concentration

The EC Merger Regulation applies to 'concentrations with a community dimension'. A concentration is defined as an acquisition of control which confers either sole control or concentrative joint control. Control in turn is defined as 'the possibility of exercising decisive influence on an undertaking' (XXI Report, p. 352). A concentration has a community dimension if (i) the aggregate worldwide turnover of all the parties taken together exceeds ECU 5 billion, (ii) the aggregate EC-wide turnover of at least two of the parties taken individually exceeds ECU 250 million, and (iii) at least one of the undertakings does not achieve two-thirds of its EC-wide turnover within one and the same member state. In addition, Article 9 of the Regulation provides member states with the possibility of asking for referral of an acquisition with community dimension to their own jurisdiction if they fear the creation or strengthening of a dominant position in a distinct market within their territory. The decision whether or not to grant the referral rests with the Commission.

3   Defining the relevant market

A relevant antitrust market is defined as the narrowest market in which a given degree of market power could be exercised. The assessment of a candidate market entails, in principle, the estimation of the own-price firm elasticity of demand faced by a hypothetical monopolist in that market. This own-price firm elasticity of demand is determined both by consumers' willingness to switch to alternative products at given prices of those products (demand substitution in our terminology) and by the reaction of competitors outside the candidate market (supply substitution in our terminology) who can either change their own pricing policy or enter the market in the short term by changing their product range. Ignoring income effects, the own-price elasticity of product demand (the reaction of consumers) can be assessed directly or through the sum of the cross-price elasticities of demand between the product considered and all the other products.

Two important issues that emerged from our discussion of market definition were: the manner in which it takes into account supply substitution, and whether the tests for product and geographic market definition are performed simultaneously or in sequence. Fishwick and Denison (1992) argue that the European practice under Article 85/6 tends to focus on demand-side substitution; we consider below whether this is also true of the analysis of mergers. As far as the procedure for product and geographic market definition is concerned, the CEC (Commission of the European Communities) clearly states that estimation occurs in sequence and not simultaneously. On page 356 of the XXIst Report on Competition Policy (1992) the wording is as follows: 'The appraisal of concentrations includes generally three steps of analysis: the determination of the relevant product market, the determination of the relevant geographic market and the assessment of the compatibility of the merger with the common market.' This approach appears to be borne out in most of the decisions we have examined. We shall review product and geographic market definition procedures in turn.

3.1   Product market definition

The CEC defines a relevant market as 'those products which are regarded as interchangeable or substitutable by the consumer, by reason of the products' characteristics, their prices and their intended use'. It has distinguished 'two grounds on which separate relevant product-markets were established' (XXlst Report, p. 357). These are 'lack of sufficient substitutability between the products concerned' and 'existence of different conditions of competition albeit the products themselves being fully interchangeable or even identical'. We discuss in turn several aspects of the Commission's approach, starting with the content given to these various terms.

3.1.1   Conditions of competition

The CEC does not specify exactly what is meant by 'conditions of competition', but clues may be gained from examining the *Magneti Marelli/CEAc* and *Varta/Bosch* cases.

A distinction was made in *Magneti Marelli/CEAc* and in *Varta/ Bosch* between the original equipment (OE) market for starter batteries for the initial equipment of new vehicles and the replacement market for starter batteries for the equipment of used cars. The distinction was made on the basis of different 'conditions of competition', which arose because supply to the OE market requires high technical capacity, intense R&D, 100 per cent reliability of the products, just-in-time delivery and supply certification granted by the car manufacturers. Supply to the replacement market, on the other hand, implies strong seasonal fluctuations in demand for a larger number of battery types. As to the nature of the product, replacement batteries can be used in some cars of different producers, otherwise OE batteries cannot. Hence a hypothetical monopoly supplier of the OE market could raise prices without encouraging suppliers on the replacement market to switch production into OE batteries. If this is the case, then different 'conditions of competition' mean here a weak response by existing producers of replacement batteries, or equivalently low supply substitution.

'Conditions of competition' might also refer here to seasonal fluctuations in demand. Seasonal fluctuations might, however, increase the probability that suppliers of replacement batteries would respond aggressively to a price increase by OE producers. Indeed, the demand for OE batteries is likely to peak in the summer, when the demand for new cars is highest, whilst demand for replacement batteries will peak in the winter. Hence the seasonal fluctuations offset each other, so that a producer of replacement batteries would have an incentive to enter into the OE market to smooth out production.

These two cases illustrate that the term 'conditions of competition' *refers to some consideration of supply substitution.* They also indicate that the Commission did not systematically define markets solely in terms of demand substitution. It seems that different conditions of competition meant in one case a probable aggressive response by competitors; it is not clear what the Commission meant by emphasizing fluctuations in demand but this could imply that a weak response could be expected from competitors outside the relevant market. In any event, it might be a useful clarification to define 'conditions of competition' in terms of competitors' responses, and to analyse different market characteristics in terms of their impact on these responses. In our opinion, it would also be useful to acknowledge explicitly the use of supply substitution as well as demand substitution in market definition.

3.1.2   Demand substitution versus supply substitution

As we have already discussed, the relevant market is the narrowest market in which significant market power can be exercised. This market power is associated with the elasticity that the dominant firm would face and this elasticity is in turn determined by the possibility that consumers might switch to competing products outside the relevant market, as well as by the reaction of the firms supplying these products.

In a number of cases, the Commission has defined markets by focusing on demand substitution, without explicit reference to 'different conditions of competition'. In such cases, some products are excluded from the relevant market but are considered again in the assessment of dominance. This practice is valid if the relevant market is determined only in terms of demand substitution, but it is inconsistent when the Commission considers both demand and supply substitution, as it does in some other cases; indeed, when the market is defined taking both demand and supply substitution into account, the assessment of dominance is solely concerned with the possibility that the merging parties could exercise the potential market power which (by construction) exists in the relevant market. That implies that products outside the relevant market are *irrelevant* to the assessment of dominance. If considering these products is deemed to be important, it means that the market has not been appropriately defined in the first place.

For instance, in *Courtaulds/SNIA* and *Metallgesellschaft/Safic Alcan*, some products are excluded from the relevant market but considered later. In the *appraisal* section of the *Sanofi/Sterling Drug* case, it is stated that there 'is some degree of substitution from alternative products not included in the operational market definition given above'. This approach is appropriate if indeed the markets are defined solely in terms of demand substitution, but not otherwise. The fact that the Commission switches from one approach to the other without warning is confusing.

The risks of an approach based solely on demand substitution are also well illustrated by the market definition in *Pepsi Co/Kas*. In this case, the Commission observed that there might be low demand substitution between different flavours of carbonated soft drinks, but a high supply substitution (switching from the production of one flavour to the other is easy in the short term). Nevertheless, the Commission decided that specific flavours were distinct markets, a particularly narrow definition. In the assessment stage, the Commission then had to consider that the market share of Pepsi Co. in the lemon market substantially overstates anticompetitive effects because of supply substitution; indeed, the Commission was trying to assess dominance in a market where there is little potential market power to start with.

However, the Commission has sometimes used supply substitution in a way which is very close to the approach that we recommend. For instance, in *Lucas/Eaton* the Commission states in paragraph 21 that supply substitution from producers of commercial brakes is unlikely within a short period of time (one year) in the market for heavy-duty brakes; quite appropriately the Commission then considers potential competition from producers of commercial brakes in the assessment of dominance.

3.1.3   Product characteristics and substitutability
The principal method used by the Commission to infer substitutability is the observation of product characteristics. The mere observation that particular products have different characteristics does not imply any particular degree of substitutability or cross-price elasticity between them. For any pair of characteristics, there will be some degree of substitutability; and the choice of relevant characteristics may sometimes be difficult. Several cases illustrate the shortcomings of the approach.

First, the lack of substitute products is sometimes defined as a product characteristic, which could be confusing; for instance, in *La Redoute/Empire* and *Otto/Grattan* the product market is defined as catalogue mail order because of certain product 'characteristics', one of which is that some people have no alternative to home shopping. If people have no alternative to home shopping, this is an indication of low demand elasticity, and should be recognized directly as such.

Goods with different characteristics may not be substitutable, but this is not always true. For example, in the *Courtaulds/SNIA* case it was stated in paragraph 14 that product characteristics indicate a distinct product market for acetate yarn. But later on, in paragraph 26, it is stated that in the event of a 'significant' price increase for 'acetate yarn, it could be expected that purchasers would at least to some extent switch to other yarns, despite their different characteristics'. Again, in the *Metallgesellschaft/Safic Alcant* case, in paragraph 13 natural rubber was not considered 'substitutable' with synthetic rubber because of different product characteristics. But in paragraph 26 it was stated that demand for natural rubber can 'at least partially be satisfied . . . by synthetic rubber'. What this case illustrates is not necessarily that the Commission is acting in an inconsistent manner (though it may be), but rather that there are strong practical limitations to a non-quantitative approach to market definition. These limitations arise from the fact that there will always exist some substitutability between products: the question is whether a given degree of substitutability is enough to restrain market power.

A recent example of the limitations of a non-quantitative approach is provided by the case of *British Airways/TAT*. The problem was to determine which bundles of routes constituted the relevant market, and in particular whether Gatwick and Heathrow should be considered in the same market for the Paris–London and Lyons–London routes. Several factors affect the amount of substitutability between the airports. These include the access facilities to London (which point to a joint market) and the possibilities for connection (which point to different markets). The Commission simply observed that 'a certain degree of substitutability . . . can be considered to exist'. This, in itself, is not very informative.

The difficulty in selecting the appropriate characteristics is illustrated in the case of *ABC/Generale des Eaux/Canal+/WH Smith TV* where it was stated that the 'value of Pay-TV to the consumer can only be determined in relation to the alternative viewing possibilities of free access channels'. But of course other forms of entertainment and leisure activity are also substitution possibilities. It might have been useful in this instance to ask consumers what their demand response would be to a given increase in the price of Pay-TV or at least to enquire about alternative substitutes.

These three cases illustrate that observation of product characteristics may not always give a good idea of demand substitution. This is because it is difficult, without having a great deal of information about consumer preferences, to know which characteristics are important, and in what proportion.

3.1.4   Consumer surveys

In the case of *Tetra Pak/Alfa-Laval*, the Commission sought more systematic information regarding anticipated behaviour by market participants. This is the only instance where the Commission sent detailed questionnaires to a large number of customers (dairies) situated throughout the Community, as well as to the principal competitors of Alfa-Laval and Tetra Pak, and to Alfa-Laval and Tetra Pak themselves. Respondents were asked to state whether, following a given rise in the price of aseptic packaging machines, they would switch demand (or expect demand to be switched) from aseptic packaging machines to non-aseptic packaging machines. Over 75 per cent of respondents considered that a price increase of greater than 20 per cent would be necessary to lead them to switch demand, indicating fairly clearly that the products were not in the same market. In this instance it could be presumed from observation of the products' characteristics that the products were not in the same market (aseptically packaged milk lasts six times longer than non-aseptically packaged milk, meaning that distribution networks must be much faster for non-aseptically packaged products). Nevertheless, the questionnaires provided strong confirmation of the market distinction.

In a number of cases, it seems that results from questionnaires could usefully have supported some assertion by the Commission. For example, in *Renault/Volvo* it is stated that certain goods are 'not normally considered by customers as substitutable'. Extra quantification may be useful here and elsewhere. It is also probable that use of questionnaires would enable greater consistency of treatment across firms, even if market definition did not follow the results of the surveys to the letter.

3.2   Geographic market definition

The CEC defines the geographic market as 'the area where the undertakings concerned are involved in the supply and demand of products or services, in which the conditions of competition are sufficiently homogeneous and which can be distinguished from neighbouring areas because conditions of competition are appreciably different in those areas' (XXlst Report, p. 358). This assessment of geographic markets has used a variety of factors including the existence of barriers to trade and imports, the possibility of transferability of demand and purchasing policies, and factors like 'substantial differences in prices' and 'significant differences in undertakings' market shares or market presence in neighbouring areas'. Here again, supply substitution has been considered in some cases but ignored in others (as in the definition of product markets). A number of comments are appropriate.

3.2.1   National preferences

National preferences are repeatedly mentioned as a factor affecting the definition of geographic markets. This is appropriate to the extent that it refers either to the unwillingness of customers to buy a product from a foreign country simply because it is produced abroad, or to the existence of barriers erected by national governments against foreign products. It is inappropriate and should be considered under product market definition when it refers to the fact that customers have tastes that lead them to prefer the characteristics of some items which happen to be produced domestically. So, for example, it is not clear why the Commission considered 'national buyer preferences' in the *Renault/Volvo* buses case under the 'geographic market' heading. Whether the Commission referred to a bias in favour of nationally produced items or to some characteristics of domestic production when it used the term 'national buyer preferences' is unclear.

3.2.2   The distinction between geographic and product market

The question of differences in tastes across national markets arises in the *Magneti Marelli/CEAc* case. Here the Commission defined the geographic market for replacement starter batteries to be France, on the basis of the fact that the same batteries are sold at different prices in France from those abroad. The Commission attributed this price differential to, among other things, consumer preferences for well-known brands (it was not specified whether or not these brands were national). A minority of the Advisory Committee on Concentrations disputed the Commission's analysis, arguing that preferences were not nation-specific and the power of buyers strong – thus suggesting that the geographic market was larger than France. The existence of differential pricing suggests that the products are in different overall relevant markets, and if we could be sure that the batteries in France and abroad were identical in all respects except for production location then there would be good grounds for believing that the geographic markets were distinct. However, the Commission's claim that there are strong preferences for brands in France implies that batteries are heterogeneous in non-locational characteristics, that there is low cross-price demand elasticity between brands and non-brands, and perhaps between different brands; and therefore that the batteries are in different product markets. The difference in opinion between Commission and Advisory Committee might have been easier to resolve had there been a sharper distinction between the concepts of geographic and product markets.

3.2.3   Consumer surveys

As with product markets, the Commission did not generally use detailed question-naires in order to assess the scope of the geographic market. One exception is the case of *Solvay-Laporte/Interox*, where the parties held a view as to the scope of the geographic market which differed from that stated in a Commission decision of 1984. Therefore the Commission conducted a survey of major producers and users of hydrogen peroxide. From the case report, it can be inferred that this questionnaire asked about market shares in different countries, prices in different countries, and the importance of imports in each country. Given that these variables are all proxies for the primary variables of transport and production costs, it might have been simpler just to ask respondents the primary question directly: namely, if the price of hydrogen peroxide was permanently increased by 5 per cent only within the UK, to what extent within a year would buyers (be expected to) shift their demand from hydrogen peroxide produced at home to that produced abroad? The Commission would then estimate whether this demand shift would be sufficient to render the original price increase unprofitable. Given that the Commission asked only for data on secondary variables, it is perhaps not surprising that the results of the survey were inconclusive.

3.2.4   Consistency across cases

Elsewhere in its analysis of geographic markets, the CEC concentrated on the height of trade barriers and the size of intercountry price differentials. These, combined with transport costs, would be the factors one would expect to be most important in determining the scope of the geographic market when cross-border mergers are involved.

However, the Commission has not always been consistent in applying these criteria. With reference to the *Eridania/ISI* case, the CEC states in the XXIst Report (1992) that from the 'demand side, the Italian market (for sugar) seemed to be a market open to imports because prices in Italy were higher than in neighbouring countries' (p. 359). This wording is odd and seems to be in contradiction with other decisions. For instance, in its outline of the concept of geographic market, the Commission indicates that price differences between two regions are a sign of *heterogeneous* conditions of competition since they point towards the existence of barriers to entry. Heterogeneous conditions of competition in turn denote different geographical markets. This principle was applied for instance in *Varta/Bosch*. In this case, the Commission observed that 'the manufacturers are able to charge in Germany and Spain for the same types of batteries different prices to those which they charge in the other member states'. This fact, amongst others, helped to establish that there were 'appreciably different conditions of competition in the various member states' and therefore that 'the replacement markets for starter batteries in Germany and Spain are . . . considered as national markets'. In the *Eridania/ISI* case, price differences are taken rather surprisingly as a sign of low entry barriers.

3.2.5   Supply substitution and geographic markets

Our argument that product market definitions will tend to be unduly narrow when supply substitution is not taken into account applies equally to geographic markets. The Commission has considered supply substitution in some cases and not in others. For instance, in *Lucas/Eaton*, the Commission considered only demand substitution and ruled that the relevant market for heavy-duty brakes was the European Community; one can reasonably wonder whether the relevant geographic market should not have included the United States in this case. (Indeed, it is stated in the description of the operation that the main clients of the joint venture will be located in the United States and Europe, and it is also reported that Lucas has significant sales in the US.) By contrast, in *Otto/Grattan*, the Commission ruled that the relevant market for mail order was the UK. In this case, the decision referred in some detail to the barriers that would make short-term reactions by competitors outside the UK unlikely. In other cases, the Commission ignored supply substitution in market definition but considered it later. For instance, in *Elf/BC/CEPSA*, the Commission decided that Spain was the relevant geographic market. However, imports from the rest of the Community were considered as a significant factor in the assessment of dominance. In some specific market segments, the Commission even considered increases in imports to be 'imminent', partly as a consequence of trade liberalization undertaken in the context of the internal market programme. Clearly, if imports were considered imminent, supply substitution from the rest of the Community should have been taken into account in the definition of markets.

3.3   Market definition: some conclusions

A number of conclusions emerge from our analysis of market definition

1 Supply substitution has been considered in some cases and neglected in others. A consistent approach should be adopted. We would strongly favour an approach based on both demand and supply substitution.

2 The shortcomings of an approach to market definition based solely on the observation of product characteristics are somewhat striking, for both product and geographic markets. Alternative approaches which directly estimate elasticities from past observations or anticipated behaviour (surveys) could usually be implemented at reasonable cost. These would not be necessary for cases that clearly raise no competition concerns even on the narrowest plausible market definitions; but for cases where the market definition might matter it makes sense to use more quantitative evidence.

3 Some terms, like conditions of competition and substitutability, have been used in a way that is confusing, if not contradictory. A more precise definition, for instance in a set of published guidelines, would be useful.

4 The definition of geographic markets has interpreted price differences across countries somewhat inconsistently. This matter could also be usefully cleared up in published guidelines.

5 Finally, product and geographic markets have been defined sequentially, rather than simultaneously; this introduces a tendency towards excessively narrow market definition.

4   Assessing dominance

The assessment of potential dominance by the Commission uses the market position of the merged firm, the strength of remaining competition, buyer power, and potential competition. We examine below the role of each factor in the decisions taken by the Commission.

4.1   Market position

The Commission takes the market share of the merging parties as its measure of concentration. This reflects the fact that the Merger Regulation does not explicitly allow for the possibility of oligopolistic behaviour, as market share measures do not allow for firm interactions. Several aspects of the use of market shares by the CEC can be singled out.

4.1.1   Market shares as necessary conditions

In evaluating the significance of market shares the Commission examines the trends of market shares, the time period over which high market shares have been held and the 'market context' (for example, the rate of growth of the market). Low market shares (normally below 25 per cent) generally lead to approval. Such a benchmark is reasonable and the great majority of cases which come before the Commission are cleared under this rule.

The CEC states in its XXIst Report that 'high market shares can be an indication of the existence of a dominant position' and that 'current market shares normally, but not necessarily, reflect future competitive strength'. Table 23.1 lists decisions in which there were substantial (over 25 per cent) market shares, and indicates whether the case was approved within a month of notification (Article 6.1b); whether it raised serious doubts (Article 6.1c) and was subsequently approved subject to remedies (Article 8.2 with cond.) or approved without remedies (Article 8.2 without cond.); or whether it was blocked (Article 8.3). The table is highly incomplete, however, because of the difficulty of obtaining market share data from the case reports.

Table 23.1 illustrates that many cases have not been blocked despite having high post-merger market shares and substantial increases in market share. Notable examples include *Alcatel/Telettra, Varta/Bosch, Du Pont/ICI, Nestlé/Perrier, Courtaulds/SNIA, Renault/Volvo* and *ABB/Brel*. The last three of these cases were approved within a month of notification. In addition, one case with high market share figures, *Aerospatiale/Alenia/De Havilland*, was blocked. This analysis clearly indicates that the Commission has taken factors other than market share into consideration. Interestingly, however, a large number of mergers have been allowed, not so much because entry was easy, but rather because actual competition was considered strong.

Table 23.1. *Market shares and decisions (in descending order of market share)*

Case (with details)	Post-merger market share	Pre-merger market share	Decision	Reasons(s) why merger approved
Air France/Sabena [Brussels-Lyons; pre-remedy]	100%	50% and 50%	6.1b	See post-remedy entry below
Tetra Pak/Alfa-Laval	90%	90% and 0%	6.1c 8.2 without cond.	No increase in market share
Alcatel/Telettra (microwaves)	83%	18% and 65%	6.1c 8.2 with cond.	Strong buyer power; potential competition
Courtaulds/SNIA [W. Europe]	65%	32%, 10%, and 23%	6.1b	Strong actual and potential competition
Aerospatiale/Alenia/de Havilland [40–59 seats]	64%	45% and 19%	6.1c 8.3	Merger blocked because high market shares; weak actual and potential competition
Magneti Marelli/ CEAc [pre-remedy]	60%	40% and 20%	6.1c 8.2 with cond.	See post-remedy entry below
Renault/Volvo [trucks]	54.3%	46.4% and 7.9%	6.1b	Strong actual competition
Air France/Sabena [Brussels-Lyons; post-remedy]	50%	50% and 50%	6.1b	Possible actual and potential competition
ABB/BREL [diesel units in EC]	50%	15% and 35% [estimate]	6.1b	Strong actual and potential competition
Nestlé/Perrier [pre-remedy]	47.5%	15.6% and 31.9%	6.1c 8.2 with cond.	See post-remedy entry below
Varta/Bosch	44%	22% and 22% [estimate]	6.1c 8.2 with cond.	Actual competition

Du Pont/ICI [pre-remedy]	43%	? •	6.1c with cond.	See post-remedy entry below
Magneti Marelli/CEAc [post-remedy]	40%	40% and 20%	6.1c 8.2 with cond.	No increase in market share
Du Pont/ICI [post-remedy]	38%	?	6.1c with cond.	Actual competition
Nestlé/Perrier [post- remedy]	36.8%	15.6% and 31.9%	6.1c 8.2 with cond.	Actual competition
Digital/Kienzle	26%	22% and 4%	6.1b	Strong actual competition: fast market growth
Alcatel/AEG Kabe	25%	12% and 13%	6.1b	Strong buyer power

The fact that market shares were not considered to provide a reliable guide to potential market power can presumably be associated with the observation presented earlier that the practice of market definition by the CEC is biased in favour of excessively narrow markets. This arises both because product and geographic markets are determined sequentially and because market definition sometimes focuses only on demand substitution in circumstances where aggressive competitor response might be important. When markets are excessively narrow, there is little market power that can be exercised to start with and the link between market share and market power is weak. The assessment of dominance through market shares and concentration indices then becomes rather uninformative.

4.1.2   Market shares and actual competition

The most common reason why a merger with high market share was nevertheless approved was because of strong actual competition. It indicates that the Commission was not satisfied with market shares. This is partly because the definitions of markets were excessively narrow but in some cases because market shares were viewed by the Commission as poor indicators of market power. It might also suggest that taking into account the distribution of competitors' market shares in a more systematic manner could be useful. It would be desirable in any case to ensure greater consistency across cases; in the current situation, arguments regarding the strength of actual competition are purely a matter of judgement and could be open to abuse. This is illustrated by a number of cases.

In *Renault/Volvo* a 54 per cent post-merger share in the market for trucks was not taken as an indication of dominance because there is effective competition from Mercedes, which supplies 18 per cent of the market. This is an illustration of why market share may not be a good measure of the strength of remaining competition: market share measures do not distinguish the competitive strength of a market with many little sellers from one with a few big sellers. The Commission assumed here that Mercedes would provide strong competition.

Varta/Bosch was another case in which a high market share was combated by actual competition. A dominant position was avoided by Fiat and Deta/Mareg each ending up with 10 per cent of the market. An important consideration here was that Fiat's access to a distribution network for a brand name meant that the 'competitive potential of the new entity will be more important than the current market shares achieved through the market share might indicate'.

One case in which market shares were taken as a sign of dominance was *Aerospatiale/Alenia (ATR)/de Havilland (DHC)*. This merger would have led to the new entity supplying 64 per cent of the 40–59 seat regional turbo-prop aircraft market. This would have entailed DHC being eliminated as ATR's strongest competitor. Fokker, the next-strongest competitor, does not have a very long order backlog;[2] and the remaining

---

[2] In principle, a long-order backlog is, however, an indication that a company is unlikely to be an aggressive competitor, because it is unable to increase supply. This argument could usefully have been qualified.

competition is weak. Thus it was not so much the market share *per se* which indicated dominance, as the fact that the characteristics of the aircraft supply market mean that strong competition can be provided only by large firms.

4.1.3   Collective dominance

As we have indicated, the EC Merger Regulation neither explicitly allows for nor rules out the possibility of collusion as a source of dominant position: it states only that a merger will be prohibited if effective competition is significantly impeded. However, the wording of the Regulation itself is restricted by the previous decisions of the European Court of Justice (ECJ). The definition of dominant position in the Merger Regulation, for example, follows that given by the ECJ for the application of Article 86. Soon after the Regulation came into force Sir Leon Brittan, the then Competition Commissioner, began indicating that the CEC would use it to control oligopolistic dominance, since he regarded the possibility of effective competition being impeded by collective firm behaviour as being a very real one (Linklaters & Paines, 1992, p. 9). Thus the Commission was seeking a test case where it could establish its *de facto* ability to control collective dominance. Although the possibility of oligopolistic behaviour was raised in *Alcatel/AEG Kabel* and *Thorn EMI/Virgin Music*, the Commission did not find such a test case until February 1992 with the arrival of *Nestlé/Perrier.*

In *Alcatel/AEG Kabel,* the Bundeskartellamt made an Article 9 request for referral on the basis that the merger would create a situation of oligopolistic dominance because three suppliers would together hold more than 50 per cent of the relevant market. In German competition law there is a presumption that three or fewer enterprises having the highest market shares are presumed each to be market-dominating if together they have a market share of at least 50 per cent (see Heidenhain, 1991). In EC law there is no such presumption, so the Commission would have to demonstrate that effective competition between the members of the oligopoly could not be expected on structural grounds. In the event, the Commission found that countervailing buyer power was strong enough for the merger not to create a dominant position, so the merger was approved (without referral to the Bundeskartel-lamt).

In *Thorn EMI/Virgin* the market share of the new entity was less than 25 per cent in most of the relevant markets affected. This, combined with the presence of other strong players on the market, meant that there was not a dominant position for the merged entity. However, the post-merger five-firm concentration ratio on the market for recorded music is 83 per cent. This, together with the fact that the market shares appear to be stable over time, led the Commission to state that there could be 'a situation of collective dominance'. It then considered the likelihood that the acquisition would create or strengthen a dominant position amongst the five major record companies taken together. This meant assessing the likelihood of effective competition between the five companies. The Commission found that a number of cooperative agreements exist in the industry involving the five major companies and that 'the scope for price competition seems to be limited'. As part of its examination the

Commission carried out a 'number of inquiries in order to evaluate the market behaviour of the main participants in the market'. These inquiries did not produce any evidence that 'the market is performing in an anti-competitive manner', and thus the merger was approved despite the high and stable market concentration, entry barriers, absence of price competition, and the existence of cooperative agreements. It is regrettable that the Commission did not give details of their inquiries in the case report. The importance of this case from a competition policy standpoint is that it was the first instance of the Commission's investigating the possibility of interactions between firms.

The oligopoly test case for the CEC appeared in July 1992 in the form of the contested takeover bid of the French bottled water group Source Perrier by the Swiss foods group Nestlé. This high-profile case gave the Commission the opportunity to establish as a precedent its ability to control collective as well as single-firm dominance. The economic details of this case are discussed in section 6.4 on remedies below, but the key question was whether post-merger relations between Nestlé-Perrier and BSN would be cooperative or competitive. The Commission found that Nestlé and BSN would become jointly dominant in the French market for bottled water. The Commission argued from the standpoint of its duty under Article 3(f) of the EEC Treaty to maintain effective competition. Since the Merger Regulation does not in so many words restrict the concept of a dominant position to that of only one firm, the Commission must apply the Regulation to dominance shared by more than one firm, since otherwise effective competition will be impeded. A minority of the Advisory Committee took the view that the Regulation does not apply at all to collective dominance. Another minority stated that it only applies where there are structural links between the firms involved.

In consequence of the joint dominant market position, the Commission concluded that Nestlé should dispose of a number of lesser brands to a single purchaser. The effectiveness of this remedy depends to a very large extent on whether a significant third force will be created.

4.1.4   Market shares and Herfindahl–Hirschman indices

Table 23.2 reports lower-bound estimates of the Herfindahl–Hirschman index for those cases which came before the CEC and for which sufficient data were available. The same comments about incompleteness that were made with reference to table 23.1 also apply here. Table 23.2 shows that on its own definition of the relevant market the CEC was more lenient in approving mergers than would be implied by the thresholds cited in the US Guidelines. However, as indicated above, the Commission's procedures for market definition may be somewhat biased in favour of narrow markets, relative to the US practice. In addition, the Federal Trade Commission is in practice considerably more lenient in applying the concentration rules than is indicated by the Guidelines. When comparing figures, it must also be remembered that the philosophy of antitrust in the United States places great emphasis on the danger of oligopoly whilst the European Commission's outlook has been to emphasize the position of single firms. Thus the HHI, which is an index of oligopolistic strength, is not a fair

Table 23.2. Lower-bound estimates of Herfindahl–Hirschman indices (in descending order of post-merger HHI)

Case [with details]	Post-merger HHI	Change in HHI	US category	CEC decision
Air France/Sabena [Brussels-Lyons; [pre-remedy]	10,000	5,000	Market power	6.1b
Tetra Pak/Alfa-Laval	8,100	0	Approval	6.1c
				8.2 without cond.
Alcatel/Telettra [microwaves]	6,890	2,340	Market power	6.1c
				8.2 with cond.
Alcatel/Telettra [line transmission]	6,560	3,280	Market power	6.1c
				8.2 with cond.
Aerospatiale/Alenia/de Havilland [60 seats]	6,350	0	Approval	6.1c
				8.3
Aerospatiale/Alenia/de Havilland [40 seats]	4,470	1,530	Market power	6.1c
				8.3
Courtaulds/SNIA [W. Europe]	4,730	2,570	Market power	6.1b
Aerospatiale/Alenia/de Havilland [40–59 seats]	4,680	1,710	Market power	6.1c
				8.3
Magneti Marelli/CEAc [pre-remedy]	4,000	1,600	Market power	6.1c
				8.2 with cond.
Renault/Volvo [trucks]	3,730	730	Market power	6.1b
Aerospatiale/Alenia/de Havilland [20–70 seats]	3,090	1,220	Market power	6.1c
				8.3
Aeróspatiale/Alenia/de Havilland [20–39 seats]	2,910	100	Market power	6.1c
				8.3
Nestlé/Perrier [pre-remedy]	2,660	1,000	Market power	6.1c
				8.2 with cond.
Air France/Sabena [Brussels-Lyons; post-remedy]	2,500	0	Approval	6.1b

Table 23.2. cont.

Case [with details]	Post-merger HHI	Change in HHI	US category	CEC decision
ABB/BREL [diesel units in EC]	2,500	1,050	Market power	6.1b
Magneti Marelli/CEAc [post-remedy]	2,400	0	Approval	6.1c
				8.2 with cond.
Digital/Kienzle	2,360	180	Market power	6.1c
Nestlé/Perrier [post-remedy]	2,310	640	Market power	6.1c
				8.2 with cond.
Varta/Bosch [pre-remedy]	2,300	970	Market power	6.1c
				8.2 with cond.
Varta/Bosch [post-remedy]	2,140	810	Market power	6.1c
				8.2 with cond.
Courtaulds/SNIA [World]	2,040	120	Market power	6.1b
Du Pont/ICI [pre-remedy]	1,850			6.1c with cond.
Du Pont/ICI [post-remedy]	1,440			6.1c with cond.
Thorn EMI/Virgin [recording]	1,380	190	Significant competitive concerns	6.1b
Mannesmann/VDO	1,360	60	Approval	6.1b
Alcatel/AEG Kabel	1,250	310	Significant competitive concerns	6.1b
Digital/Philips	850	240	Approval	6.1b
Thorn EMI/Virgin [publishing]	700	160	Approval	6.1b

basis of comparison. Nevertheless, it is probably fair to say that a merger resulting in a high measure of concentration is more likely to be blocked in the United States than in the EC.

4.2   Buyer power

Buyer power was central in the Commission's decisions in at least three cases *(Alcatel/ Telettra, Viag/Continental Can* and *Alcatel/AEG Kabel).*

We would expect that buyer power is much more effective in restraining market power when the buyer has several sources of supply and thus has the opportunity to play off suppliers against one another. An example of this point was the case of *Viag/ Continental Can,* where 60 per cent of market sales went to five buyers. The buyers have a dual/triple sourcing policy so that they can 'easily play off one supplier against another'. Consequently buyer power was important in combating high concentration.

In this light the reliance placed on buyer power in *Alcatel/Telettra,* where the merged entity has a market share greater than 80 per cent (a larger figure than that of *Aerospatiale/Alenia/de Havilland*) and the rest of the market is fragmented, seems excessive. The source of the strong buyer power is Telefonica, the national telecommunications systems purchaser. Telefonica buys 100 per cent of public switches sold in Spain, 90 per cent of the transmission equipment and 60 per cent of the microwave equipment. A remedy removed ownership links between Telefonica and Telettra (see below in the section on remedies). Telefonica was seen as being independent of the merged entity, and as being capable of switching purchases in the near future to alternative suppliers should Alcatel-Telettra raise prices. The likelihood of such switching taking place depends on both the incentives facing Telefonica and the availability of alternative suppliers. [. . .] there are transaction cost benefits for Telefonica from not switching. This also implies that the existence of pro-competitive forces in *Alcatel/Telettra* relies on keen new entrants.

4.3   Entry and potential competition

We turn now to the role of potential competition in the Commission's decisions. Entry was a particularly important factor in those cases where market shares were high, namely in the cases of *Alcatel/Telettra, Courtaulds/SNIA, Aerospatiale/Alenia/de Havilland* and *Air France/Sabena.* The Commission regards 'strong evidence of a high probability of strong and quick market entry' as a sufficient condition for a market position to be non-dominant. Whilst it is not specified what 'quick' means, these are the same criteria as those of the US Guidelines, namely likelihood, timeliness, and effectiveness.

4.3.1   Entry lags

Surprisingly, the Commission assessed entry lags explicitly in only two cases. In *Aerospatiale/Alenia (ATR)/de Havilland (DHC),* the Commission estimated that the entry lag was six to seven years because of the process of marketing research (two to three years) and R&D, production and delivery (another four years). In addition, there are sunk costs of designing, testing and gaining regulatory approval. Hence potential competition is weak, giving a firm with strong market position the chance to exercise market power.

The only other case in which the Commission explicitly estimated the entry lag was *Lucas/Eaton*, in which the time necessary to permit design and retooling work was put at two years. Despite this lag, the Commission stated that the threat of entry 'will to a certain extent constrain the competitive behaviour of existing manufacturers'. It will be recalled that two years is the threshold for entry to be 'easy' under the Department of Justice's definition. The Commission did not attempt to estimate the other two necessary conditions for entry to be easy under the US definition: likelihood and sufficiency of entry.

4.3.2 Entry barriers
A number of entry barriers were explicitly considered by the Commission, including transport costs, brand awareness and regulatory barriers.

Regulatory impediments were considered in *Alcatel/Telettra,* but only to a limited extent. Entry (by AT&T and Ericsson) was 'essential' in combating the high market share of the merged entity. Potential imports by Siemens were also important. AT&T has no sales of microwave equipment in Spain at present, though since 1988 its line transmission sales in Spain have grown strongly; the firm thinks it can expand sales in the Spanish market. Ericsson produces mainly public switching and digital transmission equipment. It has only limited production of microwave equipment but regards entry barriers as being low because no product adaptation is necessary. Siemens has only a 'marginal position' in the transmission markets in Spain, with a 9 per cent market share. It considers that the two important entry barriers are the vertical integration of Telefonica with suppliers and the fact that the Public Procurement Directive, according to which national purchasers must consider all possible domestic or foreign suppliers, will not be effective in Spain until 1996. The remedy broke the vertical ownership links with Alcatel-Telettra, though there are transaction cost reasons why Telefonica may wish to limit the number of suppliers [. . .]. With regard to public procurement, Telefonica has assured the CEC that it will technically approve new suppliers and will arrange for contacts to be made with new suppliers, be they domestic or foreign, where possible. However, given that there is no guarantee that foreign suppliers will be considered until 1996, more analysis was needed here of the likely entry lag as well as the profitability of entering a market with entry barriers. Given the small current market positions of the potential entrants and the very strong market position of the incumbent firm, more analysis was also needed of the sufficiency of entry in restraining the market power of Alcatel-Telettra.

In *Courtaulds/SNIA,* potential competition from yarn imports produced in the United States and the Far East were essential in combating high market shares. The Commission estimated the likelihood of entry by considering the costs of transport (5 per cent plus a 10 per cent EC tariff) and setting these against lower extra-EC energy and labour costs. On the basis of this calculation the Commission concluded that any attempt by the merged entity to raise prices would tend to pull in imports.

In *Alcatel/AEG Kabel* entry barriers were apparently not considered at all. Given that the relevant market was that for telecommunications cables, there would surely be some sunk costs of investment. The analysis of potential competition is also incomplete in *TNT/Canada Post et al.*, where it was stated only that entry barriers were 'considerable'. Given that the proposed joint venture has high market share, entry barriers were an important factor here and should have received detailed attention.

In *Nestlé/Perrier* the Commission indicated that brand awareness and transport costs were entry barriers. However, the Commission also observed that most of the 32.3 per cent of the French market for bottled water that is not controlled by Nestlé-Perrier or BSN is accounted for by the own-brand sales of supermarkets. Although transport costs were supposed to be high, in the last five years there have been 15 attempts at entry into the French mineral water market (Linklaters & Paines,1992). According to the Commission, a price increase by Nestlé or BSN would very probably, therefore, trigger more entry attempts. It is not clear, however, whether these fifteen attempts were successful. Some of them are bound to have failed, otherwise market shares would be more dispersed than they currently are. So barriers to entry may have been significant after all. In any event, it would seem that a more careful analysis of previous entry attempts could have yielded interesting insights.

4.4   Assessing dominance: some conclusions

Seven main conclusions emerge from our analysis of the Commission assessment of dominance:

1 A post-merger market share of less than 25 per cent is sufficient for a deal to be cleared, and normally within a month of notification. This appears sensible. In addition, and also sensibly, where market share did not much increase the merger was cleared.

2 Currently market shares do not appear to be treated as very informative indicators of market power. Market shares do not provide a reliable signal to prospective merging parties; they do not even give a particularly good indication of whether a case will require remedies. The lack of confidence that the Commission has displayed regarding the significance of market share may be associated with the observation made earlier that the definition of markets is biased towards excessively narrow markets. In those circumstances, indicators of market power lose some of their significance.

3 Market shares have been qualified in many different ways. The Commission has used a variety of additional factors associated with the structure of supply in the relevant market. At present, the additional considerations which are invoked may appear sometimes arbitrary.

4 The 'strength of remaining competitors' is most often used to complement

market share information. It would help for such considerations to be invoked somewhat more systematically.

5 The Commission is now prepared to investigate the possibility of interactions between firms. Yet the procedure to evaluate oligopolistic interactions is not systematic (as revealed for instance in *Du Pont/ICI*).

6 The Commission seems to place a good deal of faith in buyer power even when buyers face few alternative suppliers.

7 The Commission has relied heavily on entry possibilities in several cases. Yet the analysis of entry has been sketchy, for example estimating entry lag in only two cases. More systematic attention to the timeliness, likelihood and sufficiency of entry would be useful.

3.5   Efficiency: defence or offence?

It is not entirely clear whether the EC Merger Regulation allows for efficiency considerations. Efficiency has nevertheless been mentioned in a number of cases, sometimes as an offence and once as a possible defence, only to be dismissed as negligible in the case in question.

In *AT&T/NCR* possible synergies were considered under the 'Conglomerate Aspects' heading. The Commission asked whether AT&T's technical and marketing know-how could be used to 'enhance the position of NCR in the workstation market'. One mechanism through which this might occur is through a 'potential complementarity' between technical know-how and the marketing of workstations, which could give rise to 'synergies' through the possible development of 'more advanced communication features at a lower cost'. However, for 'the moment such a complementarity cannot be foreseen as there are no precise indications of concrete technical developments or possible marketing strategies'. Nevertheless, the Commission does not rule out the possibility that 'potential advantages flowing from synergies may create or strengthen a dominant position'.

Thus in this case the Commission regarded cost savings as a negative factor which could lead to the creation or strengthening of a dominant market position. Similar concerns arise in *Dräger/IBM/HMP*, *Pan Am/Delta* and *Sextant/BGT-VDO*. In those cases, the Commission seems to imply that the competitive advantage that the joint ventures might obtain is itself a matter of concern (see Jenny, 1992). There is of course sometimes a trade-off between productive and allocative efficiency, and this should be recognized; it is another matter, however, to state that improvements in productive efficiency are undesirable because they lead to allocative inefficiencies. Carried to its logical conclusion, such an argument would imply that, if only privately profitable mergers are proposed, none should be allowed. A less critical interpretation of the Commission's decision here ties in with a point made in the discussion of dominance: namely, that the Commission appears to regard the existence of small and medium-sized firms as a good thing in itself. Thus cost savings which force out small and medium-sized firms may be seen as undesirable. This decision is nevertheless slightly disturbing, and could send to other firms contemplating merger the perverse signal that cost savings are a bad thing, and will make the merger less likely to be approved.

In *Aerospatiale/Alenia/de Havilland* the parties themselves put forward an estimate of cost savings amounting to 0.5 per cent of combined turnover. These cost savings would be realized through synergies in marketing and product support, and through rationalizing parts procurement. The European Commission regarded these cost savings as 'negligible', and they were irrelevant to the final decision. The question arises whether the Commission, in its position of limited information, would have been able to detect whether more substantial claims about cost savings were realistic or not. Of course, if the firms' lawyers had been reading the *AT&T/NCR* case report, they might have concluded that they would be better off not claiming large cost savings.

References

Fishwick, F. and T. Denison (1992), 'The geographical dimension of competition in the European Single Market', mimeo, December.

Heidenhain, M. (1991), 'Merger control in the Federal Republic of Germany', in S. Cromie (ed.), *Merger Control in Europe*, London, IFR Books.

Jenny, F. (1992), 'The efficiency defence under the EC Merger Regulation', Conseil de la Concurrence, mimeo.

Linklaters & Paines (1992), *Competition Law Bulletin*, Autumn.

Index

GTE Sylvania 296–7, 304–8
Gual, J. 197, 197n, 223
Gulf & Western 71, 73

Haddock, D.H. 164, 393n
Hahn, F.H. 88n
Hamilton, J. 152n, 154n, 232n
Harman, T. 98n
Harrigan, K.R. 83, 85n, 104n, 113
Harris, R.G. 64
Harstad, R. 15, 123–51, 273–4, 279
Hart, O. 388n, 391
Hartwick, J. 319n
Haspeslagh, P. 66n
hedonic price index 198–9, 204
Heinz, 46
Hendricks, K. 36n
Herfindahl-Hirschman index 341, 362,
    369–73, 378–80, 393, 395, 398–401,
    404–8, 428–30
Higgins, R. 393n, 394
Hill, R. 86
Hobbs, B.F. 159n, 169
Hoffman la Roche 285, 289, 292
Holahan, W.L. 154
Holt, C.A. 17–19, 123n, 130, 137, 147n,
    174–87
Honda 202
Hoover, E.M. 169
horizontal merger 26–7
Hotelling, H.H. 383, 389n
Hotelling model 7n, 38, 156
Howard, M. 285
HSO (Highland Scottish Omnibuses) 278
Huang, C.-F. 83
Hurter, A.P. 159n, 169

ICI 254–64, 275, 277, 434
Icikovics, J.-P. 153n
import quota 360
industry
    aluminia refining 83
    antiknock lead additives 175
    automobile 126n, 196–231
    baby food 83
    beer 48, 60, 182n
    biscuits 59n
    books 284
    bread 54
    breakfast cereal 7, 59

bus operation 278–9
cable television 383, 387n
canned vegetables 54
chemical 13, 100–18
cigars 83
coffee 60
coffee percolators 83
confectionery 45, 60
dyestuffs 124n
flat glass 124n
flour 54
food and drinks 10, 33n, 41, 54n
frozen food 44, 58n
gasoline 21, 232–48
gasoline additives 175
instant coffee 45
integrated steelmaking 86
liquor 182n
margarine 46, 58n
mineral water 47
perfume 286
petroleum products 22, 102
pharmaceutical 10
plywood 153
prepared soup 46
rayon 83
salt 1–6, 15, 21, 24–5, 43, 54, 249–65,
    276–7
soda-ash 12, 83, 85–6, 104n
soft drinks 22, 46, 387n
soup 60
steel 16, 125, 153, 166
steel castings 86
sugar 43, 54, 60
synthetic fibres 102
titanium dioxide 10, 63–79
vacuum tubes 83
wood pulp 124, 274–5
interbrand competition 306–9
investment policy 73–5, 359
Isaac, R.M. 277

Jacquemin, A. 23, 318–24
Jefferson Parish 313–15
Jenny, F. 434
Jensen, E. 382n
joint demand 383–7
Jordan, J. 176n
Jorgenson, D.W. 209, 210, 215, 243
Joskov, P. 368n